House & Garden's
New Cook Book

House & Garden's New Cook Book

By the Editors of House & Garden

Published by The Condé Nast Publications Inc.

Book Trade Distribution by Simon and Schuster

New York—1967

The photographs in this book are by

Ernst Beadle
Fernand Fonssagrives
Bill Fotiades
Richard Jeffery
Otto Maya
Rudy Muller
Denise Otis

The drawings are by

Adolph Brotman
Tom Funk
Bill Goldsmith
Edward Kasper
Mel Klapholz
Grambs Miller
Michelle Stewart

Book designed by

Dorothea Elman

The Editors acknowledge with gratitude
the contributions of the following
expert cooks:

Elizabeth Alston
James A. Beard
Simone Beck
Iris Brooks
Helen Evans Brown
Philip S. Brown
Julia Child
Ruth Ellen Church
Craig Claiborne
William Clifford
Lelia Carson Cox
Eloise Davison
Vittoria Graham
Peggy Harvey
Nika Standen Hazelton
Barbara Poses Kafka
Dione Lucas
Tatiana McKenna
Marilyn Mercer
Kay Shaw Nelson
Elisabeth Lambert de Ortiz
Lou Seibert Pappas
June Platt
Ann Roe Robbins
Elaine Ross
Myra Waldo
Betty Wason

For allowing us to reprint their recipes,
the Editors thank

Mrs. Stewart Alsop
The Duchess of Bedford
Mrs. Hale Boggs
Miss Elizabeth Burton
Mrs. Rowland Evans, Jr.
Mr. Edward Giobbi
Mr. William Holzhauser
Mrs. William R. Merriam
Mrs. A. S. Monroney
Mr. Ted Nierenberg
Quo Vadis, New York City
Chez Camille Renault, Paris

Table of Contents

Tools, Techniques & Cooking Lore

The Cook's Tools

Like any other artisan, a cook is only as good as her tools. Blunt knives and beat-up, buckled pans, equipment of the wrong size, shape or weight are the enemies of fine cooking and all too often spell the difference between success and failure. That doesn't mean you can't improvise occasionally if you don't have the right piece of equipment on hand. An ovenproof glass bowl set over a pan of hot water can stand in for a double boiler if you're making zabaglione or Hollandaise sauce, a colander lined with cheesecloth makes a perfectly adequate strainer, and if you don't own a pan big enough to poach a whole salmon, a tin-lined copper wash boiler or a baby's enamel bathtub can be pressed into service. On the other hand, a meat thermometer is essential nowadays if your roasts are to come out to your liking every time, a chef's knife is a must for speedy, expert chopping, and your soufflés will never rise to the heights they could unless you have a copper bowl and a wire whisk for beating the egg whites to their ultimate expansion. In the long run, it is an economy to put your money into sound, sturdy equipment of the finest quality—it cooks better, lasts longer, and never lets you down. You don't have to buy everything at once. Start with the utensils, tools and gadgets you need most and add to them as you extend your range and repertoire of recipes. The following list will help you stock a well-equipped kitchen.

Apple corer.
Aspic cutters.
Au gratin dishes, round and oval, of tin-lined copper, ovenproof china.
Baking dishes, round and oval, of heavy earthenware, enameled cast iron, ovenproof glass.
Baster, bulb type.
Bread or loaf tins.
Cake pans, round, square, spring-form, tube.
Candy and deep-fat thermometer.
Casseroles, round and oval, in small to large sizes, of heavy earthenware, enameled cast iron, with tight-fitting lids.
Cocottes, round and oval, in small to large sizes, of enameled cast iron with tight-fitting lids.
Colander.

Cookie sheets.
Copper beating bowl, large, unlined.
Corkscrew, lever type.
Deep-fat fryer.
Earthenware crock or bowl, large, for marinating meat.
Electric blender.
Electric hand beater.
Electric mixer, preferably heavy-duty type with beater, paddle and dough hook attachments.
Fish cooker.
Flan rings, round and rectangular.
Fluting knife, for decorating vegetables.
Food mill, for puréeing.
Fruit juicer, electric or manual.
Graters, straight-sided and rotary types.
Ice cream freezer, electric or manual.
Jelly roll pans.
Kitchen scales.
Kitchen shears.
Knives: boning knife; chef's knife; fish filleting knife; ham slicer; paring knife; slicing knife, of carbon steel. Serrated-edge bread knife; tomato-slicing knife, of stainless steel.
Larding needles: long, wood-handled type for interior larding; smaller needles for surface larding.
Lemon stripper.
Mandoline cutter, for slicing vegetables.
Measuring cups, glass and metal.
Measuring spoons.
Meat cleaver.
Meat grinder, electric or manual.
Meat pounder or cutlet bat, for flattening scaloppine, chicken breasts.
Melon baller.
Metal kitchen spoons, plain and perforated.
Metal spatulas, narrow and broad blades.
Metal tongs, for lifting, turning food.
Mixing bowls, stainless steel and heatproof glass.
Mortar and pestle, for grinding herbs, spices, garlic.
Muffin pan.
Needle and thread, skewers, heavy white string, for sewing up and trussing poultry.
Nutmeg grater.

Oyster knife.

Pancake turner.

Pans: crêpe pan, of iron.

double boiler, preferably heatproof glass or with ceramic top.

frying pans and skillets, small to large, of heavy cast aluminum, enameled cast iron, with lids.

miniature copper pan, for melting butter, heating spirits.

omelette pan, of heavy cast aluminum or Teflon-coated aluminum.

saucepans, in sizes from 1½ quarts, of tin-lined copper, stainless steel, enameled cast iron, with lids.

sauté pan, of heavy cast aluminum, tin-lined copper.

Pastry bags, plastic-lined.

Pastry board.

Pastry brushes.

Pastry cutters, plain, fluted, fancy.

Pastry tubes, round, ribbon, star.

Pepper mills, coarse and fine grinds.

Pie plates, 9″ and 10″.

Poultry shears.

Ramekins.

Roasting rack, adjustable, V-shaped type.

Roasting pan.

Rolling pins, ball-bearing type, tapered French pastry pin.

Rotary beater.

Rubber spatulas or scrapers, small (to fit in jars, cans) and large (for mixing, folding).

Scallop shells or shell-shaped baking dishes.

Skewers, for en brochette cooking.

Soufflé dishes, 1½ and 2-quart sizes.

Soup ladle.

Steam basket, adjustable to fit different-sized pans.

Steel, for sharpening knives.

Stock pot.

Strainers and sieves, fine and coarse mesh, small and large.

Terrines, for pâtés.

Tins and molds: barquette, bombe, brioche, charlotte, coeur à la crème, cornucopia, madeleine, melon, oeuf en gelée, pâté en croute, savarin, tartlet, timbale. Decorative molds for aspics, ice cream, puddings, mousses.

Vegetable peeler.

Wire cake racks.

Wire skimmer, for lifting food from hot liquid, fat.

Wire whisks, small for sauces, large wood-handled balloon type for beating egg whites.

Wood chopping block.

Wooden spoons and spatulas, assorted sizes.

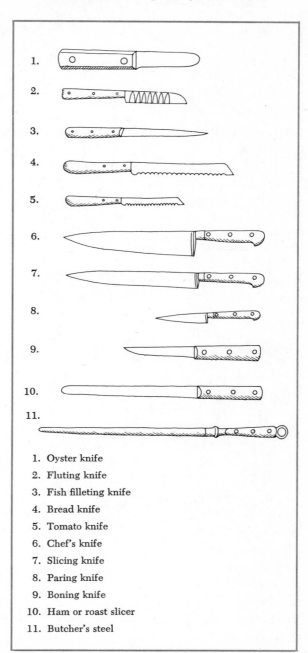

1. Oyster knife
2. Fluting knife
3. Fish filleting knife
4. Bread knife
5. Tomato knife
6. Chef's knife
7. Slicing knife
8. Paring knife
9. Boning knife
10. Ham or roast slicer
11. Butcher's steel

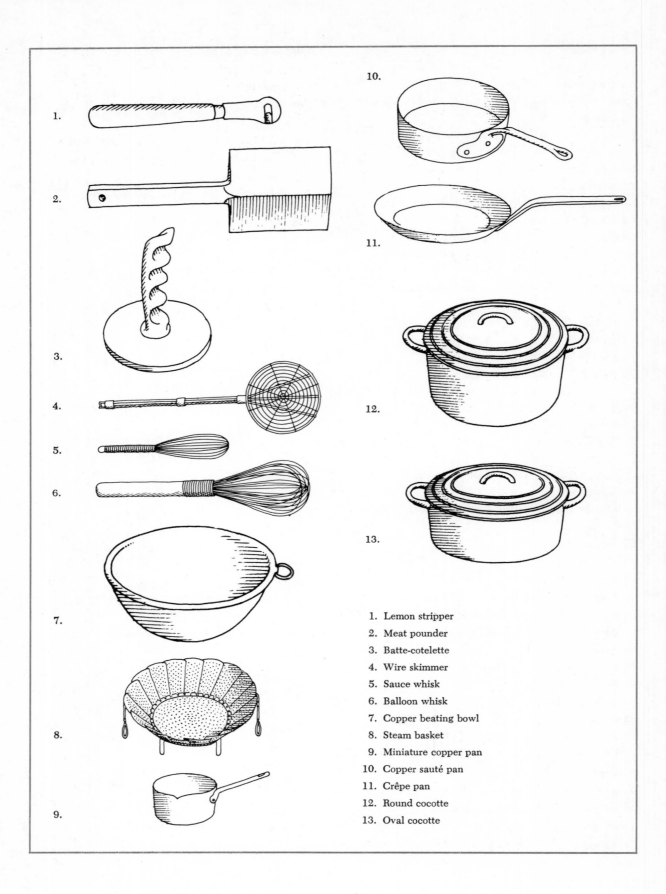

1. Lemon stripper
2. Meat pounder
3. Batte-cotelette
4. Wire skimmer
5. Sauce whisk
6. Balloon whisk
7. Copper beating bowl
8. Steam basket
9. Miniature copper pan
10. Copper sauté pan
11. Crêpe pan
12. Round cocotte
13. Oval cocotte

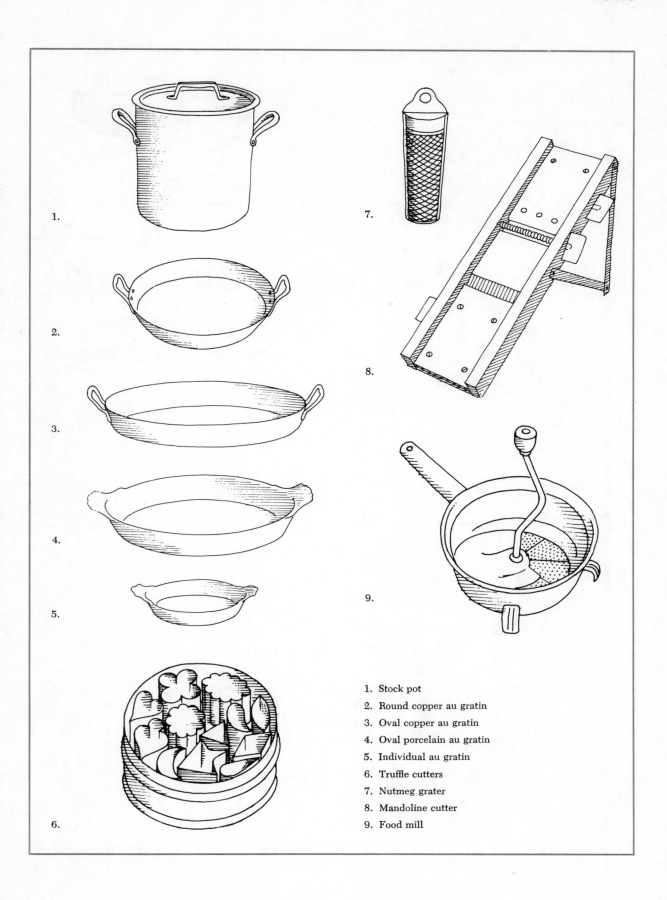

1.

2.

3.

4.

5.

6.

7.

8.

9.

1. Stock pot
2. Round copper au gratin
3. Oval copper au gratin
4. Oval porcelain au gratin
5. Individual au gratin
6. Truffle cutters
7. Nutmeg grater
8. Mandoline cutter
9. Food mill

1. Grater with three plates
2. Candy thermometer
3. Rotary egg beater
4. Kitchen scissors
5. Juicer
6. Large and small wooden spoons
7. Pastry brush
8. Rolling pin
9. Tapered French pastry pin
10. Small and large rubber spatulas
11. Broad and narrow metal spatulas
12. Electric hand beater
13. Electric mixer
14. Electric blender
15. Mixing bowls
16. Jelly roll pan and cookie sheet
17. Rectangular flan ring
18. Round cake pan with removable bottom
19. Round flan ring
20. Spring-form pan, two bottoms

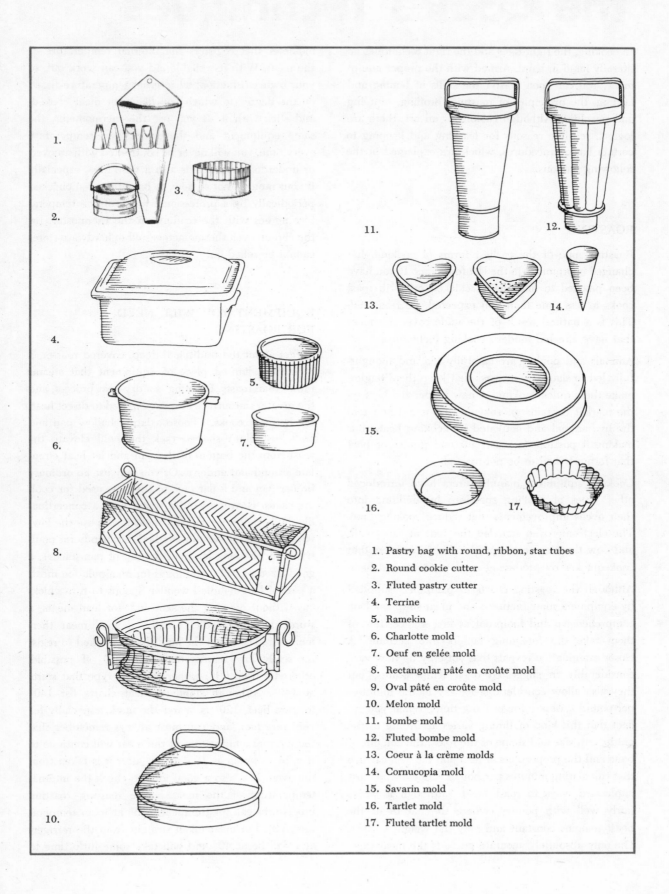

1. Pastry bag with round, ribbon, star tubes
2. Round cookie cutter
3. Fluted pastry cutter
4. Terrine
5. Ramekin
6. Charlotte mold
7. Oeuf en gelée mold
8. Rectangular pâté en croûte mold
9. Oval pâté en croûte mold
10. Melon mold
11. Bombe mold
12. Fluted bombe mold
13. Coeur à la crème molds
14. Cornucopia mold
15. Savarin mold
16. Tartlet mold
17. Fluted tartlet mold

The Cook's Techniques

In cooking, the right tools and the right techniques go literally hand in hand. Armed with the proper equipment, you can soon master the skills of boning and larding, the principles of roasting, broiling, sautéing and poaching. Although cooking is an art, there are logical, sensible reasons for learning and keeping to certain basic procedures, which are explained in the following sections.

ROASTING

Roasting, one of the earliest forms of cooking, has changed enormously in the last few years. If you have been puzzled to find that a chicken or a rib roast cooks in less time than you expected, be reassured. This is a natural result of the undercover advances that have affected modern cooking techniques.

Animals and poultry are carefully fed and thoughtfully led to slaughter in ways that keep them tender, make them quick-cooking. A new tenderized beef on the market contains an enzyme that is injected into the live animal and activated by cooking heat, thus making it possible to roast cuts and grades of beef that formerly had to be pot-roasted.

Cooking equipment manufacturers have introduced other types of cooking speed-up by building into their ovens improvements that reduce cooking time. The electronic oven signaled the start of this trend, and now there are high-speed infra-red burners that cook quicker by producing more concentrated heat.

Although the roasting charts in pamphlets supplied by equipment manufacturers and meat suppliers look comprehensive and foolproof at first glance, few of them take the foregoing factors into account. A closer examination reveals that not only do they vary considerably in suggested oven temperatures, but they also allow considerable leeway in the minutes-per-pound estimate for cooking time. When you reflect that this kind of timing varies according to the grade, cut, size and shape of the roast, the amount of bone and the proportions of lean and fat, you can see that calculating minutes per pound is one of the most haphazard ways to roast meat (although it works fairly well with poultry, where the nature of the beast remains constant and only the weight varies). The only absolutely accurate guide is the meat ther-

mometer that registers the internal temperature of the meat. With its reliable aid you can work out, to your own satisfaction, an internal temperature based on the degree to which you like your meat cooked, and stick with it. If you use the thermometer, the same equipment and the same oven temperature every time, you will never be confronted with an over- or underdone roast. It is also a wise idea, especially if your range is not so new, to have the oven checked periodically by a professional to see if the temperature agrees with the reading on the thermostat, for the clip-on oven thermometers sold in hardware stores cannot be relied on.

EQUIPMENT YOU WILL NEED FOR ROASTING

Forget about the traditional deep, covered roaster, a bulky and limited piece of equipment that steams rather than roasts. Roasting is a dry-heat process, and the greater the surface of meat exposed to direct heat, the better it cooks. Choose a large shallow pan and an adjustable V-shaped rack that will elevate the roast from the bottom of the pan and let heat circulate around and under it. Or you may use an ordinary broiler pan and a flat rack of the type used for cooling cakes. Have on hand a baster with a concertina-like bulb (not necessary for meat if you use the low-temperature, self-basting method, but handy for poultry or for drawing fat from the top of pan juices), a good-sized pair of metal tongs for manipulating meat, a pair of long-handled wooden spoons to turn chickens without piercing the skin and, for lean meats, a sturdy larding needle. Finally, a good meat thermometer. Try to get the kind that is marked to register really low temperatures (from 0° if possible, otherwise from 60°) rather than the type that starts at 140°. Although standard meat charts list 140° for rare beef, 120° is nearer the mark, especially for very rare filet, and you must always remember that the internal temperature of the meat will continue to rise, by as much as 10 degrees, after it is taken from the oven. It is also a good idea to check the internal temperature of the meat before roasting—roasting procedures call for the meat to be at room temperature, 70°, but meat taken straight from the refrigerator will be at 40° and will take some little time to reach 70°, especially if the roast is a large one.

PREPARING ROASTS FOR THE OVEN

Always let meat and poultry stand outside the refrigerator for at least an hour, preferably two, to enable them to come to room temperature. Frozen roasts or poultry taste better if thawed, although you can cook them from the frozen state if you wish, increasing the cooking time, starting the roasting at a low temperature and then stepping up the heat and inserting the meat thermometer when the inside is thoroughly thawed.

Wipe the roast with a damp cloth and dry well. Season the meat or not, as you wish. Some people prefer to season halfway through roasting, claiming that the salt draws out the juices, but this is purely a matter of opinion. If you want to flavor the roast with garlic, make tiny incisions in the meat and insert garlic slivers with the point of a knife. Place the roast fat side up on the rack in the roasting pan. Lean meats such as veal and lamb may need a covering of bacon, salt pork or suet to make them self-basting and prevent the meat from drying out. This is also advisable for birds such as chicken, turkey, squab, etc. Meats with a goodly proportion of marbling (interior fat) need no such protection. Although animal fat is shunned today because of its supposed calorie and cholesterol potential, and animals are bred to provide leaner meat, with less waste from trimming, fat keeps meat jucier, more tender, better tasting.

You can put the meat thermometer in the roast either at the beginning of roasting or when the meat has cooked a little, as you wish. Using the steel shaft of the thermometer as a measure, find the center of the meat and then insert the thermometer so that the tip is in the center of the thickest part, not touching bone, fat or gristle. If the roast is thin, insert the thermometer on a slant. For poultry, the thermometer should be inserted in the thickest part of the thigh or, if the bird is stuffed, into the center of the stuffing. If your range is equipped with a meat thermometer and cable that plugs into an oven outlet, with a separate temperature dial, set the dial knob to the required internal temperature, again remembering that it should be 10 degrees lower to allow for a temperature rise after the meat is taken from the oven.

METHODS OF ROASTING

Once it was thought that initial high-temperature searing sealed the juices in the meat, but this theory has been abandoned. The recommended method is a constant low-temperature roasting at 325°, with the temperature raised to 450° or 500° for the last 5 or 10 minutes if you want a browner exterior. Another method, recommended for very large roasts, is long, slow cooking at 200° which gives a minimum loss of juices and shrinkage. Check with the meat thermometer, and when the roast registers 10 degrees under the temperature you want, remove it from the oven, transfer it to a carving board or heated platter and let it stand for from 15 to 30 minutes. This not only finishes the cooking, but also makes carving easier as the collagen or connective tissues, softened by cooking, have time to set and the juices to settle.

When you use a standard meat thermometer, make allowance for the fact that the dial markings err on the side of overcooking and do not take into account the rise in internal temperature when the roast stands. Nowadays, many people prefer their meat under- rather than overcooked, and what would have been considered medium a few years back would now be called well done by most connoisseurs of rare roast beef or pink lamb. If you like your lamb pink, it should be removed from the oven while the needle is hovering between 130° and 135°; the dial marking for lamb, 185°, means it will be really overcooked.

Small roasts of tender meat which should be served very rare, such as a beef filet or rack of lamb, benefit from quick roasting at a high temperature. The filet should be barded, larded or smothered with butter and will take no more than 25 to 30 minutes to roast. The rack of lamb will be beautifully crisp on the outside. Roll it in a mixture of crumbs and chopped parsley before serving. Chicken will look and taste better if roasted at 400° rather than a lower temperature. It needs plenty of bacon or barding pork and should be roasted 25 minutes on one side, 25 minutes on the other, then turned breast up and basted well. With any poultry, but especially the smaller birds, one of the best tests for doneness is to move the leg up and down. If it wiggles easily, it is cooked to a turn. The following chart gives realistic roasting temperatures which you can adjust to your taste.

MEAT	OVEN TEMPERATURE	THERMOMETER MARKING (on removal from oven)
Beef, filet	500°	120°
Beef, rare	325°	120° (very rare) to 130°
Beef, medium	325°	140°
Beef, well	325°	150°
Lamb, rack of, rare	425°	120°
Lamb, rare	325°	130° to 135°
Lamb, medium	325°	140° to 150°
Lamb, well	325°	150° to 160°
Veal	325°	150° to 160°
Fresh pork or ham	325°	170° to 175° (temperature must be over 155° to kill trichinae which may lurk in underdone pork)
Chicken	350° to 400°	180° (in thigh)
Turkey	325°	180°
Duck	325°	180°
Goose	325°	180°

BROILING, GRILLING AND BARBECUING

Although broiling and grilling would seem to be one of the simplest of all methods of cooking, it is frequently misunderstood or misapplied—and the result is charred meat and dried-out seafood and poultry. Basically, broiling and grilling are the cooking of food over or under direct heat—a gas flame, electric burner or live coals. When the heat is applied by means of hot metal, it becomes pan broiling.

Although many foods can be broiled or grilled, meats, poultry and seafood remain the favorites, with beef the most popular of all. Beef lends itself to any of these forms of cooking, starting with pan broiling, a process not recommended for more delicate victuals.

PAN BROILING

Steaks of 1 to 1½-inch thickness and thick hamburgers can be pan broiled with excellent results. For pan broiling, put a heavy stainless steel, cast-aluminum or cast-iron skillet on direct heat and let it get smoking hot. No fat is added in pan broiling, but you may, if you wish, rub the pan lightly first with a piece of suet, or grease it a little. Or you can let the pan get red hot, and then cover the bottom with a thin layer of salt. Sear the salt lightly before adding the meat. Sear the meat quickly on both sides, then reduce the heat and cook until it is done to taste. This will take about 5 minutes a side for a rare steak, 8 to 10 minutes for medium rare (test for doneness by making a tiny cut near the bone). During pan broiling, turn meat so that it cooks evenly.

Two new aids to this form of cooking are a cast-iron broiler skillet and an enameled cast-iron grill which require no greasing or preparation. Ridges elevate the meat from the bottom of the pan and drain off any fat that may accumulate during cooking.

OVEN BROILING

For oven broiling, the food should be at room temperature and the broiler preheated until good and hot (5 to 8 minutes; 15 if you want your steak to sizzle and sear when it hits the rack). Without a meat thermometer that registers from 0 degrees (most start at 140), it is impossible to tell the internal temperature of meat, but it is better not to abide by the old rule-of-thumb about taking meat out of the refrigerator an hour before cooking time. A thick steak may take 1½ to 2 hours to warm up, considerably more if it has been in the cold embrace of the freezer.

If you are broiling with gas, reduce the flame from the high broil setting used to preheat to a setting that is slightly more than moderate, or about 350 degrees, for cooking. Electric broilers do not need this adjustment. Close the door on a gas broiler during cooking, but leave it slightly ajar if the range is electric. You may find some divergence in cooking times according to the type and age of the equipment you use. Electric heat that radiates down often proves to be faster than gas, where heat from the open flames tends to rise. There are exceptions. For instance, the heat emanating from infra-red ceramic gas broilers is quicker and more concentrated because it is transmitted through a screen of tiny holes.

With the standard horizontal broiling unit, meat is generally cooked with the surface at a distance of 3 inches from the heat source, although in certain instances (if a steak is very thick), it may be cooked part of the time at a distance of 5 inches.

Before broiling, grease the rack so the meat does not stick. Trim excess fat from the meat to reduce spattering of grease, and slash the remaining fat at 1-inch intervals to prevent curling. Season the meat before cooking or not, as you prefer. This does not draw out the juices, as many people believe, provided the surface is seared quickly. You might want to brush the meat with soy sauce or Kitchen Bouquet in order to add flavor to it and give it an appetizing color.

Timing, temperature and distance from the broiler all depend on the food being cooked.

Steaks for broiling should be at least 1 inch thick, preferably 1½ to 2½ inches. The exception is flank steak, a naturally thin cut. It should be placed near the flame and cooked rapidly, 4 minutes on one side and 3 on the other, until it is brown outside and juicily rare within. A 1½-inch steak cooked 4 to 5 minutes on one side, turned and cooked a further 5 minutes, will be rare. For a medium steak, increase the time to 6 to 8 minutes for each side. Sear 2 to 2½-inch steaks on each side 3 inches from the flame, then lower the meat to 5 inches and cook until done as desired.

Hamburger patties may dry out during broiling. To avoid this, shape 8 ounces of meat into patties 1 inch thick and broil 6 minutes per side, brushing with butter. A chip of ice in the center of each patty will help to keep hamburger moist.

Lamb chops, if small, may be cooked briefly under a hot broiler, 3 to 4 minutes on one side, 4 on the other. But if the chops are 3-rib or thick loin, they cook better if started in the oven at 450 degrees and finished off under the broiler.

Veal chops can be broiled successfully provided they are brushed and basted with butter, cooked slowly at a distance of 5 inches and then brought up to brown. Close cooking without added fat dries them out.

Ham steaks of the ready-to-eat variety take only a few minutes to broil. A country ham steak will require 20 minutes.

Spareribs, if meaty, need 12 to 13 minutes per side. If the ribs are not so meaty, 10 to 11 minutes will usually be sufficient.

Liver steaks between 1 and 1½ inches thick should be given 5 to 6 minutes a side.

Veal kidneys, trimmed of fat, also need quick cooking —5 minutes for rare, 8 minutes for medium.

Sausages, blanched first in boiling water, broil to a turn in 10 minutes.

Chicken is usually overcooked. For juicy chicken,

broil 13 to 15 minutes on the bone side, 12 to 15 minutes on the skin side. Increase the time if you want it more thoroughly done, and if the chicken is thicker than average, broil 5 inches from the heat, allowing 15 minutes per side, to keep the skin from charring.

Squab chicken, split and broiled, takes 7 minutes on the bone side, 6 minutes on the skin side. Start low and raise to color the skin.

Duck will be delightfully crisp if broiled bone-side up at a distance of 5 inches from the flame for 20 minutes, turned and broiled 15 minutes on the skin side, then raised very close to the flame to brown the skin, which should be pricked well first.

Lobsters of average size (1¼ pounds) should have about 10 to 11 minutes under the broiler and plenty of buttery basting.

Fish fillets are best broiled on foil, without turning. Broil for 5 to 6 minutes, or until the flesh just flakes, brushing midway with melted butter. Fish steaks 1½ inches thick will need 10 minutes.

Whole fish, if small, broil in 10 minutes; larger fish, 15 to 20 minutes.

BARBECUE GRILLING

Although the heat source here is *under* rather than *over* the food, the same principles apply. The meat should be at room temperature and the heat 350 degrees at grill level. The process of searing (and flaming, if a charred finish is desired) is controlled by adjusting the grill or the firebox so that the meat is close to the coals at first. Increase the distance for cooking. If the grill is not adjustable, you will have to control and temper the heat by spreading the coals or dousing them with a fine spray of water from a sprinkler bottle.

The fire is the heart of barbecuing. First line the bottom of the fire bowl with heavy aluminum foil. This will increase the radiant heat and catch the drippings and can be easily discarded at cleanup time. Then arrange a fire base of gravel or similar material in a level layer about 1 inch deep. This allows the fire to breathe, drawing more heat from the coals, and protects the metal and absorbs grease. The base should be renewed after six barbecues.

For fuel, charcoal briquets made from hardwood are the most readily obtainable and popular. They are clean, easy to handle and give consistent heat. Some briquets are made from anthracite and come in small bags with a starter—you only need to light the bag. This fuel is especially suitable for portable grills.

To start a fire, build a pyramid of briquets and pour about ½ cup of odorless commercial starting fluid over them. Let the liquid soak in for 2 minutes and then set alight. For a fast start to the fire, use pre-soaked briquets. Put them in a can, fill with fluid, cover and let stand at least an hour, preferably several days. Arrange the soaked briquets in a heap on the fire bed, mound unsoaked ones over them and light the saturated briquets. If you prefer, you can use one of the electric fire starters now on the market, but *never* resort to kerosene, gasoline or alcohol. These fluids are dangerous and their fumes will give the food an unpleasant taste and odor.

You don't have to load the firebox with charcoal to get a good fire. The area of the fire should be regulated by the capacity of the firebox and the size and shape of the food you are cooking. When the fire is burning well and a gray ash begins to show on the coals (after about half an hour), spread the coals evenly over the desired cooking area, leaving about an inch of space in between so drippings can fall on the gravel. Scatter new briquets around the edges of the fire so they can be pulled to the center when ignited to maintain an even heat. Sear steak quickly on both sides, close to the coals, then move it farther away from the heat and finish the cooking more slowly. If you wish to char the surface at the end of the cooking time, raise the firebox or lower the grill and, if necessary, drop a piece of suet in the fire to make it flare up.

It is almost impossible to lay down rules about barbecue cooking time. So many factors have to be taken into consideration—the size, thickness and temperature of the food, the temperature and distance from the grill of the fire, the atmosphere and the direction of the wind. Generally speaking, the timing will be much the same as for indoor broiling, perhaps a few minutes longer, but the best way to estimate when the food is done to your liking is by previous experience. If you are uncertain, test with a meat thermometer or make a small incision in the cooked food to help you to judge the state of doneness.

SPIT BARBECUING

For spit barbecuing, rake the ashy coals into two lines, one at the back and one at the front of the fire basket, and place a drip pan or pan fashioned from heavy aluminum foil in the space directly beneath the meat to catch the drippings. Or you may arrange the coals in a circle with the pan in the center. Spit the roast, making sure it is evenly balanced, insert the holding forks, tighten the screws to hold securely and put over the fire. The procedure is much the same as for broiling except that a lower temperature of 250 degrees at spit level is recommended. Insert a meat thermometer and gauge doneness with this—always remembering that with any broiled, barbecued or roasted meat or poultry, the internal temperature continues to go up *after* the food is removed from the fire. Remove the spit from the rotisserie when the thermometer registers 10 degrees less than the desired state of doneness (for a check list of recommended internal temperatures, see roasting chart). Do not leave thermometer in meat during cooking; this will ruin it. Insert only to check temperature, then remove. Let the meat remain on the spit for half an hour before carving.

Have on hand for barbecuing:

A meat thermometer to test inside temperature of roasts and thick steaks during barbecuing or rotisserie cooking, and a grill thermometer to check heat.

A bottle of water with a sprinkler top for dousing flare-ups of grease.

A long-handled basting brush.

Drip pans to catch drips from spit roasting.

Tongs for turning barbecued foods, lifting potatoes from coals.

Hinged grills to hold and turn fish fillets, hamburgers, thin steaks, chicken, shrimp, etc.

Asbestos gloves to wear while adjusting spit, grill, spreading fire.

SAUTÉING AND FRYING

Frying in all its forms, from sautéing to deep-fat frying, is more complex than it might at first appear. Sautéing, the French version of pan frying, calls for the cooking of food in a small amount of fat, usually in an open skillet. The difference is that in pan frying (or pan broiling, as it is also called) the food is allowed to brown on one side, then turned and browned on the other, whereas in sautéing, the food is kept in motion, either by shaking the pan or stirring with a wooden spoon. Sautéed food may be completely cooked through (this usually applies to fish, thin slices of meat like veal scaloppine or vegetables) or merely seared and browned, the case when beef or chicken is to be further cooked in a ragoût.

Temperatures vary according to the nature of the food. Beef must be seared at a high temperature to seal in the juices; chicken, white meats, fish and vegetables are sautéed at lower temperatures. For recipes that stipulate a *sauté blanc* (white sauté), food is cooked more slowly at a lower temperature and not allowed to reach the golden-brown color of the regular *sauté brun*. The fat must be sizzling hot (for beef, almost smoking) before any food is added and only a few pieces should be cooked at a time. Crowding the pan lowers the heat and the food steams rather than browns. It is always a good rule when sautéing meat, fish or poultry to cook at one time only as many pieces as the pan can comfortably accommodate without overlapping. The food should be absolutely dry before going into the pan or steam will develop between food and fat. Sometimes, to absorb moisture, the meat is dredged with flour, the excess shaken off. This is done just before cooking or the juices soak through the coating.

Butter is the fat most favored for sautéing as it adds flavor, but it also has a low smoking point and decomposes or burns at high temperatures. Butter is less likely to burn if the milky sediment has been removed through clarifying or if it is heated with a little oil. The rich brown glaze that forms in the bottom of the pan when food is cooked quickly in fat at a high temperature is lifted by a process called deglazing.

To deglaze a pan, you either add liquid (wine, stock, water) and stir with a wooden spoon until the glaze comes away from the pan or you blaze the pan with lighted spirits, which also lifts and liquefies the brown coating. These pan juices may be added to a ragoût or, if the meat is served right after sautéing, poured over the finished dish. As high temperature is an important part of sautéing, the pan you use should be the heavy, flat-bottomed kind that will distribute heat evenly and move easily over the burners when the pan is shaken. It should also have a tight-fitting lid, for in many recipes, slow, covered top-of-the-stove cooking follows the sautéing process.

FRENCH FRYING, DEEP AND SHALLOW

In this type of frying, where food is covered with a deep or shallow layer of fat or oil (oil, which is colorless, odorless and has a high decomposition point is usually preferred), the cooking must be quick, the temperature high and constant if the food is to be thoroughly cooked inside, crisp and brown outside and relatively free from fat absorption.

For French frying, the oil is heated to—and kept at—a temperature of between 350° and 375°. Only small amounts of well-dried food should be fried at one time as their addition causes the temperature to drop. This is especially true of things like chicken Kiev and croquettes that have been coated with flour, egg and crumbs and chilled to make the coating adhere (it is a good idea to let them warm up for an hour before cooking). Batter-dipped foods also need room to expand during cooking. Crumb or batter-coated foods should be lowered slowly into the hot oil by means of a wire basket, slotted spoon or tongs or they are apt to lose their coating. Once they have cooked to golden brown on one side, turn them with a slotted spoon. Any odd bits of batter or crumbs should be skimmed and discarded during cooking. Electric fryers and skillets are recommended for shallow and deep-fat frying. If you do use a nonautomatic pan or kettle, be sure to check the temperature with a deep-fat thermometer.

BRAISING AND STEWING

No matter how tough a cut of meat or an old bird may be, there are two allied methods of cooking that are guaranteed to turn it into a luscious mouthful—braising and stewing. In both methods (and in pot roasting, which is similar), food is cooked in liquid in a heavy covered pan or casserole at a low temperature, either in the oven or over direct heat. The combination of long, slow cooking and moisture (from the liquid and the steam that condenses under the pan lid) helps to soften and break down the connective tissue that makes meat hard on the jaws, while the low temperature prevents the liquid from reducing too rapidly and the meat from shrinking, drying out and becoming stringy. The slight difference between stewing and braising lies mostly in the amount of liquid used—more for a stew, less for braising or pot roasting where the juices should cook down to a thick, rich sauce. For this reason, braised foods are frequently cooked in a wide, shallow type of pan or covered skillet, so the liquid can reduce, while stews may be cooked in a Dutch oven, deep pan or casserole or the classic French cocotte. Fricassees and such French recipes as Estouffade de Boeuf, Boeuf en Daube, Blanquette de Veau and Navarin d'Agneau are all variations on these basic processes.

PRINCIPLES OF BRAISING AND STEWING

Although you occasionally find such delicate morsels as filet of beef being braised, mainly for the wonderfully rich flavor that results, the cuts of meat recommended for braising, stewing and pot roasting are usually those that are less tender (and less expensive) or definitely bony, such as beef eye of the round, top and bottom round, rump and chuck, flank, neck, brisket, oxtail and short ribs; pork loin or shoulder; veal shoulder, breast, shanks and neck. If you are stewing or braising poultry, you will find that roasting, stewing or frying chickens are better than young broilers, which tend to fall apart. Game and game birds also benefit from the tenderizing qualities of stewing and braising.

You may cook the meat in one piece (for pot roast or French boeuf à la mode) or cut it up, usually into cubes or sections of at least 2 inches. Whole pieces of meat should weigh about 3 pounds and have a depth of 4 inches or more, to allow for shrinkage. The flavor and texture of less choice cuts can be improved, and the meat rendered juicier and tenderer, either by larding (inserting strips of fat with a larding needle), or by marinating in a mixture of wine, vegetables and herbs (the marinade can be used later as part of the cooking liquor).

Meats or poultry to be braised, stewed or pot roasted, whether whole or cut up, should first be browned in hot fat to seal in the juices and give flavor to the cooking liquid. (An exception is the white French veal or lamb stew called a blanquette where, traditionally, the meat is blanched and then simmered in stock and flavoring vegetables, without prior browning.) If meat has been marinated, it must be drained and dried thoroughly before browning. When browning cubed meat, put only a few pieces at a time in the pan and brown them well on all sides (they should not touch each other or be in more than one layer, or the heat will drop, the juices run out and the meat steam rather than sear). If you want to eliminate the fat, you may brown the whole or cubed meat under the broiler—quickly if placed near the heat, for a longer time if put on a lower shelf—and flame it on the broiler pan. It is very important during browning not to pierce the meat with a fork, or the juices will escape. Instead, use metal tongs to turn small pieces of meat, two wooden spoons for whole cuts and birds. Occasionally a recipe will call for meat to be floured before browning, which makes it darker in color and serves to thicken the liquid.

After browning, the pan may be deglazed by flaming it with heated, lighted brandy or a similar spirit, a process that liquefies and removes the brown glaze adhering to the pan after the meat is colored. When the flames have died down, you remove the meat from the pan and add the liquid (preferably stock or a mixture of wine and stock), seasonings and flavorings. Then bring the liquid to a boil, replace the meat, reduce the heat so the liquid merely simmers and cover the pan.

To prevent a stew from becoming too liquid, put a piece of waxed paper under the lid to catch the condensing steam. Vegetables may be added, according to the recipe. You can sauté onions and carrots or mushrooms after the meat and cook them with it, or put vegetables in the pot at a later stage of cooking, or cook them separately and combine with the meat near the end of the cooking time. If you like the flavor of the vegetables to permeate a stew, but don't want them overcooked, add just one of each vegetable at the beginning of the cooking time and the rest toward the end. Once the stew, pot roast or braised dish is cooked, you should skim off any fat that has collected on the surface (with a metal spoon or bulb baster, by putting paper toweling on the surface or by chilling the liquid and then removing the fat layer) and, if necessary, thicken the sauce with beurre manié (small balls of butter and flour), potato starch, cornstarch or arrowroot mixed with a little cold water, or by reducing the liquid over high heat after the meat and vegetables have been removed with a slotted spoon. Sauces that are too thick may be thinned with a little stock. It is a good idea to check during cooking—pot roasts, which cook in a minimum of liquid, may need basting or turning, and the level of braising or stewing liquids may need bolstering. Practically all stewed, braised or pot-roasted meats improve with reheating, when the flavors have had a chance to mellow and blend, and will definitely taste better the second time around— or even cold, in the case of pot roasts. Chicken is more chancy. It requires less cooking time than meat and may disintegrate if reheated too vigorously.

THE BRAISING OF VEGETABLES

Braising applies not only to meats, poultry and game, but also to many types of vegetables, especially those that are green and leafy, such as lettuce, endive, chicory, celery and cabbage. Artichokes, brussels sprouts, chestnuts, onions, leeks and such root vegetables as carrots and turnips are also delicious braised. This is a distinctively French way of cooking vegetables and well worth trying, as the result is delicious and far different from that of simple boiling. To remove the bitterness or pungent flavor from a vegetable such as endives or old turnips, you may blanch them before braising, either by putting them in cold water, bringing them slowly to a boil, and draining, or by plunging them into boiling salted water and letting the water return to the boil for a few minutes.

Vegetables may be braised in the oven or on the range. Oven-braised vegetables are usually cooked in a shallow, fireproof covered casserole or in a baking dish large enough to hold them in a single layer with butter, seasonings and stock and covered with a piece of buttered waxed paper. Sometimes the dish is buttered and occasionally the vegetables are arranged on a bed of chopped onion and carrot with an herb bouquet and bacon, to give them a very rich flavor (this may be done with lettuce, celery or endive). Oven cooking is recommended for vegetables that need gentle heat and long, slow cooking. You can cook hardier vegetables, like onions, carrots and turnips, more quickly in a covered skillet over direct heat. In either case, after you have removed the vegetables from the braising dish, pour the cooking juices, strained, reduced and thickened if necessary, over them as a flavorful sauce.

BOILING, STEAMING AND POACHING

Boiling, steaming, simmering and poaching are allied methods of cooking with water and other liquids. Water boils when it reaches a temperature of 212° F. at sea level (the temperature decreases 1° for every 500 feet of altitude) and bubbles rise to the surface and break. There are different boils—fast, medium and slow. In a fast boil, the liquid seethes, rolls, rises and vaporizes. This kind of boil is called for when a stock has to be reduced rapidly by evaporation, or in steaming to produce sufficient volume of vapor to cook the food. With a medium boil, the heat is not so intense and the water reduces more slowly. In a slow boil, almost a simmer, the bubbles just break the surface. Simmering water, just below the boiling point, moves gently and the bubbles break below the surface. This is the temperature for cooking stews and sauces, soups and meats or poultry. In poaching, the temperature is still lower and the liquid does not bubble at all, but barely shivers—the French call this a *faible ébullition*. Fish, quenelles, eggs and other delicate foods are usually poached.

BOILING AND STEAMING

The word boiled as applied to certain foods is a misnomer. Boiled beef and chicken are not boiled at all, but simmered after being brought to a boil, for boiling would disintegrate the muscle fibers and make them dry and stringy. Fish is never boiled, but hard-shelled crab and lobster are—they should be plunged into piping hot water or court bouillon and cooked at a rolling boil. Pasta (noodles, macaroni, spaghetti) needs to be cooked in large amounts of rapidly boiling salted water so that the starch granules in the durum wheat paste have room to swell (a tablespoon of oil added to the water stops them sticking to the bottom of the pan).

Vegetables are mostly boiled uncovered in order to release in the steam strong flavors and odors and the acids liberated by cooking. Generally speaking, the amount of water used to cook vegetables is a matter of preference, but artichokes and corn need a deep pan and plenty of liquid, leaf spinach and shredded cabbage are best if cooked in minimum water (spinach only in the water that clings to the leaves after washing), while most other vegetables are cooked in water to cover. You may also steam vegetables over boiling water. This works particularly well for tender young vegetables and frozen vegetables, besides retaining the nutrients that would otherwise be transferred to the water. Herbs added to the steaming water give flavor.

Although stocks are boiled to reduce their water content and intensify the flavor, this should only be done *after* they have been thoroughly simmered, strained and degreased, or the fat and scum will be incorporated into the liquid and turn it cloudy. When the stock is clear and fat-free, you can boil it at full tilt until it becomes no more than a strong meat glaze or *glace de viande*. Mixtures of herbs and wine for flavoring sauces are also boiled down to a glaze. Thin sauces may be thickened by judicious cooking at a slow-to-medium boil over moderate heat.

Boiling—or boiling water—also figures in blanching and scalding. Blanching, in which food is immersed in boiling water and allowed to steep or cook slightly, removes strong flavors, odors and bitterness from such foods as salt pork, cabbage and endive. It also loosens the skins of nuts. Scalding, where the food is briefly submerged in boiling water, then removed and plunged into cold water, is a form of blanching used for vegetables that are to be frozen and as a means of loosening the skins of tomatoes and peaches without actually cooking them.

In steaming, the food is not cooked in the boiling liquid, but above it, either in a perforated steamer or the top of a double boiler, by direct contact with steam or the heat it generates. Steaming is a longer, gentler process than boiling. It keeps fish and vegetables firm, dries and separates the grains of rice and other cereals and opens the shells of clams and mussels without overcooking the tender meat or dissipating the juices. Puddings such as Christmas puddings, suet puddings and sponges are also steamed. For this you fill a buttered mold or pudding basin two-thirds to three-quarters full with the pudding mixture (the leeway allows for expansion) and cover it with the lid or a piece of aluminum foil. You then place the mold or basin in the top of a steamer or on a rack in a deep kettle over boiling water (if a rack is used, the water should come no more than halfway up the sides of the mold) and steam it, covered. As the water cooks away, you add more boiling water.

TWO WAYS TO POACH EGGS

To poach in skillet, have 2″ of water simmering. Break egg into custard cup, touch rim to water, slide egg in. Poach; remove with slotted spoon. For saucepan method, stir large amount of simmering water to whirlpool with spoon, slide egg into it from custard cup. To firm whites, add vinegar to water or dip unshelled egg briefly into boiling water before poaching.

SIMMERING AND POACHING

These methods are so closely related that about the best way to distinguish them is to say that in simmering the face of the water shows a grin, while in poaching there is no more than a smile. (For large fish, the water should grin, for fillets, smile.)

Poaching may be done on top of the stove or in the oven. Whole birds and fish, galantines and ballottines, gnocchi and quenelles, which need large pans and plenty of liquid, are cooked on top of the stove, so are eggs and fruits poached in wine and sugar syrup. Fish fillets are usually cooked in the oven in a buttered fireproof dish after the poaching liquid in the dish has been brought almost to a simmer on top of the stove. (Buttered wax paper on top of the fillets prevents their drying out.)

BAKING

While cooking is an art, and thrives on improvisation and adaptation, baking is a science. Inaccuracy—in equipment, measuring or methods—is the most common cause of baking flops. To begin with, your oven thermostat should be absolutely accurate. If you are at all in doubt, inquire at your local utilities company or gas appliance service organization about having your oven calibrated. Next check your measuring cups and spoons: they should be standard and accurate. And always before starting on a recipe, read it thoroughly to acquaint yourself with the steps of preparation (for instance, to see if the flour should be sifted before or after measuring), then assemble all the necessary ingredients and equipment. Unless otherwise specified, have all ingredients at room temperature. This can make a difference. Egg whites at room temperature, for example, yield a greater volume when whipped than cold egg whites. Be sure that the flour is the type called for in the recipe.

Accurate measurements are vitally important in baking. European recipes often call for dry ingredients to be weighed on scales, which gives even greater preciseness, but most American recipes are predicated on cup and spoon measures. When a level measure is called for in a recipe, use standard measuring cups and spoons and level the ingredients off with a metal spatula or knife. To measure butter or shortening by the cup, pour into the cup enough cold water to equal the difference between the amount of fat required and the full cup measure (for 1/3 cup butter, use 2/3 cup water), gradually add the fat until water reaches the cup mark, then pour off the water. When measuring sticky syrups, honey or molasses, grease the cup first and you will find that the syrup will slide out without leaving a residue behind.

Even in such an exact science as baking, there are times when you have to use your own judgment about the consistency of a dough or batter, which may be affected by ingredients, climate or altitude. If you are using very large eggs, you may have to add more flour to get the right consistency. Or, if the flour is very dry (which may happen in winter, in a warm room), the amount of liquid may have to be stepped up. In damp climates, it may be necessary to reduce the amount of water in a pie crust or cookie mix.

Other common causes of baking failures are over-beating of cake batters, overfolding and overblending. Overmixing of muffin batters makes the muffins heavy and tough; overfolding of egg whites breaks down the air bubbles that give a cake lightness. Remember that electric beaters are very fast—the ½ hour of hand beating specified in many old recipes is cut to 5 minutes with an electric beater.

EQUIPMENT

Equipment in tip-top condition is essential for good baking. Pans should be clean, bright, smooth and unwarped—and the right size. Warped pans bake and brown unevenly. If a pan is too large for the amount of batter, the cake will be pale, flat and shrunken, while too small a pan may cause overflowing. Pans of medium-weight aluminum or glass are best for baking as they conduct heat quickly and evenly.

Cast-iron popover or muffin pans, which must be preheated, should be greased with oil, rather than butter or shortening, as oil may be heated to a higher temperature. When cake pans or cookie sheets have to be prepared for baking, follow the instructions in the recipe. To grease and flour, apply melted butter with a pastry brush, then dust with flour. You can also dust cake pans with fine bread crumbs instead of flour to make the cakes come out more easily. Pans for sponge and angel food cakes should not be greased. A useful trick is to line cake pans or cookie sheets with silicone-treated parchment (manufactured in rolls and sheets by the KVP Co., and sold in household departments of stores). This prevents sticking and is especially good for torten, meringues and sweet rolls.

Pour cake batter into the prepared pans and spread evenly to the edges with a rubber spatula. Fill layer cake pans about two-thirds full and tube pans about three-quarters full.

TECHNIQUES

The basic techniques involved in baking are stirring, beating, creaming, folding, kneading and rolling. Stirring, in which ingredients are mixed with a wooden spoon or spatula until just combined, is mostly used for muffin batters or very delicate cakes or cookies. In beating, a rotary or electric beater is usually the implement, although a wooden spoon may be used if the mixture (such as a cream puff paste) is stiff. The ingredients must be thoroughly incorporated or they may separate, forming a solid layer at the bottom of the pan.

In creaming, two or more ingredients (such as sugar and eggs or butter and sugar) are beaten together with a wooden spoon or in a mixer until the mixture becomes pale yellow in color, fluffy, and forms a slow ribbon that falls back into the bowl when the spoon or beater is lifted. The sugar is added gradually to the yolks during the creaming. If you are using a mixer to cream butter and sugar, a slight degree of warmth facilitates creaming. Cut the butter into ½-inch pieces, warm the bowl in hot water, dry it and then cream the butter and sugar for several minutes at moderate speed. Folding is the gentlest way to combine ingredients and prevents the air cells from breaking down when a light, delicate ingredient such as beaten eggs or whipped cream is added to a heavier one. When both ingredients are liquid, pour the less fluffy on top of the other (the sauce base for a soufflé on to the stiffly beaten egg whites, for example). If one is dry, sprinkle it on the fluffy one and gradually fold in, with a steady but gentle down, up and over movement. Most people use a rubber spatula for folding, but your hand is just as good an implement, as you literally feel what you are doing.

Hands are also the most common tools for kneading, although some mixers do have a dough hook attachment. Kneading, a process used for making yeast doughs and—in conjunction with rolling—for puff pastry, develops the gluten in the flour and makes the dough smooth and elastic. Soft doughs may be kneaded in a wide bowl and should be worked and pulled away from the sides of the bowl until they no longer stick to either the bowl or the hands. Heavier doughs are kneaded on a flat, lightly floured surface or board by folding them over, pressing them down and pushing with the heel of the hand. They are then rotated a little, folded and kneaded again. The flour on the board should be kept to a minimum or the dough will be tough. This also applies to rolled-out doughs, the kind used for cookies and pastries. This kind of dough usually rolls better if it has been chilled and if you handle only a small amount at a time (overhandling is another cause of tough pastry). It's a good idea when working with soft, sticky doughs (yeast doughs, strudel) to roll them out on a floured cloth and use a heavy, ball-bearing rolling pin and even pressure. Cookie doughs and tart shells that are made from richer, less sticky doughs may be rolled between sheets of waxed paper (this prevents them from absorbing too much flour) with a tapered French pastry pin, not too much pressure.

TEMPERATURES

It is almost impossible to specify temperatures for baking. Certain cakes that need long, slow cooking (such as fruit cakes) may be baked at 250°, angel food cakes at 325° and other kinds of cake at 350°. Temperatures for cookies range from 325° to 400°, while breads, yeast doughs and biscuits, pie pastry and cream puffs may be baked at from 350° to 450°, according to type. To test a cake, insert a toothpick near the center. If it comes out clean, the cake is done. Or touch the top lightly with your fingertip. If the top springs back, the cake is done. It needs longer baking if the imprint remains.

Once baked, the cake should be taken from the oven and the pan put on a wire rack to cool. Don't leave the cake in the pan for more than 10 minutes; it should be removed while still warm and soft (the exceptions are delicate sponge and angel food cakes which should be cooled in the pan to keep them from collapsing). Run a spatula between the cake and the sides of the pan to loosen it. Invert the cake onto a clean towel on a wire rack, top side down, then invert onto a second rack.

TIPS

Add a pinch of salt to sugar for frosting to prevent graininess; add a pinch of salt to egg whites before beating to make them mound faster.

Unless otherwise specified, always bake on middle shelf of oven.

Never overload the oven—this will extend the baking time. If you are baking on two shelves at once, switch the pans around when two-thirds of the baking time has elapsed, to counteract any unevenness of heat in the oven. When using two pans, stagger them in opposite corners of the oven. If you are using three, place the third pan on a rack about 2 inches higher than the middle shelf, but not directly over either of the first two pans. Use top rack only for last-minute browning.

Place filled pie shells, which need more intense heat from underneath in order to bake through properly, on the lowest rack.

To prevent cream puffs from becoming soggy as they cool, puncture small puffs or split larger ones and remove uncooked center portion.

If you have difficulty removing a baked cake from the pan, place the hot pan on a damp cloth for a few seconds; steam helps release the cake.

If you have difficulty removing thin, crisp wafers from the baking sheet, hold the sheet over the range so the direct heat is under one wafer for a few seconds. This softens it enough so that it can be removed. Repeat with other wafers.

To prevent fruitcakes from overbrowning, line pan with aluminum foil, leaving an overhang on all four sides. This protects the bottom and sides during baking. Once cake has browned, draw overhangs of foil over the top to keep the crust from drying out.

As a substitute for sour milk or buttermilk, add 1 tablespoon vinegar or lemon juice to 1 cup sweet milk and let it stand for 3 minutes.

COOKING WITH FOIL

Although aluminum foil has been with us a comparatively short time—for less than twenty years—it is almost impossible to think of a kitchen without it. No other culinary development has so affected every aspect of food preparation and storage, from roasting to freezing. Not the least of the virtues of foil is the alleviation of that essential but uninspiring sequel to a meal—clean up—for almost anything can be cooked in an expendable foil package, while broilers, burners and ovens can be protected with foil liners and drip trays. Nowadays it is easy to find the size and weight of foil you need, for it comes in widths up to 18 inches as well as in small individual sheets for baking potatoes, heating rolls, covering dishes—and in two qualities, regular and super-strength or heavy-duty. Foil is acknowledged to be one of the best materials for cooking since it conducts but does not retain heat and has no flavor that might be transferred to food. Its familiar uses are manifold; in addition, a few new wrinkles have been developed.

ROASTING AND BRAISING IN FOIL

A few years back foil became famous as a brand-new method of cooking turkey under wraps—covered by either a loose tent or form-fitting jacket of foil that kept the bird juicy and flavorful. The tent, actually an improvement on the old cheesecloth-dipped-in-fat routine, is especially popular because it keeps the bird moist without the fuss of basting, but still permits some heat to flow over the bird and brown it. In the completely covered method, the turkey is encased in two large pieces of heavy foil joined with a double fold that permits it to be cooked in a quarter less time at a higher temperature. However, the result is not so crisp, and to brown the surface, the foil must be open for the last 45 minutes cooking time.

An extension of this idea led to pot roasting and braising in foil. For pot roasting, the meat is placed on a large sheet of heavy foil with a shallow pan underneath and browned on all sides under the broiler (vegetables can be added toward the end of the browning so that they also take on a little color). Then the meat is removed from the oven, wine or liquid added, the foil sealed tightly, the package returned to the oven and cooked at 300 degrees until the meat is tender—about 3½ hours for a 4- to 5-pound chuck roast.

For braising, you can follow much the same proce-

dure, apart from the initial browning. A country ham is especially delicious when braised in foil rather than cooked in water. First soak the ham. Then trim off skin and all but ¼-inch layer of fat. Place ham in the center of a large sheet of heavy foil in a roasting pan. Pour over it 1½ cups Madeira; sprinkle with seasonings. Bring up long sides of foil, overlap loosely on top of ham and close open ends by turning up to keep juices in (do not seal airtight). Bake at 350 degrees for 2½ hours for a whole ham, opening the foil and basting with the juices a couple of times.

FISH IN FOIL

Delicate fish stand a better chance of remaining intact if cooked in foil. Even large fish such as salmon are now poached whole in foil and water rather than in the traditional cheesecloth and court bouillon (with foil there is no necessity for flavored stock as fish will not come in direct contact with liquid).

Foil has also replaced cooking parchment for the classic French *en papillote* fish cookery. Heart-shaped pieces are cut from foil to enclose fish, liquid and seasonings. A variation calls for a square of foil large enough to enclose the fish envelope-style. The sides are brought up and sealed tightly with double folds and the ends secured by double folds, then turned in like an envelope.

When fish is to be broiled, put a sheet of heavy foil on the rack or in a shallow pan and grease the portion the fish will touch. Place fish on foil, brush with butter, season and broil. Thin fillets will not need turning, thicker fish steaks do. Thick fish should be arranged on a strip of foil slightly larger than the fish, which is then laid on the foil-covered rack or pan. When one side is cooked, slide a large spatula under the piece of foil the fish is resting on and flip the fish and foil over. Peel off foil and broil second side.

VEGETABLES IN FOIL

Vegetables lend themselves to foil cooking as all their natural flavor and vitamins are retained. They can be sealed in foil packages with butter and seasonings and baked like fish, or different vegetables may be boiled in one pan in separate foil packages without

WAYS TO USE FOIL

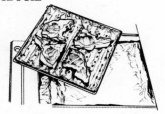

To protect broiler, mold heavy foil in bottom to catch drips. Cover broiler tray with foil, piercing it over slots to let grease drip through onto foil underneath.

To hard-cook eggs, especially cracked ones, encase in foil, bunch end into handle for removal from water.

For turkey tent, tear off sheet of heavy foil about 4 inches longer than turkey. Crease lengthwise down middle and pinch ends together. Place loosely over turkey to allow air circulation during the roasting.

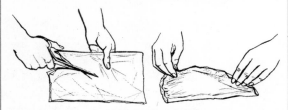

To make case for en papillote cooking, double a square of heavy foil, cut in shape of a half heart. Open up, lay food on one side, fold other side over and crimp edges, allowing some slack in middle for expansion.

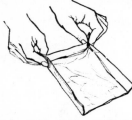

To shape pans for baking, take piece of heavy foil of desired size. Turn up the edges 1 inch all the way around, then miter the corners to keep the pan firm.

transference of flavors, each being removed as it is done. Leftover vegetables will keep their firmness and color if quickly steamed in foil on a rack over hot water until heated through. Potatoes can, of course, be baked in foil in a hot oven (don't keep them wrapped more than ½ hour after baking or they get limp). Yet another trick, if the oven is in use, is to put four layers of foil in an electric skillet, preheat to 375 degrees, add the potatoes, pricked with a fork, cover and bake for 60 minutes, turning once after 30 minutes cooking time.

BAKING WITH FOIL

If you are short on pans, foil can save the day. You can make a flan ring, for instance, by folding a long sheet of foil over and over lengthwise until you have a firm band 1 inch wide. Shape it into the desired round or rectangle and secure with a paper clip. To shape a jelly-roll pan, cover a cookie sheet or the back of a roasting pan with heavy foil and turn up the edges 1 inch all the way around, mitering the corners to make a firm pan. Different sizes of pie plates are a cinch: Roll out the pastry and cut a foil circle of the same size. Prick pastry, place on foil and turn up the edges all around, pinching at intervals to keep firm. Pie shells can be baked and served in the foil or frozen and baked later.

You can economize on cookie sheets by forming cookies, meringues or cream puffs directly on sheets of foil. To bake, slide one sheet onto a cookie sheet. When the first batch has baked, slide off the foil and slide on the next foil sheet of cookies.

You will have no trouble loosening a cake from the pan if you first put a strip of foil across the pan bottom, with one end extending up the side like a tab. As most cakes stick in the center where you cannot get at them with a spatula, all you have to do is pull on the foil tab and the cake will come away easily at the bottom.

MORE WAYS TO USE FOIL

Close the vent of poultry with crushed foil instead of skewering or sewing. It keeps stuffing in, is much easier to remove.

Protect exposed bones of meat or poultry (tips of crown roasts, drumsticks) with little foil caps to prevent charring during cooking.

Guard china dishes holding desserts to be browned with a heat-reflective layer of foil. After browning, cut away exposed foil.

Bring breads and rolls back to just-baked crispness by wrapping them in foil (add a few drops of water if very dried out), sealing and heating 30 minutes in a 350 degree oven. Or put 1 tablespoon water and four layers foil in an electric skillet, preheat to 275 degrees, add rolls, cover and heat about 15 minutes.

Section a casserole or baking dish with a liner and center division of foil, so two vegetables or mixtures can be baked at one time.

Freeze dishes made in quantity by lining a casserole with foil, adding the food, cooling, covering and freezing. Once the food is frozen, you can remove it, seal it in the foil and store it, while the casserole goes back into service. Comes time to use, you simply replace the foil package in the casserole and heat.

Make a drip pan of heavy foil to go in the oven under any food that might boil over and stick. Be sure to leave several inches between the sides of the foil pan and oven walls for air circulation. It is inadvisable to line the oven or cover the oven bottom completely as this not only causes uneven heat distribution but might, at very high temperatures, cause the foil to melt and fuse to the interior of the oven.

LARDING AND BARDING

Larding and barding, terms so similar that they are often confused, are variations of a common culinary process—the addition of fat to lean meat, poultry or game in order to give tenderness, flavor and juiciness and to prevent drying out during cooking. In larding, strips of solid fat are inserted into the center or surface of meat with sharp-pointed larding needles. The larding technique is occasionally used for purely decorative purposes, with strips of ham, tongue or pieces of truffle inserted into the center of the meat in a colorful pattern that shows up like a mosaic when the meat is sliced. For barding, thin slices of fat or bacon are tied around a roast or bird.

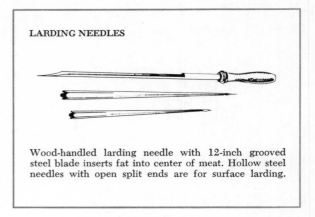

LARDING NEEDLES

Wood-handled larding needle with 12-inch grooved steel blade inserts fat into center of meat. Hollow steel needles with open split ends are for surface larding.

LARDING

Meat with plenty of fat or marbling does not need larding, but lean cuts of beef such as round, rump or chuck or a boneless veal roast cut from the leg are improved by judicious insertion of fat. Some people lard a filet of beef, but this is really painting the lily, for the meat, although it may be barded to provide a surface covering of fat, is meltingly tender and cooks rapidly. Variety meats such as a whole calf's or beef liver, beef heart or sweetbreads also benefit from the added succulence larding gives.

Large solid cuts of meat are usually larded through the center with a wood-handled, grooved larding needle. Small thinner cuts or variety meats should be larded on the surface with a slimmer, tapered needle. The surface type of larding is known as piquing, from the French verb *piquer,* to prick, sting or stick, an expressive word that calls to mind the goading jabs of the picador in a bullfight. Piquing can also be used in a slightly different although allied sense to mean the surface gashing of meat with a sharp-pointed knife, thus making little pockets into which slivers of garlic, seasonings or fat are pushed to add flavor or moisture during cooking.

Preferred fats for larding are: fatback or siding, the fresh white fat that lies between the skin and flesh of the pig's back; fat salt pork from the belly; solid pieces of fat trimmed from the fresh ham or pork loin. If you want to freshen fat salt pork and remove some of the saltiness, it can be soaked or blanched in water preparatory to cooking.

HOW TO LARD THE SURFACE OF MEAT

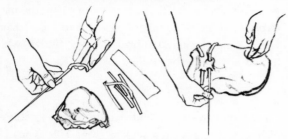

1. Cut small, thin strips of chilled fatback or salt pork. With your thumb, press tip of a strip down into the flared open end of larding needle.
2. Insert sharp point of needle through the meat, just below the surface. Pull needle forward and out, leaving fat strip threaded through the meat.

For large roast, thread short strips of fat in a double row on each side. Tie meat crosswise with string.

HOW TO LARD THE CENTER OF MEAT

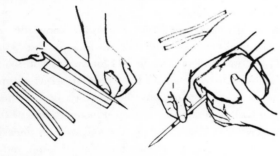

1. Measure length of meat to be larded and cut fatback into slightly longer strips to allow for overhang. Strips should be no wider than needle groove.
2. Stick larding needle through center of meat, turning to make hole. Push fat into groove with thumb, forcing it in toward handle as far as it will go.

3. Withdraw needle from meat by sliding it out backward, holding fat so it stays in meat. Repeat larding process several times; trim off overhanging fat.

HOW TO BARD BIRDS

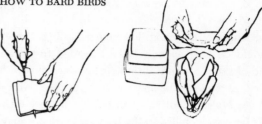

1. Cut a square of well-chilled fatback or salt pork into thin, even slices with a sharp knife. Press hand on top of the fat to steady it while slicing.
2. Truss bird in usual manner and then tuck slices of fat between the legs and breast. Cover the top of the breast and legs with more fat slices.

3. Tie fat twice crosswise with string to keep it in place while the bird cooks.
4. For large birds like pheasant, you can simply drape slices of salt pork over the breast and legs. Slit fat over the breastbone so it will drape easily.

HOW TO BARD MEAT

To bard a roast, wrap slices of bacon or salt pork around the meat and tie each slice securely in place with string. Tie meat lengthwise, also, to keep shape.

To bard tournedos (thick slices from the filet which have no fat of their own) cut long strips of fatback or salt pork as wide as the thickness of the meat. Wrap around outside edge and tie securely with string.

For larding, the chunks of solid fat are cut into thin strips or lardoons of a length and thickness determined by the type and size of larding needle and the length of the meat. For center larding, the strips should be long enough to be threaded from end to end of the meat with little tails left over. For surface larding, they can be shorter. In both cases, you will find it easier to cut and handle the slippery fat if it has been well chilled in the freezer. Lardoons may be rolled in chopped herbs or garlic or soaked in cognac or Madeira to give them extra flavor.

BARDING

While larding is confined to meat, the technique of barding can be applied to meat, poultry, and especially game. Most game birds, unless raised in the domesticity of game farms, tend to be dry and lean and need generous mantles of fat and plenty of basting. Fat for barding includes bacon, beef fat and suet in addition to pork fat, and the choice is usually determined by the nature and taste of the food to be covered—beef fat or bacon for beef, bacon for chicken or pheasant, but not for the delicate, easily overpowered quail. Fatback or salt pork is the recommended covering for birds, as it can be cut in thin sheets and draped over breasts and legs. Barding fat should be tied securely in place with string and removed before serving, although crisp salt pork may be left on roast woodcock, pheasant, partridge or other game birds when they are served for those who like to eat it.

BONING

One of the most attractive, delectable and economical ways to serve meat and poultry is to bone and stuff it. The end result looks spectacular, tastes delicious (a savory stuffing complements the flavor of the meat) and yields far more servings than the usual bone-in roast or bird. Also, if you are not to handy with a carving knife, a boned roast is much easier to slice, especially with an electric slicing knife. Classic recipes abound for stuffed and boned veal, lamb, ham, chicken, duck, goose, turkey and squab. For a spe-cial dinner party you might choose tiny stuffed squab or a stuffed gigot of lamb, baked in a pastry crust. If you are giving a buffet or open-house party, the masterpiece on the table might be a stuffed baked ham. Even a simple chicken breast tastes festive when turned into an herb-seasoned Chicken Kiev.

Considering the scope and variety of boned stuffed dishes, they are all too seldom seen. This is mainly due to the decline in artistry and professional pride among butchers and the rise in precut, prepackaged meats. While most European butchers bone meat as a matter of course, few American butchers outside the better stores in the large cities have the will or the skill, and if they do, they are apt to charge highly —anywhere from $1 to $2.50—for their time and trouble. Yet anyone with the urge to try can learn the basic techniques in a relatively short time. Although your first attempts might be botched, you will soon get the hang of it. There is nothing esoteric about boning. All you need is a good boning knife with a slim, razor-sharp blade and a pointed tip, a cleaver or poultry shears for splitting bones or cutting through recalcitrant joints, a working knowledge of an animal's anatomy and your own hands. Hands are important; fingers have to feel for you as you work, letting you know where the bones are situated and helping you to tear away the loosened flesh. Where you wish to retain the original unboned shape of the bird or roast, the bones are removed without the skin being slit. Boning methods for a leg of lamb and a chicken—plus two ways of boning a chicken breast— are illustrated in the sketches that follow. Boning a chicken breast is fairly easy and good practice.

HOW TO BONE A CHICKEN WHOLE FOR ROASTING

In this method, where you want to retain the shape of the fowl, you actually remove the entire carcass, cutting and peeling the flesh and skin back like a glove. Wings and thigh bones are also removed but the drumsticks (leg bones) are left in so the chicken can be reshaped and trussed after it has been filled with stuffing and is ready for cooking.

HOW TO BONE A CHICKEN

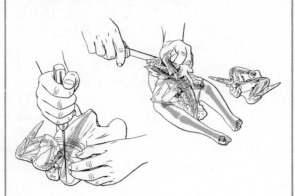

1. Start to bone at wishbone end of chicken. Cut off wings, make first incision with knife at one side of wishbone and cut around it.
2. Use knife and fingers to cut and pull away flesh, rotating bird and cutting around the carcass, keeping knife always close to bone.

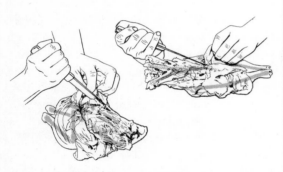

3. Continue cutting and turning, peeling skin and flesh from carcass like a glove until you reach joint where legs join body.
4. Sever connection at joint, then cut inside thigh, around bone. Cut cartilage connecting thigh and drumstick and remove thigh bone.

5. Continue cutting flesh from carcass until it can be pulled out in one piece. Chicken can now be stuffed and sewn or skewered.

TWO WAYS TO BONE A CHICKEN BREAST

As either of the following methods works perfectly well, pick the one that comes most naturally to you. The first method is the butcher's standard way of boning by simply cutting the flesh from the ribs on each side, then carefully running the knife under the skin on the ridge of the breast bone. The second method involves first cutting through the cartilage at the bottom of the breast, then snapping the joint and pushing upward to loosen the breastbone and break it in two. The meat is then cut from ribs.

HOW TO BONE A CHICKEN BREAST

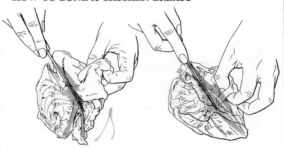

Method Number One
1. Place skin side up. Slide point of boning knife between flesh and last rib. With sawing motion, cut toward you close to ribs, working to breastbone, pulling back flesh.
2. Repeat procedure on second side of breast. Carefully slide knife blade from wishbone along breastbone, keeping the skin intact. Remove the rib cage in one piece.

Method Number Two
1. Place breast skin side down and hold rib cage open. With sharp knife, cut through cartilage below breastbone, where ribs join.
2. Hold breast in both hands and bend backward to snap the joint and flexible breastbone. Loosen flesh, pull out breastbone.

3. Turn skin side up and cut flesh from ribs with short sawing strokes as in first method. When you reach wishbone, cut away flesh.
4. Grasping wishbone with fingers, use knife point to loosen flesh around it. Now you can remove entire bone section in one piece.

HOW TO BONE A LEG OF LAMB

Here you are working in the dark, so to speak, as the bone is shrouded in meat. However, if you feel the location of the bone with your fingers as you go, and study the darkened bone section shown in the following sketches, it should not be difficult to learn.

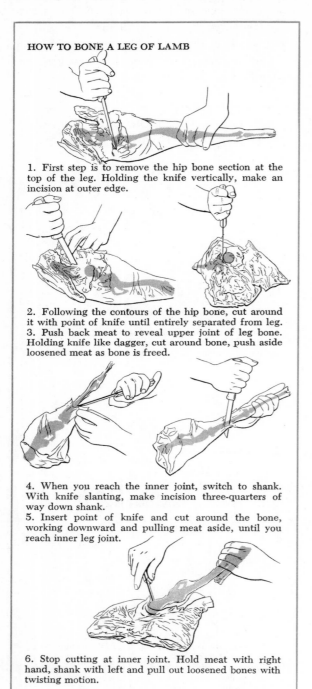

HOW TO BONE A LEG OF LAMB

1. First step is to remove the hip bone section at the top of the leg. Holding the knife vertically, make an incision at outer edge.

2. Following the contours of the hip bone, cut around it with point of knife until entirely separated from leg.
3. Push back meat to reveal upper joint of leg bone. Holding knife like dagger, cut around bone, push aside loosened meat as bone is freed.

4. When you reach the inner joint, switch to shank. With knife slanting, make incision three-quarters of way down shank.
5. Insert point of knife and cut around the bone, working downward and pulling meat aside, until you reach inner leg joint.

6. Stop cutting at inner joint. Hold meat with right hand, shank with left and pull out loosened bones with twisting motion.

BALLOTTINES AND GALANTINES

Ballottines and galantines are boned, stuffed and rolled birds or pieces of meat. They both belong to the same order of French cookery; the main distinction between them is that a poultry ballottine is generally a boned bird with the leg and small wing bones left intact and is usually served hot, whereas a poultry galantine is completely boned and always served cold. (If a ballottine is served cold, which it may perfectly well be, it is technically a galantine, according to French culinary dogma.) A ballottine can also be sewn and tied into the original shape of the bird, instead of being rolled, and braised or roasted rather than poached, the usual method. Boned meats such as a breast or shoulder of veal are also called ballottines and galantines if they are stuffed, cooked and served like poultry.

Once boned, the fowl is laid skin side down and the center of the skin covered with a layer of forcemeat. Little strips of decorative meats, truffles or pistachio nuts are then laid on top and covered with another layer of forcemeat, the idea being that when the cooked roll is sliced, a kind of mosaic pattern emerges. The loose sides and ends of the skin are wrapped over the stuffing, forming the whole thing into a shapely, even, oversized sausage, and either sewn together with thread or skewered with toothpicks (meat would be rolled up like a jelly roll to get the same effect). The roll is then wrapped in a floured cloth and the cloth tied with string at both ends and in the middle. Or, it may be wrapped in heavy foil, which doesn't need to be tied. The wrapped roll is then poached in bouillon (if in a porous cloth) or in salted water (if in foil). The best way to do this is to use a long fish boiler or large oval cocotte with handles and tie the ends of the roll to the handles so the roll is suspended and partly steamed, rather than being completely immersed in the liquid.

After cooking, a galantine is cooled with a board and weight on top to press it into shape and let the liquid drain out. The cloth and thread or toothpicks are removed and the galantine coated with aspic or chaudfroid sauce, or both, and often decorated with edible flowers made from truffles, hard-cooked eggs, tarragon leaves and chives. For a ballottine, the cloth is merely removed after cooking and the roll sliced and served hot with a sauce.

HOW TO BONE A TURKEY FOR A GALANTINE

1. Lay turkey on its side and pull back the wing to expose point at which it is joined to body. Remove the wings (they can be used for poaching stock).
2. Turn turkey breast side down and with a heavy cleaver split it straight down the backbone.

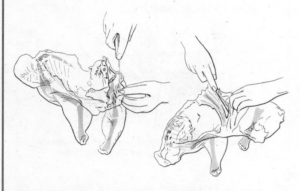

3. Spread out split turkey bone side upward. With a small, sharp boning knife, start cutting flesh from bone at the hip, working toward the breastbone.
4. Work around carcass, cutting and scraping meat from bone, pulling flesh away with fingers as you cut. Always cut close to bone; do not pierce skin.

5. Sever tendon joining legs to body. Continue cutting until you reach ridge of breastbone. Slide knife under to release carcass, but do not pierce skin.

6. To remove leg bones, slit skin down one side of leg, cut and scrape meat from bone. Pull out bones.

7. Spread boned turkey flat, skin side down. Fill with stuffing, bring skin over to enclose stuffing, shaping into long, fat roll. Sew with string thread.

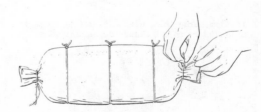

8. Envelop roll in floured cloth. Tie around center with short lengths of string. Tie ends with longer pieces of string to suspend roll from pot handles.

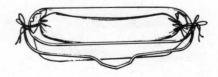

9. Tie string at ends of wrapped galantine to the handles of a long narrow fish cooker so that the roll is suspended and partly steamed in the simmering liquid.

Cooking Lore

Dried herbs yield more flavor if they are soaked in water (1 tablespoon water to 1 teaspoon herb) before being used in a recipe.

Dry mustard blends better in a sauce or dressing if combined with an equal amount of Dijon mustard.

Heavy cream whips best when it is cold. Beat in a metal bowl over ice. The cream thickens faster and holds its shape.

Chocolate needs to be melted slowly at low heat. Melt chocolate for coating on a heavy plate set on a pan of hot water over a slow fire, working it with a small palette knife. For a more liquid mixture, add water, coffee or rum, melt slowly in a heavy pan or double boiler, over low heat.

Garlic should always be fresh. Buy a little at a time and use as quickly as possible. When cooking garlic, the flavor is improved if you cook it slowly with an allied vegetable such as onion, scallion, shallot or celery. To give garlic a smooth consistency for sauces or garlic butter, chop the garlic with salt (this prevents it from sticking to the knife) and crush to a paste with a heavy knife. When the garlic is to be used merely for flavoring and later extracted, you can just bruise it with a heavy knife.

Parsley and other fresh herbs lose a lot of their flavor if they are washed. Mostly this is not necessary if the herbs are well picked over. If you have to wash parsley, the best way is to chop it first, then put it in paper towels and squeeze under running water.

HOW TO MINCE GARLIC

1. Slice garlic thin, mix with salt to keep it from sticking to knife blade during chopping.

2. Chop slices into thin slivers with up and down strokes, knife at right angle to board.

3. To mince fine, chop backward and forward as for parsley, keeping the knife tip stationary.

HOW TO CHOP PARSLEY

1. Bunch unwashed parsley and chop coarsely. Keep tip of knife steady on chopping board.

2. Hold knife tip at end. Chop quickly with length of blade in even back and forth motion.

3. To wash, twist parsley in a paper towel, hold under faucet, dry on another paper towel.

Paprika and curry powder taste raw unless cooked. Fry them slowly in fat with vegetables when making a paprika or curry sauce.

Pepper retains more pungency if you buy whole peppercorns and grind them fresh each time. Cayenne pepper and paprika, which always come ready ground, have less life than peppercorns and should be used quickly.

Vanilla bean can be used in two ways. The pod (1 or 2 inches is usually sufficient) is cooked in milk or cream for flavoring. The seeds may be scraped with the point of a knife inserted into the split pod and added to custard or whipped cream and the pod discarded (or put into a jar of sugar for vanilla sugar).

HOW TO USE A VANILLA BEAN

1. Slit the side of the vanilla bean with a sharp knife.

2. Scrape out the tiny black seeds into custard or whipped cream.

Overseason anything that will be clarified or frozen as these processes reduce the strength of flavors. This applies to flavorings in home-made ice cream.

Mushrooms lose much of their flavor if they are peeled. Wipe mushrooms with a damp cloth or, if they are on the dirty side, wash quickly in a small amount of water with lemon juice to keep them white, and dry thoroughly. Do not allow them to soak. When sautéing mushrooms, add a little lemon juice (2 teaspoons to ½ pound mushrooms) and season with salt and cayenne pepper. Cook briskly.

To skin peaches, peppers or tomatoes, plunge in boiling water, count ten, then remove to cold water and peel. Another way to skin peppers is to hold them over the gas flame until the skin is shriveled.

To remove zest from citrus fruit, remove with a potato peeler only the colored part (the zest) of the rind, none of the white pith.

To stop discoloring of cut vegetables and fruits, sprinkle with lemon juice. This applies particularly to sliced or chopped onion, celery, mushrooms, avocado, peaches, pears and apples.

To make bread crumbs, put trimmed day-old bread through the meat grinder or whirl in the electric blender. For dry crumbs, dry them in the oven at low heat. For buttered crumbs, pour cool melted butter over them, stir with a wooden spoon.

To clarify butter, melt it slowly in the top of a double boiler. Strain off butter into jars, discarding the whey (whitish sediment). Store in the refrigerator and use to brown meats and poultry, to broil and sauté fish (clarified butter is essential for sole meunière), and as an accompaniment to artichokes, asparagus, lobster.

To separate eggs, tap the center of the shell smartly against the edge of a bowl. Pour egg carefully back and forth between half shells, letting the white drop into the bowl, until only the yolk is left. You should have no egg white around the yolk, not even the glutinous thread that holds them together: carefully sever this with the edge of the shell. Leftover yolks can be stored in a jar with a little oil on top and used to enrich sauces or for mayonnaise or Hollandaise. Egg whites will keep for a week in a jar in the refrigerator or may be frozen. Add them to soufflés or use for meringue, batters.

To thicken with egg yolks, take great care not to overcook. When thickening a sauce, add a little of the hot mixture to the beaten egg, stir in well, then return to pan and gently heat through.

To beat egg whites for a soufflé, you will get the most expansion if you beat them with a large balloon whisk in a big copper bowl. The phrase "beat until stiff but not dry" puzzles many people. A simpler test is to beat until the egg whites stay in the bowl when it is turned upside down (they won't fall out if properly beaten). When adding beaten egg whites to sauce for a soufflé, be very careful just to fold in, using a rubber scraper, not a metal spoon. Do not mix in completely; lumps of white should remain in the sauce. To fold, tip up the bowl with one hand and use a cutting and smoothing motion, down, up and over with the hand holding the scraper. This should take no more than a few seconds. The less the whites are blended, the lighter the soufflé.

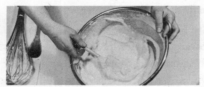

BEATING AND FOLDING FOR A SOUFFLÉ

1. Beat whites until they stay in inverted bowl.

2. Fold in soufflé sauce with up and over motion.

To line a bowl or dish for yeast doughs, wipe out the bowl with a damp cloth and then sprinkle with flour, which will cling to the side. For soufflés, butter the inside of the dish, then put in sugar (for dessert soufflés) or dry bread crumbs (for savory soufflés), roll around and tip out the excess.

LINING A SOUFFLÉ DISH

Roll dish, tipping out excess sugar or crumbs.

To make a sauce creamier but not unduly rich, substitute 1 tablespoon whipped cream, add just before serving, for each 2 tablespoons heavy cream indicated in recipe.

To make a sour cream sauce, add a spoonful of sour cream to the liquid in the pan, putting it in the very center and stirring rapidly until it is absorbed into the hot sauce. Add more as the first spoonful is mixed in. Always have a sauce thicker than you need it before adding the sour cream as this tends to dilute sauces rather than thicken them.

MAKING A SOUR CREAM SAUCE

1. To add sour cream, drop spoonful in sauce.

2. Stir quickly with whisk, blending into sauce.

If a sauce is too thick, thin with a little stock, milk or cream, whatever is indicated.

If a sauce is too thin, add small balls of butter and flour kneaded together (this is called beurre manié).

If a sauce has to stand, cover it with wax paper and the lid; the paper helps to collect moisture which would dilute the sauce.

For accurate measurements, always use standard measures and follow the same procedure.

For liquid measures, pour liquid into cup, then hold it at eye level to check amount.

For dry measures, carefully follow the stated amounts. Teaspoons and tablespoons should be evened off level, unless otherwise stated. A heaping tablespoon is just that—whereas a rounded tablespoon rises just slightly over the level of the spoon. Let flour and sugar fall into the cup when measuring. Don't shake down. The only exception to this is brown sugar, which is always measured packed down.

MEASURING SUGAR

To measure sugar, let it fall into cup.

Dry ingredients which tend to lump, such as cornstarch, potato starch, baking powder and confectioners' sugar, should be sifted before measuring for cakes. Flour is sifted only if the recipe indicates.

Substitutions:

Certain other starches may be substituted for flour in cooking but as their thickening power is greater you use proportionately less.

1 tablespoon flour equals 1 teaspoon potato starch or arrowroot or 2 teaspoons cornstarch or rice flour.

Rice flour, which has the least pronounced taste of all, is often substituted in vegetable soups.

Cornstarch is the standard thickener in Chinese recipes as it does not need long cooking.

Potato starch, which cooks clear, is often used to thicken brown sauces. It can also be added at the last minute if a sauce is too thin or shows signs of separating, as it cooks quickly and smoothly and leaves no raw taste. Potato starch does not mix well with sour-cream sauces.

Arrowroot, a thickener that is clear and almost tasteless, is useful in desserts such as blancmange.

Quick-cooking tapioca, another handy thickening agent, is good for vegetable soups and applesauce. Use 1 tablespoon to 1 pint liquid.

Wine is one of the invaluable elements in cooking. Like paprika and flour, red or white wines must be cooked or they will taste raw. Wine retains no alcoholic content after it has been cooked as the alcohol is volatilized by heat; all that remains is the flavor of the grape.

The acidity of wine helps to tenderize. This can be done during the actual cooking process or by first marinating the meat, poultry or game in a mixture of wine, herbs and seasonings. The strained marinade can be used as a liquid for the sauce or gravy.

In sauces, wine is used in various ways. To get a strong flavor, the wine may be cooked down until most of the liquid has evaporated, leaving strength rather than bulk. The wine may be cooked with water and flavoring herbs for stock, then the stock strained into the sauce (a standard way of making a white wine sauce for fish dishes). Wine is often added with other liquids to the roux for a sauce. For a richer sauce like a velouté, sherry or brandy may be mixed with egg yolk and used as a liaison to bind and enrich the cooked sauce.

Wine is frequently used to baste roasted meat or poultry. In this case, about 2 tablespoons of wine is added to the pan juices and mixed in each time the roast is basted—the cold wine should not be used for basting. For gravies, wine may be added to the pan juices with water or stock after the meat is removed to make a clear *jus* (non-thickened gravy).

Appetizer & Hors d'Oeuvre

In the anatomy of a menu there appear certain tasty morsels aptly dubbed by the French hors d'oeuvre, outside the work. These are the appetite-inciters, the palate-provokers that, like the prologue to a play, sharpen the senses for what is to come. The Romans, always prone to carry a good thing to excess, began their lengthy banquets with a gustus, or appetizer course, consisting of a truly staggering slate of foods—succulent oysters, glistening caviar, slim shrimp and plump snails, sauced eggs, spiced sausages, lentil salads and mushrooms among them.

The Greeks, another breed of stalwart eaters and drinkers, took the wise precaution of serving appetizers not only before a meal, but whenever the wine flowed freely. (Not only did they originate this prototype of the cocktail party, but a Greek poet, Antiphanes, gave the first advice to the hungover, counseling the sufferer to "Take the hair, it is well written / Of the dog by whom you're bitten.") Their "provocatives to drinking" were much like ours. Anyone desirous of duplicating an Athenian drinking party would have no trouble rounding up pistachio nuts and cheeses, olives, shrimp, caviar and goose liver pâté —even roasted grasshoppers which, in canned form, are once more classed as a "gourmet food."

Such were the noble ancestors of the Russian zakouski, the Swedish smörgasbôrd, the Italian antipasto and the French hors d'oeuvre. Now the realm of appetizers embraces the world, from the taramasalata and tirotrigona of Greece and the champignons farcis and rillettes de Tours of France to Japan's teriyaki and tempura and the empanadas and seviche of Latin America.

Whereas there was once a clear distinction between the foods eaten from a plate as the first course of a sit-down dinner or luncheon and those "thumb bits," as the Victorians called them, eaten with the fingers at a stand-up cocktail party, the passing of the old patterns of entertaining have eroded the demarcation line. Now the first course may be stuffed clams or quiche Lorraine served with drinks in the living room, while the cocktail crowd frequently feasts from a buffet table laden with such solid, serious victuals as pâtés and cold meats, smoked fish and hot sausages. The chief difference between the drinking man's and the eating man's fare is that the former is designed to appease appetite and temper thirst, while the latter must take cognizance of the courses to follow, striking a perfect balance between light and hearty, bland and spicy, plain and rich.

AVOCADO DIP

1 ripe avocado
1 teaspoon lemon juice
1 tablespoon mayonnaise
¼ teaspoon puréed garlic
½ teaspoon salt
¼ teaspoon monosodium glutamate
Dash of Tabasco

Peel avocado and mash until smooth. Combine with remaining ingredients, taste and correct seasoning to taste. Serve as a dip with potato or corn chips, crackers or raw vegetables. Makes 1 cup.

GUACAMOLE

2 large avocados
1 medium tomato, peeled, seeded and chopped
1 tablespoon finely chopped onion
2 or more canned serrano chiles, chopped
1 tablespoon finely chopped cilantro
Salt, pepper to taste
Pinch of sugar

Peel avocados and mash. Add tomato, onion, chiles, cilantro, salt, pepper and sugar. Mix well and pile into a serving dish with the avocado pit in the center to keep the guacamole from turning dark. Serve as a dip with corn chips, or as a sauce or salad with Mexican dishes. Makes about 2 cups.

MUSHROOM CAVIAR

½ cup chopped green onions, with tops
2 tablespoons butter
1 cup chopped mushrooms
1 tablespoon lemon juice
Salt, pepper to taste
⅛ teaspoon cayenne pepper
2 tablespoons chopped dill
⅓ cup sour cream
Tomato slices

Sauté the green onions in the butter for 1 minute. Add the mushrooms, lemon juice, salt, pepper, and cayenne. Sauté 4 minutes, stirring occasionally. Remove from the heat. Stir in the dill and sour cream. Serve garnished with tomato slices. Serves 2.

EGGPLANT PURÉE À LA TURQUE

2 small eggplant
1 medium onion, minced
2 teaspoons salt
¼ teaspoon black pepper
Olive oil
1 tablespoon chopped parsley
Juice of ½ lemon

Remove the stems from the eggplant and grill them whole under moderate flame. When the skins begin to split, remove the eggplant and peel them. Put them through a food mill or mash them in a bowl. Add the minced onion, salt, black pepper and beat until smooth. Add olive oil, about 2½ tablespoons, until the mixture is the consistency of mayonnaise. Sprinkle with chopped parsley and lemon juice. Serve this cold purée surrounded by rounds of black bread with which to scoop it up and eat it. If this procedure seems messy, it may be eaten with a fork. Serves 4.

TARAMASALATA

2 slices white bread, crusts removed
4-ounce jar tarama (carp roe)
¼ cup lemon juice
¼ cup finely chopped onion
1 cup olive oil and salad oil (½ cup each)
Minced parsley
Round cracker bread or sesame crackers

Dip the bread in water to moisten, then press out any extra moisture. Place the bread, tarama, lemon juice, and onion in a blender and blend until smooth. Gradually pour in the oil, blending until thick and creamy. Pour into a bowl and chill. To serve, sprinkle with parsley and accompany with Greek cracker bread, if available, or sesame crackers. Makes 2 cups dip.

Note: You may substitute a 4-ounce jar red caviar for the tarama, but in this case do not soak the bread.

CRUDITÉS WITH ANCHOVY MAYONNAISE

12–14 anchovy fillets, coarsely chopped
2 cloves garlic, finely chopped
¼ cup chopped parsley

¼ cup chopped fresh basil
1 tablespoon capers, coarsely chopped
1 tablespoon Dijon mustard
2 cups homemade mayonnaise
  Thinly sliced cucumbers, cherry tomatoes, sliced onion, whole scallions, grated carrot sticks, and other raw vegetables

Combine anchovy fillets, garlic, parsley, basil, capers, mustard and mayonnaise, and taste for seasoning. Use little salt in the mayonnaise; anchovies and capers have plenty. Arrange vegetables on a platter; dunk in anchovy mayonnaise.

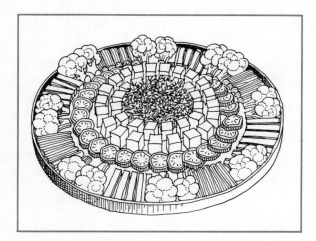

ARTICHOKES WITH OYSTER DIP

2 large artichokes, cooked and chilled
16 frozen oysters, defrosted and drained
¼ teaspoon Tabasco
2 scallions, white part only
1 tablespoon lemon juice
½ teaspoon salt
1 pint sour cream
  Paprika

Remove the artichoke leaves and place them around the edge of a round serving platter. Dice artichoke bottoms coarsely and place them in the blender with the oysters, Tabasco, scallions, lemon juice and salt. Cover and blend on high speed for 10 seconds, or until ingredients are blended to a paste. Mix paste with sour cream, pour into a serving bowl and dust with paprika. Chill until serving time. Place the bowl of dip in the center of the artichoke leaves and serve as a cocktail appetizer.

SHRIMP DIP

5-ounce can shrimp (or equal amount of cooked fresh shrimp)
1 cup sour cream
¼ cup bourbon
1 teaspoon coarsely cut parsley
½ teaspoon paprika
1 teaspoon coarsely chopped dill
¾ teaspoon salt
½ teaspoon freshly ground black pepper
1 tablespoon coarsely cut chives

Put all ingredients except the chives in blender and blend until smooth. Remove and stir in chives. Chill. Serve as a dip for a platter of raw vegetables or seafood or use as a dressing for seafood salads. Makes approximately 1¾ cups.

RUMMED CRAB SPREAD

6½-ounce can crab meat, drained and flaked
1 tablespoon capers
2 hard-cooked eggs, quartered
2 tablespoons fresh lime juice
¼ cup dark rum
2 tablespoons prepared mustard
¾ teaspoon salt
½ teaspoon freshly ground black pepper

Combine all ingredients in blender and blend until smooth. Start at low speed, increase to high. Serve as a spread with crackers or thin toast fingers. Makes approximately 1½ cups.

CHILE CON QUESO

1 large onion, minced
1 small clove garlic, minced
4 tablespoons butter
1 pound, 13-ounce can tomatoes
4-ounce can peeled green chiles, rinsed of seeds and chopped
2 tablespoons flour
1 cup cream or evaporated milk
  Salt
  Tabasco
½ pound Cheddar or Jack cheese, finely diced

Cook onion and garlic in 2 tablespoons butter until soft. Add tomatoes and simmer until thick. Then add the chiles.

Make a sauce with the remaining 2 tablespoons of butter, the flour and the cream or evaporated milk. Cook until smooth and thick. Then add to the tomato mixture. Season to taste with salt and, if you wish, Tabasco.

About 3 or 4 minutes before serving, stir in cheese until melted. Serve, keeping mixture warm in a chafing dish or a casserole over a burner. Serve with corn chips, Fritos, crackers or tostadas.

TAPENADE

18 anchovy fillets with their oil
20–24 soft black olives, pitted
3–4 cloves garlic
¼ cup olive oil
4-ounce can tuna in olive oil
28 capers
1 tablespoon Dijon mustard
¼ cup cognac
Dash lemon juice

Put the anchovies, olives and garlic in a blender with some extra oil and blend until smooth. Then add and blend the other ingredients, again with extra oil, if needed. Taste for seasoning.

Use as a dip for raw vegetables.

TANGY CHEESE SPREAD

¾ cup beer or ale
¾ pound aged Cheddar cheese, coarsely grated
⅛ pound blue cheese, crumbled
½ teaspoon dry mustard
1 tablespoon soft butter
2 dashes Worcestershire sauce
1 dash Tabasco
1 teaspoon coarsely chopped chives or onions

Put the beer or ale and Cheddar cheese in the blender and blend for 20 seconds, or until smooth. Add the remaining ingredients, except chives, and blend until smooth. Spoon into a crock or serving dish and chill. Garnish with chives. Makes approximately 2½ cups.

CELERIAC RÉMOULADE

1 pound celeriac
2 tablespoons olive oil
2 teaspoons vinegar
½ teaspoon salt
¼ teaspoon dry mustard
Dash of white pepper
Rémoulade sauce

Pare celeriac and cut into matchlike strips. Marinate overnight in olive oil, vinegar, salt, dry mustard and a dash of white pepper. Drain and mix with rémoulade sauce. For rémoulade sauce, mix into 1 cup good mayonnaise ½ teaspoon dry mustard, 1 tablespoon drained capers, 1 teaspoon chopped chives, pinches of dried tarragon and chervil or several fresh leaves of each, chopped, and a touch of garlic or shallot. Serve on a bed of lettuce. Serves 4.

CELERY VICTOR

Allow 1 celery heart for each serving. Split hearts lengthwise, trim root and lay in a shallow pan such as a chicken fryer. Cover with chicken stock, add a bouquet of bay leaf, parsley and thyme and simmer until just tender. Let cool in the stock, then drain, carefully pressing out excess stock (save the stock for soup). Arrange celery hearts on individual dishes, two halves to a serving, and sprinkle with coarsely ground black pepper, minced parsley and chervil. Make a dressing with 1 part tarragon vinegar to 2 parts olive oil and salt to taste. Pour the dressing over the celery hearts and chill thoroughly. Garnish the celery hearts with anchovy strips and pimiento strips before serving.

STUFFED CELERY

2 bunches celery
6 ounces sweet butter
½ pound blue cheese
2 tablespoons brandy
1 teaspoon freshly cracked white pepper
⅛ teaspoon Tabasco
½ teaspoon Worcestershire sauce
Rounds of buttered whole-wheat bread

Carefully wash and spread the celery stalks, keeping each one apart so they can be reshaped the same way. Wash well in ice water, dry. Cream butter in the mixer and slowly add the blue cheese. When light and fluffy, add the brandy, pepper, Tabasco and Worcestershire. Spread a little of this mixture in the hearts of the celery and continue between each stalk until you have reshaped and stuck the celery together again. Wrap in a piece of plastic wrap and chill in the refrigerator for 3 hours, or in the freezer. Remove and cut into slices about ¼″ thick. Serve on the rounds of whole-wheat bread as an appetizer.

MARINATED CARROTS

6–8 large carrots, peeled and cut into thick
   julienne strips
½ cup olive oil
¼ cup white wine vinegar
1 small onion, sliced
2 cloves garlic
1 teaspoon dried basil
1 teaspoon salt
½ teaspoon pepper
   Salad greens
   Juice of 1 large lemon

Put the carrots into a saucepan with boiling water to cover. Cook for 3–5 minutes, or until the carrots

are barely tender. Drain. Combine the olive oil, vinegar, onion, garlic, basil, salt, and pepper in a bowl (do not use aluminum). Put the carrots in the marinade and toss carefully. Refrigerate, covered, for 12 hours, or overnight. Drain the carrots, removing onion and garlic, arrange on a bed of salad greens and sprinkle with lemon juice. Serves 4–6.

ONIONS À LA GRECQUE

36–40 small white onions—identical size
   if possible
4 tablespoons olive oil
⅔ cup white wine
½ cup water
1 teaspoon sugar
1 teaspoon salt
   Sprig of fennel
½ teaspoon thyme
1 bay leaf
   Pinch of saffron
1 cup currants or sultana raisins

Peel the onions and place in a skillet. Add the oil, wine, water, sugar and seasonings, except saffron. Simmer until onions are just crisply tender. Add the saffron and currants or raisins, and cook down. Remove the onions and reduce the sauce. Pour sauce over the onions. Serve cool. Serves 6–8.

Variation: Add 1 or 2 tablespoons tomato paste.

Cold Beets in Mustard Dressing

DRAIN a ONE POUND CAN of Whole Beets. COMBINE IN A JAR: 1 TABLESPOON Olive Oil, 1 TABLESPOON VINEGAR, 1 TEASPOON DIJON MUSTARD, SALT + to taste, & ½ TEASPOON dried Mix in thyme & basil. SHAKE WELL. PUT beets in a BOWL & POUR OVER. dressing. MARINATE at ROOM TEMPERATURE for 10 to 15 minutes. SERVE COLD on TOOTHPICKS as an HORS d'OEUVRE

PARSLEY-STUFFED ARTICHOKES

6 medium artichokes
3 cups chopped parsley
1 clove garlic, minced
3 anchovies, minced (optional)
1 teaspoon salt
¼ teaspoon pepper
½ teaspoon dried basil, crumbled
1 lemon, sliced
2 tablespoons olive oil

Wash the artichokes, cut off stems at base, and pull off and discard tough outer leaves. Cut off top third of each artichoke to remove prickly tips. Spread open by placing artichoke upside down on a table and pressing stem end firmly. Dig out fuzzy chokes with a sharp knife, grapefruit knife, or teaspoon. Combine parsley, garlic, anchovies, salt, pepper, and basil. Mix well and pack into artichoke centers.

Tie a string around each artichoke (to retain shape) or place in a saucepan or skillet that is just big enough to hold them snugly. Top each artichoke with a slice of lemon. Add the olive oil to the pan and pour in 1″ of boiling water. Cook, uncovered, for 3 minutes. Simmer, covered, 20–35 minutes, or until artichokes are tender; the cooking time depends on the size and tenderness of the vegetable. Check for moisture; if necessary, add a little more water to keep at 1″ level. Serve cold as an hors d'oeuvre with a lemon juice and oil French dressing. Serves 6.

STUFFED CUCUMBER CUPS

1 pound shrimp, cooked and chopped
½ pound softened butter
1 teaspoon salt
½ teaspoon mace
Dash of Tabasco
Chopped parsley
2–3 cucumbers, unwaxed

Combine all the ingredients except the parsley and cucumbers.

Wash cucumbers, but do not peel. Cut them into ¾″ slices and use a small fluted pastry cutter to make decorative shapes. Form these into small cups by scooping out some of the seeds on one side with a melon ball cutter. Stuff with the shrimp mixture and decorate with a wreath of parsley. Chill thoroughly. Makes about 20.

LEEKS IN HAM WITH SAUCE VERTE

12 leeks
12 thin slices boiled ham
1 cup finely chopped and drained spinach
1 tablespoon chopped chives
1 tablespoon chopped parsley
1 tablespoon chopped fresh tarragon
1 tablespoon chopped hard-cooked egg
1½ cups mayonnaise
Salt, pepper to taste

Poach the washed leeks in salted water until tender. Chill. Wrap each leek in a thin slice of boiled ham and chill again. Combine the spinach, herbs and egg and add to the mayonnaise. Correct seasoning. Serve the leeks with this sauce verte. Serves 6.

LEEKS À LA GRECQUE

⅓ cup olive oil
2 tablespoons wine vinegar
1 clove garlic, chopped
½ cup white wine
1 teaspoon salt
½ teaspoon freshly ground black pepper
1 sprig parsley

Stuffed Avocados

Good pinch of thyme
12 leeks
1 tablespoon chopped parsley
Dash of Tabasco

Mix together the oil, vinegar, garlic, wine, salt, pepper, parsley and thyme to make a sauce à la Grecque. Wash the leeks and soak them well to be sure that all the grit is gone. Run them under cold water for a few minutes. Arrange the leeks in a flat pan and pour the sauce à la Grecque over them. Add enough water, or white wine and water mixed, to cover. Simmer until just tender and cool in the broth. Remove the leeks to a serving dish and cook the broth down. Add chopped parsley, Tabasco, and pour over the leeks. Chill. Serves 4–6.

CHAMPIGNONS FARCIS

1 pound extra-large fresh mushrooms
¼ cup minced onion
Butter
5 tablespoons minced clams, drained
Salt, pepper, freshly ground nutmeg to taste
1 tablespoon chopped fresh parsley

Wash and dry the mushrooms. Remove stems and mince them finely. Sauté the onion in ¼ cup butter until tender. Add the minced mushroom stems and simmer, stirring often, for 4 minutes. Add the minced

clams, salt, pepper, nutmeg, and parsley. Mix well and let cool. Brush the mushroom caps with melted butter and arrange on a shallow dish. Place in a 350° oven for 5 minutes. Fill the caps with the mushroom-clam mixture, sprinkle the tops with a little melted butter and brown them in the oven before serving. Serve hot. Serves 5–6.

SHRIMP-STUFFED MUSHROOMS

1 cup finely chopped cooked shrimp
1 tablespoon cracker crumbs
1 tablespoon minced onion
1 tablespoon minced parsley
1 tablespoon soft butter
1 teaspoon minced tarragon
Salt to taste
1 egg
1½ pounds large mushroom caps, stems removed
Buttered crumbs

Mix the shrimp, cracker crumbs, onion, parsley, butter, tarragon, salt and egg together. Fill the mushroom caps with the mixture, sprinkle with buttered crumbs and bake in a 350° oven for 15–20 minutes. Makes about 12–30 stuffed mushrooms according to size of caps.

TOMATES CHARENTAIS

5–6 beefsteak tomatoes
⅓ cup olive oil
1 teaspoon salt
1 tablespoon finely chopped fresh basil
1 tablespoon finely chopped parsley
1 teaspoon grated lemon peel
2 tablespoons cognac

Peel and thinly slice the tomatoes and arrange on a serving dish. Combine remaining ingredients and dribble over tomatoes. Let stand for at least 15 minutes before serving. Serves 4.

TOMATOES GENNARO

6 large ripe tomatoes
1 medium lobster, cooked
1½ cups mayonnaise
2 cloves garlic, crushed
1½ tablespoons tomato paste
¼ cup Pernod
6 eggs mollet (soft-cooked eggs, shelled)
1 tablespoon chopped parsley
1 tablespoon capers

Peel and scoop out the tomatoes. Turn upside down on absorbent paper and chill thoroughly. Slice lobster tail and remove meat from lobster claws in perfect sections. You will need 12 pieces of lobster. Combine mayonnaise, garlic, tomato paste, lobster tomalley and coral, if any, and blend with Pernod. Season the mixture to taste.

To serve, place an egg mollet on the bottom of each tomato and arrange lobster pieces on either side. Dress with mayonnaise mixture and garnish with chopped parsley and capers. Serves 6.

TURKISH STUFFED TOMATOES

8 medium tomatoes, ripe but firm
1½ teaspoons salt
2 cups chopped onion
6 tablespoons olive oil
1 cup uncooked long-grain rice
1 tablespoon pine nuts

2 tablespoons white raisins or currants
1 teaspoon chopped fresh dill
  or ¼ teaspoon dried dill weed
1 teaspoon chopped fresh mint
  or ¼ teaspoon dried mint
¼ teaspoon black pepper
1 cup water
1 teaspoon sugar

Cut tops from tomatoes, scoop out insides carefully so that firm shell remains. Sprinkle insides of tomatoes with ½ teaspoon salt. Force tomato pulp through sieve to remove seeds. Reserve 1¼ cups of the strained tomato pulp. Simmer the onion in the olive oil until soft and yellow. Add rice and pine nuts and stir to coat with oil. Cook 2 or 3 minutes. Add raisins, dill, mint, pepper, 1 teaspoon salt, reserved tomato pulp and water. Bring to a boil, lower heat and cook covered for 10 minutes. (Rice will still be hard.) Stir in the sugar. Fill tomatoes loosely with this mixture (the rice will swell with additional cooking). Place stuffed tomatoes in shallow baking pan, brush outside of each with oil. Bake in a 350° oven for 45 minutes. Cool the tomatoes in the pan and serve them cold. Serves 8 as a first course.

ITALIAN OYSTER PLANT HORS D'OEUVRE

⅔ cup olive oil
  Lemon juice to taste
  Salt, pepper to taste
¼ cup minced parsley
1–2 pounds cooked oyster plant

Combine the olive oil, lemon juice, salt, pepper, and parsley in a bowl. Add the cooked oyster plant and toss to coat well. Let stand for 30 minutes. Drain. Serve as an hors d'oeuvre or salad. Serves 4–6.

GARBANZO NUTS

1 pound dried chick peas (garbanzos)
¼ pound butter
4 cloves garlic, crushed
½ teaspoon dry mustard
1 teaspoon chili powder

2 teaspoons salt

1 teaspoon onion salt

1 teaspoon powdered ginger

½ teaspoon garlic salt

3 teaspoons soy sauce

Soak chick peas overnight in water to cover. Drain. Cook in well-salted water until they are nearly done but still a bit hard—about 1 hour. Drain. Divide chick peas in two portions. In two skillets, melt the butter, equally divided, and sauté two cloves garlic, put through garlic press, in each. Remove garlic and add one portion chick peas to one skillet, the rest to the other skillet. Sauté very slowly, turning and stirring often, until garbanzos begin to sizzle and turn dark golden brown. When they're crunchy on the outside and tender inside, they are done. Meanwhile, mix mustard, chili powder, salt and onion salt. Sprinkle this over one batch of the garbanzos and toss lightly until "nuts" are thoroughly coated. Mix the ginger, garlic salt and soy sauce and proceed in the same manner with the garbanzos in the other skillet.

Serve hot as soon as possible, in separate bowls, as "niblets" to accompany cocktails. They may be successfully reheated spread on baking sheet in hot oven. Put on baking sheet under broiler for 2–5 minutes, until crisp and sizzling. Makes 2–3 cups.

WHITE BEANS VINAIGRETTE

1½ cups dried flageolets or Great Northern
     beans

2 quarts water

1 teaspoon basil leaves

½ teaspoon thyme

3½ teaspoons salt

½ teaspoon pepper
     Bouquet garni of bay leaf, celery tops, parsley
     sprigs, 3 garlic cloves in cheesecloth bag

3 tablespoons olive oil

3 tablespoons lemon juice

¼ cup onion, chopped very fine

¼ cup parsley, chopped fine

Soak beans overnight in water to cover. Drain. Cook slowly about 2 hours, or until tender, in 2 quarts water with basil leaves, thyme, 2 teaspoons salt and ¼ teaspoon pepper, bouquet garni. Drain thoroughly

and chill several hours. A half-hour before serving toss very lightly with combined oil, lemon juice, remaining salt and pepper, chopped onion and parsley, reserving some of the parsley to sprinkle on top of dish or on individual servings. Mix thoroughly and return to refrigerator until serving time. Serve sprinkled with parsley, as a first course. Serves 8.

COLD CURRIED LENTILS

1½ cups lentils

4 medium onions, finely chopped

4 tablespoons butter

2 tablespoons curry powder

2 cups bouillon

2 teaspoons salt

½ teaspoon pepper

1 tablespoon lemon juice

½ cup commercial sour cream

Soak lentils overnight in 3 cups water. Cook in same water until done but still firm, and drain. Sauté onions in butter until soft, then stir in curry powder and cook over very low heat for 20 minutes, stirring frequently. Add bouillon, salt, pepper and drained lentils. Cover and simmer very slowly for about 3 hours until lentils are very soft. Though the lentils should be separate, the mixture should have nearly the consistency of a purée. Chill thoroughly. At serving time, stir in lemon juice and mix well. Serve on salad plates as a first course, in small lettuce cups or not, as you prefer. Top with a generous spoonful of sour cream. Serves 8.

This is also a delicate, delicious vegetable when served hot, omitting the sour cream. As a vegetable, it will serve 6.

CECI MARINARA

2 1-pound cans chick peas

½ cup olive oil

1 small can flat anchovy fillets, drained and
     finely chopped

½ teaspoon salt

1 teaspoon pepper

3 tablespoons parsley, chopped

Drain one can of chick peas. Combine with undrained chick peas and heat slowly in chick pea liquid. Meanwhile, heat oil and add anchovies, salt, pepper and parsley. Stir over very low heat for several minutes. Pour over heated chick peas in their saucepan, mix well and simmer slowly for 15 minutes. Chill in sauce and serve as an appetizer. Serves 6–8.

POACHED EGGS NANTUA

4 eggs
3 tablespoons butter
1 tablespoon flour
⅔ cup milk
4 ounces cooked peeled shrimp,
   roughly chopped
   Red food color (optional)
2 tablespoons whipped cream
1 cup cold madrilene

Poach eggs and slip into a bowl of cold water until needed. Melt 1 tablespoon of the butter in a small pan, remove from heat and stir in flour, then milk. Return to heat and stir until boiling. Cool a little. Place sauce in a blender with remaining butter. Blend until smooth, gradually adding shrimp. Remove from blender and color a delicate pink, if desired. Fold in whipped cream and 2 tablespoons of the cold madrilene. Divide between 4 ramekins and place a drained poached egg in each. Spoon remaining madrilene over and chill until serving time. Serves 4.

OEUFS VIGNERONNE

1 bottle red Burgundy wine
1 large carrot, scraped and diced
4 shallots, peeled and minced
1 teaspoon dried thyme leaves
1 teaspoon whole peppercorns
2 teaspoons sugar
1 teaspoon salt
6 tablespoons butter
¼ pound mushrooms, thinly sliced

¼ pound Canadian bacon, diced
8 slices narrow French bread, ½″ thick
8 eggs
4 teaspoons flour
8-ounce can snails, drained

Place wine, carrot, shallots, thyme leaves, peppercorns, sugar and salt in a saucepan and bring to a boil over high heat. Cook until reduced to ¾. Meanwhile, melt 1 tablespoon butter in a skillet and sauté the mushrooms and bacon for 5 minutes, stirring frequently. Set aside and keep warm. Sauté bread in 4 tablespoons butter until golden on both sides.

When the wine is reduced, strain it into a large skillet and heat to the simmering point. Poach the eggs in the wine, remove with a slotted spoon and keep warm. Strain the wine into a saucepan and heat. Mix the flour with the remaining butter and add this beurre manié to the wine bit by bit and cook, stirring constantly, until thickened. Add the mushrooms, bacon and snails to the sauce. Place a slice of sautéed bread on each plate, top with a poached egg and cover with sauce. Serves 8.

OEUFS POCHÉS CRESSONNIÈRE

4 eggs
2 bunches watercress
⅔ cup mayonnaise
   Cayenne pepper to taste
¼ cup heavy cream, whipped
1 tablespoon vinegar
3 tablespoons oil
   Salt, black pepper, dry mustard to taste

Poach eggs and put into cold water. Blanch ¾ of 1 bunch of cress in boiling water for 3 minutes. Drain and press to remove liquid. Put blanched cress in an electric blender with mayonnaise and blend till smooth. Season with cayenne, fold in whipped cream and taste for seasoning. Make a French dressing by whisking vinegar into oil, salt, pepper and mustard. Chop remaining watercress and mix with French dressing. Arrange down center of serving dish, drain and dry eggs and place on cress; coat with mayonnaise. Serve with thin bread and butter as a first course for a summer lunch. Serves 4.

CHEESE PINEAPPLE

> 1 pound strong New York Cheddar cheese
> ½ pound Roquefort cheese
> 2 4-ounce packages Philadelphia cream cheese
> ½ pound imported Swiss cheese
> ½ pound California Monterey Jack cheese
> ½ cup melted butter
>   Juice of 2 fresh limes
> ½ cup dry sherry
> 2 tablespoons Worcestershire sauce
> 1 teaspoon cayenne
> 1 teaspoon monosodium glutamate
> 1 teaspoon Beau Monde seasoning
>   Paprika

Grate or mash all the cheeses and mix them together in a large bowl. Add the melted butter, lime juice, sherry and seasonings, except paprika. Work the mixture together with your hands and mold it into a pineapple shape. Make a hole in the top big enough for the leafy top of a pineapple to fit into. Roll the molded cheese in paprika until completely covered. With the end of a teaspoon, indent lines on the surface to make it resemble a pineapple skin. Cut the green top off a fresh pineapple and trim it at the bottom so that it fits in the hole at the top of the cheese ball. Serve on a round platter, ringed by assorted crackers. Serves 24–30.

CAVIAR MOUSSE

> 2 tablespoons gelatin
> 2 tablespoons lemon juice
> 4 tablespoons mayonnaise
> 8 ounces caviar
>   Pinch dry mustard
> 2 tablespoons tarragon vinegar
> 2 tablespoons Worcestershire sauce
> 1 quart sour cream

Soak the gelatin in 4 tablespoons cold water. Add 1 cup boiling water and stir until gelatin is dissolved. Add remaining ingredients in the order given and blend. Pour into a shallow, rectangular dish or two dishes—the mousse should be about ¾" thick. Chill until firm. Cut into ¾" squares and serve the squares on toothpicks.

CHEESE MOLD

> ¾ pound Roquefort cheese
> 1 large package Philadelphia cream cheese
> ½ bunch celery leaves, chopped fine
> ½ green pepper, chopped fine
> ½ tablespoon minced onion
> 1 tablespoon melted butter
> 1 tablespoon Worcestershire sauce
>   Salt, pepper to taste
> ¾ pound salted pecans, chopped
>   Parsley sprigs

Mix together all ingredients except pecans and parsley and form into a ball. Roll in the pecans and chill. Garnish with parsley. Serves 6–8.

CAMEMBERT MARINÉ

> 1 whole ripe Camembert cheese
>   Dry white wine (Chablis or Sauvignon Blanc)
> ¼ pound softened butter
>   Finely chopped toasted almonds

Soak the cheese in dry white wine to cover overnight. Next morning, drain and scrape off the discolored portion, but leave some of the crust. Now mix the cheese with the butter, working well until perfectly smooth. Chill for easier handling and form into the original shape of the cheese. Cover the cheese—top, bottom, and sides—with finely chopped toasted almonds and chill, but remove it from the refrigerator about half an hour before serving. Serve with hot toasted water biscuits.

CURRY CREAM

> 1 envelope gelatin
> 2½ cups hot chicken broth
> 6 hard-cooked egg yolks
>   Curry powder to taste
>   Chutney

Soften the gelatin in ¼ cup cold water. Dissolve in the hot chicken broth. Put broth, egg yolks and 1 teaspoon curry powder in an electric blender. Blend for 30 seconds or so. Taste and add more curry if desired. Place in a well-oiled ring mold and chill. Serve as a first course with chutney in the center of the ring. Serves 8.

STUFFED CLAMS OR MUSSELS

2 dozen littleneck clams or mussels
½ cup dry white wine
Salt
1 stalk celery, finely chopped
2 green onions, chopped
3 tablespoons olive oil
½ cup white rice
3 tablespoons pine nuts
3 tablespoons currants
2 tablespoons butter

Scrub the clams or mussels thoroughly under cold running water, using a stiff brush. Place in a kettle, pour over the wine and ½ cup water and sprinkle lightly with salt. Cover and steam for 10 minutes, or until the shells open. Reserve broth. Sauté the celery and onion in the oil until soft. Add the rice and cook a few minutes.

Pour in 1¼ cups of broth drained from the clams and simmer for 20 minutes, or until rice is tender. Remove the clams from their shells and add to the rice along with the nuts and currants. Heat the butter until sizzling and lightly browned and pour over pilaff. Heat a few minutes, then fill the shells with the pilaff mixture. Serve hot. Serves 4–6.

Note: If desired, the pilaff may be prepared and placed in the shells ahead of time. When ready to serve, heat through in a 350° oven.

HERBED CLAM FRITTERS

1½ cups flour
½ teaspoon salt
8 tablespoons butter
3 eggs, separated
¾ cup beer
2 dozen fresh cherrystone clams or 2 cups canned minced clams
1 tablespoon finely chopped parsley
1 tablespoon finely chopped chives
Lemon wedges
Parsley sprigs

Place the flour and salt in a mixing bowl. Melt 4 tablespoons butter and add. Lightly beat the egg yolks and mix. Gradually add the beer and allow the batter to stand in a warm place for 1 hour.

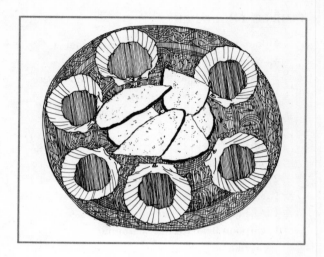

If you are using fresh clams, open them and chop them finely. Add the chopped or canned minced clams, chopped parsley and chives to the batter. Stiffly beat the egg whites and fold in. Heat remaining butter in a pan. When hot, drop in the batter by spoonfuls. Brown the fritters lightly on all sides and drain on paper towels. Serve hot, garnished with lemon wedges and parsley sprigs. Makes about 36 2½″ herbed clam fritters.

CRAB IN CLAMSHELLS

2 dozen littleneck clams
¼ cup water
1 slice onion
2 tablespoons butter
2 tablespoons flour
1 pound crab meat (fresh, canned or frozen), well picked over
Salt, freshly ground black pepper, cayenne pepper to taste
1 tablespoon cognac
Aspic

Place the clams in a saucepan with the water and onion slice. Cover and bring to the boil. Simmer 5–10 minutes, or until clams open up and release their juices. Strain the liquid; there should be about 1 cup. Remove the clams from their shells and reserve 36 half-shells. Reserve the clams for other uses.

Bring the clam juice to a boil and simmer until it is reduced to ¾ cup. Melt the butter and stir in the flour, using a wire whisk. When blended, add the clam juice, stirring vigorously with the whisk. When the mixture is thickened and smooth, add the crab meat, salt, pepper, cayenne and cognac. Spoon the mixture into the container of an electric blender and blend. Do not overblend; some of the texture of the crab meat should be preserved. Use the crab meat mixture as a stuffing for the reserved clamshells, dividing it evenly. Chill well.

Unmold the firm aspic onto a wet board and chop it with a knife. Spoon the aspic onto and around the stuffed clamshells and serve cold. Serves 4–6.

DEVILED CLAMS

24 clams on the half shell
6 tablespoons butter
3 tablespoons minced onion
1 clove garlic, minced
1 tablespoon minced parsley
¼ cup beer
4 slices crisp bacon, crumbled
4 tablespoons bread crumbs

Coarsely chop the clams. Cream together the butter, onion, garlic and parsley. Blend in the beer, then mix in bacon and clams. Fill clam shells with the mixture and sprinkle with the bread crumbs. Place on a baking sheet. Bake in a preheated 375° oven 10 minutes. Serves 4–6.

CRAB MEAT CHARENTAIS

6 tablespoons butter (approximately)
4 thin slices French bread
3–4 scallions, finely sliced
1 green pepper, finely chopped
1 tablespoon grated carrot
⅓ cup white wine
1 pound crab meat
Salt, freshly ground pepper to taste
1 teaspoon chopped tarragon leaves or
½ teaspoon dried tarragon
⅓ cup cognac
Lemon wedges
Chopped parsley

Melt the butter in a chafing dish and brown the

bread slices very quickly. Remove them to a hot platter. Add additional butter if necessary and cook scallions, pepper and carrot briskly for 2 minutes. Add white wine, crab and seasonings. Toss lightly to heat crab meat thoroughly. Heat cognac, ignite and pour flaming over the crab. Blend. Spoon the mixture over the slices of toast. Garnish with lemon wedges and chopped parsley. Serves 3–4.

LEON LIANIDES' CRAB WITH PROSCIUTTO

24 thin slices of prosciutto
12-ounce can fresh lump crab meat, picked over
1½ sticks butter
1 teaspoon Worcestershire sauce
½ teaspoon Tabasco sauce
Juice of 1 lemon
2 tablespoons finely chopped parsley
Freshly ground black pepper

Arrange 4 slices of prosciutto on a flat surface, each slice lightly overlapping the other. Place in the center a heaping tablespoon of lump crab meat. Roll the ham over the crab meat cigar-style. Repeat with remaining prosciutto and crab.

Heat the butter in a large skillet. When foaming, add the 6 ham-wrapped crab rolls. The ham will cling to the crab when heated. Turn once and cook just until ham starts to frizzle and crab is heated through. Transfer to a hot platter.

Add the Worcestershire sauce, Tabasco and lemon juice to juices in skillet. Heat. Pour over ham. Sprinkle with parsley and pepper. Serves 6.

ANGUILLES AU VERT

1 cup olive oil
3 pounds eel, cut in 1¼″ pieces
1 quart broth
½ cup chopped herbs (parsley, chervil, mint, chives, purée of spinach)
Juice of 3 lemons
1 pint white wine
Salt, pepper

Heat the oil. Sauté the pieces of eel in the hot oil for

5 minutes, turning them to cook on all sides. Add the broth, bring to a boil and cook for 5 more minutes. Add the herbs, lemon juice, wine, salt and pepper to taste and bring once more to a boil. Turn off the heat and let stand until cool. Serves 6–8.

MUSSELS EN COQUILLE

    3 quarts mussels
    1 cup dry white wine
    1 bay leaf
    4 sprigs parsley
    2 scallions, minced
    1 cup mayonnaise
    2 teaspoons Dijon mustard
    1 tablespoon drained capers, chopped
    ⅓ cup minced parsley

Scrub the mussels under cold running water and scrape off as much of the beard as possible with a small sharp knife. Bring the wine to a boil in a large pot, add the bay leaf, parsley sprigs, and scallions, and cook for 2 minutes. Add the mussels, cover the pot tightly and cook over high heat, shaking the pot frequently, for 5 minutes. Remove the mussels from their shells, discarding any whose shells have not opened. Cool and chill the mussels.

Combine the mayonnaise, mustard, capers, and 3 tablespoons of the minced parsley. Mix with the chilled mussels, divide among 8 coquilles, sprinkle with remaining parsley, and chill in the refrigerator until serving time. Serves 8.

STUFFED MUSSELS GIOBBI

    2 pounds mussels
    1½ cups fine dry bread crumbs
    ½ cup freshly grated Parmesan cheese
    ½ cup minced Italian parsley
    2 cloves garlic, crushed
    2 tablespoons olive oil
    ¼ teaspoon dried oregano

Scrub the mussels under cold running water. With a small sharp knife, pry open the shells and loosen the flesh. Perform this operation over a small bowl to collect all the juices. Discard one half of each shell. (If the mussels are very large, divide in two and place half on each half shell.) This is the preferred method, but if you find it too difficult to open the mussels, steam them open by cooking them in a large covered soup kettle over high heat for about 6 minutes, or until the shells open.

Place the mussels on the half shell in a single layer in a large shallow baking dish. Mix the remaining ingredients, and cover each mussel with a portion of the mixture. Sprinkle with the reserved mussel juice. Bake in a preheated 400° oven for 5 minutes, or until crumbs start to brown. Serve immediately. Serves 6.

OYSTERS ROCKEFELLER À LA LOUISIANE

    2 dozen oysters on the half shell
    1 pound fresh spinach, cooked and drained well
    1 tablespoon finely chopped shallots
    ½ clove garlic, finely chopped
    6 scallions, trimmed and chopped
    2 stalks celery, chopped
    ½ cup finely chopped parsley
    10 lettuce leaves
    ½ pound butter, melted
    1 cup bread crumbs
    1 tablespoon Worcestershire sauce
    1 tablespoon anchovy paste
      Tabasco to taste
    3 tablespoons Pernod
    ¾ cup grated Parmesan cheese mixed with
      ½ cup bread crumbs

Remove the oysters and any oyster liquor from the shells and put into a saucepan. Bring just to the boil, remove from the heat and reserve. Place the shells on a rack and bake in a 450° oven for 5 minutes.

Meanwhile, combine the cooked spinach, shallots, garlic, scallions, celery, parsley, lettuce and melted butter in the blender. Blend quickly, pushing the mixture down with a rubber spatula when necessary. Add the bread crumbs, Worcestershire sauce, anchovy paste, Tabasco and Pernod. Taste and if necessary, blend in salt to taste.

Place one oyster in each shell. Spoon the sauce over the oysters, sprinkle them with the grated cheese mixture and bake in a 450° oven until brown. Serve hot. Serves 4.

HOW TO CLEAN MUSSELS

Scrub mussels under running water with wire brush to remove mud, matter clinging to shell.

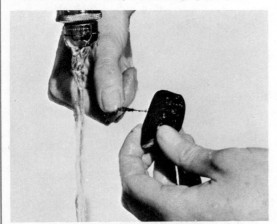

With point of small, sharp knife, remove beard (stringy piece connected to inside of shell).

BAKED OYSTERS VERA

30 large oysters
6 tablespoons butter
1 cup minced celery
3 tablespoons flour
¼ cup capers, drained and chopped
3 tablespoons cream
⅓ cup fine dry bread crumbs

Shuck the oysters, reserving the juice and 18 shells. Heat the oysters in their liquor just until they plump. Drain, and measure 1½ cups of liquor. (If necessary, add chicken consommé to make up the 1½ cups liquid.) Melt 3 tablespoons butter in a saucepan and sauté the celery over medium heat until tender but still crisp. Add the flour and stir until blended. Gradually add the reserved juice and cook, stirring constantly, until the sauce thickens. Remove from the heat, stir in the capers and cream. Chop the oysters coarsely, fold into the sauce and spoon into the reserved shells. Melt the remaining butter, mix with the bread crumbs and sprinkle over the filled shells. Refrigerate until shortly before serving time. Bake in a 450° oven for 10 minutes. Serve the oysters immediately. Serves 6.

OYSTERS ROCKEFELLER À LA FRANEY

2 dozen oysters on the half shell (and reserved oyster liquor)
5 tablespoons butter
5 tablespoons flour
1½ cups milk
Salt, pepper to taste
¼ teaspoon nutmeg
Pinch of cayenne
2 egg yolks
½ cup heavy cream
2 pounds fresh spinach
1 clove garlic, finely minced
2 tablespoons Pernod
6 anchovy fillets, finely chopped
4 tablespoons (approximately) finely grated Parmesan cheese or Gruyère cheese

Remove the oysters from the half shell. Put oysters and their liquor in a small saucepan. Bring to the boil and remove from the heat. Place 12 shells on a baking sheet and bake about 10 minutes, or until dry.

Discard the remaining oyster shells.

Melt butter in a saucepan and, using a wire whisk, blend in the flour. Add the milk, stirring vigorously with the whisk. When the sauce is thickened and smooth, continue cooking, stirring frequently, about 10 minutes. Drain liquor from oysters and add to the sauce. Season to taste with salt, pepper, nutmeg and cayenne. Combine the yolks and heavy cream. Add to the sauce, stirring rapidly with the whisk. Heat thoroughly, but do not boil.

Meanwhile, rinse the spinach well and place it in a saucepan. Cook the spinach only in the water remaining on the leaves. When it is tender, pour into a colander and drain well. Press with a spoon to remove most of the moisture. Blend the spinach with the garlic, Pernod and anchovy fillets. Cook over low heat, stirring, until spinach is somewhat dry. Spoon the hot spinach into the empty shells and top each with two oysters. Spoon a little of the hot sauce over each and sprinkle with cheese. Brown under the broiler and serve immediately. Serves 4.

PICKLED SHRIMP

Serve these iced, with cocktails, or as a first course at a summer meal. They will keep well in the refrigerator if put in covered Mason jars.

3 pounds raw shrimp, shelled and cleaned
1 cup white wine vinegar
1 cup olive oil
2 cups white wine
1 tablespoon salt
2 cups water
1 tablespoon sugar
1 large onion, chopped
6 whole cloves
2 dried hot red chili peppers
Celery leaves
Sprig of thyme
1 bay leaf
6 peppercorns

Combine all ingredients and cook until the shrimp are tender. Allow them to cool in the liquid. Serve well chilled, with or without a dunking sauce. Serves 6–8 as a first course.

MARINATED SHRIMP

1½ cups beer
½ teaspoon dry mustard
½ teaspoon celery seed
½ teaspoon freshly ground black pepper
2 pounds raw shrimp, shelled and deveined
¾ cup chopped onions
¼ cup olive oil

Combine and bring to a boil the beer, mustard, celery seed and pepper. Add the shrimp; cook over low heat 5 minutes. Cool. Meanwhile, sauté the onions in the oil; mix the undrained onions into the shrimp mixture. Marinate 24 hours in the refrigerator. Drain and pierce with cocktail picks or toothpicks.

SHRIMP MOGENS ESBENSEN

12 large shrimp
6 tablespoons butter
Salt, pepper to taste
1 tablespoon chopped fresh green onion
1 tablespoon chopped tarragon
¼ cup Pernod
1 cup Hollandaise sauce
Chopped parsley

Shell shrimp and split down the back. Heat butter in a skillet and sauté shrimp briskly until they are pink, about 3–3½ minutes. Add salt, pepper, chopped green onion and tarragon. Blaze with Pernod and add Hollandaise, being careful not to cook after Hollandaise has been added. Sprinkle with parsley. Serves 4.

SHRIMP RÉMOULADE

Court bouillon
1 dried hot red chili pepper
1 tablespoon sugar
2 pounds raw shrimp, shelled and cleaned
3 hard-cooked egg yolks
1 raw egg yolk
1 tablespoon Creole mustard (with horseradish)
or 1½ teaspoons mustard plus 1½ teaspoons horseradish

¼ teaspoon ground mace
1 teaspoon anchovy paste
1 teaspoon finely minced scallion
1 teaspoon finely minced parsley
1 teaspoon salt
½ cup olive oil
3 tablespoons tarragon vinegar
3 tablespoons white wine

Combine the court bouillon with the chili pepper and sugar, add the shrimp and boil until cooked. (This method of cooking in the Creole manner, so popular in New Orleans, is proper with this version of rémoulade sauce.)

Rub the hard-cooked egg yolks smooth in a bowl with a wooden spoon. Add the raw egg yolk, mustard, mace, anchovy paste, scallion, parsley and salt. Gradually drop in the olive oil, vinegar and wine, blending until smooth. Chill well and serve as a dunk for the shrimp, which have been speared on toothpicks, or as a sauce when they are to be served as a first course. Serves 6 as a first course.

SHRIMP WITH GREEN SAUCE

1 small onion, finely minced
3 tablespoons olive oil
1 cup minced parsley
¼ cup dry white wine
¼ cup water
  Pinch saffron
  Pinch cayenne pepper
¼ teaspoon salt
12 pitted green olives, chopped
1½ pounds raw shrimp, shelled and deveined

Cook onion in olive oil until soft, without browning. Add parsley, simmer about 30 seconds. Add remaining ingredients (except shrimp), simmer 5 minutes. Rub through sieve or purée in electric blender. Chill. Cook the shrimp in salted water until they are pink, about 4 minutes. Serve cold with green sauce as a first course. Serves 4.

SEVICHE

This pickled fish dish is a fine choice to serve with cocktails or as a first course.

1½ **pounds lemon sole, cut in thin strips**
1 **cup fresh lime juice**
½ **cup olive oil**
¼ **cup finely chopped onion**
¼ **cup finely chopped parsley**
2 **tablespoons finely chopped peeled canned green chiles**
1 **clove garlic, finely chopped**
1½ **teaspoons salt**
1 **teaspoon freshly ground black pepper**
  Dash of Tabasco sauce
  Garnish: **chopped cilantro (fresh coriander)**

Cover fish strips with the lime juice and refrigerate for 4 hours. Drain.

Blend all the remaining ingredients and toss with the fish strips. Chill. Serve with chopped cilantro as a garnish. Serves 4–6.

Variations:

1. This traditional South American dish is often made there with tiny scallops. It can also be made with crab or red snapper.
2. Avocado and whole-kernel corn may be added to the sauce.

SMOKED SALMON, SCANDINAVIAN

For each person, arrange 2–3 slices of thinly cut smoked salmon on a serving plate and garnish each with 1 tablespoon capers and 8–10 thin slices cucumber which have been scored and marinated in water, salt, sugar and vinegar with a dash of cayenne pepper. For 2 small cucumbers use 1 teaspoon salt,

3 tablespoons vinegar, 1 tablespoon sugar, 1 cup ice water and ½ teaspoon pepper. Marinate in refrigerator for several hours. Drain on absorbent towel before serving. Garnish with chopped chives or parsley and serve with 1 tablespoon of the following sauce:

Blend ½ cup sour cream with 1 tablespoon chopped fresh dill or 1 teaspoon dill weed, 1 teaspoon salt and 1 tablespoon chopped parsley. Allow to stand for 1 hour. Sprinkle with a little additional chopped dill.

Serve the salmon with thin rye bread and butter sandwiches and pass the pepper grinder.

HOT HAM AND CHEESE BALLS

>   2 cups ground cooked ham
>   2 cups fine toasted bread crumbs
>   1 cup grated Parmesan cheese
>   4 eggs, beaten
>   1 minced onion
>   4 tablespoons chopped parsley
>   Fat for deep frying

Combine the ground ham with 1½ cups of the bread crumbs, the cheese, eggs, onion and parsley. Roll into small balls and roll them in the rest of the bread crumbs until evenly coated.

Heat fat in a deep fryer to 360° and fry the ham balls until crisp and hot through. Serve on toothpicks with any or all of the following sauces for dunking: hot mustard sauce; horseradish and sour cream; puréed or finely chopped chutney; tap sauce (a spicy sauce imported from India); or an old-fashioned homemade relish or chili sauce.

KEFTETHES
(Greek Meat Balls)

>   ⅓ cup fine dry bread crumbs
>   ½ cup milk
>   4 green onions, finely chopped
>   ½ cup finely chopped parsley
>   3 tablespoons olive oil
>   2 pounds ground chuck
>   2 egg yolks
>   2 cloves garlic, minced

>   2 teaspoons salt
>   Freshly ground pepper to taste
>   2 tablespoons butter
>   3 tablespoons red wine vinegar or lemon juice
>   ½ teaspoon crumbled dried oregano

Soak the bread crumbs in the milk until soft. Sauté the onion and parsley in 2 tablespoons of the oil until limp and mix together thoroughly with the ground meat, egg yolks, soaked crumbs and milk, garlic, salt, and pepper. Shape into balls 1″ in diameter. Sauté the balls in the remaining 1 tablespoon oil and the butter in a large frying pan, turning to brown all sides. Pour the vinegar into the pan and sprinkle meat balls with the oregano. Heat a few minutes, scraping up the browned drippings. Makes about 3 dozen appetizer meat balls.

STUFFED VINE LEAVES

>   24–28 vine leaves
>   1½ cups cooked rice
>   ½ pound raw ground pork or lamb
>   ½ cup pine nuts
>   ½ cup currants or sultana raisins
>   Salt to taste
>   1 teaspoon freshly ground black pepper
>   1 egg, beaten
>   ⅓–½ cup olive oil
>   Lemon juice
>   Thyme, chopped parsley for garnish

Vine leaves in jars are available at many specialty shops. As they are packed in brine, be certain to wash them well before using. Remove the stem. If you use fresh vine leaves, soak them in olive oil to cover for 24 hours. Blanch for 2 minutes in boiling water.

Combine the cooked rice, raw meat, nuts, raisins and salt and pepper. Bind with the egg. Form into tiny balls and place one on each vine leaf. Fold and roll so that the stuffing is firmly enveloped. (If you place the ball in the center, and fold in the side points and then roll, the envelope will stay intact.)

Place the stuffed leaves in a skillet with olive oil, a little lemon juice and water to half cover. Cook gently for 15–20 minutes, turning carefully two or three times during the cooking. Remove to a rack covered with absorbent paper, or cool in the pan.

Serve cold with a little of the cooking liquid and a dusting of thyme. Or serve with yoghurt and a sprinkling of thyme and parsley. Serves 6 as a first course or accompaniment.

STEAK TARTARE

>   2 pounds filet of beef or ground top round
>   2 medium onions, finely chopped
>   ½ cup capers
>   ¼ cup chopped parsley
>   2 teaspoons (or more, to taste) Dijon mustard
>   Dash of each: Worcestershire sauce, Tabasco sauce
>   1½ teaspoons salt
>   1 teaspoon freshly ground black pepper
>   ⅓ cup cognac

The best steak tartare is made of chopped (not ground) filet. Cut the meat into finger strips and then chop it yourself, using a heavy French chef's knife. If this seems too difficult to you, buy ground top round steak. Combine the chopped meat with the remaining ingredients, mound the raw meat mixture in a bowl and serve well sprinkled with additional chopped parsley and with anchovies, Dijon mustard and toast fingers on the side.

You may, if you prefer, roll the meat mixture into small balls and then roll them in chopped nuts, or chopped parsley. Spear the balls with toothpicks. Makes about 48 balls.

HUNGARIAN HAM APPETIZER

>   ¼ cup butter
>   ¼ cup cracker crumbs
>   1 cup sour cream
>   ¼ cup grated Swiss cheese
>   1½ cups minced cooked ham
>   2 teaspoons caraway seeds
>   6 eggs, beaten until light and thick

Combine butter and cracker crumbs with sour cream, cheese, minced ham, caraway seeds and eggs. Pour mixture onto a greased cookie sheet and bake in a 375° oven until nicely browned, about 15 minutes. Cut into squares and serve hot with cocktails or salad course. Makes 24 squares.

HOW TO STUFF VINE LEAVES

Remove brine-packed leaves from the jar. Separate carefully and rinse well under cold water. Dry leaves on paper towels.

Put vine leaf flat on board, veined side upward. Form rice-meat mixture into small ball, place in center of leaf.

Fold side points of the leaf toward the center, covering the ball of filling. Roll up, starting at stem end.

Fold over point at top, like envelope flap. Place in skillet this side down so leaf does not unroll in cooking.

COCONUT MEAT BALLS WITH SWEET-SOUR SAUCE

These appetizer meat balls are equally good with or without the sauce.

>   ¾ pound lean ground round steak
>   1 teaspoon salt
>   ⅛ teaspoon black pepper
>   2 tablespoons flour
>   1 egg, slightly beaten
>   1⅓ cups flaked coconut
>   Oil for frying
>   2 teaspoons dry mustard
>   1 teaspoon vinegar
>   5 tablespoons chutney, chopped
>   ¼ cup currant jelly
>   1½ teaspoons sugar

Combine the beef, salt and pepper and shape into about 36 small 1″ balls. Stir the flour into the egg and roll meat balls in this mixture, then in the coconut. Pour oil ¼″ deep in a skillet, heat until very hot and brown the meat balls lightly. Keep warm in a 250° oven while making the sauce.

Combine the remaining ingredients in a small saucepan. Heat, stirring frequently, until the jelly is melted. Serve with the warm coconut meat balls.

TERIYAKI

>   2 pounds boneless lean pork, chicken breasts
>   or sirloin steak
>   1 cup soy sauce
>   2 cloves garlic, crushed
>   1″ piece fresh ginger grated (or 1 teaspoon dry
>   powdered ginger)
>   ½ cup dry sherry

Have the meat sliced ½″ thick and then cut into strips about 1″ wide and 6″ long. Mix the soy sauce, garlic, ginger and sherry in a bowl and marinate the meat strips. Let stand in the refrigerator for an hour.

When ready to cook, weave the strips back and forth on small individual skewers. Grill quickly, turning to cook on both sides and basting once or twice with the marinade. Chicken or steak will cook in about 3 minutes, the pork will take a little longer.

Serve teriyaki with a bowl of sesame seeds, a bowl of hot Chinese mustard and a bowl of puréed chutney for dunking. Serves 8.

RUSSIAN LIVER APPETIZER

>   1 pound calves liver
>   ¼ pound bacon
>   Herb bouquet
>   1 small onion
>   4 slices bread soaked in 1½ cups liver stock
>   2 eggs, beaten

Cook calves liver in water to cover, with bacon, herb bouquet and onion until tender. Drain; reserve stock. Grind liver and combine with bread soaked in the liver stock and squeezed dry. Add eggs and liver stock. Bake in a buttered dish in a 350° oven for 25 minutes. Serve cold and sliced, with buttered rye bread. Serves 8.

BRAINS VINAIGRETTE

>   1 pound brains, parboiled and sliced
>   ¾ cup olive oil
>   ¼ cup wine vinegar
>   2 tablespoons red wine
>   ¾ teaspoon salt
>   1 tablespoon each: chopped chives, capers,
>   green olives, parsley
>   Freshly ground black pepper to taste
>   Watercress

Arrange sliced brains neatly, overlapping, on a serving dish. Combine all other ingredients except watercress for sauce vinaigrette. Pour sauce over brains and chill. Garnish dish with cress and serve. Serves 4.

CHICKEN LIVERS GIOVANNI

>   1½ pounds chicken livers (about 24 livers)
>   ¼ cup flour
>   ½ cup olive oil
>   ¼ cup French's mustard
>   ¼ cup fine seasoned bread crumbs
>   3 tablespoons minced parsley

Pat the livers dry and coat them on all sides with flour. Heat the oil in a large heavy skillet over high heat. Fry the livers, turning constantly, until they are brown and firm to the touch. Remove livers and set aside. Mix the mustard with the pan drippings and coat the livers on all sides with the mixture. Mix the bread crumbs and parsley and coat the livers lightly. Refrigerate until serving time. (Preparation up to this point may be done in advance.) When almost ready to serve, broil the livers about 4" from the heat about 2 minutes on each side, or until brown. Serve them as an appetizer.

CHICKEN LIVER CANAPÉ

    12 thin slices Italian or French bread
    6 tablespoons butter
    ½ pound chicken livers
    2 tablespoons minced parsley
    ½ teaspoon salt
    ¼ teaspoon freshly ground black pepper
    2 anchovies, mashed
    2 tablespoons white wine

Sauté the bread in 3 tablespoons butter until browned on both sides. Wash the livers, cutting away any discolored spots. Chop very fine.

Melt the remaining butter in a skillet; sauté the livers and parsley 3 minutes, stirring almost constantly. Mix in the salt, pepper, anchovies and wine; cook 2 minutes longer, again stirring. Spread on the sautéed bread. Serves 6.

CHICKEN LIVER PÂTÉ

    ½ pound chicken livers
    4 tablespoons butter
    2 eggs
    ½ cup cognac or bourbon
    1 onion, chopped
    2 cloves garlic, finely chopped
    ½ teaspoon allspice
    1 tablespoon salt
    1 teaspoon rosemary
    ½ teaspoon freshly ground black pepper
    1 pound ground pork (sausage meat may be
      used)

    ¼ cup flour
    Salt pork strips

Sauté the chicken livers lightly in the butter until they are just firm enough to handle. Trim them and whirl in a blender with the eggs, cognac, onion, garlic, and seasonings.

Blend this mixture with the pork and the flour. Pour into a bread tin or pâté mold lined with salt pork strips and cover with a lid or with foil. Bake in a 350° oven 1½–2 hours, or until the liquid in the pan and the fat are clear. Cool for 15 minutes. Weight and cool thoroughly.

PÂTÉ MAISON

    ½ pound bacon
    ¼ cup brandy
    1½ pounds each: beef and calves' liver, ground
    ½ pound pork liver, ground
    2 eggs
    ¼ cup sour cream
    Salt, black pepper, a little crushed garlic
    3 or 4 chicken livers

Line a pâté mold with thinly sliced bacon, sprinkle with a little brandy. Mix ground livers with eggs, sour cream, and seasonings. Mix well and pour on remaining brandy, flaming. Mix well and half fill mold with mixture. Put chicken livers in row down center. Cover with rest of pâté, then cover top with bacon. Stand mold in pan of water and bake at 300° for about 2 hours, covered with foil. Remove, cool in water. Put brick on top to press down firmly and chill in refrigerator for 24 hours. Turn out and cut as many slices as needed. Arrange on a platter, overlapping, uncut piece at end. Surround with chopped aspic.

PORK LIVER PÂTÉ

This is one of the simplest forms of pâté. It may be used for hors d'oeuvre and sandwiches.

    2½ pounds pork liver
    4 eggs
    2½ pounds pork
    1 pound pork fat

2 onions, finely chopped
4–6 cloves garlic, finely chopped
1 teaspoon thyme
1½ tablespoons salt
1½ teaspoons freshly ground black pepper
½ cup cognac
½ cup flour
   Salt pork, thinly sliced

Grind the liver very fine, and mix with the eggs, or whirl a little at a time with the eggs in a blender. Grind the pork with a bit of the pork fat. Cut the remaining fat into small dice.

Blend the meat, liver, and fat. Mix well with the onions, garlic, seasonings, cognac, and flour. Line two large or several small terrines or casseroles with thin slices of salt pork. Fill with the mixture. Seal with foil and then cover with the lid. Place in a roasting pan containing boiling water, and bake in a 350° oven, allowing 2–2½ hours for large terrines, 1½ hours for small terrines. Cool 15 minutes. Remove covers and weight down the terrines while they cool thoroughly. To keep it, cover the pâté with a layer of melted pork fat.

COUNTRY PÂTÉ

2 pounds lean pork
1 pound fresh side pork with fat, diced small
2 pounds ground veal
1 tablespoon basil
1¼ tablespoons salt
1 teaspoon freshly ground black pepper
½ teaspoon Spice Parisienne or quatre épices
1 pound pork liver
6 cloves garlic
2 eggs
⅓ cup cognac
   Salt pork strips
2–3 strips bacon

Cut half the lean pork into ½" dice and grind the rest. Blend with the diced pork fat, veal, basil, salt, pepper, and spice. Divide the pork liver in half and whirl one half in the blender with the garlic and the eggs, the other half with the cognac, adding a trifle more cognac if the mixture doesn't completely cover the blender blades.

Mix all together thoroughly with your hands or with a heavy wooden spatula. Line a large round earthenware dish with strips of salt pork. Mound the mixture in it, top with bacon strips and bake in a 350° oven, uncovered, 1½–2 hours, or until the fat runs clear. Cool and chill.

FOIE GRAS AU MADEIRA

1 whole canned goose liver
Paprika
¼ cup Madeira
Thin, crisp toast

Open the can and empty the contents carefully onto a shallow baking dish. Sprinkle liberally with paprika and moisten with the Madeira. Place in a preheated 350° oven just long enough for the liver to become heated through. Serve with piles of crisp toast.

VEAL AND HAM PÂTÉ

1½ pounds ground veal
1½ pounds ground pork
1 pound pork fat, diced
2 cloves garlic, finely cut
1 teaspoon thyme
¼ teaspoon Spice Parisienne or quatre épices
1 tablespoon salt, or more
½ teaspoon freshly ground black pepper
3 eggs
½ cup cognac
1½ pounds ground smoked ham
1½ teaspoons Dijon mustard
   Pinch of ground cloves
¼ teaspoon nutmeg
¼ cup Madeira
½ cup pistachio nuts
   Barding pork
   Salt pork strips

Combine the veal, pork, and pork fat with the garlic, thyme, spice, salt, pepper, 2 of the eggs, and cognac. Mix thoroughly. Combine the ham with the mustard, cloves, nutmeg, remaining egg, and the Madeira, and blend well. Put pistachio nuts in center of the ham mixture and roll into a sausage. Wrap a piece of barding pork around it. Line the bottom of a terrine with salt pork strips and cover with a layer of the veal and pork forcemeat. Place the roll of ham in the center and enclose with additional forcemeat. Top with one or two strips of salt pork, cover, and bake in a 350° oven for 2–2½ hours, or until the fat runs clear. Cool for 20 minutes. Weight the pâté and continue cooling.

RILLETTES DE TOURS

  5–6 pounds leaf lard
  5–6 pounds pork (shoulder, loin or leg)
  Salt, freshly ground black pepper
  Chopped truffle (optional)

Render the leaf lard in a large pot. When it is melted, add the pork meat cut into fairly small pieces and 1 cup of water. Cover the pot and cook slowly on top of the stove, or in a 250°–300° oven, until the meat is so tender that it almost falls apart. This will take about 4 hours.

Remove the meat from the fat and shred it with a fork. Season to taste with salt and pepper, add some finely chopped truffle if you wish. Spoon the shredded pork into small pots with some of the fat, mashing so pork absorbs fat. Ladle enough lard on top of each to cover the meat and make it airtight. It will keep in the refrigerator for several weeks. To serve as an hors d'oeuvre, spread on toast.

RILLETTES D'OIE

  1 goose, about 8–9 pounds, roasted and cooled
  Salt
  2–2½ pounds pork kidney fat or leaf lard
  1 clove garlic
  Freshly ground pepper
  Dried herbs to taste (optional)

Remove the skin from the goose and cut the meat away from the bones. Reserve some of the goose fat from the roasting pan. Rub meat with salt and let stand for several hours. Combine with the pork fat, ½ cup water, garlic, pepper, and dried herbs, if desired, in a heavy casserole or braising pan. Add some of the reserved goose fat and cook in a 300° oven for about 4 hours, or until the goose meat has cooked down thoroughly.

Pour contents of casserole into a colander over a large pan and let the meat drain. When it is cool and drained, shred it very finely with two forks. Place in a crock and pack in, mixing well with some of the fat. Ladle fat over the top to cover. With this sealing layer of fat, the rillettes will keep for several weeks under refrigeration. Serve on bread or crackers just as you would a pâté.

TORTA RUSTICA TRATTORIA

  1 medium onion, minced
  1¼ pounds butter
  1 pound boneless pork loin
  1 pound boneless beef chuck
  1 pound boneless veal, cut from leg
  2 10-ounce packages frozen chopped spinach, cooked and drained
  1 teaspoon mashed garlic
  5 eggs
  1 cup grated Parmesan cheese
  ¼ pound ham, cut in julienne strips
  Salt, pepper
  2 tablespoons fine bread crumbs
  ½ teaspoon sugar
  4 cups flour
  4-ounce can pimiento, drained
  5 hard-cooked eggs
  1 egg yolk mixed with 1 teaspoon water

Sauté the onion in ¼ pound of the butter until transparent and golden. Coarsely grind the pork, beef, and veal together, add them to the onion, and sauté for 10 minutes over high heat, stirring constantly with a fork to break up the chunks of meat. Sauté the spinach and garlic in another skillet in ¼ pound butter for 5 minutes. Cool the meat and spinach mixtures. Beat 3 of the eggs lightly and add ½ cup of the cheese. Mix with the meats and the ham. Beat the remaining 2 eggs with the remaining ½ cup cheese and stir into the spinach mixture. Season both mixtures with salt and pepper to taste.

Grease a large loaf pan, approximately 11" by 4½" by 2¾", and sprinkle bread crumbs on the bottom.

Make the pastry: soften the remaining ¾ pound butter and combine with the sugar, ½ teaspoon salt, and ½ cup lukewarm water. Spoon the flour into a bowl, make a well in the center and pour in the butter mixture. Mix with a fork, adding a bit more water if necessary. Knead until the dough is smooth. Roll out the dough to a thickness of ⅛", and line the bottom and sides of the pan with pastry, reserving a scant ¼ for the top.

Spoon half the meat into the prepared pan and cover with half the spinach. Cut the pimiento into narrow strips and arrange it over the spinach. Cut off the ends of the hard-cooked eggs and lay them end-to-end down the center of the pan. Cover with the remaining spinach and then with the remaining meat. Cover with the reserved pastry and press the edges with a fork to seal. Brush the top of the pastry with the egg yolk mixed with water, and cut several air vents in the top. Bake in a preheated 350° oven for 45 minutes–1 hour, or until the pastry is golden. Cool the torta before turning it out of the tin. Slice and serve cold as a first course or as a light luncheon entrée. Makes 16–24 servings.

SWISSAIR TARTS

1⅓ cups flour
¼ cup ground walnuts
8 tablespoons butter, at room temperature
5 egg yolks
⅓ cup plus 1 tablespoon milk
3 ounces Gruyère cheese, coarsely grated
1 teaspoon cornstarch
3 tablespoons light cream
  Salt to taste
⅓ cup heavy cream

Mix the flour and walnuts. Add the butter and 2 egg yolks and mix with your hands until you obtain a smooth dough. Divide dough into 14–18 pieces and press each portion with lightly floured fingers over the bottom and sides of 14–18 fluted tart tins, 2"– 2½" in diameter. Prick the surface of the dough with a fork and bake the shells in a preheated 350° oven for 15–20 minutes, or until golden. Leave the shells in the tins for a few minutes, and then remove them very carefully.

Heat the milk and cheese, stirring constantly, until the cheese melts and the mixture comes to a boil.

Mix the remaining 3 egg yolks with the cornstarch and light cream. Add to the cheese mixture and heat to just under the boiling point. Remove from the heat, add salt, cool, and chill. (For fast chilling, place the mixture in the freezer.) Whip the heavy cream until stiff, fold into the chilled cheese mixture. Place the mixture in a pastry bag fitted with a star-shaped tube and pipe it into the tarts. Refrigerate until serving time. Serve them as an appetizer or as a first course. Makes 14–18 tarts.

CHEESE STICKS

2 cups sifted flour
½ teaspoon salt
2 teaspoons chili powder
1½ sticks (6 ounces) butter
1 cup grated Cheddar cheese
⅓ cup beer
4 tablespoons heavy cream
¼ cup ground nuts

Sift together the flour, salt and chili powder. Cut in the butter and cheese with a pastry blender or 2 knives. Stir in just enough beer to make particles adhere; form into ball. Chill 2 hours.

Roll out the dough ⅛" thick on a lightly floured surface. Cut into strips ½" wide by 4" long. Arrange on a baking pan; brush with the cream and sprinkle with the nuts. Bake in a preheated 425° oven 10 minutes or until browned. Cool on a cake rack. The sticks will keep indefinitely in an airtight container. Makes about 6 dozen.

GOUGÈRE EN CROÛTE

  Pastry for 9½" pie
⅔ cup milk
2½ tablespoons butter
¼ teaspoon salt
¾ cup flour
½ teaspoon dry mustard
2 eggs
3 ounces Gruyère cheese, finely diced
  Cream sauce, mixed with ½ pound cooked seafood or mushrooms

Roll out the pastry to a circle about 10½" in diameter. Line a 9½" pie plate. Flute rim.

Bring the milk and butter to a boil in a small saucepan. Add salt and flour and stir briskly until the mixture forms a ball and leaves the sides of the pan. Remove from the heat and beat in the mustard and 1 egg at a time until the dough is satiny. Fold in ¾ of the cheese. Spoon the mixture in a circle over the tart pastry, reaching about 1" from the edge and leaving a hole in the center. Sprinkle the remaining cheese over the circle of dough. Bake in a preheated 425° oven for 15 minutes. Lower the heat to 400° and bake 30 minutes longer, reducing the heat 25° every 10 minutes.

Spoon a little of the seafood or mushroom sauce in the center of the gougère and pass the rest separately. Serve as an appetizer or first course. Serves 6–8.

QUICHE LORRAINE

    2 cups all-purpose flour
    1 teaspoon salt
    1½ sticks (6 ounces) very cold sweet butter
    ⅓ cup ice water
    2 tablespoons bread crumbs
    ¾ cup freshly grated Parmesan cheese
    1 pound bacon
    2 egg yolks
    2 eggs
        Salt, cayenne pepper to taste
    1 teaspoon Dijon mustard
    ½ teaspoon dry mustard
    2 drops Tabasco
    2 drops Worcestershire sauce
    1½ cups scalded milk
    2 tablespoons chopped fresh parsley

Sift flour and salt into a large bowl. Cut the butter into small pieces and add it to the flour. Rub the butter into the flour with the tips of the fingers until it resembles coarse cornmeal. Add the ice water and work up quickly to a firm dough. Turn it out onto a lightly floured pastry board and knead to get a smooth surface. Wrap in wax paper. Chill 10 minutes. Remove. Roll out ½" thick. Line a 10" flan ring placed on a jelly roll pan. Trim off pastry neatly. Prick all over the bottom with a fork, line with a

piece of buttered wax paper. Put ½ cup of raw rice on top of the paper to keep it down while baking. Bake 30–35 minutes in a 375° oven. Take flan ring off 10 minutes before it is cooked. Remove, sprinkle the bottom with bread crumbs and grated cheese.

Cut the bacon into fine shreds and fry in a heavy frying pan until crisp. Drain. Put egg yolks and eggs into a bowl. Mix in the salt, cayenne pepper, Dijon and dry mustards, Tabasco and Worcestershire; add half a cup of grated Parmesan cheese, the scalded milk, and ½ the drained bacon. Carefully spoon this into the flan right up to the rim. Place in a 300° oven and leave for 15–20 minutes until just firm to the touch. Remove and cool a little. Sprinkle the top with the rest of the bacon, the chopped parsley and a little grated Parmesan cheese. Serves 6–8.

TIROTRIGONA

These hot, savory appetizers freeze beautifully and may be prepared in quantity ahead of time.

    1 pound feta cheese
    1 pint large-curd cottage cheese
    8-ounce package cream cheese
    3 eggs
    2 tablespoons finely chopped parsley
        Dash of pepper
    ¾ pound prepared filo dough (sold in Greek
        grocery stores)
    1 cup butter, melted

Cream together until smooth the feta, cottage cheese,

and cream cheese. Add the eggs, one at a time, beating until smooth. Mix in the parsley and pepper. Lay out filo, one sheet at a time, and brush entire sheet with melted butter. Then, cutting across the width of the dough, cut each sheet into 2″ wide strips. Place a heaping teaspoon of cheese filling on one end of the pastry strip and fold over one corner to make a triangle. Continue folding pastry from side to side in the shape of a triangle until the entire pastry strip covers the filling. Proceed in this manner with filo strips and filling until all are used. Place triangles on a buttered baking sheet and bake in a preheated 350° oven for 15 minutes, or until golden brown. Serve hot. Makes about 6 dozen.

Note: The tirotrigona may be frozen after baking. To reheat, place frozen triangles on a baking sheet and bake them at 350° for 15 minutes, or until they are heated through.

MINIATURE SHRIMP QUICHES

24 tiny tart shells
3 tablespoons grated Parmesan cheese
½ cup chopped cooked shrimp
½ cup grated Swiss cheese
3 egg yolks
¾ cup light cream
Dash of Tabasco
½ teaspoon salt

When making the tart shells, brush them with a mixture of beaten egg and milk for a brown glaze.

Divide the Parmesan cheese, chopped shrimp and Swiss cheese among the tart shells. Mix the egg yolks, cream, Tabasco and salt and fill tart shells with the mixture. Bake in a 325° oven for 15 minutes. Makes 24 miniature quiches.

RAMEQUINS

Pie or puff pastry
2 cups grated Swiss cheese
1 cup light cream
2 eggs
¼ teaspoon salt
¼ teaspoon dry mustard
⅛ teaspoon cayenne

Line 2″ tartlet or muffin pans with pie or puff pastry. Beat together cheese, cream, eggs, salt, mustard and cayenne. Spoon into lined tartlet or muffin pans, filling each about half full. Bake in a 400° oven for 15 minutes, or until golden brown. Serve very hot. Makes about 16 tartlets.

PIROSHKI

¼ cup minced onion
2 tablespoons butter
1 cup minced cooked veal, chicken or tongue
2 hard-cooked eggs, minced
2 tablespoons minced parsley
2 tablespoons fresh dill, minced
Sour cream
1 recipe cream cheese pastry (see Pastry)
1 egg, beaten

Cook onion in butter until lightly browned. Combine with veal, chicken or tongue, eggs, parsley, dill and enough sour cream to moisten slightly.

Roll out pastry very thin and cut into 2″ rounds with a pastry cutter. Put a spoonful of filling in middle of each round, moisten edges and fold up so that the seam is on top, making the piroshki boat-shaped. Brush with beaten egg and bake in a 400° oven for 10 minutes, or until brown. Makes about 2½ dozen. Piroshki may also be made with brioche dough or packaged hot-roll mix.

BASEL ONION TART

Dough:
2 cups all-purpose flour
½ teaspoon salt
½ cup butter
4 tablespoons ice water (about)
Filling:
1½ tablespoons butter
6 large onions, thinly sliced
½ teaspoon salt
⅓ cup diced bacon
2 cups milk
3 tablespoons all-purpose flour
2 eggs, well beaten
2 cups shredded cheese

To make dough, sift flour with salt. Cut in butter until particles are the size of small peas. Add ice water. Stir until a stiff dough is formed. Knead on a lightly floured board. Roll out to fit the bottom and sides of a well-buttered 10″ layer cake pan. Prick dough several times with a fork.

To make filling, heat butter in a pan and sauté onions. Add salt and diced bacon. Cook over medium heat until onions and bacon are golden brown. Add milk gradually to the flour. Stir until smooth. Beat in eggs and cheese. Add sautéed onions and bacon, including the fat in which they were sautéed.

Pour mixture into dough-lined pan. Bake at 350° for 30 minutes. Raise oven temperature to 400° and bake 5 minutes longer, or until top is browned and crisp. Cut into wedges; serve hot. Serves 6.

FRENCH MUSHROOM FLAN

20 medium mushrooms
5 tablespoons butter
1 tablespoon sherry
1 tablespoon lemon juice
   Freshly ground nutmeg to taste
2 tablespoons minced onion
2 tablespoons chopped carrot
2 tablespoons minced celery
3 tablespoons flour
   Salt, pepper to taste
2½ cups hot milk
½ teaspoon turmeric powder
¼ teaspoon paprika
1 pound shrimp, cooked and cleaned
3 eggs, well beaten
10″ pie shell, baked

Remove stems from the mushrooms. Wash and dry the caps. Melt 2 tablespoons butter in a skillet. Add the sherry, lemon juice, and mushroom caps. Sauté for 4 minutes, turning once. Drain. Sprinkle them with nutmeg and set them aside.

Melt the remaining 3 tablespoons butter in a saucepan and sauté the onion, carrot, and celery 1 minute. Blend in flour, salt, and pepper. Add the milk, a little at a time, stirring until smooth. Simmer 15 minutes, stirring often. Remove and discard vegetables.

Add the turmeric powder, paprika, shrimp, and all but three mushroom caps. Cook slowly 1 minute. Remove from the heat. Mix a little of the sauce mixture with the eggs. Add to the remaining sauce. Pour carefully into the pie shell and garnish with the three remaining caps. Bake in a 450° oven about 25 minutes, until a knife inserted in the center comes out clean. Cool for about 10 minutes before serving. Cut the flan into wedges. Serves 6.

COCKTAIL TURNOVERS

Recipe for cream cheese pastry (see Pastry)
2 eggs, beaten with cream or milk
Filling

Follow the recipe for cream cheese pastry, but quadruple the quantities, using 1 pound cream cheese, 1 pound butter, 4 cups sifted flour. Roll out to ¼″ thickness on a floured board and cut into rounds with a 3″ cookie cutter. Place one rounded teaspoon of desired filling on one side of each pastry round and fold other side over filling. Press down and press edges together with tines of a fork (a dab of water on inside edge will hold them together). Paint turnovers with egg mixture, place on a cookie sheet and bake in a 425° oven for 8–10 minutes, or until delicately golden. This amount of pastry will make approximately 80 turnovers.

FILLINGS FOR TURNOVERS

LEBANESE LAMB

3 tablespoons butter
1 cup finely ground lamb
½ beaten egg
½ teaspoon salt
⅛ teaspoon each: nutmeg, allspice, cinnamon
1–2 teaspoons beef bouillon
½ cup cooked rice

Melt the butter and add the meat and egg, tossing together with a fork until all the signs of pink have disappeared from the meat. Add the salt and spices. If the mixture looks dry, add a teaspoon or two of beef bouillon. Mix with the cooked rice. This makes enough filling for about 50 turnovers.

EMPANADA

⅓ cup seedless raisins
½ small onion, minced
1 clove garlic, minced or crushed
½ pound minced lean beef
3–4 tablespoons olive oil, heated
1 teaspoon flour
3–4 tablespoons water or beef bouillon
12 pitted green olives, chopped
Salt, pepper to taste

Soak raisins in boiling water for ½ hour. Drain well. Sauté the onion, garlic and beef in the hot olive oil. Add the flour and brown a little. Add the water or bouillon. Add the raisins, olives and season with salt and pepper. This makes enough filling for about 50 cocktail turnovers.

BEEF AND DILL

3–4 tablespoons butter
½ small onion, minced
½ pound lean ground beef
½ slightly beaten egg
Salt, pepper to taste
2 tablespoons fresh cut dill (cut with scissors and include some stems for flavor)
1–2 teapoons beef bouillon
½ cup cooked rice

Melt the butter and cook the onion 1 minute. Add the meat and egg and keep tossing together with a fork until all the signs of red have disappeared from the meat. Season with salt and pepper—season highly if the turnovers are to be eaten with cocktails. Toss with the dill. If the mixture looks dry, add a teaspoon or two of beef bouillon. Combine meat mixture with rice. Makes enough filling for about 50 turnovers.

SHRIMP AND WATER CHESTNUT

2 tablespoons butter
1½ cups minced cooked shrimp
2 teaspoons flour
½ cup (approximately) light cream
1 tablespoon tomato paste
3 tablespoons dry vermouth
1 tablespoon chopped chives
1 tablespoon chopped parsley
1 small can water chestnuts, chopped
Salt, pepper to taste

Heat the butter and sauté the shrimp a minute or two. Add the flour and cook a little. Add the cream, tomato paste and vermouth to make a smooth sauce. There should be just enough to bind the mixture. Add the chives, parsley, water chestnuts, salt and pepper. This makes enough filling for about 50–60 turnovers.

BEUREK

10 ounces feta cheese
Light cream
½ cup chopped parsley
Freshly ground black pepper

Soften the cheese with a little cream. (Feta is packed in tins and is hard and very salty. It will make a rather crumbly mixture.) Mix with parsley and plenty of black pepper. This makes enough filling for about 50 turnovers.

COCKTAIL CREAM PUFFS

Recipe for cream puff pastry (see Pastry)
Filling

Double the recipe for cream puff pastry, using 2 cups flour, 2 cups water, 1 teaspoon salt, ½ pound butter and 8 eggs. With a teaspoon, make rounded mounds of the cream-puff pastry on ungreased cookie sheets about 2″ apart. Bake in a preheated 375° oven about 15–20 minutes, or until puffed and golden with no moisture showing. Prick on bottom with tip of knife to let steam escape. Split shells or make hole in bottom of each puff and fill with desired filling, spooning it in or piping it through a pastry bag with a plain round tube. Makes about 70 puffs.

FILLINGS FOR CREAM PUFFS

ROQUEFORT-COGNAC

½ pound Roquefort cheese
3 tablespoons heavy cream

¼ pound butter, softened
¼ cup cognac
3–4 shakes cayenne pepper

Mash the cheese well with the cream until softened. Add the softened butter, cognac and cayenne pepper. Whip to a smooth fluffy mixture. Fill puffs with 1 rounded teaspoon of mixture. This makes enough filling for about 60 puffs.

CHICKEN-WALNUT MOUSSE

2 large breasts of chicken, cooked and boned
½ cup mayonnaise
1–2 tablespoons heavy cream
    Salt, pepper to taste
10 large walnut halves, chopped
6 tablespoons whipped cream

Grind the chicken breasts very fine twice. Mix with the mayonnaise and cream. Season with salt and pepper. Add the walnuts and fold in the whipped cream. This makes enough filling for 50 puffs.

SMOKED SALMON MOUSSE

8 large slices smoked salmon
4 tablespoons butter, softened
2 teaspoons prepared horseradish
    Freshly ground black pepper
½ cup whipped cream

Chop or grind the salmon to make a paste. Add the softened butter, horseradish and pepper. Fold in the whipped cream. Fill the puffs. This makes enough filling for 50 puffs.

ASSORTED FILLINGS:

1. Finely chopped chicken blended with mayonnaise, chopped toasted almonds, chopped parsley and a touch of tarragon.
2. Guacamole.
3. Deviled ham blended with a little mayonnaise and chopped pickle.
4. Deviled ham and chopped toasted filberts.
5. Foie gras or any good pâté.

PLAIN CRÊPES

¾ cup flour
⅛ teaspoon salt
3 eggs, beaten
2 tablespoons melted butter
¾ cup milk (approximately)
    Sweet butter

Sift flour and salt together into a bowl. Add beaten eggs, a little at a time and beat with an electric mixer, egg beater or wire whisk until batter is smooth. Add butter and mix thoroughly. Add milk until batter is consistency of heavy cream. Let stand at least 30 minutes. Beat again.

Heat a 6″ or 7″ crêpe pan or heavy skillet and brush with 1 teaspoon sweet butter. Pour in about 2 tablespoons batter or just enough to cover the bottom of the pan, tilting the pan so the batter covers completely. As crêpe begins to brown around edges, loosen by running a spatula around it, turn over and cook until golden on second side. Makes about 12 crêpes. Fill crêpes with any of the following fillings. Serve 1 or 2 crêpes per person as a first course, depending on rest of the menu. You may also serve these as a luncheon or supper dish. In that case, allow 3 per serving.

CHICKEN FILLING

2 tablespoons minced onion
4 tablespoons butter
4 tablespoons flour
1 cup milk
1 cup chicken stock
3 tablespoons white wine
    Salt, pepper
1 egg yolk
2 cups chopped, cooked chicken
½ cup chopped, cooked mushrooms
½ cup chopped, canned pimientos
12 plain crêpes

Sauté onion in butter till golden. Blend in flour; stir in ¾ cup milk and chicken stock and simmer, stirring, till thickened. Add wine, and salt and pepper to taste. Beat egg yolk in ¼ cup of milk and add. Bring to a simmer and let thicken, but do not boil. Set aside ½ cup of sauce.

Add chicken, mushrooms and pimiento to remaining sauce. Spread crêpes with chicken filling and roll. Tuck in ends. Place in a shallow baking dish. Mask with the reserved sauce. Put under broiler to glaze.

LOBSTER FILLING

> 4 tablespoons butter
> 4 tablespoons flour
> 2 cups milk
> 3 tablespoons white wine
> ¼ cup grated Parmesan cheese
> 1 egg yolk
> 4 tablespoons cream
>   Salt, pepper
> 2 cups cooked or canned lobster meat
> 12 plain crêpes

Melt butter; blend in flour. Add milk and wine and stir, cooking slowly till thickened. Add cheese, and stir till cheese is melted. Add egg yolk beaten with cream (to prevent curdling, pour a little hot sauce on egg-cream mixture before adding to pan). Simmer till thickened. Salt and pepper to taste. Reserve 2/3 cup of this sauce.

Add lobster to remaining sauce. Fill 12 crêpes; roll, tuck ends under and place in a shallow, greased baking dish. Mask crêpes with reserved sauce; sprinkle additional cheese on the top. Glaze under broiler.

MUSHROOM FILLING

> 1 pound mushrooms
> 4 tablespoons butter
> 2 tablespoons flour
> 1 cup milk
> ¼ cup sour cream
> 1 tablespoon parsley
>   Salt, pepper
> ⅓ cup fresh-grated Parmesan cheese
> 12 plain crêpes

Slice mushrooms and sauté in butter till tender. Stir in flour; add milk and cream. Stir over low heat till thickened. Add parsley, and salt and pepper to taste.

Spread crêpes with mushroom filling and roll. Tuck in ends. Place in shallow baking dish. Sprinkle with Parmesan cheese and place under broiler to glaze.

HAM FILLING

> 4 tablespoons butter
> 4 tablespoons flour
> 1½ cups milk
>   Salt, pepper
> 1 egg yolk
> 2 cups chopped, cooked ham
> ¾ cup chopped, cooked mushrooms
> 2 tablespoons chopped parsley
> 12 plain crêpes
> ⅓ cup grated Parmesan cheese

Blend butter and flour over heat; stir in milk and simmer, stirring, till thickened. Season to taste. Add a little hot sauce to beaten egg yolk, stirring constantly. Add to balance of sauce. Bring to a simmer and let thicken, but do not boil.

Add ham, mushrooms and parsley to sauce. Spread crêpes with filling and roll. Place in a shallow baking dish. Sprinkle with cheese, and put under the broiler to glaze. Serves 6.

CRAB MEAT FILLING

> 2 tablespoons finely chopped onion
> 4 tablespoons butter
> 4 tablespoons flour
> 1½ cups milk
> 3 tablespoons sherry
> ½ cup chicken stock
>   Salt, pepper
> 1 egg yolk
> 3 tablespoons light cream
> 2 cups crab meat, fresh, canned or frozen
> ½ cup chopped, cooked mushrooms
> 2 teaspoons chopped chives
> 12 plain crêpes
> 4 tablespoons whipped cream
>   Nutmeg

Sauté onion in butter, stir in flour, and add milk, sherry and chicken stock. Season to taste. Cook, stirring, till thickened. Beat egg yolk with cream, and add. Simmer, but do not boil, till thickened. Reserve ½ cup of sauce.

Add crab meat, mushrooms and chives to remaining sauce. Heat through. Fill crêpes, roll and tuck ends under. Place in a lightly greased baking dish. Mix whipped cream and a pinch of nutmeg with reserved sauce; mask crêpes with sauce, and glaze them under the broiler.

BLINI

> 1½ cups all-purpose flour
> ½ cup fine buckwheat flour
> 1 teaspoon salt
> 1½ cups milk
> ¼ package granulated yeast
> 1 egg, separated

Sift the white flour and the buckwheat flour with the salt into a bowl. Scald the milk and cool to lukewarm. Dissolve the yeast in 1 tablespoon of the warm milk, then add to remaining milk. Pour this onto the beaten egg yolk gradually. Add this mixture to the flours, beating all the time. Set aside and allow to rise about 2 hours. Beat well and then set aside for another 1½ hours. Just before cooking the blinis, add the stiffly beaten egg white and fold it carefully into the batter. Heat a griddle and rub it with a very little salt butter. Put on the mixture in small tablespoons and spread out a little. Brown, turn and brown on other side. Serve with the following accompaniments:

Black or red caviar, heavy sour cream, strained hard-cooked egg yolks, finely chopped hard-cooked egg white, finely chopped parsley and onion, section of lemon.

TACOS

Tacos are small (4″) tortillas stuffed with various mixtures, rolled, fastened with a toothpick, fried in lard and served with various sauces and chiles on the side, or served unfried so that they can be partly unrolled and filled with extras to individual taste. In the United States the taco is not rolled, but simply folded in half. In Mexico they are always rolled.

For a taco party set out bowls of various sauces, canned chiles, chopped lettuce, fried chopped chorizo (hot Spanish sausage), shredded chicken and pork, guacamole, frijoles refritos or some of the following taco fillings. Serve with hot tortillas (see Breads for recipe) to be filled and eaten unfried.

TACO FILLINGS

1. Tacos de Jamon: Mix together 1 cup chopped boiled ham, 1 tablespoon finely chopped onion, 3½-ounce package mashed cream cheese, 2 medium, peeled, seeded, and chopped tomatoes and chopped canned serrano or jalapeño chile to taste. Stuff 12 small tortillas with mixture. Serve with guacamole.
2. Tacos de Picadillo: Make up a recipe of picadillo (see Ground Meat for recipe). Stuff tacos in usual way and serve with guacamole.
3. Tacos de Frijol: Stuff tacos with frijoles refritos, strips of jalapeño chile, Monterey Jack or similar cheese and serve with guacamole.

TOSTADAS

Tostadas are tortillas that have been fried until golden brown and crisp in hot lard or oil, then covered with various combinations of meats, poultry, fish, sauces, chiles, etc. For appetizers use the half-size (2″) tortilla. Radishes and green olives are a favorite garnish for tostadas.

TOSTADA FILLINGS
(for 24 cocktail tostadas)

1. Tostadas Tapatias: Skin, finely chop and fry 3 chorizos. Heat 2 cups frijoles refritos. Spread beans on tostadas, follow with a layer of sausage, a layer of shredded lettuce, a little finely chopped onion, a layer of guacamole, and grated Parmesan cheese.
2. Tostadas Compuestas: Cover the tortillas with a thin layer of mashed red kidney beans. Lightly toss 1 head shredded iceberg lettuce and 2 cooked diced potatoes with a little oil and vinegar dressing. Place a layer over the beans, then a layer of shredded cooked white meat of chicken, then a layer of guacamole and grated Parmesan cheese. Place strips of chipotle on the tostadas, or serve chile separately if you prefer, as it is very hot.

NACHOS

Peel, seed and chop 1 tomato. Seed and chop two mild, pickled jalapeño chiles. Melt ½ pound coarsely grated Cheddar cheese in top of a double boiler. Add tomato and chile. Spread on tostadas.

Soup

If foods can be said to play certain roles in culinary history, that of soup would be the soother and sustainer. Thomas Fuller's remark, "Of soup and love, the first is best," could only have come from a man who had known the grinding pangs of hunger and the surcease soup can bring. Armies, marching on their stomachs, depended for sustenance on their soup kitchens and the skill with which the cooks could convert the meager ingredients to be found near the battlefield into a heartening, nourishing brew. Washington's ragged army at Valley Forge had reason to bless the Pennsylvania Dutchman who created pepper pot soup from tripe, peppercorns and the few other makings he could find.

To soup also goes the credit for adding the word "restaurant" to the language of gastronomy. In 1765, a French tavern keeper called Boulanger set a precedent by selling a choice of hot soups or restaurants (restoratives) instead of the fixed table d'hôte meal served by French inns of the day. The idea and the name caught on, and by 1794 Paris was peppered with restaurants, all superior to the humble establishment of M. Boulanger.

On the medieval table, soup was a mere by-product of stewed meat served in its own broth, but once the diners realized how fine and flavorful the broth tasted, they demanded soup for soup's sake. At the wedding feast of Henry IV, it was accorded the honor of being a separate course. By the eighteenth century, meats, vegetables and herbs were sacrificed in the noble cause of bouillon and its more raffiné relative, consommé. From this it was but a step to the ancestor of the bouillon cube, the Portable Soup originated by a Mr. Henderson of England, for which marrow-bone broth was cooked down to a jelly, then dried in the sun until hard or, as one cook book described it, "a veal glew."

In the nineteenth century, the status of soup was somewhat pompously defined thus by Grimod de la Reynière: "Soup is to dinner what a portico is to a palace or an overture to an opera. It is not only the commencement of the feast, but should give an idea of what is to follow." No mean trick when you consider that his recommended menu for fifteen guests comprised no fewer than twenty-four dishes after the soup course.

Today, in the relaxed lexicon of contemporary dining, we are more likely to think of soup as a counterpoint to the textures and temperatures of the following dishes, serving a piping-hot consommé before truites en gelée, offsetting the unctuousness of a truffled capon with the bite of a chilled watercress soup or ushering in a roast of beef with the pure, palate-cleansing flavor of a clear mushroom soup.

DOUBLE CHICKEN CONSOMMÉ

 2 pounds chicken necks
 5 pounds chicken backs
 4 quarts water
 1½ tablespoons salt
 1 onion stuck with 2 cloves
 1 or 2 sprigs parsley
 1 pound chicken gizzards
 1 egg white and shell

Put the chicken necks and 2 pounds of the backs in a kettle with the water, salt, onion and parsley. Bring to a boil, lower the heat and simmer 2 hours. Taste for seasoning and simmer a further ½ hour. Remove from heat and strain. Return the strained broth to kettle with the remaining chicken backs and the gizzards. Simmer 2 hours. Strain the broth and cool. Skim off all the fat and clarify the consommé. To do this, strain the broth through a fine linen towel. Beat an egg white until frothy and add egg white and egg shell to the broth. Return to the heat and cook a few minutes, beating with a rotary egg beater. Strain again through the towel, which has been wrung out in cold water. The egg white and egg shell gather all the impurities together and by the time the soup has been strained the second time it will be perfectly clear.

Serve the soup very hot in demitasses. If you wish an accompaniment, freshly made Melba toast sprinkled with Parmesan cheese and heated in the oven until the cheese is just melted is a delicious flavor and texture contrast. Serves 8.

CLEAR MUSHROOM SOUP

 2 pounds mushrooms
 2 quarts water
 ½ teaspoon salt
 Pepper to taste
 1 teaspoon beef extract (B.V.)
 Dry vermouth

Wash the mushrooms and chop fine, stems, skins and all. Simmer in water for 3 hours, covered. Strain, pressing the pulp dry. Discard the pulp. Reheat the broth, adding salt, pepper and beef extract. Just before serving, add dry vermouth. Serves 8.

CORN SOUP À LA CRÈME

 5 ears sweet corn
 2 medium onions, chopped
 1 green pepper, seeded and chopped
 3 tablespoons butter
 Salt, pepper to taste
 2 cups milk
 2 egg yolks
 1 cup cream
 Garnish: slivered almonds lightly browned
 in butter

Slit the corn kernels and scrape with a sharp knife. Sauté the onions and pepper in the butter. Season with salt and pepper. Add the corn and milk. Simmer for 10 minutes and put the soup through a food mill or purée in an electric blender. Beat the egg yolks. Bring the cream to the boiling point and pour this over the egg yolks, stirring briskly. Add to the hot soup and serve immediately, garnished with slivered almonds. Serves 6.

CREAM OF ONION AND CELERY SOUP

 1½ cups minced onion
 ½ cup minced celery
 1 cup hot chicken bouillon
 ½ teaspoon salt
 3 tablespoons butter
 3 tablespoons flour
 2 cups hot milk
 1 teaspoon salt
 ¼ teaspoon freshly ground pepper
 ⅛ teaspoon ground nutmeg
 ½ cup heavy cream, heated
 1–2 tablespoons chopped pistachio nuts

Combine the onion, celery, hot chicken bouillon, and salt. Simmer, covered, until the onion and celery are very soft. Rub through a sieve, put through a food mill or purée in the blender. Heat the butter in a saucepan and stir in the flour. Gradually blend in the milk. Cook over medium heat, stirring constantly, until smooth and thickened. Add the salt, pepper, nutmeg, and puréed vegetables. Cook until heated through. Stir in the hot cream. Sprinkle with chopped pistachio nuts. Serves 4.

PURÉEING SOUP VEGETABLES

1. To purée vegetable mixture for cream soups, sieve in French-style food mill over mixing bowl.

2. Rotate handle until all mixture is sieved, then scrape bottom of mill with wooden spoon.

ARTICHOKE SOUP

2 large or 3 medium artichokes, split
3 cups chicken stock
8 or 9 slices lemon
2 tablespoons minced shallots
1 cup cream
   Salt, pepper to taste

Cook artichokes in stock with 2 or 3 lemon slices until tender, about 30–45 minutes. Discard lemon and remove artichokes from stock. Reserve stock. Cool artichokes. Peel stems and mash with one of the artichoke bottoms. Dice and reserve remaining bottoms. Scrape pulp from leaves and combine with the mashed artichoke and reserved stock. Add shallots and cream. Simmer 5 minutes, strain, correct seasoning and add diced artichoke. Serve topped with a thin slice of lemon. This soup is also good iced. Serves 6.

RIPE OLIVE SOUP

2 4-ounce cans ripe olives, minced
1 small clove garlic
3 cups chicken stock
2 eggs
1 cup cream
   Salt, pepper to taste
   Minced dill for garnish

Simmer olives and garlic in chicken stock for 15 minutes. Discard garlic. Beat eggs with cream and add about 1 cup of the hot stock. Mix well, then add gradually to the remaining soup. Heat stirring until slightly thickened; do not boil. Correct seasoning and serve hot, garnished with minced dill. Serves 6.

CREAM OF JERUSALEM ARTICHOKE SOUP

2 pounds Jerusalem artichokes, peeled and sliced
2 medium onions, sliced
4 tablespoons butter
3 cups hot water
   Salt, pepper to taste
2 cups milk, heated
1 cup light cream, heated
⅛ teaspoon ground cardamom

Put the Jerusalem artichokes and onions in a saucepan with 3 tablespoons of the butter. Cover pan tightly and simmer over very low heat, stirring frequently, until the vegetables are half tender. Add the hot water, salt, and pepper. Cook, covered, until the vegetables are soft. Put through a food mill or purée in a blender. Return to the saucepan and add remaining 1 tablespoon butter, the hot milk, cream, and cardamom. Heat to the boiling point. Serves 4–6.

Variation: Substitute 1/3 cup toasted blanched almonds, chopped or cut into slivers, for the cardamom. If the almonds are salted, use less salt in the soup.

POTAGE PERRIGORDINI

6 tablespoons sweet butter
1 cup finely chopped white onions
2 tablespoons finely chopped parsley
   Salt, freshly ground white pepper to taste
½ teaspoon ground cardamom seeds
½ teaspoon sugar

3 packages large frozen peas

2 tablespoons flour

4 cups chicken stock

1½ pounds spinach

½ cup finely diced lean boiled ham
soaked in ¼ cup brandy

1 cup light cream

1 cup small croutons of bread fried in butter until golden brown

Beat the butter in a mixer until very light and fluffy. Put into a saucepan with the finely chopped onions and parsley. Season with salt, white pepper, cardamom, sugar, and cook 2 or 3 minutes without browning the onions. Then add the peas. Cover the pan. Cook slowly until the peas are quite soft. Stir in, off heat, the flour and the stock. Stir over low heat until it comes to a boil. Remove from heat and add the spinach leaves. Stir them in the soup until they wilt. Rub through a fine strainer. Return to the pan. Add the diced ham which has soaked in the brandy for a little while and the light cream. Reheat and serve the soup in cups, topped with a sprinkling of the small croutons. Serves 8.

HAZELNUT AND ASPARAGUS SOUP

½ cup hazelnuts

1 tablespoon sweet butter

1 onion, finely chopped

2 ounces boiled ham

5 cups rich chicken stock

¼ cup dry sherry
Salt, pepper to taste

½ cup heavy cream

10-ounce can asparagus tips in 1" pieces

Soak nuts briefly in hot water and remove skins. Dry, sauté until golden in butter, drain and reserve. Sauté onion until limp in the same butter, adding a little more if necessary, but do not brown. Put nuts, onion and ham into an electric blender with a little of the stock and blend to a smooth paste. Heat remaining stock, add sherry and nut mixture, stirring to blend well, adjust seasoning and simmer for 10–15 minutes. Remove from heat and beat in the cream. Add the asparagus tips. Reheat soup without allowing it to boil. Serves 6.

BOULA-BOULA

4 tablespoons salt butter

1 medium onion, finely chopped

2 packages frozen peas
Salt, pepper to taste

3 tablespoons flour
Cayenne pepper to taste

3 cups canned turtle soup

1 cup light cream

6 tablespoons whipped cream

Melt the butter in a heavy saucepan, add the onion and cook very slowly for 5 minutes without browning. Add the frozen peas, salt and pepper, and ¼ cup water. Cover and cook slowly until peas are soft. Stir in flour, off heat. Season with salt and cayenne pepper. Strain meat from turtle soup and reserve; add clear soup to pan, stirring over low heat until it comes to a boil. Reduce heat and simmer for 5 minutes. Meanwhile, dice reserved turtle meat. Rub soup through a fine strainer and return to the pan. Add the light cream and diced turtle meat and reheat. Pour soup into individual flameproof soup pots, top each serving with 1 tablespoon whipped cream and brown the surface of the cream quickly under a very hot broiler. Serves 6.

MUSHROOM-CLAM SOUP

1 pound mushrooms

3 minced green onions, with tops

4 tablespoons butter

4 tablespoons flour

4 cups clam juice
Salt, pepper to taste

⅛ teaspoon nutmeg

1½ cups light cream

Wash and dry the mushrooms. Cut off tough stem ends and slice from the round sides through the stems. Set aside. Sauté the onion in the butter for 2 minutes. Add the mushrooms and sauté 4 minutes. Stir in the flour; mix well. Add the clam juice, 1 cup at a time, stirring well after each addition. Add the sat, pepper, and nutmeg. Simmer, uncovered, 5 minutes. Add the cream and heat through. Serves 6.

POLISH FRESH MUSHROOM SOUP

½ pound mushrooms
3 tablespoons butter
¼ teaspoon caraway seeds
½ teaspoon paprika
1 tablespoon flour
4 cups chicken stock
1 egg yolk
1 cup sour cream
2 tablespoons chopped fresh dill

Wash and dry the mushrooms. Cut off tough stem ends. Slice whole mushrooms and sauté in the butter with the caraway seeds and paprika for 1 minute. Sprinkle with the flour. Blend well. Add the chicken stock, a little at a time. Simmer, covered, 30 minutes. Meanwhile, whip the egg yolk with a fork until creamy. Add sour cream and dill, mixing well. Spoon into a soup tureen and pour hot soup slowly into it, stirring with a whisk to mix thoroughly. Serves 6.

MUSHROOM AND MINT SOUP

2 ounces sweet butter
2 small yellow onions, finely chopped
1 clove garlic, finely chopped
   Salt, freshly cracked white pepper
½ pound mushrooms
1 teaspoon lemon juice
4 tablespoons rice flour or
   3 tablespoons plain flour
4 cups light chicken or veal stock
¾ cup light cream
2 tablespoons chopped fresh mint
   or 2 teaspoons dried mint soaked in
   1 tablespoon water
2 egg yolks
3 tablespoons dry sherry
4 tablespoons whipped cream

Melt butter in a heavy pan, add the finely chopped onion and garlic, season with a little salt and pepper. Cover and cook very slowly 3–4 minutes without browning onions. Put the mushrooms through a meat grinder, reserving 2 or 3 firm ones. Add to the onions and cook very slowly for another 10 minutes with the lemon juice. Stir in the flour off heat. Mix in the stock and stir over low heat until it comes to a boil. Rub through a fine strainer. Add ½ the light cream, the reserved mushrooms, finely sliced, and chopped mint. Stir over heat and reheat without boiling. Put the egg yolks in the bottom of a soup tureen. Mix in the dry sherry and remaining light cream. Slowly beat in the soup. Just before serving, float whipped cream on soup and sprinkle with chopped mint. Serves 6.

FRENCH SQUASH SOUP

1 quart milk
2 tablespoons butter
½ cup flour
2 cups cooked, mashed squash (Hubbard,
   butternut, or acorn)
1 teaspoon salt
¼ teaspoon pepper
2 tablespoons minced parsley
½ teaspoon ground nutmeg

Heat the milk. Knead together the butter and flour. Add the butter mixture to the milk in small pea-sized pieces, one at a time, stirring constantly. When the milk has thickened, gradually stir in the cooked squash, salt, pepper, and parsley. Cook, stirring constantly, until the soup thickens and is hot. Sprinkle nutmeg on top before serving. Serves 4–6.

CREAM OF LENTIL SOUP

1 cup lentils
4 cups water
1 ham bone
1 onion stuck with 2 cloves
½ cup celery leaves, chopped
1 carrot, chopped
1 raw potato, chopped
3½ cups milk
3½ tablespoons salt, or to taste
½ teaspoon cayenne pepper
Freshly ground pepper to taste
¼ pound well-seasoned salami (or cooked, smoked sausage), diced

Combine lentils, water, ham bone, onion, celery leaves, carrot and potato in soup kettle. Cover, simmer slowly for 2½ hours or until lentils are soft. Remove ham bone and press liquid and solid ingredients through a sieve, or purée them in a blender. Return purée to kettle, add milk and seasonings and let simmer slowly, without boiling, for 15 minutes or more. Serve hot, sprinkled with finely diced salami or sausage. Serves 6.

AVGOLEMONO

3 cups double chicken broth
½ cup washed rice
Salt
2 whole eggs
2 egg yolks
Juice of 2 lemons

Bring the chicken broth to a boil and add the rice. Cook until tender. Add salt, if necessary.

Beat the eggs and egg yolks until light and frothy and add the lemon juice slowly, beating it in. Add a little of the hot broth to the egg mixture, blending it in well. Slowly add the egg to the broth, stirring constantly. Heat through, but do not boil. Serves 6.

STRACIATELLA ALLA ROMANA

3 eggs
3 tablespoons freshly grated Romano or Parmesan cheese
2 tablespoons minced parsley
6 cups chicken broth

Beat the eggs until frothy. The flavor of the soup will depend principally on whether the cheese is freshly grated, so make every effort to do so. Stir the cheese and parsley into the eggs. Bring the broth to a rolling boil and pour the egg mixture into it, stirring steadily until set. Serves 6–8.

CREAM OF CRAB SOUP

2 tablespoons butter
2 tablespoons flour
2 eggs, hard-cooked
Juice and finely grated rind of 1 lemon
3 cups fish stock
2 cups milk
1 cup light cream
½ pound crab meat, flaked
Salt, pepper to taste
Dash of Angostura bitters
¼ cup dry sherry

Melt the butter in a saucepan and add the flour. Cook, stirring, for a minute or two. Remove the saucepan from the heat and add the eggs, mashing them to a smooth paste. Add the lemon juice and rind, the fish stock, milk, cream, and crab meat. Return the pan to heat and simmer very gently, stirring occasionally, for 10 minutes. Season with salt and pepper. Add the Angostura bitters and the dry sherry and reheat soup gently. Serves 6.

CLAM SOUP

> 3 pints fresh, shucked clams
> 4 cups chicken broth
> 3 tablespoons butter
> 3 tablespoons flour
> 2 cups light cream
> Salt, white pepper
> 1 cup heavy cream, lightly whipped

Pour the clams into a sieve set over a bowl to catch the clam liquid. Pick over the clams and remove black filament or spots. Roughly chop 10 of the largest and plumpest clams and set aside. Put the rest through a meat grinder or purée in an electric blender.

Bring the chicken broth to a simmer. Melt the butter in a large saucepan, blend in the flour and cook slowly, stirring, for 2 minutes without allowing flour to color. Remove from heat and beat in the simmering broth with a wire whip. Boil, stirring, for 1 minute. Add the light cream, the chopped clams, the puréed clams and the clam liquid in the bowl. (If done in advance, set aside at this point, uncovered.) Heat, stirring gently, until soup is very hot but not simmering—the clams need only be heated through. Season carefully to taste. Ladle into soup plates and top with a big spoonful of whipped cream. Serves 8.

BILLI BI

> Mussels à la marinière (see recipe in Seafood)
> Cayenne pepper to taste
> 2 cups heavy cream
> 1 egg yolk, lightly beaten

Prepare the mussels à la marinière and strain the cooking liquid into a saucepan. Reserve the mussels for another use or take them from the shells and use as a garnish for the soup. Bring the liquid to a boil, season with cayenne pepper and add 1 cup of the cream.

Blend the remaining cream with the egg yolk. Spoon a little of the hot soup into the egg yolk mixture, then pour this into the soup. Heat thoroughly until slightly thickened, but do not boil. Serve hot or cold. Serves 4.

SHRIMP BISQUE

This is a lovely soup, pale pink in color and satin-smooth in texture. This short-cut version dispenses with the classic, laborious pounding of shells, but loses nothing in the omission.

> 2 pounds raw shrimp, shelled and cleaned
> 4 tablespoons butter
> ¼ cup minced onion
> ¼ cup minced celery
> 2 tablespoons grated carrot
> 3 cups chicken stock
> Sprig of thyme
> 1 cup heavy cream
> ½ cup dry white wine
> Salt, pepper
> Lightly salted whipped cream (optional)

Grind the raw shrimp fine. Melt the butter and cook the vegetables until wilted. Add the shrimp and cook 5 minutes, stirring carefully. Add the chicken stock and thyme and cook in the top of a double boiler for half an hour. Strain, pressing as much as possible of the pulp through a sieve. Add the cream and white wine and heat over hot water. Taste for seasoning and add salt and pepper if necessary. Serve with or without a topping of whipped cream. Serves 6.

RICH OYSTER STEW

> 1 pint cream
> ½ pint milk
> 1½ pints oysters with oyster liquor
> Salt, freshly ground black pepper, cayenne pepper
> 4 or more tablespoons butter

Heat four good-sized bowls.

Heat the cream, milk and oyster liquor until barely boiling. Add salt and black pepper to taste and a touch of cayenne. Add the oysters and bring just to the boiling point again. In each hot bowl, place a good-sized piece of butter—at least a tablespoon.

Ladle the stew into the bowls and serve with hot, crunchy French bread. Serves 4.

CLAM AND OYSTER CHOWDER

6 tablespoons butter
1 tablespoon oil
1 tablespoon mixed scallion, garlic and onion, chopped
1 dozen raw oysters, cut up
1 dozen raw clams, cut up
3 cups light cream
Salt, cayenne pepper to taste
¼ cup chopped parsley

Heat in a pan 2 tablespoons butter and the oil. Add the scallion, garlic and onion. Cook slowly for 2 minutes, then add the cut-up oysters and clams. Pour on the cream and season with the salt and cayenne pepper. Bring very lightly to a boil, then add, bit by bit, the remaining butter and the chopped parsley. Simmer a few minutes and serve. Serves 4–6.

SHRIMP GUMBO

2 pounds raw shrimp
Herb bouquet (parsley, bay and thyme)
1 dried hot red chili pepper
¾ cup chopped onion
3 tablespoons ham fat
2 sprigs parsley, minced
Pinch of thyme
2 tablespoons flour
1 quart chicken stock, tomato juice or oyster liquor
1 cup or less diced cooked ham (optional)
3 tablespoons filé powder
1 pound raw rice, boiled

Boil the shrimp in salted water with the herb bouquet and chili pepper. Strain, reserving the liquor. Shell and clean the shrimp and cut each one into 2 or 3 pieces. Brown the onion in the ham fat in a large saucepan, add the parsley, thyme and flour and stir well together. Add a quart of the shrimp liquor and chicken stock, tomato juice or oyster liquor. Bring to a boil, add shrimp and, if you wish, the diced ham. Simmer for 20 minutes, taste for seasoning and correct if necessary. Add the filé powder and stir, but do

not continue cooking. Serve from a tureen into soup dishes, and pass boiled rice to be spooned into the gumbo. Serves 8.

ZUPPA DI PESCE
(Italian Fish Soup)

3 pounds sliced assorted fish (bass, snapper, whitefish, etc.)
Heads and trimmings
4 cups water
2½ teaspoons salt
½ teaspoon white pepper
1 onion
¼ teaspoon thyme
1 bay leaf
½ cup olive oil
¼ cup minced onion
2 cloves garlic, minced
¾ cup dry white wine
1 cup canned Italian-style tomatoes
¼ teaspoon saffron
Sautéed croutons

Buy at least 2 varieties of fish and have them sliced 1″ thick. You may cut each slice in half, if you like. Be sure you ask for 2 heads and the trimmings.

Combine the heads, trimmings, water, salt, pepper, onion, thyme and bay leaf in a saucepan. Bring to a boil and cook over medium heat 30 minutes. Strain and reserve stock.

Prepare the fish while the stock is cooking. Heat the oil in a saucepan; sauté the onion and garlic 5 minutes. Add the fish; sauté until lightly browned on both sides. Add the wine, tomatoes, saffron and stock. Cook over low heat 15 minutes. Serve in deep soup plates with sautéed croutons. Serves 6.

CACCIUCCO

1 live lobster
½ pound halibut or sole
1 pound sea bass or similar fish
½ pound scallops (bay, if available)
½ cup olive oil
2 cloves garlic, minced
1 tablespoon minced parsley
1¼ teaspoons salt

⅛ teaspoon crushed red chili pepper
⅛ teaspoon sage
¾ cup dry white wine
2 tablespoons tomato paste
4 cups bottled clam juice

Have the lobster cut up in the shell. Cut the fish into bite-size pieces. If bay scallops are used, leave them whole. If sea scallops, cut into 4.

Heat the oil in a saucepan; sauté the garlic and parsley 1 minute. Add the lobster, salt, red pepper and sage. Cover and cook over low heat 10 minutes. Add the wine; cook over high heat 5 minutes. Stir in the tomato paste, clam juice, fish and scallops; cook over low heat 20 minutes. Taste for seasoning. Serve in deep plates with Italian bread. Serves 4.

ONION SOUP WITH WHITE WINE

6 tablespoons butter
4 large onions, chopped very fine
3 cups chicken broth
1 cup dry white wine
  Salt, freshly ground black pepper
  Large croutons, fried in butter or oil
  Grated Gruyère and grated Parmesan cheese, mixed
  <u>Garnish</u>: chopped raw onion, chopped parsley

This is a delicate onion soup, a nice change from the heartier types which are so well known.

Melt the butter in a skillet, add the chopped onions, cover tightly and steam over a very low flame until thoroughly puréed and soft. Add chicken broth, wine and simmer for 15–20 minutes. Season to taste.

Sprinkle the fried croutons with the grated cheeses and put under the broiler flame briefly to melt the cheese. Serve the soup in a large heated tureen. Put croutons in each soup plate or bowl and ladle soup over them. Pass bowls of raw onion and parsley for garnish. Serves 6.

MINESTRONE GENOVESE

2 cups dried white beans
4 dried mushrooms
6 tablespoons olive oil
½ cup chopped onion
4 cups diced eggplant
4 cups shredded cabbage
2 cups sliced zucchini or squash
2 cups peeled diced tomatoes or canned tomatoes
2½ quarts boiling water
½ cup vermicelli
2 teaspoons salt
½ teaspoon freshly ground black pepper
¼ cup minced parsley
½ teaspoon basil
2 cloves garlic, minced
⅓ cup pine nuts or sliced blanched almonds
⅓ cup grated Parmesan cheese

Wash the beans, cover with water and bring to a boil; let soak 1 hour. Drain. Cover with fresh water, bring to a boil and cook 1½ hours. Wash the dried mushrooms, cover them with warm water and let them soak for 10 minutes. Drain well and slice.

Heat 3 tablespoons oil in a saucepan; sauté the onion 5 minutes. Stir in the mushrooms, eggplant, cabbage and zucchini until coated with the oil. Add the tomatoes, water and beans; bring to a boil and cook over low heat 30 minutes. Mix in vermicelli, salt and pepper; cook 10 minutes until vermicelli is tender.

In an electric blender, combine the parsley, basil, garlic, nuts, Parmesan cheese and remaining olive oil. Turn on blender motor and run until a paste is formed; or pound the ingredients to a paste, gradually adding the oil. Stir this *pesto* into the soup carefully so that lumps do not form. Serves 8–10.

RUSSIAN BARLEY AND MUSHROOM SOUP

    3 ounces dried mushrooms
    ½ cup chopped onion
    1 leek, chopped
    3 tablespoons butter
    1 cup diced carrots
    ⅓ cup pearl barley
    1 teaspoon salt
    4 peppercorns
    2 cups diced potatoes
    2 bay leaves
    1 cup sour cream
      Chopped fresh dill

Soak the mushrooms in lukewarm water to cover for 20 minutes. Drain, pressing to extract water. Slice mushrooms. Sauté the onion and leek in the butter in a large saucepan until tender. Add the carrots, barley, salt, peppercorns, and 2 quarts water. Bring to a boil. Lower the heat and simmer, covered, for 1 hour. Add the potatoes, bay leaves, and mushrooms. Continue to simmer until the vegetables are tender, about 45 minutes. Mix in the sour cream just before serving. Garnish with chopped dill. Serves 10–12.

LENTIL SOUP
WITH CHARD AND LEMON

    1½ cups lentils
    2½ pounds fresh Swiss chard
    ½ cup olive oil
    ¾ cup chopped onion
    3–4 garlic cloves
      Salt

1 stalk celery, chopped
¾ cup lemon juice
1 teaspoon flour

Wash and pick over the lentils. Cover them with fresh cold water and cook, covered, until tender. Wash the Swiss chard leaves and chop them. Add these and a cup of water to the lentils. Continue cooking until the Swiss chard is done, adding more water if necessary. Heat the olive oil in a skillet and add the chopped onion. Crush the garlic cloves with salt and add these and the chopped celery to the onion. Continue cooking until the onions, garlic and celery are tender and blended. Add these to the lentil mixture. Mix the lemon juice with the flour and stir it into the soup. Cook gently, stirring occasionally, until the soup is rather thick. Taste for seasoning and cool a bit.

Serve in soup bowls and pass crusty French or Italian bread to sop up the juices. Serves 6.

Variation: Spinach may be substituted for the chard. This soup may also be served cold the following day.

SCANDINAVIAN YELLOW PEA SOUP

1 pound dried yellow split peas
1 pound streaky bacon or streaky salt pork, in
   one piece
1 celeriac, peeled, or 1 large stalk celery, cut in
   1″ pieces
3 leeks, white and green parts, washed thoroughly and cut in 1″ pieces
3 medium carrots, peeled and cut in 1″ pieces
3 medium potatoes, peeled and cut in 1″ pieces
3 medium onions, thinly sliced
⅛ teaspoon thyme
1 pound Danish Canadian-style bacon (pork
   loin) or Canadian bacon
1½-pound can cocktail Vienna sausages, drained

Wash and drain peas. Cover with cold water and soak overnight or according to package directions. Drain and place in large kettle with 3 quarts water. Slowly bring to a boil. Cook covered over medium heat for 1 hour. Skim off pea skins as they float to the top. Add bacon or salt pork. (If salt pork is very salty, soak in cold water for 30 minutes, drain and pat dry.) Cover soup and simmer over lowest possible heat for about 2 hours, stirring occasionally. The peas

should be of purée consistency. Add celeriac or celery, leeks, carrots, potatoes, onions, thyme and Canadian bacon to soup during last 45 minutes of cooking time and Vienna sausages during last 15 minutes of cooking time. Stir soup occasionally and check for desired consistency; if necessary, add a little hot water. When ready to serve, remove bacon or salt pork and Canadian bacon to heated platter and slice. Serve soup and sliced meats separately. The meats may also be served cold, if so desired. Serve with a good sharp mustard, pickled beets, rye bread and sweet butter. Serves 6–8.

GARBANZO SOUP

1 large ham bone, about 2 pounds with meat on
3 quarts water
2 large onions, finely chopped
2 cloves garlic, minced
2 bay leaves
2 tablespoons salt
½ teaspoon pepper
¼ teaspoon saffron
4 peeled medium potatoes, cut in eighths
2 1-pound cans chick peas (garbanzos)
2 chorizos (or approximately ¼ pound any
   other well-seasoned Spanish or Italian-type
   sausage), sliced

Cover ham bone with water and cook with the onions, minced garlic and bay leaves for 2 hours. Add salt, pepper, saffron. Add potatoes and cook for 30 minutes. Add garbanzos, sliced chorizos. Remove meat from ham bone, dice and add. Cook 30 minutes longer, over low heat. Remove bay leaves and check seasoning. Makes 3–4 quarts. Keeps at least 2 weeks, refrigerated, and improves daily. Serves 16.

OXTAIL SOUP

1 oxtail, disjointed
   Seasoned flour
¼ cup shortening
3 quarts water
   Salt, pepper
   Herb bouquet (parsley, bay leaf, marjoram or
   thyme)

1 cup each: diced carrot, celery, onion
2 tablespoons parsley

Dust oxtail with flour and brown in shortening. Add 2 quarts water, 1 teaspoon salt, herb bouquet, and simmer until tender—3 hours or more. Skim, add 1 quart water and diced vegetables. Cook until vegetables are tender. Correct seasoning, add parsley and serve from a tureen with hot bread, preferably homemade. Meat may be removed from the bones before vegetables are added, if desired. Serves 8.

MULLIGATAWNY

1 whole chicken breast
3 cups chicken broth, skimmed of fat
1 medium onion, minced
1 stalk celery, minced
½ sweet green pepper, minced
1 tablespoon curry powder
½ teaspoon powdered cardamom
2 tablespoons vegetable oil
1 large tomato, peeled and chopped
1 teaspoon salt
1 cup boiled rice

Poach the chicken breast in the broth for 8 or 10 minutes. Drain, reserving the broth, and cut the chicken meat into fine pieces.

Fry the onion, celery, pepper, curry powder and cardamom in the oil over high heat until slightly brown. Add the tomato, salt and the reserved chicken broth. Reduce heat, cover and simmer for 1 hour. At serving time, add cooked rice and chicken pieces to each bowl. Serves 4–6.

JELLIED WATERCRESS SOUP SMITANE

1 bunch watercress
4 cups clear chicken broth (the kind that will jell)
2 tablespoons lemon juice
Sour cream mixed with pickled grated horseradish

Remove the tough stems from watercress and put it in an electric blender with 1 cup chicken broth. When blended, combine with 3 more cups chicken broth and the lemon juice. Chill until jellied, break up with a fork and serve in consommé cups garnished with a dollop of sour cream mixed with pickled grated horseradish to taste. Serves 4.

JELLIED AVOCADO SOUP

1 avocado, fully ripe
1 can jellied consommé
Lemon juice
Salt
Dash Tabasco
Sour cream
Diced avocado for garnish (optional)

Halve avocado, remove pit and peel. Rub through a sieve and combine at once with jellied consommé, or put in a blender with the consommé and whirl until smooth. Add a few drops of lemon juice, salt to taste and Tabasco. Serve topped with sour cream and, if you wish, garnished with diced avocado. Serves 3.

JELLIED CONSOMMÉ WITH CAVIAR

4-ounce jar red caviar
2 12½-ounce cans jellied consommé, or 1½ pints homemade jellied consommé, chilled until very firm
½ cup sour cream
Chopped chives (optional)

In the bottom of each cup put a teaspoon of red caviar, spoon on about ½ cup of the jellied consommé and top with a good dollop (about a tablespoon) of sour cream. You can sprinkle the top with a few chopped chives as a pleasant color contrast, if you like. Serves 6.

JELLIED MUSHROOM SOUP

1 pound fresh mushrooms, washed and chopped
1 quart fat-free consommé
2 envelopes plain gelatin
1 cup water
½ cup white wine
Salt, pepper to taste
8 tablespoons yoghurt
Chopped fresh dill or chives

Simmer mushrooms for 30 minutes in consommé. Strain, pressing all juices from mushrooms. Soften gelatin in cold water and add to hot soup. Stir until dissolved. Add wine and season with salt and pepper. Allow to set. Top each 1-cup serving with 1 tablespoon yoghurt and dill or chives. Serves 8.

CONSOMMÉ AU MUSCADET

2 tablespoons unflavored gelatin
3 cups chicken bouillon or broth, skimmed
of fat
1 cup Muscadet or other dry white table wine
Garnish: lemon twist, watercress

Soften gelatin in a little of the cold bouillon, dissolve over hot water and mix with remaining bouillon and wine. Chill until firm. Spoon into bouillon cups. Break up the jelly with a fork before serving and garnish with lemon and a sprig of cress. Serves 6.

JELLIED BORSCHT

1-pound can French-cut beets
1 envelope (tablespoon) gelatin
3 tablespoons dry sherry
1 cup beef broth
1 tablespoon lemon juice
6 tablespoons sour cream
Caviar or parsley or chives for garnish

Drain the beets, reserving juice. Soften the gelatin in the sherry in the top of a double boiler, put over hot water, add 1 cup of the beet juice and stir until the gelatin has dissolved.

Put half the beets in the blender with the gelatin mixture and purée until smooth. Remove to a bowl. Purée remaining beets with the beef broth in the blender. Combine with first purée and the lemon juice. Pour into 6 bouillon cups and chill until firm.

To serve, place a tablespoon of sour cream on each cup and garnish it with black or red caviar or chopped parsley or chives. Serves 6.

COLD SOUR CREAM SOUP

1 cup diced onion
2 tablespoons butter
4 canned peeled green chiles, rinsed of seeds
1 cup milk
Salt
1 small clove garlic, crushed (optional)
2 cups sour cream
Lemon juice
Minced cilantro or chives

Cook onion in butter until just tender. Add chiles, milk, ½ teaspoon salt and garlic. Bring to just under a boil, then whirl smooth in a blender. Stir in sour cream, then correct seasoning, adding salt if required. Add a few drops of lemon juice if needed, chill, and serve in cups, sprinkled with cilantro or chives. Serves 6.

RUSSIAN CHLODNIK WITH YOGHURT

½ cup pickled-beet juice
½ cup water
2 cups yoghurt
1 beet, cooked and chopped
1 cucumber, peeled and sliced
¼ cup diced cooked veal
¼ cup tiny cooked shrimp
1 teaspoon dried dill or 1 tablespoon fresh
chopped dill
2 teaspoons chopped green onion
Salt, pepper to taste

Combine all ingredients and chill well. Serves 6.

COLD AVOCADO SOUP

1 ripe avocado, peeled and pit removed
2 cups clear chicken broth, cold
1 cup heavy or light cream
2 tablespoons white rum
½ teaspoon curry powder
½ teaspoon salt
Coarsely ground pepper
1 lemon, quartered

Place in an electric blender the pulp of the ripe

avocado, the chicken broth (preferably homemade), cream, white rum, curry powder, salt, and a pinch of coarsely ground black pepper. Blend until perfectly smooth and serve at once in well-chilled bouillon cups. Place on the saucer of each bouillon cup a lemon quarter to be squeezed into the avocado soup at table. Serves 4.

CHILLED PUMPKIN SOUP
AU GRAND MARNIER

    1 pound soup meat and bones

    1½ pounds peeled yellow pumpkin, chopped, or 2 cups canned mashed pumpkin

    2 small raw carrots, grated

    2 medium white turnips, grated

    2 raw potatoes, chopped fine

    2 stalks celery, grated

    2 leeks, chopped fine

    ½ teaspoon pepper

    ½ teaspoon ginger

    ½ teaspoon salt

    ¼ teaspoon ground thyme

    ¼ teaspoon allspice

    2 cups light cream

    2 1-pound cans corn kernels, well drained

    ½ cup Grand Marnier

    Finely chopped candied ginger

Combine the soup meat and bones, pumpkin, the vegetables (except corn), and seasonings in 2½ quarts of water in a large pot. Cook slowly, well covered, skimming soup when necessary. After 2 hours, remove bones and pieces of meat and strain remaining mixture through a medium strainer. Allow to cool. Chill thoroughly. When ready to serve, add the light cream, corn, and Grand Marnier. Serve soup sprinkled with finely chopped candied ginger. Serves 8–10.

ALMOND AND MALAGA GRAPE SOUP

¼ pound (⅔ cup) shelled almonds
1 small 7″ loaf French bread (about 4 ounces)
1 clove garlic, sliced fine
2 tablespoons olive oil
1 tablespoon tarragon vinegar
1 teaspoon salt
¼ teaspoon pepper
¼ teaspoon ground cumin seed
¾ pound green finger or Malaga grapes
2 slices white bread
2 tablespoons butter

Blanch the almonds. Slice the French bread in 4 pieces, cover with 2½ cups cold water and soak 15 minutes. Drain off the water and save it. Place the wet bread in an electric blender, and add the almonds, garlic, olive oil, tarragon vinegar, salt, pepper and cumin seed. Run the blender at low speed for about 2 minutes, then add the water drained from the bread and run at high speed until the whole is smooth and the consistency of vichyssoise (about 5 minutes). Place in covered container in refrigerator and chill for several hours. Shortly before serving, peel the green finger or, better still, Malaga grapes, split them in two and remove seeds. Cut the white bread in tiny cubes. Melt the butter in a small heavy frying pan, add the bread and cook, stirring lightly with a fork until cubes are a light golden brown and crisp. Serve the soup in chilled plates, and pass the grapes and croutons separately to be added to the chilled soup at table. Serves 4.

POTAGE GERMINY FROID

1 bunch sorrel or watercress
1½ cups clear chicken broth
6 egg yolks
1 pint light cream
Nutmeg, cayenne pepper, white pepper
Salt to taste

Wash the greens and chop coarsely. Bring the chicken broth to a boil and add the greens. Simmer for 10 minutes.

In a small bowl beat the egg yolks with the cream, a grinding of nutmeg and pinches of both peppers. Add to the simmering broth, stirring constantly with a wooden spoon. Lower the heat and stir until thickened. Do not let the soup boil. Season to taste with salt and pour into a chilled bowl. Refrigerate. Serve in chilled soup plates. Serves 6.

BREADFRUIT VICHYSSOISE

2 tablespoons butter
2 onions, finely chopped
1 clove garlic, chopped
½ pound fresh breadfruit or ⅓ can
  (1-pound, 10-ounce) breadfruit
2 pints chicken stock
½ pint light cream
Salt, pepper to taste
Chopped chives

Heat the butter and sauté the onions and garlic until transparent. If using fresh breadfruit, peel the breadfruit, remove core, and dice. If using canned breadfruit, chop coarsely. Combine the breadfruit, onion, garlic, and chicken stock in a saucepan and cook until the breadfruit is tender. Cool. Put into an electric blender and blend until smooth, adding the cream while blending. Season with salt and pepper and chill thoroughly. If soup is too thick, thin with a little milk. Serve soup sprinkled with chopped chives. Serves 6.

NUT SUNDI SOUP

3 cups chicken or beef broth
½ cup dried salted peanuts
½ teaspoon chili powder
Salt, pepper to taste
1 cup milk

Bring the broth to a boil, add the peanuts and cook for about 5 minutes over moderate heat. Pour into blender and add the chili powder and salt and pepper. Blend until smooth. Pour into saucepan. Rinse out blender with the milk, combine with the peanut mixture, put back over heat and bring to a boil again.

Serve hot with croutons or chilled with lemon or cucumber slices floating on top. Serves 4.

QUICK BORSCHT

    1¾ cups sour cream
    1" slice of lemon, peeled and seeded
    ¼ teaspoon salt
    ½ small onion
    1 cup diced cooked beets
    1 cup crushed ice

Put the sour cream, lemon, salt, onion and beets into the blender. Cover and blend for 20 seconds, or until smooth. Add crushed ice and blend 30 seconds longer. Serve in soup cups, topped with a dab of sour cream. Serves 4.

CREAM OF CUCUMBER SOUP

    1 bunch scallions, roots trimmed
    1 tablespoon oil
    2 medium cucumbers, peeled, seeded, and cut
       into chunks
    2½ cups chicken consommé (or 3 chicken
       bouillon cubes dissolved in 2½ cups water)
    1 tablespoon fresh thyme leaves or ½ teaspoon
       dried thyme
    1½ tablespoons lemon juice
    1 teaspoon sugar
    ⅔ cup milk
    Salt, pepper to taste

Slice the scallions, including about 4" of the green leaves, and sauté them in the oil for 5 minutes over medium heat. Add the cucumbers and cook 5 minutes longer. Add the consommé, thyme, lemon juice, and sugar, and bring to a boil. Reduce the heat to medium, cover, and cook for 20 minutes or until the vegetables are very tender. Cool for a few minutes, then purée a portion at a time in an electric blender. Add the milk and season with salt and pepper. To serve hot, heat the soup just to boiling point, or chill it and serve it cold. Serves 4.

IRANIAN CUCUMBER SOUP

    3 cups yoghurt
    1½ cups grated cucumber
    ½ cup seedless raisins
    ¾ cup cold water
    1 tablespoon minced fresh dill

    3 tablespoons minced chives
    ½ teaspoon salt
    ¼ teaspoon white pepper
    2 hard-cooked eggs, chopped (optional)

Beat yoghurt in an electric mixer or with a rotary beater. Add grated cucumber and raisins. Blend and add cold water. Add dill, chives, salt and white pepper. Blend well and chill. If the soup is to be the mainstay of the meal, add the chopped, hard-cooked eggs. Serves 4–6.

ICED CUCUMBER AND MINT SOUP

    4 cucumbers, not waxed
    1 bunch green onions
    6 tablespoons arrowroot or rice flour
    3 tablespoons chopped mint
    1½ cups yoghurt or sour cream

Slice the unpeeled cucumbers and the onions (both white and green parts). Simmer together in 3 cups salted water. When the vegetables are tender, mix the arrowroot or rice flour with a little cold water and add. Stir until thick. Strain. Place the soup in a cold pan and stand the pan in a bowl containing cracked ice. Add the chopped mint and the yoghurt or sour cream and stir until blended. Garnish with mint leaves before serving. Serves 4–6.

ICED CURRY SOUP

    3 tablespoons butter
    ½ tablespoon flour
    1 tablespoon curry powder
    6 cups hot clear chicken broth
    3 egg yolks
    1½ cups light cream
    ½ teaspoon powdered ginger
    1 tablespoon chopped parsley

Melt the butter in the top part of a double boiler over low heat. Stir in the flour and curry powder. Add the hot broth gradually, bring to a simmer and cook 10 minutes. Beat together the egg yolks and cream and gradually stir into the hot broth.

Place over boiling water and cook, stirring constantly, until thickened, about 2 minutes. Remove from heat, add the ginger and stir well. Cool and refrigerate for several hours. Serve in chilled bouillon cups, garnished with parsley. Serves 6–8.

ICED BROCCOLI SOUP

> 1 pound broccoli
> 1 quart clear chicken broth
> 1 small onion, chopped
> 2 stalks celery with leaves, chopped
> 4–5 sprigs parsley, cut fine
> 1 large carrot, diced
> 1 teaspoon salt
> ¼ teaspoon cayenne pepper
> 2 tablespoons arrowroot or cornstarch
> 1 cup light cream
> 1 tablespoon chopped chives

Wash broccoli, cut off the buds and dice the stalks. Put stalks into a pot with the chicken broth, onion, celery, parsley, carrot, salt and cayenne pepper. Simmer 15 minutes and add the buds. Simmer 5 minutes and remove the buds. Add to the soup the arrowroot or cornstarch mixed with a little cold water. Simmer and stir until thick. Put through a food mill or purée in an electric blender. Chill for at least 4 hours. Add light cream. Garnish with broccoli buds and chopped chives. Serves 6.

POTAGE BATWINIA

> 6 ounces (about 1½ cups) stemmed,
>   thoroughly washed spinach
> 6 ounces (about 1½ cups) stemmed,
>   thoroughly washed sorrel leaves
> 2 tablespoons butter
> 1 small tender cucumber, peeled and finely
>   diced
> 1 small white onion or 1 large shallot,
>   finely chopped
> 2 tablespoons finely chopped fresh
>   tarragon leaves
> 7 ice cubes
> 1 cup dry white wine, chilled

> Salt to taste (about ¾ teaspoon)
> ½ teaspoon dill salt
> 2½ teaspoons sugar

Combine the spinach, sorrel leaves and butter in a covered pan and cook slowly over low heat for about 10 minutes, stirring occasionally. Cool. Place the cucumber, onion and tarragon in three separate containers and add 1 ice cube to each of the containers. Cover the containers tightly with plastic wrap and refrigerate them until ready to use.

Place the cooled greens in the electric blender and blend to a purée, or rub them through a fine sieve with a wooden spoon. Add the white wine and 1 cup cold water and stir well. Season with salt, the dill salt and sugar. Chill until ready to serve. Then add the prepared chilled cucumber, onion and tarragon with the melted ice from the containers. Crush remaining 4 ice cubes, add to soup and stir well. Serve at once in well-chilled bouillon cups. Serves 4–6.

COLD BEET SOUP

> 1-pound can small beets
> 1 quart or more fresh buttermilk, chilled ice cold
> ¾ teaspoon dill salt or to taste
> 1 tablespoon finely cut fresh dill

Place the beets, a few at a time, with their juice in the electric blender and blend to a smooth liquid. Stir in the chilled buttermilk. Season with dill salt. Mix well and chill thoroughly. To serve, pour into well-chilled cups and garnish with the finely cut fresh dill. Serves 6–8.

ICED SHRIMP SOUP

> 1 pound raw shrimp, shelled and cleaned
> 2 cups milk
> 1 cup light cream
> ¼ cup minced onion
> ½ teaspoon anchovy paste
> ½ teaspoon powdered thyme
> 1 tablespoon raw rice
>   Salt, cayenne
>   Chopped chives or parsley

Put the shrimp in the top of a double boiler with the milk, cream, onion, anchovy paste, thyme and rice. Cook over hot water for an hour, then put through a food mill, extracting all the remaining good flavor from the shrimp. Add salt if necessary and a suspicion of cayenne and chill. Serve very cold in glass bowls, with a sprinkling of chives or parsley in each serving. Serves 6.

TOMATO COB

> 6 large ripe tomatoes
> 2 medium white onions
> 1 stalk celery
> Salt, pepper
> Mayonnaise flavored with curry powder
> Chopped parsley

Scald the tomatoes, peel them and put them through the meat grinder with the onions and celery. Season to taste with salt and pepper and freeze. When the soup has frozen solid, remove it from the refrigerator and let it melt. As it becomes mushy, pour off the clear liquid. Strain this, if necessary, and serve topped with curry-flavored mayonnaise. Sprinkle with chopped parsley. Serves 4.

COLD GARDEN VEGETABLE SOUP

> ¼ cup olive oil
> 6 tablespoons packaged poultry stuffing
> 2 cups tomato juice
> 1 bouillon cube dissolved in ½ cup hot water
> 4 stalks celery, finely chopped
> 1 onion, grated
> ½ cucumber, chopped
> 3 tomatoes, coarsely chopped
> Juice of 1 lemon
> ½ teaspoon A-1 Sauce
> Salt, pepper to taste
> Chopped chives for garnish
> 8 ice cubes
> Curry-flavored mayonnaise

Combine oil, poultry stuffing, tomato juice, dissolved bouillon cube, celery, onion and cucumber. Chill.

Before serving, add tomatoes, lemon juice and A-1 Sauce. Season to taste with salt and pepper. Sprinkle with chopped chives and drop 2 ice cubes into each bowl. Float a dollop of curry-flavored mayonnaise on the soup. Serves 4.

GAZPACHO

> 1½ cups cubed white bread, toasted
> 1 tablespoon salt
> 1½ teaspoons powdered cumin
> 3 tablespoons olive oil
> 1–4 cloves garlic, peeled and pressed
> 3 cups ripe tomatoes (about 5), peeled, seeded and strained, or 3 cups tomato juice
> About 3 cups cold water
> Black pepper
> Cayenne pepper or Tabasco sauce
> 2–4 tablespoons vinegar (optional)
> 3 ice cubes
> Garnish: 2–3 cups cubed white bread, sautéed in olive oil; 2 cups each of the following diced vegetables: green peppers, celery, cucumbers, onions, tomatoes

If you have an electric blender, purée the bread with the salt, cumin, olive oil, garlic and tomatoes or tomato juice. Otherwise, mash the bread with the tomatoes or tomato juice until soft, then purée through a food mill; add the garlic, salt, cumin and oil. Add cold water, more salt as necessary, black and cayenne pepper or Tabasco, optional vinegar to taste and the ice cubes. Chill thoroughly.

Prepare the garnish and arrange in separate bowls. At serving time, ladle the chilled soup into soup dishes; pass the garnish separately so each guest may stir what he likes into his soup. Serves 8.

GREEN GAZPACHO

> 1 or 2 cloves garlic
> 2 slices white bread, crusts removed
> ¼ cup Spanish olive oil
> 6–8 medium green tomatoes
> 1 green pepper, seeded and chopped
> 1 cucumber, peeled and diced
> 1 tablespoon grated onion

½ teaspoon salt

2 tablespoons vinegar

⅛ teaspoon cumin

½–¾ cup ice water

½–¾ cup dry white wine

Garnishes: Chopped red tomato; chopped un-peeled cucumber; chopped onion; minced hard-cooked egg croutons fried in olive oil.

Put garlic through garlic press, add bread and cover with olive oil. Leave several hours or overnight. Scald tomatoes with boiling water, peel off skins and cut in quarters. Combine tomatoes, green pepper, cucumber and onion and purée in blender a little at a time. Combine the salt, vinegar, oil-soaked bread and cumin. Add half of this mixture at a time to the purée in the blender and blend until very smooth. Chill thoroughly. Just before serving, blend in ice water and white wine to desired consistency. At table, pass garnishes to sprinkle on top of the gazpacho. Serves 4–6.

GAZPACHO WITH ALMONDS

24 blanched almonds

1 tablespoon minced parsley

1 teaspoon minced fresh tarragon

1 green pepper, chopped

1 cucumber, peeled and seeded

8 scallions or 2 medium onions, chopped

2 pounds garden-fresh tomatoes, peeled and seeded, or 1-pound, 12-ounce can tomatoes

¼ cup olive oil

½ teaspoon salt, or to taste

1 teaspoon lemon juice or 1 tablespoon vinegar

12-ounce can mixed vegetable juice

3 cups clear fat-free chicken broth

Minced green pepper and cucumber for garnish

Crush almonds in electric blender, add minced parsley and tarragon, crush until paste-like. Add green pepper and cucumber to blender and run at low speed until puréed. Add scallions or onions and finally tomatoes. Blend until well puréed. You may have to do this and the following steps in two batches. Add olive oil while blender is in motion, then salt, lemon juice, vegetable juice and, if a richer red color is desired, 2 tablespoons tomato purée or paste. Mix with chicken stock. Chill for several hours in refrigerator, the longer the better. Serve with an ice cube in each dish, passing the minced green pepper and cucumber garnish. Serves 10.

Note: For a really good gazpacho, homemade chicken broth is preferable. Use garden-fresh tomatoes only if they are in season. If not, use canned tomatoes.

Seafood

The English divine and essayist, the Reverend Sydney Smith, had a penchant for summing up his ardent feelings for food in lively rhyme. About fish he wrote, "Much do I love at civic treat / The monsters of the deep to eat," a sentiment any epicure might echo. Seafood fanciers have always waxed eloquent over their preferences. To Izaak Walton, the noble salmon was the king of fish. Escoffier had a good word for the lowly salt cod, rating it among the finest of the foods caught in the ocean. Saki, the British author, declared in one of his stories, "The Matchmaker," "There's nothing in Christianity or Buddhism that quite matches the unselfishness of the oyster," while Byron, predictably, referred to the bivalve as "amatory food."

The Roman Emperor Domitian, who once interrupted a meeting of the Senate to request advice on the proper sauce to serve with turbot, would have been in total accord with the French maxim, "C'est la sauce qui fait manger le poisson" —the sauce makes the fish. Many a pisciphobe has been won over by the skilled subtleties of French fish cookery—the velvety richness of filet de sole bonne femme; those light-as-air pike dumplings, quenelles de brochet, laved in a blushing sauce Nantua; the artful simplicity of the fresh trout with a simple butter and lemon sauce that so enraptured Napoleon when he tasted it at La Belle Meunière inn at Royat.

Yet, as Grimod de la Reynière knew all too well (he described fish as "the glory of the master inspired by genius; the stumbling block of ordinary cooks"), even the most superb sauce cannot transform or disguise fish that is less than fresh, or overcooked.

The freshness of a fish can be judged by the firmness of the skin and scales, the brightness of the eyes. Once bought (or caught), it should be prepared as soon as possible with tender, loving care—gently poached (never boiled) in flavored liquid, quickly and lightly sautéed, or carefully broiled with liberal libations of butter. While freshness is a prerequisite of all fish, it is an absolute necessity with some shellfish. The buyer should beware of clams that gape and mussels that yawn, for this is a sure sign that the creature within is as dead as a doornail and should be discarded (the same applies if the shell does not open after cooking). Once a live lobster has been dismembered for cooking, it must be used with the utmost dispatch, for nothing is more moribund or gastronomically suspect than a lobster that has gone to glory twenty-four hours earlier.

BASS FLAMBÉ AUX AROMATES

½ cup butter
  Grated rind of 1 lemon
2 tablespoons lemon juice
  Oil
1 smallish bass per person (or if you can find
  good-sized stripers, allow 1 or 2 stripers for 4)
  Dried fennel branches
  Salt, pepper
⅓ cup cognac, heated
  Parsley, wet
  Dash Tabasco

Melt butter, add lemon rind and juice, keep warm.

Place foil on a broiling rack, leaving enough extra foil on the sides so that you may use it to turn the fish over midway in its cooking. Brush the foil with oil, arrange fish on top, brush fish with oil and broil about 4″ from the heating unit until it flakes easily when tested with a fork or toothpick. Cooking time depends, naturally, upon size of the fish.

Arrange dried fennel branches on a hot platter—a metal one is best for this. Remove the fish to the platter. Season it with salt and pepper, pour heated cognac over it and ignite. The dried herbs should burn and impart their flavor and perfume to the fish. Traditionally the flames are put out with wet parsley.

Serve the fish at once, with lemon butter to which you have added a dash of Tabasco.

Note: Dried fennel branches may be bought in certain specialty food shops. If not available, substitute well-dried fennel tops.

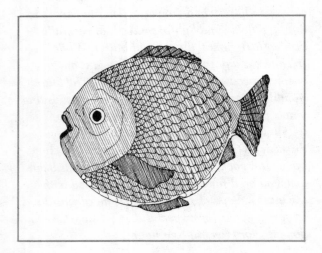

CARPE ALSACIENNE

4-pound carp, cleaned and cut into 1″ slices
½ cup chopped parsley
2 tablespoons chopped fresh chervil
  (or 1 tablespoon dried)
1 tablespoon chopped garlic
1 teaspoon dried thyme
1 bay leaf, crumbled
  Salt, pepper
2 medium onions, chopped fine
3 tablespoons olive oil
1 tablespoon flour
1 cup water
2 cups dry white Alsatian wine
  Pimiento, capers, sliced olives for garnish
Mayonnaise

Arrange carp slices on a deep platter or shallow dish and cover the slices with a mixture of the parsley, chervil, garlic, thyme, bay leaf and salt and pepper to taste (about 1 teaspoon of each). Chill the fish in the refrigerator for several hours.

To cook, brown the chopped onions delicately in the oil and when they are just golden, add the flour and blend thoroughly. When this is mixed well and has cooked for 3–4 minutes, add the water and wine. When the liquid comes to a boil, reduce the heat, add the fish slices and let them cook for about 45 minutes over very low heat. Remove fish slices to a serving dish and decorate with the pimiento, cut in strips, the capers and sliced olives. Force the sauce in which the fish cooked through a sieve or purée it in an electric blender and spoon over the fish when slightly cooled. Chill thoroughly—preferably overnight. Serve with well-seasoned mayonnaise. Serves 6.

CLAM PIE

1 carrot, cut in thin julienne strips
1 onion, cut
1 bay leaf
1 teaspoon freshly ground black pepper
2 cups white wine
2 quarts clams in shell, well scrubbed
2 cups velouté sauce (see Sauces)
1 pound mushrooms
5 tablespoons butter

Salt, pepper
3 tablepoons sherry or Madeira
1 recipe rough puff paste (see Pastry)
1 egg, beaten with a little water

Combine the carrot, onion, bay leaf, 1 teaspoon pepper and white wine in a large kettle. Add the clams. Cover and steam over medium heat until the clam shells open. Remove the clams from the shells and strain the broth through a linen cloth. Using some of the clam broth for liquid, make a velouté sauce.

Slice the mushrooms and sauté in the butter. Season to taste with salt and pepper. Mix the mushrooms and clams with the sauce and flavor with sherry or Madeira. Taste for seasoning. Pour into a baking dish or pie dish and cool. Place a support in the center of the dish to hold up the crust and top the pie with rolled out puff paste. Brush with egg mixture and bake in a 450° oven for 10 minutes. Reduce the heat to 350° and continue baking until the crust is nicely browned. With this pie, drink ice cold beer or a well-chilled white wine such as Liebfraumilch. Serves 6–8.

CLAMS AU BEURRE BLANC

2 dozen clams
8 tablespoons butter, at room temperature
2 tablespoons lemon juice
2 tablespoons finely chopped parsley
2 tablespoons finely chopped chives
⅓ cup dry white wine
1 tablespoon finely chopped shallots or
   green onions
½ clove garlic, finely chopped
1 tablespoon cognac (optional)

Have the clams opened at the fish store, or open them by hand with a knife or patented clam opener. Discard top shell. Reserve the clam liquor. Run a knife around the clams on the half shell to loosen them. Arrange close together on a jelly roll pan or any other large shallow pan. Pour the reserved clam liquor over them. Chill.

Place the butter in a saucepan in a warm place (the range pilot light will do) and beat with a wooden spoon or wire whisk until butter is soft, but not melted. Add the lemon juice, parsley and chives. Beat

until well blended. Set it aside, but do not allow the butter to melt.

Combine the wine, shallots and garlic in a saucepan. Bring the mixture to a boil and simmer one minute. Add cognac. Gradually beat this mixture into the butter. It should take on the consistency of a sauce.

Place the clams on the half shell in a 350° oven. Heat thoroughly, about 5–10 minutes, but do not overcook or the clams will toughen. Arrange the clams in piping hot soup bowls, pour the sauce over them and serve immediately with a crusty loaf of French or Italian bread and a chilled dry white wine. Serves 4.

COLD CODFISH
WITH SAFFRON SAUCE

2 white onions, sliced
2 carrots
   Several sprigs parsley
4½ cups dry white wine
4½ cups water
½ teaspoon thyme
1 bay leaf
¼ teaspoon peppercorns
4 teaspoons salt
4-pound slice fresh codfish
6 large ripe tomatoes
2 leeks
2 medium-size onions, finely chopped
6 tablespoons olive oil
2 cloves garlic, crushed
1 teaspoon coarsely ground pepper
1 teaspoon powdered saffron
2 lemons, quartered
1 tablespoon chopped parsley

Prepare a court bouillon by combining the white onion, carrots, parsley sprigs, 4 cups of the wine, 4 cups water, thyme, bay leaf, peppercorns and 1 teaspoon of the salt in an enamel fish boiler and boiling about 30 minutes. Wash the fish in cold water, wrap in cheesecloth and place in the hot court bouillon. Cook gently for about 40 minutes. Cool in the liquid. Discard cheesecloth, remove skin and all the bones, keeping the fish in as large pieces as possible. Arrange fish on a platter and cool. Wrap platter in wax paper and refrigerate until ready to serve.

To make saffron sauce, dip the tomatoes in boiling water and then remove the skins. Cut the tomatoes in half crosswise and remove the seeds. Place in a wooden bowl and chop fine. Remove green part from leeks, split white part in half lengthwise and wash carefully. Chop finely. Cook the chopped onions and leeks in the olive oil until they just begin to brown, stirring with a wooden spoon. Add the garlic and the chopped tomatoes. Cook 2 minutes, then add the remaining ½ cup white wine and ½ cup water. Season to taste with about 3 teaspoons salt, or less if you prefer, the coarsely ground pepper and saffron. Simmer 10–15 minutes, stirring occasionally. Remove the sauce from the heat and allow to cool before placing in the refrigerator to chill thoroughly.

When ready to serve, pour the cold saffron sauce over the fish and garnish with the lemon and parsley. Serve with crisp French bread, whipped butter and a good dry well-chilled white wine. Serves 6–8.

BRANDADE

Soak 2 pounds filleted salt codfish for several hours or overnight. Change the water once. Cover with fresh water, bring to the boil, and simmer for 5–6 minutes. Drain. Flake very finely. Using a mortar and pestle, a heavy saucepan and wooden spatula, or the electric mixer with a dough hook or paddle attachment, pound or work the fish, and add olive oil to it spoonful by spoonful, also adding a spoonful of warm milk or light cream from time to time until the mixture becomes well integrated. It should look rather like wet mashed potatoes. Beat in a little finely chopped garlic and chopped truffles if you wish.

Eat the brandade warm, make it into beignets, or bake in a tart shell. Additional flaked codfish, which has been soaked and cooked, may be combined with the mixture. As beignets or in tart shells, this amount of brandade will serve 4.

CODFISH MARSEILLAISE

> 1½ pounds salt codfish
> Flour
> ½ cup olive oil
> 1 large onion, chopped
> 1 garlic clove, chopped
> 5–6 medium-sized tomatoes, peeled, seeded and chopped
> Freshly ground black pepper
> Pinch of sage
> Pinch of thyme
> Salt
> 6 potatoes, peeled and quartered
> Dry white wine
> Chopped parsley

Soak the codfish for several hours in cold water, bring slowly to a boil, remove from stove and rinse in fresh water. Cut the fish into squares and roll each lightly in flour.

Heat olive oil in a skillet and sauté the fish squares until they are nicely browned. Remove them from the pan, and sauté the onion and garlic until soft and faintly colored. Add the chopped tomatoes, pepper to taste, and the sage and thyme. Simmer gently for about 15 minutes. Season to taste with salt.

Oil a casserole and arrange the quartered potatoes in the bottom. Pour the sauce over them and add enough mixed white wine and water to barely cover them. Add the pieces of codfish, cover the casserole and bake in a 350° oven for 30 minutes, or until the potatoes are tender. Remove the cover and sprinkle with chopped parsley. Serves 6.

BACALAO EN RAITO

2 pounds filleted salt codfish
⅔ cup olive oil
6 garlic cloves, chopped
3 large onions, chopped
1 fennel bulb, finely chopped (including the stems)
2 bay leaves, crushed
1 teaspoon mustard
Pinch of rosemary
Pinch of thyme
½ cup capers
½ cup chopped black olives
½ cup red wine
2 cups tomato purée
½ cup pounded or ground walnuts
A few walnut halves
Chopped parsley, capers for garnish

Soak the codfish in water for 1 hour. Change the water and soak for 8 more hours.

Heat the olive oil and sauté the garlic and onions until just soft. Add the fennel, bay leaves, mustard, rosemary, thyme, capers, olives and red wine. Simmer for 20 minutes and add the tomato purée, the ground and halved nuts and cook for 5 more minutes. Add drained codfish and cook until fish is done. Serve sprinkled with parsley and capers. Serves 6.

HAWAIIAN CRAB

2 egg yolks
Salt, cayenne pepper to taste
2 tablespoons tarragon vinegar
1 cup vegetable oil
1 teaspoon Tabasco sauce
2 teaspoons Worcestershire sauce
½ teaspoon sugar
½ cup whipped cream

½ pound crab meat
1 green pepper, finely chopped
1 red pepper, finely chopped
4 tomatoes, skinned, seeded and chopped
½ cup finely chopped onion
1 teaspoon each chopped garlic and parsley
4 small avocados
½ pound bacon, half broiled

First, make a spicy mayonnaise. Put in a bowl the egg yolks, salt, cayenne pepper and vinegar. Beat well. Then slowly beat in the oil, Tabasco, Worcestershire sauce and sugar. Mix in the whipped cream, the crab and all the other ingredients except the avocados and bacon. Arrange the mixture in a buttered baking dish. Peel and slice the avocados and arrange the slices on top. Cover with slices of the bacon and bake for 25 minutes in a 375° oven. Serve hot. Serves 4.

CRAB MEAT FLAMBÉ

12 tablespoons butter
6 tablespoons flour
3 cups chicken stock or 3 chicken bouillon cubes dissolved in 3 cups water
3 cups light cream
1½ teaspoons salt
3 pounds fresh crab meat
1 cup brandy
⅓ cup dry sherry
3 tablespoons Dijon mustard
¾ teaspoon dry mustard dissolved in 1 tablespoon water
3 tablespoons chopped parsley

Melt 6 tablespoons butter in a saucepan. Add flour and blend. Add stock and then cream, stirring constantly until sauce is smooth and thickened. Add salt. Simmer the sauce for 5 minutes. Keep warm.

In a large chafing dish over direct flame, or in a large pan on stove, melt remaining butter. Add crab meat. Heat brandy and sherry. Ignite and pour over crab meat. Stir in Dijon mustard, then most of reserved sauce. Add the dry mustard dissolved in the water, then balance of sauce. Simmer the mixture for 2 or 3 minutes. Sprinkle the top of the crab meat with the chopped parsley and serve. Serves 16.

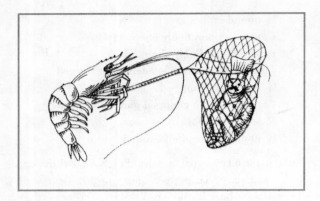

JAMES BEARD'S DEVILED CRAB

1 cup finely chopped celery
1 green pepper, seeded and finely minced
1 cup finely sliced scallion
½ cup finely chopped parsley
2 pounds crab meat, well picked over
2½ cups coarsely crushed cracker crumbs
1 teaspoon salt
1½ teaspoons dry mustard
   Tabasco sauce to taste
½ cup heavy cream
1 cup melted butter

Combine all the ingredients and pour them into a lightly buttered 2-quart baking dish. Bake in a 350° oven for 25–30 minutes. Serves 6–8.

CRAB CREOLE

6 small crabs
   Bread crumbs
3 canned pimientos, chopped fine
   Pinch of mace
1 hot red pepper, chopped, or cayenne
   pepper to taste
2 tablespoons chopped chervil
1½ tablespoons lime juice
3 tablespoons sherry
   Salt, freshly ground pepper to taste
2 cloves garlic, crushed
   Butter

Carefully remove the crab meat from the shells and chop fine. Scrub the empty shells and reserve. Mash 1½ cups bread crumbs into the crab meat until the mixture is quite smooth. Add all the other ingre-

dients except the butter, mixing thoroughly. Stuff the reserved crab shells with the mixture. Sprinkle lightly with bread crumbs, dot with butter, and bake in a preheated 350° oven for ½ hour, or until it is nicely browned. Serves 6 as an appetizer or 2–3 as an entrée for luncheon.

VIRGINIA CRAB CAKES

1 pound fresh, frozen or canned crab meat
3 eggs
½ cup mayonnaise
½ cup minced scallions, including green part
2 tablespoons minced celery with leaves
1 teaspoon Worcestershire sauce
1 tablespoon lemon juice
½ cup fresh bread crumbs
¾ cup flour
   Fine fresh bread crumbs
   Equal parts of oil and butter

Pick over the crab meat; if crab meat is canned, drain. Mix together the crab meat, 1 egg, mayonnaise, scallions, celery, Worcestershire sauce, lemon juice and ½ cup bread crumbs. Place it all in a sieve and drain.

Put the flour on one sheet of waxed paper, the fine bread crumbs on another. Beat the remaining eggs lightly. In a heavy skillet, pour oil and butter to a depth of ¼″ and heat.

Shape the crab mixture into rounded teaspoonfuls and drop into the flour. Coat with flour, then with egg, and finally with fine bread crumbs. Brown on both sides in hot fat. Serves 6.

MATELOTE OF EELS

1 onion
2 carrots
2 stalks celery
2 leeks
2 sprigs parsley
1 teaspoon dried tarragon or 1 stalk fresh
2 eels, skinned and cut in 2″ pieces
½ cup vodka
1 cup cider

1½ teaspoons salt
1 cup cream
3 egg yolks
   Dash of lemon juice

Dice onion and cut carrots, celery and leeks julienne. Arrange this mirepoix on the bottom of a heavy saucepan. Add parsley, tarragon and eels. Pour vodka and cider over mixture. Add salt. Bring to a boil, cover and simmer 20–25 minutes or until eel is tender. Remove eel to a hot serving dish.

Strain liquid. Combine 1/3 cup liquid and 1 cup mirepoix in an electric blender. Blend and pour into a saucepan. Repeat with more liquid and mirepoix. Add remaining liquid, bring to a boil and reduce slightly. Gradually stir in cream mixed with egg yolks. Stir until well blended and thickened. Correct seasoning and add lemon juice. Pour sauce over eel. Serve with fried croutons. Serves 4–6.

SPICED CRAWFISH

These tasty shellfish are available in Louisiana, Oregon, Washington, Wisconsin, Minnesota and many other parts of the country. They may sometimes be ordered from good fish stores in other areas, and are often shipped by air direct to the customer. If crawfish are not available, small lobsters or large shrimp can be substituted.

   2 quarts red wine (a good California bulk wine
      is excellent)
   1 quart water
   3 bay leaves
   4 cloves garlic
   ¼ cup Tabasco
   2 tablespoons salt
   3 sprigs parsley
   6–8 whole allspice
   1 teaspoon tarragon
   6–8 dozen crawfish

Bring the wine, water, bay leaves, garlic, Tabasco, salt, parsley, allspice and tarragon to a boil in a deep pan. Lower the heat and simmer 10 minutes. Add the crawfish and cook 8–10 minutes or until just done but not mushy. Drain. (Save the bouillon, it can be the base for a fine bisque.)

Allow 12–16 crawfish per person and serve chilled. Provide small picks to extract the meat. They are best without sauce, but you may add a bowl of French dressing or mayonnaise for dunking if you wish.

GREEK BAKED FISH

   4-pound whole fish (such as sea bass),
      or 3 pounds fish steaks
      Salt, freshly ground black pepper
      Few drops lemon juice
   ½ cup olive oil
   2 large onions, chopped
   3 medium tomatoes, sliced,
      or 1-pound can tomatoes
   2 tablespoons minced parsley
   12 stoned black Greek olives
   ½ cup white wine
   1 tablespoon soft bread crumbs
   1 lemon, sliced

Sprinkle fish with 1 teaspoon salt, pepper to taste and lemon juice. Brush some of the olive oil over the bottom of a long baking dish. Place a layer of onion and tomato in the dish and sprinkle with 1 teaspoon salt. Place the fish over the vegetables, then cover with the remaining vegetables, parsley and olives. Pour remaining olive oil and the wine over all. Sprinkle the bread crumbs over the top. Bake uncovered in a 350° oven for 45 minutes to 1 hour, basting occasionally with sauce in the dish. Serve topped with lemon slices. Serves 6.

FISH IN HAZELNUT SAUCE

   3 pounds fillets of any non-oily white fish
   2 cups white wine court bouillon
   3 ounces hazelnuts
   3 tablespoons olive oil
   1 slice thin white bread
   1 clove garlic
   1 bunch parsley
   1 teaspoon powdered saffron

Par-cook fish in the court bouillon. Soak hazelnuts in hot water for a few minutes and remove skins. Heat olive oil in a skillet and fry the bread with the garlic, being careful not to let the garlic burn. Put the bread, garlic, hazelnuts, parsley, and liquid from the poached fish in an electric blender. Blend to a smooth, medium-thick sauce. Add saffron and adjust seasoning. Put fish in a shallow casserole and cover with sauce. Heat gently to finish cooking. Serves 6.

FISH, YUCATAN-STYLE

    1 whole fish, such as pompano or snapper
    Juice of 1 lemon
    Salt, pepper to taste
    4 tablespoons olive oil
    1 onion, finely chopped
    3 ounces green olives, chopped
    1-ounce can pimiento, chopped, with liquid
    1 teaspoon annatto (achiote)
    2 tablespoons fresh cilantro, chopped,
      or 2 tablespoons chopped parsley
    Juice of 1 orange
    2 hard-cooked eggs, chopped

Marinate fish for 15 minutes in lemon juice, salt, and pepper. Heat olive oil in a skillet and sauté onion until limp. Add olives, pimiento and liquid, annatto, cilantro, salt, and pepper. Cook for a few minutes and add orange juice. Put fish in buttered casserole, cover with sauce and cook in a 400° oven for ½ hour or until tender. Garnish with chopped eggs. Serves 6.

GREEK MARINATED FISH

    2 pounds red snapper, or sole fillets,
      or halibut steaks
    Flour seasoned with salt and pepper
    ⅓ cup olive oil
    3 cloves garlic, minced
    ½ teaspoon rosemary
    ½ cup white wine vinegar

Dip the fish in the seasoned flour, coating both sides. Heat the oil in a large frying pan and fry the fish, turning to brown both sides. Remove to a hot platter. Drain off any excess oil from the pan; add the garlic, rosemary, and vinegar. Bring to a boil and let simmer a few minutes. Pour mixture over the fish and serve hot. (Equally good served chilled.) Serves 6–8.

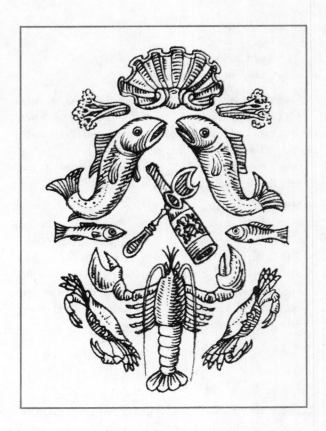

FINNAN HADDIE WITH CREAM SAUCE

    3-pound piece finnan haddie
    1 quart milk
    ¼ cup minced green onion
    ¼ cup diced green pepper
    2 tablespoons butter
    ¼ cup diced pimientos
    ½ cup butter
    ½ cup flour
    2 cups light cream
    Salt, pepper to taste
    1 cup crumbs, buttered

Cover the finnan haddie with the milk and poach gently until the fish separates easily, Drain, reserving the liquid. Separate the fish into flakes and remove any bones. Arrange in a large shallow baking dish. Sauté the onion and pepper in the 2 tablespoons butter for 3 minutes. Add the pimientos. Make a roux with the ½ cup butter and flour and add the light cream and 2 cups of the milk used for poaching. Cook, stirring, until thickened and smooth. Add the green onion-pepper mixture, season with salt and pepper, if needed, and pour over the fish. Sprinkle the top with the buttered crumbs. Serves 3.

HALIBUT PORTUGUESA

    1 pound halibut steak
        Salt, lemon juice
    1 large tomato, peeled and chopped
    1 medium onion, minced fine
    1 or 2 cloves garlic, crushed
    3 tablespoons olive oil
    1 teaspoon sugar
    ¼ cup minced parsley
    3 tablespoons tomato paste
    ½ cup white port or medium-dry sherry
    ½ cup water
    ¼ teaspoon dried mint, crushed to powder
    3 lemon slices
    1 tablespoon butter

Place halibut in an oiled shallow baking dish. Sprinkle with salt and a few drops of lemon juice. Simmer tomato, onion and garlic in olive oil until soft and golden. Add ¾ teaspoon salt, sugar, parsley, tomato paste and wine and simmer until well blended. Add water and mint, stirring to blend. Pour sauce over fish in baking dish and lay lemon slices over top of fish. Place dots of butter on fish, between the lemon slices. Cover baking dish completely with aluminum foil, wrapping foil around the bottom of dish. Bake in a 375° oven for 1 hour. Serve from the dish. Serves 3–4. (To serve 6, use 2 pounds halibut steak; the same amount of sauce will suffice.)

HARENGS CALAISIENNES

    4 small fresh herrings
    2 hard-cooked eggs, finely chopped
    2 cloves garlic, finely chopped
    2 shallots, finely chopped
    1 tablespoon chopped mixed fresh tarragon,
        parsley, thyme
        Salt, black pepper to taste
    2 slices bread, soaked in ½ cup water
    6 tablespoons butter
        Lemon juice
    1½ cups strong chicken stock

    2 peppercorns
    1 bay leaf
    1 tablespoon tomato paste
    4 ripe tomatoes, cut up
    1 clove garlic, minced
    1 small onion, very thinly sliced
    1 tablespoon flour
    1 tablespoon Tabasco sauce
    1 tablespoon Worcestershire sauce
    1 lemon, thinly sliced
        Finely chopped parsley, paprika

Remove herring heads, slit them down the back with a sharp knife and remove the bone and guts. Wash and dry well. Mix in a bowl the eggs, chopped garlic, shallots and herbs and season with salt and pepper. Squeeze water from the soaked bread and mash with a fork until smooth. Mix into ingredients in bowl. Carefully fill the herrings with this stuffing. Fold over and press down so stuffing will not come out. Make a few shallow slits on the top of the skin with a sharp knife and place herrings in an ovenproof dish. Melt 1 tablespoon butter in a pan with salt and freshly cracked pepper to taste and a few drops of lemon juice. Pour over the herrings with ¾ cup of the stock. Add the peppercorns and bay leaf. Bake in a 350° oven for 25 minutes.

Meanwhile, melt 2 tablespoons butter in a pan, add the tomato paste, tomatoes, a little salt and the minced garlic. Cook briskly for 2 minutes. Then add the remaining stock and stir until the mixture comes to a boil. Simmer gently for 10 minutes and then rub through a strainer. Return to the pan and add the sliced onion. Mix together the flour, the remaining butter and the Tabasco and Worcestershire sauces. Add to the tomato sauce and simmer 2 or 3 minutes. To serve, pour sauce on the bottom of a serving dish and arrange the baked herrings on top. Around the dish arrange the lemon slices, half of them covered with chopped parsley, the other half with covered paprika. Serves 4.

LOBSTER PROVENÇALE

    2 2-pound live lobsters
    1 medium onion
    6 shallots or small green onions
    4–6 cloves garlic

8 medium size ripe tomatoes
⅔ cup olive oil
4 tablespoons butter
4 tablespoons chopped parsley
1½ tablespoons chopped fresh tarragon (or
   1½ teaspoons dried)
1½ teaspoons thyme
1 bay leaf
2 cups dry white wine
4 tablespoons tomato purée
   Salt, black pepper, cayenne
⅓ cup cognac, warmed
4 egg yolks

Kill lobsters by inserting a sharp knife in the shell where the body and tail meet and severing the spinal cord. Flip the lobsters over on their backs and split them lengthwise. Remove sac behind eyes and intestinal vein in tail and discard. Take meat out of shells. Peel and chop the onion, shallots and garlic. Peel, seed and chop the tomatoes.

Heat the olive oil in a large skillet and add the lobster meat. Using a pair of tongs, toss the meat about in the hot oil until it is well seared on all sides. Remove the meat to a hot platter.

Add the butter to the skillet and sauté the onion, shallots and garlic until lightly colored. Add the tomatoes, parsley, tarragon, thyme, bay leaf and wine and simmer gently for 30 minutes. Stir in the tomato purée and season with salt, freshly ground black pepper, and a touch of cayenne. Pour the warmed cognac over the lobster meat and ignite.

Beat the egg yolks lightly. Take a little of the hot sauce and blend with the beaten yolks. Slowly stir this mixture into the sauce and cook and stir until smooth and thickened (be careful not to let the sauce boil or the egg yolks will curdle). Add the lobster meat and reheat. Serve over steamed rice. Serves 4–6.

LOBSTERS AU COGNAC

4 1¼-pound live lobsters
2 tablespoons butter
½ teaspoon cayenne pepper
1 tablespoon salt
   Freshly ground black pepper to taste

3 tablespoons finely chopped shallots
¼ cup plus 3 tablespoons cognac
1 cup fresh or bottled clam juice or fish stock
1 bay leaf
½ teaspoon thyme
2 sprigs parsley
2 cups heavy cream
1½ tablespoons flour

Kill each lobster by plunging a sharp knife into its thorax. Remove and crack claws. Break off the tail section and cut each tail section crosswise into 3 or 4 parts. Cut the forecarcass in half lengthwise and remove and discard the tiny inedible sac. Remove the coral (if any) and liver, place them in a small mixing bowl and chill.

Heat half the butter in a large skillet and add the claws, tail segments and forecarcasses. Sprinkle with the cayenne, salt and pepper. Cook, stirring, until shells redden. Add the shallots and ¼ cup cognac and cover immediately. Cook about 7 minutes, then add the clam juice, bay leaf, thyme and parsley. Cover and cook exactly 15 minutes. Add 1 cup cream and cook 5 minutes. Remove the lobster, let it cool slightly, then remove meat from shells. Keep the meat warm. Reserve the liquid.

Meanwhile add the remaining butter to the coral and liver and stir in the flour. Blend the mixture thoroughly with the hands or a spoon.

Bring the reserved liquid in the saucepan to a boil and cook uncovered 10 minutes. Add the remaining cream and bring to a boil. Using a wire whisk, stir in the liver mixture, bit by bit. When the mixture is thickened and smooth, strain it over the lobster. Sprinkle with remaining cognac and heat thoroughly. Do not cook further, but serve the lobster immediately with rice. Serves 4–6.

HOMARD AUX AROMATES

1 quart water
1 pint white wine
¼ cup vinegar
¼ cup and 2 tablespoons Pernod
1 carrot
1 onion stuck with cloves
   Parsley sprigs

HOW TO CUT UP A LIVE LOBSTER

1. Turn lobster on back. Kill by plunging sharp point of heavy knife into thorax. Cut through.

2. Remove claws by breaking at joints, or sever with kitchen shears, then crack hard shells.

3. With hands, bend head and tail backward to break in two. Cut tail crosswise in sections.

4. With point of small knife, carefully lift up and remove inedible sac behind eye and intestinal vein. Do not break while removing. Discard.

5. With spoon, remove and reserve coral and liver.

Salt, thyme, pepper to taste
4 1½-pound lobsters
1 cup heavy cream
Beurre manié
1 cup Hollandaise sauce
Dry bread crumbs
Fresh tarragon, chopped

Combine water, wine, vinegar, ¼ cup Pernod, carrot, onion, parsley, salt, thyme and pepper in a saucepan. Cook for 15 minutes. Add lobsters to this court bouillon and poach 12–15 minutes. Remove lobsters and cool. Split the lobsters, remove the meat, clean and reserve the shells.

Reduce court bouillon to 1½ cups over brisk flame. Strain and combine with cream. Thicken over medium flame with beurre manié and add remaining Pernod. Add lobster meat and heat. Replace in shells. Spread lightly with Hollandaise and bread crumbs. Glaze under the broiler.

Garnish with chopped tarragon. Serve with a rice pilaff and a Sancerre wine. Serves 4.

LOBSTER CARDINAL

1 cup mixed sliced onion, carrot, celery, leek
1 cup dry white wine
2½ cups water
1 bay leaf
2 sprigs fresh dill
A few peppercorns, salt, cayenne pepper
2 1¾-pound live lobsters
3 large truffles (2 diced)
¾ pound firm white mushrooms
Lemon juice
12 tablespoons sweet butter
1 teaspoon tomato paste
3 tablespoons flour
½ cup heavy cream
¼ cup freshly grated Gruyère cheese
¼ cup freshly grated Parmesan cheese

Put the vegetables in a large deep kettle with the wine, water, bay leaf, dill, peppercorns and 2 teaspoons salt. Bring all these ingredients slowly to a boil, reduce heat to a simmer, throw in the live lobsters and simmer them slowly until they blush (about 10 minutes). Cool lobsters in the liquid. When cool, remove the lobsters and carefully split them in half. Remove bag and vein. Take out tail meat in 1 piece, taking care not to dislodge the head shell from the tail. Cut off large and small claws and arrange the body shells on an au gratin dish with a slice of carrot underneath to keep them upright. Strain the fish liquid, pour a little of it over the tail meat and reserve 1 cup for the sauce. Keep in a warm place until ready to use. Remove meat from claws and cut it into small even dice. Add the diced truffle and the mushrooms which have been washed in lemon juice and water, diced thinly with the skins on and sautéed briskly in 1 tablespoon butter with salt, pepper and a few drops of lemon juice. Mix the tail meat and the mushrooms together and keep them warm, covered, while making the sauce cardinal.

Crush the small claws and shells of the large claws and the lobster livers in a mortar with a pestle until fine. Mix the tomato paste with 7 tablespoons butter, add to the crushed shells and crush together until they are all well mixed. Rub mixture through a fine sieve and then chill it.

Melt 2 tablespoons butter in a medium-sized saucepan. Stir in the flour off the heat, and season with ½ teaspoon salt and a pinch of cayenne pepper. Mix in 1 good cup of the strained fish stock and stir over low heat until it thickens and comes to a boil. Mix in the heavy cream, reboil, reduce heat to a simmer and beat in the chilled lobster butter bit by bit with a small whisk. Mix a little of this sauce with the mushroom-lobster-truffle mixture and divide it evenly between the lobster shells. Cut tail meat into even scallops and arrange on top, placing a thin slice of truffle in between the scallops. Coat the filled shells with the rest of the sauce, sprinkle the top with both cheeses and with remaining butter, melted. Brown under broiler, garnish with parsley. Serves 2–4.

LOBSTER SOUFFLÉ PLAZA-ATHÉNÉE

Sauce:

3 tablespoons butter
3 tablespoons flour
  Salt, pepper
1 cup light cream
2 teaspoons sweet butter

2 egg yolks
½ teaspoon tomato paste
2 teaspoons sherry
2 tablespoons heavy cream

Lobster mixture:

3 medium lobsters, boiled
  Cognac
  Salt, pepper, cayenne pepper
6 tablespoons butter
1 large carrot, cut in small dice
1 medium onion, diced
3 tablespoons finely chopped chives
1 tablespoon finely chopped parsley
¼ cup vegetable oil
1 cup heavy cream
½ cup dry white wine
3 tablespoons dry sherry
3 tablespoons flour
¾ cup milk
½ teaspoon Dijon mustard
¼ cup grated Parmesan cheese
¼ cup grated Gruyère cheese
5 eggs, separated
2 egg whites (from eggs used in sauce)

First, make the sauce. Melt 3 tablespoons butter in a pan, stir in the flour, season with salt and pepper to taste and pour on the light cream. Stir until it comes to a boil. Add the 2 teaspoons sweet butter, bit by bit. Mix the 2 egg yolks (reserve whites for later) with the tomato paste, 2 teaspoons sherry and 2 tablespoons heavy cream. Add this to the sauce. Set it aside in a warm place.

Remove tails from lobsters and cut each tail into three pieces. Remove meat from claws. Put tails and claw meat in a bowl and sprinkle with cognac. Season with salt and pepper to taste. Heat 3 tablespoons butter in a pan and add the diced vegetables and chives. Season with salt and pepper to taste and cook slowly, without browning, for 2 minutes. Mix in the parsley and set aside. Heat the vegetable oil in a pan, put in the lobsters, cover and cook for 2 minutes. Add the vegetable mixture. Mix in the heavy cream, white wine, sherry and 2 tablespoons cognac. Simmer gently for 12 minutes. Remove lobsters and take out meat. Cut all meat, including claw meat, into small, even pieces. Reduce liquid in pan to ¼ cup. Add the lobster meat to pan together with ½ cup of the sauce.

Butter a soufflé dish 10" in diameter and dust with bread crumbs. Tie a buttered waxed paper collar around the outside of the dish so that it rises 2" above the rim. Pour the lobster mixture into the bottom of the dish. Preheat the oven to 375°.

Melt the remaining 3 tablespoons butter in a pan and stir in, off the heat, the flour, salt and cayenne pepper to taste. Mix in the milk and stir over low heat until thickened, but do not allow to boil. Remove from heat and stir in the mustard, cheeses and the 5 egg yolks, well beaten. Stiffly beat the 7 egg whites and fold them in. Pour this soufflé mixture over the lobster in the soufflé dish (it should barely come to the top of the dish). Sprinkle top with grated Parmesan cheese and bake in a preheated 375° oven for 45 minutes. Serve immediately with the remaining sauce. Serves 6.

LOBSTER STRUDEL

For dough:

4 cups all-purpose flour
½ teaspoon salt
1 egg
  Vegetable oil
1¾ cups lukewarm water

For filling:

4 tablespoons salt butter
4 tablespoons flour
  Salt, cayenne pepper to taste
1 teaspoon Dijon mustard
1½ cups milk
¼ cup light cream
1½ cups cool melted butter
3 cups bread crumbs
1 cup grated Parmesan cheese
1 teaspoon dry mustard
  Meat of 3 boiled lobsters, cut up
1 cup grated Switzerland Swiss cheese
4 hard-cooked eggs, chopped
1½ cups sour cream
½ cup chopped parsley
¼ cup chopped chives
½ cup finely chopped shallots

2 teaspoons finely chopped garlic
  Chopped parsley
  Grated Parmesan cheese
  Béarnaise sauce

Sift the flower into a warm bowl with the salt. Make a well in the center and put in the raw egg and 4 tablespoons vegetable oil. Work up to a firm soft dough with the lukewarm water. Beat well on a marble slab or board 100 times. Sprinkle slab or board with a little flour and knead strudel dough a little to get a smooth surface on the bottom. Place on a lightly floured board, brush all over the top with vegetable oil and cover with an inverted bowl. Let stand at room temperature for 45 minutes.

Meanwhile, make sauce for the filling. Melt the 4 tablespoons salt butter and stir in the flour, off the heat. Season with salt, cayenne pepper and the Dijon mustard. Mix in the milk. Return to heat and stir until it comes to a boil. Mix in the light cream. Chill sauce in refrigerator until ready to use.

Cover a large table completely with a clean tablecloth or sheet and sprinkle the top lightly with flour, rubbing it in with your hand. Put dough on table and roll out to the size of a pocket handkerchief with a well floured rolling pin. Brush all over the top of the dough with vegetable oil. Remove any rings from your hands and lightly flour hands. With the backs of your hands under the dough, gently pull it out on all sides to the thickness of tissue paper; the stretched dough should completely cover the table and extend over the sides. Trim off thick edges with scissors and leave the dough until it feels like parchment when touched—approximately 15 minutes, although it may take a little longer if the weather is humid. Sprinkle melted butter all over the top of the dough. Mix the bread crumbs, 1 cup grated Parmesan cheese, 1 teaspoon dry mustard and ½ cup melted butter in a large bowl. Sprinkle all over the top of the strudel dough. Scatter the lobster meat over half of the dough and sprinkle the Swiss cheese and chopped eggs over the lobster. Dot with sour cream. Sprinkle with parsley, chives, shallots and garlic. Dot with the chilled cream sauce. Fold over one end of the strudel dough and sprinkle with melted butter. Fold over the sides and sprinkle them with melted butter. Roll up strudel like a jelly roll—not too tightly. Place on a buttered jelly roll pan and brush top with a little more melted butter. Bake in a preheated 375° oven for 40–50 minutes, until golden brown all over. (If the strudel is to be made in advance and reheated, remove 10 minutes before end of cooking time.) Remove and cool a little. Sprinkle the top with chopped parsley and cheese and serve on a long board, accompanied by Béarnaise sauce. Serves 8.

MUSSELS À LA MARINIÈRE

3 quarts mussels
1 cup dry white wine
3 shallots or green onions, coarsely chopped
4 sprigs parsley
½ bay leaf
½ teaspoon thyme
  Freshly ground black pepper to taste
3 tablespoons butter
¼ cup finely chopped parsley

Scrub the mussels well and remove the beard. Place mussels in a large kettle and add all ingredients except chopped parsley. Cover, bring to a boil and cook over high heat until mussels open, about 5–10 minutes. As the mussels steam, shake the kettle up and down, holding the lid in place. Discard any mussels that do not open.

Spoon the mussels into soup plates along with the cooking liquid and sprinkle with chopped parsley. Serve immediately with French bread. Serves 4.

MUSSELS LUCULLUS

2–3 quarts mussels, cleaned
1 cup white wine
3–4 pounds spinach or 2 packages frozen
  spinach
4 tablespoons olive oil
3 tablespoons butter
  Salt, pepper to taste
1 cup heavy cream
4 egg yolks
  Pinch of saffron
  Fine bread crumbs

Place mussels in a heavy pan with the white wine and steam until they open. Shell and beard the mus-

sels. Strain and reserve the liquid. If fresh spinach is used, blanch for 3 minutes in boiling water. Drain well and chop. If frozen spinach is used, thaw and drain. Chop. Heat spinach in olive oil and butter. Season with salt and pepper. Place in a gratin dish and top with mussels.

Prepare a sauce by cooking the heavy cream, ½ cup mussel liquid and egg yolks over low heat until thickened. Season to taste with salt, pepper and a pinch of saffron. Pour sauce over mussels. Sprinkle with fine bread crumbs. Glaze in a hot oven for 5–10 minutes. Serves 6–8.

MOULES À LA POULETTE
À LA MODE DE FOYOT

2 quarts mussels
1½ cups mixed diced celery, carrot, onion, leek
1 bay leaf
  Salt, pepper to taste
½ cup dry white wine
1 tablespoon sherry
¼ cup water
1 tablespoon flour
1 tablespoon butter
1 clove garlic, crushed
2 tablespoons coarsely chopped parsley
2 egg yolks
½ cup light cream

Soak the mussels in water with about 3 tablespoons dry mustard (this makes it easier to clean them). Wash in many waters and scrub well. When mussels are clean, put them in a pan with the diced vegetables, bay leaf, salt, pepper, wine, sherry and water. Cover and bring slowly to a boil and shake until the mussel shells open (discard any which do not open). Remove mussels and strain the liquid in which they cooked. Take off the top shells and arrange the mussels on a platter, scattering on top the diced vegetables with which they were cooked. Boil down the strained liquid a little. Work the flour, butter and garlic to a smooth paste and add this paste, bit by bit, to the liquid. Add the parsley and egg yolks which have been mixed into the cream. Reheat but do not boil. Pour this sauce over the mussels. Serves 4 as first course, 2 as main course.

HOW TO MAKE QUENELLES DE BROCHET

1. Take a teaspoon of the quenelle mixture.

2. Drop onto a lightly floured board and quickly roll around to form a ball.

3. With palm of the hand, gently roll back and forth into a long cork shape.

4. Roll off board onto slotted spoon to avoid fingermarks or breaking.

5. Carefully lower into a large pan of hot salted water and poach until firm.

QUENELLES DE BROCHET

    4 ounces sweet butter
    ¾ cup flour
    4 eggs
    1 cup milk
    ½ teaspoon salt
    Pinch of cayenne pepper
    1½ pounds pike, skinned, boned and put through fine blade of a meat grinder
    4 ounces finely ground beef kidney suet
    Melted butter

Sauce:

    3 tablespoons sweet butter
    3 tablespoons flour
    Salt, cayenne pepper to taste
    1 cup fish stock
    ½ cup and 1 tablespoon light cream
    2 egg yolks
    2 tablespoons dry sherry

Melt the 4 ounces butter in a small heavy pan and stir in, off the heat, the ¾ cup flour, 2 of the eggs, the milk, salt and cayenne pepper. Stir over heat until mixture thickens and comes away from the sides of the pan like a cream-puff dough. Spread this mixture (a panade) on a platter and let it get quite cold. Mix together the ground pike, ground suet and panade, then mix in the remaining 2 eggs (they should be large; if small, use 3). Rub the mixture through a fine strainer and chill a little. Form teaspoons of the mixture into cork shapes on a lightly floured board. Have ready a large pan of hot salted water which has come to a boil and then been reduced to a simmer. Carefully lower the quenelles into the water with a slotted spoon and poach in the gently simmering water, without boiling until firm to the touch, about 15 minutes.°

Meanwhile, make the sauce. Melt 2 tablespoons butter in a pan and stir in the 3 tablespoons flour, off the heat. Season with salt and cayenne pepper and mix in the fish stock. Stir over low heat until sauce thickens and then add ½ cup light cream. Stir until sauce comes to a boil and add, bit by bit, the remaining butter. Mix the egg yolks with the sherry and 1 tablespoon cream and add a little of the hot sauce to this mixture. Stir well to prevent yolks curdling, then add, to balance of sauce in pan.

Remove poached quenelles from water with a slotted spoon, draining well, and arrange on a hot flat serving dish. Pour sauce over the quenelles, sprinkle top with melted butter and brown under a very hot broiler. Serves 6.

<u>Note</u>: Finely chopped cooked lobster, shrimp or crab may be added to the sauce, or the quenelles may be served with other suitable fish sauces, such as the Cardinal sauce for Lobster Cardinal.

° Quenelles may be made hours ahead and left in the poaching water with the heat turned off, covered with paper towels. Gently reheat in poaching water before serving. They may also be frozen in the poaching liquid and reheated.

FILLETS OF POMPANO WITH ORANGE

>   4 fillets pompano
>   Bones from the fish
>   2 navel oranges
>   Juice of 1 lemon, strained
>   3 tablespoons butter
>   ⅓ cup sherry
>   1 cup heavy cream
>   Salt, pepper
>   ½ teaspoon paprika
>   3 egg yolks, well beaten
>   1 cup white wine
>   1 shallot, chopped fine

Wash the fillets in cold water and dry on paper towels. Place fish bones in an enamel pan, cover with 1 cup cold water and simmer 15 minutes. Strain and save the fish stock. Wash navel oranges, and with a sharp knife or a potato peeler cut off the orange part only of the rind. Cut in thin slivers, and cover immediately with strained lemon juice. With a sharp knife, cut off the remaining white pith from the oranges, and cut between sections to extract the pulp in neat crescent-shaped pieces.

Melt 2 tablespoons butter in the top part of small double boiler over boiling water. Add the sherry. When hot, stir in the heavy cream. Season to taste with salt and pepper and the paprika. Cook for a minute or two, then pour hot mixture over the egg yolks. Return to top of double boiler and cook, stirring constantly, until the sauce is smooth and thick like custard, about 2–3 minutes. Remove top pan and set aside to keep warm.

Put the white wine in a shallow enamel pan, add the shallot, 1 tablespoon of butter, the fish stock and the prepared orange peel, drained of lemon juice. Season lightly to taste with salt and pepper and lay on this bed the 4 fillets. Poach very gently until opaque, about 10 minutes, turning fillets over once with a pancake turner when half done. Transfer fillets gently to a hot platter and keep warm. Reduce the stock in the fish pan to 1/3 its original quantity by boiling rapidly. Add this gradually to the egg sauce, place over hot water and stir constantly until warm, not hot. Pour sauce over the fish, garnish with the orange sections and serve at once, accompanied by tiny boiled potatoes. Serves 4.

POACHED SALMON

A whole salmon of anywhere from 8–25 pounds will poach perfectly and may be eaten hot or cold.

If you do not have a large-size *poissonière*—and very few people do these days—you can find various types of vessel, including a baby's enamel bathtub, which will do the job extremely well.

You may poach the fish in salted water, or in a court bouillon. Be certain you make enough bouillon to cover the fish well during cooking.

Wrap the fish in several thicknesses of cheesecloth, leaving long ends to hang over each side of the fish cooker. Bring the water or bouillon to a boil and lower the fish into it. If you have a rack which will fit in the pan and hold the fish, it is ideal. If not, you must be careful not to split the fish when removing it from the liquid. Reduce the heat when you place the fish in the cooker so that you have what the French call a *faible ébullition,* and poach until a meat thermometer plunged into the thickest part of the fish registers 160°

Serve the poached salmon hot with lemon butter or with a Béarnaise sauce or mustard Hollandaise or a rich Béchamel sauce to which you have added chopped hard-cooked eggs and parsley. Or serve cold with a good homemade mayonnaise or mustard mayonnaise. Allow ½ pound for each serving.

Beer or a chilled Muscadet or Pinot Chardonnay go well with salmon. Cucumber salad and tiny new potatoes are good with it (chopped chives and tarragon will give the potatoes a different flavor).

BAKED SALMON

> 5-pound salmon (whole or piece), scaled and
>   fins removed
> Salt, pepper
> Flour
> 6 tablespoons butter, melted
> 1 large onion, minced
> 1 clove garlic, minced or pressed
> 1 tablespoon Worcestershire sauce
> 2 tomatoes, peeled, drained of juice, seeded, and
>   chopped, or 1¼ cups canned tomatoes,
>   drained
> ¼ cup (approximately) light cream
> Beurre manié (1 tablespoon butter and 1 table-
>   spoon flour kneaded together), if necessary
> Lemon wedges
> Parsley

Rub the salmon inside and out with salt and pepper, dredge with flour, and put into a well-greased narrow baking pan. Bake in a preheated 425° oven for 15 minutes, then add the butter, onion, garlic, Worcestershire sauce, and tomatoes, and reduce heat to 375°. Bake for 30 minutes longer, basting frequently.

A meat thermometer, inserted into the thickest part of the fish, should reach 160°. Remove fish to a hot platter and keep warm. Add a little cream, about ¼ cup, to the sauce in the pan and stir well until smooth. If sauce is too thin, thicken with beurre manié. Garnish the fish with lemon wedges and parsley and serve the sauce in a separate dish. Serves 6.

SAUTÉED SALMON FLORENTINE

> 2 salmon steaks, 1½″ thick
> Flour
> 4 tablespoons butter
> Salt, pepper to taste
> 2 cups finely chopped cooked spinach
> 1 clove garlic, crushed
> 1 tablespoon lemon juice
> 1 teaspoon crushed or chopped thyme
>   or marjoram (optional)
> 1 pound mushrooms, sliced and sautéed

Dust the steaks with flour and sauté in 2 tablespoons of the butter until done, seasoning with salt and pepper. Arrange them on a bed of chopped spinach on a heated platter and keep warm. Add the remaining 2 tablespoons butter and the garlic to the pan. Cook, stirring, until the butter has just started to color; discard garlic. Add the lemon juice and, if desired, the herb of your choice. Pour the flavored butter over the salmon, and surround with mushrooms. Serves 4.

BROILED SALMON À LA RUSSE

> 2 salmon steaks, 1½″ thick
> Salt, pepper
> Olive oil
> 5 anchovies
> 4 tablespoons sweet butter
> Paprika
> 2 tablespoons caviar
> 1 cup Hollandaise sauce

Season the steaks with salt and pepper, brush with olive oil, and broil until done. Blend the anchovies with the butter until smooth (or whirl in the blender), add paprika to give the mixture a lovely pink color, and spread this anchovy butter over the cooked steaks. Add the caviar to the Hollandaise sauce and serve with the salmon. Serves 4.

SALMON COULIBIAC

1 package granular yeast
¼ cup warm water
¼ cup lukewarm milk
2½ cups sifted flour (or more)
10 tablespoons butter
4 eggs
  Salt, pepper
2 pounds salmon fillets
1 tablespoon lemon juice
2 tablespoons minced parsley
2 teaspoons dill weed or minced fresh dill
3 cups cooked cracked wheat, kasha, or rice,
  mixed with ¼ cup melted butter
3 hard-cooked eggs, sliced

Dissolve the yeast in the warm water and stir in the milk. Add 1 cup of the flour, mix, and allow to rise until double in bulk. Soften 8 tablespoons of the butter and add to the yeast mixture with 3 of the eggs, 1½ cups of flour, and ¼ teaspoon salt. Beat hard and long in the electric mixer. Allow to rise once more, then turn out on a floured board and work in additional flour to make a soft, but not sticky, dough.

Sauté the salmon fillets in the remaining 2 tablespoons butter until lightly browned. Sprinkle with the lemon juice and allow to cool. Chop about ½ pound of the salmon, add the parsley, dill, and salt to taste, and reserve.

Roll the pastry into a rectangle about 12″ by 18″ Roll it onto the rolling pin, then unroll on a lightly floured cloth or piece of heavy foil. Spread the chopped salmon in the center of the rectangle, cover with half of the buttered cracked wheat or kasha or rice, and lay the remaining fillets over it. Now arrange the egg slices on top of the fish, sprinkle with salt and pepper to taste, and put the remaining cracked wheat on top.

Fold the ends and sides of the pastry over the filling and seal by pressing firmly together. Butter a baking sheet, invert on the filled pastry, and turn the whole thing over, cloth and all. Remove cloth, make 6 or 8 slashes in the top of the pastry and brush with the remaining egg, slightly beaten. Bake in a 375° oven for 30–40 minutes, or until brown. Serve sliced, and pass a sauce boat of melted butter. Serves 6.

Note: This glorious pastry may also be made with thick-sliced smoked salmon, but in that case be very careful with the salt.

SALMON MOUSSE

2 pounds poached salmon, boned and skinned
4 egg whites
1 cup heavy cream, chilled
  Salt, pepper
  Nutmeg or cayenne (optional)
3 tablespoons prepared mustard
2 cups cream sauce

Put the salmon through the food chopper, then pound it to a pulp in a large bowl or mortar, gradually adding 2 unbeaten egg whites as you pound. Place the bowl in a larger one containing cracked ice and work the mixture with a wooden spoon for 5 minutes, then rub it through a sieve. Return to the ice and let it stand for half an hour, stirring now and then.

Beat the remaining egg whites until stiff and gradually beat into the salmon mixture alternating with the cream. Taste for seasoning. Add salt and pepper to taste, and a little nutmeg or cayenne if you like. Turn the mixture into a well-buttered melon mold with a tight-fitting lid, or put in a fish mold, cover with buttered parchment paper, and tie in place. Put the mold in a roasting pan containing 1½″ hot water and bake in a 350° oven for about 40 minutes, or until set and firm. Remove from the oven and let stand for 5 minutes before unmolding.

Prepare a mustard sauce by combining the prepared

mustard and cream sauce. Serve with the mousse and accompany with a chilled salad of thinly sliced cucumbers with sour cream dressing. Serves 6.

SMOKED SALMON ROULADE

4 tablespoons butter
½ cup flour
2 cups milk
1 teaspoon sugar
4 eggs, separated
2 ounces cream cheese
1½ cups sour cream
6 ounces smoked salmon, cut in julienne strips

Melt butter. Blend in flour. Add milk gradually, stirring constantly until thick. Remove from heat. Add sugar and egg yolks. Stiffly beat egg whites and fold in. Grease a 10″ by 15″ jelly roll tin. Line with waxed paper. Grease paper thoroughly, dust with flour. Spread batter in lined tin. Bake in 325° oven until top is golden, about 40 minutes. Turn out on wax paper. Peel off the wax paper from the tin which is adhering to the top. Spread the surface with filling.

To make filling, blend cheese with enough sour cream to make mixture soft enough to spread easily. Add half the salmon. Mix remaining salmon with remaining sour cream to make a sauce.

Roll and place on serving platter. Serve with sauce on the side. The roll can be made in advance and reheated. To heat, cover the roll loosely with foil and place on a platter over a pot of simmering water until warmed through. Serves 6.

SCALLOPS BOURGUIGNONNE

2 pounds bay scallops
Red wine
1 teaspoon salt
½ teaspoon thyme
7 tablespoons finely chopped parsley
4 shallots, finely chopped
4 cloves garlic, finely chopped
6 ounces butter
Chopped toasted almonds or toasted sesame seeds

Poach scallops in red wine to cover, seasoned with

salt, thyme, 1 tablespoon chopped parsley, 1 teaspoon chopped shallot and 1 chopped clove garlic. The scallops will cook very quickly, in a minute or two. Do not let them shrink and get tough but scoop them out the minute they are done and arrange them in buttered individual ramekins or shells. Make beurre d'escargot by creaming the butter with the rest of the garlic, finely chopped shallots and chopped parsley. Top each ramekin of scallops with a good spoonful of the butter and sprinkle with almonds or sesame seeds. Put under broiler flame just long enough to brown well on top. Serve as a first course at dinner or a main course at luncheon. Serves 4–6. With this, drink the wine used in cooking, perhaps a Fleurie.

COQUILLES ST. JACQUES

½ cup dry white wine or dry vermouth
1 cup water
7 tablespoons butter
2 sprigs parsley
1 small onion, peeled
1 bay leaf
Pinch of thyme
1½ pounds bay scallops (if sea scallops are used, quarter them)
½ pound mushrooms, chopped
Juice of ½ lemon
Salt, freshly ground black pepper to taste
3 tablespoons flour
4 egg yolks
1 cup heavy cream
1 cup buttered bread crumbs
2 tablespoons grated Parmesan cheese

Put the wine, ½ cup water, 2 tablespoons butter, parsley, onion, bay leaf and thyme in a shallow pan and bring to the boil. Add the scallops, lower the heat and simmer until scallops are tender, a minute or two for bay scallops, about 5 minutes for sea scallops. Remove scallops. Strain and reserve broth.

Melt 2 tablespoons butter, add the mushrooms, the remaining water, lemon juice, salt and pepper and cook over medium heat 5 minutes. Drain mushrooms and set aside. Strain liquid and add to wine broth.

Melt the remaining butter and add the flour, stirring with a wire whisk. When blended, add the combined liquids, stirring vigorously with the whisk. Add the scallops and set aside to cool slightly. Beat the egg yolks with the cream and add a little to the warm sauce, stirring well. Add the remaining cream mixture and continue cooking over hot water until sauce is smooth and thickened. Do not allow to boil. Add the mushrooms. Pile mixture into individual scallop shells, sprinkle with crumbs and cheese and put under the broiler until crumbs are browned. Serve immediately. Serves 6–8.

COQUILLES ST. JACQUES PROVENÇALE

    1 pound bay scallops
    5 tablespoons butter
    1 tablespoon chopped onion
     Salt, pepper
     Large croutons of fried bread
    4 tablespoons cèpes (dried wood mushrooms)
     soaked overnight in water
    2 tomatoes, peeled, seeded and chopped
    1 tablespoon white wine
    1 teaspoon chopped chives
    1 clove garlic, minced
     Grated Parmesan cheese

Wash the scallops well. Melt 3 tablespoons butter and sauté the scallops and onion gently with a little salt and pepper for 5–6 minutes. Remove, strain excess liquid from pan and reserve. Arrange scallops on top of the croutons on a hot serving dish. Keep warm. Strain the soaked cèpes and sauté them in 2 tablespoons butter with a little salt and pepper for 10 minutes. Add the tomatoes, white wine, chives, garlic and a little extra seasoning and simmer for another 6–7 minutes. Add the liquid from the scallops. Pour the mixture over the scallops, sprinkle the tops with grated Parmesan cheese and butter, brown them quickly under the broiler and serve them immediately. Serves 2–4.

SHRIMP BORDELAISE

    2 tablespoons olive oil
    2 tablespoons finely chopped shallots
    1½ cups red Burgundy
    1 clove garlic, crushed
    1 bay leaf
    6 mixed peppercorns, black and white
    2 tablespoons salt butter
    2 tablespoons vegetable oil
    1 cup mixed sliced onion, carrot, celery, leek
    2 teaspoons tomato paste
    2 teaspoons meat glaze
    3 teaspoons potato starch
    2 cups strong chicken stock
    2 teaspoons red currant jelly
    4 marrow bones
    1 truffle, finely chopped
    2 pounds large raw shrimp, shelled and
     deveined

Heat the olive oil a little in a small heavy pan, add the shallots and cook slowly for 1–2 minutes without browning, then pour on the Burgundy, add the garlic, bay leaf and peppercorns and simmer gently for about 10–15 minutes.

Meanwhile, heat the butter and vegetable oil in another small heavy pan, add the mixed vegetables and cook slowly until golden brown. Blend in, off the heat, the tomato paste, meat glaze and potato starch. Mix in the chicken stock and stir over low heat until the mixture comes to a boil. Add the red currant jelly, marrow bones and the red wine mixture. Simmer until all is reduced to a thick rich brown sauce. Strain the sauce. Add to it the truffle and the shrimp. Extract the marrow from bones and add it also. Continue to simmer gently until the shrimp turn pink. Serve with rice. Serves 4.

SHRIMP ON THE HALF SHELL

    12 jumbo shrimp (1 pound)
    3 tablespoons oil (not olive oil;
     sesame oil is particularly good)
    1 clove garlic, finely minced
    1 teaspoon minced green ginger
    3 tablespoons minced scallions
    2 tablespoons soy sauce
    2 tablespoons whiskey
    ¼ cup chicken stock or water

Split the shrimp in half lengthwise, shells and all. Wash out the veins, but let the shrimp remain in the halved shells. Heat the oil in a heavy skillet, arrange the shrimp, shell side down, in the pan and cook gently for 5 minutes. Add the garlic, ginger, scallions, soy sauce, whiskey and chicken stock or water, cover and let the shrimp simmer gently until tender, about 10 minutes. Serve in the shells, with rice as an accompaniment. Serves 4.

SHRIMP CREOLE

  2 cups raw shrimp, shelled and deveined
  2 tablespoons butter
  2 tablespoons oil
  4 mushrooms, finely sliced
  2 tablespoons Marsala wine
  1 tablespoon mixed finely chopped red and
     green pepper
  ¼ teaspoon tomato paste
  ¼ teaspoon meat glaze
  1 cup light cream
  2 tablespoons sour cream
     Salt, cayenne pepper to taste
  ½ teaspoon dried red chili pepper
  2 onions, sliced

Toss the shrimp in 1 tablespoon foaming butter and 2 tablespoons oil for 1 or 2 minutes. Remove, add 1 tablespoon butter and the mushrooms. Cook briskly for a couple of minutes, then add the Marsala and chopped peppers. Cook until the liquid is reduced. Add a little more butter, if necessary, and stir in the tomato paste and meat glaze. Mix in, very slowly, the cream, sour cream and seasonings. Replace shrimp with the onions, which have been cooked in butter until brown and crisp. Simmer very slowly until sauce is heated through and shrimp are pink. Serve on a bed of hot cooked rice. Serves 4.

SHRIMP TARRAGON

  2 tablespoons chopped fresh tarragon
  ¼ pound butter, melted
  2 pounds raw shrimp, shelled and cleaned
  ½ cup heavy cream
     Salt

Add the tarragon to the melted butter and cook the shrimp in it until tender (from 5–10 minutes). Add the cream, bring to a boil and add salt if necessary. Serve with toast. Serves 6.

SHRIMP ITALIENNE

  2 tablespoons olive oil
  1 tablespoon vegetable oil
  4 tablespoons salt butter
  1 tablespoon finely chopped garlic
  1 tablespoon dried mushrooms, soaked in 4
     tablespoons water, drained and chopped fine
  2 green peppers, blanched, seeded and finely
     chopped
     Salt, pepper, dry mustard to taste
     A little cayenne pepper
     Paprika
  1½ pounds medium shrimp, boiled and shelled
  2 tablespoons chopped chives
  2 tablespoons finely chopped red onion

Heat the olive and vegetable oils and 2 tablespoons of the butter. Sauté the garlic and mushrooms. Add green pepper. Season with salt, pepper, mustard and cayenne pepper. Sprinkle with paprika and add the remaining 2 tablespoons butter. Add shrimp and shake over moderate heat for 5 minutes, covering them well with the sautéed mixture. Add chives and onion. Serve with saffron rice. Serves 4.

SHRIMP MARINIÈRE

    2 pounds raw shrimp, shelled and cleaned
    2 cups white wine
    2 cups chicken stock
    Herb bouquet (parsley, bay leaf and thyme)
    ⅓ cup minced shallots or green onion
    4 tablespoons butter or olive oil
    3 tablespoons flour
    Salt, pepper to taste
    ½ cup heavy cream mixed with 3 egg yolks
    12 slices French bread, toasted
    Minced parsley

Cook the shrimp in the white wine and chicken stock with the herb bouquet for 5 minutes. Sauté the shallots in the butter or olive oil. Add the flour, cook a minute or two, then add to the shrimp mixture. When smooth and thickened, add salt and pepper. Cook gently for 10 minutes and, just before serving, carefully add the cream mixed with the egg yolks. Do not allow to boil. Serve the shrimp in a shallow dish. Surround them with toasted French bread. Sprinkle liberally with parsley. Serves 6.

CURRIED SHRIMP, ICED

    1 clove garlic, crushed with flat of a knife
    ¼ cup minced onion
    ¼ cup minced apple
    4 tablespoons butter
    2 tablespoons flour
    1 cup canned tomatoes
    Salt, pepper to taste
    Curry powder to taste
    Mayonnaise
    1 tablespoon lemon juice
    2 pounds cooked cleaned shrimp, cooled
    Shaved almonds
    Sliced cucumbers

Sauté the garlic, onion and apple in the butter. When the onion is wilted, discard the garlic and add the flour, tomatoes, salt, pepper and curry powder to the pan. (In this recipe the curry powder may be added rather lavishly, as it is to be diluted later.) Cool this curry sauce and add to it an equal amount of mayonnaise and the lemon juice. Fold in the cooled shrimp, then pack into a bowl and chill for several hours before serving. Turn out on a glass plate, sprinkle the top with shaved almonds and garnish with sliced cucumbers. This is a good dish for a buffet, served, perhaps, with Virginia ham, chicken turnovers and asparagus vinaigrette. Serves 6.

SHRIMP TEMPURA

    1 pound large raw shrimp
    1 cup flour
    ½ teaspoon salt
    1 egg
    ¾ cup water or milk
    Oil for frying

Shell and clean shrimp and split part way down the back. Open and flatten slightly. Lightly mix flour, salt, egg and water or milk to a medium batter. Don't overmix. Dip shrimp in batter and then deep fry at 375° until lightly browned. Drain and serve with shoyu sauce to which grated daikon (Japanese radish) and ginger have been added. Serves 2–3.

FILLETS OF SOLE WITH LOBSTER STUFFING

    1 cup soft bread crumbs
    1 rock lobster tail, cooked, shelled and minced
    3 tablespoons olive oil
    Salt
    ¼ cup and 1 teaspoon minced parsley
    1 tablespoon minced onion
    Pinch of oregano
    6–8 toasted almonds, crushed
    6 fillets sole
    2 scallions, minced
    1 clove garlic, crushed
    2 medium tomatoes, peeled, seeded and chopped
    2 tablespoons amontillado sherry

Combine bread crumbs, lobster, 2 tablespoons oil, ¼ teaspoon salt, ¼ cup parsley, minced onion, oregano and almonds. Place 1–1½ tablespoons on each fillet and roll up. Place on individual squares of foil with overlapped side of fillet underneath. Combine scallions, garlic, tomatoes, sherry, remaining parsley and oil and salt to taste. Spoon some over each stuffed fillet. Crimp edges of foil together to seal. Bake in a 350° oven for 25–35 minutes. Serves 6.

SOLE DAHLSTROM

¼ cup (2 ounces) butter
1 teaspoon Beau Monde seasoning
12 small fillets of sole, at room temperature
1½ cups sour cream
¼ cup light cream
½ teaspoon salt
6-ounce can medium shrimp, drained
½ cup grated Parmesan cheese
9–12 pimiento-stuffed green olives, sliced

Take a flat baking dish, large enough to hold 6 fillets of sole side by side, and butter it well. Sprinkle with ½ teaspoon Beau Monde seasoning, and lay 6 fillets in it. Mix the sour cream and light cream until smooth and easy to spread, and cover the fillets with half the mixture. Sprinkle with the remaining ½ teaspoon Beau Monde seasoning and the salt. Place the drained shrimp evenly on the fillets and top with the remaining 6 fillets, making layers. Spread with remaining sour cream mixture and sprinkle with the grated Parmesan. Bake in a 325° oven for 20–25 minutes, depending upon the thickness of the fillets. (Do not overcook, as the sour cream will separate.) Remove from the oven, garnish each serving with 5 or 6 olive slices and serve immediately. This dish can be prepared an hour or so ahead of time and then gently reheated, if kept cool but not refrigerated. Serves 6.

FILLETS OF SOLE WITH WHITE GRAPES

1½ cups white seedless grapes
1 cup dry white wine
3 pounds sole fillets
4 tablespoons butter
Juice of 1 lemon
3 bay leaves
2 small shallots, peeled and sliced
12 white peppercorns
2 tablespoons flour
½ cup milk, warm

½ cup heavy cream
Salt, cayenne pepper

Peel the grapes and soak them immediately in the white wine. Preheat oven to 350°. Wash the sole fillets and pat dry. Butter a large flat ovenproof glass or enamel dish with about ½ tablespoon butter. Lay the fillets in the dish. Pour over them ½ cup cold water, the strained lemon juice and the white wine in which the grapes have been soaking. Cover the grapes and put aside until ready to use. Scatter over the fish the bay leaves, shallots and whole peppercorns. Dot with 1½ tablespoons butter. Bake in 350° oven until fish is opaque throughout, about 25 minutes, basting occasionally. When done, remove from oven and carefully strain the juices into a small pan. Keep the fish warm while you make the sauce. Make a white roux by cooking together over a very low flame 2 tablespoons of butter and the flour, stirring constantly with wooden spoon. Cook very slowly for 5 minutes, then gradually add the strained juice reserved from the fish. Continue cooking for about 5 minutes longer. Remove from fire and stir in the warm milk. Put back on fire and bring to a boil, stirring vigorously, then gradually add the heavy cream. Do not allow to boil after the cream has been added. Season to taste with salt and a very small pinch of cayenne. Add the grapes to the sauce, and pour it over the fish. Serve at once. Serves 6–8.

FILET DE SOLE MARGUERY

2 dozen large mussels, cleaned
Salt
1 cup sliced onion, carrot, celery
1 bay leaf
A few peppercorns
½ cup dry white wine
1 cup water
4 fillets of sole (and bones)
Cayenne pepper
5 tablespoons butter
6 firm white mushrooms, halved and sliced diagonally
½ teaspoon lemon juice
¼ pound small shrimp, boiled, shelled and deveined
2 teaspoons chopped parsley

3 tablespoons flour

¼ cup light cream

½ cup Hollandaise sauce

Put the mussels in a deep pan with 1 teaspoon of salt, the sliced vegetables, bay leaf, peppercorns, wine and water. Bring slowly to a boil and simmer 3 minutes, until shells have opened. Discard any that do not open. Strain liquid. Arrange sole fillets on a greased baking dish, white side (side nearest the bone) down. Season with a little salt and cayenne pepper, cut up 1 tablespoon butter and put a few dabs on each fillet. Fold fillets over lengthwise. Pour over them the strained mussel stock, cover with sole bones and poach for 15 minutes in a 350° oven. Remove and drain fillets and arrange down a hot flat serving dish. Sauté mushrooms in 1 tablespoon hot butter with lemon juice and a little cayenne pepper. Combine them with the shrimp, mussels, removed from their shells and bearded, and the parsley. Scatter this mixture over the fillets.

Melt remaining 3 tablespoons butter in a pan, stir in the flour, off the heat, season with salt and cayenne pepper to taste and strain on 1 cup of the stock from the poached fillets. Stir over low heat until it thickens, and then mix in light cream. Remove from heat and mix Hollandaise into sauce. Pour combined sauces over fillets and glaze under a hot broiler. Serves 4.

FILET DE SOLE BONNE FEMME

4 fillets of sole (and bones)

½ cup dry white wine

¼ cup water

1 bay leaf

A few peppercorns

6 firm white mushrooms, sliced and sautéed in butter

½ cup Hollandaise sauce

Follow directions for poaching fillets given in Filet de Sole Marguery, but use wine, water, bay leaf and peppercorns instead of mussel stock. Make white wine sauce with the strained stock, after poaching. Arrange poached fillets on hot serving dish and cover with sauce. Scatter sautéed mushrooms over sauce and pour Hollandaise over them. Glaze under a hot broiler. Serves 4.

ESCABECHE OF SOLE

3 tablespoons butter

¾ cup olive oil

Flour

6 small fillets sole

Salt, pepper

1 onion, thinly sliced and separated into rings

1 green pepper, cut in thin rings

1 clove garlic, finely chopped

½ cup orange juice

Juice of 2 limes

¼ teaspoon Tabasco

Orange slices

Lime slices

1 tablespoon orange zest (orange part of rind, grated or scraped)

Chopped fresh cilantro

Heat the butter and ¼ cup of the oil. Flour the fish fillets lightly and sauté them until delicately browned on both sides and just tender. Season to taste with salt and pepper.

Arrange the fillets in a flat serving dish and top them with onion rings, pepper rings and garlic. Combine the remaining ½ cup oil, orange juice, lime juice, Tabasco and salt and pepper to taste. Blend well and pour over the fish while it is still warm. Let stand in the refrigerator 12–24 hours.

To serve, garnish with orange slices, lime slices and orange zest. You may top with additional green pepper rings and chopped cilantro. Serves 6.

SOLE AND SALMON MOLD

1 quart water

2 tablespoons vinegar

12 peppercorns

½ cup dry white wine

2 bay leaves

1 teaspoon salt

4 sprigs parsley

1 onion, sliced

4 pounds sole fillets

2 7½-ounce cans salmon, drained

6 hard-cooked eggs, chopped

¾ cup chopped parsley

¾ cup mayonnaise
½ cup sour cream
1 teaspoon anchovy paste
1 small tin rolled anchovies

Make a court bouillon by bringing to boil in a large saucepan or fish poacher the water, vinegar, peppercorns, white wine, bay leaves, salt, parsley sprigs and sliced onion. Turn down heat and simmer for 15 minutes. Remove from stove. Place sole in stock and simmer just until fish flakes easily, but is not falling apart. Remove fish carefully and cool. Flake the salmon with ¼ of the poached fish. Mix with eggs, ¼ cup parsley, ¼ cup mayonnaise, ¼ cup sour cream and anchovy paste. Line bottom of a bread tin with half of the poached fillets. Spread salmon mixture on top and cover with remaining fillets. Chill at least 2 hours. Unmold on serving platter. Mix remaining cream, mayonnaise, parsley. Spread it over the top and sides of the fish mold. Garnish with rolled anchovies. Serves 12.

SKEWERED SWORDFISH

2 pounds swordfish
½ cup olive oil
¾ cup lemon juice
¼ cup grated onion
2 teaspoons salt
½ teaspoon freshly ground pepper
1 teaspoon paprika
12–16 bay leaves
2 tablespoons chopped parsley

Rinse the fish and pat dry. Cut the fish into 1½″ cubes. In a glass or pottery bowl, mix ¼ cup olive oil, ¼ cup lemon juice, the grated onion, 1½ teaspoons salt, the pepper, paprika and bay leaves. Toss the fish in the mixture, then cover and marinate in the refrigerator 6–8 hours. Turn and baste fish frequently. Drain and divide the fish among 6 or 8 skewers, putting a couple of bay leaves on each skewer. Broil 15 minutes, or until fish is browned and tender, turning the skewers so as to be sure to brown all sides evenly.

Mix together the remaining oil, lemon juice, salt and the parsley. Serve in a sauceboat. Serves 6–8.

SWORDFISH, SPANISH STYLE

1 pound swordfish, cut in very thin slices
¼ cup olive oil
2 tablespoons amontillado sherry
1 tablespoon minced parsley
1 clove garlic, crushed
½ teaspoon salt
¼ cup finely chopped onion

Arrange swordfish in large shallow pan, cover with remaining ingredients, marinate at least 1 hour. Remove from marinade, broil 4″ from heat until lightly browned on each side, using reduced flame. Serve marinade as sauce, passed separately. Serves 3–4.

BAKED TROUT MONTBARRY

6 trout (10 or 12 ounces each), washed and wiped dry
Salt, freshly ground black pepper
1 teaspoon finely chopped parsley
1 teaspoon minced onion
1 tablespoon minced chives
1 teaspoon minced chervil
3 tablespoons finely chopped mushrooms
Fresh tarragon leaves
2 tablespoons melted butter
4 egg yolks
1 ounce brandy
5 tablespoons fresh bread crumbs
5 tablespoons grated Gruyère cheese
Paprika

Season the trout with salt and pepper. Line a well-buttered baking dish with the parsley, onion, chives, chervil, mushrooms, and tarragon leaves. Put the fish on top and pour the melted butter over them. Cover the dish with buttered foil, and bake in a 400° oven for 10–12 minutes. Beat the egg yolks with the brandy. Remove the foil from the fish, pour the egg and brandy mixture over them, then sprinkle with the bread crumbs mixed with the Gruyère cheese and a little dusting of paprika. Return to the oven and bake until the crumbs are golden brown. Serve in the baking dish. The classic accompaniments are large broiled onions and thick tomato slices, grilled, with a sautéed mushroom on each slice. Serves 6.

HOW TO FILLET TROUT

1. With a sharp boning knife, slit along each side of the backbone.

2. Use boning knife like a saw to cut away flesh from bone on each side.

3. When bone is freed, pull away from body and remove entrails beneath.

4. With kitchen shears, snip bone at tail and head, cut off tail and head.

5. Lay trimmed and boned trout flat and cut lengthwise into fillets.

TROUT WITH ALMONDS

> 1 cup blanched almonds
> 18 tablespoons butter
> Juice of ½ lemon
> 8 trout (8–10 ounces each)
> 1 cup sifted flour
> Salt
> Lemon wedges dipped in finely chopped parsley

Put the blanched almonds through the food chopper, using the fine blade. Heat 6 tablespoons of butter in a small frying pan until very light brown, add the almonds and heat well, squeezing in the lemon juice toward the end. Wash the cleaned trout under running water and wipe dry with a clean cloth. Sift the flour onto a sheet of waxed paper, salt it lightly, and dredge the fish in it so that they each have a thin coating of flour.

Heat 6 tablespoons of butter in a large frying pan and when very hot, add 4 trout. (Cooking 4 at a time makes turning them easier.) Shake the pan a little as they cook to prevent sticking. Cook about 5 minutes on each side and remove to a hot platter. Add the remaining 6 tablespoons butter to the pan for the next batch. When all are cooked and arranged on the platter, pour the almond mixture over them and garnish with lemon wedges dipped in finely chopped parsley. Allow 2 trout per person. Serves 4.

TROUT MARGUERY À LA CRÉOLE

> 4 trout
> ½ cup thinly sliced onion
> 1 clove garlic
> 1 bay leaf
> 6 parsley sprigs
> 6 whole cloves
> ¼ teaspoon cayenne pepper
> Salt, pepper
> 1 tablespoon butter, cut up
> ½ cup dry white wine
> 16 oysters, poached in their juices
> ½ pound fresh mushrooms, quartered and simmered in butter and lemon juice
> 1-ounce can truffles, diced
> 4 egg yolks

½–¾ cup melted butter
¼ teaspoon Tabasco sauce
1 tablespoon minced parsley
24 cooked shrimp, shelled, warmed in butter

Have trout filleted and reserve heads, bones and skin. Simmer these trimmings with the onion, garlic, bay leaf, parsley, cloves, cayenne pepper, 1 teaspoon salt and 1 quart water in an enameled saucepan until liquid has reduced by half. Strain.

Sprinkle the 8 trout fillets with salt and pepper, lay them in one layer in a lightly buttered shallow fireproof baking dish, and dot with the cut-up butter. Pour on the fish stock, the wine and enough water barely to cover the fish. Bring almost to simmer on top of the stove, cover with buttered waxed paper, and set in lower third of preheated 350° oven. Bake for 8–10 minutes, or until a fork will pierce fish easily. Drain stock into a saucepan. Cover fish with waxed paper and set aside.

Pour the juices from the oysters, mushrooms and canned truffles into the fish-poaching stock and boil down rapidly until liquid has reduced to 1 cup. Cool slightly. Beat the egg yolks in a bowl until thick and sticky and gradually beat in the liquid. Return to saucepan and stir over low heat until lightly thickened; do not overheat or egg yolks will scramble. Remove from heat and beat in the melted butter by driblets; sauce will thicken to a cream. Beat in Tabasco sauce and parsley; season to taste.

Shortly before serving, preheat broiler to red hot. Garnish the fish fillets with the oysters, shrimp, mushrooms and truffles. Cover baking dish and heat for a few minutes over a pan of boiling water. Then spoon the sauce over the fish and garniture. Set dish so surface is 1″ from hot broiler element for 30–40 seconds, until sauce begins to brown lightly. Serves 8.

TROUT WITH VERMOUTH

2 cups dry vermouth
½ teaspoon salt
8 trout (8–10 ounces each)
8 egg yolks
20 tablespoons butter (2½ sticks),
    cut in small pieces
2 tablespoons light cream

Heat the vermouth with the salt, add the trout and poach for about 10 minutes, or until done. Remove to a heated fireproof serving dish and keep hot. Reduce the cooking liquid quickly until it becomes thick. Put it in the top of a double boiler over hot, not boiling, water. Add the egg yolks, butter, and cream, and beat well with a French wire whip until the butter melts and the sauce thickens. Do not let the water boil. Correct seasoning, if necessary, and pour over the fish. Place under the broiler for a minute or two to brown the top. Serves 4.

STUFFED TROUT BERCY

If possible, get trout weighing about a pound each for this classic dish, and serve 1 per person.

1 teaspoon minced parsley
1 teaspoon minced shallot
1 teaspoon minced chives
 Butter
2 tablespoons flour
1 cup milk
1 tablespoon anchovy paste
½ cup soft bread crumbs (approximately)
6 trout (about 1 pound each), washed
    and wiped dry
Salt, pepper
Lemon wedges
Parsley
Shoestring potatoes
Sauce Bercy

Lightly brown the parsley, shallot, and chives in 2 tablespoons butter. Sprinkle in the flour and cook, stirring, until the mixture is well blended. Stir in the milk and continue cooking over low heat until you have a thick sauce. Add the anchovy paste and blend. Bring to a boil and stir in the bread crumbs—as much as mixture will hold without becoming crumbly.

Stuff the trout with the mixture and close the openings with skewers. Season with salt and pepper, brush with melted butter, and bake in a 400° oven for about 20 minutes, turning and basting the trout frequently with melted butter. When done, arrange the fish on a hot platter and garnish with lemon wedges, parsley, and little heaps of crisp shoestring potatoes. Pass a dish of sauce Bercy. Serves 6.

HOW TO PREPARE
TRUITES FARCIES PARISIENNE

1. Roll out pastry, lay on top pattern cut to size of fish, trim pastry to shape.

2. Lay stuffed trout in center of pastry case, cover with the two sides.

3. Decorate pastry case with pastry scales (cut with fluted cutter), currant for eye.

4. To serve, lay baked trout on folded white napkin on platter, garnish with watercress.

TRUITES FARCIES PARISIENNE

6 small brook trout, ½–¾ pound each
  Lemon juice
  Cognac
  Salt, freshly ground black pepper
6 fillets of sole
3 tablespoons finely chopped shallots
3 teaspoons butter
3 small egg whites
1¼ cups heavy cream
  Nutmeg
3 tablespoons finely chopped truffles
  Béarnaise sauce

Pastry:

6 cups all-purpose flour
¾ teaspoon salt
12 ounces sweet butter
3 tablespoons oil
6 egg yolks
1½ cups ice water
3 egg yolks beaten with 6 tablespoons milk

Wash trout in lemon juice and water. If trout have not been cleaned, remove scales and cut a little off the tail fin. Remove other fins. Slit on both sides of the backbone and remove bone and guts. Wash again in lemon juice and water and dry. Season inside of each trout with a little cognac, salt and pepper. Put sole fillets through fine blade of a meat grinder twice. Place in a metal bowl over a bowl of crushed ice. Sauté shallots in 3 teaspoons butter and add to sole. Mix in egg whites. Slowly beat in heavy cream, season with salt, pepper and nutmeg to taste and add chopped truffles. Carefully spoon this fish mousse into the trout.

Make the pastry dough. Sift the flour and salt into a large bowl. Cut the sweet butter into small pieces and work into the flour until it looks like coarse cornmeal. Make a well in the center and put in it the oil, 6 egg yolks and ice water. Quickly work up to a firm dough and chill 30–45 minutes.

Roll out chilled dough ¼″ thick and on it lay a paper pattern shaped to envelop the fish completely. Cut out 6 dough cases. Enclose fish in dough and brush the top with the egg-yolk mixture. Roll out remaining dough rather thinner and cut out small fluted crescents to resemble fish scales. Put on fish, and brush again with egg mixture. Bake in a preheated 350° oven for 40–45 minutes. Serve fish on a platter garnished with watercress and serve Béarnaise sauce separately. Serves 6.

TRUITE GRENOBLOISE

>   4 trout
>   Salt, pepper
>   Salt butter
>   Flour
>   ½ teaspoon finely chopped garlic
>   2 tablespoons finely chopped shallot
>   1 small cucumber, peeled, seeded and finely
>   diced
>   3 firm tomatoes, skinned, seeded and shredded
>   (reserve seeds)
>   2 limes, peeled, sectioned and diced
>   3 lemons, peeled, sectioned and diced
>   Lemon slices
>   1 tablespoon chopped fresh parsley

Wash the trout and dry with a cloth. Season the inside of each fish with salt and pepper and put in a little butter. Reshape and dust with flour. Heat 1½ ounces salt butter in a pan and cook the fish slowly on each side. Remove and arrange on a hot flat serving dish. Add to the pan the chopped garlic and shallot, cucumber, tomatoes and the lime and lemon sections. Rub the tomato seeds through a strainer and add to the mixture. Season with salt and pepper, cover pan and cook slowly for 3 minutes. Carefully pour this mixture over the fish, surround with lemon slices and sprinkle with parsley. Serves 4.

TURBOT HOLLANDAISE

>   2¾ pounds turbot steaks
>   Lemon juice
>   1½ ounces salt butter, melted
>   A few peppercorns
>   1 bay leaf
>   Salt to taste
>   ¼ cup dry white wine

>   1 cup Hollandaise sauce
>   6 large croutons of fried bread or 6 crescents
>   puff pastry

Wash turbot in lemon juice and water and dry on a cloth. Put in a buttered baking dish with the melted butter, peppercorns, bay leaf, salt and wine. Cover with buttered waxed paper and poach for 25 minutes in a 300° oven.

To serve, carefully remove bones and arrange fish on a hot flat serving dish. Coat with Hollandaise sauce and brown under a hot broiler. Surround with croutons or pastry crescents. Serves 4.

COLD TUNA NIÇOISE

>   3–4 pounds fresh tuna
>   4–6 cloves garlic, sliced
>   12 anchovy fillets
>   Olive oil
>   2 teaspoons basil
>   3–4 onions, sliced
>   3–4 pounds fresh tomatoes or 2 1-pound,
>   13-ounce cans Italian plum tomatoes
>   2 small green peppers, chopped
>   1 tablespoon salt
>   1 bay leaf
>   1 cup red wine
>   ½ cup black olives

Make gashes in the tuna and insert garlic slices and anchovy fillets. Rub well with oil and basil and let it stand 2 hours in the refrigerator.

Sear the tuna in olive oil. Add the onions, tomatoes, peppers, seasonings and wine. Cover and braise the fish 1–1½ hours. Add olives to the sauce and serve hot. Or you may remove the fish to a serving dish, reduce the sauce and pour it around the fish. Cool and chill. Cut the fish in paper-thin slices and serve with the reduced sauce. Serves 6–8.

TUNA TART

>   Rough puff paste (see Pastry)
>   7-ounce can white-meat tuna
>   ½ pound shrimp, cooked and shelled

¾ cup tiny green olives or anchovy-stuffed
  cocktail olives
¼ cup heavy cream
1 teaspoon paprika
½ teaspoon freshly ground black pepper
¼ teaspoon Tabasco
2 cups rich Béchamel sauce

Line an 8″ tart mold that has a removable bottom
with pastry, rolled a little thicker than usual. Place
a piece of foil over the pastry and weight down by
filling with dry beans. Bake in a 400° oven for 15–20
minutes, or until the shell is nicely browned and done.
Remove from oven and take out the beans and foil.
Keep tart shell warm until ready to use.

Flake the tuna quite fine. Cut the shrimp into rather
small pieces, reserving a few whole shrimp for garnish. Mix the seafood with the olives, reserving a few
for garnish. Add the cream and seasonings and enough
hot Béchamel sauce to fill the shell. Heat to the boiling
point. Fill the shell with the mixture and decorate
with whole shrimp and olives. Serve the remaining
Béchamel sauce separately. Serves 6–8.

MATELOTE BOURGUIGNONNE

1 quart red wine
1 onion stuck with 2 cloves
¼ cup chopped parsley
1 bay leaf
3 cloves garlic, chopped
2 pounds carp, cut in small serving pieces
2 pounds pike, cut in small serving pieces
1 good-size eel, cleaned and cut in serving pieces
1 tablespoon salt
2 tablespoons beurre manié
  Garlic-flavored fried croutons

Put wine, onion, parsley, bay leaf and garlic in a
large kettle. Bring to a boil, lower heat and simmer
10 minutes. Add fish, making sure it is barely covered
by stock. Add salt and cook gently for 20 minutes.
Stir in beurre manié and cook, stirring, until blended
and thickened. Taste for seasoning. Serve in deep
plates or soup bowls and top each serving with
garlic-flavored croutons. Serves 4–6.

BOUILLABAISSE

3 tablespoons olive oil
2 tablespoons butter
4 leeks, finely diced
2 carrots, finely diced
1 small celery heart, finely diced
2 white onions, finely diced
1 fennel bulb, finely diced
2 teaspoons minced garlic
1 teaspoon grated orange rind
  Salt, cayenne pepper to taste
  Pinch of ground cloves
2 live lobsters
¼ cup brandy
2 dozen mussels, cleaned
  A little sliced mixed onion, carrot, celery, leek
½ cup dry white wine
2 cups water
1 bay leaf
  A few peppercorns
1 clove garlic, crushed
2 level teaspoons potato starch
2 teaspoons tomato paste
1½ pounds red snapper, cut into chunks
1½ pounds Spanish mackerel, cut into chunks
1 pound striped bass, cut into chunks
1 pound cod tail, cut into chunks
1 pound smoked eel, cut into chunks
1 pound ripe tomatoes, peeled and thinly sliced
10 slices blanched potato
10 eggs
  Slices of French bread, 1″ thick
¼ cup olive oil
2 teaspoons powdered saffron
½ teaspoon minced garlic

Heat the 3 tablespoons oil and 2 tablespoons butter
in a large pan. Add the diced vegetables, garlic and
orange rind. Season with salt, cayenne pepper and
ground cloves. Cover pan and cook very slowly,
without browning, for 2–3 minutes.

Split the live lobsters, remove bags and veins, claws
and feet. Put lobsters in pan shell side down, cover
and cook 2½ minutes. Flame with the brandy.
Cover and cook 2–3 minutes more. Set aside.

Put mussels (discard any that are open) in another
pan with the sliced vegetables, wine, water, bay leaf,

peppercorns, a little salt, and the crushed garlic. Cover pan, bring slowly to a boil, reduce heat and simmer 3–4 minutes or until mussels are open (discard any that do not open). Strain cooking liquid into a bowl. Mix the potato starch with 2 tablespoons cold water, blend in the tomato paste and mix into the strained mussel liquid. Pour mixture over the lobsters. Add cut-up fish and tomatoes. Bring slowly to a gentle boil. Put in the potato slices, cover pan and simmer very gently 15–20 minutes. Poach eggs in simmering liquid. To serve, transfer everything to a large pot, arrange potato slices and eggs around edge of pot and surround with slices of French bread which have been fried in the ¼ cup olive oil with the saffron and garlic until nicely browned. Serves 10.

COTRIADE

1 eel
1½ pounds haddock or cod
1–1½ pounds sea bass
4 medium onions, coarsely chopped
3 tablespoons butter or bacon fat
6 large potatoes
2 tablespoons chopped fresh mint
1 teaspoon marjoram
1 teaspoon tarragon
1 teaspoon chervil
1 teaspoon thyme
Salt, freshly ground black pepper
3 cups (approx.) white wine or dry hard cider
Chopped parsley
Garlic-flavored toasted French bread

Skin and clean the eel and cut it into 1″ lengths. Cut the haddock or cod and the sea bass into serving-size pieces.

Brown the onions well in the hot butter or bacon fat. Peel the potatoes, cut them in quarters, cover with boiling salted water and cook until just tender. Drain potatoes. Add the browned onions, the herbs, the eel and fish, salt and pepper to taste and the wine or cider. Simmer gently for about 20 minutes, or until the fish is just tender.

Pour the fish stew into a large tureen and garnish with chopped parsley. Place slices of garlic-flavored toasted French bread in the soup bowls before serving the brew. Serves 6. With this, drink a pleasant light red wine.

Note: The fish listed in the recipe above are suggestions. Choose any combination of fresh or salt-water fish or seafood that you like.

ZARZUELA

2 7-ounce rock lobster tails, frozen
6 tablespoons olive oil
1 pound halibut, cut in 1½″ cubes
1 tablespoon brandy
1 medium onion, finely chopped
2 cloves garlic, crushed
3 tablespoons crushed blanched almonds
1-pound can tomatoes
10½-ounce can undrained minced clams
1 pound well-scrubbed mussels in shell
1 tablespoon minced parsley
¼ cup white wine
1 cup water
Salt to taste
Toasted French bread

Completely defrost the lobster tails. Cut away the undershell and cut through hard shell with kitchen shears to divide each tail in thirds. Heat the olive oil in a heavy skillet, add the lobster and halibut and sauté lightly over moderate heat until the shell is bright red and the fish lightly browned. Flame with brandy. Transfer lobster and fish to a deep top-of-the-stove casserole or heavy pot. Add the onion and garlic to the oil remaining in the skillet and cook until onion is tender. Add the crushed almonds and stir until lightly browned. Add tomatoes and cook until well blended. Transfer to the casserole. Add clams and their juice, mussels, parsley, wine, water and salt. Simmer 10 minutes or until mussel shells are opened. Serve over toasted slices of French bread in soup plates. Serves 6.

Meat

The eighteenth-century wit who remarked, "Heaven sends us good meat, but the devil sends cooks," probably had reason for his quip. Even in America, a country of meat-eaters with a reputation for raising some of the world's best beef, a perfectly cooked roast, a superbly sautéed veal scallop, even a properly broiled hamburger is still something of a rarity. There are no infallible rules for cooking meat. Variations in cuts, grades, sizes and thicknesses can all affect the end result. Yet despite Brillat-Savarin, who believed that it was necessary to be born knowing how to roast meat, the skill, intuition and practised eye of the expert rôtisseur can be acquired by anyone with the will to learn.

Steak and hamburger, generally regarded as American contributions to the world's meat cookery, can claim pre-Mayflower ancestry. Strips of meat grilled on the embers were Anglo-Saxon fare and the word steak itself is believed to come from the Old Norse steikari, meaning cook, and steikja, to roast on a spit. The English lexicographer of 1753 who snidely defined a "stake" as "a small slice of meat to be broiled on or before the Fire, when a Person cannot or will not wait until the regular joint is boiled or roasted" was obviously not au courant. A London club, The Sublime Society of Beef Steaks, of which Dr. Johnson and Addison were members, had already elevated the steak to a status symbol.

Ground and chopped meats shaped into sausages, forcemeats and rissoles were among the recipes recorded by Apicius, the first epicure ever to pen a cook book. Until the invention of the fork, meat was either sliced from the joint and eaten with the fingers, or chopped, pounded and scooped up with a spoon. In the vivid vocabulary of the day, the meat was said to be frayed, teased, pulled, minced, hacked, smitten, bruised and hewed, phrases that give some indication of the lengths to which a cook had to go in order to render it palatable. By the seventeenth century, chopped meat had become much more refined, witness the "veal tosts" of Gervase Markham, concoctions of minced veal, egg, spinach and violet leaves, spread on toast and fried.

Probably the most underestimated (and frequently overcooked) of all meats in this country are those tasty morsels known to the Romans as omenta, to the Tudors as humbles (fit only to be served in a "pye" to the lower orders and unruly children, hence the phrase "to eat humble pie"), to the British as offal, to the French as abats de boucherie and to us, more euphemistically, as specialty meats. The creamy suavity of sweetbreads, the slippery succulence of tripe, the melting richness of marrow and the firm savoriness of kidneys are mainly appreciated by true gourmets and those who, while traveling in France, have happily swallowed their prejudices along with a plateful of cervelles de veau au beurre noir or tripes à la mode de Caen.

ROASTING TEMPERATURES
FOR MEAT

There was a time when roasts were put into the oven at high temperature and roasted for ½ to ¾ of an hour, at which point the heat was reduced and roasting continued until the meat was considered done. Today we find that slower cooking at one temperature makes for more even-textured, even-colored meat. You can in fact roast at temperatures as low as 180° or 200° with astonishingly good results. At these temperatures, of course, your roast will require from 1/3 to 1/2 again more cooking time.

Certain roasts may be cooked more quickly than others. For example, a leg of lamb can be cooked at 350° or 375° if you watch it carefully. Pork is best if roasted at 300°–325°, with a generous amount of cooking time, and basted to give the skin or crackling a nice flavor and texture. Veal should be roasted slowly and not be overdone. With veal, try to gauge the point where it is juicy with just a bit of firmness in it, rather than letting it go on to the stage where it is stringy and dry. Mutton, if you are fortunate enough to find a source for it, should be very well aged and cooked in the same manner as lamb.

Meat thermometers and various public agencies have perpetuated the idea that an inner temperature of 140° will yield rare beef. Inevitably it will be medium rare or even medium. If you wish to have truly rare beef, remove the roast from the oven at 120°–125°. Allow it to rest in a warm place for 15 minutes—this is nothing more than a slight cooling process—so it will become a bit firmer and easier to carve. Rare meat is pink from the outer fat to the bone or center —not bloody, but juicy and pink (or red, according to your definition of color). If you want your beef *bleu*, it should come out of the oven a few degrees before reaching the rare stage.

Lamb should be removed from the oven at 130°– 135° if you want it rare, as many people think it should be. If it is allowed to reach 160°, which is often described as "pink" lamb, it will be an unappetizing gray-brown color. The same temperature can be used for a saddle of lamb or a boned and rolled shoulder. Baby lamb, on the other hand, should be roasted until it is barely pink—to a temperature of about 150°—for best results. Again, allow your roast to rest for 10 minutes or so before carving. Veal should be roasted to an internal temperature of 150°– 160°. This temperature applies to the leg, shoulder, and saddle.

Stuffed breast of veal should be roasted to 170°, because it is a strangely textured cut of meat which requires rather long cooking to make it tender. Pork must be roasted to a temperature of 170°–175°, to the thoroughly cooked stage, for a variety of reasons. It is safer to eat (although trichinae are killed at a much lower temperature), it is easier to carve, and, quite simply, it tastes better.

If you can find a meat thermometer with a full dial, ranging from 0° up, by all means buy it. It is preferable to those that key various cuts of meat to certain temperatures. Do not leave the thermometer in the roast, but insert it only long enough to check the temperature from time to time. Some ovens, however, have a thermometer attached on a cable, which you insert and leave in the roast, and this gadget is extremely efficient. You can set the alarm for the desired temperature and check no further.

It is equally important to take the internal temperature of a roast before you place it in the oven if you want to time it properly. Obviously a roast with an icy interior will take longer to achieve the prescribed temperature than one that has been removed from the refrigerator for a period of time. It is surprising what 2 or 3 hours at room temperature will do to start the roast on its way.

PRIME RIB ROAST OF BEEF

A standing rib roast is best if it is large—at least three ribs. A five-rib or larger roast can be magnificent when presented at table. Have it cut short, and, if possible, well trimmed and tied so that carving will be easier. Never worry about leftovers, for few things are as delicious as cold roast beef. It may even be frozen after cooking and stored for several weeks.

Naturally, the roast should be either USDA Choice or Prime. There is a great difference in butchers and their treatment of a roast of beef. Some do not age beef long enough. If you have a co-operative butcher, try to order your roast a fortnight or so in advance, in order to let it hang for an extra amount of time.

To prepare the roast, score the fat and rub it well with freshly ground black pepper. Also rub some of the pepper into the flesh and on the bone side. Place the roast on a rack, rib side down. Roast at any of the following temperatures, without basting:

200°—approximately 30–35 minutes per pound.
300°—approximately 15–18 minutes per pound.
325°—approximately 13–15 minutes per pound.

For rare beef, the inner temperature should register 120°–125°. Insert thermometer into thickest part of the meat, without touching the bone.

Salt the meat during the last 15 minutes of cooking and after testing the temperature a final time. Place the roast on a platter, this time resting on its broader flesh side. Allow the meat to settle for 12–15 minutes before sending it to the table.

You may serve the pan juices with the meat or a Bordelaise or Périgueux sauce.

With the roast serve oven-browned potatoes, small buttered new potatoes, or Potatoes Anna.

ROAST SIRLOIN OF BEEF

Ask your butcher to give you a roast from the sirloin or shell, from which he cuts steaks. This is the short loin and contains some of the most expensive meat on the market. However, the fat is more perfectly distributed than on a rib roast, and the meat carves beautifully. Roast as you would a Prime rib roast. Also carve as you would a rib roast, or you may rest the sirloin on its bone side and cut straight down.

Serve with Potatoes Anna or sautéed potatoes, and perhaps petits pois. If you would like a sauce for the beef, serve one of those suggested for rib roast, or substitute a Sauce Béarnaise.

RUMP ROAST OF BEEF

This cut is not as well known in the United States as it is in Europe. However, it can be flavorful and tender, and if correctly cut, slices beautifully at table. It is not as butter-tender as the previous roasts, but it is excellent in texture and makes an interesting change from the usual cuts. The roasting rules are the same as for the rib roast. Pepper the meat well

and rub with a small amount of salt. Roast on a rack to an internal temperature of 120°–125°, salt well, and let stand for about 15 minutes before carving. A Sauce Madère would go well with this roast.

Serve with jacket potatoes and an excellent salad.

Flavor variations for these roasts:
1. Rub the roast well with rosemary and pepper before roasting.
2. Rub garlic in the fat and flesh and along the bones before roasting to perfume the roast lightly.

BEEF WELLINGTON, PÉRIGUEUX SAUCE

> 1¼ pounds mushrooms, very finely minced
> 5 shallots or green onions, very finely minced
>   Butter
> 3 tablespoons minced parsley
> 1½ cups clear beef consommé
> 1 tablespoon arrowroot or cornstarch
> 1 cup Madeira
> 3 chopped truffles
>   Salt, freshly ground black pepper
> 6 cups all-purpose flour
> 1 whole beef filet weighing 3 pounds,
>   trimmed of all fat
> 5-ounce can pâté de foie gras
> 1 egg

A good deal of the preparation for this dish can be done the day before. First, cook the mushrooms and shallots or onions in 4 ounces butter until all moisture has cooked away. Add the minced parsley toward the end. Cool the mixture, cover and refrigerate.

Next, make a Périgueux sauce by heating the beef consommé with 1-1/4 tablespoons of butter, adding the arrowroot or cornstarch dissolved in 1/3 cup Madeira and stirring, over low heat, until thick. Add the truffles. Season the sauce with salt and pepper and store it in the refrigerator.

Thirdly, make the pastry. Blend the flour and 2 1/2 cups soft butter, or half butter and half other shortening, with the fingers until a sandy mass has been obtained. Add 1 cup cold water gradually, mixing slowly, and work dough into a ball. The less water used, the better. Wrap in waxed paper and refrigerate until ready to use.

On the day of the dinner remove the duxelles (mushroom mixture) from the refrigerator. Also remove the meat and bring it to room temperature. Fold the tip back and tie it securely. Tie the other end, too, if necessary. Season the beef with salt and freshly ground black pepper.

Melt 4 ounces butter in a shallow pan which is long enough to hold the filet, but as narrow as possible. Braise the meat on top of the range for 35 minutes, turning it often with spoons. Moisten with Madeira, using about 2/3 cup, from time to time. Allow the meat to cool, but not in the refrigerator.

Add the pâté de foie gras to the duxelles, mix well and add 1 teaspoon of the Périgueux sauce. Taste carefully for seasoning.

Roll out the pastry in a rectangular shape about 14" by 9" and 1/4" thick—large enough to envelop the filet. Spread the duxelles over the pastry, leaving a border uncovered. Place the meat in the center with that side down which you want eventually to be up. Fold the pastry over the meat and seal the seam and ends with water. Place, seam-side down, on a cookie sheet and brush the top and sides with the egg, well-beaten and mixed with a little water or cream. Prick thoroughly with a fork in a crisscross design. Bake in a preheated 400° oven for 30 minutes. Serve sliced with the Périgueux sauce, hot, on the side. (Slice very thin—this is a rich dish.) Serves 8.

ELIZABETH DAVID'S SAVORY STUFFED FILET OF BEEF

    3 large onions, thinly sliced
    6 tablespoons olive oil
    4 tablespoons butter
    2 cloves garlic, minced
    18 pitted black olives, coarsely chopped
    ½ cup chopped cooked Virginia or country ham
       Freshly ground black pepper, salt
    1 teaspoon thyme
    2 egg yolks, beaten
    2 tablespoons chopped parsley
    1 filet, about 7 pounds

Sauté the onions in the oil and butter until just limp, then add the garlic, olives, ham, 1 teaspoon pepper, thyme, and 1 teaspoon salt, and cook until well blended. Stir in the beaten egg yolks and parsley, and cook for about 3 minutes.

Cut the filet not quite through in rather thickish slices, and spoon the stuffing between slices. Run a needle and string through the middle of the filet, or tie it securely. Place on a rack, brush with oil or butter, and roast in a 300° oven for about 50 minutes, or until the internal temperature is about 125°. Let it rest for 10 minutes. Salt lightly, and place on a hot platter with a garnish of perfect sprigs of watercress and tiny glazed carrots.

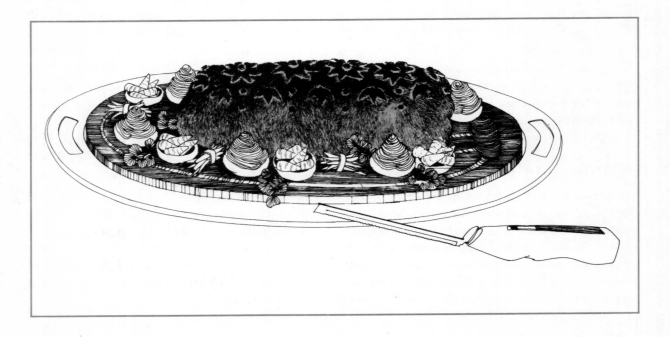

Serve with Bordelaise sauce and tiny buttered new potatoes. Serves 12.

FILET OF BEEF WITH WHITE TRUFFLES

> 5–6 pound filet
> Butter
> 5 white truffles, grated
> Freshly ground black pepper, salt

Cut the filet in 6–8 slices, not quite through, and butter each one well. Grate the truffles and add an equal quantity to each cut. Tie the filet well and rub it with softened butter. Also rub freshly ground pepper into the filet.

Roast on a rack in a 350° oven for about 45–50 minutes, or until the meat thermometer registers 125°. Baste several times with butter or the pan juices during the roasting. Salt to taste. Serve with pan juices.

Note: This particular filet can be done with a barding of fat trimmed from a cooked Virginia ham, a delicious change from any roast filet. Serves 6–8.

FILET OF BEEF TOURNELLE

> 8 large potatoes
> 10 tablespoons butter
> 2 tablespoons light cream
> 4 egg yolks
> Flour, beaten egg, bread crumbs
> Fat for deep frying
> 4 slices beef filet, cut 2″ thick
> Salt, freshly ground black pepper
> ⅔ cup Madeira
> 2–3 truffles, cut in fine julienne
> 1 tablespoon meat glaze
> Garnish: 4 slices truffle, chopped parsley

Cook potatoes in boiling, salted water until tender. Drain and peel. Put through food mill or ricer. Blend in 6 tablespoons butter, cream and, one by one, egg yolks, beating well after each addition. Shape mixture into 4 cakes same size as beef slices and 1½″–2″ thick. Let cool. Dip in flour, brush with beaten egg, dip in bread crumbs and deep fry in hot fat until browned and crisp. Drain on absorbent paper and arrange on hot platter. Keep hot.

Sauté beef slices quickly in 4 tablespoons butter until nicely browned on the outside but still rare and juicy in the center—about 5–7 minutes. Season to taste with salt and freshly ground pepper and arrange on top of the potato croquettes. To the pan in which the beef was cooked, add the Madeira, julienne strips of truffle and meat glaze. Blend and cook down for a minute. Pour sauce over meat and garnish each filet with a truffle slice and parsley. Serves 4.

BEEF SCALLOPS BLUEGRASS

> 3 tablespoons oil (or ½ oil, ½ butter)
> 12 slices beef tenderloin, ⅜″ thick
> Salt, freshly ground pepper to taste
> 4 tablespoons bourbon
> 3 tablespoons chopped shallots
> ½ cup beef broth or red wine
> 3 tablespoons tomato purée
> Dash of Tabasco
> Dash of Worcestershire sauce
> 2 tablespoons chopped parsley

You may do these at table in an electric skillet; otherwise, rush them to the table the minute they are done. Heat the oil in a skillet. When very hot, sear the beef scallops quickly on both sides. Salt these and flame with bourbon. Remove to a hot serving dish. Add shallots and finely ground pepper to the pan. Cook 1 minute. Add broth or wine, tomato purée, Tabasco and Worcestershire sauce. Pour over beef scallops. Garnish with the chopped parsley. Serve with tiny new potatoes. Serves 4.

BEEF STROGANOFF

> 2 pounds tail end beef filet
> 2 tablespoons salt butter
> 3 tablespoons brandy
> ½ ounce dried mushrooms soaked in ¼ cup water
> 1 teaspoon finely chopped yellow onion
> 1 teaspoon finely chopped garlic
> 1 teaspoon meat glaze

1 teaspoon tomato paste

2 tablespoons flour

1½ cups beef stock

  Freshly cracked black pepper to taste

1 cup sour cream

2 tablespoons chopped fresh dill

Trim off all fat from the beef filet and cut the meat into long fingers ½"–¾" thick, cutting with the grain of the meat. Heat butter in a deep heavy pan. When very hot, brown the meat a few pieces at a time. Be sure that the pieces do not touch and also that the heat of the pan remains constant. Sear the meat all over very quickly. Remove and set aside. Heat brandy, pour into the pan and stir with a wooden spoon to lift up all the glaze. Drain the mushrooms, reserving the liquid, chop them very finely and add to the pan with the chopped onion and garlic. Cook over very low heat for 2–3 minutes, then stir in, off the heat, the meat glaze, tomato paste and flour. When smooth, stir in the strained mushroom liquid and the beef stock. Season with freshly cracked pepper. Stir over low heat until thickened, then slowly and carefully beat in the sour cream. Add the dill. Just before serving put back the meat and stir it into the hot sauce off the heat—the meat should not cook any more, just reheat in the sauce. Serve with Gnocchi Voreniki. Serves 8.

BOILED BEEF WITH PLUM SAUCE

4 leeks

3 pounds center chuck of beef

1 large marrow bone

6 carrots, peeled

4 white turnips, peeled

1 onion, studded with 2 whole cloves

  Herb bouquet of parsley, ½ bay leaf and
  ¼ teaspoon thyme

  Salt, peppercorns

1 large Bermuda onion, weighing about
  9 ounces

1 pound small fresh blue plums (about 18)

1½ cups red wine

4 tablespoons butter

1 tablespoon sugar

¼ teaspoon pepper

Discard the green part of the leeks, split white part down the center and wash well. Put beef in a big pot and cover with 3 pints of cold water. Add marrow bone. Bring very gently to boiling point and skim well. Add the carrots, turnips, onion, leeks and herb bouquet and bring gently to boiling point again, skimming carefully. Season to taste with salt, add a few peppercorns and simmer gently, partially covered, for 6–7 hours.

In the meantime peel the Bermuda onion and chop, not too fine. Wash blue plums, split and remove pits. Cover with 1 cup of red wine, and stew gently for 10 minutes. Cook the onion slowly in the butter until soft, about 10 minutes, sprinkle with the sugar, ½ teaspoon salt and the pepper, add to the plums and continue cooking for 10 minutes. Add another ½ cup red wine and simmer for another 40 minutes.

When the beef is done, place it on a hot platter, cut in thin slices, garnish with parsley and serve accompanied by plain boiled potatoes and the plum and onion sauce. Serves 6.

POT ROAST, POLYNESIAN STYLE

5-pound chuck roast

  Olive oil

4 cloves garlic, finely chopped

1 cup sherry

⅓ cup soy sauce

1 teaspoon freshly ground black pepper

1 tablespoon chopped fresh ginger or 1 teaspoon
  ground ginger

1 onion stuck with 2 cloves

  Preserved kumquats, chopped cilantro

Rub the roast well with olive oil and chopped garlic. Place it in a deep bowl and add the sherry, soy sauce, pepper and ginger. Marinate for 8–24 hours, turning the meat frequently in the marinade.

Remove the meat and dry it with paper towels. Heat 5 tablespoons olive oil in a heavy pot and brown the roast on all sides. Add the onion and ½ cup of the marinade. Cover the pot and simmer for 1½ hours. Add remaining marinade and continue cooking until the meat is tender. Remove it to a hot platter and strain the juices.

Garnish the roast with preserved kumquats and chopped cilantro, if available. Italian or curly parsley may be substituted. Serve with the strained sauce, rice and a spinach salad. Serves 8.

PIÈCE DE BOEUF À LA FLAMANDE

4 tablespoons chopped beef suet
4–5 pounds top round of beef, rolled and tied
  Salt, pepper
6 medium-to-large onions, peeled and sliced
5 tablespoons butter
1 teaspoon thyme
1 bay leaf
1 pint beer
  Boiled or steamed potatoes
  Chopped parsley

Melt the beef suet and brown the meat well on all sides in the hot fat. Salt and pepper to taste. Sauté the onions separately in the butter until they are golden and season with salt and pepper. Pour off the excess fat from the meat and add the onions, thyme, bay leaf and beer. Cover the pot and simmer for 1½–2 hours, or until the meat is quite tender. Remove the meat to a hot platter and slice it neatly. Taste the sauce for seasoning and spoon it over the beef slices. Surround with the potatoes and sprinkle liberally with chopped parsley. Serve with a salad and beer. Serves 8.

ITALIAN BRAISED BEEF

1 onion, sliced
4 cloves garlic
1½ teaspoons basil
2–3 sprigs parsley
2 cups heavy red wine
5 pounds beef rump, tied and partly barded
  Beef or bacon fat
  Salt, pepper
¼ teaspoon Tabasco
½ pound ham, cut into cubes
1 calf's foot
1 Italian sausage

Combine the onion, garlic, basil, parsley and red wine to make a marinade. Place the meat in this mix-

ture and marinate for 24–36 hours, turning it several times during the process.

Remove the beef from the marinade and dry it well. Cook the marinade over a brisk flame to reduce it one half. Heat beef or bacon fat and brown the meat on all sides. Salt and pepper to taste. Place meat in a braising pot and add the hot marinade, the Tabasco, ham, calf's foot and sausage. Cover and simmer on top of the stove or in a 300° oven for 2½–3 hours, or until tender. Cooking should thicken the sauce. Remove the meat to a hot platter and skim fat from sauce. Strain sauce and serve separately.

Serve with green noodles lightly tossed with a little grated Parmesan cheese, and a romaine and raw mushroom salad. Serves 8.

SAUERBRATEN

6-pound rump of beef or rolled boned chuck
1½ cups red wine vinegar
½ cup red wine
1½ cups water
1 bay leaf
5 peppercorns
3 whole cloves
2 tablespoons salt
2 onions, sliced
4 tablespoons shortening or oil
5 tablespoons flour
4 tablespoons butter
1 tablespoon sugar
¾ cup crushed gingersnaps

It is best to have the meat in one solid piece, but if it is boned and rolled, make sure it has no added covering of suet. Combine the vinegar, wine, water and seasonings, pour this mixture over the meat. Add the sliced onions. Keep meat in the refrigerator, covered with the marinade, for 1–3 days, turning occasionally. Remove meat from marinade, wipe dry with paper towels and brown in the shortening over high heat, sprinkling with 1 tablespoon flour. Strain and add marinade, cover, lower heat and cook gently 4–5 hours, until fork-tender. Remove meat and keep in warm place. Pour off the stock. In the same kettle, melt the butter, add the remaining flour and the sugar, stirring until smooth and browned. Slowly add the stock, cooking until smooth and thickened. Add the crushed gingersnaps, and cook until dissolved. Replace meat in the sauce and cook ½ hour longer. Meanwhile, cook noodles to serve with the sauerbraten. Serves 12. This tastes better the second day.

CATALAN POT ROAST

¼ teaspoon marjoram
1 tablespoon minced parsley
2 teaspoons salt
1 clove garlic, minced
1 teaspoon cinnamon
¼ teaspoon powdered cloves
4 tablespoons olive oil
4–5 pound rump of beef
1 green pepper, minced
2 onions, chopped
2 cups canned tomatoes
1 cup red wine or orange juice
2 tablespoons vinegar, or 1 tablespoon lemon juice

With a mortar and pestle, make a paste of the herbs, salt, garlic and spices. Beat in 2 tablespoons of olive oil. Rub this into the meat on all sides and let stand at room temperature 1 hour. Heat the remaining olive oil in a kettle or pot, add the meat and brown on all sides. Add the green pepper and onions and cook about 5 minutes. Add the tomatoes, wine or orange juice and vinegar or lemon juice. Cover tightly and cook over lowest heat 3 or 4 hours. Remove meat and thicken sauce if desired with a teaspoon of cornstarch. Serve with boiled or mashed potatoes. Serves 8.

BEEF À LA MODE

6–8 strips larding pork
½ cup Scotch or cognac
4 pounds boneless rump
1 pint red wine
Salt, pepper, nutmeg
Bouquet garni (bay leaf, thyme, leek, parsley)
3 carrots, whole
Beef fat
2 calves' feet, split

Soak the larding pork in the Scotch or cognac for 1 hour. Lard the beef. Combine Scotch or cognac, wine, salt, pepper, nutmeg to taste, bouquet garni and carrots. Marinate larded beef in this mixture for 8–12 hours, turning several times.

In a heavy casserole or Dutch oven, try out enough beef fat to make 3–4 tablespoons. Add meat and brown well on all sides. Season with salt and grind a little fresh pepper on it.

Heat the marinade and pour over the beef. Add calves' feet. Cover and simmer about 2–3 hours or until beef is just tender, not mushy.

Serve hot with boiled potatoes and buttered carrots and a sauce made from the strained and skimmed marinade. Serves 6–8.

To serve cold: Place meat in a terrine. Strain and skim juices, heat. Soften 1 tablespoon gelatin in 2 tablespoons cold water. Stir into hot juices until dissolved. Pour over meat. Cover with foil. Weight with a heavy weight. Cool and chill. Slice and serve with a hot potato salad and marinated cooked vegetables.

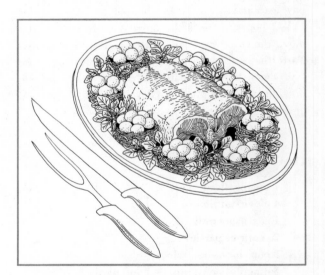

DAUBE NIÇOISE

3 pounds beef shin or chuck
1 calf's foot or 2 pig's feet
Coarse salt
6 cloves garlic
1 onion, cut in slices
A pinch each: rosemary, thyme, basil

6 peppercorns
Red wine
3–4 ripe tomatoes, peeled, seeded and chopped
⅓ pound soft black olives
½ cup chopped parsley

Rub beef and calf's foot or pig's feet with a little salt. Set aside. Combine the garlic, onion, herbs, peppercorns, salt to taste and add enough red wine to cover the meat. Bring to a boil and cook 10 minutes. Cool slightly. Pour marinade over meat, and let stand for 12–24 hours.

Remove the meat and marinade to a heavy casserole, braising pan or daubière. Bring slowly to a boil. Reduce heat so the meat cooks in the feeblest ripple of liquid. Cover.

After about 3 hours, test meat for doneness. Add the tomatoes and cook a further 45 minutes. Remove the meat and cut in thick slices. Skim excess fat from the juices. Replace the meat and cook another 15–20 minutes. Taste for salt. Add the olives and parsley.

Serve the meat and feet with a bowl of macaroni that has been dressed with the sauce. This is called macaronade. Serves 6.

BOEUF EN DAUBE PROVENÇALE

4 pounds round steak or rump steak, cut in
cubes
1 fifth red wine
½ cup wine vinegar
Freshly ground black pepper, salt
3 slices salt pork
1 cup diced ham
10 carrots, peeled and sliced
10 cloves garlic
16 small onions, peeled
5 leeks, washed and sliced
2 cloves
1 bay leaf
1 teaspoon thyme
2 pieces orange peel
1 cup tomato purée

Put the beef cubes in a deep bowl and add the wine and vinegar. Using a pepper mill, sprinkle with 12 good grinds of black pepper. Let the meat marinate in this mixture overnight.

Cut the salt pork into small dice and try it out in a large kettle. When the pork is brown and crisp, remove it and add the ham to the fat in the kettle. Toss it a little and then add the well-drained beef cubes. Cook the beef in the fat quickly for a minute or two and then add the vegetables, seasonings, orange peel and salt to taste. Pour the marinade over this, cover the pot and braise in a 350° oven for a few minutes, or until the liquid begins to simmer. Lower the heat to 275° and continue cooking 4–5 hours. Check occasionally to be sure there is enough liquid. If more is needed, add extra wine or beef broth.

Remove the pot from the oven and drain off the liquid. Reduce this over a brisk flame to about 2–3 cups and stir in the tomato purée. Pour this sauce over the meat and return it to the oven to continue cooking for 35–40 more minutes. Taste the sauce for seasoning. Serves 6–8.

Serve with macaroni tossed with butter or olive oil and a good sharp grated cheese.

Variation: Substitute 1½ pounds of tripe cut into cubes for 1 pound of the beef.

BEEF À LA GARDIEN

4–5 strips bacon, cut thick and diced
2 tablespoons olive oil
3 large onions, coarsely chopped
3 pounds chuck, cut in cubes
1 onion stuck with cloves
1 teaspoon rosemary
1 leek
1 or 2 cloves garlic
Strip of orange rind
Salt, pepper to taste
⅔ cup small green olives
1 cup black olives, pitted
3 or 4 potatoes, cut in thick slices

Try out the bacon in a heavy skillet. Add olive oil and the chopped onion. Cook until golden. Add the meat and brown on all sides. Add the remaining ingredients and about 1 cup of water. Cover. Cook slowly until meat is tender. Uncover, and reduce sauce. Serve with rice. Serves 6.

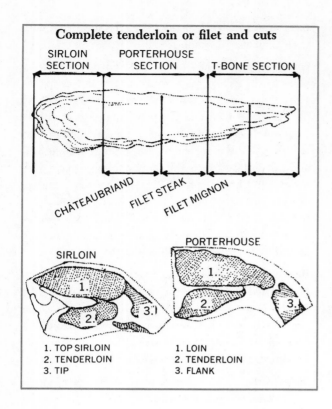

Complete tenderloin or filet and cuts

SIRLOIN SECTION | PORTERHOUSE SECTION | T-BONE SECTION

CHÂTEAUBRIAND | FILET STEAK | FILET MIGNON

SIRLOIN
1. TOP SIRLOIN
2. TENDERLOIN
3. TIP

PORTERHOUSE
1. LOIN
2. TENDERLOIN
3. FLANK

beef cubes and brown on all sides. Place a support—an inverted glass or measuring cup—in the center of a baking dish to hold up the center of the crust. As the beef cubes brown, transfer them to the baking dish. Add the sautéed shallots. Rinse the pan with a little cognac and pour the juices over the meat in the baking dish.

Slice the kidneys rather thin, dust with flour and add to the baking dish. Add the next eight ingredients and enough stock to fill the dish 2/3 full. Top with chilled, rolled crust, sealing it to the edge of the dish with cold water. Crimp with your fingers. Brush with egg mixture. You can decorate the top of the crust with rosettes and leaves cut from the pastry. Stick them on with a little water. Bake the pie in a 325° oven for 1½–2 hours, or until the meat is thoroughly tender. If the crust browns too quickly, put a piece of foil over it. Remove the pie from the oven and let it stand for 10 minutes before serving.

With the pie, serve parsley potatoes and a well-flavored cole slaw. Serves 6–8.

BEEFSTEAK, KIDNEY, AND OYSTER PIE

> 3 pounds beef chuck, cut in 1½"–2" cubes
> Flour
> Salt, pepper
> Beef fat
> ½ cup finely chopped shallots or onion
> Cognac
> 2–3 veal kidneys
> 12–14 mushrooms
> 2 onions, sliced
> 2 cloves garlic, minced
> 1 teaspoon thyme
> ½ teaspoon rosemary
> 1 bay leaf crumbled
> 1½ cans beef gravy or an equal amount of brown sauce
> 12–14 oysters
> Stock
> Rough puff paste or cream cheese pastry (see Pastry)
> 1 egg, beaten with a little water

Dust the beef cubes well with seasoned flour. Melt the beef fat and sauté the chopped shallots. Add the

STEAK À LA NORMANDE

> 2 cups sweet cider, preferably fresh
> ½ cup calvados
> ¼ cup strained lemon juice
> Rind of 1 lemon
> 4 cloves
> ½ teaspoon grated nutmeg
> Dash of cinnamon
> 4-pound round or chuck steak
> 4 tablespoons butter
> ⅔ cup heavy cream
> Salt, pepper to taste

Combine cider, calvados, lemon juice and rind and spices. Place meat in marinade. If cider has preservative added, leave at room temperature for 12 hours, turning occasionally. (If cider is fresh, marinate meat in refrigerator, turning meat and skimming marinade from time to time—it will begin to ferment. After 12 hours, remove from refrigerator and let stand at room temperature for 1 hour.) Remove meat from marinade and dry. Skim and strain marinade, reduce over high heat by half. Sauté steak in butter. While steak is cooking, add cream to marinade and cook over low heat. When steak is done, slice and season with salt and pepper. Pour sauce over steak and dust lightly with grated nutmeg. Serves 6.

MINUTE STEAK AU POIVRE À LA CRÈME

    Crushed pepper to taste
    4 minute steaks, about 1″ thick
    4 tablespoons beef fat, finely chopped
    Salt
    ¼ cup cognac
    2 tablespoons meat glaze
    1 cup heavy cream

Press crushed pepper into the steaks with the heel of your hand. Let them stand at room temperature for an hour before cooking. Melt the beef fat in a large skillet over medium heat until pan is very hot, sear the steaks on both sides and reduce the heat slightly. Continue cooking until they have achieved the state of rareness you prefer. Salt to taste. Add the cognac and ignite. When the flames die down, add the meat glaze and turn the steaks quickly to color them on the other side. Remove to a hot platter. Add the cream to the pan, let it cook down quickly and pour into a bowl. Spoon over the steaks. Serves 4.

STEAK DIANE

    For each serving:
    Rib eye or loin eye steak, ½″ thick
    2½ tablespoons butter
    1 tablespoon finely minced chives
    1 teaspoon finely minced parsley
    Salt, pepper to taste
    1 tablespoon finely minced shallot
    1 tablespoon cognac
    2 tablespoons sherry
    1½ teaspoons Worcestershire sauce (optional)

This steak is quickly and easily made at the table in a chafing dish, if there aren't too many people (each steak must be sautéed separately). It definitely requires the best grade of a tender cut of beef.

Remove any membrane or fat surrounding steak and pound as flat as possible. If meat is not tender enough to pound really thin, slice steak horizontally through middle, leaving it joined along one side, open out

and pound to flatten. Cream together 1½ tablespoons butter, chives, parsley and salt and pepper. Melt remaining tablespoon butter over medium heat with shallot, which should soften but not brown. Increase heat and sauté steak quickly—about ½ minute per side, or until just seared, remove and keep warm. Flame pan with cognac, reduce heat, add seasoned butter, sherry and, if desired, Worcestershire sauce. When blended, replace steak for an instant, turning once, then serve with sauce.

BISTECCA ALLA SALSA DI CAPPERI

    ½ cup olive oil
    2 medium onions, chopped
    4 pounds porterhouse or sirloin steak, 1″ thick, or 4 individual steaks
    ⅓ cup strained lemon juice
    5 tablespoons drained capers
    Salt, pepper

Heat oil in heavy pan. Add onions and cook for 5 minutes. Add steak, sear on both sides over high heat, reduce heat and cook until done. Remove steak and keep warm. Pour lemon juice into pan containing onions. Over high heat, carefully deglaze pan. Add capers and salt and pepper to taste (be careful with the salt—the lemon juice in part replaces it). Pour over steak and serve. Serves 4.

STEAK THULIER

For each individual serving of tournedos:

    2 tablespoons foie gras d'oie
    3 anchovy filets or 1½ teaspoons anchovy paste
    1 tablespoon olive oil
    2 tablespoons butter
    2 shallots, finely chopped
    1 tablespoon finely chopped parsley
    ¼ cup dry white wine
    1 canned black truffle, thinly sliced, and some juice from the tin
    ½ cup port or Burgundy
    1 tablespoon meat glaze
    Salt, freshly ground black pepper

In a mortar, pound foie gras and anchovies or anchovy paste into a smooth paste, or purée in an electric blender. In a skillet just large enough to contain desired number of steaks, heat olive oil and half the butter until bubbling, but not coloring. Add shallots and parsley, cook for an instant and add steaks. Cover and cook until steaks are browned on one side, turn and cook until done as desired. Remove steaks and keep warm. Add wine to pan, cook for a minute, scraping pan to raise all the glaze on the bottom. Strain mixture into a saucepan. Add thinly sliced truffle and juice, port or Burgundy and meat glaze, reduce by half over moderate heat. Add mixture of anchovy and foie gras. Season to taste with salt and pepper—you will need little salt because of the anchovies but a fair quantity of fresh black pepper. Cook, stirring, until smooth. Remove from heat and stir in remaining butter, pour over steaks and serve.

STEAK AU POIVRE, FLAMBÉ

    2 tablespoons coarsely cracked peppercorns
    1 porterhouse steak, 2½"–3" thick
    3 tablespoons butter
    1 tablespoon finely chopped shallots
    1 tablespoon finely chopped parsley
    1 teaspoon salt
    ⅓ cup bourbon

Press coarse pepper into steak with the heel of the hand. Let it stand for ½ hour. Heat a stainless steel platter until very hot. Melt butter on platter. Combine with shallots and parsley.

Broil steak to your favorite state of doneness, preferably well-charred outside and rare inside. Salt during cooking. Remove to hot platter and turn once. Add heated bourbon and blaze. Slice and serve with sauté potatoes and sauce from the platter. Serves 4.

BISTECCA ALLA FIORENTINA

    4 Delmonico (shell) steaks, 1" thick
    ¼ cup olive oil
    2 tablespoons lemon juice
    1 teaspoon salt
    ½ teaspoon freshly ground black pepper

    1 clove garlic, minced
    1 tablespoon minced parsley
    2 tablespoons butter

Trim all the fat from the steaks. Mix together the oil, lemon juice, salt, pepper, garlic and parsley. Marinate the steaks in the mixture for 2–3 hours, turning and basting frequently. Drain well.

Broil steaks to the desired degree of rareness and place a ball of butter on each before serving. Serves 4.

BISTECCA ALLA PIZZAIOLA

    3 pounds sirloin or rump steak
    4 tablespoons olive oil
    1½ pounds tomatoes, peeled and diced
    4 cloves garlic, sliced
    ½ teaspoon oregano
    2 teaspoons salt
    ½ teaspoon freshly ground black pepper
    2 tablespoons minced parsley

Cut the steak into 6 pieces, and flatten slightly by pounding. Heat 2 tablespoons oil in a saucepan; add the tomatoes, garlic, oregano, 1 teaspoon salt and ¼ teaspoon pepper. Cook over low heat 15 minutes. While the sauce is cooking, prepare the steak.

Heat the remaining oil in a skillet; brown the steak in it on both sides. Season with the remaining salt and pepper. Spread with the sauce; cover and cook over low heat 5 minutes. Sprinkle with the parsley and serve. Serves 6.

FLANK STEAK ORIENTALE

    2 flank steaks (Prime or Choice quality)
    3 cloves garlic, finely chopped
    1 teaspoon freshly ground black pepper
    ⅔ cup Japanese soy sauce
    ½ teaspoon Tabasco
    ⅓ cup sherry or vermouth
      Salt

Rub the steaks well with the chopped garlic and freshly ground pepper, place in a shallow dish and add the soy sauce, Tabasco and wine. Turn the steaks in the mixture several times. Let stand for an hour or two at room temperature, or even overnight in the refrigerator. Arrange the steaks on a broiling pan and broil at high heat close to the broiler for 3 minutes on each side for rare meat. Salt to taste and slice in thin, thin slices with a sharp knife. Hold the knife so it is almost parallel to the steak, to produce wide, diagonal slices. Serves 6.

CROWN ROAST OF LAMB

This is a very attractive roast when properly trimmed and tied. You may have a smallish crown roast or one made with a double rack. To calculate servings, allow about 2 chops per person.

Fill the center of the roast with a ball of foil to keep the crown in shape during roasting, and cover the bones with foil or cubes of fat to prevent them from charring. Season the roast well with freshly ground black pepper and tarragon, and roast on a rack in a 325° oven, allowing about 13–15 minutes per pound

for pink lamb. With a crown it is difficult to take a reading on a meat thermometer.

Let the roast stand for about 10 minutes in a warm place. Remove the covering on the ends of the ribs and replace them with paper frills. Fill the center of the crown with any of the following and serve the roast immediately:

1. Tiny new peas mixed with tiny white onions, both well buttered.
2. Rice pilaff mixed with finely cut and quickly sautéed lamb kidneys.
3. Chestnut purée, with braised chestnuts as garnish.
4. Braised chestnuts and Brussels sprouts.
5. Sautéed mushroom caps sprinkled with tarragon, parsley, and chives
6. Cracked wheat.
7. Wild rice and almonds.

Serve the pan juices, or anchovy-flavored Hollandaise sauce or a Béarnaise sauce, substituting fresh mint for the tarragon in the latter. Also serve a Bibb lettuce salad tossed with diced cooked beets.

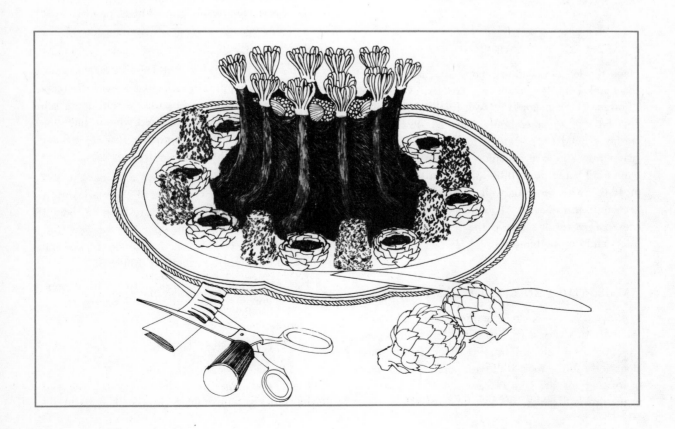

RACK OF LAMB PERSILLÉ

1 rack, about 6 chops
2 cloves garlic, very finely chopped
¾ cup bread crumbs
½ cup finely chopped parsley
 Butter
 Salt, freshly ground black pepper

Ask the butcher to cut the rack so that you can carve right through the chops without having to struggle with the bones. Trim it and wrap the bone ends of the chops with foil. Blend the garlic, the bread crumbs, and parsley. Rub the roast well with butter and freshly ground black pepper. Place on a rack in a roasting pan, and roast in a 375° oven, basting every 10 minutes. After 20 minutes, test meat for internal temperature. If it is near 130°–135°, remove from the oven. Blend the degreased pan juices with the crumb mixture, salt the roast and spread an even film of the crumb mixture over it. Dot with butter, and return to the oven until the mixture has browned nicely and the rack is done.

Serve with sautéed potatoes and broccoli au beurre noir. Serves 3.

ROAST LEG OF LAMB

Have the leg cut without chops attached and with the shank bone left intact, not cracked as one finds so often. The leg should be well trimmed and all excess fat and the membrane removed. Rub it with freshly ground pepper and a touch of rosemary and place it on a rack in a shallow pan. Roast in a 325° oven until it registers 130°–135° when tested with a meat thermometer. Salt well 15 minutes before removing from the oven. Allow to stand about 10 minutes before carving. Serve the lamb with the pan juices and tiny buttered peas.

GARLIC-STUDDED LEG OF LAMB

Peel and sliver 4–5 cloves garlic. Make incisions in the leg with a very sharp pointed knife (such as small French paring knife). Force the slivers into the incisions and rub the roast well with pepper and a touch of rosemary or tarragon. Place on a rack and roast as in the previous recipe.

Serve with white beans, blended with the pan juices, and a bit of peeled, seeded, finely chopped tomato.

Variations:

Provençal I: Cut 4–6 cloves garlic into slivers. Make fairly deep incisions in the leg and alternate garlic and anchovy filets in the incisions (you will not need to add much salt to this anchovied leg). Roast. Serve with a ratatouille.

Provençal II: Make incisions in the leg and stuff with garlic, pistachio nuts, and anchovies, pushing them deep into the incisions. Rub the leg with a touch of thyme and summer savory and roast. Salt lightly and serve with a gratin of eggplant.

MARINATED LEG OF LAMB

1 good-size leg of spring lamb, boned and tied
3 cloves garlic
 Rosemary or tarragon
2–3 onions, thinly sliced
1 bay leaf
 Few sprigs parsley
1 teaspoon salt
½ teaspoon freshly ground black pepper
 Red wine

Pique surface of meat with 2 cloves garlic (cut gashes and insert garlic slivers). Rub leg well with rosemary or tarragon and put it in a deep kettle with the onion, bay leaf, parsley, remaining garlic, salt, 1 teaspoon rosemary, pepper and enough red wine to half cover the meat. Marinate in refrigerator for 30–48 hours, turning leg several times to bathe it evenly.

To cook, put leg in roasting pan and roast at 375°, basting occasionally with some of the marinade. Allow 15 minutes per pound for rare lamb or about 18 minutes per pound for medium rare. If you use a meat thermometer, the lamb will be cooked rare when the thermometer registers 130°–135°.

Serve with boiled white beans mixed with chopped garlic, chopped parsley and olive oil. Serves 6.

ROAST LAMB CASTILIAN

5–6 pound leg of spring lamb
1½ teaspoons salt
 Freshly ground black pepper

½ cup Spanish olive oil
1 or 2 cloves garlic, crushed
10 blanched almonds
1 teaspoon paprika
½ cup dry white wine
16 small potatoes

Trim leg of lamb, cutting off all the excess fat. Dust with the salt and pepper and rub all over with olive oil. Sear in a preheated 450° oven until golden, lower the heat to 300° and roast 1½ hours or until meat thermometer registers 130°–135° (rare). Meantime, mash the garlic and almonds to a paste in a mortar and pestle (discard garlic skin). Beat in the paprika and wine. Pour this mixture over the lamb during last 10 minutes of roasting. Parboil small potatoes, peel, place in pan around meat as it roasts, turning until crisp and golden on all sides. When done, remove the lamb and potatoes, pour off excess fat, make gravy with pan drippings. Serves 8.

LEG OF LAMB WITH ARTICHOKES

5–6 pound leg of lamb
2 teaspoons salt
  Freshly ground pepper to taste
1 teaspoon crumbled dried oregano
3 cloves garlic, cut in slivers
8 medium artichokes
8 tablespoons lemon juice
1 tablespoon olive oil
  Parsley, herbs for garnish

Trim off all but a thin layer of fat from the meat. Mix together the salt, pepper, and oregano. With a sharp knife, make incisions in the meat and insert garlic slivers and the salt mixture. Rub outside of the meat with any remaining salt mixture. Place meat on a rack in a roasting pan and pour ½ cup water into the bottom of the pan. Roast in a preheated 425° oven for 30 minutes, or until meat is nicely browned. Reduce temperature to 325° and continue roasting 45 minutes longer.

Meanwhile, remove the tough outer leaves of the artichokes and cut off part of the stems. Cut ½″ off the tips, cut artichokes in half lengthwise, and scoop out the choke. Drop into boiling salted water, seasoned with 2 tablespoons of the lemon juice and the oil,

and simmer 30 minutes, or until barely tender; drain. Add the cooked artichoke halves to the roasting pan and pour the remaining lemon juice over the meat. Cover pan and roast 15 minutes longer, or until a meat thermometer registers 130°–135°.

Serve lamb on a carving board, garnished with the artichoke halves, and surround with parsley and herb nosegays. Skim fat from pan drippings and serve juices in a bowl. Serves 8.

GIGOT EN CROÛTE

5–6-pound leg of lamb, boned
  Salt, freshly cracked pepper
1 clove garlic, crushed
1 pound finely ground veal
2 egg whites
1 cup light cream
2 tablespoons finely chopped shallot
1 teaspoon finely chopped garlic
2 tablespoons finely chopped celery
2 tablespoons finely chopped parsley
1 tablespoon finely chopped dill
⅛ teaspoon nutmeg
1 pound sliced bacon
  Red wine

Pastry:

6 cups all-purpose flour
2½ cups soft butter
1 cup ice water
1 egg, well beaten

Demi-glace sauce:

2 chicken livers
3 tablespoons salt butter
2 tablespoons brandy
1 teaspoon tomato paste
1 teaspoon meat glaze
2 teaspoons potato starch
¼ cup red wine
1¼ cups chicken stock
2 teaspoons red currant jelly
  Pepper to taste
1 small truffle, finely chopped

Season the lamb well inside and out with the salt, pepper and crushed garlic. Put ground veal in a mixer, add egg whites and beat well. Slowly beat in the cream. Add shallot, garlic, celery, parsley, dill, nutmeg and salt and pepper to taste. Stuff leg with this mixture and wrap with bacon slices, tying securely with string. Put on a rack in a roasting pan and pour a little red wine and some water in the bottom of the pan. Roast at 375° for 20 minutes, reduce heat to 350° and roast for 1½ hours, basting every 20 minutes and adding 2 tablespoons wine or water each time. Remove and cool.

While lamb is roasting, make the pastry. Blend the flour and butter with your fingers until it forms a sandy mass. Add the water gradually, mixing slowly, and work dough into a ball. The less water used, the better. Wrap in waxed paper and refrigerate.

When ready to finish the lamb, roll out dough ¼″ thick and large enough to envelop the lamb completely. Place cooled lamb in center, top side down. Fold pastry over meat and seal seam and ends with water. Place seam-side down on a cookie sheet and brush top and sides with beaten egg, mixed with a little water or cream. Prick thoroughly with a fork in a criss-cross design. Bake in a preheated 400° oven for 25 minutes.

While lamb is in oven, make the sauce. Brown the chicken livers in 2 teaspoons hot butter. Flame with brandy. Remove livers and add remaining butter to pan. Stir in, off the heat, the tomato paste, meat glaze and potato starch. Mix in the wine, stock and jelly. Stir over low heat until it comes to a boil, season with pepper and simmer 10 minutes. Strain sauce and add truffle and chicken livers, finely diced.

Serve gigot on a hot serving platter, accompanied by the sauce. Serves 6–8.

GIGOT EN CROÛTE BAUMANIÈRE

> 2 or 3 lamb kidneys
> 4–5 tablespoons butter
> ⅓ cup Madeira
> 3 or 4 mushrooms, coarsely chopped
> ⅛ teaspoon thyme
> ⅛ teaspoon rosemary
> ¼ teaspoon tarragon

> Salt
> Leg of baby lamb weighing 2–2½ pounds, with leg bone removed, shank bone left in
> 1 pound rough puff paste (see Pastry)
> 1 egg, beaten with 2 tablespoons cream

Cut the kidneys into small pieces and toss them in hot butter until lightly browned. Rinse the pan with Madeira. Add the mushrooms and the herbs and season with salt to taste. Stuff the boned part of the leg with this mixture, re-form the gigot and secure it with a skewer.

Rub the outside with butter and roast in a 450° oven for 10 minutes. Reduce the heat to 375° and roast for 10–12 additional minutes. Remove from the oven and allow to cool.

Roll out the rough puff paste about ½″ thick and envelop the leg, leaving the shank bone exposed. Cut out small pastry leaves and decorate the top with them. Brush with the beaten egg and cream. Bake at 375° until the pastry is brown and crisp; 20–25 minutes should be ample. Serve the gigot with a Gratin of Potatoes. Serves 2–3.

GIGOT À LA FICELLE

> Leg of lamb, about 5 pounds, boned and tied
> 1 clove garlic, cut in slivers
> Bones from the leg
> 4 cloves garlic, crushed
> 1 bay leaf
> 1 tablespoon tarragon
> 4 tablespoons freshly ground black pepper
> 3 dried red peppers
> 2 tablespoons salt

Stud the lamb with a few slivers of garlic. Roll in a linen towel or cloth and tie securely. Combine the bones and the seasonings in a kettle with enough water to cover the leg of lamb. Bring the liquid to a boil and cook for 1 hour over medium heat. Now tie the leg of lamb to the handles of the kettle so that it does not rest on the bottom, or place it on a rack in the kettle. Bring bouillon to the boil and reduce to simmer. Allow approximately 14–15 minutes per pound boned weight for rare lamb. Remove lamb. Reserve ½ cup broth for Anchovy Sauce. Serve with sauce, tiny parslied new potatoes and petits pois with a little chopped parsley and chives. Serves 6.

ANCHOVY SAUCE

 1 clove garlic, finely chopped
 12 anchovy fillets, finely chopped
 12 black Italian or Greek olives,
   pitted and chopped
 1 or 2 tiny hot peppers, finely chopped
 2 tablespoons olive oil
 1 teaspoon lemon juice
 1 teaspoon grated lemon rind
 ½ cup lamb broth

Combine all the ingredients and stir well over medium heat until sauce mixture is smooth and heated through. Correct the seasoning. It should be very hot and the anchovy flavor quite pronounced. A dash of Tabasco may be in order.

LAMB IN A JACKET

 6 large loin lamb chops
   Salt, pepper, and oregano to taste
 2 cloves garlic, cut in slivers
 6 small carrots, peeled and halved
 6 small zucchini, halved
 6 small onions, halved
 ¼ pound feta cheese, cut into
   6 squares
   Juice of 1 lemon
 ¼ cup melted butter

Season each lamb chop with salt, pepper, and oregano, and insert slivers of garlic into the meat. Place each chop on a large square of aluminum foil and arrange on each chop 1 carrot, 1 zucchini, 1 onion, and 1 square of cheese. Sprinkle the vegetables with lemon juice, butter, and salt and pepper. Fold the squares of foil into a double fold at the top and the sides; secure sides with paper clips. Place packets in a buttered baking pan and bake in a preheated 350° oven for 1 hour. Remove the clips. Serve sealed packets on dinner plates and let each guest open his own. Serves 6.

LAMB SHASHLIK

 2 cups good red wine
 ½ cup olive oil
 1 cup sliced onion, celery, leek, a little carrot
 12 mixed peppercorns
 1 small onion stuck with 2 cloves
 1 clove garlic, bruised
   Bouquet garni
 3 pounds boned shoulder of lamb
 2 small eggplant
   Salt, freshly cracked white pepper
 12 baby white onions
 2 green peppers
 2 red peppers
   Vegetable oil, butter
 12 firm white mushroom caps
 3 firm tomatoes
   Bacon slices
 ½ cup melted salt butter
 4 cloves garlic, crushed

Combine first 7 ingredients and heat gently. Remove fat, skin and sinew from lamb and cut into large squares. Put in earthenware bowl or crock and pour heated marinade over it. Cover with a lid that is not airtight and marinate 24 hours, turning meat several times.

Cut eggplant in large squares, sprinkle with salt and allow to stand for half an hour. Wash thoroughly, drain and dry on paper towels. Blanch onions and drain. Cut peppers in 4, remove seeds, cut in 8, blanch and drain. Sauté eggplant in a little oil for a minute or two. Shake mushroom caps in seasoned butter over high heat for a minute. Quarter tomatoes.

Drain lamb well, reserving marinade. Wrap each piece in a ½ slice of bacon. Alternate lamb and different vegetables on skewers, ending with a mushroom cap. Arrange on broiling rack.
Blend melted butter with garlic, salt and pepper to taste, and brush on lamb and vegetables. Broil for 3 minutes on each side, brushing once or twice with butter mixture, or until bacon is cooked, but lamb still pink inside. Strain marinade into pan and boil until reduced a little. Serve skewers on rice or rice pilaff and pour marinade over shashlik. Serves 6.

LAMB SHISH KEBAB

¾ cup dry red wine
¼ cup lemon juice
3 tablespoons olive oil
1 teaspoon salt
  Freshly ground pepper to taste
2 cloves garlic, minced
½ teaspoon crumbled dried oregano
2 pounds boneless leg of lamb,
  cut into 1½″ cubes
1 onion, sliced
  Bay leaves
1 green pepper, cut into 1″ squares
½ pound mushroom caps
½ pound small white onions, parboiled
  Lemon wedges

Mix the wine, lemon juice, olive oil, salt, pepper, garlic, and oregano to make a marinade. Place the meat and sliced onion in a bowl and pour the marinade over them. Refrigerate overnight, or for 6–8 hours, turning once or twice. Alternate meat cubes, bay leaves, green pepper, mushrooms, and whole onions on skewers. Broil or barbecue over hot coals, basting frequently and turning once, until meat is cooked to desired doneness. Serve with lemon wedges. Accompany with Bulgur Pilaff and yogurt. Serves 6.

Variations:

1. Substitute squares of swordfish for the meat and white wine for the red.
2. Alternate lamb and bay leaves with cubes of kasseri cheese and green pepper squares.
3. Barbecue the marinated lamb without vegetables and accompany it with pilaff, sautéed mushrooms, soft round flat bread, and yogurt.

NORWEGIAN LAMB SHANKS WITH SOUR CREAM SAUCE

6 lamb shanks
  Salt, pepper
3 tablespoons butter

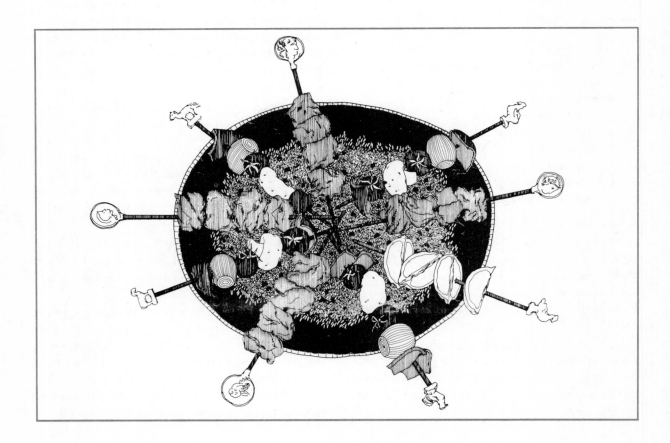

1 large onion, chopped
1½ cups dry white wine
½ cup bouillon
2 tablespoons flour
3 tablespoons water
3 tablespoons fresh dill, chopped
1 cup sour cream

Trim lamb shanks of excess fat. Rub with salt and pepper. Heat butter in skillet and brown lamb shanks on all sides. Transfer meat to casserole. Add onion to pan drippings and cook until tender. Top lamb shanks with onion. Add wine and bouillon. Simmer covered about 1½ hours, or until tender. (The meat should be well cooked.) Remove shanks to hot platter; keep warm. Strain stock and return to casserole. Mix flour and water to a smooth paste and stir into stock. Cook over low heat until smooth and thickened. Add dill and sour cream. Return lamb shanks to sauce. Heat through thoroughly, but do not boil.

Serve with steamed potatoes sprinkled with dill and a cucumber salad. Serves 6.

LAMB MARRAKECH

3 pounds lean lamb from leg or shoulder,
    cut in 1½" cubes
½ cup peanut or olive oil
2 large onions, finely chopped
3 cloves garlic, chopped
2 teaspoons salt
1 teaspoon crushed red chili pepper
½ teaspoon Spice Parisienne
1 teaspoon turmeric
3 ripe large tomatoes, peeled, seeded
    and chopped
1 cup raisins, soaked in sherry
½ cup each: toasted almonds and filberts
    Crisp fried onion rings
    Chopped parsley, cilantro (optional)

Brown the lamb in the oil. Add the onion and garlic and brown lightly. Add the seasonings, tomatoes and raisins and bring to a boil. Cover, adding a small amount of liquid if necessary, and simmer for 1½ hours, or place uncovered in a 350° oven and baste

well from time to time until the lamb is tender. If you do the latter, you may have to add more liquid or cover the pan for half the time. Add the toasted almonds and filberts, onion rings and parsley and heat through. Serve with rice, tossed with chopped parsley and chopped fresh cilantro if available. Serves 6.

ANDALUSIAN LAMB STEW

4 pounds lamb for stew, cut in serving pieces
4 teaspoons salt
2 tablespoons flour
½ cup olive oil
3 large onions, chopped
2 or 3 cloves garlic, crushed
2 ripe tomatoes, peeled and chopped,
    or 1 cup canned tomatoes
1 teaspoon powdered cumin
1 teaspoon cinnamon
¼ teaspoon ground cloves
1 cup dry sherry
2½ cups water
1 package frozen butter beans

Dust the lamb with 2 teaspoons salt mixed with the flour. Brown in the olive oil. Add chopped onion, garlic and ripe tomatoes (canned tomatoes should be added after onion is soft). Cook until onion is soft, add seasonings and remaining salt. Cook 1 minute to flavor meat thoroughly, then add sherry and water. Simmer covered 3 or 4 hours, skimming occasionally. Cool; skim off fat accumulated on top. Chill in refrigerator at least 24 hours. Reheat when needed, adding the beans. Cook the beans 20 minutes to ½ hour. Serve with saffron rice. Serves 10. This freezes well and can be made ahead of time.

HARICOT OF LAMB

1 pound pinto beans or 1 pound white beans
1 teaspoon salt
1 onion stuck with 2 cloves
1 bay leaf
3 cloves garlic
2½ pounds lamb shoulder, cut into 1½" cubes
    Flour seasoned with salt and pepper

4–6 tablespoons olive oil
3 leeks, washed and sliced
1 teaspoon thyme
   Broth or red wine
   Buttered crumbs

Soak the beans overnight in enough water to cover. Drain them and put them in a kettle with 1 teaspoon salt, onion stuck with cloves, bay leaf and 1 clove garlic. Add water, slightly more than needed to cover. Bring to a boil, lower the heat and simmer gently until the beans are just tender.

Dust the lamb cubes with the seasoned flour and brown them on all sides in the hot olive oil. Add the remaining garlic cloves, finely chopped, the leeks, thyme and just enough broth or red wine to cover. Bring to a boil, lower the heat and cover the kettle. Simmer until the lamb is tender.

In a baking dish combine the pieces of lamb, the broth from the lamb and the drained, cooked beans. Bake uncovered in a 350° oven for 45–60 minutes. Baste from time to time with additional meat broth or a little red wine. Sprinkle the top with buttered crumbs and cook for 15–20 minutes more. It should be neither too dry nor too juicy, but moist and mellow in flavor. Serves 6.

NORWEGIAN LAMB AND CABBAGE

   4 pounds boneless lamb, cut into 2″ pieces
   1 medium cabbage, cut into 1″ wedges
   1 celeriac, peeled and diced,
     or 1 cup diced celery
   1½ teaspoons salt
   ⅓ cup flour
     Boiling bouillon or water
   2 tablespoons black peppercorns tied
     in a cheesecloth bag
   ½ cup sour cream

Trim lamb of all excess fat. In heavy saucepan, place a layer of meat, fatty side down. Top with cabbage and sprinkle with some of the celeriac or celery, salt and flour. Repeat until you have at least 3 layers of meat and vegetables. Add bouillon to cover lamb and cabbage half way. Add peppercorns. Cover tightly and bring to a slow boil. Check occasionally; if necessary, add a little more bouillon. Simmer over low heat

until meat is tender, about 1½–2½ hours. Remove peppercorn bag. Stir cream into mixture and heat through, but do not boil. Serve with boiled potatoes and pickled beets. Serves 4–6.

LAMB WITH LEMON SAUCE

   4 tablespoons olive oil
   4 tablespoons butter
   1 bunch green onions, chopped
   1 head lettuce, shredded
   2 large onions, peeled and chopped
   3 pounds shoulder of lamb, cubed
     Salt, freshly ground black pepper
   1 teaspoon dill
     White wine, stock or water
     Arrowroot
     Juice of 1 lemon (or to taste)
     Rind of 1 lemon, finely chopped
   3 egg yolks

Heat the oil and butter in a large skillet. Add the green onions, lettuce and chopped onions and cook gently until wilted and tender. Add the cubed lamb and let it cook, turning the pieces frequently, until colored, but not browned. Salt and pepper to taste and add the dill. Barely cover with wine, stock or water; lower the heat, and simmer gently until the lamb is tender. Taste for seasoning.

Mix a little arrowroot with the lemon juice and lemon rind and slowly stir this mixture into the lamb stew. Cook, stirring constantly, until well blended and slightly thickened. Remove from the stove.

Beat the egg yolks slightly and add a little of the hot sauce from the stew to the eggs. Mix well, and slowly add egg mixture to stew, stirring it in a little at a time, so that it does not curdle. Serves 6–8.

CASSOULET

    1-pound package white beans
        Pork rind, rolled up and tied with string
    ½ pound salt pork, in one piece
    1 onion stuck with 4 cloves
    2 carrots
        Piece of celery
        Green part of celery, large sprig parsley,
        1 bay leaf, 1 small piece cinnamon stick,
        3 bruised juniper berries, 4 white and 3 black
        peppercorns tied in cheesecloth bag
    1 duck
    1 clove garlic, crushed
    1 quartered orange
        Salt, pepper
        Salt butter
        Red currant jelly, marmalade
    1½ pounds boned breast of lamb,
        cut in large squares
    1½ pounds boned loin of pork,
        cut in large squares
    ½ cup sherry
    1 teaspoon tomato paste
    2 level teaspoons meat glaze
    3 level teaspoons potato starch
    2 cups strong beef stock
    8 fresh pork sausages
    6 Spanish garlic sausages (paprika type)
    3 or 4 slices bacon

Put beans in a bowl, cover with water and soak overnight. Drain. Cover with fresh water in deep pan. Add pork rind, salt pork, onion, carrots, celery and herbs in bag. Simmer gently for 1–1¼ hours. Meanwhile, stuff duck with garlic and orange and season inside with salt and pepper. Tie up carefully, put on a rack, rub top with salt and pepper and brush with melted butter. Roast at 375° for 45 minutes. Baste occasionally, adding 2 tablespoons cold water to pan each time, mix with juices and use to baste. Remove duck, spread top with mixture of jelly and marmalade and glaze under a low broiler flame.

Brown lamb and pork squares quickly on each side in a little hot butter. Remove and deglaze pan with ¼ cup sherry. Stir to lift glaze and add 1 ounce salt butter. Stir in, off heat, tomato paste, meat glaze and potato starch. Pour on beef stock and ¼ cup sherry.

Season with pepper and stir over low heat until it comes to a boil. Replace meat and add the sausages. Cover pan with waxed paper and lid and simmer very gently until the meats are tender, about 35–40 minutes. When meat is cooked, remove excess fat from surface.

Carve duck into small portions and add to meat. Remove pork rind and salt pork from beans, cut rind in fine shreds, pork in dice. Discard carrot, onion, celery, herb bouquet. Carefully mix pork and rind back into beans, shaking gently so as not to mash beans. Remove any excess liquid. Put layer of beans on bottom of cassoulet pot or casserole, a layer of meat and duck on top, then a layer of beans. Continue adding layers of meat and beans until dish is full, ending with beans. Cover top with thin slices of bacon and keep warm in the oven till ready to serve. It can cook slowly an hour longer. This dish can be made ahead of time. Serves 8–10.

COUS-COUS BAUDIN

    2 pounds lamb neck
    1 boned and rolled shoulder of lamb,
        about 4–5 pounds
    3–4 cloves garlic, slivered
    1 onion stuck with 2 cloves
    2 carrots
    1 sprig parsley
    1 teaspoon rosemary
    1 hot pepper, seeded
    2 sweet peppers, seeded
        Salt
    2 1-pound, 4-ounce cans chick peas
    6–8 whole carrots
    6–8 whole onions
    6–8 white turnips
    6–8 whole zucchini
    6–8 smallish tomatoes
    1-pound package cous-cous
    2–3 hot red peppers
    3 tablespoons olive oil
    1 clove garlic, crushed
    1 teaspoon Tabasco
    ¼ cup ground walnuts

Make small gashes in the lamb neck and shoulder and insert the garlic. Put the neck in a deep pan with the onion stuck with cloves, 2 carrots, parsley, rosemary, seeded hot pepper, seeded sweet peppers, about 5 quarts water and salt to taste. Bring to a boil and simmer 3 hours. Add the lamb shoulder and chick peas. Bring to a boil, reduce heat and poach, allowing about 18 minutes per pound, keeping the liquid just below the boiling point, faintly bubbling. Cook the whole carrots, onions, turnips and zucchini separately. You may wrap them separately in foil and cook them in the same pot if you wish. Bake the tomatoes slowly.

About 20 minutes before the vegetables are ready, put the cous-cous in a colander lined with muslin and place the colander over the bubbling meat and stock—or cook it in a cous-cousière, a special type of double boiler designed for this dish. Cover and allow the cous-cous to steam.

Meanwhile prepare a piquant sauce by pounding the hot red peppers in a mortar or whirling them in a blender with 3 tablespoons olive oil. Add the crushed garlic, Tabasco and ground walnuts and blend well.

To serve, remove and slice the meat and arrange with the whole vegetables on a hot platter. Serve the cous-cous in a bowl or on a deep plate and the broth in another deep bowl. Serve the piquant sauce separately. Serves 6–8.

KADJEMOULA

>   2 pounds lamb shoulder, cut into 1½″ cubes
>   2 pounds chuck beef, cut into 1½″ cubes
>   Flour
>   3 tablespoons butter or olive oil
>   1 teaspoon salt
>   ½ teaspoon freshly ground black pepper
>   ¼ teaspoon cinnamon
>   ¼ teaspoon ginger
>   2 medium onions, peeled and sliced
>   3 cloves garlic, peeled and chopped
>   4 carrots, peeled and quartered
>   2 medium turnips, peeled and diced
>   ⅔ cup dried apricots
>   ⅔ cup dried pitted prunes
>   2–3 cups meat broth
>   1 jar quince preserves or ½ pound quince paste

Flour the lamb and beef cubes very lightly. Heat butter or oil in a large kettle and when it is bubbly, brown the meat cubes on all sides. Sprinkle the meat with the salt, pepper, cinnamon and ginger and add the vegetables and dried fruits. Pour over enough broth to cover and bring to a boil. Lower the heat, cover the kettle and simmer gently for about 2 hours, or until the meat is tender and the vegetables and dried fruits have blended down.

Remove the stew to a hot platter and surround it with mounds of steamed rice. Garnish the edges with quince preserves or slices of quince paste. Serves 6–8.

DAUBE AVIGNONNAISE

>   1 leg of lamb, boned
>   1 onion stuck with 2 cloves
>   2 sprigs parsley
>   8 cloves garlic
>   Salt
>   Strips of larding pork soaked in cognac
>   and rolled in chopped parsley
>   2 onions, sliced
>   1 carrot, sliced
>   ¼ cup olive oil
>   1 teaspoon thyme
>   1 bay leaf
>   Red wine
>   6 large onions, coarsely chopped
>   1 pig's foot, split
>   3–4 slices salt pork, diced
>   Orange rind

Save the bones from the lamb and ask the butcher for an extra one or two. Place bones in a pot with the onion stuck with cloves, 1 sprig of parsley and 2 whole cloves garlic. Add 2 quarts water, and cook down to a good broth. Season with salt to taste.

Meanwhile, cut the lamb in good-sized pieces. Lard each piece with a portion of the larding pork. Combine the sliced onion and carrot, olive oil, thyme, bay leaf, remaining parsley and 3 cloves garlic, crushed, and wine almost to cover. Marinate the lamb for several hours or overnight in this marinade.

Make a bed of the chopped onion in a deep casserole. Add half of the pig's foot, then half of the marinated meat, more onion, the salt pork, the remaining meat, and the rest of the pig's foot. Add the orange rind, strain the marinade and add the seasonings, onions, carrots and garlic from it and the remaining 3 cloves garlic. Add enough of the broth to cover. Seal the casserole with flour and water paste and cook very slowly on top of the range or in a 275° oven for 3–4 hours. This daube is delicious served with rice and a salad. Serves 6–8.

TOGGUA GRAMERUS

> 2 1-pound, 4-ounce cans chick peas
> 1 clove garlic, finely chopped
> 1 bay leaf, crumbled
> 1 clove
> 4 pounds lean breast of lamb, cut in 1″ strips
>   Flour
> ½ cup olive oil
> 4 large onions, thinly sliced
> 1 teaspoon sugar
> 1 teaspoon salt
> 1 teaspoon freshly ground black pepper
> 1 tablespoon Spanish paprika
>   Pinch of saffron
>   Broth or water

Drain the canned chick peas and mix them with the garlic, bay leaf and clove. Set aside.

Dust the meat strips lightly with flour. Heat the olive oil in a large kettle and add the sliced onions. Brown gently, sprinkling them with the sugar as they cook so that they will caramelize. Add the lamb and brown evenly. Sprinkle with the salt, pepper, paprika and saffron. Add the drained chick peas. Add just enough broth or water to cover and simmer gently for 2 hours, or until meat is thoroughly tender and the stew blended. Taste for seasoning. Serves 6–8.

HAM-LARDED LOIN OF VEAL

> 8–10 strips country ham or Smithfield ham, about 6″–8″ long and ⅜″ thick
>   Medium dry sherry
>   Double loin of veal, boned and tied
>   Ham fat, bacon, or fat pork
>   Salt
> ½ cup currants, soaked in 3 tablespoons sherry

Soak the ham strips in 1 cup sherry for 1 hour and insert them in the veal with a larding needle. If you have a whole ham, cut the fat in thin slices from the top to cover the veal.

If ham fat is not available, cover the top of the roast with bacon rashers or fat pork. Roast on a rack in a 425° oven for 30 minutes. Reduce the heat to 350°, cover with a piece of foil or parchment, and continue roasting, basting occasionally with sherry, until the roast reaches an inner temperature of 160°–165°. Remove the bacon or ham fat and the foil for the last 45 minutes and baste the roast with the pan juices and additional sherry, if desired. Salt to taste.

Remove the roast to a hot platter and allow to stand in a warm place for 10 minutes. Skim excess fat from pan and add currants and additional sherry to taste to the pan juices. Heat thoroughly and serve with the roast as a sauce.

Potatoes, thinly sliced and baked in a shallow dish with broth and butter, like scalloped potatoes, are a perfect accompaniment. Also serve with a purée of carrots dressed with butter and a touch of marjoram or summer savory.

VEAL CALVADOS

> 2½ pounds boned shoulder of veal
>   Salt crystals, cracked pepper, garlic slivers
> 6 ounces larding pork (fatback), frozen
> ½ pound bacon
> ½ cup calvados
> ½ cup water
> ½ cup heavy cream
>   Chopped parsley

Remove all skin and sinew from veal. Season inside with salt, pepper and slivers of garlic inserted into holes made with knife point. Cut larding pork into thin strips and lard meat. Flatten bacon slices with a knife blade. Bard veal with bacon, covering the top with thin overlapping slices. Tie each slice securely with fine butchers' string, then tie roast lengthwise to hold in shape.

Put veal on roasting rack and pour about 2 tablespoons calvados and 2 tablespoons water in the pan. Roast at 350° for 1½ hours, basting every 15–20 minutes with 2–3 tablespoons liquid mixed into the pan juices (reserve 2–3 tablespoons calvados for flaming). Just before veal is done, heat and flame the rest of the calvados and pour it over the veal.

Remove veal and snip off string. Put the pan on low heat and slowly mix into the pan juices ½ cup heavy cream, beating hard all the time. Add chopped parsley. Cut meat in slices, as much as required, arrange in row on serving platter with uncut piece at one end and coat with the gravy. Serves 6.

SADDLE OF VEAL PRINCE ORLOFF

This classic dish is tricky to make, but the effect is impressive if you are giving a large dinner party.

> Saddle of veal, trimmed and tied
> Bacon slices
> Salt, pepper
> 2 or more cups sauce soubise (see Sauces)
> Slices of truffle
> Grated Parmesan cheese

Wrap the saddle of veal with the bacon slices, tying them securely, and place on a rack in a shallow roasting pan. Roast in a 325° oven, basting with the pan juices from time to time, until the veal reaches an internal temperature of 165°–170°. Season with salt and pepper shortly before removing from oven.

Transfer the saddle to a hot platter or board and remove bacon. With a very sharp knife remove both filets by running a knife around the bone. Cut each filet into scallops large enough for individual servings. Brush the bone section of the saddle with sauce soubise. Replace the scallops, brushing each one with sauce soubise and placing a slice of truffle on each. Reassemble carefully so as to make a perfect saddle. Then spread the entire roast with sauce soubise, and sprinkle lightly with grated Parmesan cheese. Place under the broiler or in a very hot oven for a few minutes to glaze. Arrange a row of truffle slices along the center of the roast, and place on a hot platter with a garnish of tiny braised onions and potatoes. Serve with a string bean purée.

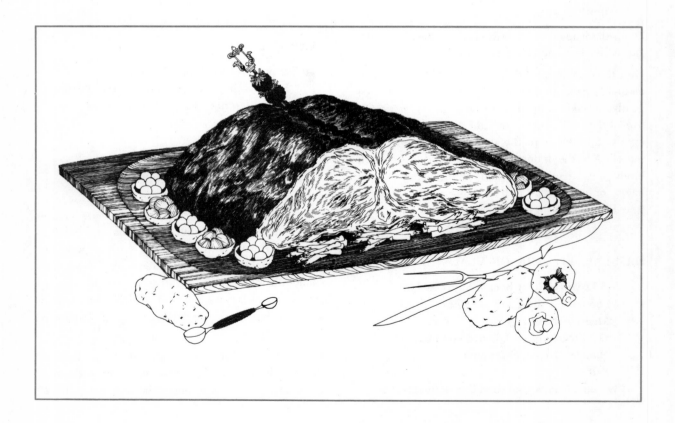

VEAL WITH LEMON

   3-pound rolled veal roast, shoulder or rump
   1 teaspoon salt
   ½ teaspoon white pepper
   ⅛ teaspoon cinnamon
   ⅛ teaspoon nutmeg
   3 tablespoons water
   Grated rind of 1 lemon
   Juice of 3 medium lemons

Remove any fat in which the veal roast may be wrapped, but keep securely tied. Rub veal with salt, pepper, cinnamon and nutmeg. Place in a heavy casserole or kettle which *must* have a tight-fitting lid. Add water, cover, and simmer over lowest possible heat for 1 hour. Add lemon rind and juice. Cover and continue simmering until veal is tender, about 2 hours. Place veal on hot platter. Slice and keep hot. Reduce pan juices to 3/4 cup. Pour over veal slices. Serve with asparagus or artichokes Hollandaise. Delicious hot or cold. Serves 4–6.

Note: Do not be disappointed if the veal does not slice well when hot. When cooking a larger roast, season and spice to taste, and count on 1 tablespoon water and the juice of 1 medium lemon for each pound of meat.

Variation: For a richer sauce, beat 2 egg yolks into 1/3 cup heavy cream. Add to reduced pan liquid and heat through, without boiling. Serve a plain green vegetable.

BRAISED BREAST OF VEAL

   4 tablespoons butter
   1 large onion, chopped
   3 cloves garlic, chopped
   ½ pound ground pork
   ½ pound ground veal
   ½ pound ground ham
   1½ cups bread crumbs
   1½ teaspoons basil
   ¼ teaspoon Tabasco
   ¼ teaspoon nutmeg
   1 teaspoon ground ginger
   4 tablespoons chopped parsley
   Salt to taste
   1 teaspoon freshly ground black pepper

   3 eggs, slightly beaten
   ½ cup sherry
   1 breast of veal cut with a pocket, flat bones
      removed
   4 thick slices tongue, cut into fingers
   Olive oil
   Pepper
   1½ cups white wine

Heat the butter and sauté the onion and garlic until nicely wilted. Combine with the ground meats, the crumbs, seasonings, eggs and sherry. Stuff the pocket in the breast of veal with this mixture, spreading half of it in first. Top this with fingers of tongue and add rest of stuffing. Place foil inside opening and sew or skewer it securely.

Rub the breast of veal with olive oil, salt and pepper. Heat olive oil in a pan and brown the veal well on both sides. When it is nicely colored, add the wine and cover the pan tightly with foil. Place in a 325° oven and cook for 2¾–3 hours, or until tender.

Serve with pan juices, or with tomato sauce, and a plain risotto. Serves 8.

VEAL MEDITERRANEAN

   4–5 pounds boneless rump of veal
   3–4 cloves garlic, cut in slivers
   8–10 anchovy fillets
   6 tablespoons olive oil
   2 medium onions, thinly sliced
   1 carrot, scraped
   1 calf's foot or pig's foot
   1 teaspoon basil
   3–4 sprigs parsley
   1 teaspoon freshly ground black pepper
   1½ cups white wine
   Cooked macaroni

Cut gashes in the meat and insert slivers of garlic alternated with anchovy fillets. No salt should be needed, as the anchovies should provide enough. Heat olive oil and brown the veal rump on all sides. Add the onions, carrot, calf's foot or pig's foot, basil, parsley and pepper. Cook for 5–10 minutes. Add the white wine, cover the pot and reduce the heat. Simmer on top of the stove or in a 300° oven for 1½–2 hours, or until the meat is tender.

Remove the meat to a hot platter. Skim the fat from the pan juices and strain. Cook down for a few minutes and pour over cooked macaroni.

Serve the veal and the sauced macaroni with ratatouille and mustard. Serves 6.

VITELLO TONNATO

Prepare the rump of veal as above and let the meat cool in the broth and seasonings. The liquid should jell. When cool, skim off the fat and combine the jellied broth with a 7-ounce can of good tuna in olive oil. Blend in an electric blender. Add finely chopped parsley, a touch of basil and capers to the sauce. Pour it over the veal and cover. Place in the refrigerator for a day before serving.

To serve, slice the meat and arrange it on a platter. Top with the sauce and decorate with anchovy fillets, additional capers, and, if you wish, homemade olive-oil mayonnaise. Serve with a salad of cold rice, finely cubed cucumber, diced tomato and green peppers, dressed with a good vinaigrette sauce. Serves 8–10.

Variation: As soon as you blend the jellied broth and tuna, slice the veal and arrange it on a platter. Top with the sauce and garnish with anchovy, capers and chopped parsley. Cover with foil and chill for 2 hours. Serve with olive-oil mayonnaise that has been lightly flavored with tuna.

TYROLEAN VEAL

> 2 pounds shoulder of veal, boned
> 2 ounces salt butter
> ½ cup brandy
> ½ cup white seedless raisins
> ½ cup finely chopped shallots
> 3 level tablespoons flour
> 1 cup coffee
> ½ cup strong chicken stock
>   Freshly cracked white pepper
> ¾ cup sour cream
> 2 teaspoons chopped fresh tarragon
> 3 small baked Idaho potatoes
> 3 egg yolks

> 3 ounces sweet butter
>   Salt, cayenne pepper
> ½ cup finely chopped yellow onion

Remove skin and sinew from veal. Cut into large squares and brown in pan, a few pieces at a time, in 1 ounce hot salt butter. Heat ¼ cup brandy, ignite, and pour over meat. Soak raisins in the rest of the brandy and, when plump, drain. Remove meat, add rest of salt butter and shallots and sauté gently for 2–3 minutes. Stir in, off the heat, the flour, brandy from raisins, coffee and chicken stock. Return to heat and stir until it comes to a boil. Season with white pepper. Simmer for a few minutes. Add the veal and raisins, cover with waxed paper and lid and cook in a 375° oven until veal is tender, about 1 hour. Remove meat and pile in the center of a round, shallow earthenware dish. Boil sauce down to about 1/3 and then carefully mix in the sour cream and chopped tarragon. Pour this over veal.

Cut potatoes carefully in half lengthwise, scoop out pulp. Rub through a fine strainer and beat in the egg yolks, sweet butter, salt and cayenne pepper to taste. Lastly mix in the finely chopped raw yellow onion. Carefully fill the potato skins. Smooth over with spatula and score top with a fork. Put under broiler for a minute or two to brown. Arrange the potatoes on a dish around the veal. Serves 6.

VEAL GOULASH

> 2 pounds veal cutlet, cut from leg
> 3 ounces salt butter
> ¼ cup cognac
> 2 cups sliced onion, carrot, celery
> 2 tablespoons Hungarian paprika
> 3 tablespoons flour
> 1 level teaspoon meat glaze
> 1 tablespoon tomato paste
> 2 cups veal or chicken stock
>   Cayenne pepper to taste
> 1 cup heavy sour cream
> ½ cup finely diced green pepper
>   Garnish: sour cream, paprika, shredded
>   pimiento

Trim skin, bone and sinew from veal and cut into large pieces 3″ long. Heat 1 ounce butter in a heavy pan and stir until on the point of browning. Brown meat well on all sides, two or three pieces at a time. Remove. Flame pan with cognac to lift the glaze. Add rest of butter, dissolve. Add onion, carrot, celery, cover and cook slowly 4 or 5 minutes. Add paprika, cook slowly 5 minutes. Add flour, cook slowly 5 minutes. Stir in meat glaze, tomato paste until smooth. Add stock. Stir over low heat until it comes to a boil. Season with cayenne. Simmer 5 minutes. Strain.

Slowly and carefully beat in the sour cream, putting a small amount at a time in the center and amalgamating with the sauce with a wire whisk. Do not add more cream until the first amount is blended in. Replace veal. Cover pan with waxed paper and lid and cook gently until veal is tender, about 20–25 minutes.

Meanwhile, blanch and drain the diced green pepper. Add green pepper to the sauce and serve from the casserole. Garnish each serving with 1 tablespoon sour cream, a sprinkling of paprika and shredded pimiento. Serve with buttered noodles, cooked in boiling salted water with 1 tablespoon oil added to the water to keep them from sticking. Serves 4.

RUSSIAN VEAL AND CHERRY CASSEROLE

This dish is best made with the dark, sour, and very flavorful Morello cherries which can be found in the better markets. Ordinary red sour cherries will do, although they are not quite as flavorful. Canned cherries must be thoroughly drained.

    ¼ cup butter
    2 pounds boneless veal, cut into 1″ cubes
    2 tablespoons flour
    4 spring onions, white and green parts, chopped
    2½ cups sour cherries, stoned
    ⅓ cup golden raisins
    ⅔ cup chicken bouillon or veal stock
    ½ cup port
    1 teaspoon ground cardamom
    1 teaspoon salt
      Freshly ground pepper to taste
    2–3 cups cooked, drained flageolet beans or
      small kidney beans

Heat the butter in a 3-quart casserole and brown the veal on all sides over high heat. Turn down the heat as low as possible and sprinkle meat with the flour. Stir until the meat is evenly coated. Add the onion, cherries, raisins, chicken bouillon, port, cardamom, salt, and pepper and mix thoroughly. Simmer covered, stirring occasionally, for 1–1½ hours, or until the veal is tender. Check for moisture; if necessary, add a little more hot chicken broth. (Different types of cherries have different moisture content which affects the thickness of the sauce.) Add the beans 10 minutes before serving time, and heat through. Serve with a hearts-of-palm salad. Serves 4–6.

Note:
1. If the cherries used make the casserole taste too sour, a little sugar may be added to taste at the end of the cooking time.
2. Morello cherries will give the casserole a rich, red color, but sour cherries may make it look too pale. A little beet juice or red food coloring may be added to deepen the color.

BLANQUETTE DE VEAU

    2 pounds veal, cut in cubes
    1½ tablespoons butter
    2 small white onions, each stuck with 1 clove
    1 or 2 carrots, cubed
    1 bay leaf
    ½ cup dry vermouth
    1½ cups water
    1 teaspoon salt
      Small thin slice of lemon peel
    ¼ pound mushroom caps, sautéed in butter
    2 egg yolks
    ½ cup heavy cream

Sauté the veal in the butter until lightly browned. Add the onions, carrots, bay leaf, vermouth, water, salt and lemon peel. Simmer covered 1 hour or until veal is very tender. Add the mushroom caps, which have been cooked separately (they retain distinctive mushroom flavor better this way). Beat egg yolks and cream. Add a little hot liquid from veal to the mixture, stirring constantly to prevent curdling. Add to liquid in the pan, stirring, and simmer until thickened, about 5 minutes, again taking care that the sauce does not boil, and that the egg yolks don't curdle. Serves 6.

HOW TO SLICE YOUR OWN
VEAL SCALLOPS

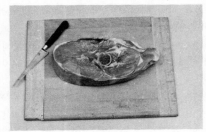

Buy a three-pound piece of veal loin which can be sliced into large and small scallops. Residue can be used for stews.

Cut out the largest lean section of meat, and trim off fat. (Small lean section next to it makes medium-size scallops.)

Press meat down firmly with flat of hand. Slice meat lengthwise with regular sawing motion as thinly as possible.

Place slices (you should get eight from this piece) between two sheets of waxed paper and pound thin with cleaver.

VEAL MARENGO

    ½ cup olive oil
    2 pounds lean boned veal, cubed
    1 cup sliced mushrooms
    12 small white onions, peeled
    1½ tablespoons flour
    2–3 medium tomatoes, peeled, seeded and
        chopped
    1 clove garlic, crushed
    ⅛ teaspoon thyme
    1 tablespoon minced parsley
    1½ cups dry white wine or dry sherry
    1½ cups hot water
    2 teaspoons salt
        Freshly ground black pepper to taste
    2 slices bread, each cut in 4 triangles

Heat the olive oil in a deep heavy pot, add the veal and brown quickly on all sides. Remove. Add mushrooms to oil, brown quickly, remove and set aside in a warm place. Add onions and pour off all but 2 tablespoons oil (save reserved oil to fry the bread triangles). Add the flour to the oil and stir until lightly browned. Add the tomatoes, garlic and herbs and cook about 1 minute. Add the wine, water, salt and pepper and replace the veal and onions in the pot. Cover and cook over very low heat until meat is very tender, 1½–2 hours. Meantime, fry the bread triangles in the reserved olive oil until lightly browned. Keep warm. When meat is tender, spoon into serving dish, arrange fried bread around the edges and mushrooms over the top. Serve with buttered noodles. Serves 6.

VEAL CURRY

    2½ pounds veal shoulder, cut into 2″ cubes
    1 onion stuck with 2 cloves
    ¼ teaspoon thyme
        Salt
    1 dozen medium mushrooms
    4 tablespoons butter
    2 medium onions
    2 teaspoons curry powder
    4 tablespoons flour
    2 egg yolks
    ½ cup heavy cream

Put the veal cubes in a kettle with the onion stuck with cloves, the thyme, salt to taste and enough boiling water to cover. Cover the kettle and simmer gently for 1½ hours, or until tender.

Meanwhile slice the mushrooms and cook them gently in 2 tablespoons of hot butter. Peel the onions and slice them very thin. Cook them in 2 tablespoons hot butter until they are almost a mush—they should not brown, but cook down to a purée. Combine the onions and mushrooms and their juices and sprinkle with the curry powder. Blend well and add the flour. If too thick, add more butter. Cook the mixture very gently for about 4 minutes.

Remove the cooked veal from the broth and keep the meat hot. Measure the broth; you will need about 2 cups. Strain the broth and add it slowly to the onion, mushroom and curry mixture. Cook, stirring constantly, until the sauce is well blended and thickened. Taste for seasoning.

Beat the egg yolks and mix with the heavy cream. Take a little of the hot sauce and stir it into the egg yolk mixture. Then add this slowly to the curry sauce, stirring and blending until smooth and thickened. Do not let the mixture boil or the eggs will curdle. Pour curry sauce over the meat.

Serve with steamed rice, a good chutney, chopped green onions, chopped toasted and salted almonds and the following egg-curry condiment: Prick 6 hard-cooked eggs with a fork and sauté them whole in 4 tablespoons butter. Add 2 tablespoons curry powder and blend well. Serves 6.

ESTOUFFADE DE VEAU

  3 pounds shin of veal, cut into 1½"–2" cubes
  Flour seasoned with salt and freshly ground black pepper
  6 tablespoons butter
  2 pounds onions, thinly sliced
  3 cloves garlic
  2 teaspoons tarragon
  Red wine
  Beurre manié (optional)

Dust the veal cubes lightly with seasoned flour. Melt the butter in a large kettle and cook the onion slices until just lightly colored, but not browned. Push the onions to one side and add the veal cubes. Brown them well on all sides. Add the garlic and tarragon and just enough red wine to cover. Put a lid on the kettle and simmer gently on top of the stove, or cook in a 350° oven for 1–1½ hours, or until the veal is tender. If you wish, you may thicken the sauce with a little beurre manié (small balls of butter and flour). Taste for seasoning.

Arrange the veal on a hot platter, cover it with the sauce and garnish with chopped parsley.

Serve with buttered noodles. Serves 6–8.

Variation: During the last 15 minutes of cooking, add 1½ cups of small green Spanish olives, black Italian olives, or red Greek olives.

VEAL SCALLOPS OPORTO

  8 large or 12 medium veal scallops, pounded thin
  Flour
  6 tablespoons butter
  3 tablespoons olive oil
  ⅔ cup port
  Salt, pepper
  ½ cup heavy cream
  Beurre manié

Flour scallops lightly and sauté in butter and olive oil, turning to brown evenly. When brown and tender, add port and cook gently for 2 minutes. Season to taste. Remove meat to a hot platter and add cream to pan. Stir to scrape up all the brown bits and thicken lightly with a little beurre manié. Taste for seasoning and pour over scallops. Serve with home-made noodles dressed with buttered crumbs. Serves 4.

ESCALOPES OF VEAL WITH SHERRY

  4 tablespoons flour
  1 teaspoon salt
  12 scallops of veal
  6 tablespoons Spanish olive oil
  2 large onions, cut in thin strips
  4 tablespoons butter
  ¾ cup and 1 tablespoon oloroso sherry
  1 cup clear chicken broth
  ⅛ teaspoon thyme

1 crushed bay leaf
1 teaspoon minced fresh parsley
Salt, pepper to taste
Toasted slivered almonds for garnish

Pound flour and salt into veal. Sauté in olive oil until golden on each side. Separately sauté the onions in the butter over low heat until tender, but not brown. Add veal to onions with ¾ cup sherry, chicken broth and herbs. Correct seasoning. Cover the pan and simmer gently 45 minutes. Serve garnished with toasted slivered almonds. Just before serving, add remaining tablespoon of oloroso sherry. Serves 6.

MME. FRAIZE'S ALOUETTES SANS TÊTES

⅔ pound ground ham, ground with 3 cloves
  garlic
3 tablespoons chopped parsley
1 teaspoon rosemary
  Sprinkle of nutmeg
  Salt, pepper
18 scallops of veal, pounded and trimmed
  Olive oil
6–7 slices bacon, cut in small pieces
  Bay leaf
⅔ cup white wine

Combine the ham, parsley, rosemary, nutmeg and salt and pepper to taste. Stuff the veal scallops with the mixture, roll up and tie firmly. Brown them in oil. Add the bacon and let it cook down. Add the bay leaf and white wine. Cook over low heat until tender, turning the rolls 2 or 3 times. You may cover the pan for part of the cooking time. The sauce may be thickened, but it is best when served over the rolls without thickening. Rice and a gratin of eggplant are perfect accompaniments. Serves 6.

VEAL ROLLS FLAMBÉ

4 thin slices veal, about 5"–6" long
4 thin slices prosciutto or Smithfield ham
  Freshly ground pepper, salt
10 tablespoons butter
¼ cup marsala
¼ cup vodka

½ pound mushrooms, sliced
1½ tablespoons flour
⅓ cup heavy cream
2 tablespoons chopped parsley
2 tablespoons cognac

Season veal and ham slices with a grind of fresh pepper. Roll veal and ham together, tie securely and slip on steel or wood skewers. Brush with a little butter. Sauté quickly in 6 tablespoons butter, turning several times. Flambé with 1/3 cup of the marsala and vodka, mixed and heated. Melt remaining butter and sauté the mushrooms, seasoned with salt and pepper, for 3 minutes. Sprinkle with the flour, blending well. Stir in cream and remaining marsala and vodka and cook until thickened. Add parsley and cognac. Remove veal rolls to a hot platter and pour mushrooms and sauce over them. Serve with spinach purée and polenta. Serves 4.

ST. GALL ABBEY MEAT PIE

1 recipe flaky pie crust for a double-crust 9" pie
8 cups soft bread crumbs
½ cup flour
2 large onions, minced
  Grated rind of 2 lemons
2 teaspoons salt
½ teaspoon pepper
⅛ teaspoon nutmeg
2 pounds veal, free of bones and gristle, cut
  into 1" cubes
1⅓ cups white wine
1 egg yolk, well beaten

Roll out ½ of the pie crust dough to fit the bottom of a well-greased spring-form pan. Blend bread crumbs with flour, onions, lemon rind, salt, pepper and nutmeg. Divide into four portions. Divide cubed veal into 3 portions. Starting and ending with the bread-crumb mixture, layer the crumbs and the meat in the pastry-lined spring-form pan. Press each layer down. Pour wine on top. Roll out remaining pie crust to fit the top of the pan. Fit crust on top of meat mixture and brush with beaten egg yolk. Place spring form on a shallow baking pan to catch spillage. Bake in a 300° oven for 3 hours. Serve the meat pie hot, with a salad. Serves 6–8.

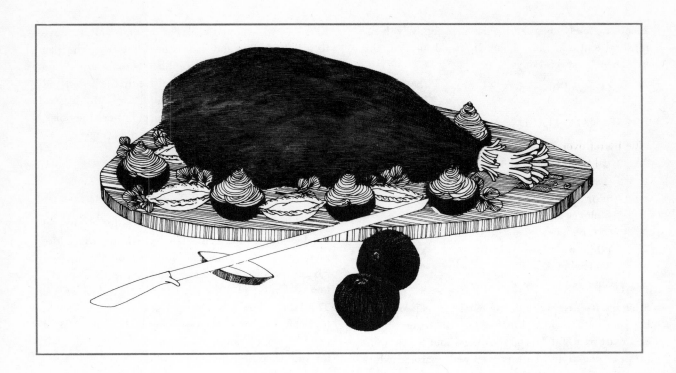

VEAL, ZURICH STYLE

    1½ pounds veal cutlet or other boneless veal
    6 tablespoons butter
    3 tablespoons minced shallots
    3 tablespoons cognac
    4 tablespoons flour
    ½ teaspoon salt
    ¼ teaspoon white pepper
    1⅓ cups dry white wine, heated, or hot bouillon
    1 cup heavy cream

Trim meat of all fat. Cut against the grain into 1″-thick pieces. Heat butter in a large skillet. Add shallots and cook 2 minutes. Add veal. Cook for 1 minute. Flame with cognac. When flame has died down, sprinkle flour over veal. Stir in salt and pepper. Add hot white wine or bouillon and cream. Cook over low heat, stirring constantly, until mixture comes to a boil and thickens. Serve with noodles or mashed potatoes and a green salad. Serves 4–6.

<u>Note</u>: If hot bouillon is used rather than wine, add 3 tablespoons of lemon juice to meat, since the dish should have a piquant taste.

ROAST FRESH HAM

The pork leg cut or fresh ham is quite versatile. It may be cooked either boned or with the bone in. Because of its size, it takes time to cook perfectly in an oven set for 325° or 300°. The fat covering eliminates the need for basting, but an occasional basting with red or white wine or broth does help the flavor and keeps a delicious moisture in the meat.

Rub the roast well with sage, freshly ground black pepper, and touch of garlic. Place on a rack in a shallow pan. Roast to an internal temperature of 175°. Remove from the oven, and allow to stand for 15 minutes in a warm place before carving. Serve with sautéed apple slices and Burgundian Mustard.

BURGUNDIAN MUSTARD

    2 tablespoons finely chopped sour pickle
    1 tablespoon finely chopped sweet pickle
    1 cup Dijon mustard
    1 teaspoon cognac

Blend the finely chopped pickles thoroughly with the mustard and add the cognac. If sealed in a jar, this will keep for several days.

FRESH HAM, ITALIAN FASHION

> 1 fresh ham, boned
> 3–4 sprigs Italian parsley
> 3–4 stalks fresh basil or 1½ teaspoons dried basil
> 2–3 cloves garlic
> Salt, pepper
> White wine
> Beurre manié
> Chopped parsley and chives

Stuff the ham cavity with the parsley, basil, and garlic. Rub with pepper. Tie securely. Place on a rack and roast in a 300° oven, allowing about 25–30 minutes per pound and basting well with warmed white wine. Salt about midway in the cooking time.

When the roast has reached an inner temperature of 175°, remove to a hot platter. Skim the excess fat from the pan juices and combine with enough additional white wine to make 2 cups. Reduce this slightly, and thicken with beurre manié (small balls of flour and butter kneaded together). Add chopped parsley and chives to the sauce. Serve the pork with this sauce, potatoes puréed with cream and butter, and broccoli sprinkled with Parmesan cheese.

FRESH HAM, NORMAN FASHION

> 1 fresh ham, about 8–9 pounds, boned
> Nutmeg, white pepper, ginger
> Sweet cider
> Salt
> ⅓ cup calvados or applejack
> 1 cup heavy cream
> 4 egg yolks

Rub the roast well with nutmeg, pepper, and a touch of ginger. Place on a rack in a shallow roasting pan, and roast in a 325° oven, allowing 25 minutes per pound, until meat thermometer registers 175°. Baste often during cooking with sweet cider, slightly warmed. Salt 15 minutes before removing from oven.

Flambé with warmed calvados or applejack. Remove to a hot platter, and skim excess fat from the pan juices. Heat juices and combine with heavy cream mixed with egg yolks. Stir until nicely thickened and smooth, but do not allow to boil. Correct the seasoning. Serve the pork with this sauce, buttered noodles, sautéed oyster plant, and candied apple rings.

ROAST LOIN OF PORK

Probably the loin of pork is the most popular cut, and the best for eating cold. This constitutes the entire rack and is usually sold in one piece or divided into rib end or loin end. You may cut the ends from the loin and roast just the rib chops or the loin chops. The bones should be cracked and the roast tied so that the carving process is easy. A loin of about 4 pounds will be ample for 4 persons, with some left for another meal.

Rub loin well with freshly ground black pepper and a little thyme, and place on a rack in a shallow pan. Roast in a 325° oven, allowing about 25 minutes per pound, until the interior temperature registers about 170°. Salt well, remove from oven, and let it rest for 10 minutes. Skim off excess fat from the roasting pan, add a cup of hot stock or broth, and let the mixture come to the boil. Simmer for a few minutes. Serve with the pork. With this have boiled potatoes whipped with butter and heavy cream and seasoned with salt and pepper and sautéed apple slices.

Variations:

1. Insert 2 or 3 garlic cloves in the pork and rub with thyme, freshly ground pepper, and salt. Roast as directed. About halfway through the roasting process, baste well with red wine. Continue basting with the pan juices and additional red wine until the roast is cooked. Serve with sautéed onions and tiny new potatoes.

2. Rub the loin with garlic. Cut a deep incision lengthwise along the top of the roast, parallel to the bone. Insert slices of truffle, cut about ¼" thick, letting them overlap. Tie the roast very tightly and sprinkle lightly with freshly ground black pepper and a bit of nutmeg. Place on a rack and roast in a 325° oven for approximately 25 minutes per pound, or until the roast registers

170°. Baste several times during cooking with Madeira or sherry. Half an hour before it is done add ½ cup stock or broth to the pan and baste again with wine. Salt the roast to taste. Remove to a hot platter and let it rest 10 minutes before carving. Heat the pan juices, after removing fat, and add 1 tablespoon finely chopped truffle. Serve with a purée of chestnuts and braised endive.

DRUNKEN PORK

    6–8 pound loin of pork roast
      Salt, white pepper, nutmeg, cloves
    ¾ cup applejack or calvados
    6 large potatoes, peeled and quartered
    6 large cooking apples, peeled and thinly sliced
      Sugar

Rub pork well with salt, ground white pepper, nutmeg and a touch of ground cloves. Place in a long dish and add enough applejack or calvados to cover the bottom. Turn pork several times and let marinate for 3 hours. Drain, reserving marinade.

Place pork on a rack in a baking dish and roast at 325° for 2 hours. Remove from oven. Pour all fat into another flat baking pan. Return pork to oven for another 30 minutes.

Meanwhile, boil potatoes in salted water for 5 minutes. Drain well and arrange in fat, turning once or twice. Salt and pepper to taste. Roast for 45 minutes in same oven with pork.

Remove pork from oven and spoon off excess fat.

Add sliced apples and sprinkle with sugar. Flame with the marinade. Return to oven for 30 minutes or until pork has reached an interior temperature of 170° on a meat thermometer and apples are soft and potatoes brown and tender. Coleslaw is good with this dish. Serves 6.

COLD BARBECUED LOIN OF PORK

    5–6-pound loin of pork roast
      Dry mustard, thyme
    ½ cup and 2 tablespoons sherry
    ½ cup and 1 tablespoon Japanese soy sauce
    3 cloves garlic, finely chopped
    2 tablespoons grated fresh ginger, or 6 pieces of
      candied ginger cut into slivers
    8-ounce jar apple or currant jelly

Have the roast boned and tied. Rub with dry mustard and thyme. Make a marinade of the ½ cup sherry, ½ cup soy sauce, garlic and ginger and pour over the pork. Marinate for about 2 hours, turning several times as it soaks. You may let it stand all night in the refrigerator and roast it early in the morning.

To cook, remove from the marinade and arrange a meat thermometer in the thickest part of the roast. Cook at 325°, allowing about 25 minutes per pound. Baste with the marinade. When the thermometer reads 175°, the pork is done.

Melt the jelly in a heavy pan over a medium flame and when it is bubbly, add the 1 tablespoon soy and 2 tablespoons sherry. Let it cook down for a minute or two, stirring constantly. Spoon over the pork and cool in a chilly room. Do not refrigerate unless the day is exceptionally hot.

Garnish with sliced tomatoes, thinly sliced onions and sliced cucumbers. Serve with a bowl of Horseradish Applesauce.

CROWN ROAST OF PORK
WITH SAUERKRAUT

The crown is sometimes made with two rib ends of the loin and sometimes with the entire loin, which makes a most spectacular roast. Wrap the ends of the rib bones with foil to keep them from charring. Rub the meat with freshly ground black pepper, a bit of sage and rosemary, or just sage and garlic. Make a heavy cushion of foil to fill in the center of the crown while roasting. Place on a rack and roast in a 325° oven, allowing about 25 minutes per pound. Baste from time to time with white wine.

While the roast is cooking, wash 3 pounds sauerkraut, and place it in a kettle lined with strips of bacon. Add 1 teaspoon freshly ground black pepper, a few juniper berries, and enough white wine to barely cover the sauerkraut. Bring to a boil and simmer. A half-hour before the roast is done add a Polish or a garlic sausage to the sauerkraut and let them cook together. When the roast has reached an internal temperature of 170°, remove it to a hot platter. Discard the foil and replace with paper frills.

Remove the foil from the center, fill the center with the sauerkraut, and garnish with slices of the sausage. Serve with boiled parsley potatoes and a salad of Bibb lettuce and grated beets.

CHOUCROUTE ALSACIENNE

    3 pounds sauerkraut
    ½ teaspoon caraway seeds
    12 peppercorns, or ¼ teaspoon coarsely cracked
       pepper
    2 carrots, scraped and cubed
    1 pound smoked pork butt (boneless), trimmed
       and thickly sliced
    4–6 pork shoulder chops, bone removed
    1 cup Rhine or Alsatian wine
    1 teaspoon salt, or to taste
    ½ pound knackwurst

Combine the sauerkraut, caraway seeds, peppercorns or cracked pepper and carrots. Place in the bottom of a large kettle. Arrange the pork butt slices and the shoulder chops over the top of the sauerkraut. Add the wine and salt, cover tightly and cook over very low heat 2–3 hours. This dish tastes best if cooked a day ahead, as it should be prepared at least 6 hours before serving time and allowed to stand. Reheat, adding knackwurst 20 minutes before serving. Serve with boiled or mashed potatoes. Serves 8.

PORK AND APPLE PIE

    4 pounds (approx.) lean pork, finely chopped
    4–5 apples, peeled, cored and thinly sliced
    2 medium onions, finely chopped
    1 teaspoon sage
      Salt, pepper
      Stock or bouillon
      Mashed potatoes
      Melted butter

Arrange alternate layers of pork and apples in a deep baking dish. Sprinkle each layer with a little chopped onion, sage and salt and pepper to taste. Moisten with a little stock or bouillon. Cover with a thick mashed-potato crust and brush well with melted butter. Bake in a 325° oven for 1½–2 hours, or until the pork is thoroughly cooked. Serve with crisp bread, pickled walnuts and beer. Serves 6–8.

RAGOÛT OF PORK WITH CHESTNUTS

    3 tablespoons pork fat, finely chopped
    3 pounds lean pork shoulder, cut into 1½″ cubes
      Flour seasoned with 1 teaspoon salt and
       1 teaspoon freshly ground black pepper
    4 medium onions, thinly sliced
    3 cloves garlic, chopped
      Red wine
    2 cups whole chestnuts (available in cans,
       packed in brine), drained
    1 teaspoon sage
      Chopped parsley

Put the chopped pork fat in a large skillet or Dutch oven and let it cook over medium heat until well melted down and crisp.

Dust the pork cubes in the seasoned flour and brown them quickly in the pork fat, turning them to color evenly on all sides. Add the sliced onions and chopped garlic and cook with the pork fat and meat cubes for a minute or two. Pour over just enough red wine to cover and bring to a boil. Lower the heat, cover the pan and simmer gently or cook in a 350° oven for 1½–2 hours.

Uncover. Add the drained chestnuts and sage and more wine if needed. Cover again and continue cooking for another 30–35 minutes, or until the pork is thoroughly tender and the chestnuts have become well blended into the sauce.

Arrange the pork and sauce in a serving dish, surround with boiled potatoes and sautéed apple rings; garnish with chopped parsley. Serves 6.

ARTICHOKE AND PORK CHOP CASSEROLE

>   2 large or 4 medium artichokes
>   Juice of 2 lemons
>   ¼ cup olive oil
>   6 lean pork chops
>   1 teaspoon salt
>   ½ teaspoon pepper
>   2 cloves garlic, minced
>   ½–1 teaspoon dried basil, or sage, or rosemary
>   1-pound, 4-ounce can Italian-style tomatoes

Prepare the artichokes as follows: slice off the stems with a sharp paring knife, leaving no more than ¼". Tear off and throw away the large outer leaves. Place each artichoke on its side and cut off the top, leaving about ½"–¾" white leaf at base; the amount depends on the size of the artichoke. Cut the artichoke lengthwise into quarters, like an apple. Drop immediately into 1 quart water combined with the lemon juice to prevent discoloring. Remove one quarter at a time. Cut out the choke, and slice, cutting small artichokes into eighths, large ones into more pieces. Replace pieces in the lemon water until needed.

Heat the olive oil in a deep skillet or shallow casserole and brown the pork chops on both sides. Pour off excess oil. Drain the artichoke slices and arrange around the pork chops. Sprinkle with salt, pepper, garlic, and desired herb. Cover with the tomatoes. Simmer, covered, for 1 hour, or until meat and artichokes are tender. If sauce looks too thin, simmer uncovered until sufficiently reduced. Serve with a salad of Belgian endive. Serves 4–6.

GENERAL INSTRUCTIONS FOR COOKING HAMS

Aged Hams

These are hams that have been cured, smoked and hung for one to seven years. As they age, they dry out and some mold forms. Do not expect a fine aged ham to be a beautiful sight before it is cooked. It needs a good scrubbing and long soaking.

First, scrub the ham thoroughly with a stiff brush. Use plenty of soap and hot water. Yes, soap. But of course you will avoid the perfumed detergents. Use plain, unperfumed household soap. Rinse the ham well and put it in a kettle with water to cover. Soak it overnight, or longer if necessary.

To cook, drain the ham and cover it with fresh water. Bring to a boil, lower the heat and cook gently. The water should not be actually boiling, but there should be some rippling on the surface. There are two methods for timing the boiling process. You may weigh the ham after it has soaked and cook it for 20 minutes per pound. Remove it from the liquid and let it cool. Or, you may simply cook it for 2½ hours and let it cool in the liquid.

After the ham has cooled, remove the skin and place the ham in a roasting pan, fat side up. Add your favorite glaze and bake in a 300° oven until well-glazed and heated through. This will take about 45 minutes to 1 hour.

A fine-flavored ham should not be drowned with too much spice and sweet. Try rubbing the ham with a little brown sugar or honey mixed with dry mustard and baste it during the baking with Madeira, sherry, rum or cognac. Or soak in Jamaica rum, rub lightly with brown sugar and mustard and baste during the baking with Jamaica rum.

Country Hams

Regional hams are produced by small smokehouses here and there across the country. The hams are usually heavily smoked and rich. Some must be soaked and boiled; others are partly cooked; some are ready-to-eat. Cooking instructions come with ham.

Tenderized and Ready-to-Eat Hams

Producers of tenderized hams state that they are ready-to-eat, but they are much tastier if they are baked and basted. Some of these hams are quite wet. If the ham seems too damp, pierce it with a fork several times as it bakes to release the excess liquid. Bake at 300° for 10 minutes per pound. Then take the ham from the oven and cut off the rind. Add your glaze and continue baking for another 10–15 minutes.

Basting these hams with sherry, Madeira or cider while they are baking gives them a fine flavor.

SUGGESTIONS FOR GLAZES

Ham with pickled peach glaze

Rub the ham with a little mustard and baste as it bakes with the juice from a large can of pickled peaches mixed with the pan juices. Remove the ham to a platter. Heat the peaches in the broiler. Skim the fat from the pan juices and add 2/3 cup of seedless raisins. Surround the ham with the pickled peaches and serve the sauce separately.

Ham with champagne glaze

Rub the ham with a little brown sugar and mustard and baste it with champagne as it bakes. Remove the ham to a platter. Skim the fat from the pan juices and cook the juices down for a few minutes. Serve this sauce separately.

Ham with paprika crust

Bake the ham plain. About 20 minutes before it is done, remove it from the oven. Mix 1 tablespoon of mustard, 2 tablespoons of paprika and 1–1½ cups of fine dry bread crumbs with enough fat from the pan to bind. Spread this paste over the top of the ham and finish cooking.

Cold ham with apricot glaze

Rub the fat with a little mustard and bake the ham plain. Remove it from the oven and arrange on a platter. Melt 1 pint of apricot jam and put it through a fine sieve. Cook down the sieved jam and add 2 tablespoons of cognac. Cool slightly and spread as a glaze over the cool ham.

Variation: Substitute grape jelly for apricot.

STUFFED HAM

> 12–14 pound ham
> 2 cups finely chopped pecans
> 1 cup fine toasted bread crumbs
> 1 cup finely chopped raisins
> ¼ cup chopped candied pineapple
> ¼ cup chopped orange peel
> ½ cup honey

> 1 teaspoon mixed ground spices: clove, ginger, cinnamon, nutmeg
> 1 cup cognac
> Cider or ginger ale
> Granulated sugar

Boil the ham and then bone it down to the shank, leaving the shank bone in. If you use a ready-to-eat ham, ask your butcher to bone it for you.

If you are using an aged ham, soak, scrub and boil. Then bone the ham down to the shank.

Combine the nuts, crumbs, fruits, honey, spices and enough cognac to moisten—about 2/3 cup. Stuff the ham with this mixture and tie it securely. Wrap the ham in foil and place it in a roasting pan with enough cider or ginger ale to cover the bottom of the pan. Bake in a 350° oven for 2½ hours. Take the ham from the oven and remove the foil. Sprinkle lightly with granulated sugar. Raise the oven temperature to 500° and return the ham to glaze.

Remove the ham from the oven and arrange it on a flameproof platter. Blaze with 1/3 cup of warm cognac. Let the ham cool, but do not chill it.

Serve with hot corn bread and a selection of salads. With this stuffed ham you may offer pickled peaches, spiced crab apples and old-fashioned relishes.

COUNTRY HAM IN CRUST

> Whole country ham
> 1 carrot
> 1 onion stuck with 2 cloves
> 2 bay leaves
> 1 cup wine vinegar
> Pastry—double the amount needed for a 2-crust pie
> Brown sugar
> Freshly ground black pepper
> Ground clove
> Ground cinnamon
> Dry mustard or Dijon mustard
> Fine dry bread crumbs
> 1 egg yolk
> ½ cup Madeira

Soak and scrub the ham. When ready to boil, cover the ham with fresh cold water and add the carrot,

HOW TO PREPARE HAM IN CRUST

Sprinkle seasonings and bread crumbs on surface of cooked ham; press in with a spatula.

Roll out pastry large enough to envelop ham, and drape over rolling pin. Unroll it over ham.

Brush top of pastry with beaten egg so decoration will stick and crust glaze while baking.

Cut rounds of excess pastry; shape into petals by pinching bottom with thumb and finger.

Decorate ham with pastry flowers, leaves, stalk (thin pieces of rolled pastry). Brush with egg.

onion stuck with cloves, bay leaves and wine vinegar. Follow directions for boiling aged ham.

While the ham is cooking, prepare a pastry dough. Regular pie pastry is excellent, or you may use a puff pastry for a truly elegant crust. Put the pastry in the refrigerator to chill.

When the ham is cooked and cooled, remove the skin and trim off all excess fat. Rub the surface with brown sugar, black pepper, a little ground clove and cinnamon, and sprinkle with dry mustard or spread with Dijon. Sprinkle dry bread crumbs over all and press them in well.

Roll out the crust until it is large enough to cover top and sides of the ham, reserving a few snippets for decorations. From the snippets of dough, cut designs: leaves, flowers, or whatever appeals to you. Cut a hole in the top center of the dough. Arrange the dough designs on the top of the ham, gluing them to the crust with a little cold water.

Beat the egg yolk with a little water and brush pastry lightly. Bake the ham in a 300° oven for 1¼–1½ hours. If necessary, raise the heat a little toward the end of the baking to brown the crust well. Remove the ham from the oven and place it on a platter. Pour Madeira into the hole in the top of the crust.

Serve with a Madeira sauce (see recipe for Jambon Braisé au Madère) and chopped spinach blended with sautéed mushrooms.

JAMBON BRAISÉ AU MADÈRE

**12–14 pound ham (ready-to-eat, country ham or
   aged ham that has previously been boiled)**
2 tablespoons granulated sugar
2 tablespoons prepared mustard (Dijon)
2¼ cups Madeira
1½ cups brown sauce or canned beef gravy
2 truffles, finely chopped

Skin the ham and rub the fat with the sugar and mustard. Place the ham in a large roasting pan and over it pour 2 cups of Madeira. Cover with a lid or foil and bake in a 350° oven. Allow 10 minutes per pound for a ready-to-eat ham. If you are using a previously boiled ham, bake it no more than 1½ hours. Combine ¼ cup of liquid from the pan in which the ham was baked with remaining Madeira and the brown sauce. Bring to a boil, lower the heat and simmer for 4 minutes. Add the truffles and simmer another minute or so.

Serve the ham with the Madeira sauce and thin slices of sautéed polenta.

Variations: Instead of Madeira, use a rich, rather sweet sherry, port, Jamaica rum or cognac.

HAM SLICES ARTOISE

    1 pound mushrooms
    6 tablespoons butter
    2 ham slices, 2″ thick
    ⅔ cup purée of foie gras or good liver pâté
    1 cup Madeira

Slice the mushrooms and sauté them in the butter. Arrange the ham slices in a baking dish and spread them with the pâté. Top with some of the mushrooms and surround with the rest. Add ¾ cup of Madeira to the pan and place in a 350° oven. Bake for 10 minutes and then pour the rest of the Madeira over the ham. Bake another 10 minutes and baste. Bake 10 more minutes and test for doneness. If not yet done, cook 5–8 minutes more.

Serve with a barley casserole with almonds added, and a good green salad. Serves 6.

HAM AND KIDNEY BEANS IN SHERRY

    5 tablespoons olive oil
    1 medium onion, finely chopped
    2 large oranges or 3 small ones, peeled and
        pith removed
    2 1-pound cans red kidney beans
    2 tablespoons prepared horseradish
    1 tablespoon salt
    2 ham steaks, 1″ thick
        Cayenne pepper
    1 tablespoon butter
    1½ cups dry sherry
        Coarse bread crumbs, butter

Heat olive oil in skillet and sauté onion slowly until limp and golden. Cut oranges into small sections and remove seeds. Drain off all but ¼ of bean liquid from each can. Lightly toss beans, horseradish, salt, oranges and oil-onion mixture together. Cut ham steaks into 8 servings. Sprinkle with cayenne on each side and sauté in butter over high heat until golden. In a shallow casserole, arrange a layer of the bean-orange combination and over this the ham slices. Top with the rest of the bean mixture and pour sherry over all. Cover and cook in a 350° oven, basting frequently, for 1 hour or until ham is tender. Remove from oven, sprinkle liberally with coarse bread crumbs, dot with butter and bake a few minutes in a 400° oven, uncovered, until crumbs are golden brown. Serves 8.

SWEDISH POTATO SAUSAGE

    1 pound lean ground beef
    ½ pound fresh ground pork
    7 cups grated potatoes
    1 finely chopped onion
    1 tablespoon salt
    2 teaspoons ground ginger

Mix all the ingredients well and stuff the mixture loosely into sausage casings. Cover the sausages with salted water and refrigerate.

To cook these delicious sausages, remove from the brine and poach in salted water for 1/2 hour. Drain. Melt 1/3 cup butter in a large skillet. Brown sausages on all sides.

ZAMPONE WITH LENTILS

    1 zampone
    1 pound lentils
    1 onion stuck with 2 cloves
    1 bay leaf
    ½ pound bacon
    ½ cup finely chopped onion
    ½ cup chopped parsley
        Sweet basil to taste

Cook the zampone, either by putting it in water to cover in a deep pan, covering it tightly with foil and placing it in a 350° oven for 2–2½ hours, or by poaching it on top of the stove for the same time.

Soak the lentils overnight. Drain. Cover with boiling water and add onion stuck with cloves and bay leaf. Cook until just soft. Do not overcook as they are to be reheated. Drain.

Cut bacon strips into small sections and try them out. Remove the bacon from the pan and keep hot. Sauté the chopped onion in the bacon fat until just wilted. Add the lentils and heat thoroughly. Add bacon, parsley and basil to taste. Cut the zampone into slices about ½″ thick and serve with the lentils and mustard fruits (available in Italian shops). Serves 6.

POLISH SAUSAGE IN RED WINE

⅔ cup chopped shallots or green onions
2½ cups red wine
1 good-sized kielbasa

Chop the shallots very fine and combine with the red wine in a heavy skillet or electric skillet. Place the sausage in the wine and bring to a boil. Lower the heat and simmer, turning several times, for 35–40 minutes or until the sausage is nicely glazed in the wine bath. Slice and serve with the juices in the pan and a hot potato salad as a first course for 6. For a luncheon dish, allow 2 sausages for 6 persons. The sausage keeps and is delicious cold.

ITALIAN SAUSAGES WITH PEPPERS

4–5 red or green peppers
12–18 Italian sausages, according to size and
    appetite
    Olive oil
2 cloves garlic, finely chopped
    Salt to taste
1 tablespoon red wine vinegar
2 tablespoons chopped Italian parsley

Although it is not necessary, this dish is far better if you take the trouble to skin your peppers. Either stick them on a fork and hold them over a flame, or place them under the broiler until they char and the skin blackens and bursts. They may then be scraped with ease. Seed the peppers and cut them in strips.

Blanch the sausages in boiling water for 6 or 7 min-

utes. Drain and brown them in 2–3 tablespoons of olive oil. Cook slowly until done.

Pour enough olive oil in a heavy skillet to cover the bottom of the pan. Heat the oil and add the finely chopped garlic and the pepper strips. Sauté gently until the peppers are just tender. If you have broiled and skinned them, they will take less cooking time than raw, unskinned peppers. You may cover the pan for part of the cooking time to tenderize the peppers. Salt to taste and just before the peppers are done, add red wine vinegar. Combine the peppers, sausage and parsley and serve with polenta or rice. Serves 6.

SAUSAGE IN BRIOCHE

The Italian cotechino or the garlic sausage from French butchers is probably the best sausage for this delectable dish. Failing one of these, you can use Polish kielbasa, or a bologna sausage.

Poach the sausage in water for 35–40 minutes. When it is cool enough to handle, remove the skin and let cool further. Cooking is not necessary with a bologna sausage but do heat and skin it.

Brioche Dough

½ cup milk
½ cup butter
⅓ cup sugar
½ teaspoon salt
¼ cup warm water
1 package dry or cake compressed yeast
1 egg yolk
3 eggs, beaten
3¼ cups sifted enriched flour

Scald the milk and cool to lukewarm. Thoroughly cream the butter and gradually add, creaming together, the sugar and salt. Measure the ¼ cup water into a bowl (use lukewarm water for compressed yeast) and sprinkle or crumble in the yeast. Stir until dissolved. Stir in the lukewarm milk and the creamed mixture. Add the egg yolk and eggs. Mix in the flour and beat for 10 minutes. Cover. Let rise in a warm place until more than doubled in bulk, about 2 hours. Stir down and beat thoroughly. Cover tightly with waxed paper or aluminum foil and chill in the refrigerator overnight. Stir down and turn out the dough on a floured board. Roll out a square ½″ thick and large enough to envelop the sausage completely. Place the cooled, peeled sausage in the center and tuck in the sides of the dough. Bring the ends together and press firmly, but let the dough be slightly loose. Turn the sausage and brioche over. Place on a buttered baking sheet. Brush the dough with a mixture of 1 egg beaten with 2 tablespoons of water so it will glaze while baking.

Bake in a 375° oven for about 30–40 minutes, or until the dough is nicely browned and puffed. Serve the sausage in brioche sliced with hot potato salad or a pungent cole slaw.

Variations:

1. Bread dough or pizza dough may be substituted for the brioche. Or for a different texture, use puff paste. (In this case, chill the roll before baking.)
2. Spread the surface of the dough with Dijon or German mustard before baking.
3. Knockwurst or large frankfurters may also be rolled in brioche. Make them into individual sausages-in-crust. They do not need pre-cooking.

PICADILLO

    1 pound lean ground round steak
    1½ tablespoons oil
    1 clove garlic, minced
    1 large onion, chopped
    12 pitted green olives
    1 cup raisins, soaked in water until plump, then
        drained
        Pinch of oregano
        Salt, pepper to taste
    1 cup red wine
    1 green pepper, seeded and chopped
        Cooked rice
        Chopped watercress

Brown the beef in the oil for 3–5 minutes. Add garlic, onion, olives, raisins, oregano, salt, pepper and wine. Simmer 20 minutes over medium heat, adding the green pepper during the last 5 minutes of cooking so that it will be crisp. Serve on a bed of fluffy rice and sprinkle with chopped watercress. Serves 4.

GERMAN MEAT BALLS WITH CARAWAY SAUCE

    1 cup coarsely grated raw potato
    1 pound lean ground round steak
        Grind of black pepper
    1 tablespoon chopped parsley
    1 teaspoon Beau Monde seasoning salt
    1 teaspoon minced onion
    1 teaspoon grated lemon peel
    1 egg, slightly beaten
    3 teaspoons arrowroot or cornstarch
    2½ cups beef bouillon
    ½ teaspoon caraway seeds

Mix the first 8 ingredients. Form into 1½″ balls and roll in 2 teaspoons arrowroot or cornstarch. Put bouillon in a deep pot with a tight-fitting cover. Bring to a boil and drop the meat balls one by one into the pot. Cover and simmer for 30 minutes. Remove the meat balls with a slotted spoon and keep hot.

Add a little freshly ground black pepper and the caraway seeds to the stock in which the meat balls were cooked. Simmer uncovered for 10 minutes. Mix the remaining arrowroot or cornstarch with 1 tablespoon of cold water and stir into the stock. Cook, stirring, until sauce has thickened. Combine with meat balls. Serves 4–6.

TURKISH MEAT AND PINE NUT BALLS

    1 pound minced lamb or beef
    2 potatoes, boiled and riced
    1 egg
    ¼ cup pine nuts
    ¼ cup currants
    1 teaspoon salt
        Pepper
    1 tablespoon minced parsley
    ¼ teaspoon cinnamon
        Oil for frying
        Tomato sauce

Combine meat, potatoes and egg. Add pine nuts, currants, salt, a little pepper, parsley and cinnamon. Mix very well and form in balls the size of ping-pong balls. Fry in oil until brown and serve with tomato sauce. Serves 4–5.

WILD WEST HAMBURGERS

2 pounds lean ground round steak
1 cup red wine
2 tablespoons drained capers
  Salt, pepper, monosodium glutamate to taste
1 medium onion, minced
1 heaping tablespoon powdered sage
1 teaspoon oregano
1 teaspoon chili powder
2 eggs
  Oil for frying

Mix the beef with all ingredients except the eggs and oil and leave at room temperature for 2–3 hours. Mix in the eggs and make 4 big patties 6″ in diameter and 1½″ thick. These require careful frying. The oil should be sputtering hot when you drop in the patties, and after 2 or 3 minutes the pan should be removed from the heat so that the first side is crusty, but the inside no more than red-pink. Turn and cook over high heat for a couple of minutes until second side gets crusty. Serves 4.

Variation: Use marjoram instead of oregano and mix in 2 tablespoons of canned shredded pineapple. Finally, just before cooking, add 2 tablespoons shredded almonds.

MEAT LOAF TANTE CLEMENTINA

1 pound lean ground round steak
1 cup plus 2 tablespoons seasoned bread crumbs
½ cup water
1½ tablespoons chopped parsley, preferably Italian
½ cup freshly grated Parmesan cheese
3 eggs
1 small onion, chopped
  Salt, pepper
4 tablespoons olive oil
¾ pound ricotta cheese or small-curd cottage cheese

Mix the beef, 1 cup bread crumbs, water, 1 tablespoon parsley, Parmesan cheese, 2 eggs, the chopped onion and salt and pepper to taste. Brush a 10″ baking dish with 2 tablespoons olive oil and sprinkle with the remaining 2 tablespoons bread crumbs. Put

half the meat mixture in the dish. Mix the ricotta or cottage cheese with the remaining egg and ½ tablespoon parsley and a pinch of salt. Spread this on the meat and cover with the remainder of the meat mixture. Press the edges of the meat layers together, brush with the remaining olive oil and refrigerate at least ½ hour, longer if possible. Bake in a preheated 450° oven for 25–30 minutes. Serves 4–6.

MEAT BALLS STROGANOV

1 pound lean ground round steak
  Salt, pepper to taste
½ cup chopped onion
1 tablespoon butter
½ pound mushrooms, sliced
½ can (3 ounces) tomato paste
2½ cups beef bouillon
1½ teaspoons celery salt
2 tablespoons bottled meat sauce
¼ cup seeded, julienne-cut green peppers
1 cup sour cream
1½ cups hot cooked noodles

Season the beef with salt and pepper and form into small balls of desired size. Sauté the onion in the butter until golden. Add the mushrooms and meat balls and brown. Add the tomato paste and bouillon and simmer 10 minutes. Add 1 teaspoon salt, the celery salt and pepper to taste. Mix in the meat sauce and green peppers and cook for 20 minutes. Stir in the sour cream and heat just to the boiling point. Serve over the hot noodles. Serves 4.

FINNISH MEAT SOUFFLÉ

4 tablespoons butter
4 tablespoons flour
2 cups hot milk
4 eggs, separated
2 cups ground meat (raw or cooked)
1½ teaspoons salt
½ teaspoon freshly ground pepper
4 anchovy fillets, minced, or more to taste

Melt butter. Stir in flour and cook until golden. Stir in hot milk. Cook, stirring constantly, until sauce is smooth and thickened. Remove from heat and beat in egg yolks, one at a time, blending well after each addition. Add meat, salt, pepper and anchovy fillets. Beat egg whites until stiff. Fold into meat mixture. Turn into greased 1½-quart baking dish. Bake in a 350° oven about 50 minutes, or until firm. Serve immediately with a green vegetable or salad as an accompaniment. Serves 4–6.

Note: This will not rise as high as some soufflés.

KIBBEE

> 2 cups cracked wheat
> 2 good-sized onions
> 1½ pounds lamb, ground twice
> 1½ teaspoons salt
> 1 teaspoon freshly ground black
>   pepper
> Dash Tabasco

Soak the cracked wheat in cold water. Drain and dry. Chop the onions very fine and blend with the ground lamb, the wheat and the seasonings. Pound and knead the mixture thoroughly. You may put it through the meat grinder, if you wish, and knead it again, adding a little ice water as you work. It should become a paste.

Form into small balls and serve raw with cocktails. Or, form into small round patties, with a chip of ice in the center. Brush well with oil and broil.

BAKED KIBBEE

> ⅓ cup olive oil
> ¼ cup chopped parsley
> 1 medium onion, chopped
> 1 clove garlic, chopped
> 1 pound ground lamb
> ⅔ cup pine nuts
> 1 teaspoon salt
> 2 dashes Tabasco
> 2·dashes cinnamon
> 1 recipe kibbee

Heat the oil and sauté the parsley, onion and garlic. Add the ground lamb and brown lightly. Add the pine nuts and seasonings and blend well.

In a well-oiled 7½″ by 11″ pan, put a layer of half the kibbee mixture. Add the ground lamb mixture and press it down evenly. Top with the rest of the kibbee and brush well with oil or melted butter, or a mixture of both. Bake in a 350° oven for about 25 minutes. Let stand a few minutes.

Cut into 6 large squares for a luncheon dish, or cut into small squares to serve as hot hors d'oeuvre.

KIDNEYS

Beef, veal and lamb kidneys are usually preferred to pork kidneys because of flavor, but all are high in nutritional value. A beef kidney weighs a little over a pound; a veal kidney half to three-quarters of a pound; lamb kidneys two to two-and-a-half ounces each. One pound of kidneys will serve four. Kidneys must be cooked quickly to be tender; when overcooked they toughen. The only exception to this is when they are used in a stew, casserole or pie that requires long, slow cooking which makes them tender again. Kidneys should be washed in cold water, the outer skin removed and the tubes and fat cut out with a sharp-pointed knife.

VEAL KIDNEYS FLAMBÉ

> 2 pounds veal kidneys, skinned and cleaned
> ¼ pound mushrooms
> 6 tablespoons butter
>   Salt, pepper
> ⅓ cup cognac, warmed
>   Chopped parsley
>   Fried toast

Cut kidneys into pieces the size of a large cherry. Slice mushrooms. Heat butter in a skillet and sauté kidneys and mushrooms for 5 minutes. Salt and pepper to taste and add warmed cognac. Ignite cognac. When flame dies down, add a liberal sprinkling of chopped parsley. Serve on fried toast with rice and asparagus dressed with Hollandaise sauce. Serves 6.

Variation: Sauté kidneys and mushrooms and flame with cognac, as above. Remove kidneys and mushrooms, turn heat low and add 1 cup sour cream to pan. Blend with pan juices and heat through but do not boil. Pour over kidneys and sprinkle with parsley.

HOW TO CLEAN LAMB KIDNEYS

Pull off outer fat; insert thumb at core and remove thin membrane around kidney.

Cut kidney in half lengthwise; scrape with knife to loosen core of fat, connecting tubes.

Turn over; cut down on slant with sawing motion while pulling core with left hand.

VEAL KIDNEYS WITH MADEIRA AND SOUR CREAM

> 3 veal kidneys, skinned, cleaned and thinly sliced
> Flour
> ¼ pound butter
> ½ cup Madeira
> ¼ cup sour cream
> Salt, pepper

Dust sliced kidneys with flour and sauté very quickly in butter, using a large skillet so all kidneys will cook in 3 or 4 minutes. Remove to a warm dish. Add Madeira to pan, carefully stir in sour cream (keep heat low so cream does not curdle). Stir, season with salt, pepper, pour sauce over kidneys and serve at once. Serves 6.

KIDNEYS WITH TOMATOES AND BASIL

> 1½ pounds veal or lamb kidneys, cut into small pieces with white tubes and skin removed
> 2 tablespoons butter or oil
> 1½ tablespoons curry powder
> 4 medium tomatoes, peeled and quartered
> 1½ teaspoons salt
> 3 tablespoons chopped fresh basil

Sauté kidneys in the butter or oil with curry powder until they are barely brown. Add the tomatoes and salt and allow to heat through. Stir in the chopped basil leaves. Serves 4–6.

KIDNEYS IN RED WINE

> 1 pound kidneys, any kind
> ¼ cup butter
> 1 small onion, chopped
> 1 cup sliced mushrooms
> ½ cup red wine
> ¼ cup stock
> Salt

Clean and slice kidneys. Brown quickly in butter. Remove and keep warm. Add onion and mushrooms to pan, adding more butter if necessary. When onion is transparent, pour in wine and stock, bring to a boil, add kidneys and salt to taste and cook a minute or less, just to heat through thoroughly. Serve at once with rice or on toast. Serves 4.

KIDNEYS BOULE D'OR

> 4 veal kidneys
> 2 tablespoons chopped shallots or green onions
> ½ pound mushrooms, sliced
> 6 tablespoons butter
> Salt, pepper to taste
> 1 tablespoon Dijon mustard

¾ **cup cream**
Beurre manié (tiny balls of butter and flour)
3 tablespoons gin

Trim most of the fat from the kidneys. Roast on a rack in a 400° oven for 18–20 minutes.

While the kidneys roast, sauté the shallots and mushrooms in the butter and season with salt, pepper and Dijon mustard. Add cream and thicken with beurre manié, if desired.

Remove kidneys from oven to a hot metal platter. Quickly remove most of the remaining fat and flambé with the gin. Slice thinly and add to sauce with juices from platter. Heat quickly and garnish with chopped parsley. Serve with rice. Serves 4–6.

GRILLED LAMB KIDNEYS

12 lamb kidneys, skinned and cleaned
½ **cup olive oil**
¼ **cup oloroso sherry**
½ **teaspoon salt**
¼ **teaspoon oregano**
¼ **teaspoon thyme**
6 slices bacon, cut in 1″ pieces

Slice the kidneys crosswise in 3 or 4 slices. Combine remaining ingredients, except bacon. Put kidneys in this marinade and leave for ½–1 hour.

Remove from marinade, arrange kidneys on skewers alternately with bacon. Place 3″ from broiler heat or over charcoal grill and cook until lightly browned, basting occasionally with marinade. Serves 4.

DEVILED LAMB KIDNEYS

12 lamb kidneys, skinned
¼ **pound butter**
¼ **cup minced onion**
1 clove garlic, pressed
Dash Tabasco
2 teaspoons prepared mustard
2 tablespoons dry sherry
¼ **teaspoon pepper**

Split kidneys and remove hard center but do not

cut completely in half. Spread flat. Mix remaining ingredients together, spread the cut side of the kidneys with the mixture and broil, spread side up, until juicy and tender—about 5 minutes. Arrange on toast, pour the drippings over the kidneys. Serves 4.

HOW TO CLEAN BRAINS

Firm brains by soaking in ice water. Starting at the loosest point, carefully peel off the covering membrane and threadlike blood clots.

BRAINS

Veal, beef, pork and lamb brains are all good to eat, and the flavor is similar. Veal brains, the most sought after, are naturally the highest in price. They weigh about a half-pound each. Beef brains weigh from three-quarters of a pound, pork and lamb brains from three to four ounces. Figure on a pound of brains for three or four servings. Brains are very perishable and should be parboiled as soon as possible after purchase. As the primary preparation for all dishes made with brains is the same, this can be done ahead of time.

TO PREPARE BRAINS

Wash brains well in cold water, then soak in salted water (1 tablespoon salt to 1 quart water) for half an hour. Remove membrane and blood clots. Simmer in salted acidulated water (1 teaspoon salt and 1 tablespoon lemon juice for each quart of water) or in court bouillon for 10 minutes. Do not boil and do not overcook lest they lose their delicate texture. Plunge immediately into cold water, cover and refrigerate until ready to use—but no longer than 1½ days.

BRAINS AU BEURRE NOIR

>2 pounds brains, parboiled
>Flour
>½ cup butter
>Toast
>Chopped parsley
>2 tablespoons vinegar
>1 tablespoon capers

Prepare brains according to directions. Dry, dust lightly with flour and brown in ¼ cup butter. Put each cooked brain on a piece of toast and sprinkle with parsley. Add remaining butter to pan and cook until a deep amber, add vinegar and capers. Pour over brains and serve at once. Serves 6.

HEART

Hearts are usually stuffed and baked or braised. A veal heart weighs close to a pound; a beef heart three to four pounds; pork heart about half a pound; lamb heart four or five ounces. A pound of heart serves two or three. Hearts should be washed thoroughly and the arteries and heavy fat removed with a sharp knife. If the heart is to be sliced it should be split first.

STUFFED BAKED HEART

>1 beef heart or 2 veal hearts
>2 cups toasted bread crumbs
>1 onion, chopped, and cooked in ⅓ cup butter
>1 egg
>Salt
>½ teaspoon rosemary
>¼ cup flour seasoned with ½ teaspoon salt
>3 tablespoons shortening
>1 cup red wine, stock or tomato juice

Wash and trim heart and enlarge opening. Make a stuffing with bread crumbs, onion, egg, 1 teaspoon salt and rosemary. Fill heart, skewer or sew opening, dust with seasoned flour and brown in shortening in a Dutch oven or casserole. Add red wine, stock or tomato juice, sprinkle with salt, cover and simmer on top of the range or bake in a 350° oven for 2 hours or until fork tender. Serves 6.

HOW TO CLEAN AND STUFF
VEAL HEART

Remove fatty covering from around heart and cut away tube at the top with scissors.

Snip away the tube and arteries from the inside, making pocket for stuffing. Fill pocket in heart with the desired stuffing.

Sew up opening with strong needle and thread, using crossover herringbone stitch.

Cut thin strips of salt pork and press into long, pointed larding needle with thumb.

Thread pork through surface of heart to keep it from drying out during cooking.

LIVER

Liver is high in minerals and vitamins as well as in flavor, but, like so many of the other specialty meats, to overcook it is to ruin it. A whole beef liver weighs about ten pounds; a calf's liver three pounds or a little more; lamb's livers are about a pound apiece. One pound of liver will serve three to four.

LIVER IN SOUR CREAM WITH DILL

2 pounds calf's liver, cut in 1″ cubes
¼ cup flour seasoned with pepper, ¼ teaspoon salt
1 large clove garlic, pressed
¼ cup butter
¼ cup stock
1 cup sour cream
2 teaspoons chopped fresh dill

Dust liver cubes with flour and cook with garlic in butter until lightly browned, but still juicy inside. Stir in stock and sour cream (keep heat low and blend in a little sour cream at a time, so it does not separate). Correct the seasoning, adding salt and pepper to taste. Add the dill. Heat the liver gently. Serve with noodles. Serves 6–8.

LIVER WITH HERBS

2 pounds calf's liver, sliced thick
¼ cup and 2 tablespoons butter
1 tablespoon each: minced parsley, chives, tarragon
2 tablespoons lemon juice

Sauté liver quickly in ¼ cup butter until brown but still pink inside. Remove to hot platter. Add to pan remaining butter, herbs and lemon juice, cook for a minute or two and pour over liver. Serves 6–8.

BEEF LIVER BOURGUIGNONNE

4 good-size slices young beef liver
Seasoned flour
12 tablespoons butter
6 slices bacon or salt pork, diced
4 medium onions, sliced
Red wine
3 cloves garlic, finely chopped
8 small croutons
Garnish: chopped parsley and chives

Dredge the liver slices with seasoned flour and sauté them in 6 tablespoons butter until nicely browned on each side and still rare and juicy in the center. Remove liver to a hot platter, cover with a hot plate and keep in a warm spot.

Sauté diced bacon or pork and onions in the pan in which liver cooked, adding more butter if necessary. When cooked, add just enough red wine to cover and simmer gently for 5 minutes.

Meanwhile sauté garlic in 5–6 tablespoons butter, add croutons and cook, turning frequently, until they are nicely browned and crisp.

When sauce has simmered for 5 minutes, add liver slices and let them cook until just heated through. Arrange liver on a hot platter, spoon some of the sauce over it, top with croutons and garnish with chopped parsley and chives. Serve the platter of liver with Potatoes Anna and rest of sauce in a sauceboat. Serves 4.

FEGATO DI VITELLO ALLA VENEZIANA
(Calf's Liver, Venetian Style)

1 pound calf's liver
6 tablespoons butter
2 cups thinly sliced white onions
1¼ teaspoons salt
¼ teaspoon freshly ground black pepper
2 tablespoons dry white wine
1 tablespoon minced parsley

The cutting of the liver is very important for this quick-cooking dish. It should be sliced paper thin and cut in finger lengths.

Melt the butter in a skillet; sauté the onions over very low heat until browned and tender. Turn up the heat and add the liver; sauté 3 minutes, stirring almost constantly. Sprinkle with the salt, pepper and wine; cook only 1 minute longer. Sprinkle with the parsley and serve immediately. Serves 4.

APPLE AND MARROW PIE

5 pounds marrow bones
Salt
2 pounds cooking apples
Pastry for 10″ pie
½ cup raisins soaked for several hours in
½ cup port

Put marrow bones in 350° oven for 15 minutes, then remove marrow, slice and sprinkle with salt. Peel, core and slice apples. Line a 10″ pie pan with pie crust, add apples, then marrow, then top with soaked raisins. Pour on any port that raisins did not absorb. Top with crust, slash, and bake in a 425° oven for 15 minutes. Reduce heat to 350° and continue baking until nicely browned. Serves 8.

OXTAIL

An oxtail weighs about two pounds and serves two or three. Oxtails make a wonderfully rich soup or stew.

OXTAIL CASSEROLE

2 pounds oxtails, disjointed
Seasoned flour
1 cup chopped onion
¼ cup butter
½ cup red wine or tomato juice
2 cups stock
Salt, pepper, rosemary
Small peeled onions, baby carrots, sliced
celery, mushrooms

Dust oxtails with flour. Cook onion in butter until wilted. Add oxtails and brown lightly. Add wine and 2 cups stock (or water). Add 1 teaspoon salt, a little pepper and a good pinch rosemary. Simmer for about 3 hours, or until almost tender. Put in a casserole with the vegetables. Cook in a 375° oven for 45 minutes, or until the vegetables are tender. Thicken sauce if desired. Serve with mashed potatoes. Serves 6.

GRILLED OXTAILS

Have oxtails disjointed, allowing 1 per person. Use only the large, meaty end. Barely cover oxtails with water, add 1 onion, a couple of cloves, some salt and a little marjoram. Cover and simmer until tender (about 3 hours or a little longer). Drain, saving stock for soup, dry, dip in melted butter and roll in fine bread crumbs. Broil until nicely browned on all sides. Serve with Sauce Diable. Supply finger bowls.

For Sauce Diable: Chop 2 shallots or green onions and cook in 2 tablespoons butter until transparent. Add 3 tablespoons vinegar, 1 teaspoon dry mustard, 1 tablespoon Worcestershire sauce, a dash of Tabasco and 2 cups brown sauce or brown gravy (you may also reduce oxtail stock, season, thicken slightly with flour and butter kneaded together and use it in place of the sauce or gravy).

OXTAIL RAGOÛT

4 pounds oxtails, cut in serving-size pieces
¼ cup flour
Salt
Dash of pepper
3 tablespoons bacon fat or rendered salt pork fat
¼ cup chopped onion
1 bay leaf
Pinch of thyme
1-pound can tomatoes
2 beef bouillon cubes
1 cup red wine
1 stalk celery, diced
2 or 3 leeks (white part only), cut in 2″ lengths
1 parsnip, peeled and cubed
1 carrot, peeled and cubed
¼ pound button mushrooms, sautéed in butter,
or 6-ounce can button mushooms

Cover the oxtail pieces with boiling water. Let stand 5 or 10 minutes; drain. Blend the flour with 1 teaspoon salt and the pepper. Dredge oxtail pieces with the seasoned flour and sauté in the hot fat in a skillet until well-browned on all sides. Transfer to Dutch oven or similar heavy pot with a cover. Add the chopped onion to the fat and cook until golden. Add onion to meat in pot with herbs, tomatoes, bouillon cubes and wine. Cover pot tightly, bring to a boil, simmer over very low heat 3 hours. Add celery, leeks, parsnip and carrot. Taste for salt and add more if needed. Cover again and cook ½ hour longer. Add sautéed or canned mushrooms to the ragoût 5 minutes before turning off heat. If possible, make the ragoût 24 hours in advance and chill in the refrigerator. It tastes better when reheated and also freezes well. Serves 5–6.

OSSO BUCO

> 6 pieces veal shank 3″ thick (the marrow bones
>   with meat around them)
> Flour
> 2 tablespoons butter
> 2 tablespoons olive oil
> 2 teaspoons salt
> ½ teaspoon freshly ground black pepper
> ¾ cup chopped onion
> ¼ cup grated carrots
> 1 teaspoon basil
> 2 tablespoons tomato paste
> 1 cup dry white wine
> ½ cup water
> 2 teaspoons grated lemon rind
> 1 clove garlic
> 2 tablespoons minced parsley

Roll veal shanks lightly in the flour. Heat the butter and oil in a Dutch oven or heavy saucepan; brown the shanks in it very well. Turn the bones upright and add the salt, pepper, onion, carrots and basil. Cover and cook over low heat 10 minutes.

Mix the tomato paste with the wine; stir into the pan with the water. Cover and cook over low heat 1¾ hours or until meat is tender. Add the lemon rind, garlic and parsley. Cook 5 minutes. Discard garlic before serving. Serve with a plain risotto or boiled rice. Serves 2–3.

SWEETBREADS

Sweetbreads are highly prized—and therefore expensive—but they have little waste. A pair of sweetbreads (one pound) will serve from two to four, depending on how they are prepared. Many connoisseurs consider them best when served simply, in cream sauce, for then their delicate flavor reigns supreme. They may also be prepared in any of the styles recommended for brains. Immediately after sweetbreads are purchased, soak them in cold water. Then simmer them for 20 minutes in acidulated water

(1 tablespoon lemon juice and 1 teaspoon salt to each quart of water). Drain, plunge immediately into cold water to stop cooking and make them firm, then clean by removing inedible parts, connecting tube and membrane. Do not remove the outer skin if you intend to cook sweetbreads whole. Veal sweetbreads are the most popular, but beef and lamb sweetbreads are also good. Beef sweetbreads require an extra 10 minutes cooking time.

HOW TO CLEAN AND SLICE SWEETBREADS

After initial cooking, remove thin membrane from center of sweetbread and the connecting tube.

With hand on top of the cooked sweetbread, cut in half lengthwise, using firm sawing motion.

SWEETBREADS ALBERT

> 1 leek, well-washed
> 3 stalks celery
> 1 green pepper, seeded
> 2 small carrots, peeled
> 6 shallots, chopped very fine
> 3 tablespoons oil
> Salt, pepper
> 2 cups white wine
> 4 pairs sweetbreads
> 1 tablespoon cornstarch
> 3 egg yolks
> Juice of 1 lemon
> Chopped parsley

Cut the leek, celery, green pepper and carrots into fine julienne strips and sauté with the shallots in oil until lightly colored. Arrange the vegetables on the bottom of a deep saucepan, season with salt and pepper to taste and add 1 cup white wine. Arrange sweetbreads (unblanched and uncleaned) on the vegetables and cover. Simmer the sweetbreads and vegetables for ½ hour over medium heat.

Remove the sweetbreads and cool them between wet towels. Drain the vegetables and save the liquid. Measure 1 cup of the liquid, add the remaining wine and the cornstarch. Simmer until the mixture is slightly thickened.

Clean the sweetbreads, adding the membranes and trimmings to the drained vegetables. Purée the vegetables in an electric blender and add to the thickened white wine broth. Beat the egg yolks lightly and add. Cook slowly, stirring constantly, until the sauce is thick, but do not boil. Add lemon juice and taste for seasoning.

Slice the sweetbreads and place them on a hot platter in the oven for a few minutes to heat through. Pour the sauce over them, reserving some in a sauceboat to be passed separately. Garnish the platter with chopped parsley. Serves 8.

SWEETBREADS AND KIDNEYS EN BROCHETTE

> 2 pairs sweetbreads, blanched, trimmed and cut in 1½" cubes
> 6 small veal kidneys, trimmed and cut in 1½" pieces
> Lemon juice
> Melted butter
> Salt, pepper
> Parsley
> ½ cup cognac

Alternate the sweetbreads and kidneys on skewers. Sprinkle lightly with lemon juice, brush well with melted butter and broil about 3" from broiling unit, turning several times and salting and peppering. Kidneys are best served rare, so figure on about 6 minutes for the broiling. Arrange on a hot platter on a bed of parsley. Flame with cognac. Serves 4.

BRAISED SWEETBREADS

> 3 pairs sweetbreads
> 2 tablespoons and ¼ cup butter
> 1 medium onion
> 1 large carrot
> 2 stalks celery
> 2 tablespoons minced ham
>   Marjoram, parsley
> 1½ cups veal or chicken stock
>   Salt, pepper
> ¼ cup Madeira

Cook sweetbreads for 5 minutes only, then plunge them into ice water. Clean. Brown dried sweetbreads lightly in 2 tablespoons butter. Chop onion, carrot, celery, add ham, a pinch of marjoram and two sprigs of parsley and put in a casserole with ¼ cup melted butter. Cook over low heat until the vegetables just begin to brown, then put the sweetbreads, whole or cut in large pieces, on top. Add stock, season with salt to taste and a little pepper, cover casserole and cook in a 350° oven for 1 hour. Put sweetbreads on toast and keep warm. Strain sauce, pressing vegetables through a sieve, and add Madeira. Reduce sauce if necessary by cooking quickly. Correct seasoning and pour sauce over sweetbreads. Serve immediately. Serves 6.

SWEETBREADS BÉARNAISE

Split cooked sweetbreads by slicing them in half lengthwise, dip them in melted butter and broil on each side until nicely colored. Serve with Béarnaise sauce and a purée of fresh peas.

TRIPE

The tripe known as "honeycomb" is the most desirable, but the other two kinds, "pocket" and "smooth," are also fine in flavor. To cook tripe, cover it with water to which salt, an onion, a stalk of celery and an herb bouquet have been added and simmer until tender—this takes anywhere from 1–4 hours, depending on how much it has been precooked before being sold.

TRIPE AND OYSTERS

1 cup minced onion
¼ cup butter
3 tablespoons flour
2 tablespoons each: chopped red and green
  pepper
1½ cups light cream
1 pint oysters
2 pounds cooked tripe, cut in 1½″ squares
  Salt, pepper to taste

Cook onion in butter until wilted, then add flour and red and green peppers. Cook a minute, then stir in cream. Cook until thickened. Meanwhile, poach oysters and add them, liquor and all, to sauce. Add tripe, correct seasoning, heat the tripe through and serve with toast. Serves 6–8.

TRIPE À LA MADRILEÑA

3 pounds fresh honeycomb tripe
3 sprigs green celery leaves, minced
2 bay leaves
½ cup minced parsley
¼ teaspoon thyme
¾ teaspoon coarsely ground black pepper
2 teaspoons salt
3 cups water
½ pound chorizo or other garlic-flavored
  sausage
6 bacon strips, chopped, or ¼ pound salt pork,
  diced
¼ cup olive oil
½ cup chopped onions
2 cloves garlic, minced
½ cup dry white wine
2 beef bouillon cubes
1-pound, 14-ounce can peeled tomatoes
4–6 potatoes, quartered
1 pound kale or Swiss chard
1 pound peas, shelled, or 1 package frozen peas

Place the tripe in a kettle with the celery, bay leaves, parsley, thyme, ½ teaspoon pepper, salt and water. Cover closely and cook 2 hours, or until tender. Drain. Cut the tripe into thin strips. Cut the sausage into 1″ pieces. Sauté the bacon in the olive oil until

fat is drawn out. Add the sausage, onions and garlic and cook over lowered heat until onions are soft. Add the wine, bouillon cubes, tomatoes, remaining pepper, tripe strips and sausage. Cover, bring to a boil and simmer over lowest heat 2–3 hours. Half an hour before end of cooking time, add potatoes, kale or Swiss chard and fresh peas. (Add frozen peas during last 5 minutes.) Serve directly from the pot or from a large earthenware casserole. This tastes better if made the day before and reheated just before serving time; it can also be frozen, but the potatoes should be removed and par-boiled potatoes added when it is reheated. Serves 6.

TRIPES À LA MODE DE CAEN

1 veal shank
4 onions, sliced
5 carrots, sliced
4 stalks celery, sliced
¼ cup butter
5 pounds tripe, cut in 2″ by 1″ strips
  Salt, pepper
  Herb bouquet of parsley, thyme, bay leaf
1½ cups white wine
1 cup calvados or applejack
  Stock

This is one of the world's great classic recipes and it requires long, slow cooking in a sealed earthenware pot to be really perfect. Put the veal shank in the bottom of a large earthen marmite, casserole or bean pot. Cook onions, carrots and celery in butter until wilted, then arrange them in layers in the pot, alternating with the tripe. Sprinkle each layer with salt and pepper and tuck the herb bouquet in the middle. Add wine, calvados and fill the pot with stock. Cover and seal the lid on with a paste of flour and water. Cook in a 250° oven for 8 hours. Remove veal shank and herb bouquet before serving. Serve with French bread. Serves 8–12.

TONGUE

Beef tongues are sold fresh, pickled, smoked, corned and, in some areas, already cooked. They weigh from two-and-a-half to five pounds. Calf's tongues weigh less, about two pounds, and are usually sold fresh. Lamb's tongues weigh about a quarter of a pound and are sold fresh or pickled. Pork tongues weigh about a pound. One pound of tongue makes three or four servings. To cook tongue, wash well and put in a large pot with water to cover, half a lemon, a sliced onion, a couple of stalks of celery and an herb bouquet consisting of parsley, bay leaf and thyme. Simmer until tender to the fork. A beef tongue will take 3–4 hours, sometimes longer. A veal tongue takes about 2½ hours, lamb tongue 1–1½ hours.

ESCABECHE DE LENGUA

This is a Mexican dish, very nice for a cold buffet or on a hot day. Cook any kind of tongue (allowing 2 pounds for 6 servings) in a court bouillon of 2 quarts water, juice of ½ a lemon, a small onion, a sliced carrot, a stalk of celery and 2 teaspoons salt. When tongue is tender, allow it to cool in the bouillon. Skin, slice and arrange in a deep platter or shallow dish, putting paper-thin slices of sweet onion and unpeeled orange and sliced ripe olives between the layers of tongue. Make a dressing with ¾ cup olive oil, ¼ cup wine vinegar, 1 teaspoon salt and plenty of freshly ground black pepper. Pour dressing over tongue and chill for 24 hours. Before serving, sprinkle with minced parsley and, if available, minced cilantro. Serve very cold.

COLD TONGUE VIN BLANC

 1 fresh beef tongue
   Sliced onion, herb bouquet
 ¼ cup butter
 ¼ cup flour
 3 tablespoons cognac
 ½ cup white wine
   Watercress
 1 cup whipped cream combined with 3
   tablespoons grated horseradish, ¼ teaspoon
   salt

Cook beef tongue in salted water to cover with onion and herb bouquet for 1 hour. Remove and skin.

Brown tongue in butter in a Dutch oven, add flour, cognac and wine and enough of water in which tongue was boiled to barely cover it. Simmer for 3 hours, or until very tender. Remove tongue and put in a dish just large enough to hold it. Strain sauce, reduce liquid to 1 cup, correct seasoning and pour it over the tongue. Chill. Serve cold, garnish with watercress and serve the whipped cream as a sauce.

TONGUE FINES HERBES

 1 beef tongue, boiled
 ¼ pound butter
 3 tablespoons each: minced parsley and chives
 1 teaspoon tarragon or marjoram or sweet basil
 ½ cup white wine
   Salt

Skin tongue and slice it about ¼″ thick, taking care not to cut through the bottom. Mix butter and herbs. Spread herb butter between slices and reshape with skewers or by tying with string. Put in a casserole with the wine, sprinkle with salt and bake in a 350° oven for 40 minutes, basting a few times. Spinach is an especially good accompaniment for tongue.

GLAZED TONGUE

 4–5 pound smoked or pickled tongue
 ½ cup sugar
 ½ teaspoon paprika
 ½ teaspoon cinnamon
 1 teaspoon mace
 1 teaspoon ginger
 1 teaspoon dry mustard
 ¼ cup light corn syrup

Place tongue in pot, cover with cold water and bring to a boil. Cover and simmer until tender, 2–3 hours. Taste water when it first boils; if it tastes salty, throw water off and cover tongue with fresh water. When tender, remove from water, skin and dry. Place in open roaster, spread with a paste made of remaining ingredients and roast in a 350° oven 1 hour, or until nicely glazed. If the tongue juices do not moisten the paste, baste with a little fruit juice or ginger ale. Makes 12 servings.

Poultry & Game

The shifting status of foods in culinary history has never affected poultry and game. From the first, their position was unassailable, their aristocracy accepted. Chicken, the oldest of the domesticated fowls, was regarded by the Romans as sacred and by the Greeks as a gift from the gods, honors which did not save the birds from being eaten. At Roman feasts chickens, plumped on a diet of barley and milk, geese, partridge and pheasant easily held their own with flamboyant peacocks, flamingos and parrots, delicate larks and nightingales. The chicken, harking from southern Asia, proved to be a true cosmopolitan, merging as gracefully with the wine and truffles of France and the rice and tomato of Spain as with the spices of the Orient. The enthusiasm of cooks for this versatile bird is summed up in the Spanish proverb, "The chicken is the foundation of a good meal." A nineteenth-century housewife was more lyrical: "Braise your chicken, fricassee it . . . convert it into a galantine, bury it in aspic, do what you will with it, so long as you do it well it can bring you but happiness and peace."

Geese and ducks, pullets and pigeons, the domesticated denizens of medieval farmyards, were joined after the discovery of America by the turkey, known to the French as the poulet d'Inde. Turkey might be said to have been admitted to the gastronomic hall of fame when Brillat-Savarin, author of La Physiologie du Goût termed it, "surely one of the finest gifts which the Old World has received from the New." Here at home Benjamin Franklin was of the opinion that the respectable turkey rather than the marauding bald eagle, which he described as "a Bird of poor moral character, like those among men who live by sharpening and robbing," should have been chosen as the national symbol.

Game, classed during the Renaissance as the meat of noblemen (beef was peasant fodder), was one of the earliest forms of sustenance in America. Pheasant and venison were as familiar a sight on the family table as chicken and steak are today.

Even now, despite the spread of urbanization, vast areas of this country still teem with wildlife, and people lucky enough to live near these regions regard game as part of the yearly food cycle, like corn on the cob and blueberry pie. For those who don't, game birds are reared on farms, much as the Romans raised wild fowl in captivity, gaining in pampered flesh what they lose in pungent flavor.

TRUFFLED CAPON

1 pound truffles
8–9 pound capon
Salt, black pepper
1 pound mushrooms
4 tablespoons cognac
3 tablespoons Madeira
2 tablespoons peanut oil
Bay leaf, thyme, mixed spices
1¼ pounds pork fat

Slice 3 or 4 of the largest truffles and slip them under the skin of the capon breast. Salt and pepper the bird inside and out and let stand, refrigerated, for 2 days so that it will be flavored by the truffles.

Wash the mushrooms and cut off the stems. Reserve stems. Cut caps and rest of truffles in quarters and put in a bowl with the cognac, Madeira, oil, a little salt, crumbled bay leaf and pinches of thyme and mixed spices. Let the mixture stand to marinate at room temperature.

Cut the pork fat into small pieces and pound in a mortar. Heat it slightly in a saucepan and add the mushroom stems, minced. Put the mixture through a food mill or rub it through a sieve. Return to very low heat and when barely warm, add the truffles, mushrooms and their marinade. Chill. Stuff the capon with this mixture. Truss the bird for roasting. Rub with oil and place breast-side up on a rack in an open roasting pan. Cover breast with aluminum foil and roast at 325° until tender, about 2½–3 hours. Serve surrounded by small, browned potatoes, with the pan juices as sauce. Serves 8.

PERSIAN ROAST CHICKEN

¼ cup cracked wheat
Salt, black pepper
1½ tablespoons butter
1 cup water
1 cup canned garbanzos (chick peas)
1 cup toasted almonds, chopped
1 young chicken (about 3–3½ pounds)
½ cup chicken stock mixed with
⅓ cup melted butter

Cook cracked wheat with 1 teaspoon salt, 1 tablespoon butter and 1 cup water in a double boiler until wheat is tender (about 1½ hours). The water should be absorbed by this time. Combine wheat with garbanzos and almonds. Add black pepper and salt to taste. Rub salt, pepper and 1 teaspoon butter on inside of chicken. Stuff chicken with dressing. Sew up cavity. Butter outside skin. Roast chicken on rack in shallow pan in a 350° oven until tender and nicely browned (about 1½ hours). Baste during roasting with mixed chicken stock and butter. Serves 4.

ROAST CHICKEN WITH VEAL STUFFING

¼ pound veal, ground
4 tablespoons butter
½ cup mushrooms, sliced
1 veal brain, parboiled and chopped
1 egg, beaten
¼ cup sherry
2 tablespoons grated Parmesan cheese
2 tablespoons parsley, chopped
1 teaspoon poultry seasoning
1 teaspoon salt
Dash pepper
1 roasting chicken (4–6 pounds)
2 tablespoons olive oil

Fry ground veal in butter and add mushrooms. Cook for 3 minutes and add parboiled, chopped brain. Cook for 1 more minute and remove from skillet. Combine mixture with egg, sherry, cheese, parsley and poultry seasoning. Add ¾ teaspoon salt, pepper and mix well. Stuff chicken cavity with dressing and tie up the chicken. Rub chicken with 1 tablespoon olive oil and sprinkle with ¼ teaspoon salt. Place chicken on a roasting rack, breast up, and cover with cheesecloth moistened with remaining oil. Roast at 325° for 1¾–2 hours, turning chicken breast down when ¾ done. Baste occasionally if chicken seems to be dry. Remove cheesecloth 15 minutes before chicken is done. Serves 4.

POULARDE FINE CHAMPAGNE, BERGONZI

2–2¾-pound roasting chicken
  Salt, pepper to taste
¼ cup melted butter
1 medium onion, sliced
1 carrot, sliced
1 stalk celery, sliced
  Pinch thyme
½ bay leaf
1 ounce cognac
½ cup dry white wine
2 cups heavy cream
  Juice of ¼ lemon

Place the chicken on a rack in a heavy roasting pan and season with salt and pepper. Pour melted butter over the chicken. Roast in a preheated 350° oven for 1 hour, basting often. After ½ hour, add the onion, carrot, celery, thyme, and bay leaf. Five minutes before removing chicken, add the cognac and wine. When ready, remove the chicken and allow the vegetables to simmer in the wine a few minutes longer. Add the heavy cream and let boil for 3 minutes. Add the lemon juice. Season to taste. Strain sauce through a sieve and pour over chicken. Serve with rice pilaf. Serves 4.

POULET PICASSO

4-pound roasting chicken
2 tablespoons olive oil
1 tablespoon butter
1 green pepper, diced
1 sweet red bell pepper, diced, or ¼ cup diced
  pimiento
⅓ cup pitted green olives, coarsely chopped
⅓ cup pitted ripe olives, coarsely chopped
¼ cup cubed baked ham
4 ripe tomatoes, peeled and quartered
  Salt, freshly ground pepper to taste
  Pinch saffron

Roast the chicken in a 350° oven for 1–1½ hours, or until done. Meanwhile heat the olive oil and butter in a heavy frying pan and add the green and red peppers. Add the chopped olives, ham, tomatoes, salt, peppers, and saffron. Cover and cook gently until the tomatoes are soft and the mixture has reduced some of the liquid. Cut roasted chicken in quarters and cover with the sauce. Serve very hot. Serves 6.

SUPRÊME DE VOLAILLE AU KIRSCH

4 chicken breasts
6 tablespoons clarified butter
½ cup cognac
½ cup kirsch
3 large egg yolks
1 cup heavy cream
  Salt, pepper
2 medium truffles, minced

Have butcher bone, skin and halve chicken breasts. Heat butter in 2 large skillets. (Two skillets are needed since 1 skillet will not accommodate the 8 pieces of chicken, which must cook without touching each other.) Sauté chicken breasts in hot butter over medium heat, about 8–10 minutes on each side, depending on size. Transfer chicken to hot serving platter. Keep hot. Combine juices from both skillets in one. Add cognac and kirsch, scraping up the brown glaze at the bottom of the skillet. Beat together egg yolks and cream. Heat skillet juices and flame. As the flame gradually dies down, lower heat. Stir cream mixture into skillet. Season with salt and pepper to taste. Heat through thoroughly over low heat, but do not boil. Pour sauce over chicken breasts and sprinkle with minced truffles. Garnish with triangles of puff paste or toast and sautéed mushroom caps. Serve with tiny buttered peas. Serves 8.

HOW TO MAKE CHICKEN KIEV

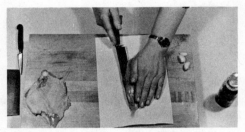

Halve chicken breast lengthwise through center.

Beat slices paper thin between wax paper layers.

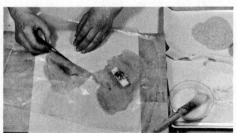

Put butter slantwise in center, roll up tightly.

After dredging in flour, brush with beaten egg.

Roll in bread crumbs. Chill before deep frying.

CHICKEN KIEV

> 4 large chicken breasts, skinned and boned
> ¼ pound sweet butter, frozen
>   Finely chopped garlic
>   Finely chopped tarragon
>   Salt, freshly cracked white pepper to taste
>   Flour
> 1 egg, beaten
>   Fine dry bread crumbs
>   Fat for deep frying
>   Watercress for garnish

Carefully cut the chicken breasts in half, slicing lengthwise. This will give you 8 pieces. Put pieces between sheets of waxed paper, cut side up, and beat with a cleaver until thin and transparent. Cut the butter into 8 fingers. Put one on each piece of chicken and top with a tiny bit of garlic and tarragon. Season with salt and pepper. Roll up to completely envelop the butter. Roll in flour, brush with beaten egg and roll in bread crumbs. Chill thoroughly in refrigerator before cooking.

Heat fat to 375° and fry chicken until golden brown. Drain on paper towels. Arrange on a serving dish and put a toothpick and cutlet frill on the end of each piece. Garnish with watercress. Serves 4.

THE SENATOR'S CHICKEN

> 4 small chicken breasts, skinned and boned
> 2 cups port wine
> 2 tablespoons brandy
>   Salt, pepper
> 6 tablespoons butter
> ½ teaspoon tarragon vinegar
> 4 tablespoons pâté de foie gras

Pound the boned chicken breasts with a mallet or underside of a heavy plate until flattened. Put the breasts into a glass, porcelain or earthenware bowl (do not use aluminum). Pour the port and brandy over the chicken. Marinate for 1 hour. Drain the chicken and reserve the marinade. Sprinkle the chicken on both sides with salt and pepper. Cream 4 tablespoons butter until soft. Beat in the tarragon vinegar. Place 1 tablespoon of the butter mixture on each chicken breast and top with 1 tablespoon pâté de foie gras. Fold over breast to enclose filling and tie with string. Brown the chicken breasts in the remaining 2 tablespoons butter. Pour marinade over the chicken and simmer covered for 30 minutes, or until tender, basting occasionally with pan juices. Remove string, place chicken breasts on a platter and spoon sauce from pan over them. If the sauce appears too thin, cook down to desired consistency after chicken breasts have been removed to a platter. Keep chicken hot while sauce is reducing. Garnish with little mounds of tiny buttered peas and broiled mushrooms. Serves 4.

CHICKEN CUTLETS BOLOGNA STYLE

4 chicken breasts, skinned and boned
2 slices white bread without crust
2 tablespoons chicken stock
¼ cup mushrooms, sliced
5 tablespoons butter
4 slices Italian prosciutto, shredded
2 tablespoons parsley, minced
¼ cup Marsala
¼ teaspoon each: salt, pepper
Flour
1 egg, beaten
¾ cup bread crumbs

Place chicken breasts between sheets of waxed paper and pound until thin. Soak bread in chicken stock and squeeze dry. Sauté mushrooms in 1 tablespoon butter for 2–3 minutes. Combine bread, mushrooms, prosciutto, parsley and Marsala and mix well. Place on each chicken cutlet a little salt and pepper and a spoonful of mixture, roll cutlets and fasten with toothpicks. Dip in flour, brush with beaten egg, roll in bread crumbs and fry in 4 tablespoons butter until golden brown. Serves 4.

BREAST OF CHICKEN SAUTÉ WITH LEMON

3 tablespoons butter
4 chicken breasts, boned and halved
Flour
Salt, pepper
⅓ cup lemon juice
Zest of 1 lemon, finely chopped

Melt butter in a skillet. Dust the chicken breasts lightly with flour and sauté them quickly, turning to brown on both sides. Reduce the heat and season to taste with salt and pepper. Cook gently for 5 minutes, turning the chicken pieces once. Add the lemon juice and simmer until just done, but not overcooked. Baste the breasts occasionally with the butter and lemon juice in the pan. The chicken should be done in about 15 minutes; 5 minutes before it is finished, add the lemon rind and check for seasoning. Serves 4.

CHICKEN IN CIDER

2 2½-pound fryers, disjointed
2 teaspoons salt
¾ teaspoon freshly ground black pepper
¼ pound butter
1½ cups chopped onions
2 cloves garlic, minced
2 green peppers, cut julienne
¼ teaspoon dried ground hot red peppers
1 cup apple brandy
1 cup cider
2 tablespoons vinegar
12 pre-soaked prunes
12 stuffed olives
12 small white onions
2 cups cubed potatoes
2 tablespoons capers
6 hot Spanish sausages

Season the chicken with the salt and pepper. Melt the butter in a casserole; brown the chicken. Add chopped onions and sauté for 10 minutes. Add the garlic, green peppers, hot peppers, brandy, cider and vinegar. Cover and cook over low heat 1 hour. Add the prunes, olives, onions, potatoes and capers. Cover and cook 15 minutes.

Slice the sausages and brown in a skillet. Drain and add to the casserole. Cook 10 minutes longer. Taste for seasoning. Serves 8.

PEPITORIA OF CHICKEN

3-pound chicken, cut up
3 tablespoons olive oil
1 large onion, finely chopped
4 tablespoons blanched almonds
3 cloves garlic
1 tablespoon minced parsley
½ teaspoon salt or to taste
2 hard-cooked egg yolks

2 tablespoons amontillado sherry
⅛ teaspoon saffron
½ cup slivered cooked ham
10–12 pimiento-stuffed olives

Place chicken neck, giblets, wing tips and boniest parts of back in 1½ cups salted water. Cover and cook 30 minutes. Drain, saving stock. Meanwhile, brown the remaining pieces of chicken in the olive oil. Remove. Add onion and sauté until soft, but not brown. Place chicken and onion in casserole. Brown blanched almonds in oil; remove, cool until crisp. Crush almonds in mortar and pestle, add garlic and parsley and crush until paste-like. Blend salt and egg yolks with this paste, moisten with a little oil, gradually stir in 1 cup of the chicken stock, the sherry and saffron. Add this to chicken in casserole. Bake in a 350° oven for 30 minutes, adding ham and whole olives during last 5 minutes of cooking. Serve with hot cooked rice. Serves 4.

TAPADO DE POLLO
(Smothered Chicken)

6 tablespoons olive oil
3½–4-pound fryer, cut in serving pieces
1 large onion, sliced
2 cloves garlic, chopped
3 large tomatoes, peeled and sliced
½ pound baby peas
1 pound zucchini or summer squash, sliced
2 cooked apples, peeled and sliced
2 pears, peeled and sliced
4 slices pineapple, cut in chunks
2 large or 4 small bananas, peeled and sliced
Salt, pepper to taste

Heat 4 tablespoons olive oil in a skillet and sauté chicken pieces until golden. Place a layer of half the chicken pieces in a heavy lidded casserole and follow with layers of half the onion, garlic, tomatoes, peas, zucchini, apples, pears, pineapple, and bananas. Season with salt and pepper and sprinkle with 1 tablespoon oil. Repeat with remaining chicken, vegetables, and fruit. Season with salt and pepper and sprinkle with remaining oil. Cover and cook on top of the stove on low heat until chicken is tender, about 1½ hours. The amount of gravy will depend on the ripeness of fruit and vegetables. Serves 6.

POLLO MESTIZO

4 tablespoons oil and butter (2 of each)
3½–4-pound fryer, cut into serving pieces
1 cup dry white wine
1 cup pineapple juice
Bay leaf
Salt, pepper to taste
6 small potatoes
2 medium tomatoes, peeled and seeded
2 cloves garlic
1 onion
6 canned pimientos
3 chorizos (Spanish sausages)
1 tablespoon capers
3 canned jalapeño chiles, or to taste

Heat the oil and butter in a skillet and sauté the chicken until golden. Remove the chicken to a covered casserole and add the wine, pineapple juice, bay leaf, salt, and pepper, leaving fat in skillet for later use. Simmer chicken until barely tender, about 45 minutes. Cook the potatoes in salted boiling water, drain, and reserve. Put the tomatoes, garlic, onion, and pimientos in a blender and blend until smooth, adding a little stock from the chicken if necessary. Skin and chop the chorizos and sauté in the oil and butter remaining in the skillet. Drain and add to the casserole. Put the blender mixture in the skillet and cook in the remaining fat for 5 minutes, stirring constantly. Add to the casserole with the potatoes and capers. Rinse the jalapeño chiles, remove seeds, if any, cut in strips and add to the casserole. Check seasoning, simmer a few minutes and serve. Serves 6.

COQ EN DAUBE

4–5-pound fowl, cut in serving pieces
2 carrots, finely sliced
1 large onion, sliced
3 cloves garlic
2 leeks, sliced
1 teaspoon salt
1 teaspoon freshly ground black pepper
Pinch each: ground cloves, ground ginger
1 teaspoon thyme
Red wine
6 tablespoons olive oil

Pig's foot or piece of pork skin
Small piece orange rind

Place chicken pieces in a shallow bowl with the carrots, onion, garlic, leek, salt, pepper, cloves, ginger, thyme and just enough red wine to cover. Marinate for 24 hours in the refrigerator.

To cook, brown the drained chicken in olive oil until nicely colored on all sides. Place in a deep casserole with pig's foot or pork skin and orange rind. Strain marinade and add just enough to cover the chicken (if more liquid is needed, add red wine). Cover casserole and simmer on top of the stove or in a 300° oven for 3—4 hours. Remove chicken to a hot platter, skim fat from juices and pour them over chicken. Serve with noodles or any pasta and asparagus or endive. To serve cold, arrange chicken in bowl, pour juices over it and chill until jellied. Serves 6.

CHICKEN CURRY

2 3½-pound chickens
Salt, lemon juice, freshly cracked black pepper
4 ounces salt butter
¼ cup olive oil
¼ cup vegetable oil
2 yellow onions, sliced
1 large carrot, sliced
2 pieces celery, sliced
1 green apple, cored and sliced with skin on
4 tablespoons Indian curry powder
4 tablespoons flour
1 teaspoon tomato paste
1 teaspoon meat glaze
2½ cups chicken stock
1 tablespoon lemon juice
1 teaspoon shredded coconut
1 tablespoon honey
2 tablespoons guava jelly
1 small stick cinnamon
1 small piece ginger root
3 crushed cardamom seeds
1 large clove garlic, bruised
1 clove
½ teaspoon dry mustard
Salt, cayenne pepper to taste

Wash and dry the chickens. Season inside with a little salt, lemon juice and freshly cracked black

pepper. Tie up carefully. Heat 2 ounces butter in a heavy cocotte. When foaming, put in the chickens breast side down. Brown them slowly, first on one side of the breast, then on the other side of the breast, then on each leg, then the wishbone and lastly the back. When the chickens are browned all over, remove and carve into serving pieces and sauté until cooked through.

Heat the olive and vegetable oils in a deep, heavy pan with the remaining 2 ounces salt butter. Add the sliced onions, carrot, celery and apple. Stir the vegetables around, then cover and cook slowly 5 minutes. Add curry powder, stir into vegetables and cook slowly 5 minutes. Stir in flour and cook slowly another 5 minutes. Then mix in, off the heat, the tomato paste, meat glaze, chicken stock, lemon juice, shredded coconut, honey, guava jelly, cinnamon stick, ginger root, crushed cardamom seeds, bruised garlic, clove, dry mustard, salt and cayenne pepper. Stir over low heat until it comes to a boil, then simmer for at least 1 hour. Rub through a fine strainer and pour over the chicken. Keep warm. (This sauce is much better when it is 1 or 2 days old.)

Serve with saffron rice and the side dishes listed below. Serves 12.

Side Dishes:
1. Peel an avocado, remove pit, cut into small dice and put into a bowl. Sprinkle with a little salt, freshly cracked white pepper and lemon juice. Shred 8 slices bacon fine and cook until crisp. Drain and mix into the avocado.
2. Cut 2 green peppers into quarters, remove seeds, cut into fine dice and put into a bowl. Sprinkle

with a little vegetable oil and lemon juice. Season with salt and a little cayenne pepper. Add the finely shredded rind and the skinned sections of 2 navel oranges.

3. Peel a Bermuda onion and cut into very thin slices. Separate the slices into rings and put into a bowl. Sprinkle with cayenne pepper and add 2 tablespoons olive oil. Mix well.
4. 1 cup shredded coconut.
5. ½ cup finely chopped parsley.
6. 1 cup blanched, shredded, browned almonds.
7. 1 cup raisins.
8. 1 cup guava jelly.
9. 1 cup Major Grey chutney.
10. 4 pieces Bombay duck, cut in ½" slices and fried in a little bacon fat until crisp.
11. 12 pappadums, fried in shallow hot oil.
12. 3 hard-cooked eggs, finely chopped.

COLD CHICKEN CURRY

> 2 young roasting chickens, 4–5 pounds, cut for fricassee
> 10 tablespoons butter
> 3 tablespoons brandy
> 2 large Bermuda onions, quartered and thinly sliced
> Salt, pepper
> 2 tablespoons curry powder
> 2 cups heavy cream
> 2 lemons, parsley for garnish

Wash and thoroughly dry the chickens. Melt 8 tablespoons of the butter in a large frying pan and brown the chicken pieces lightly on both sides. Place an iron cocotte over very low heat or, better still, on an asbestos mat over low heat and add the remaining 2 tablespoons butter. As they brown, transfer the pieces to the cocotte. When all the chicken has been transferred, heat the brandy, pour over the chicken and set ablaze. When flames die, cover the chicken with the onion and sprinkle with salt and pepper.

Add ½ cup water to the frying pan and stir over low heat to melt the brown residue in the pan to a clear gravy. Pour this over the chicken, cover tightly and simmer gently until the chicken is cooked through and about to fall off the bones, about 1¼ hours. By this time the onion should be cooked down and the chicken immersed in buttery juices. Sprinkle the chicken with the curry powder and baste well. Remove from the heat and cool until the chicken may be handled. Then remove the chicken from the cocotte and take the meat from the bones. Discard the skin, gristle and bones. Cut the breasts in half lengthwise and lay these symmetrically over the bottom of an oblong glass 6" by 10" by 2" baking dish. Distribute the rest of the meat evenly over them.

Add the heavy cream to the onion and buttery juices remaining in the cocotte. Stir well, place over low heat and heat just to the boiling point, but do not allow the cream to boil. Taste for seasoning and add more salt if necessary. When the sauce is heated through, place a colander over a large pan and strain out the onions. Press gently with a wooden spoon to extract all the cream. Pour this creamy sauce over the chicken in the dish. It should cover the chicken completely and fill the dish. Cool, cover with aluminum foil and place in the refrigerator until the sauce has jelled and set like custard.

When ready to serve, run a knife carefully around the edge of the dish. Dip the dish into a shallow pan of hot water for a few seconds to loosen the bottom, then turn out carefully onto a large oval platter. Garnish with quartered lemons and crisp parsley. Serve accompanied by a bowl of crisp romaine broken into small pieces, dressed with a good French dressing and seasoned with finely chopped fresh parsley and tarragon. Serves 6–8.·

PUNGENT FRIED CHICKEN

> 2½-pound fryer, cut into serving pieces
> 4 teaspoons grated orange rind
> ⅔ cup orange juice
> 2 teaspoons salt
> ½ teaspoon dry mustard
> Pepper
> Tabasco sauce
> ½ cup flour
> 1 teaspoon paprika
> ½ cup fat
> 1 tablespoon water

Place chicken in a single layer in a shallow dish. Combine orange rind, orange juice, ½ teaspoon salt, mustard, a dash each of pepper and Tabasco.

Pour over chicken. Marinate for 3 hours, covered, in refrigerator. Drain. Place flour, 1½ teaspoons salt, paprika and a little pepper in a bag. Add chicken and shake well to coat evenly. Sauté chicken in fat until golden brown. Remove chicken to warm platter. Pour off all but 2 tablespoons of pan drippings, and brown residue. Blend in seasoned flour remaining in bag and cook, stirring constantly, until frothy. Add marinade and water and cook until thickened. Pour over chicken. Serves 4.

CHICKEN LITCHI

> **2 egg yolks**
> **½ teaspoon salt**
> **1 teaspoon shoyu sauce**
> **⅔ cup water**
> **3 tablespoons flour**
> **2 cups cooked chicken, cut into 1½″ pieces**
> **1 cup peanut or salad oil**
> **¼ cup chicken broth**
> **1 teaspoon cornstarch**
> **⅓ teaspoon grated fresh ginger root**
> **½ cup litchi juice from the can**
> **1 cup canned litchis**

Combine egg yolks, salt, ½ teaspoon of shoyu, water and flour to make a smooth batter. Dip the chicken in the batter and fry it in the hot oil until golden brown. Drain on paper towels. Mix chicken broth and cornstarch to a smooth paste; add ginger, ½ teaspoon of shoyu and the litchi juice. Boil until the mixture thickens, add the litchis, and pour over the chicken. Serve hot. Serves 4.

PAELLA VALENCIANA

> **⅓–½ cup olive oil**
> **3-pound frying chicken, cut into 8 serving pieces**
> **Few extra chicken gizzards**
> **Salt, pepper to taste**
> **1 large onion, finely chopped**
> **1 clove garlic, chopped**
> **1½ cups rice**
> **Pinch saffron**
> **Hot chicken stock and hot water, mixed**
> **½ cup peeled and chopped tomatoes**
> **12 scrubbed, unshelled clams**
> **12 shrimps, washed and shelled**
> **1 or 2 Spanish or Italian sausages**
> **Pimiento strips**

Heat the oil in a large skillet or paella pan and add the chicken and the gizzards. Brown the chicken well on all sides and season with salt and pepper. Remove the browned chicken pieces from the pan but leave the gizzards. Add the onion and garlic to the gizzards and sauté them. Add the rice and toss in the oil for several minutes or until it turns slightly yellow. Season with salt, pepper and saffron. Pour on enough hot stock and water to cover the rice, and let it cook down gently. Add the chicken, tomatoes, clams, shrimps, sausages and more stock and water. Continue cooking until the rice is tender and the chicken cooked through and tender, adding more of the mixed hot stock and water as needed.

Serve garnished with strips of pimiento. Serves 6.

CHICKEN PIE PARISIENNE

> **3-pound fryer, cut into serving pieces**
> **¼ teaspoon salt**
> **Dash pepper**
> **½ teaspoon allspice**
> **9 tablespoons butter**
> **2 sweetbreads**
> **½ cup mushrooms, sliced**
> **4 slices lean bacon, shredded**
> **3 tablespoons cognac**
> **3 tablespoons Madeira**
> **2 cups heavy cream**
> **Rough puff paste (see Pastry)**

Season chicken with salt, pepper and allspice. Sauté in 8 tablespoons butter until golden brown and tender. Set aside. Wash sweetbreads and simmer 20 minutes in water to cover. Drain, cover with cold water and cool. Remove membrane and hard tubes and slice. Sauté mushrooms in 1 tablespoon butter and add to sweetbreads. Add bacon and mix well. Place chicken in a baking dish. Stir into the skillet in which the chicken was cooked the cognac, Madeira and cream. Cook for 1 minute, strain, add sweetbread mixture, simmer 3 minutes and add to chicken. Cover with rough puff paste and bake in a 425° oven until pastry is browned. Serves 4.

POULE AU POT

    6–7-pound fowl
      Salt, pepper
    ½ cup butter
    2 large onions, chopped
    1 teaspoon thyme
    ¼ cup chopped parsley
    1 cup finely chopped smoked ham
    2–3 cups soft bread crumbs
    6 eggs, slightly beaten
    ¼ cup cognac
    1-pound piece salt pork
    1 onion stuck with 2 cloves
    1 bay leaf
    3 tablespoons butter
    3 tablespoons flour
    1 cup heavy cream lightly beaten with
      3 egg yolks
      Dash nutmeg

Rub the fowl with salt and pepper. Heat the butter and sauté the onions until just limp. Add thyme, parsley, ham and bread crumbs and blend. Mix in the eggs and finally add the cognac. Season with a little salt and pepper. Stuff the bird with this mixture, place foil inside the vent and sew it up securely.

Put the fowl in a deep braising pot with the piece of salt pork and the onion stuck with cloves. Add the bay leaf and enough hot water to cover. Bring to a boil. Cover the pot, reduce the heat and simmer gently until the fowl is tender. This will take about 2¾ hours, or a little more. Remove the fowl to a hot platter and keep warm. Strain the stock in which the fowl cooked and skim off the fat.

Melt the butter, blend in the flour and cook for several minutes until just golden. Stir in 1 cup chicken stock, blending it well with the roux. Cook gently until smooth and thickened. Gradually add the cream and egg yolks and cook carefully, stirring constantly. Do not let the mixture boil. When well blended, taste for seasoning and add nutmeg.

Serve the fowl with the sauce, mashed potatoes, sautéed zucchini. Serves 6.

Note: The stuffing is even better cold the next day. Serve with slices of fowl dressed with mayonnaise.

ROLLED CHICKEN PÂTÉ

    8 tablespoons butter
    1 medium onion, thinly sliced
    1 stalk celery, cut in julienne
    1 carrot, cut in julienne
    1 tablespoon salt
    ¼ teaspoon Spice Parisienne or quatre épices
    2 large chicken breasts
    1 pork chop, about 6–7 ounces
    ¾ pound sweet butter, softened
    ⅓ cup cognac
    2 tablespoons shelled pistachio nuts
    1 pound prosciutto, sliced

Combine the 8 tablespoons butter, onion, celery, carrot, salt, and spice in a heavy saucepan. Add the chicken and pork chop. Cook, covered, over medium heat until tender. Do not overcook. Remove the chicken and pork from the saucepan and cool. Trim away skin, fat, and bone. Grind the meats using the finest blade. Beat into the softened sweet butter, adding the cognac and pistachio nuts as you beat. It is a good idea to use an electric mixer with a paddle attachment, if you have one.

Taste the pâté for seasoning. Turn out on a piece of waxed paper.

On two other pieces of waxed paper or plastic wrap arrange overlapping slices of prosciutto, forming two 10″ squares. Divide the chicken-pork mixture and form into two rolls. Place one roll on each of the prosciutto squares. Roll tightly, without squeezing, so the pâté is completely enveloped by the prosciutto. Place in polyethylene bags and refrigerate for 24 hours before serving. Cut in slices about ½″ thick and serve with toast and perhaps some greens.

CHICKEN SAUTÉ WITH WHITE WINE

    3½-to-4 pound chicken, quartered
      Flour (optional)
    4–6 tablespoons butter
      Salt, freshly ground pepper
    1 cup dry white wine
      Garnish: chopped parsley or chives

This is the basic method for preparing a chicken sauté to which you can add flavoring variations. You may dredge the chicken with flour if you wish. This gives a browner color, but unfloured chicken is more delicate. Brown the chicken pieces in the butter, turning each piece to color evenly. When browned, season to taste with salt and pepper and add ½–¾ cup white wine. Reduce heat and continue cooking until chicken is tender. You may cover the pan during part of the cooking time, which speeds the process, or cook uncovered. Any additional flavorings that you choose may be added during the cooking and the chicken pieces should be turned once or twice to bathe them thoroughly in the flavorings and juices. When the chicken is tender and cooked, remove it to a hot platter. Rinse the pan with remaining wine and let it cook down with the juices for a few minutes. Pour pan juices over the chicken and garnish with a little chopped parsley or chives. Serves 4.

PINK CHICKEN SAUTÉ

Sauté chicken. When the pieces are evenly browned, add 2 tablespoons finely chopped onion to the pan and let it cook down over low heat for 3 or 4 minutes. Add salt and pepper to taste, ½ teaspoon thyme and 2/3 cup white wine. Simmer gently until chicken is tender. Add ½ cup white wine and 1 tablespoon paprika and cook slowly for a few minutes. Remove chicken to a hot platter and reduce pan juices over high heat. Add 1 cup heavy cream, heat through and blend. Thicken sauce with beurre manié (small balls of butter and flour) and taste for seasoning. Pour sauce over chicken and garnish with a good sprinkling of paprika and finely chopped parsley. Serve with a rice pilaf and a crisp green salad.

MEXICAN CHICKEN SAUTÉ

Sauté chicken. When nearly browned, add 2 tablespoons finely chopped onion and cook gently until onion and chicken are browned and blended. Add salt to taste, 1 finely chopped clove garlic and 3 peeled hot green chiles (available in cans). Pour over this mixture 2/3 cup white wine and simmer gently until chicken is tender. Remove chicken to a hot platter, pour pan juices over it and garnish with chopped toasted almonds. Serve with polenta.

CHICKEN SAUTÉ FINES HERBES

Sauté chicken, add salt and pepper to taste and ½–¾ cup white wine. Cook gently until tender. Five

minutes before removing from pan, add 3 tablespoons finely chopped herbs in any of the following combinations: fresh tarragon and parsley; fresh tarragon, parsley and chives; parsley and rosemary; parsley and chervil; parsley, chives and dill. Add a little additional wine if necessary and turn the chicken pieces to bathe them well with the herb mixture. Remove chicken to platter and pour pan juices over it.

CHICKEN WITH PORT AND CREAM

> 3–3½-pound chicken, quartered, backbone removed
> Flour
> 4 tablespoons butter
> 1 teaspoon salt
> ½ teaspoon quatres épices (or Spice Parisienne)
> 1½ cups tawny port
> 1 cup heavy cream
> 3 egg yolks

Lightly flour the chicken and sauté it in the butter, turning it to color very lightly on all sides. Do not let it brown. Add salt and spice. Add 1 cup port, cover pan and simmer gently until tender. Remove chicken to a hot platter, add ½ cup port to pan juices and reduce over a high flame for 3–4 minutes. Lower heat and stir in heavy cream mixed with egg yolks. Cook very gently, stirring constantly until slightly thickened but do not let the sauce boil. Taste for seasoning. Pour sauce over chicken. Serve with a rice pilaf. Serves 4.

CHICKEN WITH LEMON SAUCE

    4-pound chicken, cut into serving pieces
    8 tablespoons butter
      Grated rind of 1 large lemon
      Grated rind of 1 large orange
    1 tablespoon Marsala
    1 tablespoon dry white wine
    2 teaspoons lemon juice
    ½ teaspoon salt
    ¼ teaspoon pepper
    1 cup sour cream
    1 tablespoon flour

Brown chicken in butter and cook until chicken is tender. Remove chicken from pan and place it in a warm dish. Add to the pan the grated rind of the lemon and the grated rind of the orange. Add Marsala and white wine. Stir, add the lemon juice, salt and pepper. Add sour cream slowly and stir in flour. Add chicken and cook 3 minutes longer. Serves 4–6.

CHICKEN WITH CHEESE

    ¼ cup butter
    3-pound frying chicken, cut up
    1 medium-sized onion, chopped
      Salt, pepper to taste
    1 clove garlic, minced
    1 tomato, peeled and cut up
    1 cup chicken broth
    ¼ pound kasseri cheese, cut into cubes

Melt the butter and sauté the chicken pieces and onion, turning the chicken to brown all sides. Season with salt and pepper. Add the garlic, tomato, and chicken broth. Cover and simmer for 30 minutes, or until almost tender. Add the cheese and cook 10 minutes longer. Serve with pilaf. Serves 4–6.

SAUTÉED CHICKEN WITH WALNUTS

    6 chicken leg and thigh joints
      Flour
    3 tablespoons oil
    3 tablespoons butter
    1 teaspoon salt
    ½ teaspoon freshly ground black pepper
    1 small onion, finely chopped

    1 cup finely chopped walnuts
    1 cup chicken broth, reduced from 1 quart
    ¾ cup halved walnuts, toasted and salted
    ¼ cup chopped parsley

Dredge the chicken joints lightly in flour. Brown them well in the hot oil and butter, and season with the salt and pepper. Add the chopped onion and nuts (these may be ground in the blender), and cover with the rich reduced broth. Simmer for 20–25 minutes, or until tender, turning once or twice. Remove to a hot platter, garnish with toasted walnut halves and sprinkle with chopped parsley.

Serve with sautéed eggplant seasoned with thyme or basil-flavored tomato sauce. Serves 6.

CHICKEN WITH MUSSELS

    ½ cup olive oil
    2 3-pound chickens, cut into serving pieces
    4 cloves garlic, unpeeled
    ¼ teaspoon dried oregano
    ¼ teaspoon dried sweet basil
    ½ teaspoon dried rosemary
    2 cups dry white wine
    1 pound tomatoes, peeled and coarsely chopped,
      or 1-pound can Italian tomatoes, coarsely
      chopped
    1 green pepper, seeded and thinly sliced
    ¼ cup minced Italian parsley
    2 pounds mussels
      Salt, pepper to taste

Heat the oil in a large skillet and brown chicken over high heat. Add the garlic, oregano, basil, rosemary and wine. Reduce heat to medium and cook 5 minutes. Heat the tomatoes and pepper in a saucepan and add to the chicken with the parsley. Reduce heat to low, cover, and simmer for ½ hour.

Scrub mussels thoroughly under cold running water and add them to the chicken. Raise heat to medium, uncover, and cook until mussels are open and chicken is tender. Remove chicken and mussels to a serving platter and keep warm. Remove and discard garlic cloves, if desired. If the sauce is too watery, reduce it over high heat. Add salt and pepper to taste. Pour over the chicken and serve immediately. Serves 8.

CHICKEN LIVER CASSEROLE

> 1 pound chicken livers
> ¼ cup butter
>   Salt, freshly ground pepper
> 1 cup rice
> 2 cups sour cream
> 1 teaspoon dried dill weed or crushed tarragon

Cut livers in half and sauté lightly in butter until blood stops running. Season with salt. Cook rice until tender, but not soggy. Season sour cream with 1 teaspoon salt, a little pepper and the dill or tarragon. Arrange a layer of rice in a buttered 1½-quart casserole, add a layer of chicken livers, then a layer of sour cream. Repeat until ingredients are used, making a top layer of rice. Cover and bake at 350° for 30 minutes or until hot. Serves 6.

SAUTÉED CHICKEN LIVERS WITH ONIONS AND APPLES

> 1 large or 2 medium red onions, thinly sliced
> 10 tablespoons butter
> 2 large apples, peeled, cored and thickly sliced
> 2 tablespoons sugar
> 1½ pounds chicken livers
> 3 tablespoons flour
> 2 cups chicken stock
>   Salt, pepper to taste

Sauté the onions in 2 tablespoons of the butter until tender. Sauté the apples in a heavy pan in 2 tablespoons butter until barely tender. Sprinkle with the sugar and continue to cook until glazed and very tender. Dry the livers thoroughly, dust with the flour, and sauté over high heat in the remaining 6 tablespoons butter until the livers are brown. Reduce the heat and add the stock gradually, stirring constantly, until the sauce thickens. Add the onions, salt, and pepper. Remove to a serving platter or chafing dish and top with glazed apples. Serves 8.

DUCK WITH CHERRIES

> 2 young Long Island ducks
>   Salt
> ¼ cup kirsch
> 1½ cups brown sauce (canned may be used)
> 1 cup sour cherries (Montmorency preferred)

Rub the ducks with salt, putting some salt inside as well. Place on a rack over a shallow pan. Roast at 350° allowing about 12–13 minutes per pound of dressed duck. Duck is done when the leg joints move easily. If a crispy skin is desired, you may increase heat to 500° for the last 15 minutes of cooking period and shorten the cooking time slightly.

Remove ducks to a hot platter. Skim off all excess fat from pan and rinse pan with kirsch. Add to brown sauce in a small saucepan. Bring to a boil and reduce for 2–3 minutes. Add cherries to the sauce and heat to the boiling point. Correct seasoning and pour sauce around duck. Serves 4–6.

DUCK WITH PEACHES

> 2 ducks
> ⅓ cup port or Madeira
> 1½ cups brown sauce
> 12 peach halves
> 6 tablespoons brown sugar
>   Butter
> ⅓ cup bourbon

Roast duck as for Duck with Cherries. Skim off fat, rinse pan with wine, add to brown sauce, bring to a boil and reduce 2–3 minutes.

While sauce is being prepared, spread peach halves with sugar and dot with butter. Broil until sugar and butter are melted and peaches heated through. Surround duck with broiled peaches, pour heated bourbon over peaches and flame as you bring it to table.

Serve sauce separately. Serves 4–6.

DUCK WITH GREEN OLIVES

> 2 ducks
>   Salt, pepper
> 12 juniper berries, crushed
> ⅓ cup gin
> ⅔ cup small green olives
> 1½ cups brown sauce

Rub ducks with salt. Put crushed juniper berries in interior of birds. Roast ducks on a rack in a 350° oven allowing about 12 minutes per pound. Increase heat to 500° for 15 minutes if a very crisp skin is desired.

Pour off excess fat in roasting pan, reserving pan juices. Flambé ducks with gin. Combine pan juices and green olives and heat for 3–4 minutes. Stir in brown sauce and simmer 1 or 2 minutes. Correct seasoning. Serves 4–6.

CANETON À L'ORANGE

> 2 4–5 pound ducks
> 2 carrots, sliced
> 2 onions, sliced
>   Thyme, bay leaf
> ¼ cup white wine
> ½ cup chicken consommé
> 2 tablespoons and ¼ cup sugar
> 1 tablespoon vinegar
>   Juice of two oranges
>   Juice of ½ lemon
> 1–2 tablespoons flour
> 1 teaspoon Kitchen Bouquet
> 2 oranges, sectioned
> 2 ounces Curaçao or Grand Marnier
> 1 ounce cognac

Prepare ducks for roasting. Place in pan with carrots, onions, a little thyme and a bay leaf. Roast at 325° for 50 minutes to 1 hour, so the meat still shows a little blood when pricked with a toothpick or skewer. Remove and keep hot. Place roasting pan on heat and cook for a few minutes. Skim off excess fat and rinse pan with white wine and consommé. Cook for 5 minutes. Strain mixture through a fine sieve. Melt 2 tablespoons sugar in a heavy pan over low heat and just as it begins to caramelize, add vinegar and fruit juices. Add strained pan juices. Bring to a boil. Skim off excess fat. Mix flour with a little water and blend with sauce; cook until thickened to a syrupy consistency. Correct seasoning. Add Kitchen Bouquet to give rich color. Garnish ducks with sections of orange. Add liqueur, ¼ cup sugar and cognac to sauce and pour sauce over and around ducks. Serves 4–6.

CANETON AU MUSCADET

> 4–5 pound Long Island duckling
>   Salt, ground ginger, ground cloves
> ⅓ cup cognac

> 1 pint Muscadet
> 2 or 3 small onions stuck with cloves
> 2 or 3 tiny carrots
> 2 tablespoons beurre manié
> 5 or 6 medium size potatoes
> 5 tablespoons butter
>   Freshly ground pepper
> ⅔ cup sultana raisins

This duck recipe is unusually light and delicate. Rub the duckling well with salt, a little ground ginger and ground cloves. Place on a rack in a roasting pan and roast in a 325° oven for 1¼ hours. Remove duck from oven and place in a deep iron casserole. Pour warmed cognac over it and ignite. Add Muscadet, onions stuck with cloves, carrots and beurre manié. Blend. Return to oven to cook for 30 minutes, basting duck occasionally with liquid in casserole.

Meanwhile peel and slice the potatoes and brown them well in the butter. They should cook until they are just soft but crisp around the edges and on the outside. Shake the pan from time to time to keep them from sticking on the bottom. Season to taste with salt and pepper.

Add the raisins to the duck mixture in casserole and cook for a further 10 minutes, basting once. To serve, arrange duck on a hot platter and surround it with the potatoes. Pour a little of the sauce over the duck and serve the rest in a sauce boat. Serves 4.

SWEET AND SOUR DUCK

> 5-pound duck
> 1½ teaspoons salt
> ¼ teaspoon freshly ground black pepper
> ¼ cup flour
> 2 tablespoons butter
> 1½ cups thinly sliced onions
> ⅛ teaspoon ground cloves
> 2 cups chicken broth
> 4 tablespoons sugar
> 1 tablespoon water
> 3 tablespoons wine vinegar
> 1 tablespoon chopped fresh mint (or
>   ½ teaspoon dried)

Wash duck. Remove as much fat as possible: dry. Rub with a mixture of the salt, pepper and flour.

Melt the butter in a Dutch oven or casserole; add the onions and duck. Brown the duck on all sides. Pour off the fat. Add the cloves and broth, cover and cook over low heat 2 hours or until tender. Turn the duck frequently. Transfer duck to a pan and place in a hot oven. Skim the fat off the gravy.

In a small saucepan, combine the sugar and water: cook over low heat until browned. Stir into the gravy with the vinegar and mint. Cook over low heat 5 minutes. Taste for seasoning—the sauce should be sweet and sour; add more sugar or vinegar, if needed.

Carve duck and serve the sauce separately. Serves 4.

ROAST ROCK CORNISH GAME HENS WITH RICE, TARRAGON AND PINE NUT STUFFING

>1 medium onion, finely chopped
>Butter
>2 cups cooked rice
>2 teaspoons tarragon
>1½ teaspoons salt
>½ teaspoon freshly ground black pepper
>3 tablespoons cognac
>¼ cup pine nuts
>4 game hens

Sauté the onion in 6 tablespoons butter, add the rice, tarragon, salt, pepper, cognac and nuts and toss well. Stuff the game hens with the rice mixture and cover each vent with aluminum foil. Place the birds on a rack in a shallow pan.

Brush well with butter. Roast in a 350° oven for 15 minutes. Baste with melted butter and turn to opposite side. Roast 15 minutes. Place on backs and baste well. Continue roasting until nicely browned and tender—about 15 minutes. Serve the roast game hens at once with pan juices. Serves 4.

STUFFED BONED SQUABS

>1 cup wild rice
>6 cups chicken broth
>1 cup chopped onions
>1 cup chopped mushrooms
>12 tablespoons butter
>¾ teaspoon freshly ground black pepper
>1 teaspoon Worcestershire sauce
>6 squabs or Rock Cornish hens
>Salt
>1 teaspoon paprika
>1 cup sliced onions
>1 cup sliced carrots
>½ cup cognac

Wash the wild rice thoroughly. Put in a saucepan with 4 cups chicken broth; bring to a boil and cook over low heat 25 minutes or until tender but still firm. Drain if any liquid remains. Sauté chopped onions and mushrooms in 6 tablespoons butter for 10 minutes. Add to the rice with ¼ teaspoon pepper and the Worcestershire sauce. Toss lightly and taste for seasoning.

Have the birds boned by the butcher or bone them yourself. Season with 1 tablespoon salt, ½ teaspoon pepper and the paprika and stuff with the wild rice. Sew up the birds securely and close the openings.

Melt remaining butter in a casserole; sauté the sliced onions and carrots for 10 minutes. Add the birds and brown on all sides. Stir in remaining broth. Cover and cook in a 350° oven 45 minutes or until tender. Remove from oven and place over direct heat. Pour the warmed cognac over the birds and set aflame. When flames die, taste sauce mixture in pan for seasoning. Thicken sauce if necessary with 2 teaspoons flour mixed with water. Serves 6.

DEVILED SQUABS WITH TARRAGON HOLLANDAISE

Split 4 young squabs and rub well with garlic, soy sauce and oil. Broil, bone side up, for about 9 minutes. Turn, salt and pepper to taste and broil, skin side up, for 7 minutes. Meanwhile heat ½ cup oil and prepare about ¼ cup bread crumbs. When broiled, remove and brush well with hot oil, press into the bread crumbs and sprinkle with oil, salt and pepper. Replace in the broiling pan, farther away from the heating unit, and broil slowly until crumbs are browned and crisp. Make Hollandaise sauce and add 2 teaspoons chopped fresh tarragon or 1 teaspoon dried tarragon. Serve with the squabs. Serves 4.

PIGEONNEAU VALLÉE D'AUGE

½ pound mushrooms, finely chopped
15 tablespoons butter
    Salt, pepper
4 squabs, split and trimmed
⅓ cup calvados or applejack
1 cup heavy cream
3 egg yolks
6 tart cooking apples, peeled and thinly sliced
    Sugar

Sauté chopped mushrooms in 4 tablespoons butter for 3 minutes. Cover and reduce heat. Simmer for 15 minutes. Salt and pepper to taste.

Melt 6 tablespoons butter in a skillet, brown the squabs lightly on both sides. Salt and pepper to taste. Flame with calvados or applejack. Add mushrooms and cook until squabs are tender, about 12–15 minutes, turning once.

Remove squabs to hot platter. Mix cream and egg yolks. Spoon mushroom mixture over squabs. Rinse pan lightly with calvados or applejack, add 1 tablespoon butter and the cream and egg yolk mixture. Stir until the sauce is just thickened. Correct seasoning and pour over squabs.

Sauté apples quickly in 4 tablespoons butter, turning carefully with spatula. Sprinkle lightly with sugar and remove to a warm serving dish. Serve apples with the squabs. Serves 4.

ROAST GOOSE WITH SAUSAGE STUFFING

7-pound goose
    Salt, black pepper
4 cups finely chopped sautéed onion
2½ pounds sausage meat, lightly sautéed
1 cup applesauce
    Goose liver, finely chopped
1 teaspoon ground sage
¼ cup brandy
    Butter

Wash the goose well. Dry thoroughly. Season inside with salt and pepper. Mix the onion, sausage meat, applesauce, goose liver, sage and brandy, season to taste with salt and pepper, stuff the goose with the mixture and tie it up securely. Place on a roasting rack and brush the top with a little melted butter, salt and pepper. Roast in a 375° oven, allowing 18–20 minutes per pound. Baste frequently, adding 1 tablespoon water to the pan each time. Serves 6.

JUNIOR GOOSE WITH FRUIT AND NUT STUFFING

1 junior goose
½ cup currants
½ cup nuts (pecans, almonds or walnuts)
2 cups chopped apple
2 eggs, slightly beaten
3 cups bread crumbs
    Cream
    Salt, pepper
    Prunes, pitted and soaked overnight in red wine

Remove liver, gizzard and heart of goose and cook in water to cover until tender, then drain and chop. (Save the stock for gravy.) Add currants, nuts, apple, eggs, bread crumbs and enough cream to moisten slightly. Season with salt and pepper to taste and stuff the goose. Fasten opening and roast in a 400° oven for 20 minutes. Prick skin, reduce heat to 325°, and continue roasting the goose for 2½ hours or until the juice runs clear when the leg is pricked. Serve garnished with prunes. Serves 6.

TIMING A ROAST TURKEY

It is almost impossible to give hard-and-fast rules about the length of time a turkey should roast. Differences in the shape and tenderness of individual birds may make it necessary to increase or decrease the cooking time, and your personal preference for a moist or well-done bird should also be taken into account. Broadly speaking, in a 325° oven a 6–8-pound turkey will take 2–2½ hours, an 8–12 pound turkey 2½–3 hours; a 12–16-pound turkey 3–3¾ hours; a 16–20-pound turkey 3¾–4½ hours; a 20–25-pound turkey between 4½ and 5½ hours. However, these timings are approximate and in no way infallible.

A more accurate way to judge whether a turkey is done is to take the internal temperature by inserting a meat thermometer into the thickest part of the thigh.

According to how well-done you like your turkey, it should register between 175° and 185°. Although the accepted internal temperature is 185°, this seems too high. Try taking the turkey out of the oven when the thermometer registers 170° and let it stand for 20–25 minutes before carving to allow the internal temperature to mount. If you do not use a meat thermometer, trust your intuition and let your fingers (protected by a paper napkin) determine the state of doneness. The drumstick and breast meat should feel soft when pressed with the fingers, and the drumstick and thigh joint should move easily. Puncture the skin at the joint of the leg and thigh to see if the juices run clear.

ROAST TURKEY
WITH PESTO-RICE STUFFING

    4 cups cooked rice
    1 cup pesto (see Stuffings)
    ½ cup pine nuts
    8–10-pound turkey
      Olive oil
      Bacon slices

Toss the rice with the pesto and pine nuts and stuff the bird lightly. Close the vent and truss the bird. Rub well with olive oil. Place the turkey on its side on a rack in a roasting pan. Cover with slices of bacon and roast at 325° for 1 hour. Turn on other side and roast for another hour. Turn the bird on its back and roast with bacon covering the breast and legs until the bird is tender and done. Baste from time to time. Serves 8–10.

ROAST TURKEY WOBURN ABBEY

This is an unusual way of serving turkey, but a pleasant change from the traditional Christmas roast turkey. For this recipe, you may use two young turkeys in preference to a large one.

    1 large onion, chopped
    5 tablespoons butter
    2 cups rice, well washed
    3 cups rich chicken or beef stock
    ½ pound cooked ham, diced
      Salt, pepper to taste
    10–12 pound turkey

Sauté the onion in the butter. Add the rice and mix well. Add the stock and simmer slowly until all the stock is absorbed, but the rice is slightly under-cooked. Add the ham, salt, and pepper. Stuff the turkey with this mixture, cover with a tent of foil and cook in a 325° oven for approximately 3 hours, or until the drumsticks move easily and the juices run clear when skin is punctured at the joint. Remove the foil for the last 30 minutes to allow the turkey to brown, and increase the heat if necessary. Serves 10–12. Serve with Sweet and Sour Sauce.

SWEET AND SOUR SAUCE

    2 slices pineapple, chopped
    1 teaspoon chopped preserved ginger (optional)
      Oil for frying
    6 tablespoons chopped onion
    1 tablespoon vinegar
    1 tablespoon tomato catsup
    1 tablespoon soy sauce
    1 teaspoon sherry
    1 teaspoon cornstarch mixed with
      1½ cups water

Fry the pineapple and ginger (if desired) in oil for a few minutes. Add the onion and fry until tender. Add other ingredients and simmer slowly 5–10 minutes.

POACHED TURKEY

    6 thin slices salt pork
    4 carrots, cut up
    3 onions, sliced
    2 leeks, cut up
    6 stalks celery, cut up
    1 tablespoon chopped parsley
      Thyme, bay leaf
    1 clove garlic, peeled and sliced
    10-pound turkey
      Salt, pepper, nutmeg
    1½ pints clear chicken broth
    1 pint dry white wine
    2 tablespoons cognac
    ½ pound butter
      Grated rind of 2 lemons
    1 tablespoon chopped chives
      Parsley for garnish

Put the salt pork on a rack in the bottom of a roasting pan with a cover. Scatter the carrots, onions, leeks, celery, parsley, a pinch of thyme, a crumbled bay leaf and the garlic over the pork.

Rub the turkey, inside and out, with salt and pepper, truss it and place it on the bed of vegetables. Pour over it the broth, wine and cognac. Cover the roasting pan and simmer on top of the stove (it's actually steaming) for about 3 hours, or until tender. Lift out the turkey, drain it and set it aside to cool a little. Strain the broth and reserve it. Discard the vegetables and clean the roasting pan.

Remove as much skin as possible from the turkey, not bothering about the back. Return the bird to the roasting pan with the broth. Keep it warm, over low heat or in a slow oven, basting occasionally.

Clarify the butter and add to it a little freshly ground black pepper and nutmeg. Add grated lemon rind and chives and heat.

When ready to serve, place the turkey on a hot platter and garnish lavishly with parsley. Pour a small amount of broth over the breast and serve the butter sauce separately. Serves 8–10.

BRAISED TRUFFLED TURKEY

    8–10-pound turkey
    Truffles, as many as possible, fresh if available
  2 pounds ground pork
  1½ pounds ground veal
  8 shallots, chopped

    Butter
    Salt, pepper to taste
  ¾ cup cognac
  2 cups fine bread crumbs
  ½ cup chopped parsley
  3 carrots, cut in fine julienne
  3 leeks, cut in fine julienne
  3 stalks celery, cut in fine julienne
    White wine
    Beurre manié (flour and butter kneaded together)
    Freshly ground white pepper

The night before you plan to cook the turkey, clean the bird, slice some truffles, and slip them under the skin. Slip several truffles into the cavity as well, wrap the bird loosely in foil, and leave in the refrigerator overnight.

Next day, prepare the stuffing. Sauté the pork, veal, and shallots in 8 tablespoons butter and blend well with salt to taste and ½ cup cognac. Do not cook completely—merely mix over heat and add the crumbs and parsley. Add seasonings to taste. Combine with the truffles in the turkey and stuff lightly. Sew up the vent and truss the turkey.

Brown the turkey well in butter or butter and oil mixed and place the bird on a bed of the julienne carrots, leeks, and celery in a large braising pan. Add the butter or butter and oil and 1½ cups white wine and turn heat to high. Cover pan, reduce heat, and cook for 2½–3 hours, basting the bird occasionally with equal parts of melted butter and white wine. When the bird is tender, remove to a hot platter and strain off the pan juices. Reduce the juices to 2 cups and thicken with beurre manié. Season to taste with salt and freshly ground white pepper and add remaining ¼ cup cognac.

Serve this delectable braised turkey with Potatoes Anna and braised celery. Serves 8–10.

TURKEY CHILI

This is not a traditional chili and has no connection with any Mexican or Texas recipe.

  5–6 pound turkey, cut in quarters
  1 onion stuck with cloves

Salmi of Cold Turkey

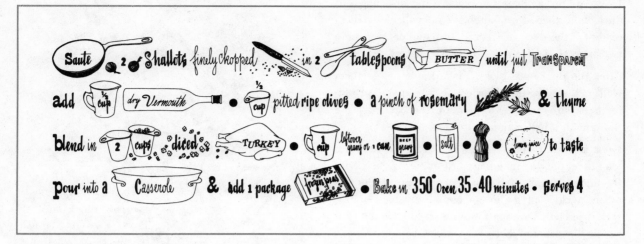

Sauté 2 of shallots finely chopped in 2 tablespoons BUTTER until just transparent • add 1/2 cup dry Vermouth • 1/3 cup pitted ripe olives • a pinch of rosemary & thyme • blend in 2 cups diced TURKEY • 1 cup leftover gravy or a can DEEP gravy • salt • • lemon juice to taste • pour into a Casserole & add 1 package frozen peas • Bake in 350° oven 35-40 minutes • Serves 4

2 stalks celery
2–3 sprigs parsley
2 small dried hot peppers
　Salt
2 tablespoons chili powder
4-ounce can peeled green chiles, finely chopped
1 cup almonds, ground or blended
½ cup peanuts, ground or blended
1 large onion, finely chopped
3 cloves garlic, finely chopped
2 green peppers, finely chopped
4 tablespoons olive oil
1 cup small green olives
½ cup blanched almonds

Cover the turkey pieces with water and add the onion stuck with cloves, the celery, parsley, and peppers. Bring to a boil. Reduce the heat, skim off any scum which may rise to the top, and cover the pot. Simmer until the turkey is tender but not falling from the bones. Remove the turkey pieces and cool until they can be handled. Remove the meat from the bones in good-size pieces.

Reduce the broth by half over a brisk flame. You should have about 4 cups broth. Strain and adjust the salt. Add the chili powder, the green chiles, and the ground nuts and simmer until the mixture is thickened, smooth and well-blended in flavor. You may find you wish to add additional chili powder. Sauté the onion, garlic, and green peppers in the olive oil. Add to the sauce and cook for 5 minutes. Add the

turkey meat and heat thoroughly. Add the olives and blanched almonds and reheat for 3 minutes.

Serve with rice or polenta and crisp French bread. A radish and cucumber salad with a vinaigrette sauce is good with this. Tortillas are excellent with the chili if you don't serve polenta and French bread. Drink beer. Serves 8–10.

SCALLOPED TURKEY

12 ounces noodles, cooked until tender
　and drained
1 cup cold turkey stuffing
2 cups diced cold turkey
1 pound mushrooms, sliced
½ cup finely chopped onion
　Butter
¼ cup chopped parsley
8 hard-cooked eggs, sliced
　Turkey gravy or Béchamel sauce
　Buttered crumbs

Make a layer of half the cooked noodles in the bottom of a deep 2½-quart baking dish. Add the stuffing and turkey. Sauté the mushrooms and onion in butter and add to the dish with the parsley and sliced hard-cooked eggs. Add turkey gravy or Béchamel sauce and top with the remaining noodles. Dot with butter and sprinkle with buttered crumbs. Cover and bake in a 350° oven for 25–30 minutes. Remove cover for last 10 minutes of cooking time. Serve with a crisp salad. Serves 6–8.

WILD DUCK

If you are not an expert in picking and drawing wild duck, take them to a butcher who will clean them ready for the oven or freezer. In game centers there are shops that offer this service to hunters.

After the ducks are picked and drawn, singe them well and, if you are a perfectionist, remove all pinfeathers with tweezers. Then rub the cavity of the ducks with a half lemon.

Duck is seldom stuffed unless it is to be roasted for a long time, but you may place seasonings in the cavity for added flavor: herbs, a few juniper berries, an onion, a clove of garlic, an orange or some orange skin. The choice is a matter of personal taste. Duck is oftened marinated before cooking. You can use a wine mixture, cognac with seasonings, or other mixtures of liquor and seasonings. Allow one duck per serving or, if they are large, a half duck. If you have teal, you may need two per serving.

QUICK-ROASTED WILD DUCK

Clean and singe the birds and rub the interiors with a cut lemon. If you wish, place a little onion and celery or several slices of orange inside each one. Or you may use a sprig of rosemary or thyme. Place the ducks on a rack over a shallow pan and roast in a 450°–475° oven, basting them well with melted butter or oil mixed with red wine, or with orange juice and melted butter. Allow 15 minutes for teal and 20–25 minutes for larger birds, depending on size. Salt and pepper to taste.

If you are an expert carver, cut the ducks in halves or quarters with a sharp knife, or use carving shears. Serve with wild rice or a barley casserole with mushrooms or almonds. An orange and onion salad with a touch of rosemary in the dressing or tiny buttered turnips are pleasant accompaniments.

Variation: Roast the ducks as above, basting with butter and white wine. Season to taste. Add 1 cup white wine and 1 cup small green olives to the pan 5 minutes before the birds are done. After you remove the ducks from the oven, flame them with ½ cup cognac. Cook the sauce down for a minute or two and add 1 cup of brown sauce. Blend well and heat through thoroughly. Serve with the duck.

BROILED WILD DUCK

This delightful way of preparing duck takes careful attention, but the result is well worth it. Split the ducks and rub them well with soy sauce and a little tarragon or rosemary. For rare duck, broil under a hot flame, watching carefully, for about 6 minutes on the bone side and about 4–6 minutes on the skin side. Be sure not to burn the skin. Baste with butter and soy or butter and white wine. Season to taste.

Serve with sautéed corn and green peppers.

Variation: Split the ducks and rub a little garlic and rosemary into the skin. Broil. When birds are done, remove from broiler and flame with gin. Serve with fried parsley and waffle potatoes.

DANISH PICKLED
WILD DUCK

An excellent and different way of preparing wild duck. Domestic duck is too fat for this method, which preserves rather than drains off the excess fat.

2 wild ducks, prepared for cooking
1 tablespoon salt for each quart of water
5 bay leaves
12 whole juniper berries
8 whole black peppercorns
1 cup red wine or ½ cup vinegar

Place ducks in deep kettle. Measure and add enough cold water to cover ducks. Add salt, bay leaves, juniper berries and peppercorns. Simmer covered until almost tender. (Cooking time depends on age of ducks.) Add wine or vinegar and simmer covered until tender. Remove from heat, cool and refrigerate in liquid for 2 days. At serving time, drain and serve cold, or reheat in liquid. Serve with creamed potatoes and pickled beets. Serves 4–6.

POTTED WILD DUCKS

1 cup chopped onion
½ pound butter
Duck giblets, chopped
4 cups cooked rice or wild rice
1 teaspoon thyme or ½ teaspoon rosemary
1 bay leaf, crumbled
1 teaspoon salt
½ cup walnuts
⅓ cup cognac
4 wild ducks
4 tablespoons oil
4 slices bacon
4 slices onion
Rind of an orange
1 cup red wine
1 cup brown gravy (canned may be used)

Sauté the chopped onion in ¼ pound butter. When nicely colored, remove and sauté the chopped giblets briefly. Mix the onion and giblets with the rice, thyme or rosemary, bay leaf, salt, walnuts, cognac and the juices from the pan in which the onions and giblets were cooked. Stuff the ducks. Secure the vents.

Melt remaining butter and the oil and heat until bubbly. Brown the ducks on all sides in the hot fat. Arrange the ducks on a rack in a roasting pan and top each with a slice of bacon and a slice of onion. Add the orange rind and wine to the pan and cover. Simmer in a 300° oven for 1¼ hours.

Remove the ducks to a hot platter and blend the brown gravy with the pan juices. Serve with the sauce, and buttered turnips mixed with sautéed mushrooms. If the ducks are very small, serve 1 per person. Larger ducks will serve 2.

This same recipe can be used for other smallish game birds that are not too tender.

SALMI OF WILD DUCK

1 or 2 ducks, cut in quarters
4 tablespoons butter
2 tablespoons flour
1 cup red Bordeaux wine
2 cups game stock or beef broth
Salt, freshly ground black pepper to taste
2 small onions, thinly sliced
1 bay leaf
2 cloves
½ teaspoon Tabasco
2 cups small Manzanilla olives
Chopped parsley

Brown the duck pieces in butter until golden. Transfer to a deep pot or casserole. Add flour to the pan and brown it well in the butter. Stir in the wine, stock and all other ingredients except the olives and parsley. Bring to a boil and simmer for 5 minutes, stirring part of the time. Pour the sauce over the duck pieces, cover the pot and simmer for 1½ hours. Taste for seasoning and add the olives and chopped parsley. If you feel this sauce is too thin, thicken it with beurre manié.

Serve with wild rice and mushrooms and braised endive. Serves 2–4.

WILD GOOSE

If young and tender, wild goose may be prepared in almost any way given for wild duck. Baste it with butter and red or white wine. Roast at 400°–425° for 35–40 minutes. Season with juniper berries, salt and pepper. A goose will serve 2–4, according to size.

Serve with red cabbage braised in red wine with apple and sautéed polenta.

TERRINE OF WILD GOOSE
OR WILD DUCK

> 1 large wild goose or 2 wild ducks
> 1 pound livers—duck, goose or chicken—or a
>   mixture, ground
> 1 pound lean pork, ground
> 6 shallots
> 1 clove garlic
> 1 teaspoon thyme
> 6 eggs, lightly beaten
> 1 tablespoon flour
> ⅓ cup cognac
> 1½ teaspoons salt
> ½ teaspoon freshly ground black pepper
>   Pork skin
>   Salt pork or larding pork

Skin the goose or ducks, reserving the skin. Cut the meat from the bones, keeping the breast fillets intact. Grind the rest of the meat and blend with the ground livers and pork. Grind the shallots and garlic and add to the meat. Add the thyme, eggs, flour, cognac and salt and pepper. If you wish to check for flavor balance, sauté a little of this farce in butter until done and taste for seasoning.

Line a terrine with the skin of the goose or ducks and some pork skin. Place a layer of farce in the bottom. Add the breast fillets and cover with the remaining farce. Top with thin strips of salt pork or larding pork and bake, uncovered, in a 300° oven for 2½ hours.

Variation: Add fingers of tongue, ham or a few truffles along with the breast meat.

WILD GOOSE GUMBO

> 1 wild goose
> 1½ teaspoons salt
> 1 teaspoon freshly ground black pepper
> ½ teaspoon Tabasco
> 2 tablespoons butter
> 2 tablespoons flour
> 1 cup chopped onion
> 4 cloves garlic, finely chopped
> 4–5 tablespoons oil
> 2 quarts water
> 2 dozen oysters and liquor
>   Cooked rice
>   Filé powder

Cut the goose into serving-size pieces and season with salt, pepper and Tabasco. Melt the butter and add the flour and cook to a dark roux. Add the onion and garlic and cook, stirring, until the onion softens.

Meanwhile brown the pieces of goose in the oil. Combine with the onion roux and add the water. Bring to a boil and simmer until the goose is tender. Add the oysters and oyster liquor and simmer 15 minutes longer. Correct the seasoning. Serve with rice and a dish of filé powder as a condiment. Serves 4–6.

SAUTÉED QUAIL

Split the birds and dust lightly with flour. Sauté in butter or oil or a mixture of the two. Cook quickly on the skin side, turn and cook on the bone side and turn again. When the birds are nicely browned, reduce the heat and continue cooking until they are tender and done. This should take from 12–18 minutes, depending on the size. Salt and pepper to taste and serve on fried toast with the finely chopped giblets which have been sautéed separately in butter.

ROAST QUAIL WITH VINE LEAVES

The French sometimes bard and wrap their quail in vine leaves. This gives the birds a distinctive flavor as well as keeping them moist. If you don't have a convenient vineyard, vine leaves may be bought in jars at shops specializing in Greek delicacies.

> 12 quail
> Butter
> Salt, pepper
> Juniper berries
> 12 slices barding pork, cut very thin
> Vine leaves
> 1 cup white wine
> 1 cup seedless grapes
> 12 pieces fried toast spread with
>   quail giblets, sautéed in butter

Rub the quail with butter, salt and pepper and place juniper berries in the cavities. Wrap each bird with barding pork and then wrap in vine leaves. Secure with twine. Roast on a rack in a shallow pan in a 400° oven for 15–18 minutes. Remove the twine and reduce the heat to 300°. Cook for 5–6 minutes.

Arrange the quail on a hot platter. Skim the fat from the pan juices and add wine and grapes. Cook 4 minutes over a brisk flame.

Serve the quail on the toast spread with giblets and pass the sauce separately. Serves 6.

QUAIL WITH SHALLOTS AND MUSHROOMS

> 8–10 shallots, peeled and chopped fine
> 12 tablespoons butter
> ½ pound mushrooms, finely chopped
> 1 teaspoon salt
> ½ teaspoon freshly ground black pepper
> 1 teaspoon Worcestershire sauce
> Dash Tabasco
> 4 tablespoons olive oil
> 1 clove garlic, finely chopped
> 6 quail, split and dredged in flour
> ⅓ cup cognac
> Broth (if necessary)

Sauté the shallots in 8 tablespoons butter. Add the mushrooms and let them cook slowly for 25 minutes, stirring from time to time. Add the seasonings and cook for 5 minutes more.

Heat 4 tablespoons butter and the oil in a large, heavy skillet and add the garlic. Add the quail and sauté until nicely browned on both sides. Flame with cognac and reduce the heat. Add the mushroom and shallot mixture and if it is too dry, a little broth. Cover the pan and simmer for 6–8 minutes, or until the birds are tender and the flavors blended.

Serve with polenta that has been cooled and then sliced and heated in butter. Serves 3.

QUAIL WITH JUNIPER BERRIES

Melt ¼ pound butter in a large skillet. When it is hot and bubbly, quickly brown 6 split quail, lightly dredged in flour, on both sides. Add 8–10 crushed juniper berries and reduce the heat. Cover the pan and cook for about 5 minutes. Flame the birds with 1/3 cup gin and cook gently for another 5 minutes, basting with the pan juices. Season with salt and pepper and serve on toast with chopped, sautéed giblets. Serves 3.

ROAST WOODCOCK

Woodcock should be cooked without drawing. The head with its long beak is often skinned and the beak skewered through the bird before roasting. Cover the breast with fat back and roast in a 400° oven for 15–17 minutes. Baste once or twice with a little red wine and melted butter. Season to taste with salt and pepper and serve on toast without removing the barding pork. Garnish with watercress. Allow 1 or 2 per serving.

Freshly made potato chips or waffle potatoes and buttered young turnips are the best accompaniments for roast woodcock.

Variation: Roast the woodcock on pieces of fried toast that are not too well browned. The juices will run onto the toast during the cooking and give added flavor. Remove the birds from the oven and flame them, using ¼ cup cognac for each woodcock. Or top the toast with a slice of foie gras and then with the woodcock.

PÂTÉ DE BÉCASSE EN CROÛTE

> 4 woodcock
> 6 tablespoons butter
>   Salt, pepper
> ¼ pound chicken livers
>   Woodcock giblets
> ½ pound fresh pork, ground
> ¼ pound veal, ground
> ½–¾ teaspoon thyme
> ½ teaspoon Spice Parisienne
> 3 ounces cognac
> 1 large or 2 small truffles, chopped
> 8 thin slices ham
> 1½ pounds (about) puff paste (see Pastry)
> 1 egg yolk beaten with 2 tablespoons cream

Bone the birds and halve the breasts, then divide each half into two pieces. Keep the leg and thigh meat intact as far as possible. Sauté the meat very gently in the butter to color it slightly. Season well with salt and pepper.

Chop the chicken livers and the giblets and season with salt and pepper. Blend with the pork and veal and add the thyme, Spice Parisienne and cognac. If you wish, cook a bit of the mixture to see if it is seasoned correctly. Add the chopped truffle.

On each slice of ham, place a piece of breast meat, some of the ground meat and a bit of leg and thigh meat. Then top with a second piece of breast meat. Fold the ham over and roll securely.

Roll out the puff paste ½″ thick. Cut 8 large pieces of puff paste that will encase the ham rolls and fold over them completely. Fold each roll in a piece of paste. Place them on a baking sheet and brush the tops with the egg yolk and cream. Bake in a 450° oven for 10 minutes, reduce the heat to 400° and cook a further 10 minutes, then reduce heat to 350° for the rest of the cooking time, about 8–15 minutes. The rolls should take about 25–35 minutes in all. Serve hot or cold. Serves 8.

SNIPE

Snipe are similar to woodcock in structure and flavor and because of their long beaks are dressed in the same manner as woodcock. The heads are skinned and the beaks skewered through the birds before cooking. They have superbly good breast meat and are delicious when roasted simply with plenty of barding pork and a liberal basting of butter.

One snipe is hardly enough for a good appetite. Two make a better portion.

ROAST SNIPE

Butter the snipe well and cover with a piece of fat back or barding pork. Roast on a rack in a 400° oven for 12–15 minutes, basting well with melted butter and red wine, half and half. Season to taste.

Serve on fried toast with pan juices. Chip potatoes and watercress are good with this.

PINTADE AU CHAMPAGNE

> 2 guinea hens
>   Thin slices salt pork
> 12 tablespoons butter
> 1 teaspoon salt
> ½ teaspoon freshly ground black pepper
> 1 pound mushrooms
> 1 cup champagne
> 3 egg yolks
> 1 cup heavy cream
>   Garnish: tiny fried croutons dipped in finely chopped parsley

Bard the guinea hens with thin slices of salt pork. Melt 6 tablespoons butter in a cocotte or casserole, arrange guinea hens in butter and season them with salt and pepper. Roast in a 375° oven for 40 minutes, basting twice with butter in pan.

Meanwhile sauté the mushrooms (sliced if they are large, whole if they are small) in remaining butter. When guinea hens are tender and brown, remove to a hot serving platter, remove barding pork and cut them in half for serving. Skim off excess fat from liquid in casserole, pour the juices into a skillet, add the champagne and reduce rapidly over high heat until liquid is half the original amount. Mix egg yolks and cream. Lower heat and carefully stir the egg-cream mixture into the hot liquid (it is a wise precaution to mix 1 teaspoon potato starch with the egg-cream mixture to prevent the sauce from sepa-

HOW TO MAKE PINTADE AU CHAMPAGNE

1. Cut a piece of salt pork into eight thin slices for barding breasts and legs of guinea hens.

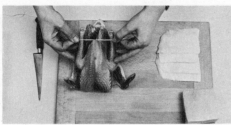

2. To tie up hen, place breast up and put thin string over legs, then bring string behind them.

3. Cross string in front by breastbone, then carry around joint of leg near body. Flip hen over.

4. Pull string up from legs and through flaps of wing joints, bringing ends together in center.

5. Tuck loose skin under string. Knot firmly. Bend back wing tips to lie flat against body.

6. Tuck salt pork slices between legs and breast. Cover tops of hens with two more pork slices.

7. Tie fat twice with string to keep it in place. Arrange barded hens in dish ready for roasting.

8. Remove roasted birds to board, slit down breast with knife, cut in half with poultry shears.

9. Arrange halved hens in serving dish and spoon sauce and mushrooms over them, coating evenly.

10. Garnish dish with a sprinkling of tiny fried croutons. Serve with a well-chilled champagne.

rating). Cook, stirring, over very low heat, being careful not to let the sauce boil. When smooth and slightly thickened, taste for seasoning and add the mushrooms with their juices. Pour the sauce over the guinea hens. Garnish with the croutons. Serves 4.

DOVES

Dove and pigeon are very popular in certain parts of the country. Doves, if delicate and tender, should be treated as if they were squab. Serve at least 1 dove per person.

DOVES COUNTRY STYLE

> **Flour**
> **6 doves**
> **6 rashers bacon**
> **Salt, pepper**
> **1½ cups heavy cream**
> **2 teaspoons chopped parsley**

Flour the birds lightly. Try out the bacon in a large skillet. Remove and keep warm. Sauté the doves in the bacon fat, browning them well on all sides. Reduce the heat and continue cooking until they are just tender, about 12 minutes. Season to taste.

Remove the doves to a hot platter and garnish with the bacon. Spoon out all but 3 tablespoons of fat. Add 4 tablespoons of flour and blend well. Cook for 3 minutes. Gradually stir in the cream and cook, stirring, until smooth and thickened. Season with salt and pepper and add the chopped parsley. Give this sauce quite a high seasoning. Serve in a sauceboat.

With this dish serve tiny new potatoes and tiny buttered peas. Serves 3–6.

ROAST PHEASANT

Pheasant has a tendency to become dry when you roast it. Here is a way to avoid this. Truss the birds and place them on their sides on a rack in a shallow pan. Lay strips of bacon or salt pork across the breasts, legs and thighs. Roast in a 375° oven for 18 minutes. Turn the pheasants onto the other side and cover with bacon or salt pork. Baste with the pan

juices or with melted butter and roast 15 minutes more. Place the birds on their backs and baste well. Cover with bacon or pork strips and roast an additional 10 minutes. Remove the bacon or pork, baste again and return to the oven for a few minutes to brown. Season with salt and pepper. A pheasant will serve 2–4, depending on size.

ROAST PHEASANT WITH SOUR CREAM SAUCE

Pluck, singe, clean and prepare two small pheasants or one medium-sized pheasant. Wipe the birds well with a damp cloth and sprinkle the cavities with a little salt. Add to the cavities as flavoring 1 whole onion, 1 stalk of celery and a sprig of parsley. Truss. Rub each bird well with butter or bacon fat and cover the breasts thoroughly with strips of salt pork or bacon. Place them in a roasting pan and add a good-sized chunk of butter.

Roast the pheasants in a 375° oven as in previous recipe, turning and basting until tender and brown.

When the birds are done, remove them to a hot platter and keep them warm. Skim the excess fat from the pan juices and place the roasting pan over a very low flame. Slowly stir in 1 cup of sour cream and blend with the juices. Taste for seasoning and add Hungarian paprika liberally. Serve separately.

With the roast pheasant and sour cream sauce, serve cabbage, sliced and steamed until just tender, and mashed buttered yellow turnips. Serves 4.

PHEASANT SAUTÉ WITH APPLES

> **2 young pheasants**
> **Flour**
> **Butter**
> **⅓ cup calvados or applejack**
> **Salt, pepper**
> **½ cup white wine**
> **1 cup heavy cream beaten with 3 egg yolks**
> **6 apples, cored and thinly sliced**
> **2 teaspoons sugar**

It is preferable to use only the breasts for this dish, although you may cook the legs and thighs separately in another skillet and offer them as a second serving for those with hearty appetites.

Remove breasts from pheasants and cut in two, removing the center breast bone. Flour each piece. Sauté very gently in 6–8 tablespoons butter until the breasts are a rich ivory color—they should not be golden brown. Flame with calvados or applejack and turn once or twice in the juices. Salt and pepper to taste and add the white wine. Simmer for about 8–10 minutes, or until just tender. Be careful not to overcook or the breast meat will be dry. Remove breasts to a hot platter and add a few drops of calvados or applejack to the pan. Slowly stir in the cream-egg mixture and cook, stirring constantly, over medium heat until the sauce is smooth and thickened. Do not allow to boil. Pass separately in a sauceboat. Garnish the platter with apple slices that have been sautéed in 6 tablespoons butter and sprinkled with the sugar to glaze them.

The legs and thighs may be floured, sautéed in butter and added to the platter if you wish. Steamed, buttered rice garnished with a sprinkling of pistachio nuts is a pleasant accompaniment to this delicious dish. Serves 4.

PHEASANT PIE

> 1 or 2 hen pheasants, depending on size
> Flour
> ¼ pound butter
> Salt, pepper
> 1 bay leaf, crumbled
> ½ teaspoon thyme
> ½ teaspoon quatre épices or Spice Parisienne
> 1 cup white wine
> 12 small white onions, peeled
> 1 or 2 slices Virginia ham (about ½ pound), cut in cubes
> ¼ pound mushrooms, sautéed in butter
> ¼ cup chopped parsley
> Rough Puff Paste (see Pastry)
> 1 egg yolk beaten with 1 tablespoon cream

Cut the bird or birds into serving pieces. Flour them lightly and brown in the butter. Season to taste with salt and pepper. Add the bay leaf, thyme and quatre-épices. Sprinkle with 1½ tablespoons flour and blend well. Add the white wine and onions. Bring to a boil, lower the heat and cover the pan. Simmer for 35–45 minutes, or until the pheasant is tender. Cool slightly and transfer to a pie dish. Add the ham, mushrooms and parsley and top with the pastry dough. Cut a vent in the top and insert a small cornucopia of paper. Brush with the egg mixture. Bake in a 450° oven for 10 minutes. Reduce the heat to 350° and bake the pie for another 10 minutes, or until crust is browned.

Serve with a barley casserole and puréed artichokes dressed with butter. Serves 6–8.

FRICASSEE OF OLD PHEASANT

> Flour
> 1 or 2 old pheasants, cut up for fricassee
> 6 tablespoons butter
> 1½ cups chicken or pheasant broth
> 1 onion stuck with cloves
> 1½ teaspoon salt
> ½ teaspoon freshly ground black pepper
> 1 teaspoon thyme
> 1 bay leaf
> Beurre manié
> 1 cup heavy cream
> ¼ cup sherry or Madeira

Flour the pheasant pieces lightly and sauté in the butter until just delicately colored. Do not brown. Add broth, onion and seasonings and bring to a boil. Cover the pan, lower the heat and simmer for 45 minutes–1¼ hours, or until the pheasant is tender. Do not overcook.

Remove the pheasant to a hot platter. Adjust the seasoning and remove the onion and bay leaf. Thicken the broth with beurre manié and finally stir in the heavy cream and sherry or Madeira. Simmer until the sauce is the right consistency. You may return the pheasant pieces to the sauce in order to reheat them for a few minutes, if you like.

Arrange the fricassee on a platter with a mound of rice in the center. Pass some of the sauce in a sauceboat. Garnish the platter with chopped parsley. Braised young carrots are a nice addition. Serves 4–6.

ALSATIAN PHEASANT WITH SAUERKRAUT

3 pounds sauerkraut
¼ pound butter
1 medium onion, chopped
2 cloves garlic, chopped
   Freshly ground black pepper to taste
12 juniper berries, crushed
1½ cups white wine
1½ cups broth
1 potato, grated
⅓ cup kirsch
1 Italian or French garlic sausage
   White or red wine
1 onion, sliced
2 pheasants
   Bacon curls

Wash the sauerkraut and place it with the butter in a large pot. Cook it gently, turning with a fork, for 10 minutes. Add chopped onion, garlic, pepper, juniper berries, white wine and broth and cover the pan. Cook in a 325° oven for 1½ hours. If it cooks dry, add more wine or broth. Add the grated potato and cook 15 more minutes. Add the kirsch and toss well. Poach the sausage in white or red wine with the sliced onion for 25–30 minutes.

Roast the pheasants.

Arrange the sauerkraut on a large platter. Carve or quarter the pheasants and place them on top. Slice the sausage. Garnish with the sausage slices and the bacon curls. Serve with boiled potatoes. The fruitiness of an Alsatian wine complements this dish perfectly. Serves 4–6.

ROAST PARTRIDGE

Wrap the breast of the partridge with thinly sliced barding pork and skewer the fat to the bird. Roast at 400° for 20–25 minutes, basting frequently. Salt and pepper to taste and serve on toast spread with the chopped sautéed giblets. You may or may not remove the barding pork before serving.

Serve the traditional accompaniments: freshly cooked potato chips and watercress. A partridge serves 1 or 2.

RACK OF VENISON

Venison can be tasty, tender and moist—or tough and dry. To be good, it must be hung for at least 1 week to 10 days; in most cases it should be marinated before cooking and treated to plenty of fat or oil to keep it moist. Ask your butcher to saw through the backbone of the venison so that each rib may be carved away easily.

4–5-pound rack or loin of venison
   Salt pork, bacon
2 chopped onions
1 sliced carrot
1 clove garlic, minced
½ teaspoon thyme
½ teaspoon oregano
4 crushed juniper berries
1 teaspoon salt
½ teaspoon crushed peppercorns
   Juice and rind of 1 lemon
½ cup olive oil
1 cup dry red wine, heated
½ cup beef stock
   Beurre manié

Make incisions in the meat with a knife or larding needle and insert strips of salt pork and bacon.

Make a marinade of the vegetables, seasonings, lemon juice and rind and olive oil, and put the meat to soak in it for 24 hours. Turn the meat frequently to be sure it is thoroughly bathed.

When ready to cook, arrange the rack of venison in a roasting pan and top it with several slices of bacon. Remove the lemon rind from the marinade and pour the marinade over the meat. Roast in a

350° oven, basting frequently with the pan juices. Allow about 20 minutes per pound for moist, rare venison. After 45 minutes of cooking, add 1 cup of heated dry red wine and continue roasting and basting until the meat is done.

Remove the venison to a hot platter and keep it warm. Skim any excess fat from the pan juices and add ½ cup of beef stock. Add a little more wine if necessary and taste for seasoning. Thicken with beurre manié (small balls of butter and flour kneaded together). Pour the sauce over the rack of venison. Carve into separate ribs and let the meat juices mix in with the sauce. Serves 4.

ROAST SADDLE OF VENISON

A young saddle is perfect roasted very rare and carved in long thin slices the length of the saddle. Do not forget to remove the filets and slice them as well to serve with the saddle.

Marinate or not, as you choose. The saddle should be roasted until it reaches an internal temperature of about 125°. Sear it first in a 425° oven for 15 minutes. Then reduce the heat to 325° and continue roasting until it reaches the right temperature. This will take about 12–15 minutes per pound.

Serve the saddle with a purée of chestnuts and sautéed string beans with almonds. Serves 4–6.

ROAST LOIN OF VENISON

    1 pint wine vinegar

    1 pint red wine

    2 bay leaves

    6 shallots

    2 carrots, thinly sliced

    1 lemon, thinly sliced

    1 tablespoon juniper berries

    1 teaspoon freshly ground black pepper

    Loin of venison

    Thickly cut bacon

    Butter

    Salt, pepper

    Beurre manié

    1 cup sour cream

Combine first 8 ingredients for a marinade. Choose a good loin that has hung for several weeks and soak it in the marinade for 2–3 hours. Remove from the marinade and wipe dry. Lard the loin with thick pieces of bacon. Arrange it in a roasting pan and spread well with butter. Season with salt and pepper. Roast in a 400° oven for 1 hour. Baste frequently with butter and some of the marinade. Reduce the heat to 325° and roast until the thermometer registers an internal heat of 120°.

Remove the loin to a hot platter. Skim the excess fat from the pan juices and add 1 cup of the marinade. Cook down to half. Add beurre manié and blend until the sauce is smooth and thickened. Stir in sour cream and heat through but do not boil. Correct the seasoning.

Serve the roast with puréed chestnuts and braised brussels sprouts. Serves 2–4, according to size.

VENISON STEAK OR CHOPS

If these are from a young deer, they need no marinating. The meat should hang for 2–3 weeks and then be properly cut by your butcher.

To cook young steaks or chops, heat a heavy skillet until quite hot and add half butter and half oil. Sauté the meat, turning it frequently to brown on both sides without charring. Salt and pepper to taste. If you like, flame the meat with cognac just before serving. If you wish to marinate the steaks or chops, use marinade given for Roast Loin of Venison.

VENISON CHILI

    4 large onions, thinly sliced or finely chopped

    2 cloves garlic, finely chopped

    ½ cup vegetable oil or olive oil

    2 pounds venison, ground

    2 tablespoons chili powder

    1 teaspoon ground coriander

    ½ teaspoon ground cumin

    Dash Tabasco

    1 cup beer

    ½ cup tomato paste

    1½ teaspoons salt

Sauté the onions and garlic in oil until they are limp and colored. Add the ground venison and break it into bits. Add the rest of the ingredients and blend. Reduce the heat and simmer for 45 minutes to 1 hour. Taste for seasoning. Add more beer if the mixture gets too dry. Cook until it is well thickened and rich in flavor. Serve with pinto or kidney beans, and rice. Serves 4–6.

Note: This makes a very tasty sauce for frankfurters. Place grilled franks in hot toasted buns and top each frank with a spoonful or so of the Venison Chili and then with a spoonful of chopped raw onion.

VENISONBURGERS

    2 pounds venison, ground
    2 cloves garlic, finely chopped
    1 tablespoon freshly chopped chives
    2 teaspoons salt
    1 teaspoon freshly ground black pepper
    Dash Tabasco
    Butter, oil
    Bourbon (optional)
    Red wine

Blend first 6 ingredients well. Form into cakes and sauté in half butter and half oil until nicely browned on both sides and still quite rare in the center. Flame with bourbon, if you like. Remove to a hot platter and rinse the pan with red wine. Pour over the venisonburgers. Serve with baked potatoes and crisp fried onion rings. Serves 4.

ROAST SADDLE OF HARE WITH MUSTARD

    2 saddles of hare
    1–1½ jars Dijon mustard
    ¼ pound butter, melted
    Heavy cream
    Salt, pepper
    4 egg yolks
    ¼ cup cognac
    Lemon juice

Spread the saddles well with the mustard—about ¼″ thick. Let them stand, covered, in the refrigerator for several hours. Place the saddles in a deep casserole that will just hold them. Spoon melted butter over them and roast in a 300° oven, basting from time to time with heavy cream. After 1½ hours, add an additional ½ cup cream and salt and pepper to taste.

When done and tender, remove the saddles to a hot platter. Mix another ½ cup cream with the egg yolks and blend into the sauce. Stir until smooth and thickened, but do not let it boil. Taste for seasoning and add the cognac and a dash of lemon juice.

Serve the saddles with puréed potatoes and glazed carrots and pass the sauce separately. Serves 4.

RABBIT OR HARE IN SWEET-SOUR SAUCE

    3-pound rabbit or hare, cut into serving pieces
    1 cup cider vinegar
    1 cup dry white wine
    2 tablespoons salt
    2 teaspoons freshly ground pepper
    2 tablespoons whole juniper berries, crushed
    1 medium onion, sliced
    1 carrot, chopped
    3 slices bacon, diced
    2 tablespoons butter

1 tablespoon sugar
3 tablespoons flour
3 gingersnaps, crumbled
½ cup sour cream

Wash the rabbit pieces in cold running water, remove the excess skin and wash again. Dry on paper towels. Put the rabbit pieces in a large, deep glass, earthenware or stainless steel bowl (do not use aluminum). Make a marinade with 2 cups water, the vinegar, wine, salt, pepper, juniper berries, onion and carrot. Pour over the rabbit pieces to cover. Refrigerate for 2–3 days, turning pieces daily. Remove the rabbit from the marinade and dry on paper towels. Strain the marinade and measure 2 cups. Cook the bacon in a Dutch oven until transparent. Add the butter and brown the rabbit on all sides in the hot fat. Add 1 cup of the marinade and simmer the rabbit, covered, over low heat for 1 hour.

Sprinkle with the sugar and flour. Gradually stir in remaining 1 cup marinade and the gingersnaps. Simmer covered, stirring frequently, for 20 minutes. Stir in the sour cream and simmer for 10 minutes. Check seasoning. Serve with hot buttered noodles sprinkled with caraway seeds. Serves 4.

RABBIT OR HARE WITH TURNIPS

1 wild rabbit or hare
Dijon or English mustard
1 onion stuck with cloves
Red wine
7 tablespoons butter
3 tablespoons olive oil
Salt, pepper to taste
1 teaspoon thyme
1 bay leaf
6–8 tender young turnips
2 teaspoons sugar
Beurre manié
Chopped parsley and tarragon
Garlic-flavored fried croutons

Cut rabbit into serving pieces, removing front and back legs and cutting up the saddle. Spread each piece liberally with Dijon or freshly made English mustard. Place rabbit in a deep bowl with onion and enough red wine to cover. Marinate in refrigerator for 24–36 hours.

To cook, melt 3 tablespoons butter with the olive oil and brown the drained pieces of rabbit on all sides. Remove them to a casserole and season with salt, pepper, thyme and bay leaf. Add strained wine from marinade, cover and cook in a 350° oven for 1 hour. Meanwhile peel turnips and brown them in 4 tablespoons butter. Shake the pan as they cook to make sure they are evenly browned. Sprinkle with sugar and shake pan to caramelize turnips all over. Cover and steam gently over very low heat until just tender. Add more butter or a little stock if necessary.

To serve, remove rabbit to a hot platter and surround with turnips. Strain sauce, add another ½ cup red wine and bring to a boil. You may thicken it, if you wish, with beurre manié. Taste for seasoning and pour some of the sauce over the rabbit. Sprinkle liberally with parsley and tarragon and serve with croutons. Pass the rest of the sauce in a sauce boat. Serves 4.

Vegetables

The Roman phrase for quick action, "in less time than it takes to cook asparagus," is an indication that they appreciated the tender nature of vegetables and had mastered the gentle art of cooking them. Then vegetables were regarded not only as splendid sustenance, but also as powerful allies. Cabbage was eaten to ward off drunkenness, onions and leeks to build up strength. Mushrooms were so highly regarded that Julius Caesar decreed the plebs unworthy of such treasures, and limited their sale to the wealthy patricians. Family names were taken from vegetables—Fabius from faba (bean); Lentulus from lenticula (lentils).

After the fall of the Roman Empire, vegetables too fell from grace in Europe. Maligned and mistreated, they were either boiled to a pulp or shunned altogether as poisonous, perilous plants. Guilt by association with the deadly nightshade family caused the eggplant of the Middle East and the tomato and potato, newcomers from the New World, to be accused of causing madness, leprosy and lust. To one Elizabethan writer, Henry Buttes, even carrots and asparagus were suspect, as capable of "provoking Venus," although he was quite ready to recommend the juice of spinach as an antidote for scorpion bites.

No such prejudices existed among the newly independent epicures of America. While Parmentier struggled to popularize the potato in France, George Washington's kitchen garden burgeoned with every known vegetable: beets and beans, turnips and squash, parsnips and peas, sweet peppers and tomatoes, and potatoes both plain and sweet. Thomas Jefferson, after his sojourn in Europe as ambassador to France, brought back asparagus and broccoli seeds to raise in his greenhouse and boldly served pommes frites with steak.

Oddly enough the English, notorious for their barbarous treatment of vegetables, produced one eighteenth-century cook—and a woman, at that—capable of going against the popular taste. Mrs. Sarah Phillips, in her book The Ladies Handmaid, advised cooking spinach without water and dressing it with butter. Of broccoli, cabbage and string beans she remarked, "They will be quickly done; take care they don't lose their fine green," advice that would be well taken today.

A virtue of vegetables too seldom exploited is their ability to merge smoothly and sensuously with foods of different persuasions and textures, with sauces and with seasonings. Braised celery topped with slivered, sautéed almonds; green beans mixed with thinly sliced water chestnuts; creamed spinach seasoned with nutmeg and studded with golden-brown pine nuts; cauliflower masked with pungent garlic sauce; braised carrots or onions kissed with Madeira; hot fava beans tossed with fresh herbs—these are everyday vegetables elevated to a delectable state that even the epicurean Romans might have envied.

ITALIAN ARTICHOKES AND PEAS

6 medium artichokes
⅓ cup minced prosciutto or lean bacon
½ small onion, minced
¼ cup minced parsley
½ clove garlic, minced
2 tablespoons butter
2 tablespoons olive oil
½ teaspoon dried basil
Salt, pepper to taste
⅓ cup hot beef or chicken bouillon
2 cups fresh shelled peas, or frozen peas, thawed

Remove tough outer leaves of artichokes and cut off all but ½″–¾″ of the stalk. Lay artichoke on its side. With a sharp knife, cut off top, leaving about 2″–3″, and slice thinly lengthwise. Drop slices into acidulated water (1 quart water and the juice of 1 large lemon) to prevent darkening. Take out one at a time, and cut out the fuzzy choke. Dry before using.

Put the minced prosciutto, onion, parsley, and garlic on a chopping board and chop together until very fine and well mixed. Heat the butter and olive oil in a heavy casserole. Add the prosciutto mixture and cook over medium heat, stirring constantly, for 3–4 minutes. Add the artichokes, basil, salt, pepper, and bouillon. Lower heat and simmer, covered, for 10 minutes, stirring occasionally. Add the peas, and if necessary, a little more hot bouillon. Simmer, covered, for 5–10 minutes longer, or until both vegetables are tender. Serves 4–6.

ASPARAGUS LOAF

1 cup coarse cracker crumbs
4 tablespoons butter
½ teaspoon grated onion
1 tablespoon chopped parsley
½ teaspoon salt
¼ teaspoon white pepper
2 eggs
2 cups hot milk
4 cups asparagus, scraped and cut into 1″ lengths
1 cup light cream sauce
Chopped chives, grated Parmesan cheese

Sauté cracker crumbs in butter with grated onion, chopped parsley, salt and white pepper for 5 minutes. Beat eggs lightly and stir into them the hot milk. Combine with asparagus and crumbs. Bake in a buttered loaf pan approximately 5½″ by 9½″ in a preheated 375° oven for 30 minutes or until set. Serve with cream sauce seasoned with chives and cheese to taste. Serves 6.

FAVA BEANS WITH FRESH HERBS

4 pounds fava beans (Italian broad beans)
6 tablespoons olive oil
1 tablespoon butter
3 cloves garlic, finely minced
½ cup minced onion
Salt, pepper to taste
1 tablespoon chopped parsley
2 tablespoons chopped fresh basil

Shell the beans and cook in boiling water until just tender. Drain. Heat the oil and butter, add the garlic, onion, salt and pepper and cook 3 minutes. Add the beans and toss well. Add the parsley and basil, toss again and serve at once. Serves 6.

Note: These beans may be served cold. Simply add more olive oil and a little vinegar.

BRAISED GREEN BEANS

2 tablespoons olive oil
1½ pounds green beans, tips cut off and sliced in half lengthwise
4 green onions, finely chopped
½ cup finely chopped parsley
1 cup Italian canned tomatoes
Salt, pepper to taste

Pour the oil into the bottom of a heavy saucepan and add the beans, onion, parsley, tomatoes, salt, and pepper. Cover and simmer slowly for 20–30 minutes, or until beans are tender. Serves 6.

YUGOSLAVIAN GREEN BEANS

1½ pounds green beans
¼ pound butter
2 tablespoons bread crumbs

½ bunch parsley, minced
1 clove garlic, mashed
Black pepper to taste
1 cup sour cream

Cook green beans by the cold water method: put beans in cold, salted water to cover, bring to a boil and simmer, uncovered, until just tender. Drain well. Melt butter in a pan and as soon as it becomes golden, add bread crumbs and let them brown evenly. Mix parsley with garlic, season with black pepper and mix with the bread crumbs. Remove the pan from the fire and combine the parsley mixture with the green beans. Put in a casserole, pour sour cream over all and bake for 15 minutes in a 350° oven. Serves 6.

POLISH BEETS

1 large bunch beets, cooked
2 tablespoons sugar
2 tablespoons butter
Salt, pepper to taste
2 tablespoons flour
1 teaspoon vinegar
½ cup sour cream

Grate cooked beets. Put them in a saucepan with sugar and butter. Season with salt and pepper. When the butter has melted, stir in flour. Add vinegar and blend. Add the sour cream and heat thoroughly but do not boil. Serve the beets with liver, roast pork or pork chops. Serves 4.

SWEDISH PICKLED BEETS

½ cup cider or white vinegar
½ cup water
¼ cup sugar
1 teaspoon salt
⅛ teaspoon freshly ground pepper
2 cups (approximately) thinly sliced, cooked
and peeled beets

Combine first five ingredients. Bring to a boil; cool. Place beets in a deep bowl and pour dressing over them. Let stand at least 12 hours before serving. Serve with fried fish, hot and cold meats or on the smörgåsbord. Makes about 2 cups.

BROCCOLI ALLA ROMANA

1 bunch broccoli
3 tablespoons olive oil
1 clove garlic
½ teaspoon salt
¼ teaspoon pepper
2 or 3 anchovies, mashed
1½ cups dry red wine

Trim tough leaves and stems from broccoli and cut into small flowerets. Wash and drain. Heat the olive oil in a deep skillet, add the garlic and cook until it is browned. Discard garlic. Add the broccoli, salt, and pepper. Cook, stirring constantly, for 3 minutes. Add anchovies and red wine and cook, covered, over lowest possible heat for 10 minutes, or until broccoli is tender. Stir occasionally with a fork, being careful not to break flowerets. Serves 4.

BRUSSELS SPROUTS
WITH EGG-LEMON SAUCE

2 pounds brussels sprouts
1 tablespoon butter
2 egg yolks
2 tablespoons lemon juice
Salt, cayenne pepper to taste

Cook the brussels sprouts in 2″ of water and the butter until barely tender. Drain sprouts, reserving liquid, and keep sprouts hot. Beat the egg yolks until thick in a deep serving dish. Beat in the lemon juice and 2 tablespoons of the reserved cooking liquid. Season with salt and pepper. Add the hot brussels sprouts and toss to coat with the sauce. Serve immediately. Serves 4–6.

RED CABBAGE WITH APPLES

1 red cabbage, thinly shredded
2 tablespoons bacon fat or lard
1 tablespoon sugar
½ cup dry white or red wine
2 tart unpeeled apples, cored and sliced
Salt, pepper to taste

Put the cabbage into a deep bowl and pour over it

boiling water to cover. Let stand 2 minutes and drain well. Heat the bacon fat and sauté the cabbage for 2–3 minutes, stirring constantly. Add the sugar, wine, and apples. Simmer, covered, for about 5–10 minutes, or until the cabbage and apples are just tender. If necessary, add a little more wine. Season with salt and pepper. Serve with roast pork, ham, duck, or goose. Serves 4–6.

SAVOY CABBAGE WITH CHESTNUTS

> 1 medium savoy cabbage, coarsely shredded
> ¾ teaspoon salt
> ¼ teaspoon pepper
> 2 cups boiling water or bouillon
> 2 cups cooked, peeled chestnuts, or canned, unsweetened chestnuts, coarsely chopped
> 2 tablespoons butter
> 1½ tablespoons flour
> ⅛ teaspoon ground cardamom

Put the cabbage into a deep saucepan. Add the salt, pepper, and boiling water or bouillon. Cook, uncovered, over medium heat, stirring frequently, until the cabbage is tender. Do not overcook. Drain and reserve cabbage liquid. Mix the chestnuts and cabbage. Melt the butter and stir in the flour and ground cardamom. Gradually add the cabbage liquid and cook, stirring constantly, until the sauce is thickened and smooth. Mix with the cabbage and chestnuts. Cook over low heat, stirring constantly, until vegetables and sauce are heated through. Serves 4–6.

CAULIFLOWER WITH PURÉE OF PEAS AND CROUTONS

> 1 medium cauliflower
> 5 tablespoons butter
> 3 slices white bread, cubed
> Salt, pepper
> 1 slice lemon
> 2 pounds fresh peas
> ½ teaspoon sugar
> ¼ cup light cream
> Milk
> Nutmeg

Cut off the cauliflower stem. Soak in cold water for ½ hour.

Melt 4 tablespoons butter in a frying pan and turn off the heat. Add the bread cubes and stir with a fork until each cube is completely saturated with butter. Turn the heat on again low, and cook the bread cubes, turning with a fork, until all are evenly brown. Drain on absorbent paper.

Pierce the stem end of the cauliflower several times and put it in enough cold water to cover. Add 1 teaspoon salt and the lemon slice. Bring to a boil, lower heat and simmer until tender.

Meanwhile cook the peas in very little water. As they cook, add 1 scant teaspoon salt and ½ teaspoon sugar. When the peas are tender, drain them thoroughly and put them in an electric blender with 1 tablespoon melted butter and the light cream. When blended, add enough milk to make a thick sauce.

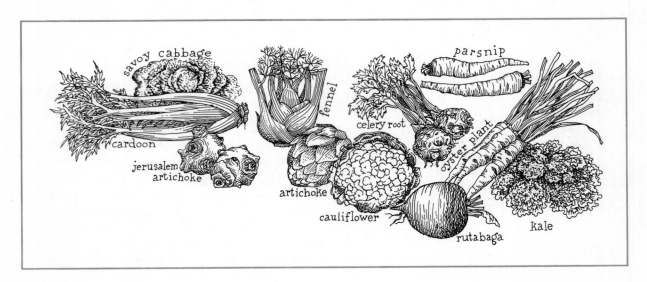

Season with black pepper, more salt if necessary, and a pinch of nutmeg. Heat through.

Drain the cauliflower thoroughly. Mask with the purée and cover with croutons. Serves 4–5.

CAULIFLOWER WITH GARLIC SAUCE

    1 head cauliflower
    6 medium potatoes (preferably the mealy kind)
    4–6 cloves garlic, mashed
    1 teaspoon salt
    ¾–1 cup olive oil
    ¼ cup lemon juice
      Sliced tomatoes
      Sliced black olives

Cook the cauliflower in boiling water until tender. Keep whole. Drain and arrange on a serving dish. Boil the potatoes in their skins. Pound mashed garlic and salt together. Peel the boiled potatoes and while still hot, mash them. Beat the garlic mixture into the potatoes, blending to a smooth paste. Gradually beat in the olive oil and lemon juice alternately, a few drops at a time. Sauce should be the consistency of thick cream. Arrange the tomatoes and olives around the cauliflower. Dribble a little sauce over cauliflower and serve remainder in a sauceboat. Serves 4–6.

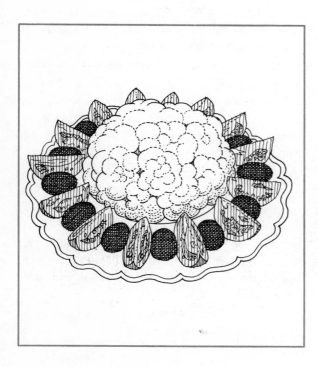

CREAMED CELERY AND ALMONDS

    4 bunches celery hearts
    2 cups clear chicken broth
      Salt, white pepper
    8½ tablespoons butter
    1¼ cups slivered, blanched almonds
    1 cup milk (approx.)
    6 tablespoons flour
    ¼–½ cup heavy cream
    ⅓ cup dry white bread crumbs

Separate the celery into stalks. Remove leaves. Wash stalks well and cut into ⅜″ dice. You should have 8 cups. Boil slowly in a covered saucepan with the broth, 1 cup water, 1½ teaspoons salt and 1½ tablespoons butter for about 10 minutes, or until celery is just cooked through but retains a suggestion of crunchiness. Drain cooking liquid into a quart measuring cup and reserve. Return celery to saucepan.

Melt 1 tablespoon butter in an 8″ skillet and stir and toss the almonds for about 5 minutes over moderate heat until they are a pale golden color. Put into saucepan with celery.

Add enough milk to the celery cooking liquid to make 3 cups. Bring to a simmer. Melt 4 tablespoons butter in a heavy-bottomed, 2-quart enameled saucepan. Blend in the flour with a wooden spoon and stir slowly over low heat until butter and flour froth together for 2 minutes without coloring. Remove from heat. Pour in the simmering liquid and beat vigorously with a wire whip to blend thoroughly. Bring to the boil, stirring, for one minute. Thin out with tablespoons of cream; sauce should be thick enough to coat a spoon fairly heavily. Season to taste with salt and white pepper, then fold the sauce into the celery and almonds with a rubber spatula. Melt the remaining 2 tablespoons butter and mix with the bread crumbs.

Spread the vegetable mixture in a lightly buttered 3-quart baking dish, 1½″–2″ deep, and sprinkle with the buttered bread crumbs. If dish is to be served immediately, set under a moderately hot broiler to reheat and brown the top. If prepared ahead, set aside uncovered; reheat for about ½ hour in upper third of a preheated 375° oven until sauce is bubbling and crumbs light brown. Serves 8.

CELERY CASSEROLE

    4 cups celery, cut in large dice
    ¼ cup chopped onion
    1 green pepper, seeded and chopped
    1 tablespoon butter
    1 small package Philadelphia cream cheese
    2 small packages blue cheese
    1 cup heavy cream

Cook celery in water until tender but still crisp. Sauté chopped onion and pepper in butter. Stir in cream cheese, blue cheese and heavy cream. Add celery and mix all the ingredients well. Put the mixture in a baking dish and heat through in a 350° oven. Serves 4.

CELERY ROOT AND POTATO PURÉE

    ½ pound celery root, peeled
    1 pound potatoes, peeled
    Boiling salted water

In peeling celery root, all external fibers must be removed. The easiest way to do this is to wash the whole root, slice it, and then pare off the skin. If the core is woody, remove it.

Cook the celery root in boiling salted water until almost tender. Add the potatoes and cook until both vegetables are done. Mash, and proceed as for mashed potatoes. This is excellent with pork and well-flavored meats. Serves 4–6.

SPANISH CARROTS

    3 tablespoons butter
    6 medium carrots, cut into ½″ slices
    Salt, pepper to taste
    ½ cup dry sherry
    1 cup chicken bouillon
    2 egg yolks

Heat 2 tablespoons of the butter and cook carrots until golden brown. Stir frequently and do not allow to scorch. Season with salt and pepper. Add sherry and bouillon and bring to a boil. Reduce heat and simmer, covered, until the carrots are tender. Remove

from heat. Melt remaining tablespoon butter and beat in the egg yolks. Stir the mixture into the carrots. Heat through, but do not boil. Serves 4–6.

COGNAC CARROTS

    12–18 young carrots
    4 tablespoons butter
    1 teaspoon sugar
    2 tablespoons cognac
    Chopped parsley

Scrape the carrots and boil in salted water until just tender. Drain. Sauté carrots in butter, sprinkling them with sugar, and add cognac. Shake pan and carefully remove to serving dish. Sprinkle with chopped parsley. Serves 6.

CORN CUSTARDS WITH FRIED TOMATOES

    1 cup scraped corn
    4 eggs, beaten
    1 teaspoon minced onion
    Salt
    Dash of cayenne pepper or Tabasco
    1½ cups milk
    6 medium tomatoes
    2 tablespoons butter
    Pepper to taste
    Pinch of chervil

Combine scraped corn, beaten eggs, minced onion, ½ teaspoon salt and cayenne pepper or Tabasco. Scald milk and add it gradually. Pour into buttered custard cups and place cups in a shallow pan of hot water in a preheated 325° oven. Bake for 30 minutes or until custard is set.

While the custards are baking, slice off the tops and bottoms of the tomatoes. Then cut each tomato into two thick slices. Fry in the butter. Season with salt, pepper and chervil. When tomatoes are dark brown on both sides remove them to a heated platter and add 1 tablespoon hot water to the liquid in the pan. Simmer and stir until reduced to a glaze. Pour over the tomatoes.

Unmold the custards or serve them in their cups, flanked by the tomatoes. Serves 6.

CUCUMBERS POULETTE

4 medium, crisp cucumbers, peeled
1 tablespoon butter
1 tablespoon flour
1 cup hot clear chicken broth
2 egg yolks
Juice of ½ lemon
Salt, white pepper
1 teaspoon minced parsley
Small lump of sweet butter

Cut the cucumbers into cubes or ½" slices and remove seeds. Cook in a small amount of boiling, salted water until barely tender. Put in a strainer, over hot water, to drain thoroughly and keep warm. Meanwhile melt the butter and stir in the flour. When the roux is smooth, add the chicken broth and cook, stirring over low heat until thick and smooth. Remove from the heat and add the egg yolks, one at a time, stirring after each addition. Stir over low heat or over hot water until thick. Remove from heat and add the lemon juice. Season to taste with salt and white pepper. Add minced parsley and sweet butter. Pour over the cucumbers. Serves 4.

Note: Other sauces which may be used with steamed cucumbers are Béchamel, or Mornay.

BRAISED ESCAROLE

2 pounds escarole
¼ cup olive oil
1 clove garlic
½ teaspoon ground marjoram
1 medium tomato, peeled and chopped
Salt, pepper to taste

Remove unsightly outer leaves from escarole, wash heads thoroughly, and dry on paper towels. Cut the heads into quarters. Heat the olive oil and brown the garlic in it. Remove and discard the garlic. Add escarole, marjoram, tomato, salt, and pepper. Simmer, covered, over medium heat about 10 minutes, or until escarole is tender, but still firm. Serve hot with plain broiled or roasted meats. Serves 4–5.

EGGPLANT ANKARA IN MOUSSAKA SKIN

1 medium eggplant
1 small onion, minced
1 tablespoon butter
½ cup chopped parsley
1 teaspoon salt
1 tablespoon flour

Eggplant in Coconut Cream

Peel & THINLY SLICE 1 large eggplant. ARRANGE in BUTTERED oven PROOF dish. Cover with three large onions FINELY CHOPPED. SPRINKLE WITH 1 teaspoon DRIED red chili Pepper, SALT & ground PEPPER to taste. POUR OVER 2 cups coconut cream. Cover dish & bake at 350° FOR 45 mins. UNCOVER & bake ten minutes LONGER. Serves FOUR to SIX.

½ cup clear chicken broth
2 sprigs fresh dill, chopped
½ cup sour cream

Cook eggplant in salted water for 10 minutes. Cut in half lengthwise and remove pulp, leaving enough for fairly sturdy shells. Keep the shells warm.

In a saucepan, sauté onion in butter. When golden, add the eggplant pulp, coarsely chopped, parsley, salt and flour. Stir over low heat and add chicken broth. Cook until eggplant is tender. Add dill and simmer 5 minutes. Add sour cream and fill the shells with the mixture. Place in baking dish and heat in a 350° oven for a few minutes. Serves 4.

STUFFED EGGPLANT

4 eggplant
Salt, freshly cracked pepper
¾ cup vegetable oil
¼ cup olive oil
1 cup bread crumbs
1 cup finely chopped onions, sautéed
2 large cloves garlic, finely chopped
2 tablespoons finely chopped parsley
2 tablespoons chopped chives
5 ounces melted sweet butter
6 tomatoes, skinned, seeded and shredded
Grated Parmesan cheese

Wash eggplant. Cut in half lengthwise. Make a few incisions wtih a sharp knife. Sprinkle well with salt and allow to stand for half an hour. Wash well with water and dry with paper towels. Fry in hot mixed vegetable and olive oil, cut side down, for 10 minutes until half cooked. Then turn over on other side and finish cooking. This should take approximately 20 minutes in all. Scrape out the pulp, leaving the skins whole, and chop finely. Mix the pulp with the bread crumbs, onions, garlic, parsley, chives, and melted butter. Lastly, mix in the tomatoes. Refill the eggplants carefully. Sprinkle the top with a few breadcrumbs, Parmesan cheese and a little melted butter. Brown under the broiler. Serves 8.

CREAMED JERUSALEM ARTICHOKES

Wash Jerusalem artichokes, scrub, and pare or scrape off skin. Place in a saucepan and cover with boiling salted water. Simmer, covered, for 25 minutes, or until tender. Drain.

Cut into slices or julienne strips. Reheat the artichokes in a Béchamel or Mornay sauce. To serve au gratin, sprinkle the creamed vegetables with grated cheese, and glaze under a hot broiler until brown and bubbly.

JERUSALEM ARTICHOKES POLONAISE

8 large Jerusalem artichokes
¼ cup butter
3 tablespoons fine dry bread crumbs
1 tablespoon minced parsley or chives

Prepare and cook Jerusalem artichokes as in preceding recipe. Cut into slices or julienne strips. Heat the butter and brown bread crumbs in it. Add the artichokes and toss until heated through. Sprinkle with parsley and serve hot. Serves 4–6.

FENNEL AND MUSHROOMS

2 large fennel
2 tablespoons butter
2 tablespoons olive oil
1 clove garlic
1 large tomato, peeled, seeded, and chopped
1 pound mushrooms, sliced
¼ cup hot chicken bouillon
1 teaspoon salt
¼ teaspoon pepper
½ teaspoon dried basil or ¼ teaspoon ground thyme

Trim green ferny tops and stems from fennel and cut bulbous lower part into thin slices lengthwise. Heat the butter and olive oil and cook the garlic until browned; discard garlic. Add the tomato and fennel. Simmer, covered, stirring frequently, for about 5 minutes, or until fennel is half tender. Add the mushrooms, chicken bouillon, salt, pepper, and basil. Simmer, covered, over low heat for about 10 minutes, or until vegetables are tender, but still firm. This dish should have just a little sauce; if there is too much liquid, simmer uncovered to evaporate. Serves 4–6.

SICILIAN BRAISED FENNEL

6 small fennel
3 tablespoons olive oil
¼ cup finely chopped onion
1 clove garlic, minced
¾ teaspoon salt
½ teaspoon freshly ground black pepper
½ cup chicken broth
4 tablespoons grated Parmesan cheese

Trim the fennel, discarding the tops, stems and tough outer leaves. Cut into 4 and wash. Drain well. Heat the oil in a skillet; sauté the onion 5 minutes. Add the garlic and fennel; sprinkle with salt and pepper. Sauté 10 minutes, shaking the skillet frequently. Add the broth; cover and cook over low heat 15 minutes or until tender. Sprinkle with the cheese and place under a hot broiler for 2 minutes to brown the cheese. Serves 6–8.

KALE WITH SOUR CREAM

3 pounds kale
1 tablespoon butter
1 teaspoon salt
¼ teaspoon pepper
⅛ teaspoon nutmeg
1 cup sour cream

Wash the kale in cold water and remove heavy stems. Put in a saucepan with boiling salted water to cover. Simmer, covered, for 15–20 minutes, or until kale is tender. Drain and chop fine. Return chopped kale to saucepan and stir in the butter, salt, pepper, and nutmeg. Heat through thoroughly. Lower heat to lowest possible and stir in sour cream gradually. Heat through, but do not boil. Serves 4–6.

LEEKS IN ARMAGNAC

12 leeks, trimmed and cleaned
3 tablespoons olive oil
1 teaspoon salt, or to taste
¼ teaspoon thyme
⅓ cup consommé
¼ cup armagnac
  Juice of ½ lemon
  Chopped parsley

Brown the leeks in the hot oil. Add salt, thyme, consommé and armagnac. Cook briskly for 10 minutes. Reduce heat and cook until just pierceable. Add lemon juice and correct seasoning. Sprinkle with chopped parsley. Serve hot as a vegetable or cold, dressed with a little additional olive oil and lemon juice, as an hors d'oeuvre. Serves 6.

LEEKS AU GRATIN

12 medium-to-large leeks
1¼ cups beef or chicken bouillon
1 cup dry white wine
¼ cup butter
¼ cup flour
½ teaspoon salt
¼ teaspoon pepper
1 cup (4 ounces) grated Swiss or Parmesan
  cheese

Trim the leeks, removing roots and all but 2″ of the green leaves. Wash thoroughly to remove all the sand between the leaves. Combine the bouillon and dry white wine in a saucepan. Bring to a boil. Lower heat and put leeks into the stock. Simmer, covered, for 7–10 minutes, or until leeks are barely tender. Drain and reserve stock—there should be about 2 cups.

Place leeks in a buttered shallow baking dish. Melt the butter in a saucepan and stir in the flour. Gradually stir in the leek stock. Cook. stirring constantly, until thickened and smooth. Stir in the salt and pepper and ¾ cup of the cheese. Cook until the cheese is melted. Pour sauce over leeks. Sprinkle with remaining cheese. Place under broiler or in a hot oven and cook until top is gold brown. Serves 4–6.

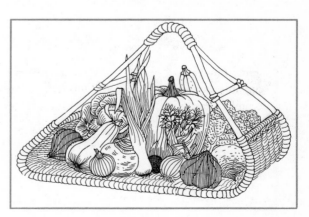

BAKED MUSHROOMS

½ pound mushrooms

2 tablespoons white wine

2 7-ounce cans artichoke hearts, drained

6 slices bacon, cooked, drained, and crumbled

2 8-ounce cans tomato sauce

2 tablespoons pine nuts

2 tablespoons chopped parsley

2 tablespoons grated Parmesan cheese

Wash and dry the mushrooms. Cut tough ends from stems. Remove stems; slice and set aside.

Sprinkle a buttered, shallow baking dish with the white wine. Arrange the mushroom caps and artichoke hearts alternately in the dish. Sprinkle with the crumbled bacon. Combine sliced stems, tomato sauce, and pine nuts; mix well. Pour over the vegetables. Sprinkle with the parsley and cheese. Bake in a 350° oven for 30 minutes. Serves 4.

GERMAN MUSHROOMS WITH SOUR CREAM

1 pound mushrooms

3 tablespoons butter

1 teaspoon onion salt

½ teaspoon salt

⅛ teaspoon pepper

2 tablespoons white wine

2 tablespoons sherry

¾ cup sour cream

1 tablespoon minced chives

3 tablespoons chopped cucumber

Wash and dry the mushrooms. Remove caps (reserve stems for another dish). Sauté caps in the butter for 4 minutes. Add the salts, pepper, white wine, and sherry. Sauté 1 minute. Stir in the cream, chives, and cucumber. Heat through. Serve on toast points, if desired. Serves 4–6.

OKRA AND TOMATOES

1 pound small, fresh okra

½ cup olive oil

3–4 onions, peeled and coarsely chopped

2 cloves garlic, peeled and chopped

1-pound, 12-ounce can tomatoes

Salt, freshly ground black pepper

1 teaspoon coriander, tied in a cheesecloth bag

Lemon wedges

Trim the cone-shaped tops from the okra, wash them and then dry them thoroughly with a paper towel.

Heat the olive oil in a large skillet and add the

chopped onion and garlic. Cook gently until the onion and garlic are tender. Add the okra, and cook, tossing lightly, until they are slightly browned. Add the canned tomatoes, salt and freshly ground pepper to taste and the cheesecloth bag of coriander. Cover the skillet and simmer gently for about 1 hour, or until the okra is tender. Remove the cheesecloth bag. Serve with lemon wedges. Serves 4–6.

BRAISED ONION SLICES

2 tablespoons olive oil
2 tablespoons butter
4 large onions, peeled and cut in 1″ slices
1 teaspoon salt
½ teaspoon finely ground black pepper
¼ cup broth
¼ cup Scotch whisky

Melt oil and butter in a heavy saucepan. Add onions and sear over high heat 2 minutes. Add salt, pepper, broth and reduce heat. Cover and simmer for 10 minutes or until just tender. Add whisky and let the sauce cook down slightly. Serve with beef, lamb or chicken. Serves 6.

Variation: Add 2 tablespoons sultana raisins previously soaked in the whisky.

PARSNIPS IN SOUR CREAM

2 pounds parsnips, peeled and cut into 1″ cubes
1¼ teaspoons salt
¼ teaspoon pepper
1 cup sour cream
¼ teaspoon ground ginger

Cook the parsnips in boiling salted water to cover until soft. Drain and mash. Beat in the salt, pepper, sour cream, and ginger. Heat the mixture through before serving. Serves 4–6.

BRAISED PARSNIPS À LA FRANÇAISE

2 pounds parsnips
¼ cup butter
¾ teaspoon salt

¼ teaspoon sugar
6 large outside lettuce leaves
3 tablespoons chopped parsley

Wash and pare the parsnips and cut lengthwise into thin julienne strips. Heat the butter in a saucepan. Add the parsnips, salt, and sugar. Wash the lettuce leaves, and leave them quite wet. Cover the parsnips with lettuce leaves. Simmer, covered, over low heat 15–30 minutes, or until parsnips are tender; cooking time depends on their texture. Check occasionally for moisture; if necessary, add a little hot water, a tablespoon at a time. Keep or discard lettuce leaves, according to taste. Sprinkle parsnips with parsley and serve hot. Serves 4–6.

PEPPERS SAUTÉ

1 clove garlic, slivered
1 medium onion, chopped
4 tablespoons olive oil
4 large green peppers, seeded and
  cut in large squares
½ teaspoon salt
3 large tomatoes, seeded and cut into squares
2 leaves fresh sweet basil (or ½ teaspoon
  dried)

Sauté garlic and onion in oil for 5 minutes. Add peppers with salt and sauté gently for 10 minutes. Add tomatoes to the peppers with sweet basil. Cover and simmer until peppers are tender. These peppers go well with all kinds of grilled meats such as steaks, hamburgers, frankfurters and ham slices. Serves 4.

STUFFED GREEN PEPPERS ROQUEFORT

4 green peppers
1 cup bread crumbs
1 cup Roquefort cheese
⅔ cup mayonnaise
⅔ cup milk
  Salt to taste

Cut peppers in half, lengthwise. Remove seeds. Cover with water and boil 5 minutes. Mix remaining ingredients and fill pepper halves. Place the peppers in a shallow baking dish with a little water in the bottom. Bake in a 350° oven for 25 minutes. Serves 4.

POTATOES ANNA

10 medium Idaho potatoes
½ pound butter, melted
Salt, freshly ground black pepper

Peel and slice potatoes into even rounds. Put in salted ice water until ready to use. Generously butter two 8″ pie plates. Dry the potatoes thoroughly and arrange them in the pie plates in a circle with the rounds overlapping. Pour melted butter over each layer, salting lightly and peppering generously. Continue until dishes are full. Preheat oven to 400° and bake potatoes until crusty and brown. Invert on round platters and cut like a pie. Serves 8.

GRATIN OF POTATOES

3–4 large potatoes, cut in thin slices
1 cup or more heavy cream
⅔ cup grated Gruyère cheese
Salt, pepper

Wash the potato slices well and dry them on a towel. Pour a thin layer of heavy cream on the bottom of a 9″ by 12″ baking dish and alternate layers of potatoes and cheese. Top with cream. Add salt and pepper to taste. Cover with foil and place in a pan of hot water. Bake at 350° until the potatoes are just tender. If all the cream has been absorbed, add more. Remove from pan of water, take off foil and replace in the oven to brown lightly. Just before serving, sprinkle with cheese and brown again. This is delicious served with baby lamb. Serves 4.

DOUBLE BOILER CREAMED POTATOES

4 large potatoes
2 tablespoons grated onion
1 small clove garlic, mashed (optional)
Salt, pepper to taste
1–1½ cups heavy cream
¼ cup salted pistachio nuts, chopped

Peel the potatoes and shred them on a grater. Squeeze out liquid. Put the potatoes in the top of a double boiler. Beat in the onion, garlic, salt, pepper, and 1 cup of the heavy cream. Cook, covered, over boiling water until the potatoes are tender and the mixture has thickened. Stir frequently. Since some types of potato absorb more moisture, it may be necessary to add another ½ cup of cream, a little at a time, to get the desired consistency. Turn into a serving dish and sprinkle with the pistachio nuts. Serves 4.

KARTOFFELROESTI
(Swiss Fried Potatoes)

2 pounds potatoes
4 tablespoons butter
¾ teaspoon salt
2 tablespoons hot water
Paprika

Boil potatoes in their skins and cool. Peel and shred, or cut into julienne strips. Heat butter in a large skillet. Gradually add potatoes and salt. Cook over low heat, turning frequently with a spatula, until potatoes are soft and yellow. Press potatoes with spatula into a flat cake. Sprinkle with hot water.

Cover and cook over low heat until potatoes are crusty at the bottom, about 10–15 minutes. Shake pan frequently to prevent scorching and, if necessary, add a little more butter to prevent sticking. Turn into a hot serving dish crusty side up, sprinkle top with paprika and serve immediately. Serves 4–6.

Variation: Add 3 slices diced bacon or ½ cup diced Swiss cheese to the potatoes in the skillet.

POMMES DE TERRE DAUPHINE

Beat together equal parts of seasoned mashed potatoes and pâte à choux. Chill. Drop by teaspoons into 370° fat and cook until puffed and nicely browned. Drain on absorbent paper, sprinkle with salt and serve immediately.

SWISS POTATOES WITH LEEKS

2½ pounds potatoes, peeled
2 tablespoons butter
¾ pound leeks, cleaned and thinly sliced
2 cups grated Swiss cheese
3 eggs, well beaten
1⅓ cups milk
1 teaspoon salt
1 teaspoon nutmeg
½ cup grated cheese

Cook potatoes until tender in boiling salted water. Drain, cool and cut into ⅛″ slices. Melt butter and sauté leeks until golden. Thoroughly butter a 2-quart casserole or baking dish, put in a layer of potatoes, then a layer of leeks, then a layer of grated Swiss cheese, ending with potatoes. Beat eggs with milk, salt and nutmeg. Pour over layers in casserole. Sprinkle with ½ cup grated cheese. Bake in a 375°

oven for 20–30 minutes, or until eggs are set and top is golden brown. Serves 6.

SWEET POTATO PUDDING

3 large sweet potatoes, grated
2 medium onions, grated or minced
1 green pepper, chopped fine
2 tablespoons melted bacon fat
¼ teaspoon black pepper
⅛ teaspoon each: thyme, marjoram, sage

Mix all ingredients thoroughly. Place in a greased casserole, cover and bake in a 350° oven for 45 minutes, or until potatoes are almost tender. Uncover and bake 15 minutes longer. Serves 6.

STUFFED SWEET POTATOES

6 medium sweet potatoes
½ pound mushrooms, sliced
6 tablespoons butter
1 teaspoon salt
¼ teaspoon freshly ground black pepper
2 eggs, beaten
⅓ cup fresh orange juice
2 tablespoons grated orange rind

Bake sweet potatoes in a 375° oven until tender, about 1 hour. Cut thin slice from top of each potato, lengthwise, and carefully scoop out the pulp. Mash. Sauté mushrooms in 4 tablespoons butter. Mix potato pulp, mushrooms, seasonings, eggs, orange juice and rind. Stuff potato shells with the mixture. Dot with remaining 2 tablespoons butter and bake in a 375° oven until brown, about 20 minutes. Serves 6.

PUMPKIN PURÉE

2 cups cooked mashed pumpkin
2 tablespoons butter, at room temperature
½ teaspoon salt
¼ teaspoon pepper
¼ teaspoon ground cardamom
¼ teaspoon ground cinnamon

⅛ teaspoon mace
1 tablespoon brown sugar
½ cup brandy

Combine all ingredients in a heavy saucepan. Cook over lowest possible heat, stirring constantly, until the purée is well blended and dry enough to keep its shape when piled in a dish. Serve with roast pork, lamb, or duck. Serves 4.

FINNISH RUTABAGA PUDDING

2 pounds rutabagas, peeled and diced
3 tablespoons light or heavy cream
5 tablespoons butter
  Salt, pepper to taste
½ teaspoon sugar
⅛ teaspoon ground nutmeg

Place the rutabagas in a saucepan. Add boiling salted water to cover by 1″. Simmer, covered, for 10–15 minutes, or until tender. Mash and put through a food mill or potato ricer. Beat in the cream, 2 tablespoons of the butter, the salt, pepper, sugar, and nutmeg. Turn into a buttered 9″ pie plate. Smooth the top with a spatula and make indentations with a spoon. Melt remaining 3 tablespoons butter and dribble over top of vegetable mixture. Bake in a preheated 375° oven fror 30 minutes, or until top is golden brown. Serves 4–6.

RUTABAGA AND APPLE WHIP

2 pounds rutabagas, peeled and diced
2 medium tart apples, peeled, cored,
  and quartered
3 tablespoons butter, at room temperature
2 tablespoons sugar
½ teaspoon salt
¼ teaspoon pepper
⅛ teaspoon ground cardamom

Place the rutabagas in a saucepan. Cover with boiling salted water and simmer, covered, for 15 minutes, or until vegetable is tender. Add the apples and continue cooking until apples are tender. Drain if necessary.

Mash the rutabagas and apples together. Stir in the butter and sugar. Season with salt, pepper, and cardamom. Whip until fluffy. Serve with pork, ham, or poultry. Serves 4–6.

ROMAN SPINACH

2 pounds spinach
2 tablespoons butter
1 tablespoon olive oil
½ cup pine nuts
1 clove garlic, mashed
2 teaspoons vinegar
  Salt, pepper to taste

Wash the spinach thoroughly, trim off tough stems, and shred large leaves. Heat the butter and the olive oil in a large deep skillet and cook the nuts in it until they are golden brown. Add the spinach, garlic, vinegar, salt, and pepper. Cook, covered, for about 4 minutes, or until spinach is barely tender. Serve very hot. Serves 4–6.

SPINACH AND MADEIRA

2 pounds spinach (or 2–3 packages frozen
  spinach)
4 tablespoons butter
1 teaspoon salt
¼ teaspoon grated nutmeg
⅓ cup crumbled crisp bacon
½ cup cooked, chopped mushrooms
1 tablespoon flour
⅓ cup Madeira
¼ cup heavy cream
  Chopped parsley

Wash spinach thoroughly and cook covered, without water, in a kettle (the moisture left on the leaves from washing is enough). Steam gently until wilted and still a bit bitey. This will only take a minute. If you use frozen spinach, be careful not to cook it too long. Drain spinach thoroughly, pressing out all excess moisture. Chop coarsely and mix with butter, salt, nutmeg, bacon and mushrooms. Sprinkle with flour and blend in Madeira and heavy cream. Reheat slightly until just heated through, heap in a serving dish and top with a good dollop of butter and sprinkle with chopped parsley. Serves 4.

SPINACH PIE

    2 bunches spinach
    1 bunch Swiss chard
    1 bunch parsley
    1 bunch green onions
    6 leaves fresh mint
    1 tablespoon salt
      Freshly ground pepper to taste
    1½ teaspoons uncooked rice
    ⅔ cup olive oil
    3 eggs, slightly beaten
    ½ pound feta cheese, crumbled
    ½ pound filo (approximately)
      Cinnamon

Wash the spinach, Swiss chard, parsley, green onions, and mint. Dry as thoroughly as possible and chop finely. Spread out on a towel and let stand at room temperature for several hours to dry completely. Put greens in a large mixing bowl with the salt, pepper, rice, 2 tablespoons of the olive oil, beaten eggs, and crumbled cheese and toss together.

Spread 6 sheets of filo with oil and line a 10″ by 14″ baking pan, letting filo come up the side of the pan. Spread tossed mixture over the dough and sprinkle lightly with cinnamon. Trim off excess filo around pan edges. Spread 6 more sheets of filo with oil and place on top of the mixture. Cut through the top layer of filo (down to the filling) making 2½″ squares. Bake in a preheated 350° oven for 1 hour, or until greens are tender. Finish cutting into squares and serve hot or cool. Makes about 24 pieces.

PURÉE OF SPINACH AND WATERCRESS

    3 bunches spinach
    2 bunches watercress
    1 clove garlic

    ¼ pound butter
      Salt, pepper to taste
      Nutmeg
      Thin slices lemon

Wash and pick over the greens carefully, keeping them separate. Cook them in two pots in the water which clings to the leaves. As they wilt, turn with tongs to get the top leaves to the bottom. When thoroughly wilted, tender and still bright green, drain thoroughly, and either chop together very fine or put through a food mill. Crush the garlic a little with the side of a knife, or make small cuts all over it with a sharp knife. Add the garlic to the hot greens and mix in the butter, salt, pepper and a grating or two of nutmeg. Remove the garlic and discard. Arrange in a serving dish and reheat in the oven if necessary. Garnish with slices of lemon. Serves 6.

ARABIAN SQUASH CASSEROLE

    3 pounds yellow squash
    1 tablespoon salt
    1½ cups grated Cheddar cheese
    1 cup cottage cheese
    5 eggs, beaten
    1 cup bread crumbs
    3 tablespoons minced parsley
    ½ teaspoon pepper
    4 tablespoons melted butter

Peel and grate the squash. Mix with the salt and let stand 20 minutes. Press all the liquid from squash. Mix together squash, Cheddar and cottage cheese, eggs, bread crumbs, parsley, pepper. Put in a buttered 3-quart casserole. Pour butter on top. Bake at 350° 1 hour. Serves 6.

STEAMED SUMMER SQUASH

    1 pound small zucchini, sliced in half lengthwise
    1 pound small yellow crookneck squash, sliced in half lengthwise
    1 medium onion, finely chopped
    1 tomato, peeled and chopped
    2 leaves mint
    2 cloves garlic, minced

Salt, pepper to taste
¼ cup olive oil

Place the sliced zucchini and crookneck squash in a saucepan, add the onion, tomato, mint, garlic, salt, and pepper, and pour the oil over. Cover and simmer for 15–20 minutes, or until vegetables are barely tender. Remove cover and cook down rapidly to reduce juices. Serves 6–8.

TOMATO SOUFFLÉS

4 large, firm tomatoes
2 cloves
1 teaspoon grated onion
Pinch of basil
1 tablespoon butter
1 tablespoon flour
½ cup hot milk or cream
2 eggs, separated
Salt, pepper
½ teaspoon cognac

Cut a 1″ slice from the tops of the tomatoes and scoop out the pulp. Save the pulp and set the tomato shells to drain, saving any further juice also. Simmer the pulp and juice with the cloves, grated onion and basil until reduced to slightly more than 1 cup. Put through a strainer, mashing so that you get everything but the seeds.

Melt the butter and stir in the flour. When smooth, add the hot milk or cream. Cook and stir until thick and smooth.

Beat the 2 egg yolks until light in color. Pour a little of the hot cream sauce into the egg yolks, then a little more, and then the lot, stirring briskly between additions. Add the tomato purée, season to taste with salt and pepper and add the cognac. Allow mixture to cool.

Beat the 2 egg whites until stiff but not dry. Stir ¼ of the whites into the sauce and then pour the sauce over the rest of the whites, folding in lightly. Cut the tiniest slice from the bottom of each tomato so that it may stand upright in the pan. Fill tomatoes ¾ full, place them in a shallow pan and bake in a preheated 375° oven for 25–30 minutes. Serves 4.

CURRIED TURNIPS

3 tablespoons butter
1 medium onion, thinly sliced
1 teaspoon ground thyme
1 teaspoon ground marjoram
1 teaspoon turmeric
½ teaspoon ground ginger
1 teaspoon salt
½ teaspoon pepper
3 tablespoons yoghurt
2 pounds white turnips, peeled and cut into 1″ cubes
1 teaspoon curry powder

Heat the butter in a large deep skillet. Add the onion, thyme, and marjoram. Cook, stirring constantly, until the onion is soft and golden. Add the turmeric, ginger, salt, and pepper. Cook over medium heat, stirring constantly, for 3 minutes. Stir in the yoghurt and cook for 3 minutes more. Add the turnips and cook, uncovered, for 5 minutes.

Lower heat. Simmer, covered, for about 25–30 minutes, stirring occasionally. Check for moisture; if necessary, add a little hot water to prevent scorching, a tablespoon at a time—the curry should be dry. When turnips are almost tender, stir in the curry powder. Cook for 10 minutes more. Serve with roast pork or ham. Serves 4–6.

GLAZED TURNIPS

2 bunches baby turnips
Lemon juice
1 tablespoon tarragon vinegar
2 ounces salt butter
Salt, black pepper to taste
¼ cup sugar
2 tablespoons honey

Peel the turnips and wash them in lemon juice and water. Put them in boiling water and add tarragon vinegar. Simmer gently until just soft. Drain. Dissolve the butter in a shallow pan and add the turnips. Season with salt and pepper and sprinkle with sugar. Add the honey and shake over a brisk fire until glazed all over. Serve in a small shallow casserole, very hot. Serves 4.

STUFFED ZUCCHINI

> 12–14 small zucchini, cut in half lengthwise
> Olive oil
> 3 cloves garlic, finely chopped
> ⅔ cup bread crumbs or croutons
> 12 black olives, chopped (preferably soft type)
> 2 tablespoons capers
> 2 tablespoons chopped parsley
> 12–14 anchovy fillets, coarsely chopped

Scoop out and discard seeds and a small amount of flesh from the zucchini. Sauté halves quickly in olive oil. Then parboil 5–10 minutes. Cool. Sauté the garlic and crumbs in 6 tablespoons oil for 2 minutes. Add the chopped olives, capers, parsley, anchovies. Stuff the zucchini with this mixture, sprinkle with additional crumbs and brush with oil. Arrange the stuffed zucchini in a baking dish and bake in a 375° oven for 20 minutes, brushing once with oil. Serve cold. Serves 12 as an hors d'oeuvre, 6 as a spicy summer luncheon dish.

ZUCCHINI-NUT CASSEROLE

> 6 medium zucchini, sliced
> 3 slices white bread, soaked in milk
> 1 egg
> Salt, pepper to taste
> ½ cup coarsely chopped almonds or peanuts
> Bread crumbs
> Butter

Place the zucchini in a saucepan with a little water and cook until tender, but still crisp. Drain and chop into small pieces. Mash the bread and combine with the zucchini. Beat the egg slightly, then stir into zucchini mixture with salt, pepper and the nuts. Pour into a buttered casserole, sprinkle with the bread crumbs, dot with butter and bake in a 350° oven until the crumbs have browned. Goes well with cold meats. Serves 4.

CASSEROLE OF EGGPLANT, SQUASH AND TOMATOES

> ½–¾ cup olive oil
> 6 onions, sliced
> 2 small eggplant, washed and diced
> 2 large zucchini, washed and diced
> 2 medium summer squash, washed and diced
> Salt, pepper, thyme, coriander
> 1 teaspoon dried basil
> 6 tomatoes, chopped

Heat the olive oil in a large iron skillet or casserole. Cook the onions on low heat until transparent, about 10 minutes. Dry the eggplant, zucchini and squash well and add to the onions. Stir well and cook covered for 20 minutes. Season with salt, pepper, a good pinch of thyme, a little coriander (just enough to cover the point of a knife) and basil. Add the chopped tomatoes and cook again covered for 20 minutes. Uncover the pan and cook 10–15 minutes, or until some of the moisture disappears. Transfer the vegetable mixture to an earthenware casserole and serve. Serves 8.

TIAN

> Olive oil
> 2 pounds raw spinach, coarsely chopped
> 2 pounds raw Swiss chard, coarsely chopped
> 6–8 finger-size zucchini, cut in small dice
> 2 medium onions, coarsely chopped
> 3 cloves garlic, finely chopped
> ½ cup basil leaves, finely chopped
> 2 tablespoons dried basil
> 1½ teaspoons salt
> 1 teaspoon freshly ground black pepper
> 8 eggs, slightly beaten
> 1–1½ cups grated Parmesan cheese
> Bread crumbs

Cover the bottom of a large skillet with olive oil and add the spinach and Swiss chard. Cook until just wilted. Remove and drain. Press out all liquid. Add the zucchini, onion and garlic to the skillet and repeat cooking procedure.

Combine the vegetables, the fresh and dried basil, salt and pepper and place in a lightly oiled heavy earthenware casserole. Pour the eggs over the vegetables and top with the cheese and bread crumbs. Bake in a 350° oven until the eggs are just set and the cheese melted and bubbly. Chill in the refrigerator and serve cold. Serves 8.

RATATOUILLE WITH FENNEL

        2 large onions, peeled and sliced
        3 cloves garlic (or more), chopped
        ⅓ cup olive oil
        2 small eggplant, cut in cubes
        4 small zucchini, sliced
        2 green peppers, cut in strips
        1 head fennel, sliced
        1-pound, 4-ounce can Italian plum tomatoes
        1 teaspoon basil
        1½ teaspoons salt
        ½ teaspoon parsley
        Freshly ground black pepper to taste

Place the onions and garlic in a skillet with the olive oil. Heat and toss until wilted. Add the eggplant, zucchini, peppers and fennel. Mix well over a brisk heat. Add the tomatoes and seasonings. Cover and simmer for approximately 1 hour, stirring occasionally. Remove cover and allow to cook down until most of the liquid has evaporated and the mixture is thick. Delicious hot or cold. Serves 6.

PERSIAN VEGETABLE PIE

        1 pound spinach, chopped, or 1 package
           frozen spinach, thawed
        2½ cups chopped scallions
        1 cup chopped lettuce
        1½ cups chopped parsley
        2 tablespoons flour
        1½ teaspoons salt
        ¼ teaspoon freshly ground black pepper
        ½ cup chopped walnuts
        8 eggs, beaten well
        4 tablespoons butter
        Yoghurt

Wash the fresh spinach and drain well, or drain the uncooked thawed spinach. Mix together the spinach, scallions, lettuce, parsley, flour, salt, pepper and nuts. Mix in the eggs.

Melt the butter in an 11″ pie plate. Pour the vegetable mixture into it. Bake in a preheated 325° oven 1 hour or until top is brown and crisp. Serve hot or cold, with yoghurt as a topping. Serves 4–6.

COLACHE

This is a sort of succotash, originally made with pumpkin, but any squash, winter or summer, will do. If hard-shelled, peel and remove seeds. Summer squash or zucchini will not need peeling unless it is large and tough.

        ¼ cup bacon fat or other shortening
        3 cups diced pumpkin or squash
        1 onion, chopped
        1 green pepper, chopped
        1 canned green chile, chopped (optional)
        1 clove garlic, minced
        3 cups stewed or canned tomatoes
        1 cup green beans, cut in ½″ slices
        Kernels of 3 ears green corn, cut from cob
        1 teaspoon salt
        Freshly ground pepper

Melt bacon fat in a heavy pan and add squash, onion, green pepper, chile and minced garlic. Cook, stirring, for about 5 minutes. Add tomatoes, beans, corn, ½ cup water and salt. Cover and simmer until the vegetables are tender. Correct seasoning, adding salt and freshly ground pepper to taste. Serves 8.

GRATIN OF VEGETABLES

        6 carrots, scraped and diced
        Best stalks from 1 bunch Pascal celery, diced
        2 leeks, white part only, sliced
        6 spring onions, white and green parts, sliced
        1 pound fresh peas
        2 eggs
        ½ cup light cream
        Salt, pepper, nutmeg to taste
        Grated Parmesan cheese
        Butter

Cook all vegetables separately in very little salted water until they are barely tender. Drain the vegetables well and mix.

Beat eggs and combine them with light cream. Season with salt, pepper and a pinch of nutmeg. Mix the vegetables into the sauce and pour into a shallow, well-buttered baking dish. Sprinkle with grated Parmesan cheese, dot with butter and cook in a preheated 400° oven until brown. Serves 6.

HARICOTS SECS À LA BRETONNE

> 1 pound dried white beans, Michigan or Great
> Northern
> 5 sprigs parsley
> 3 celery stalk tops
> 4 cloves garlic
> 2 teaspoons basil leaves
> 1 onion
> 1 teaspoon thyme
> Salt, pepper
> 3 large onions, chopped fine
> 2 cloves garlic, minced
> 2 ounces butter
> 2 rounded tablespoons flour
> 1½ cups bouillon
> 3 ounces (half a 6-ounce can) tomato paste

Soak beans overnight in water to cover. Drain. Cover with 2½ quarts water. Tie together parsley, celery tops and garlic in cheesecloth bundle for bouquet garni. Tuck into beans. Add basil, whole onion, thyme, 1 tablespoon salt, and ½ teaspoon pepper. Cook the mixture slowly 1 hour, or until the beans are almost but not completely soft.

Meanwhile, prepare the sauce. Sauté chopped onions and minced garlic in butter until golden. Sprinkle mixture with flour, stirring in gradually over low heat. When onion and flour mixture is smooth, slowly stir in bouillon, then tomato paste, 1 teaspoon salt and ½ teaspoon pepper. Simmer very slowly a half-hour or until sauce is reduced a bit.

Remove bouquet garni and onion from beans. There should be only the barest amount of liquid remaining; if there seems to be more than ¼ to ½ cup, drain it off but reserve. Add tomato sauce to beans and simmer, covered, very slowly for an hour or longer. The beans should still be slightly liquid; add a very little of the reserved bean water if liquid is needed. Serves 8.

Note: These beans are especially good with roast lamb and are even better reheated a day later. Thin with a small amount of tomato juice if necessary.

FRIJOLES

(Beans)

> 2 cups pinto, black, or red kidney beans
> 2 onions, finely chopped
> 2 cloves garlic, chopped
> Sprig epazote or 1 bay leaf
> 2 or more serrano chiles, chopped, or 1 teaspoon
> dried pequin chiles, crumbled
> 3 tablespoons lard
> Salt, pepper to taste
> 1 tomato, peeled, seeded, and chopped

Wash beans, but do not soak. Put in cold water to cover with half of the chopped onion and garlic, the epazote or bay leaf, and chiles. Cover and simmer gently, adding more water, always hot, as needed. When beans begin to wrinkle, add 1 tablespoon lard or oil. When beans are soft, almost done, add seasonings. Cook another half hour without adding more water; there should not be a great deal of liquid when beans are done. Heat the remaining 2 tablespoons lard and sauté the remaining chopped onion and garlic until limp. Add tomato and cook for 1–2 minutes, then add a tablespoon of beans and mash into the mixture, add a second tablespoon of beans without draining them so that some of the bean liquid evaporates in this cooking process. Add a third tablespoon of beans and continue to cook until you have a smooth, fairly heavy paste. Return this to the bean pot and stir into beans over low heat to thicken the remaining liquid. Serves 6–8.

FRIJOLES REFRITOS

(Fried Beans)

Cook beans as above, but when mashing them, keep adding beans until all have been mashed into lard over low heat. Add lard from time to time and cook until beans are creamy and have become a heavy, quite dry paste. You may cheat a little by using the blender to purée beans, adding them to the skillet bit by bit, and frying them dry in the hot lard.

Salad

"He who would live for aye must eat sallet in May," runs an old English proverb, while the Greeks, more concerned with intelligence than longevity, advised, "Eat cress and gain wit." The appeal of a good green salad seems to be as old as man's appetite, although accounts of the medical and magical properties ascribed to it would indicate that salad was eaten as much for what it couldn't do as what it could. At one time, lettuce was believed to make men immune to the charms of women, and sales to monasteries rose immoderately. A passage in Cogan's Haven of Health, published in 1589, makes a more modest and realistic claim: "Lettuce is much used in salats in summer time with vinegar, oyle and sugar and salt and is found to procure appetite for meats, and to temper the heat of the stomach and liver." Some of the early salads sound more likely to cause acute indigestion. In The Forme of Cury, a compendium of recipes by the cooks of Richard II of England, His Majesty's salad is loaded with parsley, sage, garlic, onions, leeks, borage, mint, fennel, cress, rue, rosemary and purslain, while a later Compound Sallet credited to Gervase Markham includes raisins, almonds, figs, capers, olives, currants, oranges, lemons, cucumber, lettuce, sage and spinach among the list of makings—compound indeed.

It was left to the horticulturist John Evelyn, author of the seventeenth-century Acetaria, a Discourse on Sallets, to reduce and refine the salad to its pure, classic proportions. His directions were both poetic and laudable: "In the composure of a Sallet, every plant should come in to bear its part without being overpowered by some herb of a stronger taste, but should fall into its place like the notes in music."

The early salads were mainly composed of leafy vegetables and herbs. During the experimental seventeenth century, chicken and seafood were introduced and fruit was quite common by the end of the eighteenth century. Today, we have a wealth of ingredients to choose from and a roster of salads both appetizing and alluring. Yet the prime favorite still remains the simple green salad, coolly glistening with honest oil and excellent vinegar. In this context, the character and consistency of the greens are all-important, and it would be well to take to heart the words of the nineteenth-century author Charles Dudley Warner, "Lettuce must be like conversation, it must be fresh and crisp, so sparkling that you scarcely notice the bitter in it."

GREEN BEAN AND TOMATO SALAD

    2 pounds green beans
    2 pounds ripe tomatoes
      Salt, pepper
    5 tablespoons olive oil
    1 tablespoon wine vinegar
    1 tablespoon Worcestershire sauce

Cook the beans in salted water until tender but still crisp, leaving them whole if they are young and slim. Otherwise, cut them as you wish. Chill.

Scald the tomatoes, peel them and cut them in eighths, removing seeds and pulp. Sprinkle with salt and pat dry with paper towels.

Put the oil, vinegar and Worcestershire sauce in a salad bowl. Mix well and add salt and pepper to taste. Add the beans and tomatoes and mix again. Refrigerate for 1 hour. Serves 6.

GREEN BEAN AND CUCUMBER SALAD

    1 pound fresh snap beans
    2 tablespoons salad oil
    2 tablespoons vinegar
    ¼ cup bouillon
    1 tablespoon finely chopped parsley
    ¼ teaspoon minced onion
    ½ teaspoon salt
    ⅛ teaspoon pepper
    1 large cucumber, sliced and lightly salted

Cook and drain beans. While still hot, add oil, vinegar, bouillon, parsley, onion and seasonings. Toss well. Chill. Add cucumber before serving. Serves 6.

BEAN SPROUT SALAD

    ½ pound bean sprouts
    ½ cup thinly sliced celery
    2 tablespoons minced green onions
    1 teaspoon grated fresh or preserved ginger
      (optional)
    ½ cup mayonnaise
    2 tablespoons soy sauce
    1 teaspoon curry powder
    1 teaspoon lemon juice
      Slivered toasted almonds (optional)

Combine bean sprouts with celery, green onions and ginger. Make a dressing with the mayonnaise, soy sauce, curry powder and lemon juice. Mix gently with the bean sprouts, arrange on lettuce and, if you wish, sprinkle with almonds. Serve with charcoal-broiled chicken or spit-roasted pork. Serves 4. This salad is also excellent mixed with ½ pound of crab meat and a little additional dressing.

ITALIAN BEET AND CELERY SALAD

    2 hard-cooked egg yolks, sieved
    1 raw egg yolk
    1½ tablespoons lemon juice
    5 tablespoons olive oil
      Salt, pepper to taste
    2 chilled celery hearts, diced
    12 walnuts
    1½ cups chilled sliced beets

Put the sieved hard-cooked yolks, raw yolk, lemon juice, olive oil, salt and pepper in a small deep bowl and beat with a wire whisk until creamy. Add the diced celery and half the walnuts, coarsely chopped. Place in the center of a round platter. Arrange the sliced beets in a circle around the celery, and top them with the remaining walnut halves. Serves 4.

RED CABBAGE SALAD

    1 medium head red cabbage
    ½ cup tarragon vinegar
      Salt, pepper to taste
    6 hard-cooked egg yolks
    1 pint heavy cream
      Lemon juice
    2 tablespoons chopped leek, chervil and fennel
    3 small cucumbers, minced
      Radishes, sliced

Remove the outer leaves from the cabbage. Wash it thoroughly, cut in julienne and blanch it briefly in salted water. Drain, chill and marinate in the vinegar, salt and pepper for 1 hour, turning frequently. Drain off marinade. Put the egg yolks through a sieve and mix them with the cream, adding lemon juice, salt and pepper to taste. Add the leek, chervil, fennel and the cabbage. Mix well. Pile on a platter and decorate the salad with minced cucumbers and sliced radishes. Serve with cold corned beef or a cold pork and ham loaf. Serves 6.

SPECIAL COLESLAW

    1 tablespoon butter
    1 tablespoon flour
    1 teaspoon sugar
    1 teaspoon salt
    1 teaspoon dry mustard
     Dash of pepper
    2 beaten eggs
    ½ pint light cream
    2 tablespoons vinegar
     Finely chopped cabbage

Cream butter with flour, sugar, salt, dry mustard and a dash of pepper. Add beaten eggs. Mix well. Add light cream. Heat vinegar, add to first mixture and cook, over a medium flame, until thick. Cool and add to finely chopped cabbage, allowing ½ cup sauce to 2 cups cabbage.

CUCUMBER-ONION SALAD

    2 large cucumbers
    1 medium-size yellow onion
    4 tablespoons sour cream
    2 tablespoons white wine vinegar
    1 teaspoon salt
    ¼ teaspoon white pepper
    1–2 tablespoons chopped fresh dill

Peel and thinly slice the cucumbers and the onion. Blend together the sour cream, vinegar, salt and pepper. Mix with the cucumbers and onion and chill for several hours in the refrigerator. Just before serving sprinkle with the chopped dill. Serves 8–10.

JAPANESE CUCUMBER SALAD

    3 cucumbers (not waxed)
    1 teaspoon salt
    1 tablespoon shoyu sauce
    ¼ cup Japanese or white vinegar
    2 tablespoons sugar
    ¼ teaspoon monosodium glutamate

Score unpeeled cucumbers with a fork or garnishing knife, leaving stripes of green. Cut in thin slices, and sprinkle with salt. Let stand an hour, then drain and press out liquid. Mix with shoyu sauce, vinegar, sugar and monosodium glutamate and chill. Serves 6.

YOGHURT-CUCUMBER SALAD

    4 cucumbers
    1½ teaspoons salt
    1 clove garlic, minced
    2 tablespoons lemon juice
    2 cups yoghurt
    1 tablespoon finely chopped dill
    ¼ cup olive oil
    2 teaspoons chopped fresh mint

Peel the cucumbers, cut in quarters lengthwise, then slice thin. Sprinkle with the salt and let stand 15 minutes. Drain well. Mix together the garlic, lemon juice, yoghurt and dill. Mix with cucumbers. Pour oil over the top and sprinkle with mint. Serve unchilled. Serves 8.

CUCUMBER AND GREEN PEPPER SALAD

    1 bunch watercress
    2 tender young cucumbers, peeled and sliced
     paper thin
    2 small green peppers
     Cracked ice
    1 cup French dressing

Wash the watercress, discard the tough stems, wrap in a wet cloth and refrigerate. Soak the cucumbers for 2 hours in ice water. Wash the green peppers; remove stem end, scoop out seeds and slice in rings. Cover the pepper slices with cracked ice until ready to serve. Add 1 tablespoon of cracked ice to the French dressing and stir well. Arrange the watercress on 6 well-chilled plates. Drain the cucumbers well and place on the watercress. Garnish with the green peppers. Pour the French dressing over all, distributing it evenly. Serve at once. Serves 6.

EGGPLANT SALAD

This is a Spanish salad. It is equally appetizing as a

first course or a luncheon entrée.

> 2 medium eggplant
> 1 teaspoon lemon juice
> 1 teaspoon minced onion
> 1 cup diced celery
> ½ cup chopped walnuts
> ¼ cup French dressing
>   Romaine or Bibb lettuce
>   <u>Garnish</u>: quartered hard-cooked eggs, olives, mayonnaise

Peel and cube eggplant. Cook in salted water with lemon juice. When eggplant is tender, drain and cool. Mix with onion, celery, walnuts and French dressing. Chill. Serve on romaine or Bibb lettuce. Garnish with quartered hard-cooked eggs and olives and top each serving with a spoonful of mayonnaise. Serves 6.

IRMA SALAD

In France, where this salad comes from, it would be served as an hors d'oeuvre, but it is excellent as a luncheon or supper dish accompanying cold meats.

Combine equal parts of sliced, unpeeled cucumbers (if unwaxed, otherwise peel them), cooked asparagus tips, cooked green beans cut in diamond shapes, and small, raw cauliflower flowerets. Mix with mayonnaise to which a little whipped cream and pinches of dried chervil and tarragon have been added. (Fresh herbs, of course, would be even better.) Heap into a mound and cover with shredded lettuce mixed with watercress leaves. Decorate with slices of radish and nasturtium blossoms.

MUSHROOM SALAD

> 1 pound mushrooms
> 1 bunch Pascal celery
> 2 tablespoons minced chives
> 3 tablespoons olive oil
> 1 tablespoon tarragon vinegar
>   Salt, pepper to taste
>   Bibb or romaine leaves
>   <u>Garnish</u>: pimiento strips and quartered hard-cooked eggs

Rinse the raw mushrooms and dry them. Slice the stems and cut the caps into cubes or pie-shaped wedges. Cube the inner stalks of the bunch of Pascal celery. Combine mushrooms and celery with minced chives and marinate the mixture in a dressing made of the olive oil, tarragon vinegar, salt and pepper. Chill for 30 minutes. When ready to serve, lift salad out of the dressing and pile it on Bibb or romaine lettuce leaves. Dust with freshly ground black pepper. Pimiento strips and quartered hard-cooked eggs may be added as garnish. Serve with squab, chops or steak. Serves 4–6.

HOT POTATO SALAD

> 24 very small new potatoes
> 12 green onions, chopped, or ⅓ cup chopped onion
> ⅓ cup chopped parsley
> ½ cup hot olive oil
> 1 teaspoon salt
> ½ teaspoon freshly ground black pepper
>   Heated wine vinegar to taste—3 tablespoons or more

Boil potatoes in their jackets. When they are tender, drain and cool until they can be handled. Peel and halve or quarter the potatoes and place them in an ovenproof dish with onion and parsley. Pour hot oil and seasonings over them and toss with heated wine vinegar to taste. Heat a few minutes before serving. Top with additional chopped parsley. Serves 6–8.

POTATO AND CELERY ROOT SALAD

> 1 pound celery root
>   Salt
> 1 pound Irish potatoes
> 1 can artichoke bottoms, drained and rinsed
> 3 cups mayonnaise
> 2 tablespoons light cream
>   Chervil
>   Capers
>   Watercress
> 1 hard-cooked egg yolk
>   Truffles or black olives, sliced

Peel the celery root, slice it crosswise ¼″ thick and

put it in a pan with cold water to cover and 1 teaspoon salt. Bring to a boil, lower the heat and simmer for 15 minutes. Drain and chill.

Peel the potatoes and cook them in salted water until tender but still quite firm. Drain and chill. Then slice them ¼″ thick.

With a cookie cutter that is approximately the same circumference as the artichoke bottoms, cut the celery and potatoes in circles.

Thin 2 cups mayonnaise with 2 tablespoons cream. Divide evenly between the three vegetables, keeping them separate. Mix each vegetable with the mayonnaise. Chill.

Arrange a layer of potatoes in the bottom of a round bowl and sprinkle them with chervil. Add a layer of celery root and sprinkle with drained capers. Add a layer of artichoke bottoms. Repeat layers until bowl is full. Chill overnight.

Unmold the salad onto a bed of crisp watercress. Mask it with the remaining unthinned mayonnaise. Rice the yolk of the egg and sprinkle over the top of the potato and celery root salad. Decorate the top with slices of truffles or black olives. Serves 6.

TOMATO SALAD

>   4–6 large ripe tomatoes
>   2 teaspoons chopped fresh basil
>   (or 1 teaspoon dried)
>   1 teaspoon salt

1 teaspoon freshly ground black pepper
6 tablespoons olive oil
¼ cup cognac
   Chopped parsley

Scald, peel and chill the tomatoes. Cut them in paper-thin slices and arrange overlapping on a dish. Pour over them a mixture of the basil, salt, pepper, olive oil and cognac. Sprinkle with chopped parsley and chill before serving. Serves 6.

TOMATOES WITH CUCUMBER ICE

Choose ripe, full-flavored tomatoes and do not peel the cucumber if the skin hasn't been waxed.

>   2 cups grated cucumber and juice (2 or 3
>   cucumbers)
>   3 tablespoons white wine vinegar
>   1 teaspoon salt
>   ¼ teaspoon pepper
>   ½ envelope unflavored gelatin
>   3 tablespoons cold water
>   6 medium-sized ripe tomatoes
>   Lettuce

Quarter cucumbers lengthwise, remove seeds and grate or chop fine in an electric blender. Add vinegar, salt and pepper. Soften gelatin in cold water and dissolve over hot water. Add to cucumber, turn into freezing tray and freeze until firm. Transfer to chilled bowl, beat well and return to tray. Freeze again. Slice tomatoes downward into 6 or 8 sections, leaving them attached at the base. Place each on a lettuce

Greek Eggplant Salad

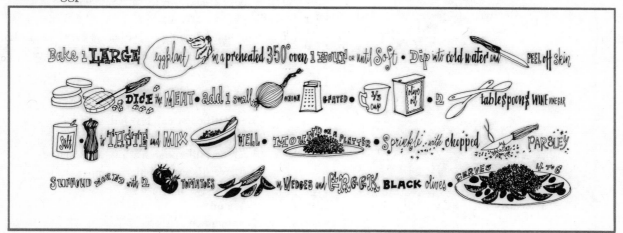

leaf and put a scoop of cucumber ice in the center of each one. Serves 6.

SPINACH AND MUSHROOM SALAD MIMOSA

2 pounds fresh spinach
½ pound raw mushrooms, thinly sliced
½ cup French dressing
2 hard-cooked egg yolks, riced

Remove leaves from spinach, discarding stems. Wash, dry and chill. Shortly before serving, toss with mushrooms and French dressing. Sprinkle with the riced egg yolk. Serves 8.

SPINACH SALAD

1 pound spinach
4 slices bacon
1 small white onion, finely minced

HOW TO PREPARE TOMATOES FOR SALADS

1. Skin tomatoes if recipe calls for it. Quarter them. Cut out the seeds and pulp.

2. To shred quarters, turn over and slice in strips, keeping knife point on board.

3. To section whole tomato slice from bottom to top. Halve slices lengthwise.

2 teaspoons salt
1 teaspoon pepper
6 tablespoons white wine vinegar

Cut off the stems of the spinach, wash leaves well and drain in a colander, then chop them up. Cook the bacon in a small skillet until browned and crisp. Remove, drain on paper towels and crumble. Add bacon to the spinach with the minced onion, salt and pepper. Add the vinegar to the bacon fat, bring to a boil, stir well and pour over the spinach. Serve immediately, while the spinach is still crisp. Serves 4.

CAESAR SALAD

2 cups croutons
Olive oil
2 cloves garlic
2 large heads romaine, chilled
Freshly ground black pepper
½ teaspoon salt
1 egg
1 lemon
4 or 5 anchovy fillets, cut in small pieces
(optional)
½ cup grated Parmesan cheese

Brown the croutons in oil flavored with 1 clove garlic. Drain and reserve. Rub a capacious salad bowl with the remaining garlic clove. Break romaine into pieces and put in bowl. Pour about ¼ cup olive oil over the romaine, add a few grindings of pepper and the salt. Mix gently until every leaf is glistening with oil. Break the egg into the center of the romaine, squeeze on the juice of ½ lemon and mix thoroughly until it looks creamy. Add the anchovies, if desired, and the cheese. Mix again and taste; you may need more oil, lemon, salt or pepper. Finally add the croutons, mix quickly and serve at once. Serves 6.

SUMMER SALAD

Leaf lettuce or oak leaf lettuce
6 scallions
1 heaping tablespoon fresh tarragon leaves
Salt, freshly ground black pepper
1 teaspoon dry mustard
Olive oil
Lemon juice

Wash the greens and dry them. Cut the scallions very fine and chop the tarragon. Blend with salt and pepper to taste, and mustard. Add ½ cup olive oil and 1 teaspoon of lemon juice. Blend and let stand for one hour to mellow. Add more oil and lemon juice (to taste) and toss with the greens at the last minute. Serves 6.

CHICORY AND DILL SALAD

2 heads chicory
2 avocado pears
6 artichoke bottoms
½ cup chopped fresh dill
½ cup vegetable oil
2 tablespoons tarragon vinegar
1 teaspoon salt
1 teaspoon white pepper
1 teaspoon chopped garlic
1 teaspoon lemon juice
1 raw egg
¼ teaspoon sugar

Wash chicory and dry well in paper towels. Roughly break with hand. Put in large shallow bowl, add the avocado pears, skinned and cut into large dice, and the artichoke bottoms, quartered. Sprinkle with dill. Put remaining ingredients in a screw-topped jar. Shake well. Pour the dressing over the salad. Toss well and serve. Serves 8.

WATERCRESS AND ENDIVE SALAD

4 bunches watercress
6 heads endive
2 tablespoons tarragon vinegar
1 tablespoon olive oil
6 tablespoons vegetable oil
1 teaspoon lemon juice
1 teaspoon salt
½ teaspoon freshly cracked black pepper
1 teaspoon Dijon mustard
⅛ teaspoon sugar
  Few drops Tabasco
  Few drops Worcestershire sauce
1 raw egg

Cut off all the hard stalks of the watercress. Separate the endive leaves. Wash them both and dry well. Put them in a large salad bowl. Combine remaining ingredients for the dressing. Just before serving, pour dressing over the salad and toss well. Serves 8.

WATERCRESS-MUSHROOM SALAD

2 cups washed watercress
2 cups sliced mushrooms
½ cup sliced radishes
⅓ cup French dressing

Arrange watercress in the center of a bowl. Cover with mushrooms and radishes, mixed together. Pour dressing over vegetables. Serves 6.

SPRING GARDEN SALAD

½ cup cooked asparagus tips or canned French
  white asparagus
½ cup sliced radishes
½ cup sliced cucumber
1 cup shredded lettuce
2 tablespoons minced green pepper
4 green onions, minced
1 tablespoon minced parsley
¼ cup grated Cheddar cheese
¼ cup French dressing

Toss all ingredients together lightly. Serves 4.

SALAD À LA VALENCIANA

1 thick slice French bread
1 large clove garlic
  Romaine and Boston lettuce

237

3 large navel oranges, peeled and sectioned
1 4-ounce can pimientos, cut in strips
1 medium onion, thinly sliced
10–12 pimiento-stuffed olives
¼ cup olive oil
    Salt, freshly ground pepper
2 tablespoons red wine vinegar

Rub the bread with the cut garlic clove. Break bread in pieces, add to salad bowl. Break washed, crisped salad greens into bite-size pieces with fingers. Combine in salad bowl with orange sections, pimientos, onion, olives and olive oil. Toss thoroughly. Sprinkle salt and grind pepper over salad. Add vinegar. Toss again. Serve at once. Serves 6. (Oranges, onion, pimientos, oil and vinegar can be mixed in advance and added to remaining ingredients at table.)

ABRUZZI SALAD

Combine in a bowl thinly sliced oranges (with rind) and Italian or Greek black olives. Add a small amount of olive oil and toss lightly.

GRAPEFRUIT-APPLE SALAD

1 medium-sized head chicory
1 medium-sized grapefruit
1 large tart, crisp apple
6 tablespoons olive oil
2 tablespoons wine vinegar
    Salt, pepper

Wash the chicory and dry thoroughly on a towel. Break into pieces in a bowl.

Peel the grapefruit and pull apart the sections. Trim or skin the membrane from each section and let the fruit drain. Cut the apple into thin, thin slices, leaving the skin on. Add the fruit to the chicory. Make a simple French dressing with the oil, vinegar and salt and pepper to taste and pour over the salad. Toss. The tartness of the fruit and the slightly bitter tang of the chicory makes this simple salad a perfect foil for the richness of ham and pork. Serves 4–6.

SALADE DE RÉVEILLON

4 navel oranges, peeled
2 grapefruits, peeled

4 medium heads Belgian endive
1 bunch watercress
    Olive oil, lemon juice, salt, black pepper
1 tablespoon grated Swiss Gruyère cheese

Section the peeled fruit and chill. Wash the endive and cut into 1"-long sections. Wash the watercress and discard the stems. Put the washed greens in the crisper compartment of the refrigerator.

Make a fairly tart dressing with oil, lemon juice and seasonings. Assemble the salad, sprinkle with the cheese and toss with the dressing. Serves 8.

ORANGE AND MINT SALAD

Peel oranges, removing all white pith. Slice, discarding ends, and arrange in overlapping slices on plates. Sprinkle with finely chopped fresh mint. Make a dressing with ¼ cup olive oil, 1 tablespoon lemon juice and 1 tablespoon cognac. Pour the dressing over the orange slices and chill well before serving. This salad is served without lettuce, although it may be garnished with a little watercress.

BASQUE EGG SALAD

2 cucumbers
    Salt, freshly ground black pepper
6 hard-cooked eggs, quartered
4 pimientos, shredded
¾ cup halved, pitted black olives
½ cup olive or salad oil
⅛ teaspoon dry mustard
1 teaspoon paprika (optional)
3 tablespoons cider vinegar

Peel cucumbers. Cut into ⅛" slices, or into chunks. Put in a bowl, sprinkle with salt and let stand 20 minutes, then drain off liquid and arrange cucumber in the bottom of a shallow serving bowl. Arrange eggs on top of cucumber. Make a border of shredded pimiento on top of the eggs, and scatter black olives in the center. Season the olive oil with 1 teaspoon salt, pepper to taste, mustard, and paprika, if desired. Beat in vinegar until the mixture emulsifies. Pour the dressing over the salad about 20 minutes before serving. Serves 4.

BACON AND EGG SALAD

  2 large or 3 medium heads romaine
  5 hard-cooked eggs
  ½ pound bacon
  4 green onions, minced
  3 tablespoons vinegar
    Freshly ground pepper

Wash and crisp the romaine. Chop the eggs. Cook bacon until crisp. Drain, saving the fat, and crumble. Break lettuce into a bowl, sprinkle with the chopped eggs, minced onions and crumbled bacon. Heat the bacon fat and add the vinegar and a little pepper. Pour over salad and mix thoroughly. Taste for seasoning and add more salt, if necessary. Mix again immediately before serving. Serves 10.

GERMAN SOUR BEAN SALAD

  3 1-pound cans limas, well drained (baby limas, preferably)
  1 medium onion, thinly sliced
  1 cup sour cream
  2 tablespoons cider vinegar
  1 tablespoon sugar
  1 teaspoon prepared horseradish
  2 teaspoons salt
  ¼ teaspoon white pepper
  ¼ cup chopped parsley

Drain limas thoroughly. Toss lightly with separated onion rings. Beat together sour cream, vinegar, sugar, horseradish, salt, pepper. Fold this gently into beans and onions. Marinate for at least 1 hour, preferably several. Serve the sour bean salad very cold, sprinkled with chopped parsley. Serves 6–8.

RED KIDNEY BEAN SALAD

  2 1-pound cans red kidney beans
  ½ cup red wine vinegar
  7 tablespoons olive oil
  1 teaspoon salt
    Freshly ground pepper to taste
  ½ teaspoon oregano
  ½ cup celery, finely diced
  ¼ cup onions, finely chopped
    Crisp lettuce leaves

Thoroughly drain kidney beans. Mix vinegar, olive oil, salt, pepper and oregano and pour over drained beans. Marinate at room temperature for 1 hour. Lightly stir in celery and onions. Chill thoroughly. Serve as a first course, or in lettuce cups as a salad. Serves 8.

CANNELLINI BEAN SALAD

  2 1-pound, 4-ounce cans cannellini (white kidney beans)
  1 slice bread
  2 cloves garlic, sliced
  ⅓ cup walnut meats
  1 cup rich chicken broth
  ½ teaspoon salt
  ½ teaspoon freshly ground black pepper
    Dash Tabasco
  1 tablespoon lemon juice
    Salad greens
    Chopped parsley
    Chopped mint

Drain the beans and set aside. Place the bread in the blender and blend to crumbs. Add the garlic, nuts, broth, salt, pepper, Tabasco and lemon juice and blend at high speed for 1 minute. Pour over the beans and toss to mix well. Line a bowl with greens and put the bean salad in the center of the bowl. Top with chopped parsley and mint and serve. Serves 6.

BEANS PRIMAVERA

  1 pound pea beans or 3 1-pound, 4-ounce cans cannellini beans
  2 7-ounce cans solid-meat tuna
  3 cloves garlic, chopped
  ¼ cup chopped parsley
  ¼ cup finely chopped fresh basil
    Olive oil
    Wine vinegar
    Salt, freshly ground black pepper

This dish may be prepared with the regular pea beans (dried white beans) or with canned cannellini beans which are available in some of the larger supermarkets or in Italian grocery shops.

If you use the dry pea beans, soak them overnight in water to cover. In the morning, drain off the water, add fresh water to cover and 1 bay leaf, 1 onion stuck with 2 cloves, salt. Bring to a boil, lower the heat and simmer until the beans are done but not mushy. Drain well and mix with the tuna, broken into pieces, the chopped garlic, parsley and basil. Add oil and vinegar to taste and season with salt and pepper. The ingredients should all be mixed while the beans are still hot. Chill well and sprinkle with chopped parsley.

If you use the canned beans, drain them well, wash them in cold water and drain again. Then mix them, as above, with the tuna, garlic, parsley, basil, oil, vinegar and salt and pepper. Let them stand for several hours to mellow before serving.

This cold bean salad may be spooned onto pieces of crisp toast or large crackers; or it may be served in hollowed-out, well-drained tomato shells. Serves 10.

LOBSTER AND POTATO SALAD

⅓ cup olive oil
2 tablespoons wine vinegar
  Salt, freshly ground black pepper to taste
3 cups boiled, sliced potatoes
½ cup peeled, finely diced cucumbers
2 1¼-pound lobsters, boiled and chilled
⅔ cup mayonnaise
3 tablespoons heavy cream
¼ cup finely chopped green onions
2 tablespoons finely chopped parsley
1 teaspoon lemon juice
  Parsley sprigs or fresh basil leaves
  Tomato slices

Pour the oil into a mixing bowl and, stirring rapidly with a fork, add the vinegar little by little. Add the salt, pepper, potatoes and cucumbers. Stir gently and let stand 1 or 2 hours. Drain.

Remove the meat from the lobsters and add to the potato mixture. Toss lightly, then add the mayonnaise, cream, onions, parsley and lemon juice. Mix well and chill until ready to serve.

When ready to serve, spoon mixture into the center of a chilled dish. Garnish with parsley or basil. Surround with tomato slices. Serves 6.

SHRIMP AND RICE SALAD

4 cups cooked rice
1 cup cooked peas
1½ cups small shrimp, cooked and cleaned
2 tablespoons minced parsley
½ cup olive oil
3 tablespoons lemon juice
  Salt, pepper to taste
½ cup sliced raw mushrooms
1 tablespoon tarragon leaves
  Lettuce leaves

Mix all ingredients, except lettuce, thoroughly. Arrange nests of lettuce on 6 individual plates, fill with the mixture and serve. Serves 6.

ENSALADA DE CAMARONES

2 cups cooked shrimp, coarsely chopped
½ cup chopped green olives
1 green chile, chopped
  Mayonnaise
  Lettuce leaves
1–2 hard-cooked eggs, sliced

Mix the shrimp, olives, chopped chile and enough mayonnaise to moisten and hold together. Serve on lettuce leaves garnished with slices of hard-cooked egg. Serves 6.

SEAFOOD RAVIGOTE

¾ cup olive oil
¼ cup wine vinegar
½ teaspoon salt
1 tablespoon finely chopped shallot
1 teaspoon finely chopped tarragon or
  ½ teaspoon dried tarragon
½ teaspoon minced chives
2 teaspoons capers
2 teaspoons finely chopped parsley
1½ tablespoons Pernod
1 pound cooked shrimp, shelled
½ pound lump crab meat, picked over
  Lettuce
  Hard-cooked eggs, sliced

Combine the oil and vinegar and add the salt, shallot, tarragon, chives, capers, parsley, and Pernod. Allow to stand at least one hour. Lightly toss with the shrimp and crab meat. Pile lightly into the center of a serving plate and garnish with lettuce and sliced hard-cooked eggs. Serves 4.

GRAPEFRUIT-CRAB LUNCHEON SALAD

1 large grapefruit
Greens
1 pound fresh cooked crab legs (or lobster)
Louis dressing

Peel and section the grapefruit. Wash the greens and dry them well. On each plate arrange a bed of greens and top with sections of grapefruit alternated with crab legs or pieces of lobster meat. Top with the following Louis Dressing:

LOUIS DRESSING

1 cup mayonnaise
2 tablespoons finely chopped onion
¼ cup chili sauce
2 tablespoons finely chopped parsley
⅓ cup heavy cream, whipped

Mix the mayonnaise, onion, chili sauce and chopped parsley and let stand to mellow for 1 hour. Fold in whipped cream and top salad with sauce. Serves 4.

SHRIMP LOUIS

Arrange cleaned boiled shrimp on a bed of shredded lettuce, garnish with hearts of artichokes, sliced hard-cooked eggs and peeled quartered tomatoes. Pour on Louis Dressing and serve well chilled.

SALADE NIÇOISE

6 medium boiled potatoes, sliced
½ cup finely chopped onion
1 tablespoon or more chopped fresh basil
3 tablespoons chopped parsley
1 teaspoon salt
½ teaspoon freshly ground black pepper
¾ cup olive oil
¼ cup wine vinegar

3 ripe tomatoes, peeled and cut into sixths
Tuna in olive oil broken into chunks
(amount to taste)
20–30 anchovy fillets
4–6 hard-cooked eggs
Rings of green pepper, sliced
Black olives
Romaine or Bibb lettuce

Toss the potatoes and onion with the basil, parsley, salt, pepper, oil and vinegar. Garnish with the remaining ingredients.

Serve additional oil and vinegar and sprinkle with more chopped parsley and basil. Serves 6 as a main course at luncheon.

SPANISH TUNA SALAD

6-ounce can white meat tuna
1 tablespoon olive oil
2 tablespoons amontillado or fino sherry
1 small onion, sliced
2 tablespoons minced parsley

Drain tuna, add olive oil and remaining ingredients, toss lightly. Chill several hours before serving. Serve on greens. Serves 2.

ANDALUSIAN RICE SALAD

3 small cloves garlic, crushed
1 teaspoon salt
1 teaspoon dry mustard

⅛ teaspoon black pepper
¾ cup olive oil
6 tablespoons vinegar
1 medium onion, thinly sliced
4 large tomatoes, thickly sliced or quartered
2 drained canned pimientos, cut in strips
3 cups cooked rice
½ cup minced parsley

Mash the garlic in a salad bowl and add the salt, mustard, pepper and olive oil. Beat to blend well. Add the vinegar, onion, tomatoes and pimientos. Marinate until serving time, then toss with rice and parsley. Serve on lettuce. Serves 4 as a luncheon dish or 6–8 as an accompaniment.

RICE SALAD ITALIENNE

3 cups cooked rice
3 pimientos, cut in strips
1 green pepper, cut in strips
12 green onions, finely chopped, or ⅔ cup
   chopped red Italian onions
1½ cups chicken or turkey breast,
   cut in julienne strips
18 large stuffed olives, sliced
18 large black olives, sliced
18 anchovy fillets, coarsely cut
1 teaspoon dried or 2 tablespoons chopped
   fresh basil
   Garlic-flavored French dressing
   Tomato wedges, quartered hard-cooked
   eggs, capers

Combine first 9 ingredients and toss with French dressing. Garnish with the tomato wedges and quartered eggs. Sprinkle with capers. Serves 6.

RICE SALAD WITH PEAS AND PIMIENTO

1½ cups long-grain rice
¾ cup French dressing
1 package frozen peas, cooked
2-ounce can pimiento

Pour 2 quarts of water into a saucepan and bring to a rolling boil. Add the rice slowly and cook for 14 minutes, or until tender, but still firm. Drain thoroughly, add the salad dressing and the peas. Drain the pimiento and cut into julienne strips, saving all the scraps. Mince the scraps, fold them into the rice, pack the rice in a bowl and chill. At serving time, unmold onto a platter and arrange the pimiento strips in a pattern over the dome of rice. Serves 8.

TABBOULEH

1 cup fine bulgur (cracked wheat)
1 pound tomatoes, chopped
2 cups chopped green onions
3 cups chopped parsley
¼ cup fresh mint
½ cup olive oil
⅓ cup lemon juice
1¼ teaspoons salt
½ teaspoon freshly ground black pepper

Wash the wheat, cover with hot water and let stand 30 minutes. Drain, then squeeze dry.

Chop together the tomatoes, green onions, parsley and mint. Beat in the oil, lemon juice, salt and pepper. Mix in the wheat until well blended. Serve in lettuce cups. Serves 6–8.

CHILEAN CREAM CHEESE SALAD

  2 cups canned, drained chick peas
  ½ cup olive oil
  ¼ cup lemon juice
  2 teaspoons salt
  ¼ teaspoon white pepper
  ½ teaspoon ground coriander
  1 onion, sliced very thin
  1 pound firm cream cheese
    Crisp, shredded lettuce leaves

Chill the chick peas several hours. Mix olive oil, lemon juice, salt, pepper and coriander together and pour over chick peas in a large bowl. Gently mix in thinly sliced onion rings, separated. Chill, covered, 45 minutes. Meanwhile, slice lengthwise in two pieces a very firm block of cream cheese, then cut these slices lengthwise in strips and then across, producing very small cubes of cheese. Separate cubes as well as possible and refrigerate immediately. At the very last minute before serving, toss them lightly with the prepared chick-pea mixture. Serve very cold on beds of finely shredded lettuce. Serves 8.

This delicious and unusual salad makes an interesting appetizer served in the same manner but naturally in smaller portions.

GREEK SALAD

  1 head iceberg lettuce
  1 head chicory
  2 tomatoes, cut in wedges
  2 green onions, finely chopped
  2 dozen Greek olives
  ¼ cup olive oil
  ¼ cup salad oil
  3 tablespoons white wine vinegar
  ½ teaspoon salt
    Freshly ground pepper to taste
  ¼ teaspoon dry mustard

  ⅛ pound feta cheese, cut into 6 squares
  6 anchovy fillets

Tear the lettuce and chicory into bite-size pieces and place in a large salad bowl. Add the tomatoes, onion, and olives. Shake together the olive and salad oils, vinegar, salt, pepper, and mustard until blended. Pour this dressing over the greens and toss. Serve on individual salad plates. Put a square of cheese on each portion and top it with an anchovy. Serves 6.

QUICK CORNED BEEF SALAD

  1 head romaine lettuce
  6 boiled new potatoes, chilled
  2 8-ounce cans corned beef, well-chilled
  4 hard-cooked eggs, quartered
  1 green pepper, sliced
  1 medium red Italian onion, sliced
  4-ounce can pimientos or green chiles, sliced
  ½ cup olive oil
  1 teaspoon Tabasco
  ½ teaspoon freshly ground black pepper
  1 clove garlic, finely chopped
  2–3 tablespoons wine vinegar according to taste
    Salt to taste
    Toasted French bread

Break the romaine lettuce coarsely and place in a chilled salad bowl. Slice the chilled potatoes and coarsely dice the corned beef. Add to the lettuce with the quartered eggs, sliced pepper, onion, and pimiento or chiles.

Make a dressing by blending the next six ingredients well and toss salad at the last minute. Serve with toasted French bread. Serves 6.

BEEF SALAD PARISIENNE

  2 cups sliced, boiled, small new potatoes
  1 cup finely cut scallions
  2 cups coarsely chopped celery, with tops
  3 cups lean boiled beef, cut in slices and then
    into 1½″ squares
  12–14 sliced sour pickles
  1 cup cherry tomatoes
  ¼ cup capers
  ½ cup green pepper strips
    Greens
  6 hard-cooked eggs

3 tablespoons Dijon mustard
1 cup olive oil
1 clove garlic rubbed into 1½ teaspoons salt
1 teaspoon freshly ground black pepper
⅓ cup vinegar
    Dash of Tabasco
    Pickled walnuts, sliced

Combine the potatoes, scallions, celery, beef, pickles, tomatoes, capers, green pepper strips, and toss together in a large bowl. Arrange on a bed of greens.

Shell 3 hard-cooked eggs, mash the yolks with a fork and work in the mustard. Stir in the olive oil, garlic-flavored salt, pepper and vinegar. Add a dash or two of Tabasco and pour this dressing over the beef salad. Garnish with 3 quartered hard-cooked eggs, the sliced pickled walnuts and the 3 egg whites, chopped. Serves 6–8.

HAM SALAD

2½ cups cubed cooked ham
½ cup chopped celery
½ cup chopped scallions
¼ cup chopped sweet pickle or chutney
    Mayonnaise flavored with Dijon mustard
    Romaine
    Hard-cooked eggs, finely chopped parsley

Combine the ham with the celery, scallions, pickle and bind with the mustard mayonnaise. Heap on a bed of romaine, surround with halved hard-cooked eggs and garnish with chopped parsley. Serves 6.

SPANISH SALAD

3 medium-size potatoes
    French dressing
1 pound peas
1 small white onion
2 hard-cooked eggs
¼ pound cooked ham, in one piece
    Mayonnaise

Cook the potatoes in their jackets in boiling salted water until tender, about 25 minutes. Drain and when cool enough to handle, remove the skins. Cut into small neat dice, marinate in a little French dressing, and let stand until cool. Meanwhile cook the peas until tender, 10 minutes or so, drain and

cool. Peel and finely chop the onion. Cut the hard-cooked eggs into small cubes. Cube the ham, cutting the pieces no larger than ¼". Combine all the ingredients and blend with mayonnaise.

The salad may be chilled or not, as you wish. Serves 4 as a main course.

SWEETBREAD SALAD

Cut cooked sweetbreads in small pieces and for each cup sweetbreads add 1/3 cup diced celery, 2 tablespoons finely minced green onions, 1/2 cup halved seedless grapes, 1/4 cup sliced blanched and toasted almonds. Mix. Dress with mayonnaise that has been combined with a little unsweetened whipped cream.

CHICKEN AND LOBSTER SALAD

1 whole chicken breast, cooked
½ pound lobster meat
    French dressing
3 hard-cooked eggs
1 cup finely chopped celery
1 cup mayonnaise
2 tablespoons chili sauce
1 tablespoon chopped chives
    Salt
½ cup whipped cream
2 cups shredded cabbage or lettuce

Cut the chicken meat into neat julienne strips and dice the lobster. Marinate in a little French dressing with the chopped egg whites and the celery for about an hour. Prepare and chill the following dressing. Mash or sieve the egg yolks and blend with the mayonnaise, chili sauce, chives and a little salt. Fold in the whipped cream. To serve, make a bed of the cabbage or lettuce in a salad bowl. Mix together the chicken and lobster and the dressing, and place in the bowl. Serves 4–6.

MACADAMIA CHICKEN SALAD

2 cups cold white chicken meat
1 tablespoon fresh finely chopped tarragon
    or 1 teaspoon dried tarragon soaked in
    2 tablespoons white wine
1 cup mayonnaise

½ cup sour cream
 Salt, pepper
⅔ cup Macadamia nuts
 Salad greens
4 hard-cooked eggs, quartered
¼ cup capers

Combine the chicken with the tarragon. If you use dried tarragon, soak it for 45 minutes in the white wine. Add mayonnaise to sour cream and beat well. Correct seasoning. Reserve some of the mayonnaise mixture for garnish. Toss the rest with the nuts and chicken. Arrange on a bed of greens. Garnish with mayonnaise, the eggs and capers. Serves 4–6.

CHICKEN AND BACON SALAD

3 cups cooked, diced chicken
½ cup bacon, fried until crisp and crumbled
1 cup cooked, sliced new potatoes
¼ cup diced celery
1 tablespoon capers
 Salt, pepper to taste
 French dressing
 Salad greens

Combine chicken, bacon, potatoes, celery and capers. Season with salt and pepper, add French dressing and serve on salad greens. Serves 4–6.

CHICKEN AND RICE SALAD

1 cup cooked rice
2 cups cooked, diced chicken
1 cup diced melon
1 cup fresh cream
1 teaspoon lemon juice
 Salt, pepper to taste
 Salad greens

Combine all the ingredients and serve on a bed of salad greens. Serves 4.

TURKEY SALAD

¼–½ cup cold turkey meat, cut in good-sized
 cubes
6–8 black Greek olives, pitted
 Salad greens
1 teaspoon capers
1 tomato, cut in sections

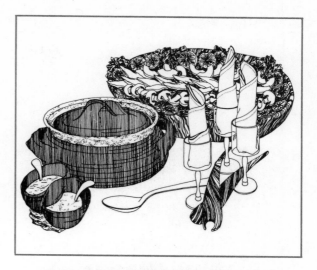

1 hard-cooked egg, sliced or quartered
 Mayonnaise, made with olive oil
 Finely chopped parsley

Combine the turkey with the pitted olives. Arrange on a bed of greens and garnish with the capers, tomato sections, and egg.

Spoon mayonnaise over the salad and add a sprinkling of finely chopped parsley. Serves 1.

DUCK AND ASPARAGUS SALAD

1 large bunch asparagus
½ cup French dressing
3 cups cooked, diced duck
1 head lettuce
⅓ cup mayonnaise
2 tablespoons chopped parsley
 Pimiento strips
3 hard-cooked eggs, sliced

Break off the tough ends of the asparagus. Cut off 3″ pieces with tips and tie them into 6 bundles for individual servings. Cut the rest into 1″ pieces. Cook until tender in boiling salted water. Drain thoroughly and marinate and chill in the French dressing. Just before serving, mix the duck with the 1″ pieces of cut-up asparagus. Make a bed of shredded lettuce in the middle of a large round platter and put the duck mixture on it. Cover with mayonnaise and chopped parsley. Surround with the bundles of asparagus tips, bound with strips of pimiento, alternating with rows of slightly overlapping egg slices. Serves 6.

Egg & Cheese

When you consider that the famous French gastronome Grimod de la Reynière once totted up 685 ways to serve forth an egg (and he probably wasn't even trying), it is obvious that no cook with eggs in the refrigerator need be at a loss for a delectable, spur-of-the-moment dish. On its own, an egg may be boiled, poached, fried, scrambled, coddled, baked, or turned into an omelette. With the help of other ingredients, it can appear in many guises, from the rib-sticking solidity of an Italian frittata or Spanish tortilla (a relation in name only of the familiar Mexican pancake) to the unctuous richness of a zabaglione or crème caramel. Without doubt, the modest, inexpensive egg is the most protean of foods, and the kitchen would be a sorry place without it. It lends the thickening, binding qualities of its yolk to sauces, the leavening of its white to soufflés. Without eggs there could be no baked Alaska, no angel food cake, no mayonnaise, Hollandaise or avgolemono. Eggs combine superbly with almost any other food you can name, from meat, fish and poultry to vegetables, fruits and cheese—especially cheese, for there seems to be some close kinship and natural affinity between these products of the hen's and cow's generosity.

Cheese, poetically described by Clifton Fadiman as "milk's leap toward immortality," is one of the most venerable of all processed foods, with a history that reaches back to about 9000 B.C. Wealthy Romans had special kitchens for making cheese, Lucullus was proud to serve it to his discriminating guests, and the Greeks not only had a word for it, formos (from which came the Italian formaggio and French fromage), but considered it a worthy offering to the gods on Mount Olympus. During the Middle Ages, French monks further refined the cheese-making process and developed those subtle, soft-ripening cheeses that have become one of the greater glories of that gastronomic paradise. Cheese is a food of many facets. It can be sharp or bland, hard or soft, overpoweringly pungent or practically odorless. There is a world of difference between the innocent freshness of a ricotta and the ripe decadence of a well-aged Gorgonzola, yet both are members of the same family. While the majority of cheeses are best eaten in their natural state, with the good companionship of bread and wine, or fruit, there are others that have successfully infiltrated the kitchen, notably the invaluable Parmesan, Cheddar, Swiss, Gruyère, mozzarella, the cream and cottage cheeses and the blues. These are the friends of the cook, adding their flavor and texture to appetizers and soups, sauces and salads, entrées and desserts and providing the raison d'être for such national dishes as Swiss fondue, British rarebit, French coeur à la crème and American cheesecake. For however it is served, cheese is a never-failing delight that has given rise to many a complimentary proverb and saying, from the rapturous simile "Grapes with cheese taste like a kiss" to the more prosaic but equally telling remark of a character in Treasure Island, "Many's the long night I've dreamed of cheese—toasted mostly."

SCRAMBLED EGGS
(Oeufs Brouillés)

Choose a thick pan and spread melted butter over bottom of it before adding well-beaten eggs. For creamy, even scrambling, stir the eggs constantly over moderate heat and remove pan from heat just before eggs are cooked enough; heat retained in pan will finish cooking. A worthwhile refinement when scrambling eggs is to strain the beaten eggs into the pan, thus removing the little white threads that hitch the yolk to the white.

OEUFS BROUILLÉS XÉRÈS

    1 carrot
    1 orange
    2 tablespoons butter
    ¼ cup medium dry sherry
    2 tablespoons light cream
    4 eggs, beaten
    4 slices buttered toast
      Watercress for garnish

Cut carrot lengthwise in slices 1/8″ thick, discarding any yellow core. Cut slices into needle-size strips. Pare orange rind using vegetable peeler and cut into strips of similar size. You should have 1/4 cup loosely packed orange strips and 1/3 cup carrot strips. Put orange rind in a small pan of boiling water and boil for 5 minutes to remove the strong flavor; drain rind and rinse with cold water. Melt half the butter in a heavy pan and stir in the orange rind and carrot. Put a piece of foil on them and cover the pan and cook without browning for 7 minutes. Add sherry and simmer uncovered 5 minutes to reduce. Add remaining butter to pan. Combine cream with beaten eggs, pour into pan and stir very gently until creamy and set. Spoon onto hot buttered toast and garnish with small bouquets of watercress. Serves 4.

EGGS WITH CACTUS LEAVES
(Huevos con Nopales)

    8-ounce can nopalitos
      (tender, young cactus leaves)
    3 tablespoons butter
    2 tablespoons heavy cream

    6 eggs, lightly beaten
    Salt, pepper to taste

Rinse cactus pieces well with cold water and drain thoroughly. Heat butter in a skillet and sauté the cactus lightly. Add heavy cream to the eggs and season them with salt. Scramble the eggs into the cactus. Season the scrambled-egg mixture with freshly ground pepper. Serves 6.

EGGS DIANA

    2 tablespoons butter
    2 scallions, sliced
    2 ounces Provolone cheese, finely diced
    2 teaspoons grated Parmesan cheese
    6 large black olives, halved and pitted
      Freshly ground black pepper to taste
    4 eggs, beaten
    Salt

Heat the butter in a skillet, add the scallions and soften for a few minutes. Add cheeses, olives and black pepper to eggs; pour into skillet. Stir over low heat so cheese melts as eggs scramble. Taste for salt; the amount will depend on the olives. Remove from heat while eggs are still creamy. Serve for lunch, with garlic bread. Serves 4.

CARACAS EGGS

    2 tablespoons butter
    1½ ounces dried beef
    1 teaspoon chili powder
    8-ounce can peeled tomatoes
    3-ounce package cream cheese
    6 eggs, beaten
    ¾ teaspoon salt

Heat a little of the butter in a skillet and quickly brown the beef slices. Remove and set aside. Melt remaining butter and cook chili powder very slowly for 3 minutes to mellow the flavor. Add tomatoes and cream cheese, heat and stir until smooth and bubbling. Stir in eggs, salt and about two-thirds of the dried beef. Scramble. Serve with remaining dried beef scattered on top. Serves 6.

EGGS WITH CORN

> 1 ear corn
> 2 tablespoons butter
>   Salt, pepper to taste
> 4 eggs, beaten
>   Fresh chopped chives

Boil corn in salted water 3–4 minutes. Drain and remove kernels with sharp knife. Melt butter in small skillet, add corn, salt and pepper. Stir for a few minutes while corn absorbs some of the butter. Pour eggs into skillet; stir over moderate heat until scrambled. Serve sprinkled with chopped chives. Serves 2.

SCRAMBLED EGGS WITH OYSTERS

> 4 eggs
>   Salt, pepper to taste
> 3 tablespoons butter
> 6–8 oysters, each cut in 3
>   Hot buttered toast

Beat eggs, salt and pepper. Melt butter in a skillet and sauté oysters for ½ minute. Pour in eggs and stir over moderate heat until creamy. Spoon onto hot buttered toast and serve at once. Serves 4.

FRIED EGGS
(Oeufs Sautés)

A little melted butter or oil lining a moderately hot pan will eliminate sticking. Break eggs in directly from shell, or pour from cup. Pan should be hot enough so white sets speedily, but not so hot that white burns or sticks. Choose a flexible spatula for turning; tip the pan slightly toward the spatula so that the egg almost slides onto it.

OEUFS AU BEURRE NOIR

> 4 eggs
> 6 tablespoons butter
> 2 teaspoons cider or wine vinegar, or
>   lemon juice
> 1 tablespoon capers

Fry eggs in two tablespoons of the butter. Cook remaining butter in small pan until deep nut-brown in color. Remove from heat, stir in vinegar or lemon juice and capers; pour foaming over the fried eggs. This makes a very nice change from the more usual breakfast eggs. Serves 4.

EGGS PRINCESSE

> 4 mushrooms
> 3 tablespoons butter
> 4 ounces cooked ham or tongue, chopped
> 1 tablespoon freshly chopped parsley
> 3 tablespoons light cream
> 1 egg yolk
>   Pinch of cayenne pepper
> 1 teaspoon lemon juice
>   Salt
> 4 eggs, fried in butter

Wipe and slice mushrooms; sauté in 1 tablespoon butter in a skillet; add ham or tongue and about ⅔ of the parsley. Heat through on low flame. Mix light cream, egg yolk, remaining butter, pepper and lemon juice in a double boiler. Stir with a spoon or whisk until thick, then season to taste with salt. Heap ham mixture in serving dish and arrange eggs on top. Spoon sauce over eggs and sprinkle with remaining parsley. Serves 4.

EGGS VALENCIANA

> 3 tablespoons butter
> 1 cup rice
> 2 cups stock or broth
>   Salt, freshly ground black pepper to taste
> 2 medium onions, sliced
> 1 green pepper, sliced
> 2 tablespoons olive oil
> 2 large tomatoes, skinned, seeded and chopped
> 2 tablespoons slivered almonds
> 2 tablespoons raisins
> 2 bananas, sliced
> 4 eggs
>   Oil for frying

Melt 2 tablespoons butter in a heavy pan, stir in rice and cook slowly about 5 minutes. Add stock, salt (amount will depend on stock used) and pepper. Bring to a boil and simmer 20 minutes, until the rice is just tender, adding more liquid if needed. While the rice cooks, sauté the onions and green pepper in the oil in a skillet until quite soft and delicately brown. Add the tomatoes and cook a few minutes. Combine this mixture with the almonds and raisins. Wipe out the skillet with a paper towel. Melt the remaining butter in the skillet and fry the bananas briefly. When rice is tender, stir in vegetable mixture with a fork and then add the bananas. Fry eggs. Heap rice down the center of a serving dish and place the eggs on top. This makes a hearty dish for a winter lunch. Serves 4.

EGGS, RANCH-STYLE
(Huevos Rancheros)

> **Lard**
> **1 large onion, finely chopped**
> **1 clove garlic, chopped**
> **1 pound tomatoes, peeled and chopped**
> **Salt, pepper to taste**
> **½ teaspoon sugar**
> **¼ teaspoon oregano**
> **3 or more canned serrano chiles, chopped**
> **12 tortillas**
> **12 eggs**
> **Cooked black beans or frijoles refritos, heated**

Heat 2 tablespoons lard in a skillet and fry onion and garlic until limp. Add tomatoes, salt, pepper, sugar, oregano, and chiles. Simmer this sauce gently for about 15 minutes. Heat 3 tablespoons lard in a skillet and fry the tortillas on both sides until limp or, if preferred, until quite crisp. Place 2 tortillas side by side on each plate and keep warm. Fry eggs in lard, or butter if preferred. Slide an egg onto each tortilla. Pour sauce over eggs and serve with a couple of tablespoons of hot beans or frijoles refritos on the side. Serves 6.

OEUFS MOLLETS AND
HARD-COOKED EGGS

Take eggs from refrigerator at least 20 minutes before cooking to prevent shells cracking. Place eggs in fast boiling water and time them from the moment the water reboils. A frying basket is an asset for lowering a large number of eggs into a pan at one time. When the time is up, plunge eggs immediately into cold water to prevent further cooking. Boil eggs for oeufs mollets (shelled soft-cooked eggs) for 6 minutes only, so white is set and yolk still creamy. When cooked, shelled oeufs mollets may be kept warm or reheated in a bowl of hot water. Hard-cooked eggs should not be boiled for more than 12 minutes; this avoids the ugly black ring so often found around the yolk. If eggs are to be stuffed, turn them three or four times during cooking so yolk will set in the center.

EGGS MOLLET WITH HADDOCK

> **4 eggs mollet**
> **2 tablespoons butter**
> **2 tablespoons flour**
> **1 cup milk**
> **½ cup light cream**
> **Salt, pepper**
> **2 cloves garlic**
> **1 tablespoon oil**
> **2 cups cooked, flaked haddock**

Keep the shelled eggs mollet warm in a bowl of hot water. Melt butter in a good-sized pan. Remove from heat and stir in flour, then milk. Return to heat and stir until boiling. Add cream and boil rapidly for 5 minutes. Season to taste with salt and pepper. Chop garlic finely, sprinkle with ¼ teaspoon salt and crush until smooth with the blade of a knife. Cook crushed garlic in oil in a saucepan for a few minutes, then add cooked haddock. Beat over heat, gradually adding ¾ of the cream sauce; check seasoning. Turn haddock mixture into warm serving dish. Remove eggs from water, drain well and arrange on top. Coat eggs with remaining cream sauce and serve for brunch with toast or garlic bread. Serves 4.

OEUFS MOLLETS EN SOUFFLÉ SURPRISE

> **4 eggs mollet**
> **¼ cup each: diced onion, carrot and celery**
> **¼ cup chopped leek, white part only**
> **3 tablespoons butter**
> **3 tablespoons flour**
> **2 cups milk**
> **¼ teaspoon salt**
> **10 peppercorns**

Pinch mace
3 eggs, separated

Keep shelled eggs mollet in warm water until needed. Cook vegetables in 1 tablespoon butter in a covered pan. When soft but not brown, add remaining butter, remove pan from heat and stir in flour, then milk. Season with salt, peppercorns and mace. Stir over heat until boiling, reduce heat and simmer gently for 20–30 minutes, covered. Butter a 1½-quart soufflé dish. Strain sauce into a bowl and stir in egg yolks. Whip egg whites stiffly and fold in. Pour about 1/3 of mixture into the soufflé dish, lay well-drained eggs mollet on this, then add rest of mixture. Bake in a 325° oven for 20–25 minutes or until brown and well risen. Serve at once. Serves 4.

OEUFS SOLEIL D'OR

1 teaspoon curry powder
1 tablespoon oil
½ cup dry white wine
½ cup mayonnaise
 Salt, pepper, lemon juice
¼ cup heavy cream, whipped
6 hard-cooked eggs
1 tablespoon chopped chives
 Lemon wedges

Cook the curry powder in the oil over low heat for 5 minutes. Add the wine and simmer until reduced to 2 tablespoons. Cool slightly, then stir gradually into the mayonnaise. Season to taste with salt, pepper and lemon juice, adding a pinch of sugar if needed. Fold in the whipped cream. Chill. Cut the eggs in half lengthwise. Press yolks through a strainer onto waxed paper; sprinkle with salt and pepper. Rinse and dry egg whites and slice. Arrange on a small platter, spoon strained yolks over whites and scatter chives on top. Chill. Serve very cold, passing lemon wedges and chilled sauce separately. Perfect for a spring or summer luncheon. Serves 4.

EGGS SOUBISE

2 tablespoons butter
2 bunches scallions, cut in 1″ pieces
2 tablespoons flour
2 cups milk

½ teaspoon salt
 Freshly ground black pepper to taste
6 hard-cooked eggs
½ cup grated Cheddar cheese

Melt butter in a saucepan, stir in scallions, cover tightly and cook until scallions are quite soft, but not at all brown, at least 15 minutes. (If scallions are not thoroughly cooked, the sauce will curdle.) When scallions are soft, remove from heat, stir in flour, then milk. Bring to a boil, simmer for 2 minutes, then add salt and pepper. Cut eggs in half, remove yolks. Slice whites and put in bottom of fireproof dish. Press yolks through a strainer and scatter over whites. Now spoon onion sauce over the eggs, sprinkle top with grated cheese and brown in a 400° oven about 10 minutes. Serves 4. Delicious for supper or as a main course for luncheon.

HIGHLAND EGGS

6 hard-cooked eggs, shelled
¾ pound pork sausage meat
1 beaten egg mixed with 1 tablespoon water
¼ cup fine dry bread crumbs
 Deep fat for frying

With moistened hands, enclose each egg in a portion of the sausage meat. Dip into the egg-water mixture and then into the crumbs. Make sure to coat the sausage meat completely. Deep fry at 370° for 5–6 minutes, or until brown on all sides. Drain on absorbent paper and serve immediately. Serves 3 as a main course.

OEUFS À LA CHIMAY

9 hard-cooked eggs
7½ tablespoons butter
4 tablespoons flour
1½ cups boiling milk
 Salt, pepper
¾–1 cup light cream or milk
1¼ cups finely minced mushrooms
1½ tablespoons minced shallots or green onions
3 tablespoons minced fresh green herbs (parsley
 and chives or chervil, or parsley and tarragon)
½ cup plus 2 tablespoons grated Swiss cheese

Shell the eggs and halve them lengthwise. Rub the yolks through a sieve with a wooden spoon and place in a bowl. Shave a sliver off the bottom of each half egg white, if necessary, to prevent them from rocking. Set the halves aside.

Melt 3 tablespoons butter in a heavy enameled 6-cup saucepan and blend in the flour. Stir with a wooden spoon over low heat until the butter and flour froth together for 2 minutes without coloring. Remove from heat. Vigorously beat in the boiling milk with a wire whisk, then season with ¼ teaspoon salt and a pinch of pepper. Boil, stirring, for 1 minute. The sauce will be very thick. Stir 4 tablespoons of sauce into the sieved egg yolks. Clean off the sides of the saucepan, float ¼ cup light cream or milk over the top of the sauce and set aside.

Twist the mushrooms, a handful at a time, in the corner of a kitchen towel to extract their moisture. Melt 1½ tablespoons butter in an enameled skillet and sauté the mushrooms over moderately high heat with the shallots or onions for 6–8 minutes, stirring frequently, until the pieces begin to separate from each other. Season lightly with salt and pepper and add to the egg-yolk mixture. Vigorously beat in the minced herbs and 2 tablespoons of the butter, softened. Season to taste. Dome the mixture into each half egg white.

Bring the sauce to a simmer again, beating. Thin out with spoonfuls of the remaining light cream or milk until it is just thick enough to coat the eggs. Correct seasoning, remove from heat, and beat in ½ cup of the grated cheese. Spread ¼ of the sauce in a lightly buttered baking dish, just large enough to hold the eggs, and arrange eggs, filled side up, over the sauce. Spoon remaining sauce over them, and sprinkle on the remaining 2 tablespoons grated cheese. Dot with remaining 1 tablespoon butter, cut into small pieces.

The dish may now be set aside until 20–30 minutes before serving time, if desired. To reheat, put dish in upper third of a preheated 375° oven and bake until sauce is bubbling and top has browned lightly. Follow same procedure if dish is to be served immediately, but cut down on cooking time. Serves 6.

Variations: Instead of mushrooms, use 1/2–2/3 cup cooked and minced asparagus tips, artichoke hearts, ham, poultry, chicken livers, shellfish, tuna or salmon for filling, with appropriate herbs and seasonings.

CURRIED EGGS

- 2 medium onions, minced
- 1 clove garlic, minced
- 1 small ginger root, sliced
- 3 tablespoons butter
- 1 tablespoon curry powder
- 3 tablespoons flour
- 2 cups chicken bouillon
- 3 cups milk
- 1 cup seedless raisins
- 1 small apple, peeled, cored and chopped
  Juice of ½ lemon
- 1 strip lemon peel
  Salt, pepper
- 1½ dozen hard-cooked eggs

Sauté the onions, garlic and ginger in the butter until brown. Stir in the curry powder (you may use more if you wish) and the flour. Gradually add the chicken bouillon and milk, which have been heated together. Stir and simmer until smooth. Strain into a double boiler. Add the raisins, which have been soaked in tepid water and drained, the apple, lemon juice and peel. Cook slowly over hot water for 10 minutes. Season to taste. Peel and slice the eggs and add them to the curry sauce. Serve on English muffins or with fluffy rice. Serves 12.

SWEDISH EGGS WITH MUSTARD SAUCE

- 2 tablespoons butter
- 2½ tablespoons flour
- 1⅓ cups milk
- 4 teaspoons French's mustard
- 8 hard-cooked eggs
- ¼ cup finely diced drained herring in wine

Melt the butter in a small saucepan over medium heat. Add the flour and stir until smooth. Gradually add the milk and cook, stirring constantly, until the sauce thickens. Remove from heat and add mustard.

Cut the eggs in half lengthwise. Mash the yolks, add ¼ cup of the mustard sauce and the diced herring. Mound the mixture in the egg whites and place in an ovenproof dish that can come to the table. Spoon the remaining sauce over the eggs and bake in a preheated 450° oven for 6 minutes, or until hot. Serves 4–6.

SPECIAL STUFFED EGGS

> 24 eggs
> 1 tin mousse de foie gras or 1 cup homemade
>   liver pâté
> 1 tablespoon sour cream
> 2 tablespoons chopped parsley
> 1 truffle, finely chopped
>   Salt, freshly ground pepper
>   Cognac
> 24 truffle slices

Cook the eggs until just hard; remove the shells and cool. Cut a thin slice from the broad end of each egg to enable eggs to stand upright on serving dish.

Slice off the small ends of the eggs so that you can scoop out the yolks. Mash the yolks well and mix with the mousse de foie gras or pâté, sour cream, parsley, chopped truffle and salt and pepper to taste. Add enough cognac to make a good paste. Using the rosette tube of a pastry bag, force the yolk mixture back into the eggs and finish off the top of each egg with a decorative swirl. Top each with a slice of truffle and chill well. You may also glaze the eggs with aspic. Serve as an appetizer.

Variation: Mash the egg yolks and blend them with 3 tablespoons mayonnaise. Add 1 tin boneless and skinless sardines, mashed, ½ cup finely chopped chives, ¼ teaspoon Tabasco, 1 teaspoon lemon juice and salt and freshly ground pepper to taste. Mix thoroughly and pipe this filling into the eggs, using directions above. Top with chopped chives or parsley.

POACHED EGGS
(OEUFS POCHÉS)

Fill a pan three-quarters full of water and bring it almost to boil. Add salt or vinegar to improve flavor of eggs and help firm the whites. Poach only a few eggs at a time so they do not stick together. Slip eggs into almost simmering water one at a time, from the shell or from a cup. Keep water just below boiling

HOW TO FRENCH POACH AN EGG

1. With spoon, stir water to whirlpool.

2. Slide egg from cup into moving water.

3. Poach. White forms bag around yolk.

4. Remove to bowl of water with a spoon.

point for 4–5 minutes, then remove poached eggs with slotted spoon. Trim any ragged edges, then hold spoon over absorbent paper briefly to blot up water from the egg. To French poach: Stir water around and around with a fork until a whirlpool appears in center of water. Stop stirring, and when water is moving quite slowly, slide egg into center. The white will wrap around the yolk in perfect shape. To keep poached eggs hot: Slip cooked eggs into bowl of fresh hot water. Eggs will keep perfectly until needed. Renew hot water if necessary.

EGGS WITH CRAB MEAT, MORNAY SAUCE

    2 tablespoons butter
    1 tablespoon flour
    1¼ cups milk
    ¼ bay leaf
    1 cup grated Cheddar cheese
    ½ cup freshly grated Parmesan cheese
    ¼ teaspoon dry mustard
        Salt, pepper to taste
    8–12 ounces picked-over crab meat
    2 tablespoons dry sherry
    4 poached eggs

Melt 1 tablespoon butter, remove from heat and stir in flour, then milk and bay leaf. Bring to boil and simmer 2–3 minutes; remove bay leaf. Stir in grated cheeses and mustard. Season with salt and pepper. Keep this Mornay sauce warm without boiling. Melt remaining butter in a skillet, add crab meat and heat through over a low flame. Warm sherry, set alight, and pour over crab meat as the flames die down. Heap crab meat down a serving dish, lay poached, drained eggs on top and coat them with Mornay sauce. This is a good, quick dish for either lunch or supper. Serves 4.

PERUVIAN EGGS

    1 pound fresh cod
    1 cup milk
    ½ teaspoon salt
    6–8 ounces cooked peeled shrimp
    1½ cups grated Gruyère or Switzerland Swiss
        cheese
    6 poached eggs

Using top pan of a double boiler, simmer cod with milk and salt for 15 minutes, uncovered. When cod is cooked, place pan on the bottom of the double boiler filled with hot water. With a fork, stir in shrimp, then cheese. The mixture should be hot enough to melt cheese and thus thicken the milk, but not enough to harden cheese. Spoon fish mixture into serving dish. Drain the eggs well, arrange on top of the fish and serve. Serves 6.

OEUFS À LA REINE

    1 chicken breast
    1 cup chicken stock
    3 tablespoons butter
    1 tablespoon flour
    6 mushrooms
    1 truffle, diced
    2 egg yolks
    ¼ cup light cream
    2 tablespoons lemon juice
    6 poached eggs

Poach chicken breast in chicken stock until tender, about ½ hour. Drain and cut in julienne strips. Melt 1 tablespoon of the butter, stir in flour off the fire, then stock from cooked chicken. Stir until boiling, then simmer sauce about 5 minutes, uncovered. Meanwhile, slice the mushrooms and cook in remaining butter, add truffle and cooked chicken and keep warm. Beat egg yolks, cream and lemon juice, add some of the hot sauce to this mixture, then return to balance of sauce in pan. Stir over heat a few minutes to let egg yolks thicken the sauce; do not let boil. Moisten the chicken mixture with 3 tablespoons of the sauce, heap onto a serving dish. Lay poached eggs on top and coat with remaining sauce. This is an elegant lunch or brunch dish, especially for spring or summer. Serves 6.

OEUFS SUR LE PLAT

For this splendid method of egg cookery the eggs are baked in the dish or dishes in which they will be served. Heat dish in oven with a little butter. Remove from oven and spread the butter over bottom of dish before breaking eggs in. Sautéed mushrooms, cooked kidneys, asparagus or other ingredients may be put underneath the eggs. Sprinkle a little melted butter or cream over each yolk to keep moist.

OEUFS SUR LE PLAT LORRAINE

> 6 strips lean bacon, cut in 1½″ pieces
> 6 thin slices Gruyère or Switzerland Swiss cheese
> 6 eggs
> Salt, black pepper
> ¼ cup light cream
> 1 tablespoon finely chopped parsley

Cook bacon in boiling water for 4 minutes, then drain thoroughly. Arrange in the bottom of a fireproof dish and cover with the cheese slices. Break eggs into dish and sprinkle with salt and pepper. Pour cream over egg yolks, sprinkle with parsley and bake in a 325° oven for 15–20 minutes or until egg whites are set. This is a quick and easy dish for a weekend brunch or breakfast. Serves 6.

EGGS WITH ANCHOVIES

> 1 cup long-grain rice
> 2 tablespoons butter
> 8-ounce can peeled tomatoes
> 1 tablespoon tomato paste
> 1 clove garlic, crushed with ½ teaspoon salt
> Small bay leaf
> 4 anchovy fillets, rinsed
> 4 eggs
> 2 tablespoons grated Parmesan cheese

Cook rice in plenty of boiling salted water about 12 minutes (or until tender), drain and rinse with a cup of hot water. Melt butter in pan rice was boiled in, toss rice in butter. Stew tomatoes with tomato paste, garlic and bay leaf. Cut anchovy fillets in half lengthwise. Heap rice in fireproof dish, make a hollow for each egg. Spoon tomato mixture (bay leaf removed) over rice. Break an egg into each hollow, and place anchovy strips crisscross on each egg. Sprinkle grated cheese over all and bake in a 325° oven until egg whites are set, about 15 minutes. Delicious for supper. Serves 4.

Note: Some brands of anchovies have a strong fishy taste, unpleasant in this dish. It is best not to bake these anchovies on the eggs, but to lay them on just before serving.

EGGS À LA FLAMENCA
(Huevos à la Flamenca)

> 1 large onion, sliced or chopped
> 2 cloves garlic, crushed
> 2 tablespoons olive oil
> ½ pound chorizo or similar garlic-flavored sausage, cut in slices
> 1 teaspoon minced parsley
> 2 pimientos, diced
> 1 medium can (1 pound) tomatoes
> ½ teaspoon salt
> 8 eggs
> 1 cup shelled peas or ½ package frozen peas, cooked, or 8 cooked asparagus spears

Sauté onion and garlic in olive oil until soft; add sausage and cook until lightly browned. Add parsley and pimientos and cook 2 minutes. Add tomatoes, cutting them into small pieces, and cook until thickened. Add salt. Divide sauce between 4 shallow ramekins. Break two eggs into each. Arrange cooked peas or asparagus around eggs, covering with sauce. Bake in preheated 350° oven until eggs are just set, about 15 minutes. Serve at once. Serves 4.

SPINACH AND EGGS, GRANADA STYLE
(Huevos con Espinacas à la Granadina)

> 1 pound spinach
> 20 almonds, blanched
> 1 or 2 cloves garlic
> ½ teaspoon powdered saffron
> 1 whole clove
> 2 peppercorns
> 2 cumin seeds or 1 pinch powdered cumin
> 2 slices bread
> 2 tablespoons olive oil
> 1 cup beef or chicken bouillon
> 6 eggs
> ½ pound lean, cooked ham, cut julienne

Thoroughly wash the spinach, cook 2 minutes, drain

and chop. Coarsly chop the almonds (if a blender is used, turn on at low speed, turn off, turn on again). Mash the garlic thoroughly with a mortar and pestle, then discard skins. Mash the saffron, clove, peppercorns and cumin to a paste with the garlic. Add a little water to make a thick sauce. Crumble bread, discarding crusts, and brown in the olive oil with the chopped almonds. Add the garlic mixture, then add all this to the spinach with the bouillon. Purée in a blender. Divide spinach purée between 6 individual ramekins or casseroles, forming a well in the center. Break an egg into each. Lay ham strips over eggs. Bake in 350° oven until egg white has just set, about 15 minutes. Serves 6.

NELLE SAVOYARDE

> 10–12 thin slices ham (cold cooked, Virginia or
>   prosciutto)
> 4 tablespoons butter
> 4 tablespoons flour
> 1 pint milk
>   Salt, freshly ground black pepper
>   Dash of nutmeg
> ¼ pound grated Gruyère and Parmesan cheese
>   mixed
> 6 eggs, well-beaten
>   Tomato sauce

Line a charlotte mold with the ham slices. Melt the butter and blend in the flour. Gradually add the milk and cook and stir until the sauce is smooth and thick. Season to taste with salt, pepper and nutmeg and stir in the grated cheese. Remove from the heat and add the eggs.

Pour the sauce over the ham and place foil on the mold, tying it down firmly. Steam in a steamer for 1¼ hours. Remove the mold from the steamer and take off the foil. Cook in a 350° oven for 15–20 minutes. Unmold and serve with tomato sauce. Serves 4.

FRENCH HAM AND EGG RING

> 14 eggs
> 2½ cups finely chopped cooked ham
>   Salt, freshly ground black pepper
>   Grilled or sautéed mushrooms
>   Hollandaise sauce

Butter a ring mold well and break 6 eggs in the bottom very carefully so that the yolks are not broken. Cover the eggs with the chopped ham and season lightly with salt and pepper. Add 8 more eggs to the top and season again.

Stand the ring mold in a pan of water and cover the top with foil. Bake at 350° for ½ hour, or until the eggs are set. Unmold the ring on a platter and fill the center with the grilled or sautéed mushrooms. Serve with Hollandaise sauce. Serves 6–8.

<u>Variation</u>: Fill the center of the ring with a well-seasoned tomato sauce, surround it with pieces of frizzled ham and sprinkle chopped parsley and chives over all.

HINTS FOR OMELETTE MAKING

First, buy an omelette pan of very heavy porous metal, either cast iron or cast aluminum, about ½″ thick, approximately 10″ in diameter at the top, curving to about 8″ at the bottom. Before use, rub the inside well with steel wool, wipe out, and season the surface by heating a little cooking oil slowly in the pan. Wipe out with paper towels.

The pan should never be washed. If food sticks, clean thoroughly with steel wool and rinse with vegetable oil. Wipe with paper towels.

It is very important to heat the omelette pan to the correct temperature before putting in the egg mixture. Let the empty pan heat slowly over moderate heat. Do not overheat. Test by rubbing a small lump of firm salt butter on the pan. If it sizzles briskly without discoloring, the pan is ready. If the pan is not hot enough, clean it immediately with a paper towel and continue heating. (Do not allow the butter to remain in the pan while heating.) After use, wipe the pan with paper towels, cool and put away in a dry place.

A scant ½ ounce of salt butter is sufficient to cook the omelette. If you want a richer omelette, put tiny pieces of butter in the egg mixture.

The eggs should always be fresh, and water, not milk or cream, should be added to them as this makes a lighter mixture. Do not overbeat the egg mixture. Beat only until it is blended with the water and salt and is slightly frothy.

Do not add pepper to the omelette until it is being served as it tends to discolor the eggs. Always warm the serving dish.

PLAIN OMELETTE

> **3 eggs, very fresh and chilled**
> **1 teaspoon cold water**
> **⅛ teaspoon salt**
> **½ ounce salt butter**
> **A little sweet butter**
> **Freshly cracked black or white pepper**

Break eggs into a bowl with water and salt and beat with a rotary whisk until frothy. Heat omelette pan over medium heat until hot enough for butter to sizzle without browning. Pour egg mixture quickly into sizzling butter and stir, using a fork with even tines, at the same time shaking pan with left hand so as to fill in any holes made by fork. Stir until eggs begin to set, allow to set for 20 seconds, then take off heat. Slide fork carefully around edge and fold sides in. Take handle of pan in left hand, tip pan toward you and fold omelette over. Turn out on hot serving dish, rub top with sweet butter, sprinkle with pepper and serve immediately.

The following omelettes, except where noted, serve 2 as a first course or 1 as a main course.

FINES HERBES OMELETTE

> **2 tablespoons very finely chopped fresh parsley**
> **2 teaspoons finely chopped fresh aromatic herb such as: tarragon, chervil, dill, rosemary, basil, marjoram**
> **1 teaspoon finely chopped white onion**
> **¼ teaspoon finely chopped garlic or 2 teaspoons finely chopped shallots**
> **Plain omelette mixture**

Chop the herbs together very finely again, and use ½ ounce more salt butter in pan when making the omelette. Put the herbs, onion and garlic or shallots in omelette pan just before adding the egg mixture. Cook. Turn out on hot serving dish and spread sweet butter on top of omelette.

HOW TO MAKE A PLAIN OMELETTE

1. Heat omelette pan slowly. Pan is ready when butter on fork sizzles.

2. As butter melts, add beaten eggs.

3. Stir eggs rapidly in circles with fork, shaking the pan back and forth.

4. As eggs begin to set, smooth over with fork; run it around the edges.

5. Fold in sides. Roll with fork. Tilt pan so omelette rolls over on itself.

6. With thumb at top of handle, tip pan forward, roll omelette onto dish.

CHEESE OMELETTE

½ teaspoon dry mustard
2 teaspoons dry sherry
  Plain omelette mixture
3 tablespoons freshly grated Gruyère cheese
  Sweet butter
  Freshly cracked pepper
1 tablespoon freshly grated Parmesan cheese

Add the mustard and sherry to the egg mixture and make the omelette as usual. Just before folding, put in the grated Gruyère cheese, fold over and turn out on a hot serving dish. Mark the top with red hot skewers, rub with a little sweet butter and sprinkle pepper and the grated Parmesan cheese over the top of the omelette.

GRILLED KIDNEY OMELETTE

2 lamb kidneys
1 tablespoon salt butter
4 small mushrooms, sliced
4 small white onions, blanched and drained
4 small cocktail sausages
1 tablespoon brandy
½ teaspoon meat glaze
¼ teaspoon tomato paste
½ teaspoon potato starch
1 tablespoon red wine
¼ cup chicken stock (scant)
  Plain omelette mixture
½ teaspoon finely chopped parsley
  Salt, freshly cracked pepper
  Lemon juice

Skin kidneys and cut in half. Carefully remove the fat and core. Heat the butter in a small heavy skillet, add the kidneys, cut side down, and brown them quickly on each side.

Brown mushrooms, onions and sausages in the same pan. Remove, add brandy and stir to remove glaze from bottom of pan. Stir in, off heat, the meat glaze, tomato paste and potato starch. When smooth, add wine and chicken stock and bring to a boil over low heat. Slice kidneys and sausage and halve onions and add to the sauce along with the mushrooms.

Make the omelette and put half the kidney mixture in the center. Fold and turn out on a hot serving dish. Place remaining kidney mixture on top and add the chopped parsley mixed with salt, pepper and a drop of lemon juice.

OMELETTE PAYSANNE

⅓ cup diced bacon, ham or salt pork
2 tablespoons butter
¾ cup cooked, diced potatoes
6 eggs, lightly beaten
½ cup cooked sorrel
1 teaspoon finely chopped parsley
1 teaspoon finely chopped chervil
  Salt, pepper to taste

Parboil meat for a few minutes and drain well. Sauté meat until lightly browned in 1 tablespoon butter. Remove. Add potatoes to pan and sauté until golden brown all over. Return meat to pan with the beaten eggs. Add well-drained sorrel, parsley, chervil and salt. Stir the mixture with a fork, shaking the pan in a circular motion at the same time. When the mixture begins to set, add another tablespoon of butter. When it starts to brown lightly, fold over, turn out and sprinkle with pepper. Serves 2 as a main course.

OMELETTE BASQUE BAYONNAISE

2 tablespoons olive oil
1 shallot, finely chopped
1 small green pepper, finely chopped
1 small sweet red pepper, finely chopped
1 clove garlic, chopped
1 tablespoon finely diced smoked ham
1 tablespoon tongue, diced
1 large tomato, skinned, seeded and coarsely
  chopped
  Plain omelette mixture
1 tablespoon salt butter
  Oregano

Heat the olive oil in a pan and add the chopped shallot, peppers and garlic. Cook briskly for 2 or 3 minutes, and then add the meats and tomato. Cook down slowly for about 30 minutes, until practically no juice is left.

Make omelette and spread mixture in the center, leaving about a ½" margin around edge. Fold and turn out onto a hot serving dish. Rub top with salt butter. Sprinkle with oregano.

CRAB MEAT OMELETTE

2 teaspoons chopped fresh tarragon
1 tablespoon finely chopped parsley
3 teaspoons finely chopped shallots
2 tablespoons creamed sweet butter
½ cup cooked crab meat, boned and flaked
4 tablespoons heavy cream
1 tablespoon dry sherry
    Plain omelette mixture
    Sweet butter
    Garnish: fresh tarragon leaves, heavy cream

Add the chopped herbs and shallots to the creamed butter. Stir over very low heat until butter begins to dissolve and then add the crab meat. Heat without browning and lastly add the cream and sherry. Cook over high heat for a minute or two to reduce cream. Make omelette and put in filling. Fold over, turn out onto a hot dish and brush top with sweet butter. Put under broiler for one minute to brown. Garnish with fresh tarragon leaves and a spoonful of heavy cream.

ROE OMELETTE

1 small shad roe, or 2 small flounder roe
2 tablespoons salt butter
1 tablespoon finely chopped shallot
½ cup raw fish, ground
    Salt, cayenne pepper to taste
2 tablespoons sweet butter
1 teaspoon lemon juice
    Nutmeg
2 tablespoons sour cream
    Plain omelette mixture
8 anchovy fillets and 2–3 tablespoons oil from
    anchovies
¼ cup capers

Blanch roe in boiling water for 4–5 minutes. Drain,

cool and carefully remove any membrane and skin. Mash well with a fork. Put 1 tablespoon salt butter in a pan with shallot and raw fish, season with salt and pepper and cook 3–4 minutes, stirring constantly. Add roe, rest of salt butter and cook another 2–3 minutes, stirring constantly. Add sweet butter and lemon juice and season to taste with nutmeg. Mix in the sour cream. Add this filling to prepared omelette and turn out onto a hot, flat serving dish. Brush the top with a little anchovy oil, cover with strips of anchovy and scatter capers over the omelette just before serving.

FOIE GRAS OMELETTE

3 ounces pâté de foie gras
2 truffles, chopped
2 tablespoons sweet butter
    Salt, freshly cracked pepper to taste
    Plain omelette mixture
6 tablespoons Madeira

Dice the foie gras. Warm the chopped truffles in the sweet butter and add to foie gras. Season with salt and a little pepper. Make a plain omelette and fill with foie gras mixture. Fold and turn out on a hot serving dish. Heat the Madeira, ignite and pour around the omelette. Serve.

MOUSSELINE OMELETTE

3 eggs
    Salt, cayenne pepper to taste
2 tablespoons heavy cream
2½ tablespoons salt butter

This very delicate creamy omelette, a variation of the plain omelette, is not to be confused with the fluffy dessert omelette.

Separate the eggs. Beat the yolks until thick and pale with salt, cayenne pepper and the heavy cream. Beat the whites stiff but not dry and blend with the yolk mixture. (If a larger omelette is desired, use 4 yolks and 3 whites.)

Heat the omelette pan. Add the salt butter, pour in the egg and proceed as for a basic omelette, but cook

HOW TO MAKE A FILLED
MOUSSELINE OMELETTE

1. Put desired filling and butter in pan.

2. Use spatula to pile fluffy egg mixture on top.

3. Stir with fork, shake as in plain omelette.

4. Turn out, add mushroom, brown butter.

over lower heat. Do not overcook. Fold and turn out onto a hot serving dish. A mousseline omelette may be plain, or have a filling such as mushrooms and garnish of mushroom cap, brown butter.

GERMAN OMELETTE

2 tablespoons flour
3 eggs
½ cup cream or milk
  Salt, pepper, nutmeg to taste
4 teaspoons salt butter

Put the flour in a bowl. Beat in eggs one at a time with a whisk. Add milk or cream, season with salt, pepper and a little nutmeg. Let mixture chill in the refrigerator about half an hour before using.

Heat the omelette pan and dissolve about ½ teaspoon of salt butter. Pour in half the egg and spread out so it makes a very thin omelette or pancake. Cook slowly until lightly browned on one side. Turn over and brown other side. Turn out on a plate and roll up like a cigar. Make up the second omelette in the same way. Pour over remaining butter, browned. Omelettes may be filled with mushroom, chicken, etc.

The omelettes can also be cut into strips, rolled in granulated sugar and served with fresh berries, or used plain as a garnish for consommé.

SPANISH PEASANT OMELETTE
(Tortilla)

2 medium potatoes
1 large or 2 medium onions
4–6 tablespoons olive oil
½ teaspoon salt
4 or 5 eggs, well-beaten

Peel and chop potatoes and onions. Cover bottom of omelette pan or heavy skillet with olive oil, add chopped potatoes and onions. Cook over very low heat until vegetables are tender, but do not allow to brown at all. Chop with sharp knife as they cook, to make them like hash, turning occasionally with a spatula to prevent sticking. When very tender, sprinkle salt over the top, stir once to blend salt through vegetables and drain off excess oil. Add one-third of the beaten eggs to the pan, lifting so moist egg can run under. When egg has become solid, add another third, and finally the last third of the eggs. When golden crust has formed on bottom, loosen carefully with spatula, invert plate over top of pan, turn out upside down. Scrape out any bits of vegetable sticking to pan, add a little more oil, slip tortilla back with moist side down. Cook as before until solid and invert on plate. If not solidly cooked, slide back into pan once more. The omelette has a delightfully nutty flavor and is very hearty fare for 3 or 4 persons. On the first try, this may seem tricky, but once you learn it, this typically Spanish omelette is easy to prepare and makes a good dish for a simple lunch or supper.

FRITTATA OF ARTICHOKE HEARTS

⅓ cup oil
1 clove garlic, finely chopped
2 packages frozen artichoke hearts, thawed
6 eggs
2 tablespoons water
1 teaspoon salt
½ teaspoon freshly ground black pepper
Grated Parmesan or Romano cheese

Heat the oil in a large iron or heavy aluminum skillet. Cook the garlic for 3 or 4 minutes. Add the thawed artichoke hearts, toss them in the oil and heat thoroughly (they are cooked before freezing, so they merely need heating). When they are heated through and tender, beat the eggs slightly with the water, the salt and pepper, and pour this mixture over the artichoke hearts. Cook for a few minutes on top of the stove until the eggs begin to set. Sprinkle lavishly with grated cheese and place under the broiler, about 3″ from the flame, or in a 450° oven for a few moments, just enough to brown the cheese and set the eggs on top. Serves 6.

ZUCCHINI FRITTATA

6–8 small zucchini
3 tablespoons olive oil
2 tablespoons butter
8 eggs
1 teaspoon salt
½ teaspoon freshly ground black pepper
½ cup grated Parmesan cheese

Wash but do not peel the zucchini. Cut into ¼″ slices and cook slowly in the oil and butter until just tender. Beat the eggs with the salt and pepper and pour gently over the zucchini. Cook until just set. Sprinkle the cheese on top and run under the broiler to brown lightly. Let the frittata stand for a minute or two, and then cut in wedges and serve. Serves 6–8.

FRANKFURTER FRITTATA

1 medium onion, thinly sliced
½ green pepper, finely chopped
6 tablespoons butter
4–5 frankfurters, cut in shreds
6 eggs, beaten
½ cup grated Parmesan cheese
¼ cup chopped parsley
1 teaspoon salt
¼ teaspoon Tabasco

Cook onion and green pepper in butter until onions are just tender and not colored. Add frankfurters and cook until delicately browned and cooked through— about 4–5 minutes. Add eggs, cheese and parsley which have been well mixed with the seasonings. Cook until eggs are just set. You may place under the broiler for 3–4 minutes to give the top a delicate brown if you wish. Cut frittata in wedges and serve with potato salad or cole slaw. Serves 4.

Note: Thin slices of salami or summer sausage or knockwurst may be used instead of the frankfurters.

SWISS FONDUE

In Switzerland, this most glorious of all dunks is made on the kitchen stove in a "caquelon," a heavy earthenware or cast-iron casserole that holds the heat. It is then placed on a warmer (for the fondue must be kept hot) in the middle of the table for serving. A heavy chafing dish is good for making fondue, which must be cooked over very low heat or the cheese will become stringy.

1 pound natural Switzerland cheese
   (Emmenthal, Gruyère or a mixture of both)
2 tablespoons flour
1 clove fresh garlic, cut
2 cups dry white wine
3 tablespoons kirsch
   Nutmeg, pepper and salt to taste
2 loaves crusty Italian or French bread, cut into
   bite-size pieces, each with some crust

Shred cheese or cut into small, transparent slices. Dredge cheese with flour. Rub the cooking utensil with the cut sides of the garlic. Pour in wine, set over low heat. When wine is heated to the point that air bubbles rise to the surface, add cheese gradually, stirring constantly with a wooden spoon. Stir until cheese is melted. Stir in kirsch, and a pinch of nutmeg, pepper and salt. Keep fondue hot, but below the simmering point. If the mixture becomes too thick, thin with a little wine, a tablespoon at a time. Serve with the bite-size pieces of bread, which are speared on special two-pronged forks (or ordinary forks) and dipped into the fondue. Serves 4–6 as a meal, more as a dunk.

FONDUTA

1 pound Fontina cheese,
   or ¾ pound Mozzarella cheese and
   ¼ pound Swiss, diced
1 tablespoon potato or corn starch
1 cup milk
2 tablespoons butter
½ teaspoon salt
¼ teaspoon white pepper
4 egg yolks, beaten
1 can white truffles, sliced

In the top of a double boiler, combine the cheese, potato or corn starch mixed with the milk, the butter, salt and pepper. Place over hot water and cook, stirring constantly, until the cheese melts and is very smooth. Gradually beat in the egg yolks, stirring steadily until thickened, but do not let the mixture boil. Pour into a heated serving dish or individual dishes and sprinkle with the truffles. Use as many as you can. Surround the fonduta with slices of sautéed bread and serve at once. Serves 4–6.

LONDON RABBIT

2 tablespoons butter
1 pound (4 cups) Cheddar cheese, grated
¾ cup beer
½ teaspoon salt
1 teaspoon dry mustard
   Dash of cayenne pepper
1 teaspoon Worcestershire sauce
1 egg yolk

Use a chafing dish or double boiler with hot water underneath. Melt the butter in the top part and add the cheese; stir occasionally until melted. Stir in the beer, salt, mustard, cayenne pepper and Worcestershire sauce until smooth.

Beat the egg yolk in a bowl; gradually add a little of the cheese mixture, stirring steadily to prevent curdling. Pour back into cheese mixture. Stir until thickened, but do not let boil. Serve on buttered toast or English muffins. Serves 4–6.

LAYERED CHEESE AND SPINACH TART

½ cup plus 1 tablespoon fine bread crumbs
⅓ cup freshly grated Parmesan cheese
2 tablespoons butter, melted
1 pound ricotta or cottage cheese
1 cup sour cream
2 tablespoons flour
2 eggs
   Salt to taste

10-ounce package frozen chopped spinach,
   cooked and well-drained
¼ pound cooked ham, diced
¼ teaspoon Lawry's Seasoned Pepper

Mix ½ cup of the bread crumbs with 2 tablespoons of the grated Parmesan cheese. Blend in the melted butter, and press the crumb mixture onto the bottom and sides of a 9″–10″ pie plate. Place the ricotta or cottage cheese, remaining Parmesan cheese, 2 tablespoons of the sour cream, flour, and eggs in the large bowl of an electric mixer. Beat at high speed until the mixture is smooth. Add salt.

Mix half the cheese mixture with the spinach and spread evenly in the prepared pie shell. Add the ham to the remaining cheese mixture and spread carefully over the spinach-cheese layer. Sprinkle the seasoned pepper and the remaining crumbs on top. Bake in a preheated 350° oven for 40 minutes. Serve immediately and pass the remaining sour cream separately as a sauce. Makes 6 servings.

CHEESE SOUFFLÉ IN A TART SHELL

    Pastry for 10″ pie
2 tablespoons flour
⅛ teaspoon nutmeg
½ teaspoon prepared mustard
1 cup milk
¼ pound Gruyère cheese, coarsely grated
¼ cup freshly grated Parmesan cheese
4 eggs, separated
    Salt to taste
¼ teaspoon cream of tartar

Prepare the pastry, roll it out, and fit it into a 10″ pie plate. Flute the rim and prick the surface with a fork. Bake in a preheated 450° oven for 15 minutes. Combine the flour and nutmeg in a saucepan. Add the mustard and milk and bring to a boil, stirring constantly. Cook until the sauce thickens and remove from the heat. Add the cheeses, replace over the heat and cook, stirring constantly, until the cheeses are melted. Remove from the heat and add the egg yolks and salt. Beat the egg whites until foamy, add the cream of tartar, and beat until stiff. Fold into the cheese sauce, and pour into the partially baked tart

shell. Bake the tart in a 375° oven for 25 minutes, or until the soufflé filling is puffed and golden in color. Makes 5–6 servings.

CHEESE SOUFFLÉ

4 tablespoons butter
4 tablespoons flour
1 teaspoon salt
¼ teaspoon dry mustard
1 cup light cream
1 cup beer or ale
½ pound (2 cups) grated Cheddar cheese
5 eggs, separated
    Grated Parmesan cheese

Melt the butter in a saucepan; blend in the flour, salt and mustard. Gradually add the cream and beer, stirring steadily until it reaches the boiling point; cook over low heat 5 minutes. Mix in the cheese until melted. Beat the egg yolks in a bowl; add to the cheese mixture slowly, stirring steadily to prevent curdling. Cool.

Butter a 2-quart soufflé dish, dust with grated Parmesan cheese and tie a wax paper collar around it.

Beat the egg whites until stiff but not dry; fold in the

HOW TO MAKE A CHEESE SOUFFLÉ

1. Butter soufflé dish well inside. Tie collar of buttered wax paper around outside of the dish.

2. Dust inside with grated Parmesan cheese, turning dish to coat evenly. Tip out excess.

3. Mix beaten egg yolks with cooked sauce.

4. In copper bowl, beat egg whites with large whisk in figure eight pattern until they are stiff.

5. Carefully spoon cooled cheese mixture onto the egg whites, trying not to break them down.

6. Fold in the cheese mixture with slow up and over motion until just incorporated with whites.

7. Stand soufflé dish in pan of water; fill with mixture. Smooth over top, sprinkle with cheese.

8. Bake until cooked, well-risen and browned.

cheese mixture carefully. Pour into soufflé dish, stand dish in a pan of water and bake in a preheated 375° oven 40 minutes or until puffed, set and browned on the top. Serve at once. Serves 4–6.

MÜNSTER CHEESE BATTER PUDDING

  1 egg
  ¾ cup flour
  1 cup milk
  ½ teaspoon salt
    Dash cayenne pepper
  ¼ pound Münster cheese

Beat the egg lightly in a bowl with a whisk. Add the flour and half the milk and beat until smooth. Stir in the remaining milk, the salt and cayenne pepper. Let the batter stand for 1 hour. Coarsely grate the cheese and stir half of it into the batter. Grease an 8″ Pyrex pie plate, pour the batter into it and bake in a preheated 425° oven for 30 minutes, or until puffed and brown. Scatter the remaining cheese on top and bake just until the cheese is melted. Cut into 24 narrow wedges and serve as an appetizer.

CHEESE TIMBALE

  6 tablespoons butter
  8 tablespoons flour
  1 small can evaporated milk
  1 cup milk
  1¼ pounds grated Swiss cheese
  12 eggs, separated
    Salt, pepper
    Fine bread crumbs
  1 pound mushrooms, sliced
  1 cup cream

Melt 4 tablespoons butter. Add 6 tablespoons flour. Add evaporated milk and ½ cup milk gradually, stirring constantly until thickened. Add cheese, stirring until melted. Remove from fire. Add egg yolks. Season to taste with salt and pepper. (The amount

of salt depends on the cheese.) Beat egg whites stiff. Fold into cheese mixture. Grease two 2-quart pudding molds and dust with bread crumbs (or use 4 coffee tins). Divide cheese mixture between them. Place in pots of simmering water that reaches no more than half way up the sides of the molds. Cover pots tightly and steam 1½ hours for pudding molds, 1 hour for coffee tins. Remove from pots. Wait five minutes before turning out on serving platters. Sauté mushrooms in remaining butter for 5 minutes. Sprinkle with remaining flour. Add ½ cup milk and cream gradually, stirring constantly until thickened. Add salt and pepper to taste. Spoon a little mushroom sauce over each timbale, serving balance in a sauceboat. Serves 12.

GNOCCHI VORENIKI

  1 pound cottage cheese
  ½ pound cream cheese
  2 eggs, beaten
    Flour
    Salt, cayenne pepper
  6 ounces sweet butter
  ½ cup fresh grated Parmesan cheese

Strain cottage and cream cheeses through a very fine strainer. Put into a bowl and slowly mix in the beaten eggs. Add just enough flour to bind, approximately two level tablespoons. Season with salt and cayenne pepper to taste. Cover bowl and chill mixture for at least half an hour in the refrigerator. Have ready a large pan of boiling salted water. Reduce the heat to a slow simmer. Put in the cheese mixture in small teaspoonfuls and allow to poach without boiling for 20 minutes or until they come up to the surface of the water and are firm to the touch. (Gnocchi may be made in advance, left in the cooled water and gently reheated without boiling.) Slowly dissolve the butter and season it with salt and pepper. Brush the bottom of an au gratin dish with a little of the butter. Carefully drain the gnocchi and place in the dish. Sprinkle them well with the Parmesan cheese and the rest of the butter. Serves 8.

Rice, Grain & Pasta

According to ancient myth, grain was a gift of the gods. The Egyptian deities Isis and Osiris were credited with originating cereals and agriculture, while in ancient Greece and Rome Demeter, or Ceres, was the goddess of grain. On our own continent, corn had a mystic significance for the Indian tribes, whose word for it meant "she who sustains us." Grain has indeed been the great sustainer of life throughout the world, transplanted by exploration and trade from continent to continent. Rice, migrating from the Orient, spread slowly to the great Mediterranean civilizations of Egypt, Greece and Rome. The Moors carried it to Spain and the Spanish to the New World where, with the wheat and barley brought by Colonial settlers, it flourished in the good company of the native grains—Indian corn or maize and the wild rice of the Great Lakes.

Every country has evolved indigenous grain dishes, from the pellao of India to kasha, the Russian stand-by, and the cracked wheat or bulgur of the Middle East. In Italy, two types of grain dishes predominate—risotto and pasta—with each accorded the status of a separate course. Risotto was Asia's contribution to Italian cooking; pasta, mistakenly assumed to have been imported from China by Marco Polo, is the true native dish. The museum at Pompeii shows the equipment for making, cooking and serving what the Romans called laganum, a form of tagliatelle. By the thirteenth century, the rich inventiveness of pasta cooks had widened the range to include "maccheroni" with sweet and savory fillings, fetching little shapes like wagon wheels and cock's combs. Naples established itself as the great pasta center and professional mangia macarone held contests where they wolfed down as much as six pounds of the stuff in a single, non-stop gobble. Although pasta was accounted a humble food in Italy, it rated as an expensive imported delicacy in Restoration England, when Italian modes were all the fashion, and macaroni passed into the language as a synonym for a fop. The word reached America before the food. When Americans sang of the Yankee Doodle Dandy who stuck a feather in his cap and called it macaroni, pasta was an unknown quantity.

Now there is no variety of grain on which we cannot draw to enrich our menus and complement our food. We partner poultry or game with a barley casserole, sausage or pork dishes with cornmeal polenta, beef stroganoff with kasha and lamb shish kebab with bulgur pilaff, giving thanks to those early travelers who recognized and distributed the largesse of grain.

STEAMED RICE

1 cup rice
½ teaspoon salt
Butter
Water or stock

Wash the rice. Put rice and salt into a heavy skillet lightly greased with butter. Pour on enough water or stock to come 1½" above the rice. Cover tightly and bring to a rapid boil very quickly. Lower the heat and let the rice cook very slowly until all the liquid is absorbed. This should take about 15–20 minutes. Do not remove cover during cooking time. Fluff up rice with a fork and serve. Serves 4.

Variations:

1. Substitute chicken broth for the water or stock. When cooked, toss with toasted buttered almonds and melted butter.
2. Mix steamed rice with mushrooms sautéed in butter.
3. Mix steamed rice with crisp bacon bits and chopped, sautéed onions.

BROWN RICE WITH NUTS

1 cup California brown rice (or white rice)
½ cup chopped walnuts, almonds, pecans or filberts
¼ cup butter

Cook rice according to directions on the package. It should be dry and flaky. Brown nuts in butter. Mix with the cooked rice and serve at once. This is particularly good as an accompaniment to poultry or game. Serves 4–6.

RICE WITH PINE NUTS

1 cup finely chopped onion
1 cup pine nuts
1½ teaspoons paprika
½ teaspoon Tabasco
½ cup olive oil
4 cups hot cooked rice
Salt, pepper
Chopped parsley
2 pimientos, chopped

Sauté the onion, pine nuts, paprika and Tabasco in the olive oil for 6–8 minutes. Toss with the hot rice, using two forks. Season to taste with salt and pepper. Garnish with the chopped parsley and chopped pimientos. Good with lamb dishes or with braised chicken. Serves 4–6.

FRIED RICE ORIENTALE

⅓ cup peanut oil
½ cup finely sliced green onions
1 cup julienne strips Smithfield or country ham
3 cups cooked rice
½ cup sliced water chestnuts
2 eggs, slightly beaten
3 tablespoons soy sauce
Chopped cilantro
Salt, pepper to taste

Heat the peanut oil and lightly sauté the onions and ham. Blend in the rice and water chestnuts. Stir in the beaten eggs and the soy sauce and cook until the eggs are thoroughly mixed with the rice and other ingredients. Taste for seasoning.

Spoon the mixture into a bowl or a charlotte mold, pressing it down well with the back of the spoon. Unmold onto a hot platter. Garnish with chopped cilantro if available, or with parsley and shredded green onions. Serves 4–6 as main course.

Note: You may substitute julienne strips of turkey, chicken or pork for the ham, or you may use part ham and part chicken or turkey.

ARROZ À LA MEXICANA
(Mexican Rice)

2 cups rice
1 large onion
2 cloves garlic
4 cups stock
4 tablespoons olive or salad oil
1½ cups peeled, seeded and puréed tomato
Salt, pepper to taste

½ cup cooked green peas
Fresh red peppers, cut into rings
Fresh cilantro
1 large avocado, peeled and sliced

Cover rice with hot water and let stand for 15 minutes. Drain and rinse in cold water until final water is clear. Drain and dry. Put onion and garlic in an electric blender with a little stock and blend smooth. Heat oil in a skillet and sauté rice until it is golden. Transfer rice to a saucepan, add onion, garlic, tomato, stock, salt and pepper. Bring to a boil, cover, lower heat and cook until rice is almost done. Fold in the peas and continue cooking until rice is tender and all liquid absorbed. Serve garnished with peppers, sprigs of cilantro, and slices of avocado. Serves 6.

SAFFRON RICE

½ cup mixed vegetable and olive oil
1½ ounces salt butter
2 finely chopped white onions
Salt, cayenne pepper to taste
2½ cups long-grain rice
5 cups chicken stock
½ teaspoon saffron

Heat the vegetable and olive oils and butter in a deep pan. Add finely chopped onions with a little salt and pepper. Cook slowly without browning for three minutes. Stir in the rice, mix in chicken stock. Dilute saffron in a tablespoon of cold water and add it to the rice. Stir over high heat until it comes to a slow boil. Reduce the heat to a simmer, cover with lid and cook without removing lid for 25 minutes. Remove; fluff the rice with a fork and serve in a casserole. Serves 8–10.

CASSEROLE OF TURKEY WITH RICE

2 medium onions, chopped
Butter
½ pound sliced mushrooms
2 cups diced cold turkey
½ cup diced ham

1 cup crumbled leftover turkey stuffing
2 tablespoons chopped parsley
Pinch of thyme
Salt, freshly ground black pepper to taste
1 tablespoon curry powder
1 cup rice
2 cups hot turkey or chicken broth

Sauté the onions in butter until just tender. Add the mushrooms, and sauté for 2 minutes or so. Combine in a casserole with the turkey, ham, stuffing, parsley, thyme, salt, and pepper.

Add an additional tablespoon of butter and the curry powder to the skillet used for sautéing the onions and lightly sauté the rice. Add to the casserole and pour in the hot broth. Place in a preheated 375° oven and cook until the rice is tender and the liquid is absorbed. Add more heated broth if necessary to finish cooking the rice. Serves 4–6.

ARTICHOKE AND RICE CASSEROLE

3 tablespoons butter
2 tablespoons olive oil
2 large artichokes, sliced and choke removed
1 large tomato, peeled, seeded, and chopped
½ clove garlic, minced
½ teaspoon dried basil
2 cups (approximately) hot chicken bouillon
1 cup long-grain rice
1 teaspoon salt

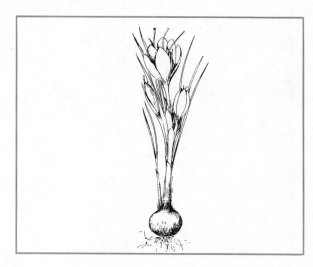

½ teaspoon pepper
¼ cup minced parsley
Freshly grated Parmesan cheese

Heat 2 tablespoons of the butter and the olive oil in a heavy saucepan. Add the artichokes. Cook, stirring constantly, for 3 minutes. Add the tomato, garlic, basil, and ½ cup of the bouillon. Simmer, covered, over low heat until the artichokes are half tender. Heat the remaining tablespoon of butter in a 1½–2 quart casserole. Add the rice and cook over medium heat, stirring constantly, until the rice is yellow and transparent. Add the remaining 1½ cups bouillon, the salt and pepper.

Simmer, covered, over lowest possible heat until the rice is three-quarters cooked. Check for moisture; different kinds of rice will absorb less or more liquid and a little more bouillon may have to be added. (For this dish, the rice should be on the dry side when completely cooked.) Add the artichoke mixture to the rice and mix well. Simmer, covered, until both rice and artichokes are tender, but still firm. If necessary, add a little more hot bouillon to prevent scorching. Sprinkle with parsley and serve with plenty of freshly grated Parmesan cheese. Serves 4–6.

BRAZILIAN CASSEROLE

7 tablespoons butter
3 cups rice
6 cups chicken stock or 6 teaspoons chicken
    concentrate dissolved in 6 cups water
½ cup grated Parmesan cheese
½ cup catsup
16 eggs
8 bananas, halved lengthwise
1 canned pimiento, cut into strips

Melt 4 tablespoons butter. Add rice. Stir until rice is glazed. Add stock. Bring to boil. Turn flame low, cover pot and cook for 20–25 minutes, until rice is tender and liquid absorbed. Remove from flame. Stir in cheese and catsup. Spread 1" deep in shallow oven-proof casseroles. This preparation may be done in advance. About 25 minutes before serving time make 16 shallow depressions, evenly spaced, in rice. Break an egg into each, being careful not to break yolk. (If you break the egg into a saucer and then tip it into rice, you take no risk.) Bake in a preheated 400° oven until white is set, about 15 minutes. Meanwhile, melt remaining butter in large pan. Sauté banana halves until golden on all sides. Remove baked eggs from oven. Arrange bananas and pimiento on rice between eggs. Serves 8–16.

Green Rice Casserole

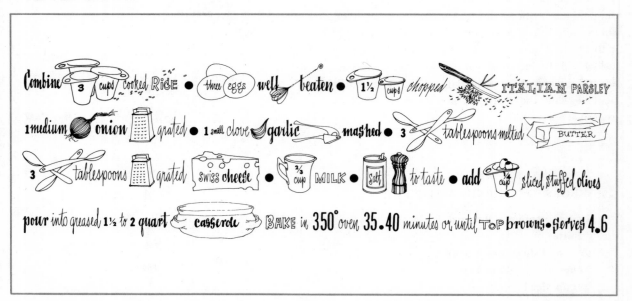

Combine 3 cups cooked RICE ● three eggs well beaten ● 1½ cups chopped ITALIAN PARSLEY 1 medium onion grated ● 1 small clove garlic mashed ● 3 tablespoons melted BUTTER 3 tablespoons grated swiss cheese ● ⅔ cup MILK ● salt to taste ● add ¼ cup sliced, stuffed olives pour into greased 1½ to 2 quart casserole BAKE in 350° oven 35.40 minutes or until TOP browns ● Serves 4.6

RISI E BISI

  1 small onion, finely chopped
  5 tablespoons butter
  ½ cup shredded smoked ham
  1 package frozen peas, thawed
  3–4 cups chicken or beef stock
  1½ cups rice
  3 tablespoons grated Parmesan cheese

Sauté the chopped onion in 2 tablespoons butter. Add the ham and the thawed peas. Mix in 1 cup of stock and bring to a boil. Add the rice and then 2 cups of boiling stock. Cook until all stock is absorbed. If more liquid is needed, add another cup of boiling stock. Cook until the rice is just dry, but not too soft. Stir in the remaining 3 tablespoons butter and the Parmesan cheese. Serve at once. Serves 4.

RISOTTO ALLA MILANESE

  5–6 tablespoons butter
  1 small onion, finely chopped
  2 cups rice
  ½ cup white wine
  3 or more cups hot stock

  1 teaspoon salt
  Saffron
  Grated Parmesan cheese

Melt 3 tablespoons butter in a heavy skillet. When it is bubbling, add the onion. Cook for 2–3 minutes, do not allow the onion to brown. Add the rice and stir it well with a spatula; do not allow it to color. Be certain that the onion and rice are well coated with the butter. Add the wine and let it almost cook away. Start to add stock, a cup at a time. Let each cup of stock cook away before adding more. As the rice becomes tender, stir it with a fork to keep it from sticking to the pan. Add salt and a touch of saffron. When the rice is done, stir in the remaining 2–3 tablespoons of butter and a little grated Parmesan cheese. Serve at once. This is usually offered as a first course in Italy but may be served with certain meats, if you wish, or as a main course at luncheon. Serves 4 as a main course.

Variations:

1. Before adding the wine, add 4–5 slices poached marrow.
2. Add a little dry sherry, about 1/3 cup, to the risotto when you add the stock. If you are serving the risotto with a veal or chicken dish, use hot

tomato juice instead of stock and add a little chopped basil.

3. Garnish the cooked risotto with thinly sliced white truffles.

VENETIAN SHELLFISH RISOTTO

1½–2 pounds cooked shellfish (shrimp, clams, lobster, scallops, any combination you like)
Shells from shrimp and lobster
Fish bones and heads
1 recipe Risotto alla Milanese
1 clove garlic, chopped
6–7 tablespoons butter
Salt, pepper
3 tablespoons chopped parsley
Grated Parmesan cheese

Make a rich fish stock with the shells, fish bones and heads. Follow the recipe for risotto but add chopped garlic with the onion, and cook the rice in the strained hot fish broth.

Heat the cooked shellfish in 4 tablespoons butter, season to taste and toss with the chopped parsley. Mix into the cooked risotto and add the remaining butter and grated Parmesan cheese. Serves 6.

RISOTTO ALLA CREMA DI FORMAGGIO

3 tablespoons butter
3 tablespoons minced onion
2½ cups white rice
¼ cup cognac
4½ cups hot chicken broth
Salt, pepper to taste
2–3 tablespoons dry bread crumbs
2 cups cream sauce
¼ pound (about 1 cup) grated Fontina cheese or mixed Swiss and mild Cheddar
2 tablespoons grated Parmesan cheese
2 tablespoons minced truffles (1-ounce can)

Melt the butter in a heavy saucepan and sauté the onion 2–3 minutes. Add the rice and stir over medium heat until it is well coated with the butter. Add the cognac and let it almost cook away. Stir in 1½ cups of the broth (you may also use the liquid from the canned truffles) and let simmer slowly, stirring occasionally until liquid has almost evaporated, then add another 1½ cups and repeat. Add the final 1½ cups of broth, cover the rice and simmer slowly for 5 minutes. Uncover and stir constantly until liquid has been absorbed completely. Correct seasoning. (Cooking should take about 20 minutes in all.)

Pack into a buttered 8-cup ring mold which has been lightly dusted with the bread crumbs. Cover with waxed paper and bake for 15 minutes in a preheated 350° oven. Heat the cream sauce, stir in the cheese and simmer slowly for 10 minutes, stirring frequently. Unmold the rice on a hot platter, pour the cheese sauce in the middle, sprinkle with Parmesan cheese and truffles. Serves 8.

RISOTTO PANCAKES

2 tablespoons butter
1 cup rice
1 small onion
3 cups highly seasoned chicken stock
½ cup flour
2 eggs
2 tablespoons chopped parsley
Salt, pepper
¼ cup shortening

Melt butter. Add rice. Stir until rice is glazed. Add onion. Add 2 cups stock. Cover and cook over low flame for 20–25 minutes until rice is tender and liquid absorbed. Remove from flame. Discard onion.

Blend flour and eggs thoroughly. Add remaining stock and parsley. Stir in cooked rice. Adjust seasoning. Melt some of shortening in large heavy frying pan or on griddle. Fry thin pancakes about 3″ or 4″ in diameter. Note: These may be made in advance or even frozen. Reheat in pan or oven.

WILD RICE

Bring 4 cups of salted water to a rapid boil. Slowly add 1 cup of wild rice. Be sure that the water does not stop boiling. When all the rice is added, cover the pan and cook for 15–20 minutes, or until the rice is tender, but not mushy. Drain thoroughly.

Serve with any of the following:
1. Melted butter.
2. Crisp buttered crumbs.
3. 1 cup chopped toasted almonds and melted butter.
4. ½ cup pine nuts, melted butter.
5. ½ cup sliced mushrooms, sautéed in butter.

WILD RICE AND OYSTER CASSEROLE

½ cup butter
¾ cup minced shallots, or mild onion
¾ cup minced celery
3 cups cooked wild rice
1 pint oysters with liquor
  Milk
1 teaspoon salt
¼ teaspoon pepper
¼ teaspoon ground cardamom
1 cup grated Swiss cheese

Heat ¼ cup of the butter in a skillet and cook the shallots and celery until soft and barely golden. Combine with the wild rice. Grease a 1½- or 2-quart casserole and arrange alternate layers of rice and drained oysters in it, ending with a layer of rice. (Reserve oyster liquor and add enough milk to it to make ¾ cup liquid.) Add salt, pepper, and cardamom to the milk and oyster liquor and pour it over mixture in casserole. Top with grated cheese. Melt remaining ¼ cup butter and sprinkle over cheese. Bake, covered, in a preheated 400° oven for 25 minutes. Serve with broccoli vinaigrette. Serves 4.

WILD RICE AND TURKEY CASSEROLE

1 cup wild rice
1 pound mushrooms, sliced
1 onion, chopped
6 tablespoons butter
2 teaspoons salt
¼ teaspoon freshly ground black pepper
3 cups diced cooked turkey
½ cup blanched sliced almonds
3 cups turkey or chicken broth
1½ cups heavy cream
3 tablespoons Parmesan cheese

Wash the rice thoroughly and cover with boiling water. Let soak 1 hour. Drain well.

Sauté the mushrooms and onion in 1 tablespoon butter for 10 minutes. In a greased casserole, combine the rice, sautéed vegetables, salt, pepper, turkey and almonds. Add the broth and cream. Mix lightly. Cover and bake in a 350° oven 1½ hours. Remove cover; sprinkle with the cheese and dot with the remaining butter. Turn oven up to 450° and bake 5 minutes. Serves 6–8.

KASHA

1 cup buckwheat groats
1 egg
2 cups stock
  Salt
4–6 tablespoons butter

Heat a heavy skillet with a tight-fitting lid. Add the groats and stir in the raw egg. Continue cooking and stirring until thoroughly blended and cooked dry. Add the stock and salt to taste, cover, lower the heat and simmer very gently for about ½ hour, or until the groats are cooked and the broth is absorbed. Mix with the butter. Serve with ragouts and stews, beef stroganoff and other sour cream dishes, with moussaka, etc. Serves 4.

BULGUR PILAFF

> 2 tablespoons butter
> 1 tablespoon chopped onion
> 1 cup bulgur (cracked wheat)
> ½ teaspoon salt
>   Freshly ground black pepper
> 2 cups (approximately) chicken
>   stock or bouillon

Melt the butter in a skillet and add the onion. Let it cook for 2–3 minutes and add the bulgur. Stir until the grains are well coated with butter. Add the salt, pepper to taste and the stock. Bring to a boil, lower the heat and cover the pan. Cook gently for 13–15 minutes, or until the wheat is done and the liquid absorbed. Serves 4.

Variations:
1. Add toasted sliced almonds to pilaff after it is cooked.
2. Add ½ cup sliced mushrooms, 2 tablespoons butter with onion.

BARLEY CASSEROLE

> ½ pound mushrooms
> 4–5 tablespoons butter
> 1 large onion, chopped very fine
> 1 cup pearl barley
>   Salt, pepper
> 2–3 cups boiling beef or chicken broth

Slice the mushroom caps and chop the stems. Heat the butter in a skillet and add the chopped onion. Cook for 3 or 4 minutes and add the mushrooms. Cook another 4 minutes, stirring occasionally. Add the barley and brown it lightly, mixing it well with the onions and mushrooms. Season to taste with salt and pepper and pour into a buttered casserole. Add enough boiling broth to cover the mixture and come ½″ above it. Cover the casserole tightly and bake in a 350° oven for 25 minutes. Taste the barley for doneness. Add more broth, if necessary, and continue cooking until the liquid is absorbed and the barley tender. Serve as an accompaniment to duck, game, goose, squab and other kinds of poultry—wherever you would use wild rice. Serves 6.

Variations:
1. Add finely slivered buttered almonds to the barley just before serving.
2. Cook chicken gizzards in a well-seasoned broth and use the broth to cook the barley. Add the thinly sliced gizzards at the last minute.
2. Add sautéed chicken livers and some chopped fresh parsley to the barley casserole just before serving.
4. Substitute ½ cup finely chopped green onions for the onion and add ¼ cup finely chopped celery and ¼ cup thinly sliced water chestnuts. Season the broth with a few dashes of soy sauce. Serve this oriental version of barley casserole topped with a sprinkling of chopped parsley.

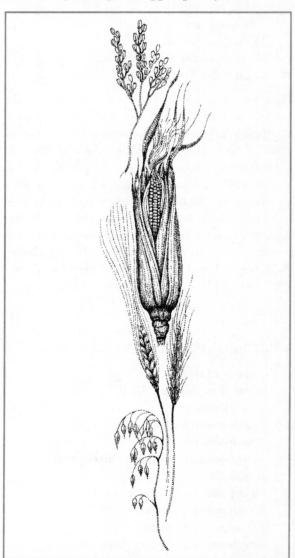

FINNISH BARLEY PUDDING

> 1⅓ cups barley, large-grain variety
> 6 cups boiling milk
> 1 teaspoon salt
> ½ teaspoon pepper
> ⅓ cup butter

Soak barley overnight, or according to package directions, in 4 cups water. Cook in same water. As barley begins to absorb the water, gradually add the boiling milk and seasonings, stirring constantly. Cook barley over very low heat about 30 minutes, stirring frequently to prevent scorching. Transfer to buttered 1½-quart or 2-quart baking dish. Dot with butter and bake in 250° oven until golden brown, about 2 hours. Serves 4.

POLENTA

> 1½ cups cornmeal
> 1 teaspoon salt
> 2 ounces butter
> Grated Parmesan cheese

Put the cornmeal in the top of a double boiler and stir in 1 cup water. When well mixed, stir in 3½ cups boiling water. Cook over a very low flame, stirring constantly, until the mixture comes to a boil. Add salt. Place over hot water and continue cooking for 35 minutes to 1 hour.

Add butter and a lavish sprinkling of grated Parmesan cheese. Or grate the cheese over the polenta just before serving. Serve the polenta with game, pork or with spicy Mexican food. Serves 4.

POTATO AND SEMOLINA GNOCCHI

> 1½ pounds mealy potatoes
> 1 teaspoon salt
> ½ teaspoon freshly ground black pepper
>   Pinch of mace
> 1½ cups milk
>   Semolina
> ½ cup grated Gruyère cheese
> 2 eggs, beaten
>   Melted butter
>   Grated Gruyère or Parmesan cheese

Peel and quarter the potatoes and cook them in boiling, salted water until tender. Drain and mash. Add the salt, pepper and mace. Gradually beat in the milk, using an electric mixer or a wooden spatula. Place over a medium flame and slowly add enough semolina to make a very stiff mixture. Add the ½ cup grated Gruyère cheese and remove from the stove. Beat in the eggs. Pour into a buttered flat tin and let stand for 12–24 hours.

Form the dough into small balls and drop into boiling salted water. Cook for 4 minutes. Remove the gnocchi from the water with a slotted or perforated spoon and keep them warm. Arrange in a well-buttered au gratin dish, drizzle with melted butter and sprinkle with grated Gruyère or Parmesan cheese. Place in a 375° oven to heat through. Serves 4 as a main dish or 8 to accompany a highly seasoned tomato dish.

EGG PASTA
(for ravioli, cannelloni, noodles)

> 2 cups sifted flour
> 2 eggs
> ½ teaspoon salt
> 2 tablespoons cold water

Sift the flour into a bowl; make a well in the center. In it place the eggs, salt and water. Work in the flour with the fingers until a ball of dough is formed. If too dry, add a little more cold water. Knead the dough on a board until very smooth and elastic. Cover with a bowl and let rest 15 minutes, while preparing the filling.

RAVIOLI

> 1 cup ground cooked beef or chicken
> ¼ cup finely chopped ham
> 1 egg, beaten
> ¼ teaspoon minced garlic
> ½ teaspoon salt
> ¼ teaspoon freshly ground black pepper
> ¼ cup grated Parmesan cheese
> 1 recipe Egg Pasta

Mix together the first seven ingredients for the filling. Divide the dough into 2 pieces, one slightly larger.

HOW TO MAKE EGG PASTA
AND RAVIOLI

1. Put sifted flour, eggs, salt, water in a bowl. Mix until dough forms a stiff ball and comes away from sides.

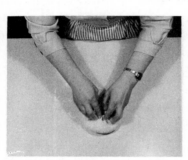

2. Turn out on floured pastry board and knead until smooth and elastic. Cut in two pieces, one slightly larger.

3. With long, thick pin, roll out each piece of dough paper thin. Flour pin and board to prevent dough sticking.

4. Brush smaller piece of dough with beaten egg. With wet hands, roll filling into balls, place at 2″ intervals.

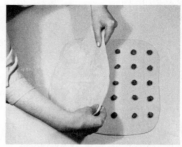

5. Fold larger piece of two in half, lift up and unfold over bottom piece. Trim edges of dough with knife.

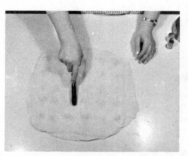

6. With handle of spatula, pat between rows, vertically and horizontally, so layers of dough adhere.

7. Stamp out ravioli with round fluted cutter. To produce square ravioli, cut out with a ravioli wheel.

8. Expel air around filling by pressing gently with smaller cutter (do not pierce dough). Let dry 1 hour.

Roll out each piece paper thin. Lift dough and sprinkle board and rolling pin with flour when necessary. Brush the smaller piece with beaten egg and, at 2″ intervals, place a little of the filling. Cover with other piece of dough. Cut into shapes with a pastry wheel, knife or fluted round cutter, then gently press out air with smooth top of smaller cutter. Be sure the edges are sealed. Let dry for 1 hour.

Cook in deep boiling, salted water about 7 minutes, or until they rise to the surface. Drain and serve with melted butter and grated Parmesan cheese, or with tomato sauce. Serves 4–6.

CANNELLONI

   1 recipe Egg Pasta
   1 cup cooked spinach
   1 cup ricotta cheese
   2 tablespoons melted butter
   ½ cup grated Parmesan cheese
   ½ cup tomato sauce

Prepare the egg pasta and roll into 2 paper-thin sheets, well sprinkled with flour. Cut into 3″-by-4″ rectangles, then let dry 1 hour. Cook a few pieces at a time in boiling, salted water 5 minutes. Drop into cold water. Drain and dry on a clean towel.

Purée the spinach in an electric blender or chop very fine. Mix with the ricotta cheese, butter and ¼ cup Parmesan cheese. Spread on the cooked dough pieces and roll up like a jelly roll.

Spread half the tomato sauce on the bottom of a buttered baking dish. Arrange the cannelloni in it; cover with the remaining tomato sauce and sprinkle with the remaining Parmesan cheese. Bake in a 450° oven 10 minutes. Serves 6.

SPAGHETTI WITH PORK

   ⅓ cup olive oil
   ½ pound lean pork, cut julienne
   1½ pounds tomatoes, peeled and diced
   1¼ teaspoons salt
   ¼ teaspoon crushed red chili peppers
   1 pound spaghetti, cooked and drained
   Freshly grated Parmesan cheese

HOW TO MAKE CANNELLONI

1. Roll pasta dough into a thin sheet; cut into 3″ x 4″ rectangles and allow to dry for 1 hour.

2. Mix cooked spinach, butter, ricotta and Parmesan cheeses. Spread mixture on each rectangle.

3. Roll up rectangles like jelly rolls and put in oval baking dish on a layer of tomato sauce.

4. Pour tomato sauce over top of cannelloni and sprinkle with cheese. Bake 10 minutes at 450°.

Heat the oil in a skillet; brown the pork in it very well. Stir in the tomatoes, salt and red peppers. Cover and cook over low heat 20 minutes. Pour over the spaghetti. Serve with grated cheese. Serves 4–6.

SPAGHETTI ALLA CARBONARA

2 tablespoons butter
¼ pound bacon, cut in matchstick lengths
½ cup chopped onion
¼ cup dry white wine
3 eggs
½ cup freshly grated Parmesan cheese
½ teaspoon freshly ground black pepper
2 tablespoons minced parsley
1 pound spaghetti, cooked and drained

Cook the butter, bacon and onion until lightly browned. Add the wine; cook over low heat until the wine evaporates.

In a large bowl, beat the eggs, cheese, pepper and parsley. Mix in the spaghetti and coat well as quickly as possible; then pour in the bacon mixture, stir quickly and serve immediately. Serves 6.

SHRIMP MARINARA AND SPAGHETTI

1 cup chopped onion
1 clove garlic, puréed
¼ cup olive oil
6 tomatoes, peeled and diced
  Salt, pepper
  Sugar
  Basil
1 cup white wine
1 pound raw shrimp, shelled and cleaned
1 pound spaghetti or other pasta, cooked

Cook the onion and garlic in the olive oil until golden. Add the tomatoes and cook slowly for half an hour or so. Season to taste with salt and pepper, a speck of sugar and as much sweet basil as you like. Add the white wine and shrimp, bring to a boil, and cook about 8 minutes, or until shrimp are done. Serve over cooked spaghetti. Serves 6.

SPAGHETTI ALLA SICILIANA

½ cup olive oil
½ cup minced onion
2 cloves garlic, minced
3 cups peeled diced eggplant
1 cup julienne-cut green peppers
3 cups peeled diced tomatoes
½ teaspoon basil
6 anchovies, shredded
1 tablespoon capers
½ cup Italian black olives, pitted
  Salt, pepper
2 tablespoons parsley
1 pound spaghetti, cooked and drained
2 tablespoons melted butter
4 tablespoons grated Parmesan cheese

Heat the oil in a saucepan; sauté the onion 10 minutes. Add the garlic, eggplant and peppers; sauté 5 minutes. Add the tomatoes and basil; cover and cook over low heat 30 minutes, stirring frequently. Mix in the anchovies, capers and olives; taste for seasoning. Cook over low heat for 10 minutes. Mix in the parsley.

Toss the spaghetti with the butter and cheese. Then pour the sauce over it. Serves 4–6.

SCAMPI WITH FETTUCCINE

1 cup chopped onion
½ cup butter
2 pounds raw scampi or jumbo shrimp,
  shelled and cleaned
¼ cup cognac
¼ cup flour
1 cup clam juice
1 cup light cream
½ cup tomato purée
  Salt, pepper to taste
1 pound fettuccine, cooked
  Melted butter
  Grated Parmesan cheese

Cook the onion in ¼ cup butter until wilted; add the shrimp and cook 5 minutes. Remove from heat, add the cognac and flame. Make a sauce by melting the remaining ¼ cup of butter, adding the flour and mixing well for a minute or two, then adding the clam juice, cream, tomato purée, salt and pepper. Cook slowly for 5 minutes, or until thick and smooth. Combine with the shrimp. Toss the cooked fettuccine with melted butter and pour the shrimp mixture over it. Pass freshly grated Parmesan cheese. Serves 8.

SPAGHETTI WITH TRUFFLES

    6 anchovies
    ¼ cup olive oil
    2 cloves garlic, split
    2 tablespoons tomato paste
    ¼ teaspoon freshly ground black pepper
    2 truffles, chopped
    ½ pound spaghetti, cooked and drained

Wash and drain the anchovies; chop. Heat the oil in a saucepan; cook the garlic in it until browned and remove. Add the anchovies and mash in the oil with a wooden spoon. Mix the tomato paste with 1 cup water, and add with the pepper. Cook over low heat 15 minutes. Taste for seasoning and stir in the truffles. Pour over the spaghetti. Serves 2–3.

LASAGNA SCARPELLINO

    2 pounds Italian sausage, sliced
      Olive oil
    2 1-pound, 13-ounce cans Italian plum tomatoes
    6-ounce can tomato paste
      Salt, pepper, oregano to taste
    2 cloves garlic, halved
    1 pound lasagna noodles (Italian kind with
      rippled edges)
    1 package sliced mozzarella cheese
    1 package ricotta cheese
    1 egg, beaten

Cook the sausage with a little olive oil in a heavy saucepan until brown. Add the tomatoes and tomato paste. Season with salt, pepper and oregano. Add garlic, cover and simmer for 2 hours. Remove garlic.

Cook the noodles for 20 minutes in plenty of salted water. Run cold water over them and spread them out, one by one, on a clean cloth.

In a rectangular baking dish arrange layers in the following order: noodles, slices of mozzarella, the ricotta which has been mixed with the beaten egg, and the tomato sauce. Repeat until the dish is full, ending with noodles and sauce. There will be some sauce left. Reserve it.

Refrigerate overnight. Next day bake in a 375° oven for 25 minutes. Heat extra sauce and put some on top of each portion. Serves 6.

BRAINS WITH LASAGNA

    ½ pound ground beef
    ½ pound ground veal
    2 tablespoons butter
    1 pound brains, parboiled and chopped
    1 cup chopped cooked spinach
    ¼ cup grated Parmesan cheese
    1 tablespoon minced parsley
    2 teaspoons salt
    ½ teaspoon crushed rosemary
      Pepper to taste
      Light cream
    6 ounces cooked lasagna
      Butter or olive oil
      Grated Parmesan cheese

Cook beef and veal in butter until lightly browned. Add brains, spinach, cheese, parsley, seasonings and enough cream to make mixture soft. Arrange a layer of lasagna in a buttered casserole, add a layer of meat mixture and continue in that order until casserole is full, making top layer lasagna. Brush top with butter or oil, sprinkle with grated cheese and bake in a 350° oven for 20 minutes. Serves 6.

SHELLFISH WITH LINGUINE

    3 pounds mussels
    2 tablespoons finely chopped shallots or green
      onions
    ½ clove garlic, finely chopped
      Pinch of thyme

½ bay leaf
  Salt, freshly ground black pepper to taste
½ cup dry white wine
1 teaspoon butter
18 raw shrimp, shelled and deveined
½ pound scallops
1 cup cream
2 egg yolks
1 teaspoon lemon juice
1 pound linguine, cooked

Scrub the mussels thoroughly and place them in a deep kettle. Add the shallots, garlic, thyme, bay leaf, salt, pepper, wine and butter. Cover and steam the mussels until they open, about 5 minutes. Discard any mussels that do not open. Remove mussels from their shells and keep warm. Strain the liquid in which they cooked.

Add the shrimp and scallops to the mussel liquid and cook gently about 5 minutes. Remove the shrimp and scallops and keep warm with the mussels.

Reduce the cooking liquid by half and add ½ cup of the cream. Season to taste with salt and pepper and simmer 3 minutes. Return the mussels, shrimp and scallops to the sauce. Blend the yolks with the remaining cream and add a little of the hot sauce. Stir well and return to the balance of the sauce. Heat thoroughly, but do not boil. Add lemon juice and serve with linguine or thin spaghetti cooked according to package directions. Serves 4–6.

CASSEROLE OF VEGETABLES AND PASTA

1 pound small pasta (elbow macaroni, shells or
  whatever shape you like)
2 tablespoons butter
2 tablespoons olive oil
1 cup minced parsley
1 clove garlic, sliced
3 medium onions, sliced
  Pinch of oregano, salt, pepper
3 medium tomatoes, peeled and cut in eighths
3 medium zucchini, sliced ¼″ thick
  with skins on
1 cup clear chicken or beef broth
  Butter, grated Parmesan cheese

Cook pasta according to package directions, but slightly underdone. Drain and keep hot.

Heat butter and oil in a large iron or earthenware casserole. In this, sauté the parsley, garlic, onions with a pinch of oregano. When the onions are golden, add the tomatoes, zucchini and chicken or beef broth. Season to taste with salt and pepper. Cover and cook until zucchini is tender.

Combine with the pasta which has been lightly buttered. Cover with grated Parmesan cheese, dot with butter and brown under the broiler. Hot French or Italian bread, a good *vin ordinaire* and a salad should accompany this hearty dish. Serves 6.

PASTA WITH BEANS

1 pound dried cannelini or pea beans (or 2 to
  3 cups canned cooked white beans)
1 cup parsley, chopped
3 cloves garlic, pressed
2 large onions, finely chopped
2 medium carrots, finely chopped
¼ pound bacon, finely chopped
2 tablespoons dried basil leaves
1 teaspoon oregano
¼ cup olive oil
3 large tomatoes, peeled and chopped
½ cup bouillon
1 tablespoon salt
1 teaspoon pepper
4 tablespoons butter
1 pound ditalini or elbow macaroni, cooked
  according to package directions
  Grated Parmesan cheese
  Chopped parsley

If dried beans are used, soak overnight in water to cover. Drain. Simmer slowly 1–2 hours, or until nearly tender. Drain. If canned beans are used, drain only. Combine parsley, garlic, onion, carrots, bacon, basil leaves and oregano, and sauté in hot olive oil in large kettle until all are limp. Add tomatoes, bouillon, salt and pepper. Cover, and simmer the mixture slowly, stirring, for about 10 minutes or until all the vegetables are tender.

Add cooked, drained beans. Simmer very slowly for 20–30 minutes. Just before serving, melt the butter and toss cooked pasta lightly with butter and ½ cup grated cheese. At serving time, combine with other mixture and serve sprinkled liberally with parsley and with more grated cheese. Serves 8.

MACCHERONI CON LE SARDE

This is a delicious Sicilian dish which is unusual in many ways and a real show-stopper whenever it is served. The recipe calls for fresh sardines, but if you cannot get them, you might use smelts.

1 pound fresh sardines
1 large onion, chopped
  Olive oil
6 tomatoes, peeled, seeded and chopped
½ cup sultana raisins
½ cup pine nuts
1 tiny envelope (about ¼ teaspoon) saffron
½ teaspoon basil
1 small can anchovy fillets, finely chopped
  Flour
  Salt, pepper
1½ cups bread crumbs
2 heads fresh fennel
1 pound good semolina macaroni

Skin and fillet half the sardines and cut into small pieces. Sauté the onion in ¼ cup olive oil. Add the tomatoes and the cut-up sardines. Cook until soft. Add the raisins, pine nuts, saffron, basil and the anchovies. Cook this sauce down for 3–4 minutes.

Flour the remaining sardines and sauté in olive oil until brown and crisp. Salt and pepper to taste.

Heat the crumbs with ¼ cup oil, or more if they absorb it all. Wash and slice the fennel very thinly, and cook in 2½ quarts salted water. When nearly tender, add the macaroni and cook until done.

Drain the macaroni and fennel and blend with the sauce. Butter a baking dish and make a layer of the macaroni-fennel mixture, a layer of crumbs and a layer of the sautéed sardines. Top with macaroni. Strew the top with crumbs, and sprinkle with oil. Bake at 350° for 20 minutes. Serves 4.

BAKED MACARONI AND TOMATOES

4 cups cooked elbow macaroni (2 cups uncooked)
4–6 medium tomatoes, peeled and sliced
¾ teaspoon salt
1½ teaspoons sugar
½ teaspoon basil
¼ cup flour
2 tablespoons heavy cream
½ cup soft white bread crumbs
1 tablespoon butter

Grease or oil a 1½-quart casserole. Arrange a layer of cooked macaroni over bottom and add a layer of sliced tomatoes. Combine salt, sugar, basil and flour and sprinkle tomatoes with half this mixture. Add more macaroni, more tomatoes and remaining seasoning mixture. Pour cream over top, then add crumbs and dot with butter. Cover casserole and bake in a 375° oven for 45 minutes. Uncover the casserole during the last 15 minutes to allow the crumbs to brown slightly. Serves 4.

MARVELOUS MACARONI AND CHEESE

2 cups elbow macaroni (8 ounces)
3 tablespoons butter
¼ cup chopped onion
3 tablespoons flour
½ teaspoon salt
⅛ teaspoon pepper
1 cup heavy cream
½ cup dry white wine
2 cups grated sharp Cheddar cheese (about 8 ounces)

Cook the macaroni according to package directions. Drain and reserve. Heat the butter and cook the onion until tender. Stir in the flour, salt, and pepper. Slowly add the cream and wine and cook over low heat, stirring constantly, until thickened. Add the cheese and stir until melted. Mix together the macaroni and cheese sauce. Put into a greased 1½-quart casserole. Bake in a preheated 350° oven for 15 minutes, or until thoroughly heated through. With this, have buttered fresh leaf spinach. Serves 4.

Sauce & Stuffing

Throughout the centuries, stuffings and sauces have served as the handmaidens of cuisine, giving to other foods the savor and substance they lack, dressing up the drab and disguising the occasional imperfection. The spendthrift Romans employed stuffings more to astonish the eye than pleasure the palate, and the more expensive the hidden cargo, the greater the status of the host. The censors finally clamped down on one particular piece of ostentation—the "Trojan pig," packed with thrushes, ortolans and figpeckers, in simulation of the armed men in the Trojan horse. While cooks of the sixteenth and seventeenth centuries were occasionally called on to produce similar ludicrous "surprises," such as pies filled with live birds or frogs, or chickens with unexpected interior trimmings, most stuffings were both edible and suitable—fruit in duck, oysters in capon, chestnuts in suckling pig. Many of the old recipes are surprisingly long-lived. The veal olaves in Gervase Markham's The English Housewife, published in 1651, are none other than our veal birds or the French alouettes sans têtes (the English, rugged traditionalists, still call stuffed meat rolls "olives").

The great sauces of the world are mainly French inventions or adaptations. Their names roll like a parade of Gallic history—Soubise, Mornay, Talleyrand, Béchamel, Colbert, Chateaubriand, Mayonnaise—for the French believed that men and battles are best immortalized in the deathless language of gastronomy. Nor were they loath to credit their sources. When the Dutch idea of serving fish with a lavishment of melted butter was carried one step further by the French, the simple beurre Hollandaise, thickened and transmuted with egg yolks, became the glorious Hollandaise sauce. The annals of cuisine are full of such memorable moments. Tomato sauce was the inspiration of a chef at the Spanish court who audaciously combined the strange fruit with onions and olive oil. Duxelles resulted from La Varenne's infatuation with the ineffable flavor of mushrooms.

Today, we cull our sauces and stuffings from the four corners of the world, using them to lend a touch of the exotic to everyday foods—the velvety tartness of avgolemono, the Greek national sauce, on a plain green vegetable; the sweet-and-salty savor of Japanese sashimi sauce with clams; the rum-soaked fruitiness of a Haitian Kenscoff dressing in a roast bird; the delicate crispness of a Chinois dressing filling out a baked fish.

Allow roughly 1 cup of stuffing per pound of poultry, and rather more than ½ cup per pound for meat and fish. Some stuffings bulk more after cooking, so you will find this a fairly generous estimate. Stuff lightly. Any excess stuffing can be baked in a greased casserole and basted with pan drippings or melted butter. As seasoning is a matter of taste, precook a tiny bit of stuffing, taste, and adjust the seasoning to suit. Be sure to stuff just before cooking, so there is no chance of the mixture spoiling.

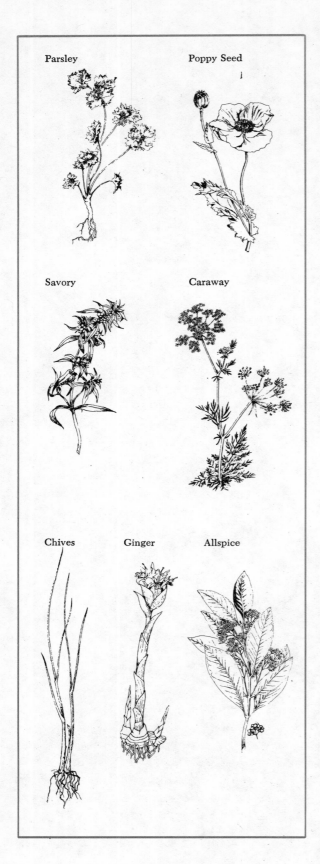

Parsley Poppy Seed

Savory Caraway

Chives Ginger Allspice

BASIC BREAD STUFFING

A basic bread stuffing is exceedingly accommodating because it lends itself to all kinds of additions and flavorings. Fresh bread crumbs, made in the blender or on a rather coarse grater, are preferable to commercially packaged crumbs. For a dry stuffing, the crumbs may be made from homemade Melba toast.

> ½ pound (or more) butter
> 1 cup finely chopped shallots, onions,
>   or spring onions
> 8 cups (approx.) fresh bread crumbs,
>   crusts and all
> 1 tablespoon fresh tarragon (or more to taste)
>   or 2 teaspoons dried tarragon, moistened
> 1 cup finely chopped parsley
> 1 tablespoon salt, or to taste
> 1½ teaspoons freshly ground black pepper

Place the butter, shallots, or onions in a saucepan, and allow the butter to melt over low heat. Do not sauté the shallots. Combine with the crumbs and other ingredients and toss lightly. Add more melted butter if needed, and taste for seasoning. This makes enough stuffing for a 10-pound bird.

Herb Variations: Instead of tarragon you can use any of the following herbs to taste. (It is better not to mix herbs, except for the addition of parsley, but mix if you must.)

1. About 1½ teaspoons dried thyme, soaked in a little white wine for an hour.
2. Sage. Use with discretion, or it smothers all other flavors in the stuffing.
3. Summer savory. This has a delicious flavor for turkey and is less known than most herbs.
4. Basil. The fresh is delicious, but it is only available in summer, when it is superb in the stuffing of a spitted bird. If fresh is not available, use about 2 teaspoons of dried basil, soaked in white wine.

Another way to give the flavor of fresh basil to your dressing is by adding pesto, the Italian sauce normally used with pasta. Again, pesto can be made only in summer, when fresh basil is in the market or in your herb garden, but fortunately it freezes rather well, so it is possible to have it at any time of year. Add about 3 tablespoons of pesto or more to the basic bird stuffing.

PESTO

>   2 cups fresh basil leaves
>   3 cloves garlic
>   1 cup parsley
>   ⅔ cup pine nuts
>   Olive oil, about 1 cup

Blend all ingredients in a blender, or pound in a mortar until they form a soft paste. The amount of oil used depends on the method. If you use the blender, it is best to make the pesto in two batches, using enough oil each time to cover the blades of the blender—about ½ cup. In the mortar method, add the oil a little at a time, until the paste has reached the proper consistency. It should not be too runny. Makes about 1¼ cups.

To store unused portion of pesto, place in a jar and cover the surface with a film of olive oil. Wrap in foil or plastic wrap. Keep in refrigerator, or freeze.

Additives for Basic Bread Stuffing

You will have to reduce the amount of crumbs, depending upon the quantity of additive.

1. 1½–2 cups coarsely broken cooked chestnuts. (These may be purchased in tins.)
2. 1 cup or more toasted salted filberts.
3. 1 cup or more toasted unblanched almonds.
4. 1 cup or more salted pecan halves.
5. 1½–2 cups toasted walnut halves.
6. 2 cups finely diced celery. This makes a delicious change in the stuffing and is also good in goose.
7. 1½ cups of finely diced fennel bulb. Omit any other herb save parsley.
8. A head of finely shredded Boston lettuce. Added to the basic stuffing at the last minute, this is surprisingly good. You may need additional salt.

SAUSAGE STUFFING

You may, if you like, stuff the body cavity of the bird with the bread stuffing, using one of the variations given above, and the neck cavity with the following very highly seasoned sausage meat stuffing.

>   2 pounds shoulder or loin of pork (about 60 per cent lean, 40 per cent fat), ground coarsely
>   1½ teaspoons salt

>   1 teaspoon freshly ground black pepper
>   ½ teaspoon ginger
>   1 teaspoon or more of desired herb
>   Large dash Tabasco
>   ½ teaspoon crushed anise seeds

Blend all ingredients for the stuffing lightly but well. Makes 3 cups.

CORN BREAD STUFFING

>   ¼ pound (or more) butter
>   1¼ cups finely chopped onion
>   1 cup finely diced celery
>   ½ cup chopped celery tops
>   1½ teaspoons thyme
>   1 pound small link sausages or chipolatas, lightly browned
>   1 tablespoon salt or more, to taste
>   1½ teaspoons freshly ground black pepper
>   6–8 cups coarse corn bread crumbs
>   ¾ cup Madeira

Melt the butter in a saucepan with the chopped onion. Add the celery, celery tops, and thyme. Sauté the sausages gently or broil them. Add the salt and pepper to the crumbs and mix with the onion-celery mixture, the sausages, and the Madeira. Add more melted butter or some of the rendered sausage fat, if needed. Taste for seasoning. Makes enough stuffing for a 10-pound bird.

Variations:

1. Omit sausages and add 1 cup whole kernel corn and ½ cup finely chopped green chiles (or 1 cup, if you like the taste of chiles). Substitute ½ cup cognac for the Madeira.
2. Omit sausages. Sauté ½ pound sausage meat with the onions, breaking it up well. Add to the stuffing with 1 cup pecans.
3. Omit sausages. Add 1½ cups finely shredded Smithfield ham to the stuffing. Sauté the onions in ham fat instead of butter.
4. Omit sausages. Add 2 cups crisp crumbled bacon to the stuffing. Sauté onions in bacon fat.
5. Omit sausages and celery. Add 2 cups coarsely chopped Smithfield ham and 2 cups coarsely chopped, roasted and salted peanuts or toasted and salted filberts.

6. If you like oysters in a stuffing, add about 2 dozen oysters with their liquor.

LANCASTER COUNTY STUFFING

A Pennsylvania Dutch specialty particularly suitable for goose, duck, or a fat capon.

> 1 large onion, sliced in eighths
> 1 small clove garlic, minced
> ⅓ cup rendered poultry or bacon fat
> 6–8 ounces any liver, chopped
> ⅓ cup chopped celery
> 2½ cups mashed potatoes blended with
>   ½ teaspoon baking powder
> 4 cups croutons
> 2 teaspoons chopped parsley
> 2 teaspoons salt
> ½ teapoon poultry seasoning
> ¼ teaspoon pepper
> ⅛ teaspoon each: savory, sage
> Dash rosemary

Sauté the onion and garlic in a large covered skillet in the fat until golden brown. Add the liver and cook, stirring, until it loses color. Add the celery and cook, covered, about 3 minutes. Scrape the bottom of the skillet well, and add the sautéed mixture with the drippings to the mashed potatoes. Add all other ingredients and blend thoroughly. Cool before using. Makes a generous 9 cups.

PORT-AU-PRINCE DRESSING

An unusual stuffing for turkey or other birds, veal, tomatoes, cucumbers, squash, chayote, rutabagas, onions, peppers, beets, and cabbage rolls.

> ½ pound dried black mushrooms
> ½ pound pork loin or shoulder, diced fine
> ¼" slice salt pork, diced
> 3 kosher frankfurters, sliced
> 1 clove garlic, minced
> 1 tablespoon oil
> 3 scallions, including tops, minced
> 1½ teaspoons salt
> ¼ teaspoon each: Tabasco, thyme
> 1 cup raw rice
> 1 medium green pepper, cut julienne

Snip the mushrooms into bits with kitchen shears. Cover with 2½ cups hot water and soak 30 minutes, squeezing occasionally to darken the water. Sauté meats and garlic in oil in a large skillet until browned. Add the softened mushrooms in their liquor and the remaining ingredients. Bring to a boil, then lower heat, cover, and simmer until liquid has been absorbed, about 15–20 minutes. Cool dressing before using. Makes approximately 8 cups.

BACON AND CHESTNUT DRESSING

A hearty stuffing for turkey and other poultry; or for flank steak, beef heart, breast of veal, cabbage, turnips, tomatoes, peppers, and mushrooms.

> 3 medium onions, minced
> 1 stalk celery, chopped
> ½ pound slab bacon, diced
> 10 slices day-old bread, toasted and diced
> 1 pound chestnuts, cooked and coarsely chopped
> 1 teaspoon salt
> ½ teaspoon poultry seasoning
> ⅛ teaspoon each: thyme, pepper
> ⅔–¾ cup broth or water

Sauté the onion, celery, and bacon until golden. Drain off all but 3 tablespoons of drippings and add contents of pan to the bread, chestnuts, salt, poultry seasoning, thyme and pepper. Mix thoroughly, adding enough broth or water to bring the dressing to the desired consistency. Makes about 7 cups.

FARCE HENRY IV

A delicate dressing for boiled or braised chicken, a whole head of cabbage, or vegetables.

> 2 cups stale bread crumbs
> ½ cup warm milk
> 1 set giblets, minced (optional)
> ¼ pound boiled ham, chopped fine
> ¼ cup chopped celery
> 4 large mushrooms, chopped
> 1 teaspoon salt
> ½ teaspoon pepper
> Dash each: sage, thyme, mace
> 1 egg, well beaten

Soak the crumbs in the milk for 20 minutes. Add remaining ingredients and mix all together well. Makes a good 3 cups.

CHATEAUBRIAND STUFFING

This traditional stuffing for goose is equally good for turkey and savoy or red cabbage.

> 3 pounds pork sausage meat, fresh or smoked
> 1 large onion, chopped
> 1 clove garlic, minced
> 1½ dozen chestnuts, cooked and halved
> ¼ cup cognac
> ¼ cup diced black truffle
> 2 teaspoons salt
> ¼ teaspoon each: pepper, nutmeg

Brown the sausage meat, onion, and garlic lightly. Add with 3 tablespoons of the pan drippings to the remaining ingredients. Mix well.

Use white wine or a dry apple cider for basting goose, and for added bounce, flame after roasting with calvados or applejack. Makes about 12 cups.

FARCE CHAMPENOISE

A classic stuffing, excellent for chicken or a wine-basted cabbage head, or for cucumbers, rutabagas, turnips, summer squash, chayote, or mushrooms.

> 1 medium onion, chopped fine
> 1 clove garlic, minced
> 2 teaspoons minced shallot
> 3 tablespoons butter
> ¾ cup flat champagne or other dry white wine
> 2 chicken livers, minced
> 1 pound pork sausage meat
> 1 tablespoon minced parsley
> 1 teaspoon salt
> ⅛ teaspoon pepper

Sauté the onion, garlic, and shallot in the butter in a large skillet until soft and faintly colored. Drain, add the wine and simmer until the mixture is reduced by half. Cook livers and sausage meat in another skillet for 5 minutes, and pour off all but about 3 tablespoons fat. Combine with the onion-wine mixture

and remaining ingredients and mix together thoroughly. Makes about 5 cups.

RELLENO CRIOLLO

A south-of-the-border favorite that is especially good with any of the drier game birds or Rock Cornish hens, the coarser fish, and veal, eggplant, tomatoes, squash, onions, and peppers.

> 1½ cups diced, cooked ham
> 3 cups crumbled corn bread
> 1 small onion, grated
> 2 tablespoons chopped parsley, or 1 tablespoon
>   each: chopped parsley, cilantro
> 1 tablespoon chili powder
> 2 teaspoons salt
> ⅛ teaspoon each: cumin, pepper
> 1 egg
> ¼ cup melted butter

Combine ingredients in order given. Toss lightly. Makes a scant 5 cups.

EASTERN SHORE DRESSING

A perfect stuffing for turkey and almost any other kind of bird.

> ½ pound pork sausage meat, preferably smoked
> 1 set giblets (from turkey or selected
>   bird), ground
> 1 cup minced green pepper
> 1 cup minced celery
> ½ cup minced onion
> ½ cup minced shallot
> 1 large clove garlic, minced
> 1 cup finely chopped walnuts
> ½ cup minced mushrooms
> 4 hard-cooked eggs, riced
> 2 teaspoons each: chopped parsley,
> • celery leaves
> 6 cups crumbled corn bread
> 2 tablespoons salt
> ½ teaspoon pepper
> 1 large bay leaf, crumbled
>   Broth or boiling water

Sauté the sausage meat and ground giblets 4 minutes

HOW TO MAKE STUFFED CABBAGE ROLLS

Cut hard core from blanched leaf.

Overlap cut edges. Put stuffing in the center. Pull top of leaf over it.

Roll up, tucking in leaf at sides.

Push loose end inside as you roll.

Cabbage roll ready to pack in pan.

in a large skillet, then remove. Add to the pan drippings the pepper, celery, onion, shallot, and garlic, and sauté 5 minutes. Add the walnuts, mushrooms, eggs, parsley, celery leaves, corn bread, and seasonings. Mix well, then add enough broth or boiling water to bring dressing to desired consistency. Makes about 14 cups.

OYSTER STUFFING

Superb for the Christmas turkey.

> 11 tablespoons butter
> 3 pounds chestnuts, cooked and riced, or 2½–3 cups canned unsweetened chestnut purée
> 2 teaspoons salt
> ¼ cup heavy cream
> 1 cup chopped celery
> 1 large onion, minced
> 8 cups day-old bread crumbs
> ¼ teaspoon each: pepper, sweet paprika
> ⅛ teaspoon thyme (optional)
> ¼ cup chopped parsley
> 2 dozen large oysters, shucked, coarsely chopped

Melt 8 tablespoons of the butter and beat into the riced chestnuts with the salt and heavy cream to make a fluffy purée. Sauté the celery and onion in the remaining 3 tablespoons butter until limp. Add the remaining ingredients and mix all together well. Makes about 16 cups.

RHUMBA DRESSING

Despite its Cuban name, this dressing comes from Hawaii, where it is a favorite for small suckling pigs. It may also be used for crown roast of pork, zucchini, eggplant, and artichokes.

> 6 cups soft bread crumbs
> ⅔ cup minced onion
> 4–6 anchovy fillets, minced
> ¼ teaspoon salt
> ⅛ teaspoon pepper
>   Dash Tabasco
> 1 cup claret
> ¼ cup melted butter

Combine ingredients in a bowl in order given and toss lightly. Makes about 6 cups.

RELLENO À LA ZARAGOZANA

This delicious stuffing for fish is named for the Havana café whose specialty it was.

    1½ cups flaked lobster or crab meat,
       or chopped raw shrimp
    2 tablespoons lime juice
    2 tablespoons light Bacardi rum
    1 tablespoon grated onion
    1 tablespoon capers
    1 teaspoon Tabasco
    ¼ cup diced hard ripe avocado
    ¼ cup chopped mushrooms
    1 egg beaten with 1 tablespoon olive oil
    ¾–1 cup fine cracker crumbs
    Pinch each: dry mustard, mace, basil

Combine the seafood, lime juice, rum, onion, capers, and Tabasco and let stand 3 hours in the refrigerator. Drain slightly and add all remaining ingredients, using sufficient crumbs to make consistency desired. Makes about 3 cups.

YANKEE CLAM DRESSING

A Down-East favorite for fish, but also good for onions, tomatoes, cucumbers, or eggplant.

    ½ cup chopped clams
    2 cups fine cracker crumbs
    2 tablespoons melted butter
    2 tablespoons lemon juice
    2 teaspoons chopped sweet pickles or gherkins
       or Indian relish
    ½–⅔ cup clam liquor or water
    1 egg (optional)
    ¼ teaspoon salt
    ⅛ teaspoon black pepper or cayenne

Combine ingredients in order given and mix lightly, adding egg if a firmer dressing is desired. Makes about 2½ cups.

SHRIMP DRESSING OLIVETTE

A versatile dressing for veal birds or fish, for avocado, eggplant, chayote, onions, tomatoes, squash, cucumbers, and peppers.

    2 tablespoons butter
    1 teaspoon anchovy paste
    1 heaping cup soft bread crumbs
    ¾ cup minced, cooked shrimp
    2 tablespoons chopped green or ripe olives
    1–2 tablespoons grated onion
    4 teaspoons lime juice
    ½ teaspoon Tabasco

Heat the butter, anchovy paste, and 1½ teaspoons water until the butter melts, then blend smooth. Add to bread crumbs and blend well. Add remaining ingredients. Makes a scant 2 cups.

EAST INDIAN DRESSING

A spicy stuffing for fish, particularly sea bass, snapper, and carp; also for chicken, crab shells, Chinese cabbage rolls, tomatoes, peppers, and cucumbers.

    2 6½-ounce cans crab meat
    1 cup stale bread, pulled into pieces
    ½ cup minced onion
    ½ cup grated coconut
    1 clove garlic, minced
    2 tablespoons peanut oil
    1 tablespoon curry powder
    1 teaspoon salt
    Dash each: turmeric, ginger
    1 tablespoon chopped cilantro
    ½ cup drained bean sprouts
    1 egg

Drain the crab meat, reserving the liquid; pick over to remove any cartilage, then shred. Pour the reserved liquid over the bread, add a bit of water, if necessary, and let soak 10 minutes. Squeeze fairly dry and crumble. Sauté the onion, coconut, and garlic in the oil with the spices and cilantro until golden. Add the bean sprouts and cook about 1 minute more. Combine with the crumbled bread and egg and toss all ingredients together. Makes about 4 cups.

CHINOIS DRESSING

The subtle oriental flavor makes this a good dressing for duckling or fish (basted with dry vermouth), tomatoes, Chinese cabbage rolls, peppers, mushrooms, or Bermuda onions.

> 1 medium onion, minced
> 1½ cups diced celery
> 3 tablespoons peanut oil
> 1½ cups boiled rice
> 1 cup chopped water chestnuts
> 2 teaspoons grated green ginger
> 1–2 teaspoons shoyu or soy sauce
> ⅛ teaspoon pepper
> Dash sugar
> Dash dry mustard
> 1 tablespoon chopped cilantro (for fish)

Sauté the onion and celery in the oil until pale gold. Drain and add remaining ingredients. Mix well. Makes approximately 4 cups.

STUFFING À LA RUSSE

This rich filling is equally good for birds, meat, fish, or vegetables.

> 1 pound narrow egg noodles, cooked and cooled
> 1 egg beaten with ¼ cup sour cream
> ½ pound mushrooms, sliced
> 2 tablespoons butter
> ¼ teaspoon sweet or hot paprika
> Dash nutmeg
> ¼ cup fine dry bread crumbs
> Grated zest of ½ lemon
> 1 tablespoon minced parsley and/or chives
> 1 teaspoon salt
> ⅛ teaspoon pepper (omit if hot paprika is used)
> Dash beefsteak or Worcestershire sauce

Mix the noodles thoroughly with the egg and cream mixture. Simmer the mushrooms in the butter 15 minutes, seasoning with paprika and nutmeg. Stir in all remaining ingredients. Toss thoroughly with noodle mixture. Makes approximately 7 cups.

MACADAMIA STUFFING

A delicious dressing for chicken, white meats, bland vegetables, flounder, or red snapper.

> 1½ cups chopped celery
> ½ cup minced onion

> 1 clove garlic, minced
> 5 tablespoons butter
> ⅔ cup coarsely chopped Macadamia nuts
> 4 cups crushed baking-powder biscuits
> ½ cup milk or broth (optional)
> 1½ teaspoons salt (or less, if nuts are salted)
> ½ teaspoon marjoram or poultry seasoning
> ¼ teaspoon black pepper or cayenne to taste

Sauté the celery, onion, and garlic in the butter until the celery is slightly soft and the onion is transparent. Add the nuts and toss thoroughly. Combine with the crushed biscuits, adding liquid, if desired, and the seasonings. Makes 6 cups.

ORANGE-CRESS STUFFING

A very tasty stuffing for rich fowl like goose and duck, meat, or oily fish such as mackerel and blue (omit nuts when using for fish). It is also excellent in baked pumpkin, winter squash or onions, basted with bacon fat.

> ½ cup minced onion
> ½ cup broken walnuts (optional)
> ¼ cup butter or bacon fat
> 6 cups toasted bread cubes or 3 cups each shredded stale bread and crushed shredded-wheat biscuits
> 2 cups orange sections, halved and seeded
> 1 cup chopped watercress (leaves only)
> 1½ teaspoons salt
> 1 teaspoon grated orange zest
> ½ teaspoon sweet paprika
> Generous dash hot red chili pepper, crushed

Sauté the onion and walnuts, if used, in the butter or fat until slightly golden. Add with the pan drippings to the remaining ingredients, combining thoroughly. Makes about 8 cups.

PARMENTIER DRESSING

A hearty potato stuffing for birds, rolled beefsteak or a beef heart, pork, or veal.

> 6 large potatoes, peeled
> 2 medium onions
> ½ celery root

2 tablespoons butter
½ cup melted poultry fat or drippings
¼ cup chopped parsley
1 teaspoon each: salt, poultry
　　seasoning (optional)
½ teaspoon sweet paprika
¼ teaspoon pepper

Put the potatoes, 1 onion, and the celery root through the coarsest blade of a food chopper. Dice the remaining onion and sauté in the butter until lightly browned. Add the melted fat, parsley, and seasonings, and cook 2 minutes. Drain the potato mixture and combine thoroughly with the other ingredients. Makes about 4 cups.

MUSHROOM DRESSING FINES HERBES

This stuffing might be called the "universal dressing." It is easy to prepare and good with any bird, any meat, any fish, any seafood, and any vegetable.

　　1½ cups coarsely chopped fresh mushrooms
　　2 tablespoons minced shallot
　　¼ cup butter
　　2 cups stale crumbs (any bread, baking powder
　　　　biscuits, corn pone, etc.)
　　2 heaping tablespoons each: chopped parsley,
　　　　chives, any fresh herb
　　1 small bay leaf, crumbled
　　1 scant teaspoon salt
　　½ teaspoon sweet paprika
　　⅛ teaspoon each: mace, pepper
　　　　Dash nutmeg

Sauté the mushrooms and shallot in the butter for 5 minutes. Add to the remaining ingredients. Toss thoroughly. Makes approximately 4 cups.

MUSHROOM-RICE STUFFING

　　¼ pound mushrooms
　　2 tablespoons butter
　　1 medium onion, chopped
　　1 tablespoon red wine
　　　　Salt, pepper to taste
　　6 slices bacon, cooked, drained, and crumbled
　　½ cup chopped pecans

2 tablespoons chopped dill
2 cups cooked rice

Wash and dry mushrooms. Cut off stem ends. Slice.

Melt the butter in a skillet. Add the onion and sauté until tender. Add the mushrooms, wine, salt, and pepper. Sauté 5 minutes. Add the bacon, pecans, dill, and rice. Mix well. Use to stuff tomatoes, poultry, eggplant, rolled meat slices, or fish. Makes 4 cups.

DUXELLES

　　1 pound mushrooms
　　3 tablespoons minced onions
　　3 tablespoons minced shallots
　　4 tablespoons butter
　　2 tablespoons oil
　　　　Salt, pepper to taste
　　1 teaspoon chopped fresh parsley

Wash and dry the mushrooms and cut off tough stem ends. Chop mushrooms as fine as possible. Press in a cloth to remove any moisture. Sauté the onions and shallots in the butter and oil over a high flame for 1 minute, stirring constantly. Add the minced mushrooms and lower the flame. Sauté over low heat until all the moisture has evaporated and the mixture is quite dark. This may take an hour or more. Season with salt and pepper and mix in the parsley. Makes 2 cups.

Note: This classic mushroom mixture freezes well and may be used in many interesting ways. Here are some suggestions:
1. Use as a filling for mushroom caps.

2. Use to stuff scooped-out vegetables such as tomatoes and onions.
3. Mix with herb-flavored bread crumbs and use as a stuffing for chicken or game.

PARSNIP STUFFING

An unusual and interesting dressing for chicken, Rock Cornish hens, squab, pork chops, or onions.

> 3 parsnips, peeled and shredded
> ½ cup chopped celery leaves
> 1 small onion, grated
> ⅓ cup butter
> 3½ cups toasted bread cubes
> 8 cardamom seeds, pounded
> 1 teaspoon salt
> ⅛ teaspoon each: mace, pepper

Cook the parsnips, celery leaves, and onion in the butter over low heat, stirring, about 4 minutes. Add remaining ingredients and mix. Makes a scant 5 cups.

FARCE MIRABELLE

An unusual dressing for a holiday goose, duckling, breast of veal or beef.

> 8 cups crumbled white bread or white corn pone
> 1½ cups canned purple plums, drained and cut into eighths
> ⅔ cup minced celery
> ⅔–1 cup orange juice
> 2–3 tablespoons brown sugar (optional)

> 1 egg
> 1 scant tablespoon grated orange rind
> 1½ teaspoon salt
> ¼ teaspoon each: ginger, cinnamon, pepper

Toss the bread with the plums and celery. Blend the orange juice with the sugar, if used, and the egg, and pour over the bread mixture. Add the orange rind and seasonings and toss thoroughly. Let stand about 20 minutes before using. Makes about 10 cups.

KENSCOFF DRESSING

This is a Haitian favorite traditionally used for guinea fowl. Try it, too, for squab and small game birds, spit-roasted and basted with a spicy blend of lime juice, rum, and Tabasco.

> 2½ cups ¼″ croutons
> 2 cups banana purée
> 1 tablespoon each: lime juice, grated lime zest
> 1 tablespoon dark rum
> ½ teaspoon salt
> ⅛ teaspoon Tabasco
> Generous dash each: nutmeg, cinnamon, cloves

Mix all ingredients thoroughly. Makes about 4 cups.

FESTIVE STUFFING

A delicious holiday mixture for any bird or a crown roast of pork.

> 1½ cups cranberries
> 4 cups cooked wild rice
> ⅓ cup melted butter
> ⅓ cup golden corn syrup
> 1 small onion, grated
> 1 shallot, minced
> 1 teaspoon salt
> ½ teaspoon marjoram
> ⅛ teaspoon pepper
> General dash each: dry mustard, mace, basil

Grind the cranberries through coarsest blade of food chopper into a large saucepan. Add the remaining ingredients and cook 10 minutes, stirring frequently. Cool before using. Makes 7 cups.

Kingston Stuffing

MINTED APPLE STUFFING

A delicious choice for duck or goose, mutton chops, boned lamb shoulder, pork shoulder, or a head of cabbage, especially if they are basted with cider.

> 6 cups diced day-old bread
> 2 cups chopped greenings (tart apples)
> 2 tablespoons chopped mint
> 1½ teaspoons salt
> ¼ teaspoon each: sweet paprika, pepper
> 2 teaspoons lemon juice

Toss all ingredients together. Makes about 8 cups.

APRICOT STUFFING AMANDINE

Delicate and not too sweet for a bird, or a breast of lamb or veal. Try it also for Bermuda onions with an apricot-juice glaze.

> 1 cup dried apricot halves
> 2 tablespoons lemon juice
> 1 tablespoon brown sugar
> 1 teaspoon salt
> ½ cup blanched, chopped almonds
> 5 cups diced, day-old cracked-wheat bread
> ½ cup melted butter

Bring apricots to a boil with the lemon juice, brown sugar, salt, and 1 cup water. Simmer 5 minutes, then drain, reserving liquid. When cool enough to handle, cut each apricot half into 3 or 4 strips. Mix with remaining ingredients, adding reserved liquid to bring

to proper consistency. Makes about 7 cups.

BEEF STOCK

> 3 pounds crossrib of beef
> 1 pound neck of veal
> 2 pounds beef knuckle and marrow bones
> 2 onions, sliced
> 2 leeks, sliced
> 1 teaspoon sugar
> 6 quarts water
> 1 small yellow turnip
> 2 white turnips
> 3 carrots
> 1 parsley root
> 4 stalks celery
> 2 tomatoes
>   Handful of parsley
> 4 bay leaves
> 6 peppercorns
>   Salt

In a large soup kettle, brown beef and veal in their own fat. Add bones, sliced onion and leeks. Sprinkle with sugar and stir until all have a rich, brown color. Add water, bring to a boil, skim off scum. Turn heat low and simmer, covered, for 1 hour. Pare turnips, scrape carrots and parsley root and slice all vegetables. After 1 hour, skim off scum again, add the vegetables, parsley, bay leaves and peppercorns. Simmer 3 hours longer. Bring to a boil and reduce stock to half. Strain, reserving meat for other use, and add salt to taste. Cool liquid and skim off fat. Reduce

further if a more concentrated stock is needed; add more water if a less concentrated flavor is desired. Makes about 3 pints.

CHICKEN STOCK

1 fowl
2 onions
2 leeks
1 celery root (celeriac or knob celery)
2 stalks celery
2 carrots
1 small parsnip
1 small parsley root
Rind of ¼ lemon
4 peppercorns
Salt

Put fowl in soup kettle with all vegetables, cleaned and sliced, lemon rind, peppercorns, and water to cover. Bring to a boil, skim off scum, turn heat low, cover and simmer for several hours, until chicken is tender. Remove chicken, reduce stock to half, strain, add salt to taste. Cool, skim off fat. Makes 2–3 pints.

COURT BOUILLON

1 pint water
1 pint white wine
Herb bouquet (parsley, bay, and thyme)
1 carrot, sliced
1 small onion, sliced
2 stalks celery
6 peppercorns

Combine all ingredients in a saucepan and simmer for 15 minutes before using. If preferred, the white wine may be omitted, and a tablespoon of vinegar added to a quart of water instead. Makes 1 quart. Increase quantity for cooking large fish.

WHITE WINE FISH FUMET

1½ pounds fish bones, heads, and trimmings
1½ quarts water
1 quart dry white wine
1 teaspoon dried thyme
2 medium onions stuck with 3 cloves each
2 carrots, sliced
1 clove garlic, crushed
1 bay leaf
Salt, pepper to taste

Cook the fish bones, heads, and trimmings in the water for half-an-hour, then strain through a fine cloth. Add all other ingredients, bring to a boil, and simmer for 20 minutes before adding the fish to be cooked. Makes 2 quarts.

RED WINE FISH FUMET

1½ pounds fish bones, heads, and trimmings
1½ quarts water
1 quart red wine
Herb bouquet (parsley, bay, and thyme)
2 stalks celery
1 onion stuck with 3 cloves
2 carrots, sliced
Salt, pepper

Proceed as for White Wine Fish Fumet, substituting red wine for white. Makes 2 quarts.

VELOUTÉ SAUCE

4 tablespoons butter
4 tablespoons flour
2½ cups chicken or fish stock

Melt the butter in a heavy saucepan and stir in the flour. Cook over very low heat, stirring constantly, for about 3 minutes. Gradually mix in the stock (chicken stock for poultry or meat dishes, fish stock for fish dishes) and cook over low heat, stirring constantly, until sauce comes to boiling point. Cook 20 minutes, stirring occasionally. Makes about 2 cups.

BÉCHAMEL SAUCE

3 cups milk
2 tablespoons minced onion
4 tablespoons butter
⅓ cup flour
½ teaspoon salt
Dash of white pepper

Bring the milk and onion to a boil, then let stand 10 minutes. Strain. Melt the butter in a heavy saucepan and stir in the flour. Cook over very low heat, stirring constantly, until the flour turns golden. Gradually mix in the milk and cook over low heat, stirring constantly, until sauce comes to boiling point. Cook over low heat for 20 minutes, stirring the sauce frequently. Makes about 2 cups.

Note: Béchamel sauce may be used wherever a white sauce or cream sauce is called for. You may substitute chicken or fish stock for half the milk in chicken or fish dishes. For a rich sauce, add 1 egg yolk, beaten with 4 tablespoons heavy cream, for each cup of sauce, first adding a little of the hot sauce to the egg mixture before mixing it into balance of sauce.

MORNAY SAUCE

Add 2–3 tablespoons grated Swiss or Parmesan cheese (or a mixture of the two) to each cup of Béchamel sauce. Heat until cheese is melted.

SAUCE SOUBISE

Add ½ cup grated Gruyère cheese, ¼ cup grated Parmesan cheese and 1 cup cooked puréed onion to 1½ cups Béchamel sauce. Season with salt and pepper to taste. Heat until all the flavors are blended and the sauce is smooth.

WHITE WINE SAUCE

4 tablespoons butter
1 tablespoon flour
1 cup white wine fish fumet or strong fish broth

½ cup dry white wine
1 tablespoon onion juice
1 tablespoon chopped sautéed mushroom
Salt, pepper
1 tablespoon lemon juice
1 teaspoon minced parsley

Melt 1 tablespoon of the butter, add the flour, and cook for 3 or 4 minutes, stirring. Let cool somewhat and add the fumet. Simmer and stir until thick and smooth. Add white wine and simmer until as thick as desired. Add remaining ingredients, finally beat in rest of the butter, a little at a time. Serve with baked, poached, or boiled fish. Makes about 1½ cups.

SAUCE BERCY

1 tablespoon minced shallot
2 tablespoons butter
½ cup dry white wine
½ cup fish fumet or fish stock
½ cup velouté sauce (made with fish stock)
Finely chopped parsley

Sauté the shallot in 1 tablespoon of the butter until it begins to brown. Add the white wine and fumet, mixed together, and the velouté sauce. Bring to a boil and let mixture simmer very slowly for a few minutes, stirring frequently. When ready to serve, add the remaining 1 tablespoon butter and a little chopped parsley. Serve with fish. Makes 1½ cups.

BROWN SAUCE OR SAUCE ESPAGNOLE

½ cup minced onion
¼ cup minced carrot
¼ cup minced celery
2 slices lean bacon, diced
6 tablespoons beef drippings
½ cup flour
8 cups beef stock
½ cup white wine
1 tablespoon tomato paste
6 sprigs parsley
6 peppercorns
2 bay leaves
2 teaspoons salt
¼ teaspoon thyme

Sauté onion, carrot, celery and bacon in beef drippings in a large saucepan over medium heat for 5 minutes. Add flour, blend until smooth. Gradually add beef stock, stirring constantly with a wire whisk. Remove from heat, stir in wine and remaining ingredients. Replace over heat and bring to a boil. Turn heat low and simmer until reduced to half, stirring occasionally. Skim off fat, strain, and adjust seasonings. Makes 4–5 cups.

QUICK BROWN SAUCE

    3 shallots or scallions, finely chopped
    3 tablespoons butter
    1 cup red wine
    10½-ounce can beef bouillon (not consommé)
    1 teaspoon tarragon
     Pinch of thyme
     Salt, freshly ground pepper to taste
     Beurre manié

Sauté the shallots or scallions in the butter. Gradually add the wine and bouillon and bring to a boil. Add the seasonings. Cook down for a few minutes. Thicken to taste with beurre manié. Let simmer for a few moments and strain. Makes about 1½ cups.

SAUCE PÉRIGUEUX

Add finely chopped truffles to the brown sauce.

SAUCE DIABLE

To 1 cup brown sauce add 1 tablespoon Dijon mustard and a few dashes of Tabasco. Mix well.

BORDELAISE SAUCE

Add a little poached marrow to the brown sauce. Correct seasoning. Add a bit of chopped parsley.

SAUCE MADÈRE

To each cup of brown sauce add ¼ cup Madeira.

MUSHROOM-MADEIRA SAUCE

    ½ pound mushrooms
    2 tablespoons butter
     Salt, pepper to taste
    ½ cup Madeira
    1 cup beef stock
    2 egg yolks, well-beaten
    1 tablespoon chopped chives

Wash and dry the mushrooms. Remove stems and cut caps into thick slices. Melt the butter in a skillet. Add the mushrooms, salt, and pepper. Sauté 1 minute. Add Madeira and cook 3 minutes. Add stock and simmer, covered, 5 minutes. Remove from the heat. Stir in the egg yolks and chives. Makes 2 cups. Serve with steak, chops, poultry, or cold roast meat.

SALSA BOLOGNESE

    2 tablespoons butter
    ¼ cup diced ham
    ½ cup chopped onion
    ¼ cup grated carrots
    ¼ cup chopped celery
    ¾ pound ground beef
    ¼ pound ground pork
    ½ cup dry white wine
    2 tablespoons tomato paste
    3 cups beef stock
    ½ teaspoon each: salt, black pepper

⅛ teaspoon nutmeg
¼ pound mushrooms, sliced

Melt the butter in a saucepan; lightly brown the ham. Add the onion, carrots and celery; cook over low heat 5 minutes. Add the beef and pork; cook, stirring almost constantly, for 5 minutes. Mix in the wine; cook until evaporated. Stir in the tomato paste, 1 cup stock, the salt, pepper and nutmeg. Cook over low heat 15 minutes. Add mushrooms, remaining broth; cover; cook over low heat 45 minutes. Taste for seasoning. Serve with pasta. Makes 4½ cups.

TOMATO SAUCE

¼ cup olive oil
1½ cups sliced onions
½ cup grated carrots
1 clove garlic, minced
2 pounds tomatoes, diced
½ cup beef stock
1 teaspoon salt
½ teaspoon freshly ground black pepper
½ teaspoon basil
2 tablespoons minced parsley

Heat the oil in a saucepan; sauté the onions 10 minutes. Add the carrots and garlic; cook 5 minutes. Mix in the tomatoes, stock, salt, pepper, basil and parsley. Cover and cook over low heat for 1¼ hours. Purée in an electric blender or force through a sieve. Taste for seasoning. Makes about 2½ cups.

For Neapolitan-style tomato sauce, use 2 extra garlic cloves, and a 29-ounce can of Italian-style tomatoes in place of the fresh tomatoes.

SICILIAN SPAGHETTI SAUCE

2 cloves garlic, chopped
16–20 anchovy fillets, cut in pieces
½ cup olive oil
⅓ cup sultana raisins
⅓ cup black walnuts
¾ teaspoon basil
½ teaspoon freshly ground black pepper
  Salt

Heat the chopped garlic and anchovy fillets in the olive oil, then add the raisins, walnuts and basil. Season with the pepper and salt if needed. Spoon over spaghetti or other pasta, and sprinkle with chopped parsley. Makes about 1½ cups.

ITALIAN DRIED MUSHROOM SAUCE

1 ounce dried mushrooms
2 tablespoons olive oil
1 medium onion, minced
1 clove garlic, crushed
3 tablespoons tomato paste
1 cup cooked tomatoes
1 cup white wine
1 cup bread cubes
½ teaspoon salt
  Freshly ground pepper
¼ teaspoon marjoram
3 tablespoons chopped fresh parsley

Soak the mushrooms in lukewarm water to cover for 20 minutes. Drain, press to extract water, and chop. Heat the oil in a saucepan. Sauté the onion and garlic for 1 minute. Add the tomato paste, tomatoes, white wine, bread cubes, salt, pepper, and marjoram. Simmer, covered, for 10 minutes, until sauce is thick. Add the mushrooms and simmer 5 minutes. Stir in the parsley. Serve with pasta. Makes 2 cups.

HOLLANDAISE SAUCE

2 large egg yolks
2 teaspoons tarragon vinegar

2 tablespoons light cream
    Salt, cayenne pepper
¼ pound sweet butter, cut in 8 pieces
2 drops lemon juice

Put egg yolks in glass heatproof bowl (or top of double boiler) and beat in the vinegar and cream. Season with salt and a little cayenne.

Stand bowl in pan of hot water (or top of double boiler over hot water) over low heat and beat with a small wire whisk until the mixture is as thick as heavy cream. It is important that the water should not boil; add cold water if it gets too hot.

Beat in the sweet butter, piece by piece, adding another piece only when the previous one has been absorbed. When all the butter is absorbed, add lemon juice. To hold, stand bowl in a pan of lukewarm water, cover top with foil. Makes 1 cup.

BÉARNAISE SAUCE

2 tablespoons tarragon vinegar
2 shallots, chopped fine
½ teaspoon minced tarragon
3 egg yolks
½ teaspoon salt
    Dash of cayenne pepper
¼ pound sweet butter, cut in 8 pieces

Heat the vinegar and cook the shallots until vinegar is absorbed. Add the tarragon.

Put the egg yolks, seasonings and shallot mixture in a small heatproof glass bowl in a pan of hot water (or in the top of a double boiler over hot water) on very low heat. Beat with a small wire whisk until it thickens, as for Hollandaise, then beat in the butter gradually, bit by bit. When thickened, remove from heat. Sauce can be kept over warm (not hot) water until serving time. Makes 1 cup.

SALTSA AVGOLEMONO
(Lemon Sauce)

This refreshing, classic sauce enhances soups, stews, and casseroles.

2 eggs
    Dash salt
    Juice of 1 lemon (3 tablespoons juice)
1 cup boiling broth or stock

Beat the eggs until light; add salt and beat in the lemon juice. Gradually beat in the hot broth, beating constantly. Then stir sauce into a stew or soup and heat gently, stirring, until sauce is thickened. (Do not boil, or sauce may curdle.) Makes 1 cup.

Note: This is the traditional way of preparing lemon sauce. For a fluffy variation, separate the eggs. Beat the whites with salt until they form soft points; add egg yolks one at a time and beat in lemon juice. Gently fold in the hot broth, then stir sauce into stew and heat until thickened.

MAYONNAISE

2 egg yolks
½ teaspoon dry mustard
1 teaspoon Dijon mustard
1 level teaspoon salt
⅛ teaspoon cayenne pepper
½ teaspoon lemon juice
1 tablespoon tarragon vinegar
¼ cup olive oil
1 cup vegetable oil

Beat the egg yolks, seasonings, lemon juice and vinegar in a mixer until light and fluffy. Very slowly add the olive and vegetable oils, drop by drop at first, beating all the time. As the oil begins to take and the mayonnaise thickens, pour more quickly. This mayonnaise will keep well in a screw-top jar in the refrigerator. If you want to thin for use, add light cream until mayonnaise reaches the desired consistency. Makes about 1½ cups.

GREEN MAYONNAISE

1 cup homemade mayonnaise
½ cup mixed finely chopped herbs and greens
    (parsley, tarragon, watercress, spinach)

Mix the mayonnaise with the desired selection of chopped fresh herbs, which will lend a delicate green color and a good flavor.

BASIC FRENCH DRESSING

> 1 level teaspoon salt
> ½ teaspoon cracked black pepper
> ¼ teaspoon dry mustard
> ¼ teaspoon Dijon mustard
> Few drops lemon juice
> 2 tablespoons tarragon vinegar
> 6 tablespoons vegetable oil
> 2 tablespoons olive oil
> Chopped garlic to taste (optional)

Put all ingredients into a screw-top jar and shake vigorously to blend.

VINAIGRETTE DRESSING

To Basic French Dressing add finely chopped onion, parsley and tarragon. Finely chopped green olives and capers may also be added.

SALSA CRUDA
(Uncooked Tomato Sauce)

This sauce appears on Mexican tables almost as often as salt and pepper. It is served with meats, poultry, fish, and eggs, in tacos and tostadas.

Mix together 2 ripe large tomatoes, peeled and chopped fine; 2 or more canned serrano chiles, chopped; 1 small onion, finely chopped; 1 tablespoon cilantro, chopped; a pinch of sugar, and salt and pepper to taste. Makes about 1 cup.

SALSA VERDE
(Green Sauce)

Drain liquid from a 10-ounce can of Mexican green tomatoes and mash them with 1 small white onion, finely chopped; 1 clove garlic, chopped; 2 or more canned serrano chiles, chopped; 6 sprigs fresh cilantro, chopped; and salt and pepper to taste. Or mix and whirl for a second or two in an electric blender. Serve like Salsa Cruda. Makes about 1 cup.

SAUCE VERTE

> 1½ cups walnuts
> ½ cup chopped chives
> ¼ cup chopped parsley

> 2 tablespoons chopped tarragon
> ½ cup olive oil
> Salt
> Freshly ground black pepper
> 1 tablespoon lime or lemon juice

Grind the walnuts or chop them in an electric blender. Mix with the chives, parsley, tarragon and add the oil. Season to taste with salt and pepper and blend in the lime or lemon juice. If all the oil is absorbed by the nuts, add a little more—enough to make a smooth paste. Makes about 3 cups.

MIGNONETTE SAUCE
(for raw oysters and clams on the half shell)

> 1 tablespoon coarsely ground white or black peppercorns (vary amount according to taste)
> ½ cup white or red wine vinegar
> 2 tablespoons finely chopped shallots or sweet onions
> Salt to taste

Combine all ingredients and chill. Serve with chilled oysters or clams on the half shell. Makes about ½ cup.

SASHIMI SAUCE
(for raw clams)

> ½ cup soy sauce (preferably an imported brand)
> ½ cup lemon juice
> Grated horseradish to taste

Combine the soy sauce and lemon juice and add the

den. Add the cubed eggplant, tomato, tomato paste, garlic, pepper, sugar, and stock and simmer, covered, for ½ hour, or until the vegetables are very tender. (Add more liquid if necessary during cooking.) Stir in the cheese, remove from the heat, adjust seasoning and cool. Blend in the mayonnaise and chill. Serve as a thick sauce for cold roast veal or other cold meats. Makes 4 cups.

HORSERADISH SAUCE

Add 2 tablespoons prepared horseradish and ½ teaspoon salt to 1 cup sour cream. Mix well. Serve with roast beef.

HORSERADISH APPLESAUCE

Combine 2 cups applesauce and 6 tablespoons fresh grated horseradish or 4 tablespoons bottled horseradish, drained. Blend well and chill. Vary the amount of horseradish to make the sauce hotter or milder. Serve with roast pork.

horseradish. Pour the mixture into small individual bowls to use as a dip for clams on the half shell. This makes an interesting change from the usual cocktail sauce. Makes 1 cup.

ITALIAN SAUCE

    1 medium eggplant, sliced ½″ thick
    1 teaspoon salt
    ⅓ cup olive oil
    1 medium onion, peeled and chopped
    1 green pepper, seeded and coarsely chopped
    1 tomato, peeled, seeded, and coarsely chopped
    2 tablespoons tomato paste
    1 clove garlic, very finely minced
    ¼ teaspoon coarse black pepper
    ½ teaspoon sugar
    1 cup chicken, meat, or vegetable stock
    3 tablespoons freshly grated Romano cheese
    ⅓ cup mayonnaise

Sprinkle the eggplant with salt and let stand for ½ hour. Wipe the slices dry and sauté them in ¼ cup of the oil until slightly brown on both sides. Remove the eggplant, cut into cubes and reserve. Sauté the onion and pepper in a large, heavy skillet in the remaining oil over medium heat until the onion is gol-

CRANBERRY SAUCE DE LUXE

    4 dozen almonds
    1 pound fresh cranberries
    2 cups granulated sugar
    6 tablespoons orange or citrus marmalade
    Strained juice of 2 lemons

Blanch almonds by pouring boiling water over them. Let them stand a few minutes, then pour off the water, rinse in cold water and pinch off the skins. Cover with cold water and place in refrigerator for several hours.

Wash and pick over cranberries. Moisten granulated sugar with 1 cup of cold water, stir, bring to a boil, skim carefully and boil 5 minutes. Then add the cranberries and cook 3–5 minutes longer or until they have all popped open and become transparent. Remove from fire and add 6 generous tablespoons of orange or citrus marmalade. Stir, and add the lemon juice. When cold, add the blanched almonds, which have been well drained. Serve this cranberry sauce chilled with cold roast chicken, turkey or pheasant.

CHOCOLATE SAUCE

> 6 ounces dark sweet chocolate
> 1½ cups light cream
> 3 teaspoons sweet butter
> 2 tablespoons plain flour
>   Pinch of salt
> 2 tablespoons granulated sugar
> 3 tablespoons whipped cream
> 2 teaspoons vanilla

Cut the chocolate in small pieces and put into a pan with the light cream. Stir over very low heat until dissolved. Melt the sweet butter in a pan and stir in, off the heat, the flour and pinch of salt. Slowly add the chocolate cream and stir over low heat until it comes to a boil. Add the sugar and allow to simmer very gently for 10–15 minutes. Slowly mix in the plain whipped cream and the vanilla. Serve with steamed puddings, soufflés, etc. Makes 2 cups.

ICED CHOCOLATE AND MINT SAUCE

> 6 ounces dark sweet chocolate
> ½ cup water
> 1 cup light cream
> 1 teaspoon strong peppermint flavoring
> ½ cup heavy cream
> 3 teaspoons confectioners' sugar
> 1 pint vanilla ice cream
> ½ cup hard crushed peppermint candy

Grate chocolate on the coarse side of grater, put into a pan with water and light cream. Stir over low heat until dissolved and simmer 10–15 minutes until fairly thick. Add peppermint flavoring. Stir over a bowl of ice until well chilled. Beat heavy cream with a wire whisk in a metal bowl over ice until it begins to thicken, add confectioners' sugar and continue beating until thick. Stir slowly into chilled chocolate sauce. Beat vanilla ice cream until smooth and mix into sauce. Just before serving, add the candy. Serve with ice cream or sundaes. Makes 4 cups.

CHOCOLATE WALNUT SAUCE

> ½ cup butter
> 2 cups chopped walnuts
> 2 cups semi-sweet chocolate pieces

Melt the butter in a heavy skillet. Add the walnuts and cook over a medium heat, stirring constantly, until lightly browned. Remove from heat, add the chocolate pieces and stir until smooth. Serve warm over ice cream or plain cake. Makes 2½ cups.

MANGO MACADAMIA SAUCE

> 14-ounce can mangoes in syrup
> ⅔ cup sugar
> ½ teaspoon vanilla
> 1 cup Macadamia nuts

Combine mangoes, sugar and vanilla, and cook down over medium heat for 10 minutes. Cool and add Macadamia nuts. Makes about 2 cups. Serve cold on vanilla or coffee ice cream or on raspberry sherbet.

COFFEE SAUCE

> 3 cups strong Italian or French dark-roast coffee
> 6 tablespoons granulated sugar
> 1 teaspoon lemon juice
>   Grated rind of ½ lemon
> 2 tablespoons arrowroot
> ¾ cup heavy cream
> 1 tablespoon confectioners' sugar

Put the coffee in a pan with 4 tablespoons of the sugar, the lemon juice and rind and bring to a boil. Simmer very briskly until reduced by half. Chill. Mix the arrowroot with 3 tablespoons of the cold coffee mixture. When quite smooth, stir in the rest of the coffee mixture and half the heavy cream. Stir over low heat until it comes to a boil and then add the rest of the granulated sugar. Simmer for about 10 minutes. Chill a little. Whip the remaining cream in a metal bowl over ice. When it begins to thicken, add the confectioners' sugar and continue beating until stiff. Mix this slowly into the coffee sauce. Serve with steamed puddings or soufflés. Makes 3½ cups.

HARD SAUCE

> 1 cup butter
> 1 cup confectioners' sugar
> ¾ cup brandy

Beat the butter well. Add the sugar gradually, then the brandy. Chill well. Serve with plum pudding. Makes 2½ cups.

Aspic

Aspic is to haute cuisine what jewels are to haute couture—the final glittering touch that spells elegance. Yet there is more to an aspic than meets the eye. A means of preventing cooked dishes from spoiling in the days before refrigeration, aspic seals in the succulence of cooked cold foods and keeps them from drying out. Armored in shining aspic, a whole salmon retains its moist texture on the buffet table, an oeuf mollet remains as fresh as when peeled from the shell, and a molded jambon persillé stays invitingly cool and shapely. Although flavored jellies count as aspics too, an aspic is basically a stock that can stand up for itself. Classically, its backbone comes from the gelatinous parts of meat, poultry and fish, boiled with liquid and flavorings to a concentrated bouillon that is then clarified, and chilled until set, but now a quick version of aspic can be concocted by dissolving powdered gelatin in stock.

Aspics were counted among the glories of the tables of the past. The first printed cook book, by a Renaissance author under the nom-de-plume of Platina, had the engaging title of De Honesta Voluptate (which might be translated as Permissible Pleasures). Included among these pleasures was a pesce in gelatina. Two earlier, hand-written cook books from the English and French courts of Richard II and Charles V, The Forme of Cury and Le Viandier, show how akin the royal kitchens were. Both list aspics of meat and fish with just the slightest variation in spelling—galantines in French, galantynes in English.

Legend has it that the chaudfroid was born, rather than made, by one of those happy accidents that seem to abound in gastronomic history. Called from his table and his guests to receive a message from Louis XV, the Maréchal de Luxembourg returned to find the chicken cold in its own jellied cream sauce, tasted it and pronounced it delicious.

For centuries, aspic was made the lengthy, laborious way. A seventeenth-century French physicist had invented a machine he called a "steam digester" that extracted gelatin in its pure form, but his invention went virtually unnoticed until the Napoleonic Wars were ravaging Europe when his compact form of instant protein was found to be invaluable in saving off starvation. But it was left to a perspicacious nineteenth-century salesman in New York State, Charles B. Knox, to capitalize on the possibilities of concentrated gelatin. Through astute merchandising and demonstrations, he publicized the virtues of this short-cut to gleaming aspics, molded salads and desserts, and made America the world's most gelatin-conscious country.

Batches of aspic, made the classic or the quick way, keep for at least two weeks in the refrigerator. Flavoring wine should be added after clarifying and straining, or the aspic will be cloudy rather than the crystal-clear covering that reveals and enhances the food beneath. Set aspic, chopped on a board covered with waxed paper, makes a splendid, glittering garnish, but if the serving platter is silver, it is advisable to protect it with plastic wrap for aspic has one bad habit—it stains metal.

To clarify aspic, beat until liquid boils and stiff egg white rises to surface.

BASIC MEAT ASPIC

1 small boiling fowl
1½ pounds beef (eye of round)
2 cracked knuckles of veal
3 marrow bones
2 leeks
1 carrot
2 stalks celery
2 white onions
2 tomatoes
Herb bouquet (tarragon, parsley, bay leaf, celery leaf)
Small white onion studded with 4 cloves
1½ dozen mixed (black and white) peppercorns
2 tablespoons salt
2 tablespoons Italian tomato paste
8 tablespoons plain gelatin
4 egg whites, stiffly beaten
½ cup dry sherry

Tie up the fowl and put into a large earthenware, cast-iron or aluminum pot with the beef, veal knuckles and marrow bones. Add 3 quarts water and bring slowly to a boil. Reduce heat and remove all the scum with a metal spoon. Cut the leeks, carrot and celery in thin slices, the onions in half and the tomatoes in quarters. Add to the stock with the herb bouquet (tied in a piece of cheesecloth) and the onion studded with cloves. Tie the bouquet to the handle of the saucepan so it can be easily removed. Add the peppercorns and salt and simmer gently for 1½–2 hours. Allow to cool. Strain stock through a fine strainer lined with cheesecloth. Discard vegetables and bones. Reserve beef and chicken for other uses.

Put the strained stock into a large tin-lined or stainless-steel pan, add the tomato paste, gelatin and beaten egg whites. Beat with a large whisk over low heat until the liquid comes to a rolling boil. Draw aside and let stand for 15 minutes without disturbing. Wring out a fine cloth in ice water and chill it in the freezing compartment of the refrigerator. Line a fine chinois strainer with the cloth and strain the liquid through it (the iced cloth catches and holds any fat). Add the dry sherry to the strained aspic. Chill and use as required. Makes about 10 cups.

BASIC CHICKEN ASPIC

This is made in the same way as the meat aspic, except that a 3-pound roasting chicken is substituted for the beef. The cooked chicken can be used for chicken à la king, or chicken stuffing for crêpes.

QUICK CHICKEN ASPIC

1½ pints double-strength clarified chicken broth
¼ cup white wine
3 envelopes unflavored gelatin dissolved in ¼ cup cold water

Heat the broth and wine to boiling point. Add the dissolved gelatin. Stir until gelatin has melted. Cool. Makes 3¼ cups.

BASIC FISH ASPIC

1 small fish head, well washed and scraped
4 sole bones, edges well trimmed, heads removed, washed and dried
1 cup mixed sliced onion, carrot, celery, leek
2 tomatoes, sliced
Herb bouquet (bay leaf, parsley, celery leaf)
10 mixed peppercorns (black and white)
1 cup dry white wine
1 teaspoon salt
1 tablespoon tomato paste
5 tablespoons plain gelatin
3 egg whites, stiffly beaten
¼ cup brandy

Put the fish head and bones in 2 quarts of water and bring slowly to the boil. Remove all scum, add the sliced vegetables, herb bouquet, peppercorns, white wine and salt. Simmer gently for ¾ hour. Strain the stock through a sieve lined with a damp cloth. Chill thoroughly. Put stock in a stainless-steel or tin-lined pan, add the tomato paste, gelatin and egg whites. Beat over low heat with a wire whisk until it comes to a rolling boil. Draw aside and let stand, undisturbed, for 15 minutes. Pour through a strainer lined with a fine cloth wrung out in cold water. Add brandy. Chill until ready to use. Makes about 8 cups.

BASIC CHAUDFROID SAUCE

4 tablespoons vegetable oil
12 tablespoons water
12 tablespoons flour
4 tablespoons plain gelatin
2 teaspoons salt
⅛ teaspoon cayenne pepper
4 cups milk
1 cup light cream

In a small heavy pan, heat the oil and water a little. Thoroughly mix together the flour, gelatin and seasonings and stir into the oil and water, off the heat. Mix in milk and stir over low heat until the mixture comes to a boil. Remove, add the cream and stir over ice until on the point of setting. Makes about 6 cups.

SET MAYONNAISE

2 egg yolks
1 teaspoon Dijon mustard
1½ teaspoons salt
Pinch of cayenne pepper
2 teaspoons tarragon vinegar
1 teaspoon Tabasco
1¾ cups oil
½ cup light cream
1½ tablespoons plain gelatin
5 tablespoons milk

Beat the egg yolks, Dijon mustard, salt, cayenne pepper, tarragon vinegar and Tabasco with an electric mixer. Slowly beat in the oil. Mix in the light cream. Put the gelatin and milk in a small pan and stir over a very slow fire until the gelatin is dissolved. Cool a little and carefully stir into the mayonnaise. Makes about 2¾ cups.

OEUFS POCHÉS BEAU-RIVAGE

6 artichoke bottoms
1½ cups shrimp, boiled, shelled, and deveined
1 cup pea purée
2 cups Set Mayonnaise
6 poached eggs
1 cup chicken or meat aspic

Carefully drain the artichoke bottoms, dry on paper towels and arrange on a rack over a jelly roll pan. Dice the shrimp, reserving three of the best. Mix the pea purée with mayonnaise on the point of setting. Bind the chopped shrimp with a little of this sauce. Put some of the shrimp mixture on each artichoke bottom and top with a drained, dried poached egg. Coat with remaining mayonnaise mixture on the point of setting. Carefully cut the three whole shrimp in half lengthwise and place one half on each egg. Put to set in refrigerator. When set, coat with aspic on the point of setting. Serve surrounded by the remaining aspic, set and chopped. Serves 6.

OEUFS POCHÉS FROU-FROU

6 poached eggs
3 cups chaudfroid sauce
3 hard-cooked egg yolks, finely strained
¼ cup heavy cream
6 thin slices truffle
2 cups chicken or meat aspic
2 cups cooked, drained asparagus tips, chilled
2 cups cooked, drained peas, chilled
2 cups cooked, drained string beans, cut in 1″ pieces, chilled
2 cups set mayonnaise
Asparagus tips, pimientos for garnish

Place drained, dried eggs on a rack over a jelly roll pan. Make chaudfroid sauce according to directions. When it comes to a boil, add the strained egg yolks which have been mixed with the heavy cream. Stir sauce over ice until it coats the back of a silver spoon. Coat the eggs with the sauce and chill until set in the refrigerator. Put a thin slice of truffle on each and coat with aspic on the point of setting. Chill.

Meanwhile, put the chilled vegetables in a bowl and mix them with mayonnaise on the point of setting, using two forks. Fill a deep charlotte mold with vegetable mixture, put to set in the refrigerator. To serve, unmold on a cold, flat dish, place poached eggs at equal distances around the top of the vegetable mold. Chop the rest of the set aspic, put in a pastry bag with a round tube and pipe a ribbon of chopped aspic around each egg. Place between eggs small bundles of asparagus tips with a thin strip of pimiento around the center. Serves 6.

OEUFS POCHÉS À L'ESTRAGON

    1 teaspoon salt
    ½ cup tarragon vinegar
    8 fresh eggs
    6 cups chicken or meat aspic
    16 perfect tarragon leaves
    1 cup diced cooked string beans
    1 cup diced cooked carrots
    1½ cups diced cooked young white turnips
    Watercress for garnish

Fill bottom of a double boiler ¾ full of water, add salt and tarragon vinegar and gently poach the eggs, one at a time, for 3½ minutes. Remove with a slotted spoon and chill in bowl of ice water. Thoroughly chill 8 small oval molds. Dissolve 1½ cups aspic over low heat, stir over ice till on the point of setting and put about ¼″ of the aspic in the bottom of each mold. Chill until set. When set, decorate by arranging two tarragon leaves, dipped in aspic on the point of setting, criss-cross in the center. Carefullly drain poached eggs, trim, and dry on paper towels. Put an egg in each mold and fill with aspic on the point of setting. Chill until aspic is set.

Meanwhile, drain and thoroughly chill the vegetables. Put them in a large bowl and mix carefully with two forks. Pour over them ¾ cup of aspic on the point of setting. Rinse a 9″ layer cake pan with ice water. Fill with the vegetable aspic. Chill until set.

To serve, carefully slide a thin bladed knife around the edge of the vegetable aspic and invert on a flat serving dish. Rub top quickly with a hot damp cloth and lift off the mold. Turn out the eggs in the same way and arrange in a ring on top of the vegetable aspic. Decorate dish with watercress sprigs. Serves 8 as a first course.

HOW TO MAKE OEUF POCHÉ A L'ESTRAGON

Put ¼″ aspic on point of setting in mold. Chill. Decorate with tarragon.

Add egg. Fill with aspic. Chill until set.

To loosen aspic, slide knife around mold.

Rub bottom of mold with hot cloth.

Unmold egg in aspic, ready to serve.

STUFFED CRAB

>   2 large crabs, boiled
>   2 cups fish aspic
>   1 cup carrots, diced, cooked and drained
>   1 cup turnips, diced, cooked and drained
>   1 cup baby lima beans, cooked and drained
>   1 cup string beans, diced, cooked and drained
>   1 cup set mayonnaise
>   2 tomatoes, thinly sliced
>   2 hard-cooked eggs, sliced
>   2 gherkins
>   Sprigs of parsley

Remove large claws of crabs and carefully take out meat. Empty crab shell and discard inedible portions. Dice meat and mix with a little aspic on the point of setting. Fill small upright dariole molds with the mixture and put to set in the refrigerator. Put all the cooked, drained vegetables in a large bowl and mix carefully with a fork. Stir in mayonnaise on the point of setting. Fill the empty crab shells with this vegetable mixture and cover it with thin slices of tomato, overlapping. Put a slice of hard-cooked egg on each tomato slice and put a round of gherkin in the center of each. Give each filled crab shell a coat of aspic on the point of setting. Chill. To serve, arrange on a platter on a bed of parsley. Run a sharp-bladed knife around the inside edge of the dariole molds and rub the outside with a hot damp cloth. Turn out on the serving dish and arrange in a circle around the shells. Serves 4.

TIMBALES DE FILET DE SOLE

>   12 medium size fillets of sole
>   Lemon juice
>   1½ pounds salmon
>   2 egg whites
>   1¼ cups light cream
>   Salt
>   2 pinches cayenne pepper
>   2 large truffles, finely chopped
>   ¼ cup dry white wine
>   8 cups fish aspic

Wash the fillets in lemon juice and water and dry on paper towels. Chill well. Skin and bone the salmon and put it through a fine meat grinder. Put ground salmon and egg whites in a mixer and beat well. Slowly add the cream, 3 teaspoons salt and cayenne pepper. Divide the mousse mixture in half and add the finely chopped truffle to one half. Cover the darker side of 6 fillets (the side which was next to the skin) with the salmon-truffle mixture, about ¼″ thick. Spread the other 6 fillets with the plain salmon mixture. Roll up like little jelly rolls and fasten with toothpicks. Place in an ovenproof glass baking dish with the wine, about 1 cup water, a squeeze of lemon juice and a little salt. Cover with waxed paper and poach in a 350° oven for about 20 minutes. Remove and allow to get quite cool in the liquid. Drain carefully and dry with paper towels. Cut each fillet into 4 round slices. Place on a rack over a cookie sheet and coat with fish aspic on the point of setting. Thoroughly chill a 10″ ring mold and pour about ½–1 cup of aspic on the point of setting in the bottom. Chill in the refrigerator until set. Remove and arrange in the bottom of the mold the slices of sole, overlapping, and cover them with a little aspic on the point of setting. Arrange other slices, not overlapping, around the sides of the mold. Fill up the mold with aspic and put in the refrigerator to chill and set. To serve, just loosen the edge of the aspic from the mold with a sharp knife and invert on a platter. Cover top of mold with a hot cloth and unmold. Serves 8.

OYSTERS IN ASPIC

>   1 pound button mushrooms
>   Lemon juice
>   ½ cup heavy cream
>   ¼ cup port wine
>   Salt, cayenne pepper
>   3 tablespoons sweet butter
>   3 tablespoons flour
>   1 teaspoon meat glaze
>   1 cup light cream
>   3 ounces foie gras
>   3 dozen freshly opened oysters with their liquor
>   ½ cup dry white wine
>   1½ envelopes plain gelatin
>   5 tablespoons water
>   Set fish aspic
>   Watercress, endive for garnish

Cut off the mushroom stalks level with the cap. Wash caps in lemon juice and water and dry well. Put the caps in a heavy skillet with the heavy cream and port wine, season with salt and a little cayenne pepper and cook over high heat, stirring constantly, until the liquid is thick enough to coat the mushrooms. Remove pan from heat.

Melt the sweet butter in a small pan and stir in the flour, off the heat. Season with salt and a little cayenne pepper and mix in the meat glaze and light cream. Stir over low heat until the mixture comes to a boil. Chill well. Mix this cold sauce with the foie gras until well blended and smooth. Correct seasoning.

Stir the cooled sauce into the mushroom mixture. Put the freshly opened oysters (minus shells) and their liquor in a small saucepan and add the white wine. Cook over low heat until the liquid boils. Remove from heat. Stir the gelatin, water and 2 teaspoons lemon juice in a small pan over low heat until dissolved. Add this to the hot oyster mixture and stir well until blended. Blend mushroom and oyster mixtures and pack into a mold rinsed out in cold water. Chill until completely set. To unmold, slide a thin-bladed knife around the inner edge of the mold and invert on a flat silver dish. Cover the mold with a hot cloth for a minute to free the aspic. Remove the mold. Garnish with chopped set fish aspic, sprigs of watercress and endive leaves. Serves 6.

MOUSSELINE DE SAUMON A LA CHANTILLY

    ¾ pound salmon
    1 onion
    1 carrot
    1 bay leaf
    ¼ cup dry white wine
    15 tablespoons sweet butter
    3 tablespoons flour
    1 cup milk
      Salt, pepper
    2 tablespoons sherry
    2 tablespoons heavy cream
    1 cup fish aspic
      A few sprigs parsley
    1 tomato

Put the salmon, onion, carrot and bay leaf in a pan with the white wine and a little water. Bring slowly to a boil. Simmer for 15–20 minutes. Cool in stock. Skin and bone salmon.

Melt 3 tablespoons butter in a pan and stir in the flour, off the heat. Stir until smooth, add the milk, season with salt and pepper to taste. Stir over low heat until mixture boils. Pour onto a plate to cool.

Pound the salmon in a mortar with 12 tablespoons butter and the cooled sauce. When well pounded, add the sherry, cream and a little more seasoning. Fill a soufflé dish almost to the top with the mixture, smooth over and put in a cool place.

To garnish, melt a little fish aspic in a pan and stir over ice until on the point of setting. Put a thin coat of the still-liquid aspic on top of the salmon mousse, dip a few sprigs of parsley into the aspic and arrange these at even intervals on top of the aspic. Peel the tomato, cut the skin into small flowerpot shapes, dip these in aspic and put one at the bottom of each parsley sprig. Put in a cool place, then fill the dish to the rim with more aspic on the point of setting. Chill in the refrigerator until set. Serves 6. (This mousse can be made with ham, chicken or veal in place of the salmon, and coated with chicken aspic.)

PÂTÉ OF SALMON

    1 large onion
    2 stalks celery
    1 carrot
    1 bay leaf
    2 slices lemon
      Salt, pepper
    2 pounds salmon in one piece
    ¼ cup butter
    1 envelope unflavored gelatin
      Hard-cooked eggs
      Ripe olives

Make a court bouillon with the onion, celery, carrot, bay leaf, lemon, and enough water to cover the fish. Salt and pepper to taste. Poach the fish for about 10–15 minutes, or until it flakes easily when tested with a fork. Remove the fish and cool. (Strain and reserve the broth.) Flake the fish and either pound in a mortar or work with a wooden spoon in a bowl until it is finely crumbled. Cream the butter well, incorporate the salmon, and correct seasoning.

Dissolve the gelatin in ¼ cup cold water. Add 1 cup boiling fish broth. Pour a layer in a 1-quart mold and chill in the refrigerator until firm. Place the salmon mixture on the gelatin and press down well. Chill for 12 hours. Unmold the salmon, and decorate with eggs and olives cut with little truffle cutters, or garnish according to your own imagination. Serve the salmon pâté with a dill mayonnaise.

LOBSTER ASPIC À LA RUSSE

    3 cups fish stock
    3 live lobsters
    3 cups set mayonnaise
    2 large truffles, sliced
    3 pimientos, sliced
      A few sprigs of fresh dill
    6 cups fish aspic
    2 cups cooked asparagus tips
    3 cups diced artichoke bottoms

Heat fish stock in a large kettle. Add live lobsters, cover and cook gently until they blush, 12–15 minutes. Allow to get cold in the stock. Remove. Carefully remove tail and claw meat without breaking (to remove meat whole from claws, cut the side of claws with sharp scissors). Cut the tail meat into neat scallops, place on a rack over a jelly roll pan and coat with mayonnaise on the point of setting. Decorate the center of each scallop with a slice of trufflé, a slice of pimiento and a sprig of dill. Put to set in the refrigerator. Pour 1½ cups of fish aspic on the point of setting into a 10″ ring mold. When lobster has set, line the mold with the tail meat scallops, decoration side down. Fill mold with aspic and put to set in the refrigerator. Carefully mix the asparagus tips and artichoke bottoms with the rest of the mayonnaise. Fill with this mixture a deep charlotte mold that will fit into the center of the ring. Put to set in the refrigerator. To serve, unmold the aspic ring on a flat round silver serving platter, unmold vegetables in the center. Garnish with claw meat and chopped set aspic. Serves 6.

TRUITES À LA GELÉE

    8 trout (8 or 10 ounces each)
    1 quart rich white wine fish fumet (see Sauces)
      Tarragon leaves, blanched
      Thinly sliced truffles or large ripe pitted olives
      Thinly sliced lemon

Butter a shallow baking dish and arrange the trout in it. Pour the fumet over the fish and poach gently for 5 minutes. Turn carefully with a spatula and poach on other side. Turn off heat and cool in the liquid. Remove trout from liquid, reserving liquid. Remove skin, arrange trout nicely on your prettiest serving platter, and decorate tastefully with blanched fresh tarragon leaves and thin slices of truffle or pitted ripe olives. The fish fumet should be rich enough to jell, but if it isn't, cook it down some more or, as a last resort, add an envelope of unflavored gelatin, softened in a little water. When the fumet has almost jelled, spoon it carefully over the fish and put in the refrigerator to chill. Garnish the platter with thin slices of lemon. Serves 8.

SALMON IN ASPIC

> 8–10-pound whole salmon
> Court bouillon
> 1 egg white, slightly beaten, and egg shell
> 2 envelopes unflavored gelatin
> 2 hard-cooked eggs, sliced
> Stuffed green olives, sliced
> Fresh tarragon leaves (if available)
> ½ pound cooked shrimp, cleaned
> Parsley

Poach the fish in court bouillon until done; skin and chill. Reheat the court bouillon, add the egg white and egg shell, let come to a boil, then remove from heat. Let it stand for a few minutes to settle, then strain through a linen cloth wrung out in cold water. There should now be 4 cups of very clear liquid. Dissolve the gelatin in ½ cup cold water, add to the hot clarified bouillon, and allow to cool. When the aspic starts to congeal, brush the salmon with a thin coating, then decorate with hard-cooked egg slices, stuffed olive slices, and tarragon leaves, and chill again until they stay firmly in place.

Now pour the rest of the aspic evenly over the fish, covering it completely with a shimmering transparent coat. Garnish prettily with the cooked shrimp and put a wreath of parsley around the edge of the platter. For a finishing touch, make more aspic, pour it into a shallow pan to set, then dice small and strew around the fish. Serves 15–20, depending upon the number of accompanying vegetable dishes.

This pretty dish is spectacular as the main event at a large buffet or smörgåsbord. Be sure to include a cucumber salad as one of the accompaniments—delicate salmon and cucumber have a natural affinity.

QUAIL WITH WHITE GRAPES

> 4 quail
> Salt, black pepper
> ½ cup Madeira
> 6 ounces pâté de foie gras
> 4 slices fat salt pork
> 2 white mushrooms, sliced
> 1½ cups strong chicken stock
> 1½ cups chaudfroid sauce
> Thin slices of truffle
> 1½ cups chicken aspic
> 2 cups skinned seedless white grapes

Remove heads of quail, split them down the back and carefully remove the breast bones. Sprinkle cavities with a little salt and pepper and a few drops of wine. Beat the foie gras until light and creamy, season well with salt, pepper and a little wine. Divide mixture evenly between the four quail, fill the cavities, fold over the skin and sew up with fine thread. Wrap quail in salt pork slices and put into a pan with the sliced mushrooms, the stock, remaining wine, quail heads and a little salt and pepper. Bring slowly to a boil and simmer very gently for half an hour. Allow to get cool in the liquid. Unwrap. Discard salt pork. Carefully remove thread. Wipe quail dry with paper towels and put them on a rack over a jelly roll pan. Coat with chaudfroid sauce, chill until set in refrigerator, remove, coat and chill again. When set, decorate with thin slices of truffle and glaze with chicken aspic on the point of setting. Return to refrigerator until well chilled and set. To serve, arrange quail down the center of a flat serving dish, pile skinned white grapes at each end and garnish with chopped set chicken aspic. Serves 4.

SUPRÊME DE VOLAILLE PARISIENNE

 3 large chicken breasts
 1 cup mixed sliced onion, carrot, celery
  Sprig of tarragon or bay leaf
  Peppercorns, salt, cayenne pepper
 2 2-ounce cans liver pâté
 3 ounces sweet butter, creamed
 2 tablespoons brandy
 2 cups chaudfroid sauce
  Garnish (tarragon leaves or mushroom
  slices, or truffles)
 3 cups chicken aspic

Put the chicken breasts, sliced vegetables, herb, a few peppercorns, 1 teaspoon salt and 4 cups water in a pan. Bring slowly to a boil and simmer gently for 25 minutes. Let chicken breasts cool in stock. Drain, skin and bone them and cut each boned half-breast almost in two lengthwise, leaving it joined at the outer edge. Mix together the liver pâté, butter and brandy, season to taste with salt and cayenne pepper. Put this mixture into a pastry bag with a plain round tube and pipe it carefully into the half breasts. Reshape them. Chill. Arrange on a rack over a shallow pan. Stir chaudfroid sauce over ice until on point of setting. Coat chicken with sauce. Put in refrigerator to set. Remove and decorate with tarragon leaves, or slices of mushroom (cooked in a little lemon juice and water and well drained) or shapes cut from truffles. Coat with aspic on the point of setting. To serve, arrange on a flat silver platter and surround with chopped set aspic. Serves 6.

JELLIED DUCK À L'ORANGE

 2 Long Island ducks, 5–6 pounds
  Salt, coarsely ground pepper
 3 navel oranges
  Juice from 1 large lemon
 12-ounce can madrilene
 12-ounce can clear chicken broth
 1½ tablespoons unflavored gelatin
 1 bunch watercress

Clean the ducks and wipe inside and out with a damp cloth or paper toweling. Sprinkle the cavities with salt and pepper. Preheat oven to 350°. Place ducks

HOW TO PREPARE
SUPRÊME DE VOLAILLE PARISIENNE

Cut pocket in cooked, boned chicken.

Pipe in pâté, moving tube up and down.

Press gently, smooth with spatula.

Coat with sauce, using side of long spoon.

Place decoration carefully on set sauce.

Coat again, with aspic on point of setting.

side by side in a roasting pan and roast until very tender, about 2½ hours. Pour off the fat after they have cooked 1 hour and again in another hour. Remove from pan when done and cool; then remove all the meat from the bones in as large pieces as possible, cutting each breast into 4 pieces. Discard all skin, fat and undesirable pieces. Sprinkle lightly with salt, cover with a plate, and chill.

In the meantime, remove the thin outer rind from 1 of the navel oranges, using a sharp knife. Place it in a cup and pour the lemon juice over it. Cover and place in refrigerator until ready to use for flavoring the aspic. Remove white pith left on the orange and cut the rind and white pith from the 2 remaining oranges. Then cut between the sections of the 3 oranges with a sharp knife, removing the pulp in half-moon-shaped pieces. Chill.

Heat together the madrilene and chicken broth. Soften the gelatin in 3 tablespoons cold water, add to the heated broth and stir well. Strain the reserved orange-flavored lemon juice into it. Add salt, if necessary, and cool. Arrange the orange pieces around the edge of a large glass pie plate, and pour just enough of the cooled aspic over them to cover the bottom of the plate with a ¼"-thick coating. Place in the refrigerator to set.

Garnish the center of the aspic-covered plate with a pattern of watercress leaves and cover the whole with the pieces of duck, placing the most perfect pieces in the center and the bits around the edge and on top. Pour the remaining aspic over all and refrigerate until firm. When ready to serve, run knife around the edge of the plate, dip the bottom of the plate in hot water, and turn out on a large round serving platter. Serve at once accompanied by a watercress salad with a sharp dressing made from lime or lemon juice, salt and a very little olive oil or peanut oil. Serves 6–8.

GALANTINE OF DUCK

    4½ pound duck
    3 tablespoons brandy
      Salt, pepper, nutmeg
    4 tablespoons sour cream
    1 pound sausage meat
    2 large slices boiled ham
    ½ pound boiled smoked tongue, sliced
    2 hard-cooked eggs
    4 chicken livers
    2 ounces blanched pistachio nuts
    2½ cups chaudfroid sauce
      Meat aspic

Bone the duck. Reserve the liver. Spread boned duck flat on a board, skin side down and brush the inside with 1 tablespoon brandy. Season with salt and pepper. Mix together the sour cream, sausage meat, remaining brandy with salt, pepper and a little nutmeg to taste. Spread ¾ of the stuffing on the duck, cover with the slices of ham and tongue and spread the remaining stuffing on top. Arrange on top of this the hard-cooked eggs, chicken livers, duck liver and pistachio nuts. Fold the skin over the stuffing, shaping it into a thick symmetrical roll (be careful not to break the skin). Sew the overlapping edges of skin with fine thread. Roll in waxed paper and aluminum foil, then in a clean white cloth. Fasten each end tightly with string and suspend the duck in a deep oval cast iron pan by tying the string to the handles at each end. The duck should not touch the bottom of the pan. Pour in water to cover. Bring to a boil and simmer gently for 1½ hours. Remove, cool a little, place in an oblong bread tin and put on top a heavy weight like a brick. Chill overnight in the refrigerator. Unwrap and rub off all the fat with a paper towel. Stand on a rack over a flat baking pan and coat all over with the chaudfroid sauce. Coat the duck as smoothly and evenly as possible, put in the refrigerator to set, then coat and set once more. Stir the liquid aspic over ice until on the point of setting. If desired, decorate the duck with flowers made from tiny rounds cut from hard-cooked egg white, hard-cooked egg yolk mixed with a little shortening and piped through a wax cornucopia, chives, tarragon and dill for stalks and leaves, designs cut from truffles or pimiento. Dip each piece in aspic on the point of setting so that it sticks to the sauce. When the design is firmly set, coat duck with a thin layer of aspic on the point of setting, put to set in refrigerator. To serve, arrange on platter bordered with chopped aspic. Serves 8.

DUCK WITH PINEAPPLE

    2 4–5-pound ducks
    ¼ cup brandy
    2 teaspoons salt
    1 teaspoon freshly cracked white pepper
    2 chicken breasts
    1½ pounds ground veal
    3 egg whites
    2 cups light cream
    ¼ teaspoon cayenne pepper
    ½ pound boiled tongue, cut in strips
    2 hard-cooked egg yolks
    2 truffles, coarsely chopped
    ½ cup pistachio nuts
    2½ cups chicken aspic
    1 small pineapple

Carefully bone both ducks by splitting down the center of the back, and, with a small, sharp knife, removing all meat from the carcass, taking care not to make any holes in the skin. Spread skin side down on a board, sprinkle with a little brandy and season with a little salt and freshly cracked white pepper.

Skin and bone the chicken breasts and put them through a meat grinder. Put ground chicken and ground veal in a mixer, beat in the egg whites and slowly add the light cream. Lastly, add remaining salt and cayenne pepper and beat well. Allow to stand for 10 minutes. With a spatula spread ½ the mixture on each duck, leaving a ¼" margin all around. Press on top strips of tongue, put an egg yolk in the center and scatter chopped truffle and pistachio nuts over all. Sprinkle with remaining brandy. Fold over skin and sew up ducks with fine thread. Place ducks on a rack in a roasting pan and pour a little water in the pan. Roast at 350°–375° for 1½–2 hours. Baste frequently, adding a little more water when necessary. About ½ hour before end of cooking time, cover ducks with aluminum foil. When cooked, remove from pan, wrap in fresh foil and chill completely with weight on top. When cold, remove all excess fat with a paper towel wrung out in cold water. Dry well. Put the shapelier of the ducks on a rack and cover with chicken aspic on the point of setting. Put in refrigerator to set. Remove, coat again, rechill. Repeat until there is a good ¼" thickness of aspic over the top of the duck.

Peel pineapple, remove the eyes and cut in half lengthwise. Remove hard core and cut in ¼" thick slices. Dry thoroughly between two or three thicknesses of paper towels. Overlap slices on top of duck and coat two or three times with aspic, chilling in between each coat. Scatter a little chopped set aspic on the bottom of a chilled flat silver platter and place the duck in the center. Insert two toothpicks where the duck's legs would have been and cover the ends with two large cutlet frills.

Put a little more chopped set aspic down each side of the platter and garnish with slices of the other duck. Chill thoroughly before serving. Serves 12.

TERRINE OF DUCK À L'ORANGE

    6-pound duck
    ¼ pound baked ham
    ¼ pound pork fat
       Salt
    ¼ teaspoon Spice Parisienne or quatre épices
    ⅔ cup Grand Marnier
    ½ pound lean pork
    ½ pound veal
    ½ pound fresh pork siding or fat pork
    2 cloves garlic
    2 teaspoons tarragon
    1 bay leaf, crushed
    ½ teaspoon Tabasco
    2 eggs
       Salt pork strips
    2 cups chicken aspic
       Juice of 1 orange
    1 orange, thinly sliced

Bone the duck completely, remove the breast meat, and save the skin. Cut the breast, the ham, and the pork fat into ½" cubes. Add 2 teaspoons salt, the spice, and 1/3 cup of the Grand Marnier. Marinate in this mixture for 2 hours.

Grind the lean pork, veal, fat pork, and the rest of the duck meat with the garlic, 1 tablespoon salt, tarragon, bay leaf, and Tabasco. Beat the eggs lightly and add to the mixture. Combine with the cubed meats and the marinade, and mix thoroughly. Line a terrine with a few strips of salt pork, add the meat mixture, and cover with the duck skin. Bake in a 350° oven for 1½–2 hours, or until the liquid and fat are completely clear. Cool 15 minutes. Weight the terrine and let it cool until the next day.

To serve, remove the weight and unmold the terrine. Carefully remove all the fat from the terrine and the pâté. Save the natural jelly. Replace the pâté in the terrine. Add the jelly to the aspic with the orange juice and remaining 1/3 cup Grand Marnier. Cover the pâté with orange slices, and then spoon the aspic over it. Chill thoroughly. Serve from the terrine or on a platter decorated with orange slices which have been dipped in aspic and chilled.

TURKEY EN CHAUDFROID

> 8–10-pound turkey, poached or roasted, chilled
> 4–5 cups chaudfroid sauce
> For decoration: tarragon leaves; green tops of leek and scallion; sliced truffles; black or stuffed olives; pimiento; green pepper; hard-cooked egg
> Meat aspic

Arrange the chilled turkey on a rack over a large pan. You may skin the turkey or leave the skin on. If you wish to carve the bird and put the pieces back in place before adding the decorations, remove the skin and breast fillets whole, slice very carefully and replace on the bone. You may also slice the thigh meat if you wish, but for this dish it is better to leave the thighs whole.

Spoon the chaudfroid sauce, which should be all but congealed, over the entire surface of the chilled bird, being careful to cover all visible parts.

When it is completely covered with the sauce, decorate according to your own fancy. Leaves of tarragon or leaf shapes cut from leek or scallion green, truffle slices, flowers cut from pimiento and green pepper can be combined in effective designs. The white of hard-cooked eggs, truffles, and other decorative ingredients may be cut into fancy shapes with truffle cutters or vegetable cutters. It is best to work out the design ahead of time and lay out the ingredients you will use for decorating.

When the turkey is decorated, chill again and then brush with or carefully spoon over aspic, which should be syrupy and just about to set. Cool until serving time, arrange on a platter and decorate the platter with chopped set aspic and any greens you desire. Tiny tomatoes stuffed with Salad Russe and glazed with aspic, or stuffed eggs filled with a mixture piped through a pastry bag with a rosette tube, make a pretty, edible decoration.

Serve the Turkey en Chaudfroid with cold ham and tongue and a selection of vegetables vinaigrette.

BOEUF À LA MODE FROIDE

4 pounds rump of beef
12 strips larding pork
2 tablespoons chopped parsley
2 bay leaves
  Salt to taste
2 teaspoons cracked black and white pepper
½ teaspoon nutmeg
1 small onion, finely sliced
1 small carrot, finely sliced
½ teaspoon thyme
3 cloves
2 sprigs fresh tarragon
8 peppercorns
1¼ cups brandy
3½ cups red Burgundy
¼ cup bourbon
1 tablespoon bacon fat
2 calves' feet, blanched
1 clove garlic, finely chopped
  Herb bouquet (bay leaf, parsley, celery tops)
12 each: baby carrots, baby white onions,
  baby turnips, baby mushrooms
½ pound salt pork, diced, blanched and drained
3 tablespoons plain gelatin
2 cups meat aspic

With a larding needle, lard the beef with the strips of pork. Place beef in a deep earthenware crock. Sprinkle with parsley, 1 crushed bay leaf, salt, cracked pepper, nutmeg, onion and carrot slices. Add thyme, cloves, whole bay leaf, tarragon, peppercorns, 1 cup brandy, 1½ cups Burgundy and bourbon. Marinate for 24 hours, turning once or twice. Remove, drain and dry meat well, heat bacon fat in a large cast iron kettle and brown meat on all sides over high heat. Remove meat from pan and lift glaze with ¼ cup flaming brandy, stirring all the time. Return meat to pan with marinade, calves' feet, remaining Burgundy, garlic and herb bouquet. Cover and bring to a rolling boil. Cook in a 350° oven for 4 hours, turning meat once or twice.

Remove beef to another kettle with a close-fitting lid. Remove all fat from gravy and strain over the meat. Add vegetables, diced salt pork, and meat trimmed from calves' feet. Cover and cook in a 350° oven for 1 hour. Let meat get quite cold in the liquid. Remove, place on a heavy board, place a heavy weight on it and let it chill for a few hours. Cut meat into very thin slices. Arrange them overlapping on a flat glass or silver dish. Strain the gravy, mix it with the gelatin and stir over ice until it is on the point of setting. Coat the meat slices with this sauce and chill in the refrigerator. Arrange vegetables down each side of dish and coat with meat aspic on the point of setting. Serves 8.

COLD JELLIED BEEF PÂTÉ

2 calves' feet, cracked
1 pig's foot, cut in 4
2 pounds beef chuck, sliced
2 pounds pork, sliced
  Salt, freshly cracked pepper
2 white onions, skinned and finely sliced
3 carrots, peeled and finely sliced
2 cloves garlic, finely chopped
½ cup chopped parsley
2 crushed bay leaves
2 cloves
1 teaspoon chopped rosemary
½ teaspoon each: cinnamon, nutmeg, ginger
  Bacon slices
1 cup red Burgundy
¼ cup brandy
2 cups meat aspic

Put the calves' feet and pig's foot in a Dutch oven. Then alternate layers of beef and pork, seasoning each layer generously with salt and pepper and putting between each layer thin slices of onion and carrot, and all the other herbs and spices. Cover with bacon slices, add the wine and brandy and simmer gently for 6 hours. Remove only the meat. Finely chop or coarsely shred meat and pack into a 2-pound bread tin or terrine. Strain the juices through a fine cloth and pour over the meat. Chill, but do not allow to set and then add 1 cup of aspic on the point of setting. Chill until set. Unmold and decorate with remaining set aspic, finely chopped.

HOW TO PREPARE HAM
GLAZED WITH ASPIC

Coat surface of cooked ham with chaudfroid sauce on point of setting, pouring from
side of spoon so surface is coated evenly.

Stamp out truffle rounds and crescents with
circular cutter. Decorate ham sides with
crescents, overlapping rounds down center.

Carefully and quickly spoon aspic on the
point of setting over the surface, pouring
from side of spoon so ham is evenly coated.

Arrange ham on platter, border with chopped
aspic. Fold sheet of white paper in half, snip
edge, tape into frill for bone.

HAM GLAZED WITH ASPIC

**10–12-pound country ham, ready-to-eat or
previously boiled**
1 pint sherry
4–5 cups chaudfroid sauce
Meat aspic
Truffles

Place the ham, with skin on, in a roasting pan and
add the sherry. Cover and bake in a 350° oven,
allowing 10 minutes per pound for a ready-to-eat
ham, or 1½ hours if you are using a ham that has
been previously boiled.

Allow the ham to cool and carefully remove the skin
and trim off excess fat. The surface should be a thin
layer of perfectly smooth white fat. Stir chaudfroid
sauce over ice until on point of setting, then carefully
coat ham with sauce. Put in refrigerator to set.

Chill part of the aspic very firm and leave the rest
in a semi-jellied state, about the consistency of egg
white. Cut thin slices of truffle and, using a truffle
cutter, shape them into interesting patterns. Attach
the truffle shapes to the ham with semi-jellied aspic.
Chill thoroughly. Spoon the rest of the semi-jellied
aspic over the ham, spreading it evenly. Put in refrigerator until serving time.

When you are ready to serve, place the ham on a
platter, put a paper frill around the shank bone and
surround the ham with mounds of chopped firm
aspic. This is a spectacular centerpiece for a buffet.

HAM MOUSSE

4 ounces salt butter
¾ cup flour
Salt, cayenne pepper
½ teaspoon nutmeg
2 eggs
1 cup milk
6 ounces sweet butter
1½ pounds boiled ham
1 teaspoon tomato paste
½ cup heavy cream, whipped
2 egg whites, stiffly beaten

4 cups meat aspic
4 ounces sliced tongue
1 small truffle, sliced
1 bunch watercress

Dissolve salt butter in a small heavy saucepan, mix in the flour, off the heat, and season with salt, cayenne and nutmeg. Add the two beaten eggs, mix in the milk, and stir over low heat until mixture comes clean away from the sides of the pan. Spread sauce on a plate and chill well.

Cream sweet butter until very light and fluffy in a mixer. Put the ham through a fine meat chopper three times, beat it slowly into the creamed butter, add the tomato paste and season well. Mix in chilled sauce, then the whipped cream and lastly the stiffly beaten egg whites. Well chill a ring mold. Pour in the bottom 1½ cups aspic on the point of setting. Chill until set in the refrigerator. Cut out small rounds of boiled tongue, and cut a smaller round from the center of each. Fill hole with a round of truffle cut the same size. Dip this decoration in aspic on the point of setting and place at even distances in the ring mold. Pour over the decoration a little more aspic on the point of setting and chill again. When set, carefully fill the ring mold with the ham mousse and, on top of the mousse, a little more aspic on the point of setting. Chill until set, then unmold on a round platter and decorate with sprigs of watercress and chopped set aspic. Serves 6–8.

JAMBON PERSILLÉ

Boil a small ham in half water and half Alsatian wine until tender. Remove it from the broth and cool. Cut into uneven dice.

Chop a lavish amount of parsley. You will want at least half as much parsley as you have ham. Arrange the ham mixed with the parsley in a mold and cover with meat aspic. Place a double layer of foil over the top and weight the ham down with canned goods until cooled. Serve in thin slices. Serves 10–12.

HAM CORNUCOPIAS IN ASPIC

Slice boiled ham or canned ham into thin uniform pieces. Roll each piece into a cornucopia. Put purée of foie gras in a pastry tube and stuff each cornucopia. Top each one with a thin slice of truffle.

Arrange the stuffed cornucopias in a shallow serving dish or platter, placing them in a fan-shaped pattern, a rosette pattern, or any decorative pattern that you wish. Melt meat aspic and cool it until half solid. Spoon a little of the aspic over the cornucopias and chill until firm: add more aspic and chill again. Continue until the cornucopias are completely glazed.

BEET JELLY

2 packages lemon gelatin
2 cups boiling water
1 cup sugar
½ cup cold water
1 cup wine vinegar
  Salt
2 cups chopped, cooked beets
1 tablespoon pickled grated horseradish
1 teaspoon grated onion
  Mayonnaise

Dissolve lemon gelatin in boiling water and add sugar. Stir until dissolved. Add cold water, vinegar and salt to taste. Chill until a soft jelly. Add beets, horseradish and onion. Pour into a mold which has been rinsed with cold water. Chill. Serve with mayonnaise. This goes well with cold roast fowl. Serves 4.

CUCUMBER JELLY

2 tablespoons unflavored gelatin
2 tablespoons cold water
1½ cups clear chicken broth
1 slice onion
1 stalk celery
1 sprig parsley
  Salt
2 cucumbers

Soften the gelatin in the cold water. Bring the chicken broth to a boil with the onion, celery and parsley. Add the gelatin, ¼ teaspoon salt, strain and cool. Cut 4 thin slices from the unpared cucumbers and put one in the bottom of each of 4 individual molds. Pare and chop fine the rest of the cucumbers. Add to the jelly and pour into the molds. Serve this cucumber jelly with fish. Serves 4.

Pastry, Cake & Cookie

Sweet are the uses of baking. The Egyptians honored Isis with horn-shaped cakes, and the Saxons hailed their goddess Eastre with similar delicacies. The Greeks offered up flaky pastries to the deities of Mount Olympus whenever it seemed that the divine humor was in need of a little sweetening, and their passion for cheesecakes was so inordinate that islands from Samos to Crete vied in the creation of these little niceties. (Some cooks were inspired to mold the matchless cheesecake into an equally splendid form— that of a woman's breast.)

The skill of the baker and pastry cook was never underestimated, and seldom unrewarded. Sugared pièces montées, known as sotelties were the high spot of the coronation feast of Henry V and his fair Catherine. Louis XIV elevated a country cook to the royal kitchens for inventing petits fours, while Madame Du Barry, a woman of many talents, earned her Cordon Bleu from Louis XV by preparing him an epicurean dinner that ended with a superb peach cake. Even the young Queen Victoria, casting about for ways to please her beloved Albert, set queenly hand to stove and baked one of his longed-for German foods, gingerbread. To Richard Baddeley, an eighteenth-century pastry cook turned actor, there could be no better way to perpetuate his name than to leave 100 pounds, invested at three per cent, for a Baddeley Cake to be eaten annually in his memory by "His Majesty's Company of Comedians" in the Green Room at Drury Lane theatre.

Pastry is a malleable, magical medium that allows of infinite variations, from the sturdy crust that supports a pie filling to the aptly name pâte feuilletée, with multiple layers crisp as autumn leaves, and the even flakier tissue-thin strudel— descended, it is said, from the baklava the Turks brought to Budapest. No alchemy is needed to turn a simple paste of flour, water and shortening into a glorious confection, only the light hand of a careful cook and the hot breath of the oven.

Although in the nineteenth century America was to take over the title of land of cakes, cookies and pastries, it was the English who were the original sweet tooths, going so far as to name one part of Cheapside market Pye Corner. The names of their pastries range from the prosaic to the poetic —shoestrings, maids of honor, love's wells. Henry VIII was the first to taste sweet potato pie, and the Elizabethans doted on those made with apples. ("Thy breath," sighed one swain to his lady, "is like the steame of apple pyes.") Americans who share this devotion to the fruit planted by Johnny Appleseed might well understand the reproachful comment of Lord Dudley, Victorian diplomat and pastry fancier, after a profuse banquet, "Bless my soul! No apple pie."

BASIC PIE PASTRY

> 1 cup flour
> ¼ teaspoon salt
> 6½ tablespoons vegetable shortening
> 2 tablespoons water

Place the flour and salt in a bowl. Cut in the shortening with a pastry blender or 2 knives until the mixture forms fine crumbs. Sprinkle the water over the crumbs very gradually, stir and press down with a fork until the dough begins to hold together. Shape it into a ball with your hands. Chill until ready to use.

PÂTE À FONCER
(Short Pastry)

> 2 cups flour
> ¾ cup butter or lard
> 1 egg
> ½ teaspoon salt

Sift the flour onto a pastry board or work table and make a well in the center. Put the butter, egg and salt in the well. Working quickly with your finger tips, blend the pastry into a ball. Wrap it in waxed paper and chill for 1½–2 hours.

ROUGH PUFF PASTE
OR ENGLISH PUFF PASTE
(for many meat, poultry and game pies)

This dough is not as delicate as French puff pastry, but it is exceedingly good.

> 2¼ cups flour
> ¼ teaspoon salt
> ¾ cup lard or butter
> Dash lemon juice
> Ice water

Sift the flour and salt and add the lard or butter, cut into pieces the size of large cherries. Mix and blend well. Make a well in the center and add the lemon juice and just enough ice water to make an elastic dough. Press into a ball and chill for 15 minutes.

Place on a floured board and roll into a long strip. Fold away from yourself into three folds. Seal the edges with the rolling pin and turn the pastry around so that the folded edges are to your right and left. Roll again and fold. Chill for 15 minutes. Repeat the process and chill another 15 minutes. Then repeat once more and chill the dough until needed.

BASIC PÂTE À PÂTE
(for pâté en croûte)

> 4 cups flour
> ⅔ cup butter
> ⅔ cup lard
> ½ teaspoon salt
> 2 egg yolks

Combine all ingredients, adding water if necessary to make a fairly stiff dough. Roll the pastry dough in small pieces with the heel of the hand and then form it into a single firm ball. Chill for several hours before using. Makes enough pastry for a loaf-sized pâté.

CREAM CHEESE PASTRY

> 1 cup flour
> ¼ pound cream cheese
> ¼ pound butter

Work all together in a mixing bowl. Pat into a ball, wrap in waxed paper, and chill in the refrigerator for several hours or overnight. If left overnight, let stand at room temperature for an hour or so before rolling out. Good for any pie, or to cut in small shapes as appetizers.

PÂTE SUCRÉE

(for any sweet pie, and for making shells for fruit tarts)

1 cup flour
2 ounces butter
¼ cup sugar (4 tablespoons)
2 egg yolks
Few drops vanilla or little grated lemon rind

Put the flour on a marble slab or on a pastry board. Make a well in the center, and in it put the other ingredients. With your finger tips, work them into a smooth paste. Then push the flour gently over the paste and work it in with the heel of your hand. When the mixture will form a smooth ball, wrap it in waxed paper and chill in the refrigerator for at least ½ hour before rolling out.

GRAHAM CRACKER CRUST

1½ cups graham cracker crumbs
¼ cup sugar
½ cup melted butter

Roll the crumbs very fine with a rolling pin. Blend them with the sugar and butter. Press evenly on the bottom and sides of a 9″ pie plate (an 8″ tin placed over the crumbs and pushed around the edge helps distribute them evenly).

Chill 2–3 hours in the refrigerator before filling.

RICH PASTRY

(for flans and tarts)

2 cups unsifted flour
3 tablespoons sugar
3 hard-cooked egg yolks, mashed
2 raw egg yolks
¾ cup butter, or ½ cup butter plus ¼ cup
  vegetable shortening, firm but not icy
1 teaspoon grated lemon rind
½ teaspoon salt

Put the flour on a marble work top, a table or in a bowl and make a well in the center. Put all the rest of the ingredients in the well. Working quickly with your finger tips, mix the flour with the other ingredients. When the dough is well blended, break off small bits and rub them on the work top with the

heel of your hand. This mixes the dough thoroughly. Press the dough together and chill for at least 1/2 hour before using. Roll it out between two sheets of waxed paper. Roll away from yourself and then toward yourself; turn the dough, loosen the paper and roll again. Repeat process until dough is size you need. This dough should be rolled at least 1/3″ thick.

PÂTE SABLÉE

(for fruit flans, tarts or for lining barquette tins)

¾ cup butter
⅓ cup sugar
1 egg
2 cups flour
½ teaspoon salt

Cream the butter and sugar and add the egg. Blend well. Sift the flour and salt and gradually blend into the sugar-butter mixture. If the paste is too stiff, add a little ice water, but this is seldom necessary. The pastry should be the consistency of a good cookie dough. Mold into a flan ring or pan, or roll out and fit into the pan. Chill. Bake in a 375° oven for about 20 minutes. Cool before filling.

MAKING FLAN SHELLS

Flan rings are available in shops that specialize in equipment for the serious cook. They can be round, square or oblong. The standard oblong ring is about 12″ by 4″. Round rings vary from 4″–12″ in diameter. Square rings come from 6″–12″ in size.

To make a flan shell, set the ring on a baking sheet. Roll out the dough to fit the ring and carefully lift it into the ring so that the dough falls to the bottom, trying not to break it too much. Then, with the sides of your hands, press it in. Run the rolling pin across the top rim to give an edge to the dough and to cut off any excess.

If you plan to fill the flan with pastry cream and fruit or just with fruit, you must bake the shell first. Cover the dough with a piece of foil and fit it in loosely. Fill it with dry beans and bake as directed, or until the shell is just baked and delicately browned. Remove the beans and foil (you can save the beans and use them over again for the same purpose) and cool the shell on the baking sheet.

HOW TO MAKE A FLAN SHELL

1. Roll out dough. Turn it a little after each rolling to keep even circle.

2. Roll until dough will cover flan ring. Hold ring on dough to check size.

3. Working toward you, carefully roll up dough from board onto rolling pin.

4. Lift and gently unroll dough away from you over ring on baking sheet.

5. Carefullly press the dough snugly against sides and bottom of flan ring.

6. Run the rolling pin over the rim of flan ring to remove any excess dough.

7. Crimp dough edge to make fluted rim; prick bottom of pastry with fork.

8. Cut circle of foil to fit flan shell; weight with rice to keep pastry flat.

FILLINGS FOR FLAN SHELLS

1. Fill with pastry cream. When the cream is set, cover with ripe strawberries or raspberries and glaze with melted currant jelly.
2. Omit the pastry cream and simply pile high with berries and glaze.
3. Fill with poached peaches or apricots and cover with a raspberry or apricot glaze.
4. Melt a 6-ounce package of semi-sweet chocolate bits and combine with ¼ cup finely chopped filberts or walnuts. Spread on the bottom of the flan ring. Cover with poached pear halves and top with an apricot glaze.
5. Fill flan rings with split seeded grapes, alternating black grapes with green, or purple with red. Brush with currant glaze and serve with whipped cream.

GLAZES FOR FLANS

Currant glaze: Melt a 1-pound jar of currant jelly over medium heat and boil down for 1 minute.

Apricot glaze: Melt a 1-pound jar of apricot jam and bring to a boil. Add 2 tablespoons of cognac and boil down for 2 minutes.

Raspberry glaze: Melt a 1-pound jar of raspberry preserves. Bring to a boil and stir in 2 tablespoons of crème de cassis. Strain.

PASTRY CREAM
(Crème Pâtissière)

    2 cups milk
    4 egg yolks
    ½ cup sugar
    ½ cup flour
    ½ teaspoon salt
    1 teaspoon vanilla

Scald the milk. Beat egg yolks and sugar together with a wire whisk. Add flour mixed with salt. Slowly pour on the hot milk, stirring constantly. Stir over a slow fire until the mixture thickens. Remove and pour into a cold mixing bowl—or if you are in a hurry to use the cream, into a large shallow enamel pan. When cool, add the vanilla.

Pastry cream may be flavored with rum or kirsch instead of vanilla.

Coffee Pastry Cream: Blend in 1–2 teaspoons of instant coffee dissolved in a little hot water instead of the vanilla.

Chocolate Pastry Cream: Add 1–2 tablespoons of cool melted chocolate.

FONDANT ICING

    2½ pounds sugar
    ½ cup corn syrup
        Pinch cream of tartar
    2 cups water

Put all the ingredients into a saucepan. Bring rapidly to a boil, stirring until the sugar is dissolved, and cook to 240° on candy thermometer. Pour on a moist marble slab. When cool, work with a heavy wooden spoon or metal scraper until the fondant becomes white and opaque. Store in a screw top jar in the refrigerator. When ready to use, warm the amount you need over very low heat.

It may be flavored with vanilla extract, instant coffee dissolved in a little hot water, or melted chocolate.

GLOSSY CHOCOLATE FROSTING

    4 squares chocolate, melted
    3 cups sifted confectioners' sugar
    ⅜ cup boiling water
    1 tablespoon butter
    1 teaspoon vanilla

Melt the chocolate. Sift the sugar into a mixing bowl, pour on the boiling water, and stir until the sugar is thoroughly dissolved. Blend in the chocolate, butter and vanilla. If too stiff, add a little more hot water.

CONFECTIONERS' VANILLA FROSTING

    2 cups sifted confectioners' sugar
    ½ teaspoon vanilla
        Dash salt
    3–4 tablespoons boiling water

Sift the sugar into a mixing bowl. Add the vanilla and salt, then stir in the boiling water. Mix all the ingredients together thoroughly.

BASIC STEPS IN MAKING
PUFF PASTRY

1. Roll pastry dough into a rectangle.

2. Put chilled butter in the center.

3. Fold over ends and sides. Chill.

4. Roll dough, folded side up, in quick back and forth strokes away from you.

5. Still rolling away from you, make long strip. Reverse dough during rolling.

6. Lay strip across board and fold in thirds. This is called a turn. Roll again.

MOCHA FROSTING

2 squares chocolate
3 tablespoons butter
3 cups sifted confectioners' sugar
¼–½ cup hot coffee
1 teaspoon vanilla

Melt the chocolate with the butter and a pinch of salt. Beat in the sugar alternately with the hot coffee until smooth and of a good spreading consistency. Lastly add the vanilla.

PUFF PASTRY
(Pâte Feuilletée)

Pâte feuilletée (leafy pastry) is one of the finest of all pastries. Delicate flaky light layers are characteristic of puff pastry, and although it is not easy to make, and is time consuming, by taking proper precautions and following the rules, you should be successful. The principle is not complicated. You make a dough with flour and water, fold it around butter, and then roll and fold it several times, always enclosing the butter, and keeping in air. Each time, fold the dough in 3 parts, making 3 layers the first time, 9 layers the second time, 27 the third and so on. At the end of the required 6 rollings and foldings (called turns), you will of necessity have numerous layers. If the butter has not broken through, and if the oven is hot, the paste rises phenomenally. A hot oven is vital for the initial baking.

To keep the butter trapped and solid, you must have cool working conditions and you must work quickly. The kitchen should be cool (which makes puff paste a difficult summer project), the ingredients and utensils chilled, and the dough thoroughly chilled after you cut it out and before you bake it. If you can, let the dough rest in the refrigerator overnight before the final rolling and baking, giving it the last 2 turns before the final rolling. When working with the dough, if it softens, put it in the refrigerator.

PÂTE FEUILLETÉE

½ pound sweet butter
2 cups flour
⅔ cup ice water

Knead and squeeze the butter in very cold water to force out any moisture that may be in the butter. Shape butter into a rectangle ½″ thick, wrap in wax paper and refrigerate.

Put the flour in a mixing bowl. Gradually add the ice water, mixing with the fingertips to make a dough. Roll out on a lightly floured board into a rectangle a little more than twice as large as the butter. Place chilled butter in center, fold over ends and sides, seal edges well and refrigerate for 20 minutes. Place dough on board with the folded edge nearest you. Press lightly with rolling pin over entire surface of dough, then roll out away from you in a series of quick, light, back-and-forth rolling movements, so as not to permit the butter to break through the surface. When the dough is ½″ thick, fold the third furthest away from you toward the center, then fold the third nearest you over it, making three layers in all. Turn the dough one-quarter way around, so that the open edge is nearest you. Repeat the rolling and folding. Chill for 30 minutes in the refrigerator or 15 minutes in the freezer, repeat the two rollings and foldings, chill again, roll and fold twice more. Use as little flour on the board as possible, brushing any excess flour from dough before folding. Chill in the refrigerator for 15–30 minutes before using. Roll out the dough and use as directed.

NAPOLEONS

Cut 2 strips of puff paste, ¼″ thick, 2½″ wide and as long as a cookie sheet (usually 15″). Rinse the cookie sheet with cold water, place the strips on it, and chill in the refrigerator for at least 30 minutes. Bake about 15 minutes in a 425° oven, until well risen and nicely browned, then turn over and bake another 15–20 minutes at 350°. Remove and cool. Cut each piece in half, making 4 layers. Put aside the best looking piece for the top. Place one layer, cut side up, on a long wooden board or serving platter. Cover with pastry cream. Place the next 2 layers over this, both cut side up, both filled with pastry cream. Put the top layer on a cake rack, brown side up. Spoon confectioners' vanilla frosting over the top, using half the given recipe. Let cool and set in the refrigerator. Melt 1 square of chocolate with a teaspoon of butter and just enough water to make it smooth—1–2 tablespoons. Make a small cone with double thickness waxed paper, securing it with a paper clip. Put the chocolate in it, and pipe 3 very narrow lines lengthwise down the white icing. Immediately draw a toothpick across the lines at ½″ intervals, reversing the direction every other time. This will give you a nice professional looking topping. Place it on top of the other layers, and smooth the sides. Chill. After half an hour it is ready to be served. Cut into 2″ slices.

Chicken Napoleon: Sandwich the puff paste slices with creamed chicken and garnish the top of the pastry with sautéed mushroom caps or slivered browned almonds.

VOL-AU-VENT AND BOUCHÉES
(Large and Small Patty Shells)

When rolling puff paste for patty shells, it is important to have it of even thickness, or your shells may be lopsided. In rolling, there is a tendency to use one hand more heavily than the other, causing unevenness. To correct this, turn the paste occasionally when rolling it. Also feel it, to be sure it is the same thickness all over.

Vol-au-Vent: Roll out puff paste ¼″ thick. Cut into two 8″ rounds. Cut a 3″ round out of the center of one round. Make diamond-shaped cuts in the 3″ round with a sharp knife. Brush a cookie sheet with water. Place the 3″ round and the large whole round on it. Brush the outside 2″ of the large round with cold water, and place the second 8″ round on top, fitting exactly. Press down lightly. Make diagonal cuts on the second round, and straight shallow cuts down the sides of both, at ½″ intervals. Brush the small round, and the top of the second round with beaten egg, taking care not to go over the edge, since this would hinder rising. Chill 30 minutes in the refrigerator. Bake in a 450° oven about 10 minutes, until puffed and lightly browned. Reduce heat to 375° and cook an additional 25–30 minutes. Remove, scoop out any uncooked part in the middle, and fill with savory mixture. Top with the small round.

Bouchées: These are small vol-au-vents. Use 3″ fluted cutters with the center cutter 2″ and plain.

PALMIERS
(Palm leaves)

Roll puff paste ¼″ thick, covering the board or slab with granulated sugar instead of flour. Sprinkle half the paste with sugar, fold and press the edges together. Roll, sprinkle with sugar, fold and press, 3 times. Then roll into a strip as long as the cookie sheet—about 15″—and 8″ wide. Sprinkle well with sugar. Make a 2″ lengthwise fold on each side, toward the center. Moisten the center lightly with water, fold one side over the other, and press down. The strip now has 4 layers. Sprinkle a cookie sheet with sugar. Cut the strip crosswise into pieces ½″ thick. Place them cut side up about 2″ apart on the cookie sheet, since they will rise sideways rather than up. Press down with a spatula and sprinkle with sugar. Chill for at least 30 minutes in the refrigerator. Bake in a 400° oven for about 10 minutes, just until golden brown on the bottom. Turn each with a spatula. Cook another 10 minutes or so. Palm leaves have to be carefully watched as sugar caramelizes and may burn.

CREAM HORNS

Roll a piece of puff paste ⅛″ thick, and about 12″ long. Cut into lengthwise strips ¾″ wide. Brush a strip with water, cut off one end at an angle, pinch the strip onto one end of a metal horn cone, and roll it around the cone, moistened side up, slightly at an angle, with each row overlapping the last row a little. Press end in, and place on a greased cookie sheet, with the end underneath. Sprinkle lightly with sugar. Let chill for at least 30 minutes in the refrigerator. Bake in a 400° oven for 20–30 minutes. Remove horns from the cones while hot or they may stick. When cool, fill with sweetened flavored whipped cream or flavored pastry cream.

CROISSANTS

2 envelopes or cakes yeast
¼ cup lukewarm water
4 cups flour
½ teaspoon salt
1 teaspoon sugar

1½ cups milk
¾ pound butter
Little beaten egg yolk mixed with cold milk

Soften the yeast in lukewarm water in a mixing bowl. Add 1 cup flour and stir to form a smooth firm ball. Cut a cross in the top, cover with a dry towel and set in a warm place to rise until double in bulk.

Sift into a bowl 3 cups flour mixed with the salt and sugar. Gradually add the milk, stirring to make a smooth dough. Combine this dough with the sponge (the yeast mixture), beating well. Cover with a towel and let rest for 10 minutes. Then chill for 1/2 hour.

Roll out the dough into a long rectangle about 1/2″ thick. Work the butter into a flat cake and place it in the center of the dough. Fold 1/3 of the dough over the center 1/3 and fold the remaining 1/3 on top to make 3 layers. Turn the folded dough so that the open ends face you. Roll out, fold over as before and turn. This whole operation is called a turn. Make another turn and place the dough in the refrigerator for several hours or overnight, well wrapped in freezer wrap and a cloth. Next day roll out, fold and turn. Repeat operation, making 2 more turns.

Chill the dough in the refrigerator for 1 hour. Then roll it out 1/8″ thick and cut it into 6″ squares. Cut each square diagonally into 2 triangles. Starting with the longest side of the triangle, roll loosely to form a cylinder thicker in the center than at the ends. Shape into crescents, place on wet cookie sheet, cover with cloth stretched over two glasses like canopy and allow to rise in warm place till double in bulk. Brush lightly all over with beaten egg and milk (which must not touch the cookie sheet), bake at 425° for 15–20 minutes. Remove and serve hot.

APRICOT DANISH PASTRIES

1 package granular yeast
¼ cup warm water
¼ cup milk, scalded
2 eggs, lightly beaten
6 tablespoons sugar
½ teaspoon salt
½ teaspoon almond extract
2 tablespoons soft butter
2 cups all-purpose flour

10 tablespoons cold butter, sliced thin
20 large dried apricot halves
¼ cup apricot jam
1 tablespoon apricot brandy

Dissolve the yeast in the warm water. Pour the scalded milk into a bowl. Reserve 2 tablespoons of the beaten eggs and add the remainder to the milk with 4 tablespoons sugar, the salt, almond extract and soft butter. Cool to lukewarm. Add the dissolved yeast and 1¾ cups of the flour. Beat thoroughly. Place the remaining 1/4 cup flour on a pastry board, turn the dough out on top of it and knead until the dough is smooth and all the flour absorbed. Let the dough rest for ½ hour.

Flour the board lightly. Roll out the dough to a rectangle 1/3″ thick with a floured rolling pin. Place half the butter slices on the center third of the dough. Fold one end of the dough over the butter. Place the remaining butter on that third of the dough, then fold over the other end of the dough. (You now have 3 layers of dough with butter between each layer.) Pinch the open edges of the dough together to enclose the butter completely. Flatten the dough slightly with the rolling pin (press down, do not roll) and place the dough in a freezer for 15 minutes.

Flour the board lightly again. Place the dough on the board with the folded edge nearest you. Press lightly with the rolling pin all over the surface of the dough, then roll out away from you in a series of quick, light back-and-forth rolling movements, to keep the butter from breaking through the surface. When the dough is 1/3″ thick, fold the right-hand third toward the center, then fold the left-hand third over it, making 3 layers again.

Turn the dough 1/4 way around so that an open edge is nearest you. Repeat this rolling, folding and turning until the butter is blended smoothly into the dough. (If the butter starts to ooze out during the rolling, chill the dough in the freezer for a few minutes before proceeding.) Chill the dough for 3/4 hour. While the dough is chilling, make the filling: Simmer the apricots in water to cover for 1/2 hour, or until soft. Drain, mash the fruit, and stir in the remaining 2 tablespoons sugar, the jam and brandy. Chill.

Roll out the dough to a square 1/4″ thick on a lightly floured board. Cut the dough into 16 squares and place a portion of the filling on the center of each square. Bend each corner of the square almost to the center and press down very gently so that the filling does not spread. Place 1½″ apart on greased baking sheets and set in a warm place to rise for 1½ hours, or until double in bulk. Dilute the reserved 2 tablespoons beaten egg with 1 tablespoon cold water and brush on the top of each pastry. Bake in a preheated 400° oven for 15 minutes, or until golden. Serve warm or reheated. Makes 16 pastries.

CREAM PUFF PASTRY
(Pâte à Choux)

Choux paste is used for large cream puffs, small ones (profiteroles), éclairs and other variations. It is one of the easiest of all pastries to make and handle successfully if you follow a few simple rules. The method is quite different from other pastries, since the flour is added to a boiling liquid, and the eggs beaten into the hot mixture. The oven temperature is one key factor for success. The finished products are similar to popovers, firm dry hollow shells. The leavening is steam, produced by the rather large quantity of liquid, and a high heat is needed in the beginning to form steam quickly. Once the mixture has risen and browned, the heat should be lowered; slower baking is required so that the insides dry out, the shells get firm and crisp, to prevent shrinking and collapsing on cooling.

PÂTE À CHOUX

> **1 cup sifted flour**
> **1 cup cold water**
> **½ teaspoon salt**
> **½ cup (¼ pound) butter**
> **4 large eggs**

Measure flour and put it by the stove. Bring the water, salt and butter rapidly to a boil in a deep medium-size (6-cup) saucepan, stirring occasionally with a wooden spoon. As soon as the mixture comes to a good boil, add the flour all at once, take the pan off the fire, and stir hard until the batter stiffens and draws away from the sides of the pan, forming a compact ball. This happens quickly, in less than a minute. Put the pan back over the heat and stir vigorously for another minute. (This stage of cooking the flour is important, because if it is not cooked long

enough, it won't absorb enough moisture to exert the necessary binding power. Don't overcook though, or the butter may start oozing out, and the mixture won't puff as it should.) Remove and let stand for 2 or 3 minutes to cool. Then beat in the whole eggs, one at a time. Beat 1 minute with electric mixer after each addition, 2 or 3 minutes by hand. After all have been added, beat for 5 minutes. When the first eggs are added, it may seem that they are not thoroughly incorporated, that the batter is slippery and separated, but by the time the last egg is beaten in, the batter will be smooth, shiny and stiff—stiff enough in fact to stand up on the baking sheet. Let stand for at least an hour in a cool place before making and baking puffs. Cook on a lightly greased cookie sheet (the temperatures for individual uses follow). Place the cookie sheet on the center rack so that the bottoms and tops will brown evenly. The puffs are done when the shells feel firm and dry; if they are soft, they will collapse after you take them out of the oven. Cool thoroughly before using, and fill just before serving so that the shells won't get soggy.

Note: 4 teaspoons of sugar may be added for a slightly sweet batter along with the salt and butter. For extra shiny puffs, brush before baking with an egg lightly beaten with a fork.

CREAM PUFFS

Use the basic choux paste recipe, adding 4 teaspoons of sugar if you wish. Pipe into 2″–2½″ rounds on a lightly greased cookie sheet, using a pastry bag and large plain tube. Finish with a quick twist for center higher than the sides. (Or you can use a rounded tablespoon of the paste, scraping it off with another spoon and swirling the top a little.) Make puffs 2″ apart. Bake in a 450° oven for 20 minutes, reduce heat to 350° and bake another 20–30 minutes. When cool, make a hole in the bottom with a small knife and, using a pastry bag with a small plain tube, fill with pastry cream or with sweetened whipped cream flavored with vanilla. Or cut the puffs in half and sandwich them. Dust with confectioners' sugar, or top with chocolate, vanilla or mocha frosting. Cream puffs may also be filled with ice cream and served with chocolate sauce. The basic recipe makes about 15 large cream puffs.

HOW TO MAKE CROQUEMBOUCHE

1. Spear cream puffs on knife, dip in hot caramel. Cool on oiled cookie sheet.

2. Put 8½″ high bombe mold on cookie sheet. Oil it to prevent caramel sticking.

3. Clip excess caramel from bottom of puffs. Make ring of largest around mold.

4. Dip tops of puffs in caramel so they stick together. Pile them in a pyramid.

PROFITEROLES

Use the basic choux paste recipe to make tiny profiteroles. Drop them by half teaspoons on a lightly greased cookie sheet, or pipe into 1″ rounds with a pastry bag and small plain tube. Bake in a 450° oven for 15 minutes, reduce heat to 350° and bake another 20 minutes or so, until firm and dry. Let cool before filling. Makes about 35–40.

Small cream puffs are often used as canapés, filled with savory cheese mixtures, pâté de foie gras, or chicken, lobster, crab meat or shrimp salad.

Profiteroles au chocolat: Fill the little cream puffs with sweetened whipped cream, flavored with vanilla or brandy. Make a small hole in the bottom of each one and pipe the whipped cream in with a pastry bag and small plain tube. Pile the profiteroles on a silver platter, and dust well with sifted confectioners' sugar. Serve hot chocolate sauce separately in a silver bowl.

CROQUEMBOUCHE

> **Double recipe pâte à choux**
> 1 egg, beaten
> 2 whole eggs
> 2 egg yolks
> 6 tablespoons sugar
> 6 tablespoons flour
> 1 tablespoon gelatin
> 1½ cups milk, scalded
> 2 egg whites
> 2 cups whipped cream flavored with
>   2 tablespoons rum or 2 teaspoons vanilla

Caramel syrup:
> 2 cups sugar
> 1½ cups water
> ½ teaspoon cream of tartar

Make choux paste and pipe small profiteroles through a pastry bag with a small plain tube onto a lightly greased cookie sheet. You will need about 65–70 profiteroles. Brush tops with beaten egg. Bake according to directions for profiteroles. The puffs should be golden brown and firm to the touch.

Meanwhile, make filling for the puffs. Put the whole eggs and egg yolks, 6 tablespoons sugar and 6 tablespoons flour in a bowl and beat well with a wire whisk. Add gelatin and pour on 1½ cups hot milk. Stir over low heat until just on the point of boiling. Remove and stir over ice until cold. Stiffly beat the egg whites and fold them in. Fold in the flavored whipped cream.

When puffs are baked, remove from oven and cool. Make a small hole in the bottom and fill with the cream mixture, piping it into the puffs through a pastry bag with small plain tube.

Make a caramel syrup by putting the sugar, water and cream of tartar in a heavy pan, bringing it slowly to a boil and cooking to a deep caramel color. Remove from heat and stand in a bowl of ice so the caramel does not get any darker. Pierce bottom of puffs with point of a small knife and dip them into caramel, one at a time. Put on an oiled cookie sheet to set. Oil a tall conical metal mold and pile puffs in a pyramid around it. When completely set and hard, remove mold. Put croquembouche on a platter.

Note: Do not touch puffs while caramel is hot or it will burn you.

GÂTEAU SAINT-HONORÉ

> 1 recipe pâte sucrée
> 1 recipe pâte à choux
> 1 egg, lightly beaten
> 1 recipe pastry cream
> 1 recipe caramel syrup (see Croquembouche)
> 1 tablespoon gelatin
> ¼ cup cold water
> 2 egg whites
>   Pinch salt
> ½ cup sugar

Roll out pâte sucrée to a 10″ circle, ¼″ thick, and place on a lightly greased cookie sheet. Put half the choux paste into a pastry bag with a large plain tube and pipe a rim crown around the edge of the circle. Brush with beaten egg and bake in a 400° oven until pastry is lightly browned, about 40 minutes. Remove and cool. With remaining choux paste, make walnut-sized profiteroles. Bake, cool, and fill with some of the pastry cream. Dip tops in caramel syrup, following directions for croquembouche and place these around the choux-paste rim. Soften gelatin in cold water and dissolve over hot water. Add to remaining

pastry cream (cream should be hot when gelatin is added). Cool. Beat egg whites with salt until stiff, then beat in sugar, a tablespoon at a time. Fold into cool pastry cream. Fill center of ring with mixture.

FRUIT PUFF

Make a choux paste with half the basic recipe. Place it in a buttered 9″ deep pie plate, smoothing it with a rubber scraper, leaving the sides slightly lower than the center. Bake in a 400° oven for 40–50 minutes, until golden brown and firm. The edge will puff up in a high ring. Remove and cool on a cake rack. Just before serving, carefully remove the top of the center and fill with pastry cream, or with flavored whipped cream, or with vanilla ice cream. Cover with 2 cups of slightly sweetened strawberries, raspberries or blueberries. Replace the top and serve at once.

ÉCLAIRS

The standard size for éclairs is about 4″ long, and ¾″–1″ wide. However it is nice to make smaller ones, about 2½″ long and offer a choice of flavors. Pipe choux paste on a lightly greased cookie sheet in a straight line, using a pastry bag and a large plain tube. Bake for 20 minutes in a 450° oven, reduce heat to 350° and bake another 20–30 minutes. When cool, make a hole at one end and pipe in flavored pastry cream or sweetened flavored whipped cream. Top with vanilla, mocha or chocolate frosting.

BEIGNETS SOUFFLÉS

To serve 5 or 6 people, make half the basic choux paste recipe, adding 2 teaspoons of sugar to the water, salt and butter. Let stand at least an hour. Drop by teaspoons into 370° deep fat, cooking only 3 or 4 at a time. The beignets will slowly swell and brown and automatically turn themselves over when the underside is cooked. They are done when golden brown all over. Remove with a slotted spoon, drain on absorbent paper, sprinkle with sifted confectioners' sugar, and serve immediately while hot and crisp.

BASIC STEPS IN
MAKING STRUDEL

1. Work strudel mixture with hand until it holds together.

2. On lightly floured board, knead and slap the dough.

3. Using flailing motion, slap dough down hard on board.

4. After dough has rested, roll it out on floured sheet.

5. Before stretching, brush surface with melted butter.

6. Put back of hands under dough and pull out gently.

7. Trim off thick overhanging, brush with butter.

8. Sprinkle filling over strudel, covering three quarters.

9. Lift up edge of sheet and roll up strudel like jelly roll.

10. Before baking, brush with butter to make crisp.

STRUDEL DOUGH

1 egg
2 tablespoons melted butter
2 cups sifted flour
¾ cup warm water

Have all the ingredients at room temperature. Beat the egg slightly with a fork in a large mixing bowl. Add the melted butter and flour and blend with a fork. Work in the water with your fingers, a little at a time. As soon as the mixture holds together, turn it out on a lightly floured wooden board (enamel or marble are too cool). Knead about 10–15 minutes, slapping the dough down hard on the board occasionally. When you are through it should not be a bit sticky, and should be very elastic. Cover with a warm bowl, which should not touch the dough, and let rest for at least 30 minutes while preparing filling.

Cover a table measuring about 30" by 48" with a clean cloth, large enough to hang over the edges. Sprinkle cloth lightly and evenly with flour. Place the dough in the center and roll it out with a rolling pin as far as it will go easily. Brush with melted butter. Take off your rings and flour your hands. Start pulling the dough very gently with the back of your hands. Begin in the middle and work slowly all around. It takes a little time, but hurry or carelessness may cause holes. When the dough is fairly thin, you can anchor it to one corner of the table, then pull until it completely covers the table and hangs over the edge. (It should be so thin and transparent that you could read a newspaper through it.) Brush with melted butter and let stand for 10–15 minutes to dry a little. (All this brushing with butter may make the strudel crisp rather than very flaky, but much easier to handle.) Cover with desired filling.

Pull or cut off the thick edges below the table top. Roll the strudel by lifting the cloth at the filling end, fold the dough over the filling, then hold the cloth high and the strudel will roll over itself like a huge jelly roll. Roll onto a greased large shallow baking pan. Brush with butter and bake in a 425° oven for half an hour. Brush occasionally with melted butter. Serve warm. If the strudel is made ahead of time, reheat it in a slow oven for 10–15 minutes.

STRUDEL FILLINGS

Flaky strudel dough lends itself to both sweet and savory fillings and can therefore be served either as a main dish or as a dessert.

CHERRY FILLING

2 cups dry bread crumbs
3–4 tablespoons butter
½ cup chopped almonds
2 cups pitted dark sweet cherries, chopped
½ cup sugar
½ teaspoon grated lemon rind
3-ounce package cream cheese
1 cup sour cream

Fry the bread crumbs in butter until nicely browned. After the dough has been stretched, brushed with melted butter and rested, sprinkle the crumbs evenly over ¾ of it. Cover with the almonds, cherries, and sprinkle with the sugar mixed with the lemon rind. Dot with small bits of cream cheese and sour cream.

CABBAGE FILLING

1 medium cabbage
2 teaspoons salt
1 teaspoon sugar
3 tablespoons butter, melted
2–3 tablespoons sour cream (optional)

Core and finely chop the cabbage. Mix with the salt, sugar and butter. Place in a shallow baking pan and cook in a 350° oven for ½ hour. Cool. Spread on the strudel dough. Dot with sour cream if you wish.

APPLE FILLING

1 cup dry bread crumbs
3–4 tablespoons butter
4–6 large cooking apples
½ teaspoon grated lemon rind

½ cup seedless raisins
½ cup chopped walnuts
1 cup sugar
2 teaspoons cinnamon

Fry the bread crumbs in butter until nicely browned. Peel and core the apples, cut into small dice, and mix with the grated lemon rind. After the dough has been stretched, brushed with melted butter and rested, sprinkle ¾ of the surface evenly with the fried crumbs. Cover with the apples, then the raisins and nuts, and lastly the sugar which has been mixed with the cinnamon.

SOUR CREAM FILLING

1 cup bread crumbs
6 tablespoons butter
4 tablespoons sugar
4 eggs, separated
½ teaspoon grated lemon rind
1 cup sour cream
½ cup seedless raisins
½ cup chopped almonds

Fry the bread crumbs in 2 tablespoons of butter until nicely browned (the bread crumbs help keep the dough dry and the filling from soaking into it). After the dough has been stretched, brushed with melted butter and rested, sprinkle ¾ of it with the crumbs. Cream the sugar and remaining 4 tablespoons butter. Blend in the egg yolks and lemon rind. Stiffly beat the egg whites and fold in alternately with the sour cream. Place over the crumbs and sprinkle over the top the raisins and almonds.

BAKLAVA

(Honey and Almond-filled Pastry)

This famous pastry is at its best when made with toasted almonds and drenched in a honey syrup, rather than a sugar-based one.

1½ pounds blanched almonds,
  finely grated or ground
1 cup sugar
  Grated peel of 1 orange
1 teaspoon cinnamon

1½ cups sweet butter, melted
1 pound prepared filo dough
  (available at stores that sell Greek foods)
  Whole cloves
1½ cups honey

Toast the grated or ground almonds in a preheated 300° oven for 10 minutes, or until lightly browned. Mix with ½ cup of the sugar, orange peel, and cinnamon. Butter a 10″ by 14″ baking pan and spread butter on the filo sheets. Line the pan with 3 buttered sheets, cut to fit the pan. Sprinkle lightly with some of the nut mixture and repeat, alternating 2 sheets of buttered filo and the nut mixture, ending with filo. Cut into 1″ by 1½″ triangles. Insert a whole clove in the center of each triangle. Bake in a preheated 325° oven for 50 minutes, or until golden brown. Meanwhile, bring to a boil the remaining ½ cup sugar, and ½ cup water. Add the honey, and let simmer a few minutes; then cool. Cut through pastry diamonds completely, and while hot, pour over cool honey syrup. Makes about 4 dozen pieces.

RICH PUMPKIN PIE

1 recipe pâte sucrée
2 cups cooked puréed pumpkin
1 cup brown sugar
6 eggs, lightly beaten
2 cups cream
½ teaspoon salt
1 teaspoon cinnamon
½ teaspoon ground cloves
½ teaspoon mace
⅓ cup cognac
4 tablespoons finely chopped candied ginger

Line a 9″ pie tin with the pastry and place foil on top. Fill with dry beans and bake in a 400° oven for 10 minutes. Remove the beans and foil.

Combine the pumpkin with the sugar, eggs, cream, seasonings and cognac and blend well. Pour through a strainer into the pie shell. Sprinkle with chopped candied ginger and bake in a 375° oven for 30–35 minutes, or until the pumpkin is set. Serve slightly warm with cheese or whipped cream. Serves 8.

TART OF LES DEMOISELLES TATIN

> **Butter**
> **Sugar**
> **12–14 green apples**
> **1 recipe rich pastry**
> **1 egg beaten with a little water or cream**

Blend 4 tablespoons butter and ½ cup sugar in a heavy pie tin and cook over medium heat until the mixture is thick, syrupy and lightly browned. Peel, core and slice apples. Arrange them on top of the butter-sugar syrup in layers. Dot each layer with butter and sprinkle with a little sugar. Build the apple slices up in the center to come above the rim of the pan. Cover with rich pastry rolled 1/3″ thick. Brush with egg. Bake in a 450° oven for 10 minutes. Reduce the heat to 375° and continue cooking until the apples are soft and the crust cooked through.

Let the tart cool slightly and then carefully invert it onto a serving plate. The apples should have caramelized with the sugar-butter mixture, making a delicate brown top for the tart. Serve warm or cold with cream. Serves 8.

PARISIAN PEACH AND WALNUT TART

> **⅔ cup plus 2 tablespoons flour**
> **⅔ cup sugar**
> **4 tablespoons butter**
> **1 egg yolk**
> **1½ pounds peaches, peeled and sliced**
> **3 eggs**
> **½ teaspoon vanilla**
> **¾ cup ground walnuts**
> **Confectioners' sugar**

Place 2/3 cup flour, 2 tablespoons sugar, butter, and egg yolk in a bowl. Mix the ingredients with your hands until they form a smooth dough. Press the dough evenly over the bottom and sides of a 9½″ pie plate. Bake in a preheated 375° oven for 15 minutes, or until pale gold. Cool for 15 minutes.

Arrange the peaches in the pastry shell. Beat the remaining sugar with 1 whole egg and 2 egg yolks until thick and light. Beat in the vanilla, nuts, and remaining 2 tablespoons flour. Beat the 2 egg whites until

stiff, but not dry, fold into the batter, and pour over the peaches. Bake in a 350° oven for 1 hour. Cool and dust with confectioners' sugar. Makes 8 servings.

ORANGE-ALMOND FLAN

> **1 recipe rich pastry**
> **Marmalade**
> **4 eggs**
> **⅔ cup super-fine sugar**
> **4 ounces ground almonds**
> **⅓ cup candied orange peel, finely chopped**
> **1 teaspoon almond extract**
> **Apricot glaze**
> **Whipped cream flavored with sugar and grated orange rind**

Roll out pastry about ⅜″ thick. Line a 9″ flan ring with pastry. Freeze. When well frozen, spread the pastry with marmalade. Beat the eggs and sugar and add the almonds, orange peel and almond extract. Blend thoroughly and pour over the marmalade. Bake in a 350° oven for about 30 minutes, or until the flan is set and nicely browned. Cover the top with apricot glaze.

Serve the flan with whipped cream, sweetened to taste and flavored with grated orange rind. Serves 6.

CALIFORNIA DEEP-DISH APPLE PIE

> **¼ cup almonds, blanched or unblanched**
> **¾ cup butter**
> **¼ cup lard**
> **½ teaspoon salt**
> **1½ cups flour**
> **4 pounds tart apples**
> **1 cup sugar**
> **Juice and grated rind of 1 orange**
> **2–3 tablespoons rum**
> **Thick cream**

To make the crust, put almonds in blender and whirl until fine. Mix with ¼ cup of the butter, lard, salt, flour and enough water to hold the dough together. Form in a ball, wrap in waxed paper and refrigerate while preparing the apples.

Peel and slice apples into a baking dish about 2″

deep. Melt the remaining butter and combine with the sugar and the orange juice and rind. Pour mixture over the apples and mix in. Roll out almond dough to fit over the top of the dish (use it all; you don't want the crust too thin). Cut 2 or 3 holes in the dough, then cover the apples, pressing crust down at edges. Bake in a preheated 450° oven for 10 minutes, then reduce heat to 325° and cook until the apples are tender (prod with a skewer through one of the holes). Pour rum through one of the holes and tilt pie back and forth so that it will be evenly distributed. Serve warm with thick cream. Serves 8.

KEY LIME PIE

> 3 egg yolks
> 1 can sweetened condensed milk
> ¾ cup fresh lime juice
> 9″ pie tin lined with graham cracker crust
> 3 egg whites
> 3 teaspoons sugar
> Pinch salt

Beat the egg yolks until light and frothy and add the milk and lime juice gradually, beating them in until the mixture is smooth. Fill the pie shell.

Beat the egg whites until they form into soft peaks. Beat in the sugar and salt gradually and continue beating until the meringue is firm. Spread evenly over surface of filling. Bake in a 350° oven until the meringue is set and lightly browned. Serves 6.

CHEESE PIE

> ½ teaspoon butter
> 3 tablespoons graham-cracker crumbs
> 1¾ cups cream-style cottage cheese
> 4 teaspoons cornstarch
> 5 tablespoons sugar
> 1 teaspoon vanilla
> Grated rind ½ lemon
> 2 eggs, separated

Butter a 9″ pie plate with the ½ teaspoon butter and sprinkle with the graham-cracker crumbs. Place the remaining ingredients, except the egg whites, in an electric mixer and beat until smooth. Beat the egg whites until stiff, but not dry, and fold into the batter.

Pour into the pie plate and bake in a preheated 350° oven for 25 minutes. Cool the pie, but do not chill. Makes 4–6 servings.

VERY RICH BLUEBERRY PIE

> 9″ pie tin lined with graham cracker crust
> 2 pints fresh blueberries or 2 15-ounce cans
>   blueberries in heavy syrup
> 1 cup granulated sugar
> ½ cup cold water
> ½ cup (1 stick) butter
> 1 cup powdered sugar
> 2 eggs
> 1 teaspoon vanilla
> 1½ cups heavy cream

Bake crust about 6–8 minutes in a 350° oven. Set aside to cool.

If using fresh blueberries, pick over and wash them. Drain well. Moisten granulated sugar with ½ cup cold water. Bring to a boil, skim carefully, add the berries and cook 15 minutes or until juice is well reduced and thick. Cool and chill.

In the meantime, cream the butter and gradually add the powdered sugar. When light and fluffy, add the eggs, one at a time, beating well each time. Flavor with vanilla. Chill until ready to assemble the tart, shortly before serving.

Beat heavy cream until very stiff. Spread over the bottom of the cooled tart shell an even coating of the butter-sugar-egg mixture. Cover this with the cooked blueberries or substitute the 15-ounce cans of blueberries in heavy syrup. Cover blueberries completely with the beaten cream and serve at once. Cut at the table in 8 pie-shaped pieces. Serves 8.

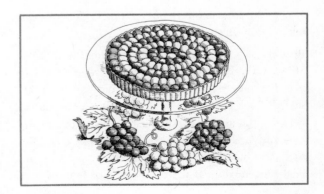

CHOCOLATE BUTTER CREAM CAKE

For cake and decoration:

7 eggs
1 cup granulated sugar
8 ounces dark sweet chocolate
5 tablespoons strong coffee
¼ cup cool melted butter
   Grated rind of 1 lemon
1 cup plain cake flour (without baking powder)
   Pinch salt
   Confectioners' sugar

For Chocolate Butter Cream:

3 egg yolks
1 cup granulated sugar
½ teaspoon cream of tartar
½ cup water
½ pound sweet butter
½ cup vegetable shortening
8 ounces dark sweet chocolate
4 tablespoons strong coffee
2 tablespoons dark rum
   Pinch salt

Butter a 9″ spring-form cake pan, line the bottom with a round of waxed paper and butter again. Dust with flour. Put the 7 eggs and 1 cup granulated sugar in an electric beater and beat until mixture holds its shape. Cut 4 ounces of the chocolate in small pieces, put in a heavy pan with the coffee and stir over low heat until chocolate is dissolved. Pour the cool melted butter and melted chocolate on the beaten eggs and sprinkle on the lemon rind. Sift in the flour and salt. Fold in carefully until blended, breaking down the mixture as little as possible. Pour into cake pan and bake for 50 minutes in a 350° oven, or until cake tester comes out dry and cake begins to come away from sides of pan. Remove, slide a thin-bladed knife around the edge and turn out on a rack. Cool at room temperature until ready to frost.

Beat the egg yolks in a mixer until light and fluffy. Stir the sugar, cream of tartar and water in a pan over low heat with a metal spoon until sugar is dissolved. Cook until the mixture will spin a fine thread between thumb and forefinger. Pour onto the beaten egg yolks and continue beating until thick and quite cool. Add butter and vegetable shortening bit by bit. Beat until mixture is the consistency of butter.

Put 8 ounces dark chocolate and the coffee in a pan over low heat and stir until dissolved. Stir over ice until it begins to cool. Add to the butter cream. Add rum and a pinch of salt and stir over ice until firm enough for frosting.

Completely cover cake with the chocolate butter cream. Put remainder in a pastry bag with a star tube and decorate edge of the cake with rosettes. Cut the remaining 4 ounces of chocolate in pieces and put on a plate over a pan of hot water on low heat. Work with a spatula until the chocolate dissolves. Cut small rounds of waxed paper about 1½″ in diameter and spread the chocolate evenly on them. Refrigerate on a cooky sheet until set. When set, carefully peel off paper. Stick rounds on sides of cake, slightly overlapping.

Dust the top of the cake with confectioners' sugar and chill well before serving. Serves 8.

COFFEE HONEY CAKE

2 cups flour
   Pinch salt
6 ounces sweet butter
1 egg
1 egg yolk
3 hard-cooked egg yolks, strained
2 tablespoons strong coffee
½ cup opaque honey
1 cup honey butter spread
2 tablespoons instant coffee
   Grated rind of 1 lemon
1 tablespoon lemon juice
   Confectioners' sugar

Sift the flour and salt into a bowl. Cut the butter in small pieces and chill thoroughly. Add to the flour and rub in quickly with your fingertips. Add the egg, egg yolk, strained hard-cooked egg yolks, coffee and honey and work up quickly to a dough. If too stiff, add a few drops of ice water. Turn out onto a lightly floured board and knead a little to get a smooth surface on top. Wrap in waxed paper; chill at least ½ hour. Remove. Divide dough into thirds. Roll out each third in an 8″ round and trim edges (use an 8″ saucepan lid as a guide). Put on a lightly floured cooky sheet and prick the top of the dough with a fork. Bake in a 375° oven until a light golden brown, about 15 minutes. Remove, chill.

Cream the honey butter, add instant coffee, lemon rind and juice. Beat well. Chill until firm. Sandwich the cake rounds with this filling, reshape cake and dust the top with confectioners' sugar. Chill before serving. Serves 8.

WALNUT CAKE

 1½ cups egg whites
   Pinch salt
 2 cups sugar
 10 egg yolks
 2 tablespoons dry cocoa
 1½ cups ground walnuts
 2½ cups sifted flour
 2 teaspoons vanilla

Beat the egg whites and salt until foamy. Gradually beat in 1½ cups sugar until the meringue is very stiff and glossy. Beat the egg yolks with the remaining ½ cup sugar until they make a ribbon when the beater is lifted. Add the cocoa to the yolks. Pour the yolks into the meringue and fold in with the walnuts and flour. Fold in the vanilla.

Line large and small well-buttered spring-form pans with waxed paper and butter the paper. Pour in the batter and cut through it with a silver knife to eliminate air pockets. Bake for 1 hour in a preheated 350° oven. Test by pressing gently with a finger. When the cake is done, the top will be springy. Invert pans on racks. Cool. Unmold. Cut cakes in half and fill with Mocha Butter Filling and frost with White Icing. Serves 8.

MOCHA BUTTER FILLING

 1¾ cups sugar
 4 egg yolks
 ¼ cup very strong coffee
 2 tablespoons powdered cocoa
 16 tablespoons sweet butter

Make a syrup with 1¼ cups water and the sugar by boiling 5 minutes, or until a candy thermometer registers 240°. Beat the egg yolks until light and thick. Pour the syrup onto the egg yolks, beating all the time until cool. Beat in the coffee and cocoa. Cream the butter until fluffy. Gradually work in the egg-syrup mixture, beating all the time. Spread thickly between layers of the cakes.

WHITE ICING

 4 cups sugar
 ¼ teaspoon cream of tartar
 2 cups boiling water
 2 cups confectioners' sugar

Boil the sugar, cream of tartar and water in a saucepan until it makes a thin syrup. Cool a little and add enough confectioners' sugar to make an icing that will pour. Place smaller cake on top of large one on a cake rack over a platter. Pour icing over the cakes. Scrape up icing from the platter and soften over warm water until all the icing is used. If this cake is not used for a wedding, the recipe may be halved and the icing may be chocolate or mocha.

PAIN DE GÊNES
(Almond Cake)

- 1 cup blanched almonds
- 9 tablespoons sweet butter, softened
- ¾ cup granulated sugar
- 3 large eggs (1 ounce each)
- Salt
- ⅓ teaspoon double-action baking powder
- ¼ teaspoon almond extract
- 1 tablespoon kirsch or orange liqueur
- ¼ cup sifted cake flour

Pulverize the almonds, ¼ cup at a time, in an electric blender, then rub them through a coarse sieve. Put any unsieved pieces into the blender with the next batch to be pulverized. Measure out ¾ cup of the pulverized almonds and reserve.

Preheat oven to 350°. Take 1 tablespoon softened butter. Butter the interior of an 8″ cake tin, 1½″ deep, cut a round of waxed paper to fit the bottom and smooth it evenly into the tin. Butter the paper.

Put remaining 8 tablespoons of the softened sweet butter and the sugar into the bowl of an electric mixer and beat together at speed 6 until light and fluffy—2 or 3 minutes. Continue beating and add the ¾ cup almonds, 2 tablespoons at a time, then beat for 1 minute. Break 1 egg into the mixture and beat at speed 6 for 1½ minutes, follow with the remaining two eggs, beating for 1½ minutes after each addition. The mixture will be light, creamy and ivory colored. Continue beating while adding a pinch of salt, the baking powder, almond extract, and liqueur. Beat 1 minute more, then remove bowl from stand. Sprinkle a spoonful of the cake flour over the mixture and fold it in delicately with a rubber spatula. Continue with the rest of the flour. Immediately turn the batter into the prepared tin, filling it about ¾ full. Spread the batter almost up to the rim of the tin, then tap bottom of tin on table to level the mixture.

Immediately set the cake in the middle level of the preheated oven. In about 20 minutes the cake will have risen to the top of the tin, and in a total of 40–45 minutes it should be a nice golden brown. It is done when it falls a little and is just beginning to show a faint line of shrinkage from the edges of the tin. Run a knife around the inside edge of the tin, turn a rack over the tin, reverse the two, giving a sharp, downward jerk to dislodge the cake. Peel off the paper and reverse the cake onto another rack. Cool before serving. This cake will keep well for a week or more in a tightly closed tin. Serves 8.

AUSTRIAN NUT CAKE

- 3 ounces sweet butter
- ⅓ cup plus 1 tablespoon granulated sugar
- 1 egg, separated
- 1½ ounces ground filberts
- ¾ cup all-purpose flour, sifted
- 1 tablespoon instant coffee
- 1 teaspoon baking powder
- 2 tablespoons milk
- 6 green apples
- ½ cup apricot jam
- Grated rind of 1 lemon
- ½ cup light brown sugar
- ½ pound dark sweet chocolate
- 5 tablespoons strong coffee
- 1 teaspoon vegetable oil
- 8 walnut halves

Cream the sweet butter well. Add the granulated sugar and beat until white. Beat in the egg yolk, then mix in the ground nuts, sifted flour and instant coffee. Beat for a few more minutes. Beat the egg white until stiff. Fold into the batter with the baking powder and milk. Grease a shallow cake tin and line with a round of waxed paper. Butter the paper and dust lightly with flour. Fill with mixture, spread evenly, and bake in a 350° oven for 20–25 minutes or until the cake comes clean away from the side of the tin. Remove, slide a thin-bladed knife around the edge, and turn out onto a rack to cool. Peel, core and quarter the apples and cut them into thick slices. Add the jam, lemon rind and brown sugar. Cook until soft, but not too mushy. Spoon onto a platter and allow to get quite cool. Split cake and sandwich with apple filling. Chill a little. Place cake on a rack over a jelly roll pan. Cut up the chocolate and put it into a pan with the strong coffee and oil. Stir over a slow fire until it dissolves and reaches the consistency of heavy cream. Cool by stirring over ice and then pour over the cake, completely covering it.

Leave for a few minutes to set and decorate around edge with halved walnuts. Serves 8.

Alternate filling: Whip ½ cup heavy cream over ice until it begins to hold its shape. Stir in 2 tablespoons confectioners' sugar and beat until stiff. Fold in 1 beaten egg white and 2 teaspoons vanilla extract.

INDIO DATE CAKE

> 1 teaspoon baking soda
> ¼ teaspoon salt
> 1 cup boiling water
> 1½ cups dates, pitted and finely cut
> 3 tablespoons butter
> 1 cup sugar
> 1 egg, separated
> 1½ cups flour
> ½ cup walnuts, chopped
> Powdered sugar

Add baking soda and salt to boiling water. Pour over dates. Let stand 20 minutes. Meanwhile, cream together butter and sugar. Beat in egg yolk, flour and the date mixture. Combine thoroughly, then add walnuts. Finally, beat the egg white until stiff but not dry, and fold into the mixture. Pour into a buttered 8″ by 12″ baking pan and bake in a 350° oven for 30 or 40 minutes, or until it shrinks away from the edges of the pan. Cool, sprinkle top with powdered sugar, and cut in squares to serve. Serves 6–8.

KENTUCKY BOURBON CAKE

> 4½ cups sifted cake flour
> ½ cup (4-ounce jar) finely chopped citron
> ½ cup finely chopped candied pineapple
> ½ cup finely chopped candied orange peel
> ½ cup finely chopped walnuts
> 1 pound butter, softened
> 2 cups sugar
> 10 eggs, slightly beaten
> 1 cup bourbon

Combine ½ cup flour with fruits and walnuts. Cream butter until light; gradually add sugar and beat until very light and fluffy. Gradually add eggs, beating until very light after each addition. Beat remaining 4 cups flour into batter gradually, beating until light. Fold in fruit mixture. Turn batter into greased and floured 10″ tube pan. Bake in 325° oven about 2 hours, or until cake tests done. Remove cake from oven and place on cooling rack. Pour bourbon over cake. Allow to cool thoroughly, about 1½ hours. To store, cover cake and keep in cool place (refrigerator if necessary). Serves 8.

DOBOS TORTE

For cake:

> 6 eggs
> 9 ounces granulated sugar
> ¼ teaspoon salt
> 7½ ounces flour
> 1½ times recipe for Chocolate Butter Cream*
> Garnish: 1½ cups coarsely grated dark sweet chocolate

For caramel glaze:

> 1½ cups granulated sugar
> ¾ cup water
> ½ teaspoon cream of tartar

To make the cake batter, beat the eggs, sugar and salt in a mixer until the mixture holds its shape. Sift in the flour and fold in carefully. (It is important to weigh, rather than measure, dry ingredients to get the right batter consistency.) Grease 7 heavy cooky sheets and dust with flour. Using a 9″ saucepan lid as a guide, draw 9″ circles on center of each cooky sheet. Pour 2 heaping tablespoons of batter on each circle and spread evenly with a spatula. Bake in a 350° oven for about 15 minutes or until golden brown. Remove and loosen at once with a thin-bladed spatula. Place 9″ saucepan lid on top of the circles and trim evenly with a sharp knife. Chill cake rounds on racks. Sandwich 6 of the rounds with chocolate butter cream, and spread it smoothly around the sides of the cake. Reserve one round.

To make the caramel glaze, stir the sugar, water and cream of tartar in a pan over a slow fire until it is dissolved and the syrup is a clear amber. As soon as the syrup reaches this point, put pan in a bowl of cold water to stop cooking. When bubbles have subsided, spread syrup evenly on top of reserved cake round with a lightly oiled spatula. Allow to set just a little, then mark off 8 lines with an oiled knife blade to indicate where cake will be sliced. Repeat several times to make impressions deep enough. Trim off any surplus caramel around edge with scissors.

Put caramel-glazed top on cake and fill in any holes around edge with chocolate butter cream. Cover sides with coarsely grated chocolate, and pipe small rosettes of butter cream around the edge. If possible, freeze for about 1 hour, then chill 2 hours before serving. Serves 8.

*Follow directions given for Chocolate Butter Cream Frosting in Chocolate Butter Cream Cake but use 4 egg yolks, 10 ounces dark sweet chocolate, 6 tablespoons coffee and 3 tablespoons rum.

LINZER TORTE

 2 cups flour
 ½ cup granulated sugar
 1 teaspoon salt
 4 ounces firm sweet butter
  Strained yolks of 2 hard-cooked eggs
  Grated rind of 1 lemon
 1 level teaspoon ground cinnamon
 1 level teaspoon nutmeg
 ½ cup unblanched almonds, ground
 2 eggs, beaten
 1 cup bread crumbs
 3 cups concentrated raspberry preserve
 1 tablespoon lemon juice
  Granulated sugar
 1 cup red currant jelly
 2 tablespoons sherry
  Confectioners' sugar

Sift flour, sugar and salt into a large bowl. Cut the butter into small pieces and add it to the flour. Rub the butter into flour with tips of your fingers until it resembles coarse cornmeal. Then add the strained hard-cooked egg yolks, lemon rind, cinnamon, nutmeg and nuts. Lastly, add the beaten eggs. Work up quickly to a firm dough with one hand (a tablespoon of ice water may be added to the ingredients if the pastry is too firm). Then turn the dough out on a lightly floured pastry board and knead a little to get a smooth surface on the bottom. Wrap in a piece of wax paper, chill half an hour. Remove, cut off ¾ of the dough and roll it out ¼" thick. Line a small flan ring on a jelly roll pan, trim off and sprinkle the bottom with a few bread crumbs; mix the rest of the bread crumbs with the raspberry preserve. Add the lemon juice and pour into the flan. Roll the rest of the dough to the same thickness and cut into long narrow strips. Cover the top of the flan criss-cross with these strips. Sprinkle the top with a little granulated sugar. Bake in a 425° oven 35–40 minutes or until golden brown on the top. Remove, loosen flan ring and chill. Remove flan ring and place torte on a flat serving dish. Put red currant jelly and sherry into a small pan. Heat, strain, and cool. Brush it over the top of the torte. Sprinkle the edge with confectioners' sugar. Serves 8.

TEXAS PECAN TORTE

 3 cups pecans
 6 eggs, separated
 1½ cups sugar
 3 tablespoons flour
 1 teaspoon salt
 3 tablespoons Jamaica rum
 ½ cup heavy cream
 2 tablespoons powdered sugar
 1 cup semi-sweet chocolate bits
 ½ cup sour cream

Put pecans in the blender (1 cup at a time) and whirl until very fine. Beat egg yolks until very light, then beat in sugar, flour, salt, 2 tablespoons rum and nuts. Mix well, then fold in egg whites that have been beaten until stiff but not dry. Pour into three 8" or 2 10" layer-cake pans that have been lined with waxed paper and buttered. Bake in a preheated 350° oven until a gentle finger pressure fails to leave a mark, about 25 minutes. Cool and remove from pans. A few hours before serving put together with filling of the cream whipped with the powdered sugar and 1 tablespoon of Jamaica rum. For icing, melt the semi-sweet chocolate bits, fold in the sour cream and spread over the top of the cake. Serves 8–10.

HOW TO MAKE AND
DECORATE DOBOS TORTE

1. Grease and flour cookie sheet. With 9″ pan lid as your guide, mark off a circle.

2. Put 2 heaping tablespoons cake batter on circle. Spread evenly to edges with spatula.

3. As soon as each layer is baked, loosen quickly from sheet, taking care not to break.

4. Trim cake edges with a knife. If rounds get too crisp, put in warm oven a minute.

5. Put layers together with butter cream. Protect plate with triangles of waxed paper.

6. When six layers are sandwiched, cover top and sides evenly with the butter cream.

7. Put seventh layer on oiled cookie sheet. Pour on caramel, spreading with oiled spatula.

8. Oil knife blade (so caramel won't stick); mark slices. Repeat until marks are deep.

9. Top cake with trimmed layer. Press grated chocolate around the sides of the cake.

10. Remove waxed paper and excess chocolate. Pipe butter cream rosettes around edge.

HOW TO CHOP WALNUTS

Use a heavy chef's knife. Keep knife point on board.
Move blade up and down, backward and forward.

TORTA LAMPO

2 squares (2 ounces) unsweetened chocolate
½ cup blanched almonds
¼ cup walnuts
5 eggs, separated
¾ cup sugar
½ cup strong coffee
Whipped cream, optional

Melt the chocolate over hot water. Chop both the
almonds and walnuts very fine by hand or in an electric blender. Beat the egg yolks lightly, adding the
sugar, nuts, melted chocolate and coffee. Mix well.
Beat the egg whites until they stand in peaks when
you lift up the beater, then fold gently but thoroughly
into the chocolate mixture. Pour into a 9″ cake pan
that has been previously greased and dusted with a
light film of flour. Bake in a 350° oven for 1 hour.
Cool the cake before serving. Serve with or without
whipped cream. Serves 6–8.

HAZELNUT TORTE

¼ cup butter
½ cup sugar

8 eggs, separated
4 ounces semi-sweet chocolate
2 teaspoons grated lemon rind
½ cup fine dry bread crumbs
1 cup toasted hazelnuts, ground
2 cups heavy cream, whipped, sweetened
    to taste

Cream the butter until soft. Add the sugar and beat
well. Beat in the egg yolks, one at a time, beating
well after each addition, until the mixture is thick
and lemon colored (it is best to use an electric
beater). Melt the chocolate over hot water. Stir the
chocolate into the egg mixture. Beat in the lemon
rind, bread crumbs and ½ cup of the hazelnuts. Beat
the egg whites until very stiff and fold into the batter.
Grease three 8″ layer-cake pans and line the bottoms
with wax paper. Spread batter evenly in the pans.
Bake in a preheated 325° oven about 30 minutes, or
until a light touch with the finger leaves no depression
in the dough. Turn out on a wire rack and cool. Do
not remove wax paper until ready to frost. Fill and
frost with the whipped cream. Sprinkle with the remaining hazelnuts. Serves 8–10.

SWEDISH OPERA TORTE
A handsome, delicate cake that is at its best if served
very cold, almost frozen.

Cake:

2 cups sifted confectioners' sugar
1⅓ cups sifted cornstarch
6 eggs, separated
¼ teaspoon cream of tartar
4 tablespoons water
1 teaspoon vanilla

Filling:

3 teaspoons unflavored gelatin
4 tablespoons cold water
4 egg yolks
6 tablespoons sugar
3 tablespoons cornstarch
2 cups milk
1 tablespoon vanilla
1 cup heavy cream, whipped
3 tablespoons cognac (optional)

Almond Paste:

    1 cup blanched almonds
    2 cups confectioners' sugar
    1 teaspoon almond flavoring
    2 egg whites, slightly beaten
    Green food coloring

Topping:

    ½ cup sifted confectioners' sugar

Preheat oven to 350°. Grease four 8″ layer-cake pans and line the bottoms with waxed paper.

To make the cake, sift together 3 times 1 cup confectioners' sugar and the cornstarch. Beat the egg whites, cream of tartar and water in a large bowl until the mixture forms soft peaks. Gradually beat in remaining cup confectioners' sugar, a little at a time. Continue beating until stiff peaks form when beater is raised. Add egg yolks and vanilla; beat in just until well blended. Fold in sugar-cornstarch mixture a little at a time, and blend thoroughly. Divide batter between pans and bake about 30 minutes, or until top of cake springs back when touched lightly with finger. Cool before removing from pans.

Meanwhile, make the filling. Soften gelatin in cold water. Combine egg yolks, sugar, cornstarch and milk in top of double boiler. Cook over simmering, not boiling, water until mixture is smooth and thick. Stir constantly. Remove from heat and beat in gelatin and vanilla. Cool, beating occasionally to keep smooth. Fold in whipped cream and cognac. Chill before using.

While filling chills, make almond paste. Put almonds through nut grinder twice or grind fine in electric blender. Combine with sugar, almond flavoring and egg whites. Work with spoon until smooth. Stir in a few drops of green food coloring to color the paste light green. Knead almond paste with hands until it is very smooth and the sugar has been completely absorbed. This may take from 5–10 minutes. Roll out on waxed paper in an 8″ circle.

To assemble the torte, neatly spread filling on cake layers; the top layer should also be spread with filling. Put layers together. Place almond paste over filling on top layer. Sift confectioners' sugar through a paper lace doily on almond paste to form decorative pattern. (To do this, place paper doily on almond paste, sprinkle with sugar, remove doily carefully.) Makes 10–12 servings.

ICEBOX CHEESECAKE

    3 cups zweiback crumbs
    1½ cups granulated sugar
    1 teaspoon cinnamon
    1 teaspoon nutmeg
    ¾ cup cool melted sweet butter
    2 envelopes gelatin
    ½ cup boiling water
    4 eggs, separated
    ¾ cup light cream
    1 pound cream cheese
    Grated rind of 1 lemon
    1 cup heavy cream

Grease the inside of a 9″ spring-form cake pan with a little vegetable shortening. Put the zweiback crumbs in a bowl with 1 cup sugar, the cinnamon and nutmeg. Mix well and stir in the cool melted butter. Stir until they resemble very rich crumbs. Put ¾ of these crumbs into the greased cake pan. Then with the back of a tablespoon, press completely and evenly against bottom and sides to line the cake pan—about a little under ½″ thick all over.

Mix the gelatin into the boiling water, leave until entirely soft. Mix the ½ cup sugar into the egg yolks in a heatproof glass bowl and beat in well. Then put the bowl in a pan of boiling water over low heat. Beat with a whisk until thick. Mix in the dissolved gelatin and the light cream. Beat the cream cheese in a mixer until light and fluffy. Add the grated lemon rind and slowly and carefully mix in the ingredients from the bowl. Stiffly beat the egg whites, remove the cream cheese mixture from the machine and carefully fold in the beaten egg whites. Put the heavy cream in a metal bowl over another bowl of ice, beat with a whisk until thick. Fold this carefully into the cream mixture. Put into the lined cake pan and carefully and evenly cover the top with the rest of the crumb-crust mixture. Cover with a piece of plastic wrap and put into the freezer for two hours. Remove and leave at room temperature for half an hour. Carefully remove from pan. Serves 10.

TORTA DI RICOTTA

    1½ pounds ricotta cheese
    1⅛ cups very fine sugar

4 tablespoons crème de cacao

⅓ cup chopped candied fruit

12 lady fingers or 1 sponge cake

Beat the cheese, sugar and crème de cacao until very smooth and fluffy. Add the candied fruit.

Split the lady fingers, or cut the sponge cake into thin strips the shape of lady fingers. Line the bottom and sides of a buttered 1½-quart round mold with them; fill with the cheese mixture. Cover with ladyfingers and chill overnight. Turn out; decorate top of cake with candied fruits, if desired. Serves 6.

CHOCOLATE JELLY ROLL

4 large eggs

1½ cups granulated sugar

½ cup potato starch

3 tablespoons Dutch cocoa

2 teaspoons baking powder

 Unsweetened cocoa

¼ cup strong coffee

¼ teaspoon cream of tartar

½ cup egg whites

 Pinch salt

Put the 4 eggs and ¾ cup sugar into a mixer and beat until white and fluffy. Sift together the potato starch, cocoa and baking powder. Carefully fold this into eggs, about 1/3 of the quantity at a time. Grease a jelly roll pan and line with waxed paper so that it extends at least 2″ over each end. Heavily butter the paper and spread the mixture evenly on it. Bake in a 425° oven for 5–6 minutes. Remove, loosen from the tin, sprinkle the top with a little unsweetened cocoa and turn out, waxed paper side up. Carefully peel off waxed paper and leave to cool partially with a damp cloth over the top. Put the coffee, ¾ cup sugar and cream of tartar into a small pan over a slow fire. Stir until the sugar dissolves and then cook until the syrup is heavy enough to spin a thread between finger and thumb. Beat the egg whites until stiff with a pinch of salt and slowly pour the coffee syrup over them. Continue beating until mixture holds its shape. Spread onto the chocolate roll, roll up like a jelly roll and wrap in waxed paper. Chill for 2–3 hours before cutting. Serves 6.

ALMOND ROLL

½ cup sifted cake flour

¼ teaspoon salt

3 eggs, separated

1 teaspoon cider vinegar

¾ cup sugar

¾ teaspoon almond extract

 Confectioners' sugar

3½-ounce can blanched almonds

¾ cup heavy cream

Grease a jelly roll pan, line with wax paper and grease the wax paper. Sift the flour and salt together and set aside.

Beat the egg yolks with an electric mixer for a good 10 minutes. This long, hard beating is essential to achieve a light and beautiful cake. Beat the egg whites until they are frothy, then mix in the vinegar and gradually beat in ½ cup sugar. Continue beating until the mixture is satiny and holds a stiff point when you lift up the beater. Stir in ¼ teaspoon almond extract and fold very gently into the beaten egg yolks. Sift the flour over the surface and fold in until batter is well blended.

Pour into the jelly roll pan and bake in a preheated 350° oven for 12–15 minutes, or until the cake begins to leave the sides of the pan. Take care not to overbake it. Invert on a clean dish towel sprinkled lightly with confectioners' sugar and pull off the wax paper very carefully.

Roll up the cake lengthwise. Leave towel around cake to keep its cylindrical shape as it cools.

While the cake is cooling, chop the almonds coarsely and toast in a 350° oven until golden. Beat the cream until it is very thick and heavy, then stir in the remaining ¼ cup sugar and ½ teaspoon almond extract and the almonds. Unroll cooled cake, spread almond filling over the surface and re-roll. Chill before serving. Serves 6.

LEMON SPONGE ROLL

4 eggs, separated

¼ cup sugar

¼ cup flour

¼ **cup cornstarch**
½ **teaspoon vanilla**
½ **teaspoon grated lemon rind**
Lemon Butter Cream

Beat the egg whites until they form soft peaks. Gradually add the sugar, beating constantly, and continue beating until firm and stiff.

Beat the egg yolks lightly and stir in 1 cup of the egg-white mixture. Pour this blend over the remaining egg-white mixture and fold it in.

Sift the flour and cornstarch and fold this into the eggs with the vanilla and lemon rind.

Grease an 11″ by 16″ baking pan and line it with buttered paper. Pour the batter into the pan and bake at 400° for 10 minutes. Dampen a large cloth and spread it on a work table. Put on top a large piece of wax paper. Turn the sponge out upside down onto the paper, remove buttered paper from top and, carefully taking the edge of the wax paper in your fingers, roll up the cake. Cool. Unroll and spread with the following filling:

LEMON BUTTER CREAM

½ **cup plus 2 tablespoons granulated sugar**
¼ **cup water**
Pinch cream of tartar
5 egg yolks
½ **pound creamed butter**
3 tablespoons lemon juice

Blend sugar, water and cream of tartar. Boil until it reaches 238°, or until syrup spins a thread.

Beat the egg yolks in a mixer until they are light and fluffy. Pour the syrup onto the egg yolks slowly in a thin stream, beating constantly. Continue beating until the mixture is cool. Blend with the butter and lemon juice and spread on the sponge roll. Roll up the cake and dust lightly with powdered sugar. Serves 6.

ALMOND-ORANGE RIND MACAROONS

Finely shredded rind of 1 large orange
8 ounces finely ground almonds
½ **cup sugar**
2 tablespoons flour
2 egg whites

Combine the orange rind, ground almonds, sugar and flour and mix well. Beat the egg whites until stiff and fold into the almond mixture. Form into small balls, handling very lightly, and arrange them on a greased baking sheet, spacing them well apart to allow for some expansion. Bake in a 350° oven for 5 minutes and then increase the heat to 400°. Finish cooking until lightly browned and done.

Variation: These macaroons are exceptionally good made with tangerine rind.

HOW TO BLANCH AND SLICE ALMONDS

1. Soak almonds in boiling water to soften skins. Holding almond tip outward, rub between thumb and forefinger. The skin will slip off very easily.

2. Slice almond lengthwise with small, sharp knife. For slivered almonds, lay the slices flat on chopping board and cut in lengthwise strips.

MARQUISETTES

¾ cup chocolate morsels
7 tablespoons butter
4 eggs, separated
½ cup sugar
1½ tablespoons flour, sifted
4 tablespoons sweet butter
¼ ounce bitter chocolate, grated

Melt the chocolate morsels in the top of a double boiler and pour into the bowl of an electric mixer. Add the butter, egg yolks, sugar and flour and beat until light and fluffy. Beat the egg whites until stiff, but not dry and fold into the batter. Reserve 1 cup batter. Spread the remainder in a greased and floured 9″ square baking pan and bake at 350° for 30 minutes. Cool in pan.

Cream the sweet butter, fold into the reserved batter and beat in the electric mixer until thick and light in color. Spread the butter cream on the surface of the cooled cake, sprinkle with the grated chocolate and chill until firm. (The cake sinks as it cools, leaving a high rim of cake around the edges. When you frost the cake, do not attempt to cover that rim, but spread the frosting evenly, leaving the top of the rim exposed.) Dip a sharp knife in hot water and cut into 25 squares. Refrigerate until serving time.

MINCEMEAT COOKIES

1¼ cups sifted flour
2½ teaspoons baking powder
¼ cup shortening
½ cup sugar
1 beaten egg
1 cup mincemeat

Sift the flour again, with the baking powder. Cream the shortening, gradually adding the sugar and stirring. Add the egg and mix well. Add the mincemeat alternately with the flour mixture, beating after each addition. Drop by teaspoonfuls on a greased cookie sheet. Bake in a 350° oven for 10–12 minutes.

CASHEW SHORTBREAD

2 cups sifted cake flour
½ teaspoon baking powder
1 cup softened butter
½ cup confectioners' sugar
1 cup chopped salted cashews

Sift the flour and baking powder together. Work the butter and sugar together until mixture is as smooth as possible. Mix in the flour and cashews thoroughly. Refrigerate for at least an hour before baking.

Divide the dough in half. On a lightly floured board, roll out one portion at a time (keep remaining portion in refrigerator) about 1/3″ thick. Work fast because of the richness of the dough. Cut into 2″ squares. Bake on an ungreased cookie sheet in a 375° oven for 15 minutes. Makes about 3½ dozen.

SWEDISH SHORTBREAD

½ cup sweet butter
⅓ cup confectioners' sugar
½ teaspoon vanilla
¼ cup cornstarch
1½ cups sifted flour

Cream butter and sugar until light and fluffy; beat in vanilla. Sift together cornstarch and flour and add to butter mixture. Mix or knead until smooth. On waxed paper, roll dough into a square ¼″ thick, then cut into 1½″ squares with pastry wheel or knife. Bake on buttered cookie sheets in a 350° oven about 10–12 minutes, or until golden. Makes about 30–40 pieces of shortbread.

KOURABIEDES

    ½ **pound sweet butter**
      Confectioners' sugar
    2 egg yolks
    2 tablespoons brandy
    2 tablespoons orange juice
    ⅓ **cup finely chopped blanched almonds**
    2¼ **cups flour**
    ½ **teaspoon baking powder**

Cream the butter with ½ cup confectioners' sugar until very light and fluffy. Add the egg yolks, brandy, orange juice and almonds and stir until smooth. Sift the flour with the baking powder, add to the first mixture and beat until the dough is well blended.

Break off walnut-sized pieces of dough and roll between your palms into small cylinders with pointed ends. Shape into crescents and place them ½″ apart on greased baking sheets. Bake in a preheated 350° oven for 20 minutes, or until the undersides of the crescents are golden and the edges begin to color. Sift a thin layer of confectioners' sugar on a board. Place the hot cookies on the sugar, sift additional sugar on top and leave until cool. Store in an airtight tin. Makes about 4–5 dozen cookies.

FESTIVE LEBKUCHEN

    2 eggs, separated
    ⅔ **cup sugar**
    2½ **cups ground almonds**
    ¼ **teaspoon powdered cardamom**
    ¼ **teaspoon powdered cloves**
    1 teaspoon cinnamon
    3 tablespoons minced candied cherries
    ⅓ **cup confectioners' sugar**
    1 tablespoon rum
    8 candied cherries, quartered

Beat the egg yolks with the 2/3 cup sugar. Beat the whites until stiff, but not dry and fold half the whites into the yolk-sugar mixture. Mix the nuts with the spices and fold into the batter. Add the minced cherries, and lastly fold in the remaining egg white.

With moistened hands, shape into walnut-sized balls and place them 1″ apart on greased baking sheets. Bake in a preheated 325° oven for 13 minutes, or until the top looks dry but the cookies still feel soft. Remove to a rack. Mix the confectioners' sugar with the rum and frost the tops of the lebkuchen while still warm. Before frosting stiffens, place a quarter cherry on top of each cookie. Store in an airtight tin in the refrigerator. Makes about 2½ dozen.

FRESH LEMON COOKIES

    1 lemon, peeled and seeded
    1 egg
    1 tablespoon sour cream
    ¼ **pound butter**
    1 cup sugar
    1½ **cups flour**
    ¼ **teaspoon baking soda**
    ½ **teaspoon baking powder**
    ¼ **teaspoon mace**
    ⅓ **cup confectioners' sugar**
    1 teaspoon lemon juice
    Candied lemon peel, cut in small squares

Cut the lemon pulp into pieces and place in the container of an electric blender with the egg, sour cream, butter and sugar. Whirl in the blender, scraping down the sides with a rubber spatula, until the mixture is smooth. Sift the flour, baking soda, baking powder and mace into a bowl, add butter mixture and stir until blended.

Drop rounded half-teaspoons of the batter 1″ apart on greased cookie sheets. Bake in a preheated 350° oven for 12–15 minutes, or until light brown around the edges and on the bottom. Cool on a board. Mix the confectioners' sugar and lemon juice and drop a little on the center of each cookie. Place small squares of candied lemon peel on the frosting. Allow to dry before packing in airtight tins. Store in tins for a few days. For longer storage, put these lemon cookies in the freezer. Makes about 5 dozen.

CARRIE GUILD'S MACADAMIA NUT COOKIES

½ cup butter
5 tablespoons powdered sugar
1 teaspoon vanilla
1¼ cups sifted flour
1 cup grated Macadamia nuts

Cream butter, sugar and vanilla; add flour and nuts and mix well. Roll into pencil-thin rolls about 3″ long, put on a cookie sheet, and form into crescents. Bake in a 350° oven until light brown (10–15 minutes). Let cool slightly, remove carefully. You may sprinkle the Macadamia nut cookies with powdered sugar while still warm. Makes about 5 dozen.

COFFEE COOKIES

1½ cups all-purpose flour
½ cup granulated sugar
1 teaspoon instant coffee
½ teaspoon salt
  Grated rind of 1 lemon
7 ounces sweet butter
2 strained hard-cooked egg yolks
2 egg yolks
2 tablespoons very strong coffee
1 teaspoon lemon juice
3 ounces honey (cloudy, not clear)
  Confectioners' sugar

Sift the flour, granulated sugar, instant coffee and salt into a bowl. Add the lemon rind. Chill 4 ounces sweet butter, cut it into small pieces, and add to the flour. Work with the fingertips until it resembles coarse cornmeal. Add the strained hard-cooked egg yolks, raw egg yolks, and liquid coffee. Work up quickly to a firm pastry. If too dry, add a little more coffee. Turn out onto a lightly floured board and knead a little to get a smooth surface on the bottom. Wrap in a piece of waxed paper and chill for ½ hour.

Roll out dough about ¼″ thick and cut into rounds with a plain cooky cutter 1½–2″ in diameter. Place on an ungreased cooky sheet and bake in a 425° oven for 15 minutes. Remove and chill. Meanwhile, beat the remaining butter to a cream, slowly add the lemon juice and honey. Sandwich the cooled

cookies with this filling and dust the tops with a little confectioners' sugar. Chill. Makes about 2 dozen.

FLORENTINES

½ cup sugar
⅓ cup heavy cream
⅓ cup honey
4 tablespoons butter
4 ounces ground candied orange peel
6 ounces blanched sliced almonds
3 tablespoons flour
8 ounces semi-sweet chocolate melted with
  2 tablespoons butter

Combine the sugar, cream, honey and butter in a saucepan and boil until the candy thermometer registers 240°, or until a firm ball is formed. Stir in candied orange peel, almonds and flour.

Drop small teaspoons of this batter on well-greased cookie sheets, leaving at least 2″ between cookies. Flatten each cookie with a fork dipped in milk. Bake in a 400° oven 8–10 minutes, or until cookies look golden. Immediately upon removing from oven, shape each cookie with a greased round cutter. When firm.

remove from sheets and cool. Coat back of each cookie thinly with melted chocolate and butter. Place in refrigerator briefly. Makes about 14–16.

MINIATURE FRANSKE VAFLOR

1 cup flour
¼ pound plus 6 tablespoons sweet butter
3 tablespoons cream
9 tablespoons sugar
1 egg yolk
½ teaspoon vanilla

Beat the flour, ¼ pound sweet butter and the cream in the small bowl of an electric mixer at low speed until the dough is well blended. Chill in the freezer for 15 minutes, or until firm enough to roll. Roll out the dough ⅛″ thick on a lightly floured board. Cut out rounds of dough with a cookie cutter or glass 1½″ or 2″ in diameter.

Spread 6 tablespoons of sugar on the pastry board over an area large enough to accommodate 4 or 5 rounds of dough side by side depending on size. Press 4 or 5 rounds of dough into the sugar, coating them on both sides and place them side by side on the same sugared board. Roll the rounds of dough once with a spiked rolling pin, turn them over and roll them again. (A small, spiked meat tenderizer may be substituted for the spiked rolling pin. However, with the rolling pin you roll 4 or 5 rounds of dough at a time; with the tenderizer, you can only do one at a time.) Repeat until all remaining rounds have rolled in sugar. Place the rounds ¼″ apart on well-greased cookie sheets. Bake in a preheated 450° oven for 7 minutes, or until caramelized on the underside. Cool.

Beat the egg yolk in the small bowl of an electric mixer. Cook the remaining 3 tablespoons sugar with 2 tablespoons water in a small saucepan over high heat, stirring constantly until the sugar dissolves. Boil rapidly until the syrup spins a thread, and pour slowly over the egg yolk, continuing to beat rapidly. Beat in the 6 tablespoons sweet butter, bit by bit, and add the vanilla. Chill until firm enough to spread. Sandwich in pairs with the butter cream. Store in the refrigerator for a few days, or in the freezer for longer periods. Makes about 30 1½″ or 2″ paired cookies.

HOW TO MAKE FRANSKE VAFLOR

1. Roll out dough on lightly floured board and cut out 1½″ or 2″ rounds with a plain cookie cutter.

2. Spread granulated sugar on pastry board. Press cut-out cookies into the sugar, coating both sides.

3. Pound sugared surfaces with spiked meat tenderizer, making waffle design. Bake in a 450° oven.

ALMOND KISSES
(Almendrados)

2 egg whites
1 cup sifted confectioners' sugar
2 tablespoons crushed almonds
½ teaspoon cinnamon
Grated rind ½ orange

349

Beat egg whites until very stiff, then beat in sugar until glossy. Finally fold in crushed almonds, cinnamon and orange rind. Drop by spoonfuls on greased baking sheet. Place in a preheated 400° oven. Turn off heat and leave in oven 4 hours.

CHOCOLATE LEAVES

¼ cup butter
⅓ cup very fine (or super-fine) granulated
  sugar
1 egg
¾ cup flour
⅓ cup ground walnuts
½ teaspoon orange extract
¾ cup chocolate morsels
1½ teaspoons vegetable shortening

Cream the butter, sugar and egg in the small bowl of an electric mixer. Add the flour, walnuts and orange extract and beat until smooth. Grease 2 cookie sheets. Dip a metal leaf stencil in cold water. Shake off excess water. Hold firmly on sheet and spread a rounded teaspoon of dough over stencil with a spatula dipped in cold water. Carefully lift stencil and scrape off excess dough. (The most practical stencil has a couple of 2½"-long leaf cutouts, making it possible to spread 2 leaves at a time.) Repeat with remaining dough, wiping the stencil frequently with a paper towel. Bake in a preheated 350° oven for 8–9 minutes, or until golden around edges. Cool on board.

Melt the chocolate morsels with the vegetable shortening over hot (not boiling) water. Spread on the underside of the leaves and mark the veins with the edge of a spatula or knife. Allow to dry at room temperature for several hours. Pack in an airtight tin with waxed paper between layers. Makes about 4½ dozen.

SWEDISH BRANDY RINGS

1⅓ cups sweet butter
¾ cup sugar
1 egg yolk
¼ cup brandy
3¼ cups sifted flour

**HOW TO MAKE
CHOCOLATE LEAVES**

1. Dip leaf stencil in cold water. Hold stencil flat on greased cookie sheet. Spread dough over stencil.

2. Carefully lift up stencil so dough shapes remain on sheet. Scrape excess dough from stencil.

3. When leaves are baked, remove from sheet. Spread undersides with the melted chocolate.

4. Use edge of spatula to mark veins on chocolate. Let chocolate leaves dry at room temperature.

Cream butter and beat in sugar, a little at a time. Beat mixture until light and fluffy. Beat in egg yolk and brandy. Blend in flour and mix thoroughly. Chill dough. To shape cookies, use a little of the dough at a time, keeping remainder in refrigerator for easier handling. With floured hands, shape dough into rounded strips 5″ long and ¼″ wide. Twist two strips together to make a rope. Shape each rope into a ring. Bake on a buttered and floured cookie sheet in a 350° oven about 10–12 minutes, or until golden yellow. Makes about 50–60.

Note: This dough may also be shaped any other way, into plain rings, crescents, etc. The cookies should be thin, or they won't be as crisp. Eat while fresh.

HAZELNUT BAGUETTES

    ¼ **pound butter**
    ⅔ **cup sugar**
    2 **eggs, separated**
    1 **cup fine dried bread crumbs**
    1 **cup ground hazelnuts**
    1 **teaspoon vanilla**
    3 **tablespoons chopped hazelnuts**

Cream the butter and sugar until light and fluffy. Add the egg yolks and continue beating. Add the bread crumbs, ground hazelnuts and vanilla and mix until well blended. Beat the egg whites until stiff, but not dry and mix half into the nut batter. Fold in the remaining stiffly beaten whites. Pinch off generous marble-sized balls of dough and roll them between the palms of your hands, making baguettes about 1½″ long with tapered ends. Dip the tops of the baguettes into the chopped hazelnuts and place them 1″ apart on greased cookie sheets. Bake the cookies in a preheated 350° oven for 14 minutes, or until the underside is golden brown. Cool on racks. Store in an airtight tin. Makes about 4 dozen.

CIGARETTES

    6 **tablespoons sweet butter**
    ½ **cup confectioners' sugar**
    1 **egg yolk**

HOW TO MAKE CIGARETTES

1. For filling, squeeze packaged liquid or melted chocolate into butter cream. Beat in; chill well.

2. Drop 12 scant teaspoons cookie dough, evenly spaced, on ungreased cookie sheet. Bake.

3. Roll each warm cookie over handle of a small wooden spoon and press down where it overlaps.

4. Hold rolled cookie in place for a few seconds until it stiffens. Slide cookie off handle and cool.

5. Put chilled filling in pastry bag with small star tube. Pipe rosettes at the ends of each cylinder.

> 1 foil packet liquid unsweetened chocolate or
> 1 ounce semisweet chocolate, melted and cooled
> 3½ tablespoons butter
> 3½ tablespoons sugar
> 1 egg
> 5 tablespoons flour

Cream the sweet butter, confectioners' sugar and egg yolk until light and fluffy. Beat in the chocolate. Chill this butter cream in the refrigerator until it is firm enough to hold its shape.

Meanwhile, cream the butter and sugar until light and fluffy. Beat in the egg, then stir in the flour. Drop 12 evenly spaced scant teaspoonfuls of dough on an ungreased cookie sheet. Bake in a preheated 350° oven for 8 minutes, or until golden brown around the edges. Leaving the pan in the oven and the oven door open, remove one wafer at a time. Roll the wafer over the handle of a wooden spoon, press down where it overlaps and hold for a few seconds until the roll stiffens. Slide off the handle. Roll the remaining wafers. (If a wafer stiffens before you can roll it, replace it in the oven until it is soft.) Bake the remaining batter. Repeat the rolling. Cool rolled wafers.

Spoon the chilled butter cream into a pastry bag fitted with a small star-shaped tube and pipe rosettes at both ends of the cylinders. Store in airtight tins in the refrigerator for a few days, or in the freezer for extended storage. Makes about 32.

TOTENBEINLI

> ¾ pound almonds
> 1 cup butter
> 1 cup sugar
> 3 medium eggs
> 1 tablespoon rose or orange water
> 2½–3 cups all-purpose flour
> ½ teaspoon salt
> ⅓ cup candied citron, chopped
> 2 egg yolks, beaten with 1 tablespoon cold water

Blanch almonds. While still moist and warm, cut into slivers with a sharp knife. There should be about 3¾ cups. Cream butter with sugar. Beat in eggs,

one at a time, beating well after each addition. Stir in rose or orange water. Beat in 2½ cups flour and salt. The dough will be sticky, but if it is too sticky to handle, beat in an additional ½ cup flour, a little at a time. Knead dough on lightly floured board or kitchen table. Knead in slivered almonds and citron. Wrap dough in waxed paper and chill for 2 hours.

Shape into finger-length rolls and place on greased and floured baking sheets. Preheat oven to 375°. Paint cookies with beaten egg yolk. Depending on size of cookies, bake about 10–15 minutes, or until golden brown. Cool for 2 minutes on baking sheets, then remove cookies with spatula. Makes about 40.

Note: Since many ovens tend to overheat, any second and subsequent batches of cookies may take less time to bake. Watch them carefully.

TUILES

> 3 egg whites
> ¼ cup confectioners' sugar
> ⅓ cup sifted flour
> ¼ teaspoon salt
> 3 tablespoons butter, melted
> 1 teaspoon vanilla
> 1 teaspoon cognac
> ⅔ cup coarsely chopped almonds or hazelnuts

Beat the egg whites until they form soft peaks and beat in the sugar a little at a time until the whites are stiff and the sugar is well blended. Add the flour, salt and melted butter and fold in well. Add the vanilla, cognac and nuts. Fold lightly.

Drop by teaspoons on a buttered cookie sheet. Bake in a 350° oven approximately 9–10 minutes, until they are brown around the edges. Remove from the pan with a spatula and fold around a rolling pin to bend slightly. Cool on a rack. Makes 24–28.

ZIMTWAFFELN

> 1 egg, well beaten
> 4 tablespoons butter, softened
> ½ cup sugar
> 6 tablespoons flour
> 1 tablespoon cinnamon

Mix all the ingredients in a bowl. Heat a gaufrette iron over medium heat until a drop of water bounces on contact with the iron. Drop rounded half-teaspoons of the batter on the iron, close the iron and bake for a half minute or less, or until cinnamon-brown on the underside. Turn the iron and bake for an additional half minute or less, or until cinnamon-brown on both sides. Remove the waffeln with a broad spatula and place on a board to cool and crisp. Two waffeln may be baked at one time.

Turn the iron frequently—at least once between each two or three bakings. This prevents one side from heating more than the other. Often a few crumbs adhere to the iron after the waffeln have been removed; they should be brushed off. If the first waffeln are not perfect, don't be alarmed as this is to be expected. Store in an airtight tin. Makes about 4 dozen.

Note: Gaufrette irons, similar to miniature waffle irons, are available in shops specializing in cooking equipment or in good housewares departments. If you do not have a gaufrette iron, you can make the cookies by dropping the batter by rounded half-teaspoons, 1″ apart, on ungreased cookie sheets. Bake at 350° for 8–9 minutes and then remove the zimtwaffeln to a board to cool and crisp.

HOW TO MAKE ZIMTWAFFELN

1. Heat gaufrette iron on medium heat until drop of water bounces on contact. Drop on two half teaspoons of batter.

2. Close iron and bake for half a minute or less, first on one side, then on the other, or until cooked cinnamon brown.

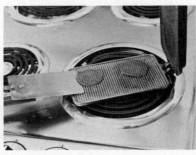

3. Remove the waffeln with a broad metal spatula and place on a board.

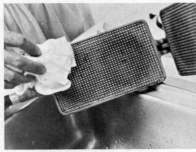

4. Remove any crumbs adhering to iron by brushing with a paper towel. This will prevent waffeln sticking.

Bread & Sandwiches

Paradoxical as it may sound, there is often more true satisfaction—and cachet—in serving a crusty, golden loaf of bread still warm from the oven than in presenting the most spectacular culinary tour de force. For bread and the honest smell of its baking are as old as civilization and as elemental as hunger. To the Egyptians, Greeks and Romans bread, the giver of life, had a powerful and mystical significance. Bread figures were made to honor the gods and the dead, a practice that still survives in many Catholic countries, where the old pagan rituals involving bread became transformed into Christian festivals—All Soul's Day, Easter and Christmas. The shaping and decoration of bread is fraught with early symbolism. Bread baked in a ring suggests the continuity of life, egg-encrusted Easter breads denote fertility, the braided rope of the Jewish challah stands for a ladder to heaven. Friends break bread together, and it is from cum panum (with bread) that the word "companion" comes.

In medieval times, bread was not only food, but platter as well. Hunks of meat, hacked from the joint, were eaten on thick slabs of bread that soaked up the rich juices. Antedating cutlery, bread in one of its many indigenous forms was the logical wrap-around for food in parts of the world as far apart in culture or customs as Mexico and Persia, long before the days of the gambling earl who gave the sandwich its name.

The outdoor lunch of the French peasant, a long, crusty loaf stuffed with all manner of inviting tidbits, was the European ancestor of our "poor boys," a specialty of nineteenth-century New Orleans. Nuns doled out French loaves stuffed with meat and cheese to the children who came begging for pourboires and the anglicized version of the name passed into the argot as a synonym for sandwich. Another New Orleans favorite was the wife-pacifier, a hollowed-out French loaf filled with luscious hot oysters with which tardy husbands appeased (or at least stemmed the reproaches of) their angry spouses.

Today we have sandwiches to suit any occasion, any time of year. Grilled or toasted sandwiches are great for snacks; tiny, thin sandwiches make a bon bouche with tea or cocktails; the tempting Danish open-faced sandwiches known as smørrebrød qualify as a lunch in themselves.

Good bread is not only the foundation, but also the raison d'être of the sandwich. Although there are many highly acceptable commercial breads, few can rival the unparalleled freshness of the home-baked variety. A selection of breads makes for more interesting sandwiches—brioche bread for melting little morsels of onion and mayonnaise; wafer-thin white for cucumber or chicken tea sandwiches, hearty corn bread to complement the flavor of fine Virginia ham.

"All sorrows," said Cervantes, "are less with bread." To which any bread-lover would add the rider "and all joys greater."

HOW TO MAKE CHALLAH

1. Beat dough with a wooden spoon, adding flour until too stiff to beat.

2. Put rest of flour on board. Turn out dough, knead until smooth. Let rise.

3. When dough is tripled in bulk, punch down and cut into 12 portions.

4. Roll each portion toward you under palms, making rope of 1″ diameter.

5. Line up three ropes and braid together to make 1 loaf of challah.

6. When ropes are braided, pinch ends together so they won't untwine.

7. Pick up bread and push into shape fat enough to fit into greased pan.

8. Leave until risen. Brush with egg, sprinkle with poppy seeds. Bake.

BASIC WHITE BREAD

> 2 packages granular yeast
> 1¼ cups warm water
> 1 cup lukewarm milk
> 3 tablespoons sugar
> 2 teaspoons salt
> 2 tablespoons vegetable shortening
> 1 tablespoon soft butter
> 7 cups all-purpose flour

Dissolve the yeast in 1/3 cup of the warm water. Combine the remaining water, milk, sugar, salt, shortening and butter in a large bowl. Add the dissolved yeast and enough of the flour to make a soft, sticky dough. Place the remaining flour on a pastry board, turn the dough out on top of it and knead until the dough is smooth and the flour absorbed. If the dough is still sticky, add a little more flour. Place the dough in a greased bowl and turn once to bring the greased side on top. Cover and let rise in a warm spot for 1 hour, or until the dough doubles in bulk.

Punch down, turn dough again and let rise for ½ hour, or until almost double in bulk. Divide the dough in half and let rest for 10 minutes. Shape each half into a loaf and place in a well-greased 5″ by 9″ loaf pan. Cover and let rise in a warm spot for 1/2 hour. Bake the loaves in a preheated 425° oven for 25 minutes, or until they sound hollow when tapped. Remove to racks to cool. Makes 2 loaves.

CHALLAH

> 2 packages granular yeast
> 2½ cups warm water
> 6 tablespoons sugar
> 2 teaspoons salt
> ⅓ cup salad oil (not olive oil)
> 4 eggs
> 8⅔ cups all-purpose flour
> 1 egg yolk mixed with 1 teaspoon cold water
> 4 teaspoons poppy seeds

Dissolve the yeast in the warm water in a large bowl. Add the sugar, salt, oil, eggs and 6 cups of the flour. Beat thoroughly with a wooden spoon. Gradually add more flour until the dough is too stiff to beat with a spoon. Place remaining flour on a pastry board, turn the dough out on top of it and knead until the dough is smooth and all the flour absorbed. If the dough is still quite sticky (this may happen if you use very large eggs), you may find you have to add a little more flour to get the right consistency.

Place the dough in a very large covered bowl and let rise in a warm place for 1½ hours, or until triple in bulk. Punch the dough down, and divide it into 12 portions. Shape each portion into a rope about 1″ in diameter on a lightly floured board. Braid 3 ropes together. Repeat with the remaining ropes. Place each braid in a well-greased 4½″ by 8½″ loaf pan and let rise in a warm place for ¾ hour, or until almost triple in bulk. Brush the tops of the risen dough with the egg wash and sprinkle with the poppy seeds. Bake in a preheated 375° oven for 25–30 minutes, or until the breads are golden brown. Remove to racks to cool. Makes 4 loaves.

BRIOCHE BREAD

> 2 packages or cakes yeast
> ½ cup lukewarm water
> 4 cups flour
> 1 tablespoon sugar
> 1½ teaspoons salt
> 7 eggs
> 10 ounces creamed butter

Dissolve the yeast in the warm water and add 1 cup of flour. Turn out, knead into ball, slash top criss-cross with knife and drop into lukewarm water. Leave until dough rises to top.

Blend the rest of the flour with the sugar and salt and beat in the whole eggs. Continue stirring until the mixture is smooth and slowly add butter. When dough is smooth, add drained yeast sponge. Mix in well. Cover with plastic wrap and a cloth. Set in warm spot to rise until double in bulk. Punch down dough. Refrigerate dough until you are ready to bake. When you are ready to use the dough, turn it out onto a floured board and shape into loaf to fit into a well-buttered bread tin. Let rise for 20 minutes at room temperature. Bake in a 375° oven for 40–45 minutes, or until the loaf is browned and done.

Brioche bread is particularly good for little hors d'oeuvre onion sandwiches.

HOW TO MAKE QUICK FRENCH BREAD

1. Beat ingredients with dough hook in mixer.

2. Turn out, knead, pulling edges in to middle.

3. Put dough in bowl, brush with oil, let rise.

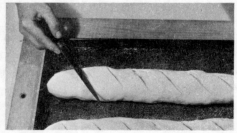

4. Shape into long oval, cut into two loaves.

5. Before baking, slash diagonally along top.

QUICK FRENCH BREAD

> 1 cake or package yeast
> 2 cups lukewarm water
> 1¼ tablespoons salt
> 1 tablespoon sugar
> 5–6 cups flour
> Oil, cornmeal

Add the yeast to the warm water and add the salt and sugar. Stir until the yeast dissolves. Beat the flour in, a cup at a time, using a wooden spoon or the dough hook on your electric mixer. Add as much flour as you need to make a smooth dough. Knead until smooth. Brush top and sides with oil. Cover the dough with a towel and stand in a warm place to rise until double in bulk.

Turn the dough out onto a floured board and shape into two long French loaves. Place the loaves on a baking sheet sprinkled with cornmeal and let stand to rise for 5 minutes.

Slash the tops of the loaves in several places, brush them with water and place in a cold oven. Set the oven for 400° and start it. Place a pan of boiling water in the oven with the loaves and bake them for 40–45 minutes, or until crusty and done.

MABELLE JEFFCOTT'S GRAHAM BREAD

> 1 large can evaporated milk
> Equal amount hot water
> ¼ cup melted butter
> 3 tablespoons sugar
> 1 tablespoon salt
> 1 cake or package yeast
> ½ cup warm water
> 3 cups coarse graham flour
> 5–6 cups white flour

Mix the milk, hot water, melted butter, sugar and salt and let stand until lukewarm. Dissolve the yeast in the ½ cup of warm water and add this to the milk mixture. Add the graham flour, beating it in with a wooden spoon, and then enough white flour to make a smooth dough. Or use the dough hook on your electric mixer and add first the graham and then the white flour. Continue mixing until the dough is elastic and satiny. Or turn it out on a floured board and knead until it is elastic and satiny.

Put the dough in a bowl, cover with a towel and place in a warm spot to rise until doubled in bulk. Turn it out onto a floured board and divide into 3 or 4 parts. Mold into loaves and put into buttered tins. Cover again and stand in a warm spot to rise but only until half again as bulky. This bread should be very firm in texture.

Bake in a 375° oven for about 1 hour or until browned and done.

THIN CORN BREAD

> ½ cup sifted flour
>
> 1½ cups cornmeal (yellow or white)
>
> 1½ teaspoons salt
>
> 1 teaspoon sugar
>
> 2 teaspoons double-action baking powder
>
> 3 eggs
>
> 1 cup cream
>
> ⅓ cup melted butter

Mix the dry ingredients. Beat the eggs with the cream and add them to the cornmeal mixture. Stir in the melted butter and blend thoroughly. Spread the batter in a well-buttered jelly roll tin and bake in a 400° oven for 15–18 minutes, or until lightly browned and done. Cut the hot corn bread into squares and split and butter them at once.

INDIVIDUAL CRACKED WHEAT LOAVES

> ½ cup fine cracked wheat
>
> 1½ cups boiling water
>
> 1 package granular yeast
>
> ⅔ cup warm water
>
> ¼ cup vegetable shortening
>
> 2 teaspoons salt
>
> 2 tablespoons light molasses
>
> 2 tablespoons honey
>
> ⅔ cup milk
>
> 1 cup whole-wheat flour
>
> 4 cups (approximately) all-purpose flour

Cook the cracked wheat in the boiling water for 20 minutes, stirring occasionally. For the last few minutes, raise the heat and stir constantly until all the water has evaporated. Meanwhile, dissolve the yeast in the warm water. Add the shortening, salt, molasses, honey, and milk to the cooked cracked wheat, stir and cool to lukewarm. Combine with the dissolved yeast, stir in the whole-wheat flour and 2½ cups of the all-purpose flour. Gradually knead in as much of the remaining flour as is necessary to obtain a smooth dough that has lost most of its stickiness. (It may even be necessary to use more flour than stipulated. The amount depends on the moistness of the cooked cracked wheat.)

Place the dough in a bowl, cover, and let rise in a warm place for 1½ hours, or until double in bulk. Punch it down and divide into 8 equal portions. Shape each portion into a small loaf and make 6 evenly spaced diagonal slits in the top of each loaf with sharp knife. Place in greased 6″ by 3¾″ by 2″ aluminum foil pans, cover and let rise for 1 hour, or until double in bulk. Bake in a preheated 375° oven for 35 minutes, or until the loaves sound hollow when tapped on the bottom. Cool loaves on a rack. These loaves may be frozen.

BANANA BREAD

> ½ cup butter
>
> ¾ cup sugar
>
> 3 mashed ripe bananas (1½ cups)
>
> 2 beaten eggs
>
> 1½ cups flour
>
> 1 teaspoon baking powder
>
> 1 teaspoon salt
>
> ¾ cup chopped macadamia nuts (optional)

Cream butter and sugar, add bananas, eggs and dry ingredients sifted together. Mix just enough to moisten flour, fold in nuts if used, and pour into a well-buttered loaf pan. Bake in a 300° oven for 1–1¼ hours, or until a tester comes out clean. Cool before slicing. This is even better on the second day, and freezes nicely. Sliced thin it makes delicious tea sandwiches. It is also good toasted, for breakfast.

PISTACHIO BREAD

> 1¼ cups milk
>
> 1 package granular yeast
>
> Sugar
>
> ¼ teaspoon salt

Melted butter, about ¾ cup

4 cups all-purpose flour

¾–1 cup coarsely chopped pistachio nuts

1 egg, well beaten

Heat the milk to lukewarm. Sprinkle the yeast over ¼ cup of the milk to soften, then combine the remaining milk with ½ cup sugar, the salt, ½ cup melted butter and about half the flour. Beat until smooth. Add the yeast and remaining flour, continuing to beat until dough is smooth. Cover with a dish towel and let rise in a warm place until double in size. Turn out on a lightly floured board and knead until smooth.

Cut dough in half and roll each half into a thin rectangle. Brush surface with melted butter and sprinkle generously with sugar and nuts. Beginning with long edge of each rectangle, roll dough like a jelly roll. Join the ends to form a ring and place both rings on a greased baking sheet. Snip top into slices with scissors or knife but do not cut through the roll completely. Spread or separate the slices, pressing one slice toward the center of the ring, and the following slice toward the outside edge. Let rise in a warm spot until almost double in size. Brush with well-beaten egg and bake in a preheated 375° oven for 25–30 minutes.

LIMPA

1½ cups beer

2 tablespoons fennel seeds

1 tablespoon white vinegar

¼ cup molasses

¼ cup dark corn syrup

2 teaspoons salt

2 packages granular yeast

2 tablespoons butter, softened

4 cups fine sifted rye flour

1¾–2 cups sifted flour

Heat beer to lukewarm. Combine in large bowl with fennel seeds, vinegar, molasses, corn syrup and salt. Sprinkle yeast into lukewarm liquid and stir until dissolved. Beat in butter. Stir in rye flour and 1½ cups flour, a little at a time, and mix well. Use some of the remaining flour to sprinkle on baking board.

Turn dough onto baking board and knead with floured hands until smooth and elastic, and no longer sticky. Place dough in a greased bowl and turn to grease on all sides. Cover and let rise in warm place until double in bulk, about 1¾–2 hours. Punch down, pull edges toward center and turn dough in bowl. Let rise again until almost double in bulk, about 45 minutes.

Turn dough out onto floured board and divide into two portions. Knead for 2 minutes and shape each portion of dough into a round loaf. Place on a buttered cookie sheet and let rise again until double in bulk, or about 50 minutes. Bake in a 350° oven for about 35–40 minutes.

BLACK WALNUT BREAD

3 cups sifted all-purpose flour

4½ teaspoons baking powder

½ cup sugar

1 teaspoon salt

1 cup chopped black walnuts

2 eggs

1 cup milk

¼ cup butter, melted

Sift the flour, baking powder, sugar and salt together into a mixing bowl, then stir in the nuts. Beat the eggs, milk and melted butter. Add to the flour mixture and stir until very well mixed, but don't attempt to beat out all the lumps. Spoon into a greased loaf pan and bake in a preheated 350° oven for 1 hour. Turn out of pan and cool before serving.

SAFFRON BUNS

1 cake or package yeast

¼ cup warm water

1 cup milk

⅛ teaspoon powdered saffron

Sugar

1 teaspoon salt

¼ cup (2 ounces) butter

2 eggs

3½ cups flour

½ cup raisins or currants

Crumble yeast cake into the warm water and stir, or dissolve the package of yeast in the water. Warm the milk with the saffron and combine with 3 tablespoons sugar, the salt and butter. Stir until the butter has melted. Beat 1 egg and add to milk mixture with 1 cup flour and the yeast mixture. Beat well, then add raisins or currants and enough additional flour (about 2½ cups) to make a soft, but not sticky, dough.

Knead lightly, put into a greased bowl, turn dough upside-down so the top will be greased, too. Cover with a cloth and allow to rise until double in bulk.

Knead down, turn out on a lightly floured board and form into a long roll. Cut into 18–24 pieces, depending on how large you want the buns, and form into smooth balls.

Put on buttered baking sheets, flatten slightly and let rise until double in size. Brush tops with remaining egg, slightly beaten, sprinkle with sugar and bake in a preheated 375° oven for 20 minutes or until nicely browned. If preferred, the dough may be baked in muffin tins.

VERA'S ROLLS

 4 teaspoons granular yeast
 ⅓ cup sugar
 2 tablespoons warm water
 ¼ pound butter, cut into pieces
 5 tablespoons margarine, cut into pieces
 1½ cups milk, scalded
 2 eggs, lightly beaten
 1 teaspoon salt
 1 teaspoon powdered cardamom
 4 cups all-purpose flour
 2 tablespoons butter, melted and cooled
 1 egg yolk mixed with 1 teaspoon cold water

Dissolve the yeast and 1 teaspoon of the sugar in the warm water until the mixture starts to bubble. Meanwhile place the butter and margarine pieces in a large mixing bowl, pour the scalded milk over them and let cool to lukewarm. Add the eggs, remaining sugar, salt, cardamom and dissolved yeast. Gradually beat in the flour, beating until the dough is smooth and leaves the spoon and sides of the bowl clean. Cover the bowl and refrigerate the dough overnight. The next day, turn the dough out onto a lightly floured board and knead well, adding a little flour if the dough is sticky. Divide the dough in half and roll out each half into a 5″ by 10″ rectangle. Brush

the melted butter over the dough. Starting from a long side, roll up each piece of dough jelly-roll fashion. Cut each roll into 24 equal slices, and place cut side down and 1″ apart on greased baking sheets. Cover lightly and set in a warm place to rise for 1–1½ hours, or until the dough doubles in bulk. Brush the tops of the rolls with the egg wash. Bake in a preheated 350° oven for 10–15 minutes, or until golden. Remove to racks to cool. Makes 1 dozen rolls.

PARMESAN BREAD STICKS

 1 package granular yeast
 ½ cup warm water
 ⅓ cup milk, scalded
 1 teaspoon butter
 1 teaspoon sugar
 ½ teaspoon salt
 ⅓ cup grated Parmesan cheese
 2 cups all-purpose flour

Dissolve the yeast in the warm water for 5 minutes. Pour the scalded milk into a bowl and add the butter, sugar, salt and cheese. Cool to lukewarm and add the dissolved yeast and 1½ cups of the flour. Beat with a wooden spoon until the dough is smooth. Place the remaining ½ cup flour on a pastry board and turn the dough out on top of it. Knead until the dough is smooth and all the flour has been absorbed. Place in a covered bowl and let rise in a warm place for 1 hour, or until double in bulk.

Divide the dough into 36 equal-sized pieces and roll each piece under the palms of your hands into a rope 4″–4½″ long. Place the pieces 1″ apart on greased baking sheets and let rise for ¾ hour, or until double in bulk. Bake in a preheated 400° oven for 15 minutes. Turn off the heat and open the oven door for 5 minutes. Close the door and leave the bread sticks in the oven for 1 hour, or until dry and crisp. Store in an airtight tin. Makes 3 dozen bread sticks.

SESAME WAFERS

 1 cup all-purpose flour
 2 teaspoons sugar
 1 teaspoon baking powder
 ½ teaspoon salt
 2 tablespoons wheat germ

¼ **cup rye flour**
2 **tablespoons butter**
2 **tablespoons vegetable shortening or lard**
2 **tablespoons sesame seeds**
2 **tablespoons honey**
¼ **cup milk**

Combine the all-purpose flour, sugar, baking powder, salt, wheat germ and rye flour in a bowl. Cut the butter and shortening into the dry ingredients with a pastry blender or 2 knives until the mixture forms coarse crumbs. Add the sesame seeds, honey and milk and stir with a fork until the dough holds together. Roll out the dough 1/16″ thick on a lightly floured board. Cut the dough into 1″ by 2½″ rectangles with a pastry wheel and place them ½″ apart on greased baking sheets. Gather the scraps of dough together, roll and cut as before. Bake in a preheated 350° oven for 13 minutes, or until nut-brown around the edges. Remove to a rack to cool. Makes about 50 wafers.

TORTILLAS

2 **cups Quaker masa harina**
1⅓ **cups warm water**
1 **teaspoon salt**

Mix the ingredients to form a soft dough. Divide into balls the size of a small egg and flatten on a tortilla press between two sheets of plastic or waxed paper to a thin pancake about 4″ across. If the tortilla sticks, the dough is too moist. Scrape it off, add a little more masa harina to the dough and begin again. It does not hurt the dough to handle it.

Place ungreased griddle over medium heat and cook tortillas one at a time, about 2 minutes on each side, or until the edges begin to lift and they are very slightly browned. Makes 1 dozen small tortillas.

Note: Tortillas can be kept warm for several hours. Preheat oven to 150°. Have ready a cloth napkin or kitchen towel wrung out in hot water. As you make the tortillas, wrap them first in paper towels and then in the napkin and put in the oven. When there are a dozen stacked up, dampen the napkin again, wrap the lot in aluminum foil and keep in the oven until needed. Cold tortillas can be reheated over direct heat, turning them constantly. If they have become dry, pat them with damp hands.

Large tortillas, about 6″ across, are mostly eaten as bread with meat dishes, as are the small 4″ tortillas, which are also used for made-up dishes. Use a ball of masa about the size of a large egg for the 6″ tortillas. To make tiny tortillas for appetizers, use a walnut-sized ball of dough.

BATHED BREAD

Olive oil
1 **loaf French bread**
Salt, freshly ground black pepper
4 **medium tomatoes, sliced**
1 **green pepper, seeded and shredded**
6 **scallions, cut into pieces**
12 **anchovies**
1 **celery heart, shredded**
1 **pound pitted black olives**
12 **fresh mushrooms, sliced (optional)**

Cover a baking sheet with olive oil. Split the loaf of bread in half and place the two halves, cut sides down, on the oiled surface. Let them stand to soak for a half hour.

Place the oiled bread halves, cut sides up, on a working table, or large platter. Season one half well with salt and freshly ground black pepper. On it arrange the sliced tomatoes, shredded green pepper, scallions, anchovies, shredded celery, olives and sliced mushrooms, if you like. Top with the other half of the loaf and press down firmly. Weight the stuffed loaf of bread with heavy objects, such as cans of food. Let it stand under the weights for an hour or more. Cut into 12 finger-sized slices. This can also be made on individual size French rolls.

ANCHOIADE

This Mediterranean sandwich has a filling of ingredients that are chopped and blended to make a spread. Here are three versions:

1. Chop 24 anchovy fillets very fine and work in 1 finely chopped garlic clove, 1 tablespoon of tomato paste, 2 tablespoons of finely chopped parsley and blend all together thoroughly. Spread on the oiled lower half of a loaf of French bread. Top with upper half of bread. Press together firmly. Chill or heat in the oven and slice.

2. Chop 36 anchovy fillets with 2 cloves of garlic and ½ cup of pine nuts. Blend with 4 tablespoons of fruity olive oil and a few drops of lemon juice. Butter the lower half of a split loaf of French bread and spread with this mixture. Top with a layer of sliced hard-cooked eggs and a layer of pimientos. Brush the top half of the bread with oil and press the bread together. Chill and slice.

3. Chop 24 dried figs very fine. Chop 20 anchovy fillets, 2 garlic cloves, 24 walnuts. Blend all together. Mix in 4 tablespoons of finely chopped parsley and enough olive oil to make a paste. Spread on the oiled lower half of the bread and top with the upper half. Press together firmly and heat in a 375° oven for 15–20 minutes, or until the bread is crisp and the filling heated through. Slice and serve very hot.

PAN BANIA

Split a crisp, crusty French or Italian loaf of bread (the long, slender type) the long way and brush each half with butter or olive oil. Spread with any of the following fillings and press the two halves together. Chill well and cut into 4–6 individual sandwiches.

Suggested fillings:

1. Spread in layers on the bread 2 sliced ripe tomatoes, 2 green peppers cut in julienne strips, 12 anchovy fillets (or more, to taste), 2 small thinly sliced onions, 24 pitted black olives (Greek or Italian), salt and pepper to taste, a squeeze of lemon juice.

2. On lower half of the bread place a layer of anchovy fillets, a layer of sliced hard-cooked eggs, a layer of sliced onion, a sprinkling of 2 tablespoons of chopped fresh basil, chopped capers and a layer of sliced cucumbers. Top with a bit of wine vinegar and rub top half of bread with garlic.

3. Spread the lower half of the bread loaf with oil and add a layer of chopped onions (scallions are an excellent choice), then a layer of tuna fish, a layer of sliced hard-cooked eggs, a layer of thinly sliced tomatoes and a layer of pitted black olives.

4. Spread the lower half of the bread with oil and add a layer of fresh, raw fava beans, a layer of thinly sliced onions, a layer of sliced tomatoes and a layer of sardines. Sprinkle with chopped tarragon, chopped Italian parsley, chopped capers, and add a dash of lemon juice and some freshly ground black pepper. Rub the top half of the bread loaf with garlic-flavored oil.

5. Marinate sliced, cooked potatoes in a good vinaigrette sauce (3 parts olive oil to 1 part wine vinegar, salt and pepper to taste) with 2 chopped cloves of garlic and 2 tablespoons of finely chopped parsley. Spread on the split loaf a layer of the marinated potato slices, a layer of onions, a layer of paper-thin slices of salami and a layer of pitted black olives.

ITALIAN HERO SANDWICHES
(also called Grinders or Poor Boys)

A properly made hero sandwich combines a careful selection of foods with complementary flavors. Use French or Italian bread—either a long or a round loaf. Split the loaf and butter both top and bottom halves. Put the filling on the bottom half and press the loaf together. Slice long loaves, cut round loaves into wedges.

Suggested fillings:

1. Spread the bread with a good layer of mustard-seasoned butter. Add a layer of thinly sliced skinned Mortadella, a layer of thinly sliced onion, a layer of prosciutto, a layer of thinly sliced Provolone cheese and a few hot peppers.

2. Butter the bread halves. On the bottom half place a layer of thinly sliced *mostardi frutti* (available in jars), a layer of prosciutto, a layer of cold cooked cotechino, a layer of thinly sliced salami, a layer of sliced Provolone and top with another layer of sliced *mostardi frutti*.

3. Butter the bread and on the bottom half place a layer of thinly sliced salami, a layer of sliced tomatoes, a layer of sliced Mortadella, a layer of hot peppers, a layer of pepperoni and a sprinkling of chopped Italian parsley.

4. Use a long loaf of Italian bread, split and buttered. Place first a layer of sliced onions and season with salt. Add a layer of sliced Provolone cheese, a layer of sliced Mortadella, a layer of pickled olives, pitted, and a layer of sliced salami.

5. Use a long loaf of bread, split and spread with mustard-flavored butter, or with butter and mus-

tard. Add a layer of sliced salami, a layer of sliced Gruyère cheese, another layer of salami, a layer of sliced hard-cooked eggs, a layer of sliced Provolone and a layer of prosciutto.

6. Use a long loaf of Italian bread. Split the loaf, rub each half with garlic and brush with olive oil. Add a layer of Italian tuna fish (packed in olive oil), a layer of sliced onions, a layer of Italian anchovies, a layer of hot peppers, a sprinkling of chopped Italian parsley, a layer of sliced tomatoes, a sprinkling of chopped fresh basil and a little lemon juice. Dot with pitted olives.

OYSTER LOAVES

Use long French rolls. Cut a slice off the top and scoop out the inside crumbs. Butter the inside of the roll and toast it lightly. Fill with crisp fried oysters and season with a dash of Tabasco and a dash of lemon juice. Replace the top of the roll and serve at once.

Note: If the oysters are very large, cut them in pieces before dipping them in crumbs and frying.

CROQUE MONSIEUR

Lightly butter a slice of bread and on it arrange 2–3 thin slices of Virginia ham or country ham. Add 2 slices of Gruyère cheese, or, if not available, Emmenthal cheese. Top with another buttered slice of bread and press the sandwich together firmly. Butter the outside of the sandwich on both sides, trim off the crusts, and sauté gently in a buttered skillet, or toast under the broiler. Turn the sandwich once or twice during cooking to toast it nicely on both sides.

CROQUE MADAME

Proceed as for Croque Monsieur, but substitute sliced white meat of chicken for the sliced cheese. You may brush the bread with a little Dijon mustard before adding the ham and chicken.

BEEF SANDWICH ORIENTALE

First prepare a mustard spread: Blend 1 tablespoon of water with a heaping tablespoon of marmalade or kumquat syrup and 2 teaspoons of dry mustard. Mix until smooth.

Butter thin slices of bread. On half the slices spread a film of the mustard mixture and add several thin slices of very rare roast beef. Top with the rest of the buttered bread slices and press together firmly. Trim the crusts, butter the outside of the sandwiches and sauté them in a buttered skillet until crisp and brown on both sides. Serve with crisp pickles.

CHEESE SANDWICHES

1. Sausage-Cheese Sandwich: Butter a slice of white bread and arrange 3–4 slices of garlic sausage or garlic salami on top. Add thin slices of Swiss cheese or mozzarella. Top this with another buttered slice of bread and press together. Cut off the crusts and butter the outside of the sandwich. Sauté in butter or broil until brown on both sides and oozing with melted cheese.

2. Onion-Cheese Sandwich: Butter a slice of white bread and on it place a slice of onion ¼″ thick and several slices of mozzarella. Add a dash of salt and some freshly ground black pepper. Top with a slice of buttered bread and press together. Trim the crusts, butter the outside and sauté in butter or broil until the cheese melts and the sandwich is brown. Serve with pickled hot peppers.

3. Corned Beef-Cheese Sandwich: Use buttered white, rye or pumpernickel bread. Spread with a savory mustard or with freshly grated horseradish. Add a good slice of cold corned beef and a slice of Emmenthal, mozzarella or Monterey Jack cheese. Top with buttered bread, press together and butter the outside. Sauté in butter or broil. Serve with crisp dill pickles.

GRILLED CHEESE AND PROSCIUTTO SANDWICHES

1 large loaf French bread
Fontina cheese, sliced
Thinly sliced prosciutto

Split the loaf of bread the long way and arrange slices of the cheese and ham on the bottom half. Top with the other half of the bread and press it together firmly (or slice the loaf diagonally and make sandwiches of the sliced cheese and ham). Broil quickly, turning to cook on both sides, until the bread is lightly toasted and the cheese melted.

TOASTED TARTAR SANDWICH

Spread bread with butter and add a bit of English mustard, a small grating of fresh horseradish and a thin slice of onion. Cover with a thin layer of raw chopped beef and season to taste with salt and pepper. Top with a buttered slice of bread and press together. Brush with butter and sauté in butter or toast under the broiler.

These are excellent with cocktails or beer. Pass pickles and relishes, if you like.

Variation: Add a thin slice of Swiss cheese.

TOASTED SHRIMP SANDWICH

>   ½ cup chopped cooked shrimp
>   1 teaspoon anchovy paste
>   3-ounce package cream cheese
>   2 tablespoons butter
>   14 thin slices bread

Mix together the shrimp, anchovy paste, cream cheese and butter. Spread on thinly sliced bread, trim crusts, roll and fasten with toothpicks. Toast under the broiler. Serve at tea or with cocktails.

CHICKEN SANDWICH VITTORIA

>   2 slices white bread, toasted
>   1 teaspoon creamed butter
>   2 slices white chicken meat
>   1 slice Italian prosciutto
>   4 slices cucumber
>   Salt, pepper to taste

Spread bread with creamed butter. Place a slice of chicken on bread, top with a slice of prosciutto, then with slices of cucumber. Top with second chicken slice. Season with salt and pepper and cover with second slice of bread.

LOBSTER ROLLS

Poach lobsters, shell and clean. Cut the meat into chunks. Mix 1 pound of lobster meat with 1 finely

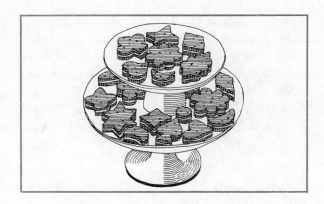

chopped hard-cooked egg, ½ cup of finely chopped celery, a pinch of tarragon, salt and freshly ground pepper to taste and enough mayonnaise to bind.

Split French rolls almost in half, but do not cut through completely. Fill the rolls with the lobster mixture and garnish with chopped ripe olives and chopped pimiento. Excellent for an outdoor snack or for the picnic basket.

CHICKEN AND CREAM CHEESE SANDWICH

>   1 teaspoon creamed butter
>   2 slices whole-wheat bread
>   1 teaspoon sour cream
>   1 tablespoon cream cheese
>   ¼ teaspoon caraway seeds
>   2 slices white chicken meat
>   Salt, pepper to taste

Spread butter on bread. Mix sour cream with cheese and add caraway seeds. Place one slice of chicken on bread and spread with cream cheese. Season with salt and pepper, top with second slice of chicken and cover with second slice of bread.

BRIOCHE-ONION SANDWICHES

>   1 loaf brioche bread
>   Mayonnaise
>   48 thin slices white onion
>   Salt
>   Chopped parsley

One loaf of brioche bread, cut into 24 slices, should give you 48 small round sandwiches. Cut 4 rounds from each slice of bread. Spread the rounds generously with mayonnaise. On half of the rounds, place a thin slice of white onion (use small white onions about the same size as the bread rounds). Season lightly with salt and top with the rest of the rounds. Press the little sandwiches together firmly. Roll the edges in mayonnaise and then in chopped parsley.

Wrap these brioche-onion tidbits in foil and refrigerate until thoroughly chilled.

ONION SANDWICHES

Use homemade bread or the very best bakery bread you can find. It should not be too fresh—about a day old is right. Spread thin slices of the bread with butter and top with thin slices of red Italian onions or yellow globe onions. Salt well and top with another slice of buttered bread. Cut into fingers.

Variations:
1. Marinate the onions in a good French dressing with a touch of fresh dill for an hour or so. Drain well before using.
2. Chop 12 green onions with a small bunch of chives and bind with a homemade mayonnaise. Use as sandwich filling.
3. Spread the bread with butter and a thin coating of cream cheese. Add slices of red Italian onions or yellow globe onions. Salt to taste.

CUCUMBER SANDWICHES

Cut cucumbers into thin slices and remove the seeds. Soak the sliced cucumbers in water seasoned with a little salt and sugar for an hour or two. Drain thoroughly. Cut thin slices of bread and butter well. Arrange the cucumber slices on the bread and season with salt and freshly ground black pepper. Top with another buttered slice of bread, press the bread together, trim sandwiches and cut into shapes.

Variations:
1. Marinate the cucumbers in a pungent French dressing.
2. Combine 2 peeled, seeded and sliced cucumbers with 1 thinly sliced onion. Marinate in 4 tablespoons of olive oil, 2 tablespoons of wine vinegar, 1 teaspoon of salt and 1 teaspoon of freshly ground black pepper. Let stand for 1 hour. Drain well.

CUCUMBER AND ONION SANDWICHES

Spread slices of white, whole-wheat or oatmeal bread with butter. Add thin slices of seeded cucumbers and thin slices of red Italian onions. Season to taste with salt and freshly ground black pepper and brush with a little mayonnaise. Top with buttered bread and cut the sandwiches into shapes.

TOMATO SANDWICHES

Spread paper-thin slices of white or whole-wheat bread with basil-flavored sweet butter (blend ¼ pound of soft butter with 2 tablespoons of finely chopped fresh basil, or 2 teaspoons of dried basil). Add finely cut peeled and seeded tomatoes. Salt to taste. Cover with sliced buttered bread and cut into fingers. Wrap in aluminum foil and chill.

Variations:
1. Spread white or graham bread with basil butter and top with thinly sliced tomatoes.
2. Spread thin slices of bread with a good homemade mayonnaise. Mix chopped, peeled and seeded tomatoes with a little chopped chives and basil. Spread on the bread and season to taste with salt.

WATERCRESS SANDWICHES

Spread thin slices of white bread with sweet butter and add sprigs of watercress. Top with more slices of bread, well-buttered, trim and cut into shapes.

Variation: Spread thinly sliced white or brown bread with sweet butter and cut into strips. Place sprigs of watercress on each strip and roll it up, letting a bit of the leaves peek out at the ends of each roll. Chill.

CHOPPED CORNED BEEF SANDWICHES

Chop 1 pound of corned beef with 1 or 2 small sweet gherkins. Blend in 1½ tablespoons (or to taste) of Dijon mustard. Spread on thin slices of well-buttered rye or pumpernickel and top with another slice. Cut into fingers and chill.

GREEN PEPPER SANDWICHES

Chop 3 green and red sweet peppers (seeded) rather fine and blend with a little homemade mayonnaise. Season to taste with salt and freshly ground pepper and use as a sandwich spread on thin slices of buttered white, whole-wheat or oatmeal bread.

Variation: Combine the spread with a little cream cheese and use as a filling for rye bread.

VEAL AND ANCHOVY SANDWICHES

Blend ¼ pound of soft butter with 6 chopped anchovy fillets, a bit of freshly ground black pepper and a squeeze of lemon juice. Spread thin slices of white bread with this mixture and add thin slices of roast veal. Top with more slices of bread with anchovy butter and press together firmly. Cut into shapes and chill.

Variation: Spread rounds of bread with anchovy butter, top with sliced veal and add a dash of paprika. Cover with aspic and chill. Serve open faced.

OPEN-FACED SANDWICHES OR SMØRREBRØD

These Danish sandwiches are time-consuming to make, because they must be decorative. If you have the patience, here are suggestions:

First of all use good white, rye or pumpernickel bread. The slices should not be too large. These are snacks, generally eaten without cutlery, and the bread is meant as a plate for the food on top. Use good sweet butter, of course.

SHRIMP

Tiny shrimp from Denmark, Iceland and Alaska are available frozen. On sliced buttered bread, arrange these little morsels in a neat geometrical design. Add a bit of chopped dill or parsley and a touch of mayonnaise, if you like.

RARE ROAST BEEF

Spread buttered bread with mustard and add thin slices of very rare beef. Top the beef slices with crisp fried onion rings.

HERRING TIDBITS

On buttered bread make a decorative arrangement of cut herring bits. Add onion rings and chopped dill.

EGG AND ANCHOVY

Spread buttered bread with anchovy paste and arrange sliced hard-cooked eggs on top. Garnish with anchovy fillets.

SMOKED SALMON

Place thin slices of smoked salmon on the buttered bread and garnish with onion rings, chopped hard-cooked eggs and capers.

HAM AND SALMON

On half of the buttered slice of bread place thin slices of good ham; on the other half, thin slices of smoked salmon. Garnish with fresh dill, mustard sauce and chopped hard-cooked egg.

PÂTÉ

Use any favorite liver pâté or tinned pâté. Spread on buttered bread and garnish with truffles cut into designs with a truffle cutter. Brush with aspic and chill.

TONGUE AND CHICKEN

Use dark bread, well-buttered. Alternate thin slices of smoked tongue and thin slices of chicken brushed with mayonnaise. Garnish with sliced gherkins and a touch of mayonnaise.

MUSHROOM

Marinate thinly sliced raw mushrooms in your favorite French dressing for 1 hour. Drain and arrange them on buttered bread. Garnish with chopped herbs and a thin julienne of ham.

CAVIAR

Do not use the best caviar for this sandwich. Use pressed caviar or red caviar. Spread on buttered bread and garnish with chopped onion and chopped hard-cooked egg.

HOW TO MAKE WATERCRESS SANDWICHES

1. Cut whole bread into thin slices, using knife with a serrated blade. Trim crusts from bread.

2. To halve sliced bread, press flat with hand, work knife back and forth with a sawing motion.

3. To keep slices moist until needed, put between layers of dampened paper towels. Wrap in foil.

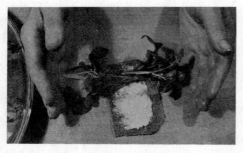

4. For rolled watercress sandwiches, put sprig at each end of slice, roll up like a sausage.

SALAMI

Arrange overlapping thin slices of salami on buttered bread and garnish with sliced hard-cooked eggs and sliced sweet gherkins.

TOMATO

Cover buttered bread with thin slices of tomato, garnish with onion rings, crumbled bacon.

LOBSTER

On buttered bread, arrange thin slices of cold poached lobster tail. Garnish with mayonnaise mixed with chopped parsley, chives and dill, and top with a slice of hard-cooked egg.

SMOKED SALMON AND CHEESE

Use thickish slices of heavy dark rye or pumpernickel. Butter the bread and spread with cream cheese. Add a layer of thinly sliced onions, a layer of thinly sliced smoked salmon, some capers and chopped parsley.

Variation: Substitute smoked sturgeon or smoked eel for the salmon.

ROAST BEEF AND POTATO SALAD

Thickly butter thin slices of dark rye bread. Place on each slice of bread a large enough piece of roast beef, very thinly sliced, to more than cover the bread, curling the beef up on one end so that it does not lie flat. Place curls of lettuce behind the curl of beef to hold it in place. Place a spoonful of potato salad over the beef. Make tomato twists by cutting tomatoes in thin slices, cutting halfway through each slice and twisting each to form "legs." Stand tomato twists on top of the potato salad. Put dabs of mayonnaise on either side of the tomato twist, sprinkle the mayonnaise with minced parsley.

HANS CHRISTIAN ANDERSEN

Thickly butter white bread; spread liver pâté over the butter, then arrange crisp cooked bacon on the liver pâté. Top the bacon with tomato twists. Sprinkle minced parsley over the tomato.

TOMATO AND EGG

Thickly butter white or pumpernickel bread; arrange overlapping slices of hard-cooked egg over the butter to the very edges of the bread. Place a tomato twist over the egg slices. Arrange raw onion rings, watercress and parsley on either side of the tomato.

HAM AND TOMATO

Thickly butter white or rye bread; arrange two very thin slices of ham on the bread, with each slice curling up at one end. Slip a lettuce curl under the curled end of the ham to hold it upright. Arrange a tomato twist over the ham. Place dabs of sour cream blended with horseradish on either side of the tomato. Sprinkle minced parsley over the sour cream.

MACKEREL AND TOMATO

Make a pâté of boned tinned fillet of mackerel by mashing it until smooth. Spread white or pumpernickel bread thickly with butter, then spread the mackerel pâté over the butter. Arrange alternate twists of tomato and cucumber over the top of the pâté. Garnish with dabs of mayonnaise; sprinkle minced dill over the mayonnaise.

SANDWICH BUTTERS

Here are some seasonings and flavorings to add to sweet butter for sandwich fillings:

1. Horseradish: To ¼ pound of softened butter add 2 teaspoons of freshly grated horseradish, or 2 teaspoons of drained commercial horseradish.
2. Mustard: To ¼ pound of butter add 1 teaspoon each of Dijon mustard and dry mustard, or 2 teaspoons of mild prepared mustard, if you prefer a less hot spread for your sandwiches.
3. Tarragon: To ¼ pound of butter add 1½ teaspoons of dry tarragon rubbed to a powder in the palm of your hand.
4. Garlic: To ¼ pound of butter add 2 mashed cloves of garlic.
5. Shallot: To ¼ pound of butter add 3 finely chopped shallots.
6. Anchovy: To ¼ pound of butter add 3 coarsely chopped anchovy fillets.
7. Shrimp: To ¼ pound of butter add 5–6 finely chopped shrimp, salt and pepper to taste.
8. Dill: To ¼ pound of butter add 1 teaspoon of finely chopped fresh dill and a touch of salt.
9. Caper: To ¼ pound of butter add 1 tablespoon of chopped capers.
10. Chutney: To ¼ pound of butter add 1½ tablespoons of chopped chutney.
11. Sardine: To ¼ pound of butter add 2 tablespoons of mashed boneless, skinless sardines and a dash of lemon juice.

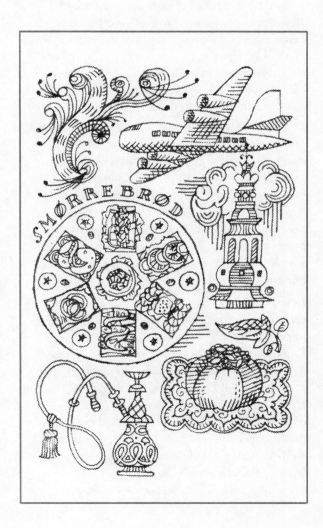

Dessert

It was a taste for honey that first introduced the western world to the temptations of dessert. Honey flavored the cakes of the Greeks and Romans, the baklava of the ancient Persians. The cane sugar of Asia was a costly (and coarse) form of sweetening only kings could afford until the thirteenth century, when the wily Venetian traders found a better way to refine it—and a fortune in the process.

One form of dessert that could be enjoyed by both king and commoner was fruit, a sweetmeat in itself. Recipes for apples and pears, quinces and oranges, poached or in pies, are common in early cook books. The Emperor Tiberius loved melon. King James I of England craved figs. Napoleon, brooding in exile on Saint Helena, was cheered by his cook's fritters of rum-marinated bananas, a dish that must surely have called to mind his one-time empress, the Martiniquaise Josephine.

Royal marriages were responsible for culinary trades that have become history. Zabaglione, imported to the French court of Henry II by his bride, Catherine de' Medici, with other Italian delicacies such as sherbet and "iced cream," was adopted by the French as sabayon. The alliance of Henry VIII's daughter Mary and Philip II of Spain delighted the sweet-toothed but predominantly Protestant English on one count only—it brought them sherry-soaked bizcocho borracho which remained, in literal translation, tipsy cake until some nineteenth-century

prude gave it the innocuous name of trifle.

Fashions in desserts are long-lived, and reveal much about national attitudes. The English, inventors of the portly plum pudding, have a weakness for this form of noble stodge, perhaps as insulation against the rigors of winter. The French, who not only gave dessert its title, but also originated many of its greater glories, prefer the dulcet lightness of dishes enriched with eggs—crèmes and crêpes, soufflés and meringues. Americans, introduced to the frosty delights of ice cream by Thomas Jefferson, who learned to make it in France and served it at a state banquet, audaciously encased in hot, crisp pastry, soon allied it to the continent's distinctive, home-grown flavor, chocolate.

With the current emphasis on calories, desserts have fared badly, a fate both undeserved and unnecessary. A sherbet or granité, poached pears or peaches, or a soufflé made chiefly of puréed fruit and egg whites are no more fattening than a wedge of Brie cheese or a second cocktail. Even a judicious sampling of the richer desserts is permissible in the context of a well-balanced meal, when preceded by two high-protein courses—oysters, perhaps, and roast filet. To round out a meal with a taste of honey makes sense. It assuages any lingering vestige of appetite and brings the dinner to a felicitous conclusion for, as the old saying has it, " 'Tis the dessert that graces all the feast; an ill end disparages the rest."

COMPOTE OF FRESH FRUIT

1½ dozen almonds

4 ripe peaches

4 tablespoons or more powdered sugar

2 ripe pears, peeled, quartered and cored

4 ripe apricots, peeled, pitted and quartered

4 ripe plums (preferably Ace plums)

1 cup hulled, washed and halved ripe
strawberries

1 cup ripe raspberries

1 cup seedless white grapes

2 ripe bananas

1 ounce kirsch

1 ounce maraschino liqueur
Sugar wafers or lady fingers

To make almonds taste like fresh green almonds, cover with boiling water, allow to stand a few minutes, pinch off the brown skins, rinse in cold water and soak in ice water. Peel and slice peaches into a large bowl, and sprinkle with 1 tablespoon or more of powdered sugar. Add pears and apricots to the peaches and sprinkle with another tablespoon of sugar. Peel plums and slice them into the rest of the fruit and sprinkle with another tablespoon of sugar. Add strawberries and washed ripe red or black raspberries. Peel seedless white grapes (a bore but worth the bother), sprinkle immediately with another tablespoon of sugar, and add to the rest of the fruit.

Lastly, peel and slice bananas into the fruit. Add a little more sugar if you like and pour the kirsch and maraschino liqueurs over all. Toss very gently, place in glass or crystal bowl inside a larger matching bowl. Surround with cracked ice. Garnish with the blanched well-drained almonds and serve with sugar wafers or lady fingers. Serves 6–8.

PINEAPPLE, KUMQUAT AND GINGER BAKED COMPOTE

12 slices unsweetened canned pineapple (3 14-
ounce cans)

12½-ounce jar preserved kumquats

9 pieces preserved ginger in syrup
Juice from canned pineapple
Syrup from kumquats

3 tablespoons ginger syrup

6 tablespoons dark brown sugar

1 cup heavy cream, whipped with
¼ cup sugar or 1 pint sour cream mixed with
¼ cup brown sugar

Arrange pineapple slices in shallow, ovenproof dish that is suitable for serving. Place kumquats on top. Sliver ginger and scatter over all. Combine juice, syrups and sugar. Pour over fruit and bake uncovered in a 300° oven for 1¾ hours. Serve at room temperature with a bowl of sweetened whipped cream or sour cream. Serves 12.

COMPOTE OF PEARS

1 dozen baby winter pears

2–3 slices lemon

6 crushed cardamom seeds

2 cups granulated sugar

½ cup honey

¾ cup water

Finely shredded rind of 1 orange, 1 lemon,
1 lime

1 clove

12 sticks preserved pineapple

Carefully peel pears, plunge them in boiling water with the slices of lemon. Simmer until half cooked. Put into a pan the cardamom, sugar, honey, water and finely shredded rind of the orange, lemon and lime. Stir over low heat until the sugar dissolves, then cook to a light syrup without stirring. Drain the pears carefully and stick one of them with the clove. Remove the cores with a potato parer, keeping the pears whole. Replace the cores with the pineapple sticks. Place in a deep earthenware casserole and pour the syrup over them. Cook in a 300° oven for 1½ hours. Baste the pears occasionally. Serve the pears warm or cold as desired. Serves 12.

DESSERT COMPOTE

4 Valencia oranges

2 crisp, juicy apples, cored

½ cup kirsch

Chill the fruit. Peel the oranges and remove all the white membrane. Divide the oranges into sections,

HOW TO CUT AN ORANGE INTO SECTIONS

1. With sharp chef's knife, slice off peel, pith.

2. To section, cut on each side of membrane.

holding them over a bowl to catch all the juice, and remove the membrane from each section. Drop the sections of fruit into the bowl with the juice. Leave the peel on the apples and cut them into neat dice. Add these to the orange sections. Add the kirsch and chill in the refrigerator for 1 hour. Serves 6.

COLD POACHED ORANGES WITH ALMONDS AND COINTREAU

> 8 large navel oranges
> 2½ cups sugar
> ½ cup Cointreau or orange liqueur
> ¾ cup blanched, slivered almonds

Peel the whole oranges with a knife, removing the rind and pith and exposing the pulp. Remove all pith from the orange rind and cut rind into fine julienne with a sharp knife. Make a syrup by boiling the sugar and 2 cups water and poach the rind for 30 minutes. Poach the oranges in the syrup just long enough to give them one rolling boil. Do not let them get limp.

Arrange oranges in a serving dish. Add orange liqueur to the syrup and pour over the oranges. Sprinkle with the slivered almonds. Chill well before serving. Serve the cold poached oranges with Chocolate Leaves. Serves 8.

FRUIT THAÏS

Use assorted fruits—peaches, apricots, pears, pineapple, cherries and bananas. Use canned fruits if the fresh are not available—be sure to get home-style peaches, if canned. Arrange the fruit in layers in a baking dish. Sprinkle each layer with brown sugar, slivered almonds and dabs of sweet butter. Pour ½ cup of sherry, or more if you are making a large amount, over all and cover with crushed macaroons. Bake 20 minutes in a 350° oven.

BAKED BANANAS FLAMBÉ

> 4 large bananas, peeled
> ½ cup brown sugar
> 3 tablespoons lime juice
> ½ cup light rum
> 1 teaspoon ground allspice
> Butter

Cut the bananas lengthwise, then in half across. Arrange in a well-buttered baking dish. Sprinkle with the sugar, lime juice, ¼ cup of the rum, and the allspice. Dot with butter. Bake in a 350° oven for 30 minutes, basting two or three times during cooking. Just before serving, heat the remaining ¼ cup rum, pour over the bananas, and set aflame. Serves 4.

FIGS WITH CREAM

> 1 quart fresh figs (making about 2½ cups pulp)
> 3–4 tablespoons dark rum
> Granulated sugar to taste
> 1 cup chilled heavy cream
> 1 cup chilled sour cream
> Confectioners' sugar

Skin the figs and mash the pulp in a serving bowl with a fork. Stir in rum and sugar to taste. Beat the chilled heavy cream in a chilled bowl with a chilled beater until beater leaves light traces on the cream. Fold the sour cream into the whipped cream, fold in confectioners' sugar to taste, then fold the cream into the fig mixture. Chill until serving time. Serves 6.

BAKED TEMPLE ORANGES WITH TANGERINE CUSTARD SAUCE

> 6 temple oranges
> 2 tablespoons butter
> 6 tablespoons sugar
> ½ cup orange juice

Peel the oranges and arrange them in a shallow baking dish. Loosen the sections slightly and pull them apart at the top. Dot with the butter and sprinkle with the sugar. Pour the orange juice over them and bake in a 350° oven for 40 minutes, basting occasionally with the pan juices. Cool and serve with Tangerine Custard Sauce.

TANGERINE CUSTARD SAUCE

> 2 eggs
> 2 tablespoons sugar
> ⅛ teaspoon salt
> 1 cup scalded milk
> 6 tablespoons frozen tangerine juice, undiluted
> 2 tablespoons Curaçao

Beat the eggs slightly and add the sugar and salt. Put this mixture in the top of a double boiler and slowly add the scalded milk, stirring constantly. Cook over hot, not boiling, water, stirring constantly, until the mixture has thickened enough to coat the spoon. Cool and add the undiluted tangerine juice and Curaçao. Chill and serve on the baked temple oranges. Serves 6.

PEACHES À LA BORDELAISE

> 4 large ripe peaches
> ¼ cup powdered sugar
> 1¼ cups red Bordeaux wine
> ½ cup granulated sugar
> 2″ stick cinnamon

Immerse peaches in boiling water while you count twenty slowly. Peel immediately, cut in half, remove pits and place cut side up in shallow dish. Sprinkle with powdered sugar. Refrigerate for one hour. Place red Bordeaux wine in enamel pan and add granulated sugar and cinnamon stick. Boil 1 minute and add the peaches and their juice. Cook until peaches are tender, about 10 minutes. Place in serving dish. Continue cooking syrup 5 minutes longer, then pour it over the peaches. Serve hot or ice cold. Serves 4.

PEACHES WITH RASPBERRY SAUCE

Purée 2 packages frozen raspberries, after you have poured off some of the liquid. Flavor lightly with eau-de-vie de framboise or kirsch.

Blanch, do not cook, 12 ripe peaches in boiling water for 5 minutes. Peel and arrange in a serving dish. Sprinkle lightly with sugar and some of the same eau-de-vie you used for the purée. Spoon purée over peaches. Serve very cold with ice cream or whipped cream. Serves 6–12.

POIRE AU CHOCOLAT

> 6 ripe pears (or 6 firm green apples)
> 1 cup apricot jam
> Grated rind and juice of 1 lemon
> 1 cup and 8 tablespoons granulated sugar
> ¾ cup water
> ¾ cup candied fruits, finely chopped and soaked in ¼ cup cognac
> 6 ounces dark sweet chocolate, cut in small pieces
> 3 egg whites

Carefully peel whole pears, keeping stalk on top. Remove core with a potato peeler. (If apples are used, prepare in the same way, but use an apple-corer.) Put the jam, lemon juice, lemon rind, 1 cup sugar and water into a large heavy pan. Stir over low heat until it dissolves and becomes a thick syrup. Simmer pears or apples gently in the syrup until just soft but not mushy, turning them to cook evenly. Chill in the syrup. Remove. Fill cavities with the finely chopped soaked candied fruit and arrange on a baking dish.

Add the cut-up chocolate to the syrup and stir slowly over low heat until dissolved. Pour this around the fruit. Beat the egg whites until stiff and slowly add the 8 tablespoons of sugar, beating all the time. Continue beating until the meringue holds its shape. Fill into a pastry tube with a large star tip, and cover the pears (or apples) with the meringue. Sprinkle the top with granulated sugar and put in a 350° oven until meringue is golden brown, about 5–6 minutes. Serve immediately. Serves 6.

PINEAPPLE PUDDING

> **2 cups finely chopped fresh pineapple**
> **4 ounces ground almonds**
> **4 egg yolks, lightly beaten**
> **½–1 cup sugar, depending on sweetness**
>   **of pineapple**
> **½ cup dry sherry**
> **¼ teaspoon ground cinnamon**
> **12 lady fingers**
>   **Apricot jam**
>   **Sour cream**
> **1 ounce slivered almonds**

Mix pineapple, ground almonds, egg yolks, sugar,

half the sherry, and cinnamon. Cook over low heat, stirring constantly until thickened. Cool. Split the lady fingers and spread with a thin layer of apricot jam. Place half the lady fingers in the bottom of a serving dish. Sprinkle with half the remaining sherry. Spread with half the pineapple mixture. Add second layer of lady fingers, the rest of the sherry, and the remaining pineapple mixture. Chill, spread with sour cream, and stick with almonds. Serves 6–8.

ALICE B. TOKLAS' PRUNES WITH CREAM

> **3 dozen prunes (pitted, extra-large variety)**
> **4 cups port**
> **1 cup sugar**
> **1 piece vanilla bean**
>   **Whipped cream, macaroons, candied violets**

Soak prunes for 24 hours in 2 cups port. Then add 2 more cups port, sugar and vanilla bean. Simmer gently about ½ hour. Cool and refrigerate for 3 days.

To serve, put in a decorative bowl and cover with whipped cream. Sprinkle whipped cream with a thick layer of powdered macaroons and garnish with candied violets. Serves 6–8.

RASPBERRIES WITH BLANCHED CREAM

3–4 small boxes ripe raspberries
¾ cup powdered sugar
⅓ cup kirsch
2 cups heavy cream
2 tablespoons granulated sugar
6 egg whites
1 teaspoon vanilla
2 teaspoons orange flower water (optional)

Wash berries and drain well. Place in serving dish, and sprinkle with powdered sugar. Pour kirsch over them and refrigerate for at least 1 hour. Serve with blanched cream made as follows: Scald 1-1/3 cups heavy cream in top part of double boiler. Sweeten with granulated sugar. Beat together the egg whites and 2/3 cup heavy cream for 100 turns of hand rotary beater. Add gradually to scalded cream, stirring constantly. Continue cooking over boiling water, stirring continuously, until well thickened, about 4–5 minutes. Remove from fire and cool, stirring occasionally. Flavor the cooled blanched cream with vanilla and orange flower water and chill. Serve with the raspberries. Serves 4.

STRAWBERRY FLUFF WITH KIRSCH

1 quart ripe firm strawberries
1 cup and 2 tablespoons sugar
⅓ cup kirsch
10 egg whites
Whipped cream

Pick over the berries. Sprinkle with 2 tablespoons sugar and kirsch. Let stand ½ hour.

Caramelize ½ cup sugar and line a 1½-quart soufflé dish with the caramel. Beat the egg whites very stiff to make a meringue, adding the remaining sugar by spoonfuls. Fold in the drained strawberries and pour into the caramelized soufflé dish. Stand in a pan of hot water and place in a 375° oven. Bake until puffy and lightly browned.

Serve at once with whipped cream which has been delicately flavored with a little kirsch and sugar. Serves 4–6.

STRAWBERRIES ROMANOFF IN MERINGUE SHELLS

8 individual meringue shells
2 quarts ripe strawberries
Sugar
6-ounce can frozen orange juice concentrate
1 cup port
3 tablespoons Mandarine liqueur
2 cups heavy cream
Pistachio nuts

Buy meringue shells at a bakery or make your own.

Hull the berries and sugar them if needed. (Remember the wine and the orange concentrate have sugar, as does the liqueur.) Add the orange concentrate and port and let the berries mellow in this mixture for 2 hours. Toss them carefully several times. Add the Mandarine liqueur. Whip the cream just before serving. Fill the meringue shells with berries, top with whipped cream and garnish with chopped pistachio nuts. Serves 8.

HOT COFFEE PUDDING

½ pound sweet butter
½ cup (scant) granulated sugar
6 ounces blanched ground almonds
4 tablespoons very strong coffee
1 teaspoon instant coffee
3 eggs
¾ cup sifted flour
Confectioners' sugar, ground coffee

With hand, cream butter well in a bowl. Clean off hand with rubber scraper. Slowly beat in the granulated sugar with a wooden spoon; beat until sugar is blended into butter. Slowly mix in the ground almonds. Add the liquid coffee and instant coffee. Beat in the eggs, one at a time. Slowly add the flour. Butter an 8″ cake tin or soufflé dish, line with waxed paper, butter again. Fill with the mixture and bake in a 350° oven for 45 minutes. Test with a cake tester. When baked, carefully slide a thin-bladed knife around the outside edge. Turn out, dust with confectioners' sugar and ground coffee. Serves 4–6.

GINGER PUDDING

½ cup butter
¾ cup sugar
1 egg, slightly beaten
2½ cups flour
3 teaspoons baking powder
  Pinch salt
1 teaspoon ground ginger
3 tablespoons finely chopped candied ginger
1 cup milk

Cream the butter and sugar and when smooth, add the beaten egg. Sift the dry ingredients and mix 1 tablespoon with the chopped candied ginger. Add the rest to the butter mixture a bit at a time, alternating with the milk. When the dough is well mixed, add the candied ginger. Pour into a buttered 1½-quart mold and cover tightly. Steam for 2 hours. Serve with whipped cream. Serves 6.

MARRON PUDDING

2 pounds fresh chestnuts in shell, or 1 pound
  dried chestnuts, or 1 large can whole
  chestnuts in brine
2½ tablespoons cocoa
1½ cups confectioners' sugar
8 tablespoons butter
½ cup blanched almonds, coarsely chopped
¼ cup Grand Marnier, Cointreau, or other
  orange-flavored liqueur
2 cups milk
1 cup sugar
1 teaspoon vanilla
2 tablespoons flour
4 egg yolks
¼ cup Marsala wine
  Candied fruits

To prepare fresh chestnuts in the shell, cut a cross with a sharp knife on the flat side of each chestnut. Place in a saucepan and cover with cold water. Bring to a boil and remove from heat. Take out only a few chestnuts at a time and peel off outer and inner skins while still hot. Cover the shelled chestnuts with water and simmer until tender. Drain. To prepare dried chestnuts, cover with boiling water to which ¼ teaspoon baking soda has been added and soak over-night. Boil the chestnuts in the soaking liquid until tender. If canned chestnuts are used, heat them to the boiling point.

Force the chestnuts through a sieve or food mill while they are still hot and blend thoroughly with the cocoa and confectioners' sugar. Cream the butter well. Beat into the chestnut mixture with the almonds. Beat well, then add the Grand Marnier, Cointreau, or other orange-flavored liqueur. Pour into a buttered charlotte mold or small soufflé dish. Cover with foil and chill in the refrigerator for several hours.

Meanwhile prepare a pastry cream: combine the milk, sugar, and vanilla, and heat to the boiling point. Blend with the flour and egg yolks and cook over low heat, stirring constantly, until the mixture thickens and just begins to boil. Add the Marsala wine and simmer, stirring, for a few moments. Cool. To serve, unmold the chestnut pudding on a serving dish. Decorate with candied fruits and serve with the cooled pastry cream. Serves 8–10.

CLAFOUTIS

2 cups stemmed fresh dark cherries
2 tablespoons butter
½ cup granulated sugar
1½ cups milk
2 eggs
6 tablespoons flour
  Confectioners' sugar
½ pint heavy cream

Preheat oven to 400°. Wash, stem and pit the cherries. Butter a 9½″ ovenproof glass pie plate with 1 tablespoon butter. Sprinkle the cherries with ¼ cup of granulated sugar, mix and spread over the pie plate. Make a smooth batter of the milk, eggs, 1 tablespoon melted butter, flour and ¼ cup granulated sugar. If you use an electric blender, place the ingredients in the glass container in the order given and run at low speed while you count twenty. Pour over the cherries. Bake at 400° about ½ hour, reducing the heat to 325° the last 10 minutes if necessary to prevent over-crisping. Serve at once, sprinkled copiously with confectioners' sugar and accompanied by heavy cream. Serves 4–6.

HOW TO PREPARE CRÊPES DIRECTOIRE

1. Heat crêpe pan. When hot, rub the pan with butter (it should sizzle on touching).

2. Quickly pour in ladleful of batter, tilt and shake so batter covers bottom in thin layer.

3. When crêpe begins to brown at edges, loosen it with spatula and quickly flip over.

4. Pat turned crêpe flat with fingers, brown second side. Gently remove with a spatula.

5. Spread cooked crêpes on lighter (second) side with thin layer of cooled pastry cream.

6. Put baked banana on each crêpe, sprinkle with almonds, and roll up like a fat cigar.

DESSERT CRÊPES

    ⅞ cup flour
    ¼ cup sugar
    ⅛ teaspoon salt
    3 eggs
    2 tablespoons cognac or rum
      A little scraped vanilla bean or 1 teaspoon
      grated lemon rind
    2 tablespoons melted butter
    Milk

Sift the dry ingredients together and add the eggs one at a time, mixing well. Mix until there are no lumps—an electric blender at low speed is excellent. Add the flavorings and the melted butter and gradually stir in just enough milk to give the batter the consistency of thick cream. Let the batter rest for an hour or two before baking.

Make the crêpes in a well-buttered 6″ pan over a fairly brisk heat. Pour a little of the batter in the pan and tip so that it runs over the entire surface. When done, turn and brown lightly on the other side. Keep hot in a low oven or over hot water, wrapped in foil until ready to use. This makes 12 small crêpes. Allow 2–3 per serving.

Crêpes may be kept several days in refrigerator in foil. They may also be frozen.

Variations:

1. Raspberry Crêpes: Bake crêpes. Spread with a good raspberry preserve and roll up. Flambé the rolled crêpes with framboise.

2. Peach Crêpes: Flavor thinly sliced peaches with sugar and bourbon. Bake crêpes and place a layer of peaches on each. Arrange a stack of 8 or 10 crêpes, topped with a plain crêpe. Heat and blaze with bourbon. Serve with whipped cream.

3. Strawberry Crêpes: Slice strawberries and marinate in sugar and kirsch. Roll in baked crêpes and flambé with kirsch. Serve with whipped cream.

4. Pineapple Crêpes: Spread baked crêpes with pineapple preserves or with fresh pineapple. Roll and flambé with rum or cognac.

CRÊPES NORMANDES

    8 cooking apples
    6 tablespoons butter
    1 teaspoon vanilla
    12 crêpes
    3 tablespoons calvados or applejack

Peel and core the apples and cut in sixths. Melt butter in a heavy skillet, add apples, cover and shake pan. After several minutes, add vanilla. Cook until apples are soft, but not mushy. Add sugar if necessary. Keep hot.

Sauté crêpes in crêpe pan in a little butter and spread each one with apple mixture. Sprinkle with sugar and a few drops of calvados or applejack. Pile one on top of the other, finishing with a plain crêpe. Heat in oven for a minute. Blaze with cognac or calvados. Serve with sweetened whipped cream.

CRÊPES MONTAIGNE

    8 egg yolks
    ¾ cup sugar
    ⅓ cup flour
    2 cups hot milk
    1 teaspoon vanilla
    12 crêpes
    ½ cup slivered toasted almonds
    ¼ cup kirsch
    ½ cup heavy cream, whipped

Beat egg yolks and sugar until light and lemon-colored. Mix in flour and gradually add milk. Add vanilla. Cook over medium heat, stirring, until thickened. Cool. Spread crêpes with some of this pastry cream and roll up. Place in a lightly sugared baking dish. Combine rest of pastry cream with the almonds, kirsch and whipped cream. Top rolled crêpes with this mixture, sprinkle with a few slivered almonds and put in a 450° oven for a few minutes to glaze.

CRÊPES DIRECTOIRE

    6 large unpeeled bananas
    Pastry cream
    (see recipe for Crêpes Montaigne)
    ⅓ cup sugar
    ½ cup Grand Marnier

    12 small crêpes
    ¾ cup blanched, shredded (or chopped)
    almonds
    ⅓ cup cognac, warmed

Bake bananas in skins in a 350° oven for 15–18 minutes, while preparing pastry cream. Heat sugar and Grand Marnier in a shallow, flameproof serving dish, caramelizing it slowly over very low heat. Spread each crêpe with pastry cream, top with a halved banana and sprinkle liberally with almonds. Roll up crêpes and arrange them in pan with caramelized sugar. Sprinkle with a little sugar, add a dash or so of Grand Marnier and heat through quickly in the oven or on top of the stove. Pour cognac over crêpes and ignite. Spoon juices over crêpes and serve.

CHOCOLATE SOUFFLÉ OMELETTE

    1½ ounces semi-sweet chocolate
    1 tablespoon water
    4 egg yolks
    ½ cup granulated sugar
    6 egg whites
    Fine granulated sugar

Melt the chocolate with the water in a small pan over low heat. Set aside to cool. Beat the egg yolks with the sugar until thick and pale. Add the chocolate. Beat the egg whites until stiff but not dry and carefully fold into the yolks as for a soufflé.

Butter an oval flameproof omelette dish and pour in the egg mixture all at once, reserving a little for decoration. Fill a pastry tube with this and pipe rosettes across the top of the mixture, which has been rounded with a spatula. Put into a 350° oven for 25–30 minutes. Just before it is completely cooked, sift over it fine granulated sugar and return to oven to give a light golden glaze (turn up heat and glaze for about 5 minutes). Be careful not to overcook—omelette should be creamy inside. Serve at once. Serves 4.

ORANGE SOUFFLÉ OMELETTE

    6 egg yolks
    1¼ cups fine granulated sugar
    Grated rind and sections of 1 orange
    8 egg whites
    Confectioners' sugar

Beat together the egg yolks and sugar until mixture is light and thickened. Add the grated orange rind. Beat the egg whites and fold into the yolk mixture. Pour into a buttered and sugared soufflé dish, piling the egg mixture higher in the center. Bake in a 450° oven for 20 minutes or until the soufflé is well puffed. Sprinkle with confectioners' sugar and put under the broiler to glaze for about one minute. Arrange the orange sections around the edge of the soufflé and serve at once. Serves 4.

SWEET OMELETTE

> 2 eggs, very fresh
> 2 level teaspoons sugar
>   Pinch of salt
> 1 teaspoon water
> 1½ teaspoons salt butter
> 3 tablespoons confectioners' sugar

Allow the pan to get a little hotter than for a plain omelette. Separate the eggs, add sugar to the yolks and beat with a small wire whisk until very light and fluffy. Add salt and water to the egg whites and beat until stiff. Carefully fold in the yolks. Rub the omelette pan with salt butter and spread the egg mixture carefully on top. Allow to cook without stirring until edges are light brown. Fold in half and turn out onto a hot flat dish. Sift the confectioners' sugar on top of the omelette and sear with red-hot skewer. Serves 2.

STRAWBERRY OMELETTE

> 1 cup each: sliced strawberries, whole strawberries
>   Juice of ½ lemon
>   Confectioners' sugar
> ¾ cup heavy cream
> 1 teaspoon vanilla
> 1 recipe Sweet Omelette
> ½ cup dissolved and strained red currant jelly
>   Kirsch

Sprinkle sliced strawberries with lemon juice and a little confectioners' sugar. Chill well. Beat heavy cream in a small bowl over a bowl of ice until it begins to thicken. Add vanilla and 2 tablespoons con-

HOW TO MAKE A SWEET OMELETTE

1. Fold beaten egg yolks into whites.

2. Pour mixture into hot omelette pan.

3. Smooth top; cook without stirring.

4. When edges are light brown, run fork around sides to loosen and fold in half.

5. Tilt pan over dish, flip omelette out.

6. Sift confectioners' sugar all over top.

fectioners' sugar and continue beating until stiff. Mix in the sliced strawberries. Make sweet omelette, fill with strawberry cream mixture, fold and turn out on a hot silver or copper serving dish. Dip whole strawberries into jelly and arrange around the omelette. Sprinkle top of omelette well with confectioners' sugar and mark top with a red-hot skewer. At the table, pour flaming kirsch or any other desired liqueur over omelette. Serves 2–3.

MARMALADE WITH RUM OMELETTE

> 1 recipe Sweet Omelette
> ¼ cup marmalade (or apricot or peach jam)
> Granulated sugar
> 2–3 ounces rum

Make a plain sweet omelette, fill with the marmalade, fold and turn out onto a hot platter. Sprinkle lightly with the fine granulated sugar. Ignite the rum and spoon over the omelette. Serve at once. Serves 2.

SOUFFLÉ ORIENTALE

> 11-ounce can mandarin oranges
> 1¾ cups sugar
> 1 cup preserved kumquats in heavy syrup
> 1-pound, 13-ounce can peach halves, well drained
> 1 tablespoon lemon juice
> 3 tablespoons grated orange rind
> 1 tablespoon butter
> 1 tablespoon Grand Marnier
> 9 egg whites, at room temperature
> ½ teaspoon cream of tartar
> 1 cup heavy cream

Combine the mandarin oranges and their juice and 1½ cups sugar in a saucepan. Bring to a boil over high heat, stirring frequently, and boil until the syrup spins a thread. Add the kumquats, peaches, lemon juice and orange rind and purée the mixture, a portion at a time, in an electric blender. Chill well. Butter two 6-cup soufflé dishes, dust each dish with 1 tablespoon sugar, and sprinkle the Grand Marnier over the bottom of the dishes. (Preparation up to this point may be done in advance.)

Preheat the oven to 400° 30 minutes before serving time. Beat the egg whites until foamy, add the cream of tartar and continue beating until stiff. Thoroughly fold half the whites into 3½ cups of the fruit purée (reserve balance of purée and use as sauce for ice cream), then lightly fold in the remaining egg whites. Pour the soufflé mixture into the dishes and bake for 22–25 minutes. Whip the cream until stiff with the remaining sugar and place in a serving bowl. Serve the soufflé on warm plates. Pass the sweetened whipped cream separately. Serves 8.

LEMON SOUFFLÉ

> 4 tablespoons sweet butter
> 5 rounded tablespoons granulated sugar
> 3 rounded tablespoons flour
> 1 cup milk
> Pinch of salt
> Grated rind and juice of 2 lemons
> 4 eggs, separated
> 2 egg whites
> Confectioners' sugar

Butter the inside of a 1½-quart soufflé dish with 1 tablespoon sweet butter and dust inside with 1 rounded tablespoon sugar, knocking out excess. Tie a buttered wax-paper collar around outside of dish to extend about 2″ above rim. Preheat oven to 350°. Melt remaining 3 tablespoons butter in a pan and stir in flour, off the heat. Mix in milk and salt. Return to heat and stir until sauce thickens. Mix in grated lemon rind, juice and remaining sugar. Mix in egg yolks, one at a time. Beat in well. Beat the 6 egg whites until stiff, but not dry. Pour sauce mixture onto egg whites and carefully fold in with a rubber scraper. Pour mixture into prepared soufflé dish and dust top with granulated sugar. Stand soufflé dish in a pan of hot water and bake at 350° for 40–45 minutes. Remove. Remove paper collar, dust top with confectioners' sugar and serve immediately. Serves 4.

SOUFFLÉ FRANGIPANE, DEMOULÉ

> 6 tablespoons softened butter
> Granulated sugar
> 10½-ounce can crushed pineapple (¾ cup fruit, ½ cup syrup)

5 eggs
3 tablespoons flour
⅓ cup ground blanched almonds
¼ teaspoon almond extract
1 cup boiling milk
5 tablespoons dark rum
1 egg white
   Salt
⅔ cup apricot preserves, forced through a
   sieve
10–12 toasted almonds

Preheat oven to 350°. Using 1 tablespoon butter, heavily butter a 2-quart charlotte mold 4″ deep. Coat the bottom well so that the soufflé will unmold easily. Roll sugar around the mold to coat the bottom and sides. Knock out excess.

Drain the pineapple. Boil the syrup in a small saucepan for 5 minutes, then add the pineapple and boil 5 minutes more. Drain. Reserve fruit for the soufflé, syrup for the sauce.

Put in a large mixing bowl 1 egg, 1 egg yolk (save the white for the soufflé mixture) and ½ cup granulated sugar. Beat with a wire whisk or electric beater for several minutes, until mixture is pale yellow and drops back onto the surface in slowly dissolving ribbons when beater is lifted. Beat in the flour, ground almonds and almond extract. Finally, beat in the hot milk by driblets. Pour mixture into a heavy 2-quart saucepan and stir slowly with a wire whisk over moderately high heat. As the cream comes to a simmer and turns lumpy, beat vigorously to smooth it out. Cook, stirring, over moderately low heat for 2 minutes. Remove from heat.

Separate the remaining 3 eggs, dropping the whites into a beating bowl. Beat the yolks into the almond cream with a wooden spoon. Then beat in 3 tablespoons butter and 3 tablespoons rum. Add the reserved egg white and 1 more egg white to the beating bowl and beat with a pinch of salt until soft peaks are formed, using a wire whisk. Stir ¼ of the egg whites into the almond cream, then pour the cream over the ¾ egg whites, using a rubber scraper to get all the mixture out of the pan. Delicately fold the whites into the almond cream with the scraper. Turn 1/3 of this mixture into the prepared mold and spread over it ½ the crushed pineapple. Cover with ½ the

remaining soufflé mixture, the rest of the pineapple and then the last of the soufflé mixture. The mold should be about 2/3 full. Set mold in a roasting pan and pour in enough boiling water to come halfway up the outside of the mold. Place in lower third of preheated oven and bake for 1¼ hours, regulating heat so water in pan never quite simmers. The soufflé must cook slowly. It will rise about ½″ above the rim of the mold and the top will brown. It is done when a straw or long knife, plunged down through the side of the puff, comes out clean.

While soufflé is baking, prepare the sauce. Beat the pineapple syrup, apricot preserves, and remaining 2 tablespoons rum in a small saucepan until blended. Remove from heat and beat in remaining 2 tablespoons softened butter just before serving the soufflé.

To serve, turn a warm, lightly buttered serving platter upside down over the mold and reverse the two, giving a sharp downward jerk to dislodge the soufflé. Decorate top of the unmolded soufflé with almonds and pour sauce around it. Serves 8.

<u>Note</u>: When the soufflé is cooked, it may remain in the turned-off oven in its pan of hot water for half an hour before it is unmolded and served.

APRICOT SOUFFLÉ

   1 cup apricots soaked in sherry, with a little
     of their marinade
   1 cup sugar
   ½ teaspoon salt
     Cognac or apricot liqueur
   5 egg yolks
   6 egg whites
   1 pint high-quality vanilla ice cream

Blend the apricots, sugar, salt, 1/3 cup cognac or apricot liqueur and egg yolks in a blender, or force the apricots through a fine sieve and then blend with the sugar, salt, cognac and egg yolks. Beat the egg whites until stiff, but not dry and fold into the mixture. Pour into a buttered and sugared 1½-quart soufflé dish and bake in a 400° oven for 25–28 minutes. Serve with a sauce made by melting down the ice cream and blending in a little of the same liquor used in the soufflé. Serves 4.

HOW TO PREPARE
SOUFFLÉ FRANGIPANE, DEMOULÉ

1. To make unmolded soufflé, heavily butter charlotte mold and coat inside with sugar.

2. Spoon alternate layers of soufflé mixture, pineapple into mold until it is two-thirds full.

3. Set filled mold in pan of hot water. Bake. Put serving plate over the baked soufflé.

4. Reverse plate and soufflé together. Give sharp downward jerk to dislodge the soufflé.

5. Decorate unmolded soufflé with toasted almonds and pour the rum-fruit sauce around it.

MINCEMEAT SOUFFLÉ

2 cups egg whites
½ teaspoon salt
1½ cups honey
2 cups mincemeat
1 ounce cognac

Beat the egg whites with the salt until they are stiff, but not dry. Slowly add the honey, beating constantly. Continue to beat until whites stand in peaks.

Put the mincemeat in a bowl and stir in the cognac. Pour the whites over the mincemeat and fold in lightly. Pour into a 2-quart soufflé dish and bake in a preheated 250° oven for 35 minutes. Serves 8.

MONTE CARLO SOUFFLÉ

8 tablespoons granulated sugar
2 teaspoons plain gelatin
¼ cup lemon juice
5 tablespoons water
6 egg whites
Grated rind of 2 lemons
Praline powder (see recipe for Coffee-Praline Ice Cream)
Caramel Sauce

Measure out the sugar onto a paper towel. Put the gelatin, lemon juice and water into a small saucepan and stir over a slow fire until it dissolves. Beat the egg whites in a mixer until they begin to peak. Slowly add the measured sugar, continuing to beat all the time and beat about 3 minutes after all the sugar has been added. Remove, sprinkle the grated lemon rind on top and carefully fold in the melted gelatin. Tie a band of oiled paper around the outside of a soufflé dish 6½″ in diameter. The band should come about 2″ above the rim of the dish. Fill with the soufflé mixture which should be about 1½″ above the rim. Put to set in the freezer for 1½–2 hours.

Sprinkle the top of the soufflé with the praline powder. (Any leftover powder may be stored in a screw-top jar in the refrigerator where it will keep for many months. It can be sprinkled over ice cream or other desserts or mixed into the pastry cream base for open strawberry or apricot tarts.) Serves 8.

Serve the Monte Carlo soufflé with Caramel Sauce.

CARAMEL SAUCE

    1¼ cups granulated sugar
    ½ teaspoon cream of tartar
    ½ cup water

Put ingredients in a heavy pan. Stir with metal spoon until sugar dissolves. Allow to cook over low heat without stirring until dark brown. Place pan in a bowl of cold water to stop further cooking. When bubbles have settled, stir in half a cup of cold water. Chill sauce and serve separately in a bowl.

COLD ORANGE SOUFFLÉ

    1 cup cold water
    2 envelopes unflavored gelatin
    8 eggs, separated
    ½ teaspoon salt
    2 6-ounce cans frozen orange juice concentrate
    1 cup sugar
    1 cup heavy cream

Place water in the top of a double boiler and sprinkle the gelatin over the surface to soften. Beat the egg yolks lightly and add them with the salt. Mix well. Place over boiling water and cook, stirring constantly, until the gelatin dissolves and the mixture thickens a bit, about 4 minutes.

Remove from the double boiler and stir in the orange concentrate. Chill until the mixture drops from a spoon into soft mounds. Beat the egg whites until stiff, but not dry. Gradually beat in the sugar and continue beating until the egg whites are stiff. Whip the cream. Fold the whites into the orange mixture and then fold in the cream.

Arrange a collar of doubled waxed paper around a 2½-quart soufflé dish. The collar should come 2″ above the top of the dish. Fasten it with gummed tape. Pour the mixture into the dish and chill until firm. Remove the collar and decorate with orange sections, if you like, before serving. Serves 8–10.

NORMANDY CHOCOLATE MOUSSE

    1 pound dark sweet chocolate, cut up
    2 ounces bitter chocolate, cut up
    7 tablespoons strong coffee
    2 tablespoons kirsch or rum
    5 eggs, separated
    2 ounces sweet butter
    1 cup heavy cream
    2 dozen lady fingers
    Whipped cream, shredded chocolate

Put sweet and bitter chocolate and coffee in a heavy pan over low heat. Stir until the chocolate is dissolved, then add the kirsch or rum. Remove from heat. Add the egg yolks, one at a time, then add the butter bit by bit. Beat the cream over a bowl of ice until thick. Add slowly to the chocolate. Fold in the stiffly beaten egg whites.

Lightly butter a 9″ charlotte mold and line with split lady fingers. Fill with the mousse and chill in the freezer overnight. Remove and allow to warm slightly at room temperature. Wrap a hot towel around the mold and slide a thin-bladed knife around the edge of the mousse. Turn out onto a flat serving dish. Decorate with whipped cream and shredded chocolate. Serves 8–10.

MOCHA MOUSSE

    6 egg yolks
    ¾ cup granulated sugar
    1½ cups strong coffee
    2 envelopes gelatin
    1½ pints heavy cream

Make a soft custard with the egg yolks, sugar and coffee. Add the gelatin, which has been softened in ½ cup cold water. Stir and cool. Whip the cream and fold it in. Pour into a 2-quart melon-shape mold and chill.

Unmold and pour Sauce Tia Maria over the mousse before serving. Serves 8.

SAUCE TIA MARIA

    3 cups strong coffee
    1½ cups sugar
    2 tablespoons arrowroot
    2 ounces Tia Maria liqueur

Heat the coffee with the sugar. Stir the arrowroot

into ¼ cup cold water and add. Simmer and stir until thickened. Add Tia Maria and chill.

Note: Whenever a sauce should be clear, as in this case, arrowroot is preferable to cornstarch. Cornstarch may be substituted if arrowroot is not available. Kahlua may also be substituted for Tia Maria.

FROZEN RASPBERRY AND MACAROON MOUSSE

1 quart fresh raspberries
1 cup sugar
1 cup macaroon crumbs
  Pinch of salt
⅓ cup framboise
1 quart heavy cream, whipped

Purée the raspberries and blend with the sugar. Add the macaroon crumbs, salt and framboise. Blend with the cream, pour into a mold and freeze until mushy. Mix well and freeze until solid. Serves 8.

MOUSSE D'ABRICOTS PROVENÇALE

1 lemon
1 pound dried apricots, soaked in water
8-ounce jar applesauce
  About ½ cup sugar
4 egg whites
  Toasted slivered almonds

Pare rind from lemon with a vegetable peeler. Squeeze lemon. Simmer apricots, applesauce, lemon rind and juice for 30 minutes, uncovered. Drain off any excess juice and press the mixture through a sieve, or purée in an electric blender. Let cool, then add sugar to taste. Whip the egg whites stiffly, then put beater in the apricot purée. Whip purée, gradually incorporating egg whites. Heap mousse into serving dish. Chill. Garnish with almonds. Serves 8.

GLACE AUX MARRONS

1 ounce rum
1 cup granulated sugar
1 teaspoon vanilla

1 can (2 cups) puréed, unsweetened chestnuts
4 egg whites
2 ounces butter, melted
11-ounce bottle marrons glacés

Mix the rum, sugar and vanilla with the puréed chestnuts. Beat the egg whites until stiff, but not dry, and fold them in. Add the butter and 3 marrons glacés, broken into small pieces. Place in a 1-quart mold and chill for at least 4 hours. Unmold and decorate with halved marrons glacés. Serves 8.

LEMON CREAM

3 eggs, separated
1 cup sugar
1 envelope unflavored gelatin
  Juice of 2 lemons
  Juice of 1 small orange
1 teaspoon grated lemon rind
1 teaspoon grated orange rind
1 cup heavy cream, whipped

Beat the egg yolks and sugar until thick and lemon colored. Soften the gelatin in ½ cup cold water, dissolve over hot water and stir into the egg mixture. Add the lemon juice, orange juice and grated lemon and orange rinds. Mix well. Chill until the mixture begins to thicken, resembling unbeaten egg white. Beat the egg whites until they stand in stiff peaks. Fold the whipped cream and lastly the beaten egg whites into the lemon-egg mixture. Pour the lemon cream into a glass or silver serving dish and chill until set and firm. Serves 4.

POTS DE CRÈME CAFÉ

2 cups light cream
1 tablespoon instant coffee
6 egg yolks
½ cup granulated sugar
½ cup heavy cream
  Pinch salt
2 tablespoons confectioners' sugar

Scald the light cream with all but ½ teaspoon of the instant coffee. Cool slightly. Beat the egg yolks with the granulated sugar until very light and lemon colored. Slowly mix in the scalded cream, stirring constantly. Strain through a fine sieve into 6 pots de crème. Stand the pots in a pan of water. Bake in a 300° oven for 35–40 minutes or until a knife inserted in the center comes out clean. Remove to refrigerator and chill in the water. Beat the heavy cream and salt over ice until it begins to thicken. Add the confectioners' sugar and continue beating until cream holds its shape. Fill a pastry tube with the whipped cream. Pipe a large rosette on each pot, sprinkle with the remaining instant coffee. Serves 6.

OEUFS À LA NEIGE AU CAFÉ

> 14 tablespoons granulated sugar
> 6 eggs, separated
> ½ cup very strong dark-roast coffee
> 1½ cups light cream
> 1 cup heavy cream, whipped
> 1 quart skimmed milk
> ½ cup lump sugar, rubbed on skin of an
>   orange
> ¼ cup water
> ¼ teaspoon cream of tartar

Beat 10 tablespoons sugar and the egg yolks in a mixer until very light and fluffy. Combine coffee and light cream in a pan and slowly bring to a boil. Mix into egg yolk mixture and cook over low heat, stirring with a silver spoon, until mixture coats the back of the spoon. Remove pan from heat and stir over ice until mixture begins to cool. Mix in 2 stiffly beaten egg whites and the whipped cream. Pour mixture into a shallow glass serving dish and chill. Scald the skimmed milk in a shallow pan. Beat remaining egg whites until stiff, fold in 4 tablespoons sugar. Take up mixture with 2 tablespoons, cupping one over the other to form meringues. Slide them into milk and poach 3 minutes on each side. Chill in milk; drain with a slotted spoon and arrange on the coffee custard. Put the lump sugar, water and cream of tartar in a pan and stir over a low fire until the sugar dissolves. Cook to the hard crack stage (300°– 310° F). Dip a fork into the caramel and dribble it over the meringues in a design of spun sugar threads. Serve chilled. Serves 8.

**HOW TO MAKE
OEUFS À LA NEIGE AU CAFÉ**

1. Cook coffee custard slowly in a pan, stirring, until it is thick enough to coat the back of a metal spoon (do not use a wooden spoon for testing).

2. Chill custard or stir over ice until cooled. With wire whisk, first fold in stiffly beaten egg whites and then whipped cream. Refrigerate custard.

3. Scald milk in a shallow pan. Warm two large metal spoons in milk. Take up big spoonful of meringue mixture, smoothing it to form shape of egg.

4. Lower spoon to surface of milk and slide in meringues. Poach 3 minutes on each side. Remove with slotted spoon.

5. Put custard in glass bowl. Arrange meringues on top like star. With fork, dribble threads of caramel over them.

CRÈME BRÛLÉE

1½ quarts heavy cream
12 egg yolks
6 tablespoons sugar
2 teaspoons vanilla extract
Dark brown sugar

Preheat oven to 375°. Scald the cream. Beat together the egg yolks, 6 tablespoons of sugar and vanilla. Add to the cream and mix well. Strain into a buttered 2-quart baking dish, stand dish in a pan of hot water and bake in a 375° oven for 40 minutes, or until set. Cool for ½ hour or longer. Lightly sprinkle a ½"-thick layer of dark brown sugar over the surface of the crème. Put under hot broiler, 4" from the heat, until the sugar begins to caramelize. (If necessary, turn the dish to ensure even caramelizing. Watch carefully for burning.) Chill for 4 hours or more before serving. To serve, shatter the caramel with a spoon. Serves 8–10.

COLD ZABAGLIONE

6 egg yolks
2 whole eggs
½ cup granulated sugar
½ cup Marsala or sweet sherry
¼ cup brandy
Pinch of cinnamon
½ teaspoon vanilla

Place egg yolks and whole eggs in top of a deep 2-quart enamel double boiler and beat with a rotary beater until light, about 3 minutes. Gradually beat in granulated sugar. Add, little by little, Marsala or sherry, then brandy and flavor with cinnamon and vanilla. (At this point the mixture will not be as thick as before, but this is all right.) Place pan over boiling water and continue beating with rotary beater until it foams up almost to the top of the pan, about 3–4 minutes. Be careful not to overcook. Remove from heat and continue beating with a spoon, scraping the thickest part into the rest until smooth. Pour immediately into 8 glasses or custard cups of ½-cup capacity. Cool and refrigerate until ready to serve, at least 2 hours. Serves 8.

AVOCADO ICE CREAM

2 egg yolks
¾ cup sugar
2 cups thin cream
½ teaspoon salt
½ teaspoon vanilla
2 ripe avocados, mashed smooth
½ teaspoon almond extract
1 teaspoon lemon juice

Beat egg yolks. Add ¼ cup of sugar and cream, a little at a time. Cook over low heat until slightly thickened. Add salt and vanilla; chill. Add remaining sugar to avocado pulp and flavor with the almond extract and lemon juice. Add custard mixture and freeze in a crank freezer, using 1 part rock salt to 8 parts crushed ice. Serves 6.

TANGERINE ICE

3 tangerines, peeled and sectioned
1 quart water
2 cups granulated sugar
3 cups tangerine juice
¼ cup lemon juice
Grated rind of 2 tangerines
Chopped pistachio nuts

Chill the tangerine sections until ready to use.

Boil the water and sugar together for 5 minutes. Add the tangerine juice, lemon juice and tangerine rind and mix thoroughly. Remove from the heat and cool. Pour the mixture into ice trays and freeze. When it starts to ice, remove from the freezer and beat thoroughly; then return it to the freezer until solid.

Serve the tangerine ice garnished with the tangerine sections and chopped pistachio nuts. Serves 8.

MACADAMIA NUT ICE CREAM

6-ounce can Macadamia nuts (slightly salted)
1⅔ cups milk
½ cup sugar
2 eggs, separated
1 teaspoon vanilla

1 cup heavy cream
3 tablespoons rum

Place the nuts in the electric blender, turn the blender on and then off immediately to reduce the nuts to a coarse powder.

Heat the milk in top of a double boiler over simmering water. Add the sugar and stir well. Beat the egg yolks and gradually add part of the hot milk. Stir this mixture into the remaining hot milk and cook, stirring constantly, until slightly thickened. Cool, add the vanilla, the unbeaten egg whites and the heavy cream. Place in an electric automatic ice cream freezer in freezing compartment of the refrigerator and freeze for about 1 hour. Scrape down the sides and bottom and continue freezing about 1 hour longer. Remove the dasher and stir in the rum and about half of the coarsely ground nuts. Continue freezing until stiff, about 3 hours. Half an hour before serving, remove freezer from the freezing compartment and place in the refrigerator to soften slightly. To serve, place in a well-chilled serving bowl and sprinkle with the remaining nuts. Serves 6.

GINGER ICE

½ cup sugar
¼ cup white corn syrup
½ cup water
¾ cup orange juice
⅓ cup lemon juice
¼ cup syrup from preserved ginger
2 tablespoons chopped preserved ginger

Cook sugar, syrup and water together for 5 minutes. Cool. Add fruit juices, ginger syrup and ginger. Pour into a crank freezer and freeze, using 8 parts of ice to 1 part of rock salt. Serves 6.

FRESH PEACH ICE WITH PEACHES

5 pounds (approx.) ripe peaches
1½ pints heavy sugar and water syrup
2 tablespoons lemon juice
⅓ cup cognac
6–8 ripe peaches, sliced and sugared

Mash the 5 pounds of ripe peaches and force them through a fine sieve or a food mill. You will need 4 cups of this purée. Combine it with the sugar and water syrup, lemon juice and cognac and freeze in an old-fashioned freezer or in your freezing unit. If you freeze the latter way, freeze the mixture to a mush, remove it and beat it up for 2 or 3 minutes and return to the freezer. Serve this ice with the sliced sugared peaches which have been flavored with additional cognac. Serves 8.

MANGO ICE CREAM

2 soft ripe mangoes
Strained juice of 1 lemon
¾ cup granulated sugar plus 2 tablespoons
2 eggs, separated
1 cup heavy cream
½ teaspoon almond extract

Peel mangoes and cut pulp away from pits. Mash with potato masher (you should have 2 cups mashed pulp). Add the strained lemon juice and ¾ cup granulated sugar. Mix well. Place in shallow ice tray in refrigerator freezing compartment and freeze for about 1 hour.

Beat the egg whites until stiff with the 2 tablespoons granulated sugar. With the same beater, beat the yolks until light and fold them into the whites. With another beater, beat the heavy cream until it is as thick as custard, but not stiff, and fold into the egg mixture. Scrape the frozen pulp mixture into a bowl. Add the cream-egg mixture and almond extract. Mix lightly but thoroughly, place the mixture in a deeper freezing tray and freeze until stiff, stirring once or twice during the process. In about 2½ hours the ice cream should be ready to serve. Serves 6.

CAFÉ GRANITÉ

1½ cups drip-grind Italian-roast coffee
2 quarts boiling water
1½ cups granulated sugar
2 cups cold water
2 or more cups heavy cream
1 cup crème de cacao liqueur

Make very strong, clear, drip coffee with the coffee and boiling water. Strain through cheesecloth. Moisten the sugar with the cold water and stir. Place over heat and boil for 3 minutes without stirring, counting from time the mixture first comes to a boil. Add the coffee. Cool. Place in refrigerator freezing trays, turn control to coldest and freeze, stirring frequently, until mushy (about 1 hour).

Have ready 6–8 chilled parfait glasses and a pitcher of heavy cream. When ready to serve, scrape the café granité with a sturdy spoon and fill the glasses ¾ full. Rush them to the table accompanied by the cream and a small pitcher of the crème de cacao, to be poured over the café granité. Serve with lady fingers. Serves 6–8.

COFFEE-PRALINE ICE CREAM

  5 egg yolks
  1½ cups granulated sugar
  ½ teaspoon cream of tartar
  ⅔ cup strong espresso coffee
  1 cup strong coffee, boiled down with 6 lumps
    of sugar to ¼ cup essence
  1 quart light cream
  1 cup heavy cream, whipped
  ¾ cup blanched almonds
  2 teaspoons light rum

Beat the egg yolks in an electric mixer until light and fluffy. Put ¾ cup sugar, ¼ teaspoon cream of tartar and the strong coffee in a pan and stir over heat until it dissolves. Cook until mixture will spin

a thread between thumb and finger. Pour slowly onto the beaten egg yolks, beating all the time. Continue to beat until very thick and quite cold. Add the strong coffee essence and slowly mix in the light cream. Lastly, add the whipped cream. Pour into an electric ice cream freezer and turn for 10 minutes, or until quite set. Put the blanched almonds, remaining ¾ cup sugar and ¼ teaspoon cream of tartar into a heavy pan and cook over moderate heat, stirring occasionally, until the syrup is a dark caramel brown. Pour onto a lightly oiled tin and leave until quite set. Put through a coarse nut mill or crush in an electric blender. Carefully open the top of the ice cream freezer, add the rum and the praline powder, give one or two turns to mix in. (Anything crunchy should be added to the ice cream at the very end so that it keeps its crispness. This also applies to liquor or candied fruits.) Serves 6.

SNOWBALL SURPRISE WOBURN ABBEY

  2 quarts vanilla or coffee ice cream
  9″–10″ round sponge cake layer
  1 tablespoon butter
  1 tablespoon brown sugar
  6 tablespoons rum
  4 bananas, chopped
  4 egg whites
  1 cup sugar

Press the ice cream into a bowl or deep mold, slightly smaller in diameter than the sponge layer, leaving a hollow in the center. Freeze until firm. Melt the butter and add the brown sugar and 2 tablespoons of the rum. Pour over the bananas and leave for 1 hour. Twenty minutes before serving, whip the egg whites until foamy, gradually add the sugar, and continue beating until stiff. Put the banana mixture into the hollow of the ice cream. Dip mold into hot water for a few seconds and loosen around edges with a sharp knife. Cover bottom of mold with sponge cake layer and place a flat cookie sheet over it. Invert to unmold ice cream onto the sponge round. Cover completely with the egg white, making sure all the ice cream is covered. Bake in a 425° oven for 5–8 minutes. With aid of two spatulas, slide onto serving dish. Heat remaining rum, ignite, and pour over top. Serve flaming. Serves 8.

Index

Index

Index